Business, Banking, and Politics

The Case of British Steel, 1918–1939

Steven Tolliday

D1393946

Harvard University Press
Cambridge, Massachusetts
London, England   1987

Library of Congress Cataloging-in-Publication Data

Tolliday, Steven.
    Business, banking, and politics.

    (Harvard studies in business history; 39)
    Includes index.
    1. Steel industry and trade—Great Britain—
History—20th century.   I. Title.   II. Series.
HD9521.5.T64   1987   338.4′7669142′0941   86-31944
ISBN 0-674-08725-9 (alk. paper)

Editor's Introduction

ONE of the major challenges facing business historians is to describe, analyze, and attempt to explain the larger institutional framework in which business enterprises and business leaders operate. Over the years business historians have concentrated on telling the story of individual companies or persons, usually indicating how they respond to changing markets and technologies. Obviously these responses of individual corporations or entrepreneurs also reflect the activities of enterprises and institutions external to the corporation—particularly those of competitors, financial intermediaries, and the state.

In this history of a major British industry during the interwar years Steven Tolliday emphasizes that "the institutional structures of firms, banks, and government were crucial in developing the steel industry." By examining and analyzing business and industrial decision making within this broader institutional context, Dr. Tolliday has pioneered in developing a new approach to business and economic history.

During the 1920s, the "black decade" of the British steel industry, nearly everyone connected with that industry agreed that its revival depended on replacing old and increasingly obsolete equipment with modern, best-practice technologies of production essential to increase productivity and decrease costs. Despite such agreement, these goals were rarely reached. Existing institutional barriers were too great. The conflicting interests within the firm—family owners, creditors, and managers—and among the different competitors prevented a meeting of the minds concerning what to build and where, and particularly how to finance new or improved facilities. Nor were the major institutions outside of the industry—the banks and the state—able to apply the pressure or provide the incentives necessary to achieve reorganization and modernization. The large commercial banks to which the weakening firms turned for short-term working capital, as well as long-term investment capital, had their own particular interests; and the central bank had neither the skills nor the personnel to implement the broad plans proposed by its governor, Montagu Norman. Moreover, as Tolliday explains, the "visible hand" of the state reinforced the structural deadlock of the industry. It too had goals and interests different from those of the financiers and the industrialists. The result, in the words of K. Warren, another historian of the industry, was that "despite the achievements, the most distinctive legacy of the inter-war years in steel was in problems unsolved and possible solutions compromised" (quoted from Neil K. Buxton and Derek K. Aldcroft, eds., *British Industry between the Wars: Instability and Industrial Development, 1919–1939* [London: Scolar Press, 1979], p. 125). Once wartime and postwar reconstruction needs were met, the British steel industry continued its steady decline.

Tolliday tells this story in three parts. The first covers the structure of the enterprises and the structure of the industry in which they operated and the impact both had on decision making. Part II reviews those comparable structures within the banking system that affected the decisions about modernizing the industry. Part III does the same for government institutions. This institutional approach, based as it is on a rich, detailed narrative, provides massive amounts of new information and so becomes an innovative and authoritative history of the British iron and steel industry during the interwar years. The book's information, insights, and analyses have significant implications for declining industries in other economies and in other times. Its relevance for steel and other depressed industries in the United States in recent years will be apparent. Of even more importance, this study provides a model for future scholars to place the history of businesses and of industries in their larger institutional setting.

Alfred D. Chandler, Jr.

Acknowledgments

I SHOULD like to thank the British Steel Corporation, the Bank of England, and the Public Record Office for permission to consult and use material in their possession. In particular, I am grateful to the staff of the BSC's regional record centers, especially John C. Drew at Irthlingborough and Carl Newton at Stockton-on-Tees. At the Bank of England warm thanks are due the archivist, Henry Gillett, for his valuable assistance; and in Scotland Peter Payne of the University of Aberdeen generously allowed me full access to the papers of the Scottish steel companies that were in his possession. The Department of Trade and Industry made available to me the papers of the Import Duties Advisory Committee, which were at that time closed to the general public. I owe a special debt to Michael Moss, archivist at the University of Glasgow, both for his assistance in consulting that archive and for his personal help and suggestions, which enabled me to take a number of important steps forward in my research. In addition I should like to thank the staffs of the Cambridge University Library and the Library of the London School of Economics for their work and attention throughout the preparation of this book.

I have benefited greatly from discussions with and comments from Joseph Melling, Alastair Reid, and Jonathan Zeitlin, and from the encouragement and guidance of Leslie Hannah. Donald Coleman and Sidney Pollard also made helpful comments.

Finally, I thank my family and friends for their patience and encouragement, and Sophie Cox for her love and support.

S.T.

Contents

Tables

Figures

Maps

Introduction

Explanations of the decline of the British economy are constantly shifting as the dimensions of the decline seem to change. At one time the crisis was seen as one of poor economic management—the failure of economic policy and investment strategy to take advantage of the opportunities of the post-1945 boom. More recently economists and historians have begun to stress the long-term structural and historical roots of that decline. In this context it has been frequently noted that the competitive and specialized system of manufacturing that suited the period when Britain dominated the world economy proved resistant to adaptation to changed conditions of international markets and competition. In recent years much attention has been focused on the cultural and psychosocial aspects of this inadaptability.[1] However, less attention has been paid to the constraints on economic reorganization that derive from the structural rigidities in the economic and political institutions that grew up on the basis of the nineteenth-century economy.

The standard textbooks on the interwar years by such writers as Derek Aldcroft, Harry Richardson, Alexander Youngson, William Ashworth, and, to a lesser extent, Bernard Alford[2] concentrate primarily on supply and demand and pay little attention to the structures and processes of decision making at the level of the firm or the role of economic and political institutions like the banks and government beyond their macroeconomic effects on the economy through fiscal and monetary policies. This book attempts to show the importance of taking institutional structures seriously in analyzing the development of the economy by focusing on a case study of one of Britain's most important industries, steel. Maps 1 and 2 show the major areas with which we shall be concerned. No attempt is made to present a

1

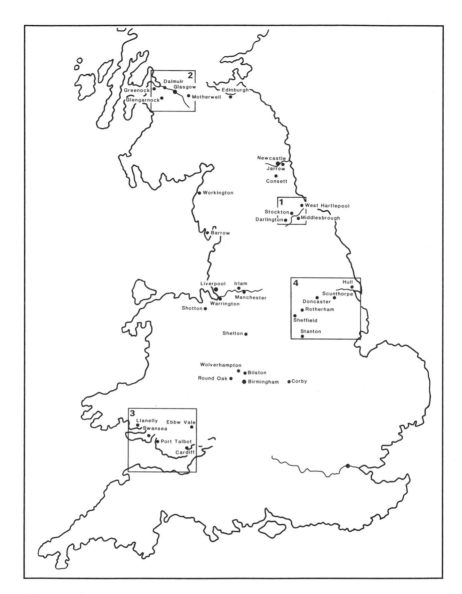

Map 1   The major steelmaking areas

1. Teesside

2. Clydeside

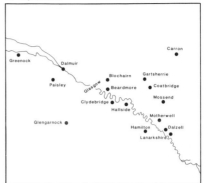

3. South Wales – Tinplate Industry

4. Sheffield/Scunthorpe

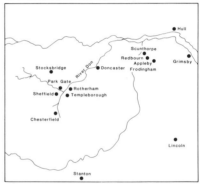

Map 2   Steelworks referred to in the text, by area

consecutive and comprehensive history of the industry. Instead the book presents a thematic analysis of a number of important issues concerned with the problems of restructuring declining sectors of a major capitalist economy.

The first theme is the impact of corporate structures and decision-making processes on economic change: To what extent did the institution of the firm itself condition the possibilities for effective industrial reorganization? How did such institutional factors interact with the constraints of the market? In particular the book takes issue with two common approaches to the issue of industrial decline. On the one hand, it criticizes the use of supply and demand models that treat the firm and the entrepreneur simply as transmission belts for the operation of wider market mechanisms. On the other hand, it criticizes a tendency to import uncritically the concept of the managerial "visible hand" as the crucial key to modern corporate growth, which Alfred Chandler has developed in relation to a historical study of the American economy. The Chandler thesis argues that changing markets and technology require businesses to pursue new strategies such as continuous mass production and the integration of production and distribution. The problems arising from these developments induce the formation of new organizational structures, particularly bureaucratic hierarchies, which coordinate economic activities in place of the "invisible hand" of the market.[3] Much of the most interesting business history of recent years has been stimulated by the Chandler thesis,[4] but while accepting the correctness of Chandler's stress on institutions, strategies, and structures, the argument developed here questions the elements of functional determinism in his ideas and the extent to which the theory can be applied to an economy whose history and structure are so different from those of America.

Part I analyzes the interaction of company decision-making processes and institutional structures with economic and technical constraints and places it in the context of these theoretical issues. This analysis is based on three major case studies of companies in action set against the background of the market environment and industrial structure of the industry. On the Northeast Coast intense rivalry between historically competing firms and the development of powerful factions and interest groups within the firms made strategic long-term decision making an impossibility and paralyzed the fragmented structure of firms and production. In Scotland a similar paralysis was overcome by a powerful alliance of bankers and shipbuilders (the industry's major customers in this area); but although regional reorganization of firms was achieved, it did not produce the restructuring of production that expert opinion desired. In South Wales one giant firm (Richard Thomas and Co.) was slowly able to emerge in the tinplate industry, which was characterized by a mass of small firms. But in the process of breaking out of the mold of small-scale production by investing in new capital-intensive technology, the company ended up losing its independence to bankers and boardroom control to its rivals, who were more concerned to control its expansion than to pursue rapid modernization. In each of these cases outcomes were strongly conditioned by the dynamics of the business institutions concerned, and, it is argued, this was not a feature confined to steel but a widespread phenomenon that shaped the development of large parts of British industry in this period.

In view of the importance of the structural and institutional logjams prevalent at the level of the firm, the rapidly rising costs of the old market structures, and the inability of the existing institutions of management and corporate organization to deal with perceived needs for industrial reorganization, the potential importance of central action to curb the costs of the market and promote coordinated development becomes a critical issue. Parts II and III show that such attempts by banks and government in the interwar years were much more extensive than has generally been thought and that they make up a vital part of the prehistory of developments such as nationalization and the growing role of financial institutions in industry since the Second World War.

Part II focuses on the implications for industrial restructuring of the frequently noted conflict between the City and industry in Britain and attempts to shift this debate onto new terrain. Most of the discussion of this relationship has concentrated on issues such as the gold standard, the sterling question, or balance of payments matters. Instead, we shall examine the nature and limitations of the power of the banks in British industry by direct analysis of their interaction with a major industry. The economic crisis of the interwar years weakened the traditional mutual autonomy of British banking and industry, although it did not overturn it. The potentiality of banking action as a "strategic" sector of capital in restructuring other parts of the economy came to the fore, and the Bank of England in particular began to develop its interventionist role for the first time, both to prevent state intervention and in the interests of efficiency as it saw it. Steel was the leading case of these developments. The book presents a detailed analysis of the industrial policy of Montagu Norman, governor of the Bank of England, in both its political and economic aspects. On the one hand, the Bank aspired to a directive and rationalizing role; on the other, it remained contained within its traditional framework of banking aims and objectives and a political outlook opposed to increased state action. Norman sought to encourage the development of coordinated action for industrial reorganization, but he wanted it to emerge from within the industry; he did not want to take on primary managerial or financial responsibility for it himself. In the event, the Bank found itself continually buffeted around as a third party in struggles between conflicting capitalist interests and was unable to utilize the potential power it had over the industry because of the weakness of its policy, institutions, and managerial capabilities. The banking sector, contrary to the traditional view, became intimately involved in the fate of key sectors of British industry, but the banks were unable to transform their financial powers into effective managerial control.

The problems that confronted the bankers also defeated the government. In Part III I argue that state action in the 1930s had an important impact on the outcome of efforts to restructure important sections of British industry. Most attempts to understand the increase of state intervention have interpreted it either as a vehicle of system-maintenance essentially functional for capitalism or as a series of unpatterned ad hoc interventions. The evidence presented here suggests that state action was both more sustained and more important than is often argued and that its effects were highly contradictory. For most of the 1920s successive governments shied away from responsibility for the reorganization of industry, but starting with the issue of the tariff and fiscal protection for ailing industries, the state followed the banks into the affairs of the steel industry in the 1930s. The government saw itself as the partisan of supramarket coordination and reconstruction, but in practice the policy makers sought to achieve this by establishing a collaborative relationship with the owners in the industry. In an industry so internally divided and conflict-ridden as steel, this inevitably meant compromise and developed into government support for industry-wide cartelization whereby owners sought to protect themselves from the rigors of the market. Despite its aims, the contribution of the state was to help freeze the industrial structure and foster defensive federations under a state umbrella rather than promoting change and restructuring. The government helped to reinforce the backward structure of the industry with a new layer of powerful institutions that embodied the existing structural problems rather than counteracted them. At the same time, the government played a major role in making possible the emergence of an organized and coherent corporate interest group from among the traditionally individualistic steelmakers which provided the basis for the effective and vigorous resistance to nationalization in the 1940s. Yet the government itself had contradictory economic, political, and social aims, and in addition to the areas of conflict and discontent in its relationship with industry there were also important developments that led to a new framework for cooperation between government and private industry.

The failure of banking and government actions highlights some intractable problems of the transition from market to corporate forms in a mature economy. Britain's traditional industries depended on a market that was breaking down. Yet the institutions that had the potential to intervene had been formed by the same historical developments that shaped the crisis in which they were intervening. Britain's early start and the long span and relatively slow pace of its industrial and commercial development had resulted in the development of particular political and financial—as well as managerial—institutions that were intimately connected to and as resistant to change as the structure of production itself. Consideration of the problems associated with restructuring and intervention leads outward from the particular industry to wider political and economic structures and raises questions of power relations and business politics as well as the issues of markets, demand, and choice of technique that more usually hold the center of the stage.

PART I

The Steel Companies in the Interwar Years

Market Environment, Industrial Structure, and Decision Making, 1918–1939

1.

Decision Making, Entrepreneurship, and the Theory of the Firm

Like the contemplation of imminent death, the study of the decline of the British economy has wonderfully concentrated the minds of economists and economic historians. In contrast, however, leading business historians have devoted their most intensive efforts to the study of the rise of large and successful companies and paid much less attention to the experience of crisis and decline that has been so prominent a feature of recent British industry.[1] At the same time, the accumulation of an impressive corpus of company biographies has had little input into wider analytic or theoretical concerns. It has proved difficult to widen the interpretative focus and relate the company to the wider economy, and historians have confined themselves to reiterating their conviction that entrepreneurship and corporate organization are major and systematic determinants of economic performance without being able to develop compelling explanatory models.[2] In part this is a result of the theoretical legacy that historians have generally drawn on, which, insofar as it goes beyond a simple empiricism, centers on hypotheses derived from neoclassical and Keynesian theories. Yet both of these theoretical traditions are notoriously weak on the issue of the firm.

In neoclassical equilibrium theory the firm does not really figure. As George Archibald put it, "In perfect competition, firms have so little to do . . . that there is nothing worthy of a separate title."[3] In fact, the neoclassical theory of the firm is only the inverse of the neoclassical theory of value and price: it assumes that businessmen strive to maximize money profits subject to the constraints of technology and the prevailing pattern of demand. The traditional theory turns the decision maker into a cipher for the hidden hand of the market. For business economists, therefore, if perfect knowledge and competition are assumed, questions about the actual behavior of particular firms become irrelevant and confusing and little more than "mere cataloguing."[4]

Yet neoclassical theory and its assumptions provide the foundations for the highly influential approach of New Economic Historians such as Donald McCloskey, Lars Sandberg, and Roderick Floud, whose work, especially on the reinterpretation of the late-nineteenth-century British economy, has dominated the scene for more than a decade. Although their focus has been on the "redemption" of late Victorian entrepreneurs, their methodology leaves little room for—and implicitly attributes little value to—the microeconomic study of individual enterprises. Their analyses of coal, steel, textiles, and engineering proceed primarily at the level of the aggregate sector, using total factor productivity indices to examine the hypothesis of failure. On this basis they have attacked the whole notion that there was any economically relevant failure or missed opportunities to be explained. They argue that, in general, British entrepreneurs pursued their comparative advantages and that growth was as fast as factor endowments allowed. In this context entrepreneurship is both everything and nothing. As McCloskey puts it, "In a competitive situation market resources tend to find their way into the hands of men with the best idea of how to use them,"[5] and, elsewhere, "in a competitive milieu, even a brief period of irrationality would be eroded by the expansion of better managed firms."[6] Clearly, against a background of such assumptions, the behavior of particular businesses is not a central concern: they constitute only the tendential operation of more fundamental processes.

But the validity of this methodology depends on certain crucial assumptions. The core of these is that every economic unit is a profit maximizer operating in conditions of atomistic competition, homogeneous products, transparent markets, free information, universal rationality, unitary decision-making structures, and free markets. However, as Stephen Nicholas has argued, once these assumptions are relaxed, the whole theoretical basis of the approach becomes fundamentally ragged and perhaps unsustainable.[7] In practice, the closed system of this old "high theory" has lacked conviction since it was disrupted fifty years ago under the impact of world depression and related theoretical shifts. The work of Piero Sraffa and others in the 1920s undermined many of the central tenets of the old orthodoxy,[8] and theoretical debates entered what Brian Loasby has called a prolonged "paradigm crisis" that is still with us in the theory of the firm.[9] The old theory was not adequate to cope with the problems of oligopoly, market segmentation, uncertainty, imperfect information, bounded rationality, and the multivariate preferences of actors that confronted it.[10]

Such perceived weaknesses of equilibrium analysis have not resulted in its abandonment, however. For some, like J. R. Hicks in the 1930s, confronted as he saw it by "the threatened wreckage of the greater part of general equilibrium theory," the only solution was for economists doggedly to continue to assume that competition is perfect. "At least," he noted, "this get-away seems well worth trying."[11] Others like Fritz Machlup have defended it as having a weakly predictive value for certain aspects of firms' behavior,[12] and Keynesian and marginalist theorists like Ronald Coase have attempted to deal with the inability of equilibrium theory to deal with the growth of firms over time. But, as Philip Andrews and Elizabeth Brunner have argued, they made little significant advance, because "despite all the grand passages in the General Theory where Keynes discusses the effect upon business affairs of the uncertainty which surrounds business operations, he yet, when it comes to the point, resolves that uncertainty into the formal equivalent of certainty."[13]

Three main lines of criticism of neoclassical theory relating to the firm particularly concern us here. In the work of George Shackle and Loasby equilibrium analysis has been rejected primarily because of its inability to take account of the environment of pervasive uncertainty and incomplete knowledge within which all economic decisions are made.[14] Parallel to this, behavioral and organizational theorists such as Herbert Simon, Robin Marris, Richard Cyert, and James March have focused on the area of discretion that monopoly or oligopoly power introduces into business decisions.[15] Some have emphasized that firms can pursue a variety of objectives, ranging from growth to "psychic income," whereas others have stressed the prevalence of "satisficing" policies. Like Shackle and Loasby, they stress the high costs of uncertainty in decision making in a partially known environment, particularly "information costs" and the problems of "bounded rationality." Oliver Williamson's "markets and hierarchies" paradigm is the most rigorous attempt to specify this approach in a quantifiable model: like the neoclassicists, he assumes rationality in the face of costs, but he expands the range of costs to include those of bounded rationality, imperfect information, and a whole range of "transaction costs." Different economic institutions have different patterns of costs and benefits. The classic instance is the role of transaction costs in determining the shifts from putting out to the factory system or from markets to managerial hierarchies.[16]

At first sight this approach appears to break away from the study of abstract markets and to open up new theoretical issues in the analysis of the firm. In fact, as M. Bauer and E. Cohen note, Williamson's theory simply slams the doors shut again.[17] Rather than exploring uncertainty, power, and preferences, he seeks to incorporate them into the neoclassical model by effectively substituting the minimization of transaction costs for the maximization of profits. He stresses that in the long run competition will restrict the pursuit of noneconomic goals and reduce the scope of economic institutions to a very restricted feasible range of choices. His work remains a variation on older forms of structural-functionalist equilibrium theory.[18]

All of these lines of approach, however, have directed attention away from the economy as a whole and toward the nature and characteristics of the decision-making agents and the importance of the institution of the firm. But it is the third line of criticism of traditional theory that has been most influential in the field of historical writing. This line of thought, which can arguably be traced back to the economics of Joseph Schumpeter, stresses the innovative role of entrepreneurship. Whereas in the neoclassical scheme firms are more or less powerless, Schumpeter argued that market and technical conditions are not given but rather are changed through innovative leaps by entrepreneurs who thus achieve "entrepreneurial profits" and drive other entrepreneurs to emulate them. The entrepreneurial function is central to the dynamics of growth and the course of business cycles under capitalism.[19]

Many historians who have attempted to trace the sources of British economic decline have had a similar model implicit in their work. Aldcroft, for instance, asserted that "changes in economic variables stem largely from entrepreneurial decisions"; he concentrated on analyzing the "entrepreneurial variable" largely in terms of the speed with which British entrepreneurs took up best-practice modern technological innovations (and on criticizing them for their failure to do so).[20] McCloskey quite correctly denounced this method for "[descending] to summary judgements of good and bad entrepreneurs the way the parody of schoolbook history chronicles Good and Bad Kings";[21] he insisted that technical changes and innovations should not be assessed as measures of performance in their own right but only in relation to demand conditions and the market they faced. McCloskey went on to argue that, in effect, little else was possible within the framework of the market and that British entrepreneurs could not be blamed for economic decline. More recently, however, William Lazonick has reconstructed the critique of British entrepreneurship in a more explicitly Schumpeterian framework: demand is something to be made as well as submitted to; markets may well constrain the feasibility of technical change, but markets themselves are susceptible to entrepreneurial action. Lazonick takes up the Schumpeterian distinction between "entrepreneurial" and "managerial" activity within the firm: managerial activity optimizes subject to market and technical constraints; entrepreneurial activity transforms the constraints. He goes on to argue that "British businessmen performed admirably as neo-classical managers: they took the conditions facing them as given and tried to do the best they could, subject to those constraints. As entrepreneurs, however, they failed precisely because as individualistic managers in a highly competitive and vertically specialized structure they were powerless to alter the organizational constraints that determined feasible technological choices and profitable opportunities."[22]

Lazonick's critique is greatly strengthened by his assimilation of the work of Alfred Chandler into his argument and because he shifts the focus from Aldcroft's concern with technology to wider questions of the organization of production. Chandler has argued persuasively that the key to the development of the modern American corporate economy was the supersession of the market by the visible hand of modern corporate organization. Administrative coordination permitted greater productivity, lower costs, and higher profits than could be achieved by coordination through the market. The corporation internalized what were previously market transactions and instead allocated funds and coordinated processes of production and distribution by administrative actions implemented by a professional managerial hierarchy.[23]

Lazonick and Bernard Elbaum have gone on to argue that the prolonged delay of British industry to move from the "competitive capitalist firm" to Chandler's "corporate capitalist firm" was at the root of the failure of so much of British industry to modernize effectively. In Germany, Japan, and the United States corporate capitalism developed based on oligopoly, managerial hierarchies, the vertical integration of production and distribution, direct managerial control of the labor process, and the integration of financial and industrial capital. But "Britain was impeded from making a successful transition to mass production and corporate organization in the twentieth century by an inflexible nineteenth century institutional legacy of atomistic economic organization."[24]

This view correctly maintains that the market does not automatically restructure production in response to competitive shifts as in neo-classical economics and that the structures within which decisions are taken play a vital intermediate role. The firm is a social phenomenon within which outcomes are determined by the interplay of complex forces and interests rather than a simple mechanism, and it is an important element in economic change. It is therefore right to pose the problem of whether firms could have changed the constraints they faced rather than simply obeying them. But there are also problems in applying the Chandlerian yardstick to evaluate the structural development of British enterprise, as a number of historians have done recently.[25]

Chandler himself takes a rather more cautious view of the implications of his work. In general terms he sees changing business organization as a functional response to market opportunities and technical change. The role of entrepreneurs is to devise suitable structures to take advantage of the changing environment of demand and available technology. The structure of organizations, therefore, usually follows from the strategic needs of the company, although the response may be delayed and/or inefficient depending on the quality of entrepreneurship. Structure follows strategy more or less quickly, and the speed of the change depends on how quickly opportunities that exist in the market are seized.[26] It is not clear to what extent Chandler believes that corporate structures could themselves transform the market. His paradigm is the convergence of modern corporate economies on the multidivisional form of company organization because, for him, the single high road to economic growth is mass production and distribution operating close to the frontier of new technology. The relative delay in the emergence of this form of organization in Britain is explained by the differences in markets and the related restriction of opportunity to develop mass production and distribution techniques. Hence, the lag in Britain is seen as a transition period.[27]

The convergence of capitalist economies toward a "Fordist" or mass production norm is being increasingly questioned,[28] and in any case it is apparent that in Britain such a transition spans a very long historical period. It is an open question whether British steel, motors, or engineering can or could emulate the course pursued by American mass manufacturing and mass marketing. And if it is not simply a question of different routes and different chronologies on the way to the same goal, we need a much more open-ended view of the role, limitations, and possibilities of business organization. Firms and industries are not simply subordinate to the market, although it is necessary to be wary of the more "voluntarist" notions of Schumpeterian economics. The determinants of their development are social and institutional as well as market and technical. A firm may as easily be "overcommitted" to certain ownership, financial, or political structures as to particular patterns of capital investment. As Barry Supple has put it: "Power as well as profit and efficiency, determines choice and . . . power relationships in business have proved more resistant to theoretical analysis than have profit orientations."[29]

I have noted the weaknesses of various theoretical approaches in coming to terms with these power relationships. The argument of this book is that the institutional structures of firms, banks, and government were crucial in shaping the development of the steel industry, and it attempts to provide a properly historical account of these forces in action and to describe the process of interaction of institutional structures with technical and market constraints. In Part I this interaction is examined by considering the market environment of the steel industry and the responses of three distinct subgroups of steel producers to this environment: what were the implications of the structures of ownership, management, and decision making for the course of development of the industry? In the later parts we shall analyze the impact of external institutional forces, the banks and the government, on these outcomes. In the course of these studies we are also attempting to shed light on the wider historical picture of the relationship between business organization, financial structures, and politics during a crucial period in the history of the British economy.

2.

The Economics of Steelmaking: Market Environment and Industrial Structure

Elements of decline and expansion were both present in the British steel industry in the interwar years.[1] During the period as a whole output increased and there was a marked shift to newer products; yet for most of the period the industry was characterized by features of depression and decline. Fluctuations in output and demand were sharp, exports stagnated, there was much excess capacity and high unemployment, and technical and structural weaknesses remained unchanged. But steel fed into both declining trades like shipbuilding and railways and rising trades like automobiles and new consumer goods. Opportunities for modernization and revived prosperity stood alongside structural deficiencies and problems of the world market that were outside the effective control of British firms or entrepreneurs. Options were limited, but steel was not yet in the grip of terminal decline.[2] This book focuses on how the internal dynamics and interaction of companies, banking institutions, and the government structured responses to options that existed; this chapter sketches the broad determinants of the context in which they operated.

World steel output had expanded at an average rate of 4% per annum with only moderate cyclical fluctuations during its long wave of expansion between 1880 and 1913. This expansion was closely linked to technical innovations, expanding demand, and the substitution of steel for wrought iron and new ore discoveries. But by 1900 the forces of innovation and substitution were nearly exhausted, and the continuation of expansion depended mainly on rising demand.[3]

In the interwar years there was no new technological impetus toward cost reduction in common-grade steelmaking to offset the lack of growing markets. After the 1880s no radically new techniques of production were pioneered. Technical changes were confined to two major categories. The first lay in the field of power generation, particularly in the areas of application of electric power to steel mills and to the development of complex systems of gas interchange and heat economies. The second area of innovation was adaptations of open-hearth practice in relation to varying configurations of raw material costs, notably the Talbot tilting furnace and the duplex process. But these changes probably had considerably less impact on overall productivity than the innumerable detailed changes introduced piecemeal over the period, especially those relating to materials handling, selection, and preparation: layout of plant; heat conservation; instrumentation and process control; and the use of coke-oven gas in the open-hearth furnace.[4]

This situation of relatively static demand, costs, and technology followed a long period of upswing and heavy capital investment, and overcapacity was an inevitable consequence once the interwar depression set in. The traditional mechanisms of competition could not effect rapid adjustment in industries like steel where capital invested in plant was heavy and the sensitivity of demand to changes in price was low. The aggregate steel output of the four major European producers did not move significantly above 1913 levels until 1937 in response to growing demand from the consumer goods sector and the enormous stimulus of European rearmament.[5]

In certain respects steel mirrored the general interwar stagnation of the European producer goods sector. Yet world steel as a whole did not stagnate in this period. Rather, European stagnation took place in the context of moderate long-term world steel growth. World production of steel grew by 75% from 1913 to 1937, but European production rose by only 35%. The major European steel producers were unable to capitalize on this channel for expansion because in these years most of the substantial extra-European consumers (United States, USSR, Canada, Japan, India, Australia, and South Africa) were able to develop largely self-sufficient steel industries by autarchic policies.[6] This was not because these industries could produce steel competitively with Europe; in fact, it is an indicator of the relative competitiveness of the European industries that they actually increased their share of the less developed markets at the expense of their largest non-European competitor, the United States, over this period (see Figure 1). Rather, steelmaking was undertaken in these countries because of broad political and geographical or geological determinants, and this development led to fundamental and possibly irreversible changes in the world steel economy. In the face of such a situation Britain could not regain its previous position in world steel trade whatever its competitive performance.

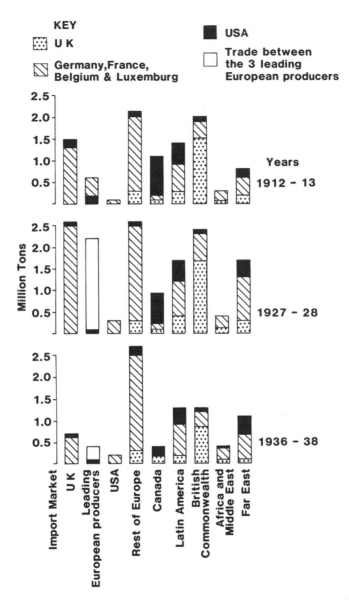

Figure 1 Relative shares of the world import market held by the leading producers in selected years, 1912–1938. *Source:* United Nations, *Statistics of World Trade in Steel, 1913–1959.*

Two main factors underlay this change. First, because the raw materials for steel are widespread and fairly easily accessible, changing
global patterns of procurement made possible the rise of new steel-
producing nations, either through using domestic resources, as in the
cases of India and Brazil, or on the basis of coastal locations and cheap
assembly of materials on a worldwide mineral market, as in the case
of Japan.[7] Seen in this context, Europe's primacy was historically
specific and vulnerable. Europe is not really a mineral-rich part of the
world. Europe west of the Urals has only one major rich iron ore
field—that of Swedish Lapland. The Jurassic ore fields of Germany,
Britain, and Lorraine are large, but their ores are lean and phosphoric.
Historically the European industries developed first because of the
conjunction of these ores with good (although in the long term limited) coking coals. Hence their capacity clustered around these coal/
ore fields, but later, from the interwar years on, their lack of sufficient
coastal locations prevented them from taking advantage of the richer
and more prolific resources available from the increasingly unified
world ore market.[8]

Second, more and more governments around the world were becoming willing and able to shoulder certain economic costs for the
strategic benefits of self-sufficiency in steel. In India, for instance, the
nascent steel industry was able to get off the ground when political
concessions by the British to the rising nationalist movement made
infant industry tariff protection possible. Aided by the political situation and by the willingness of local investors to accept lower rates
of return on their investments than European investors, the Tata Iron
& Steel Co. was able to establish itself, reduce its costs, and capture
73% of the Indian steel market by 1939.[9] Comparable developments
took place in Australia, South Africa, and Brazil.[10]

The pattern of development in these markets made world trade in
steel more static than the upward trend of world consumption might
suggest. Only the USSR emerged as a major new steelmaking nation
in this period. But several smaller nations such as India and Australia
were able to produce a considerable proportion of their own needs.
Meanwhile, the relative shares of the leading European producers in
the available world import market remained fairly steady. The only
major exception to this rule was the British import market: in the
1920s it was by far the world's largest unprotected market, and correspondingly much of the continental competitive effort was turned
in that direction. Belgium carved itself a particular niche in this unique
arena, supplying 60% of British semifinished and finished steel imports in the late 1920s and early 1930s.[11] Although Belgium expanded
its sales at the expense of British makers in that period, it suffered

most from the loss of this market in the 1930s. The export-dependent development of its steelmaking meant that Belgium was bypassed by the domestically based revivals of its more solidly based European competitors in the 1930s. The penetration of the British market in the 1920s did not reflect any clear long-term cost differentials, and with the establishment of tariffs the anomalous position was rapidly redressed. This is not to deny internal competitive weaknesses in the British steel industry but to stress that they were not out of proportion to those of Britain's major rivals. In fact, between the wars Britain had a more rapid rate of growth of overall steel production than its European competitors: between 1913 and 1936–37 total European output increased by only 36.5% (from 39.1 to 53.4 million tons), and that of Germany by 36.4% (from 14.3 to 19.5 million tons); British output increased by 61.5%, from 7.8 to 12.6 million tons.

The course of British growth was rather different. Britain's major export outlets were concentrated on the Commonwealth markets which, as Figure 1 shows, were stagnating in the 1920s but which did not collapse as dramatically as the key European outlets, namely Britain and its rival European producers' domestic markets, in the depression. This provided a significant element of export stability which many continental producers lacked. The continental producers, however, were favored by the expansion of imports to the south and east of Europe, which they dominated economically and politically. These markets were the most important areas for investment outside the British Empire and Latin America once the Russian market had been lost. But as Alice Teichova has shown, competition in this region was dominated by the rivalry between Anglo-French and German financial groups operating in a cartelized and restricted market in which political leverage often had greater impact on market shares than prices or efficiency.[12] Such political constraints reduced still further the gains to be made through direct competition for shares of the world market.

Britain in the 1920s could have gained a significantly enlarged outlet by closing its domestic market to imports: taking two-thirds of that production would have given Britain two million tons of production per annum worth some £16 million. Apart from that, even reversing the shares of "neutral" markets held by Britain and its competitors would not strikingly have increased potential output. As Figure 1 shows, reversing the British and German shares of these markets would give Britain only an additional 1.1 million tons in 1927–28. Overcapacity, protectionism, and the shifting structure of world markets combined progressively to marginalize the international steel trade between the wars.

In the 1920s this took the form of the breakdown of the high degree of uniformity between national and international prices that had existed before the First World War. Countries like Germany, which exported 30% of its output, employed sharp price differentiation between its home and export markets as a competitive weapon to maximize its outlets. From 1926 on it backed this up with cartelization and a series of bilateral agreements on reserved markets. This was followed by what Svennilson has called the "virtual abolition of the competitive market" for European steel during the crisis years of 1931–1933. Britain's abandonment of free trade provided the final cornerstone of this cartelization process. After joining the European cartel Britain could raise its domestic prices to the high levels of those of France and Germany; trade between cartel countries declined rapidly, and the flexibility of international trade between members virtually ended.[13] Shifts in distribution in the 1930s could only be won by bargaining within the cartel. The trade map became increasingly politically determined as government-industry cooperation became entrenched as a major feature of cartel operations. Cartel price policy was deliberately employed to prevent the further development of national steel industries outside their own domestic markets by dual pricing systems and "penetration" agreements.[14]

The upshot of this was that patterns of European steel development became almost totally dominated by the trajectory of the domestic economy. For Britain, whose world trade position in the nineteenth century was largely based on the international division of labor and mutual trade under the umbrella of her hegemonic political and informal imperialism, the implications were complex. As that system broke down, Britain suffered from its great specialization.[15] This meant that in the 1920s Britain failed to share fully in the world upswing of 1925–1929 because of the predominance of the old export staples in her economy. But the weakness of the upswing had its counterpart in the comparative moderation of Britain's slump.[16] The depression was based on the collapse of incomes in the primary producing countries and was transmitted to Britain via its export sector, a declining sector that was shedding investment, causing intense regional depression; at the same time, the impact was cushioned for the economy as a whole by the scissors movement of the terms of trade with the primary producing countries, which kept world commodity prices falling faster than the income of most employed workers.[17]

In the years before the First World War more than 40% of British steel production was exported each year, and through its use as the principal raw material for shipbuilding and engineering, British steel was even more involved in the world economy. Between 1910 and 1913 the value of British steel exports was four times that of its imports;

but by 1928–1931 exports were little more than double the value of imports, and by 1936–1938 exports had fallen to 12% of total steel production.[18] This trend implied a drastic reorientation. Contrary to the prognoses of most businessmen in the 1920s, British recovery did not depend on the revival of world trade but on the stimulus of the domestic economy and import substitution. Consequently, the iron and steel revival of the 1930s was based on three parallel movements: first, a shift from the international to the domestic market; second, a slow shift within that market toward finished and especially flat rolled products oriented toward the consumer rather than the producer sector; and third, the intense stimulus of rearmament to the older sectors. The second shift was of considerable importance, but it must be kept in perspective. The rise of flat products as a proportion of all steel products was considerably slower in Britain and Europe than in the United States. Indeed, in Europe as a whole, flat products as a proportion of all products were static from 1929 to 1938. The prewar dominance of automobile-related demand in the U.S. economy was a result of the very special conditions of demand on that continent.[19]

The contrast between the United States and the European product market lies behind the prolonged and difficult takeoff of new thin flat product technology in Britain from the 1930s to the 1950s. In Britain,

Table 1   Distribution of finished steel by markets, 1924–1937 (percentages)

Market	1924	1930	1935	1937
Shipbuilding and marine engineering	19.0	16.1	8.3	10.1
Building and constructional engineering	13.7	16.8	21.2	20.8
Mechanical engineering	16.0	15.0	13.5	14.3
Electrical engineering	2.1	2.2	2.8	2.8
Motors, cycles, and aircraft	3.8	5.0	6.9	7.0
Railways and rolling stock	12.3	10.3	9.4	9.2
Collieries	4.1	4.6	5.1	4.4
Hardware, holloware, etc.	7.2	9.1	10.5	9.5
Rivets, bolts, nuts, springs	8.2	8.2	7.8	7.6
Wire and wire manufactures	6.2	5.5	6.2	6.0
Others	7.4	7.2	8.3	8.3

Source: Ingvar Svennilson, *Growth and Stagnation in the European Economy* (Geneva: United Nations Economic Commission for Europe, 1954), table 70, p. 228.

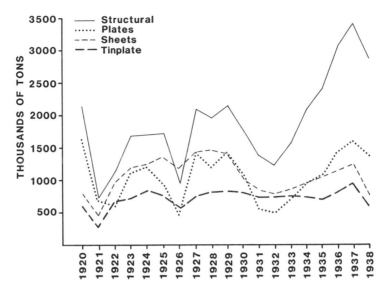

Figure 2 Comparative output of major finished steel products, 1920–1938. *Source:* BISF statistics.

the prominence of shipbuilding demand and its armament-based revival from the mid-1930s to the mid-1940s, together with the growth of constructional uses of steel, maintained continuity in demand patterns throughout the period. As Table 1 shows, the British product market remained fairly heterogeneous and above all lacked a really dynamic leading sector. There was not yet any equivalent to automobiles in the United States. In 1937 motors, cycles, and aircraft together accounted for only 7% of national output, less than the 9.5% accounted for by hardware and holloware. This demand provided a basis for significant development in sheet and tinplate but only in conjunction with a continuing export demand for these products. Nevertheless, the consumer goods sectors followed a rather different cyclical trajectory to the capital goods sectors in the interwar years, and the sheet, tinplate, and tube trades benefited as a result.

Within this framework the cyclical movements of steel demand and output are fairly clear. Output was at a peak in 1920, a reflection of the postwar boom, but it collapsed sharply in the slump of 1921 and recovered only slowly until 1924. The General Strike produced a very sharp fall in 1926, but the recovery that followed lasted until 1929 when output was again nearing its 1920 peak. This boom was then checked and the following downswing continued through 1930 to reach a nadir in 1931–32. When recovery began again, it was rapid:

Table 2   Percentage rates of profit[a] of selected steel companies, 1920–1938

Year	Dorman Long & Co.[b]		Bolckow Vaughan & Co.[b]		South Durham/ Cargo Fleet[b]		Consett Iron Co.[b]	
	(1)	(2)	(1)	(2)	(1)	(2)	(1)	(2)
1920	11.4	12.3	17.5	12.5	—	19.3	17.1	17.1
1921	4.9	5.0	9.6	7.6	—	7.0	10.2	10.2
1922	1.9	1.6	−0.8	−2.1	—	4.8	−3.0	−3.0
1923	2.3	2.0	−4.0	−13.0	10.7	12.6	4.9	5.3
1924	4.2	3.7	−0.4	−6.8	8.0	4.8	8.4	9.5
1925	1.9	−0.7	−1.5	−4.8	5.4	2.3	3.5	2.9
1926	−1.4	−5.5	−0.4	−3.5	−0.6	−5.4	−2.3	−8.2
1927	2.2	0.5	2.3	0.8	5.1	−1.5	−0.6	−5.3
1928	2.9	0.4	2.7	1.2	7.5	6.8	5.0	4.3
1929	3.6	1.5	—	—	7.1	3.1	5.2	4.7
1930	2.9	0.2	—	—	6.4	0.8	7.8	9.1
1931	2.4	−2.5	—	—	5.3	1.4	4.8	3.9
1932	0.9	−4.6	—	—	—	—	1.0	−2.5
1933	1.3	1.5	—	—	—	—	1.5	−1.7
1934	3.0	1.1	—	—	—	—	3.2	1.2
1935	—	—	—	—	—	—	—	7.5
1936	13.5[f]	—	—	—	7.4[f]	—	9.6[f]	11.4[f]
1937	—	—	—	—	—	—	—	—
1938	—	—	—	—	—	—	—	—

by 1934, 1929 levels were again being reached and by 1937 new record levels of output were being achieved. Output fell off temporarily in 1938, but the trend was upward and this was confirmed with the onset of the Second World War.

A disaggregation of this overall picture by products, as shown in Figure 2, shows considerable differential movements within this pattern of output. The heavy steel products fell sharply from their 1920 peak, and both plates and structural steel oscillated in tandem at quite low levels throughout the 1920s, recovering somewhat toward 1929. But in the trough of the early 1930s plates fell to a greater extent, and after 1934 the two products diverged notably when structural steel, benefiting from a wider variety of demand including house and factory building, boomed dramatically. By 1937 structural output was double the 1920 peak whereas plate output even in 1937 never re-

Table 2, continued

Year	United Steel Companies Ltd.[c]		Stewarts & Lloyds[d]	Richard Thomas & Co.[d]		Guest Keen and Nettle- folds Ltd.[d]
	(1)	(2)	(2)	(1)	(2)	(2)
1920	—	8.4	14.4	—	10.2	8.4
1921	—	5.2	18.0	—	5.7	7.2
1922	—	−3.2	12.8	—	4.9	4.9
1923	—	2.7	11.2	—	6.3	7.4
1924	—	2.8	8.7	—	7.2	7.0
1925	—	0.4	5.4	—	3.8	7.6
1926	—	−1.5	3.5	—	0.1	7.6
1927	—	−3.4	8.2	—	0.1	7.3
1928	—	−2.9	7.5	—	0.7	7.7
1929	—	−0.5	9.1	—	0.4	7.6
1930	—	—	—	—	—	—
1931	—	0.7	—	—	—	—
1932	—	3.1	—	—	—	—
1933	—	5.8	—	—	—	—
1934	—	15.8	—	—	—	—
1935	—	18.6	—	—	—	—
1936	12.6[f]	15.8[f]	—	9.6[f]	—	—
1937	—	—	—	—	—	—
1938	—	—	—	—	—	—

gained its 1920 level. Within heavy steel overall these trends are damp- ened down by a third product, rails (not shown on the graph), which maintained a steady low demand in the 1920s but did not share in the recovery of the 1930s. The 1937 output of rails and sleepers was still below the average for that product in the mid-1920s.[20]

The lighter products, sheet and galvanized steel, which reached only half the plate output at the peak of 1920, grew steadily through- out the 1920s in contrast to the depressed plate sector and went through only a moderate trough in the early 1930s. Between 1922 and 1935 sheet and galvanized output never fell significantly below that of plates. The cycle was much more moderate, but correspondingly sheet did not expand as dramatically in the 1930s, and from 1935 plates again began to move ahead. Tinplate likewise had a fairly gentle rising trend. After some expansion in the early 1920s it was charac-

Table 2, continued

Year	Baldwin's Ltd.[d] (1)	(2)	Forty-three selected companies[e] (2)	Fourteen largest steel firms[f]	All steel industry[g]
1920	—	12.0	—	—	9.9
1921	—	5.8	—	—	7.9
1922	—	1.7	—	—	6.6
1923	—	3.7	—	—	8.5
1924	—	3.8	—	—	7.5
1925	—	−0.1	—	—	4.7
1926	—	0.8	1.9	—	3.6
1927	—	−1.2	2.9	—	4.6
1928	—	0.1	3.1	—	5.3
1929	—	1.0	3.3	—	5.6
1930	—	—	4.4	—	6.8
1931	—	—	2.4	—	4.5
1932	—	—	1.8	—	3.7
1933	—	—	2.6	—	4.6
1934	—	—	4.3	—	6.9
1935	—	—	5.4	—	8.3
1936	11.2[f]	—	—	10.5[f]	10.5
1937	—	—	—	—	13.2
1938	—	—	—	—	11.9

Sources: See footnotes b through i.

a. Because the return on long-term debt and preference stock does not fall when profits fall, the fluctuation in the rate of return on shareholders' assets is greater than that on net assets. (1) Income from trading divided by year-end book value of net assets (equal to book value of shareholders' capital, ordinary and preference, plus book value of long-term loans and debentures). (2) Rate of return on ordinary shareholders' assets. This is identical to the rate of profit on net assets except that interest on long-term debt and preference capital is subtracted from the profit figure and the book value of these items is subtracted from the assets figure.

b. Company records.

c. Philip W. S. Andrews and Elizabeth Brunner, *Capital Development in Steel: A Study of the United Steel Companies Ltd.* (Oxford University Press, 1952).

terized by a long flat output plateau which barely wavered in the slump but hardly increased in the 1930s until a marked acceleration took place in 1936–37.

Movements in profits corresponded closely with these movements. The figures for the profit rates of major companies given in Table 2

Table 2, continued

Year	All manufacturing industry[h]	Steel gross profit index numbers[i]	Benchmarks for annual gross profit in industry (£m)[e]
1920	7.6	102	—
1921	6.8	65	—
1922	10.2	44	—
1923	11.1	54	—
1924	11.4	46	—
1925	11.6	26	—
1926	11.4	18	—
1927	12.5	36	11.44
1928	12.7	34	—
1929	13.2	45	—
1930	13.0	38	—
1931	12.1	24	—
1932	10.3	24	7.31
1933	11.6	37	—
1934	13.7	64	—
1935	15.4	78	—
1936	16.4	100	23.87
1937	16.2	—	—
1938	15.1	—	—

d. *Stock Exchange Official Intelligence* and *Wheeler's Company Tables.*

e. Ronald H. Coase, R. S. Edwards, and R. F. Fowler, *The Iron and Steel Industry, 1926–1935: An Investigation Based on the Accounts of Published Companies* (London and Cambridge Economic Service, Special Memorandum no. 49).

f. See Table 19.

g. Figures for the rate of profit of all iron and steel industry calculated from gross profit/first cost value of all fixed assets in current prices. From P. E. Hart and J. E. Bates, *Studies in Profit, Business Saving and Investment in the U.K.*, 2 vols. (Cambridge University Press, 1965–1968), II, 274.

h. Hart and Bates, *Studies*, II, 231.

i. Hart and Bates, *Studies*, I, 81.

are somewhat fragmentary, but they clearly suggest the overall swings and the differing experiences of various sectors of the industry. Particularly noticeable are the rather different profit records of companies such as Richard Thomas, Stewarts and Lloyds, and GKN, which specialized in the more highly finished tinplate, tube, and wire-based products, from those of the other companies, which were primarily centered on heavy steel products. (For details of the size of these concerns see Table 4).

As Table 2 shows, the relationship of financial structure to profit swings was vital. The sharper fluctuations of column (2) in relation to column (1) show how high gearing could accentuate profits crises. Firms with high levels of fixed interest were vulnerable to collapse but those with more flexible capital structures could sit out depressions with a degree of comfort.

There were opportunities for successful growth in the lighter products, but even so the path ahead was by no means clear and easy; in the heavy products the situation was more problematic but there was a fair degree of resilience in the trade. In both sectors the fairly sharp cyclical movements made it hard to see a clear way forward. In this context capital investment at the right time was of immense importance, and mistiming or the inability to invest because of financial burdens could be decisive. Despite its problems, steel was still an industry with important future prospects for growth and development, but the paths to success remained rather uncertain.

Against this background of a fluctuating and segmented market with limited overall growth, there was only a weak tendency toward increased industrial concentration between the wars. Table 3 shows the changing patterns of industrial concentration. Table 4 shows the share of total output of the firms producing 80% of that output in 1920, 1929, and 1937, the peak years of each cycle. Output is a good indicator of the relative weight of firms within a sector. Capitalization is notoriously deceptive because it is not necessarily related to current performance or productive strength.[21]

The tables deal only with *steel ingot* output. It must be stressed that most firms produced steel only as part of a wider range of products, and this table shows not the absolute size of firms but only the size of the steel sector of their business. Firms like the armaments concerns, Vickers, John Brown, Beardmore, and Cammell Laird, had enormous power and resources in other areas even though they were only medium-sized steel producers. In addition, many of the other firms were major coal and iron producers—notably Dorman Long, United Steel, Bolckow Vaughan, Consett, Richard Thomas, and Partington—and there was a wide divergence in the extent to which the various firms carried the further processing of their steel. Value of output of all finished and semifinished steel products leaving the firm might be a better indicator, but the figures are not available.[22]

The first year chosen (1920) represents a date at the end of a period

Table 3 Concentration in steel, 1920, 1929, and 1937

Year	Percentage of total output			Number of firms producing 80% of total output
	Top three firms	Top five firms	Top ten firms	
1920	25.9	36.4	57.5	34
1929	28.5	38.2	57.2	27
1937	36.4	47.0	67.9	17

Source: Table 4.

of significant change in concentration. In 1913 the share of the three largest firms (Colvilles, Dorman Long, and South Durham and Cargo Fleet at that time) was only about 17% as against 25.9% in 1920, and of the top five (Steel, Peech and Tozer plus John Summers in addition) less than 25% as against 36.4% in 1920.[23] The three largest firms of 1920 and the Guest, Keen & Nettlefolds Ltd. (GKN)/John Lysaght & Co. combination (which is the fifth) were all products of the wave of growth and amalgamation of the war and postwar years. But in the static market that followed this rapid expansion, the larger firms were unable to realize significant economies of scale or organization and tended to be outpaced by smaller units during the next fifteen years. Concentration increased only marginally in the 1920s. In fact, the share of output of the top firms was maintained only by mergers. No size-class enjoyed a clearly better performance than the others. Within the broad middle band of firms performances were very uneven: some firms closed down, others increased their share, depending on their particular local or sectoral conditions.

Concentration increased more markedly in the 1930s, and over the period as a whole the share of the top three firms increased from a quarter to a third and of the top ten from a half to two-thirds. In both decades a number of moderate- to small-size firms were eliminated, although the broad slowly flattening base of smaller firms persisted strongly. But of the fourteen firms of the 1920 top thirty-six that disappeared by 1937, only three closed down altogether and broke up their plants. The other eleven all went out as part of mergers. Three of the disappearances are accounted for by the creation of the English Steel Corporation out of the de-merger of the steel sections of several armaments combines and their recombination. Likewise, Partington disappeared into the Lancashire Steel Corporation out of the breakup of the vertical Armstrong Whitworth combine. These four exits took place in the late 1920s.[24] The rest are accounted for by

Table 4 Industrial concentration in steel: size of firms by output (in thousands of tons of steel ingots per annum), 1920, 1929, and 1937

1920		1929		1937	
Firm	Output	Firm	Output	Firm	Output
David Colville and Sons	829	United Steel Companies Ltd.	1,112	United Steel Companies Ltd.	1,675
Dorman Long & Co.	780	Dorman Long & Co.	941	Colvilles Ltd.	1,556
United Steel Companies Ltd.	745	David Colville and Sons	698	Dorman Long & Co.	1,500
South Durham Steel and Iron Co./Cargo Fleet Iron Co.	550	Guest Keen and Nettlefolds Ltd./John Lysaght & Co.	498	Guest Keen Baldwins Ltd.	692
Guest Keen and Nettlefolds Ltd./John Lysaght & Co.	400	Richard Thomas & Co.	441	Richard Thomas & Co.	675
John Summers & Sons	360	South Durham Steel & Iron Co.	413	Stewarts & Lloyds Ltd.	652
Steel Company of Scotland Ltd.	297	English Steel Corporation Ltd.	400	South Durham Steel & Iron Co.	630
Bolckow Vaughan & Co.	280	John Summers & Sons	380	John Summers & Sons	630
Baldwin's Ltd.	220	Stewarts & Lloyds Ltd.	330	English Steel Corporation Ltd.	430
Richard Thomas & Co.	205	Consett Iron Co.	300	Lancashire Steel Corporation Ltd.	382
Consett Iron Co.	200	Baldwin's Ltd.	270	Consett Iron Co.	360
Stewarts & Lloyds Ltd.	193	Steel Company of Scotland Ltd.	249	Guest Keen and Nettlefolds Ltd./John Lysaght & Co.	360
Ebbw Vale Steel, Iron & Coal Co.	180	Lancashire Steel Corporation Ltd.	180	Barrow Hematite Steel Co.	254
Cammell Laird & Co.	180	Park Gate Iron & Steel Co.	150	Park Gate Steel & Iron Co.	200
Lanarkshire Steel Co.	164	Round Oak Co.	140	Round Oak Co.	150
Partington Iron & Steel Co.	150	Skinningrove Iron Co.	135	Thomas Firth & Sons and John Brown Ltd.	140
Park Gate Iron & Steel Co.	150	Thomas Firth & Sons and John Brown Ltd.	130	Partridge Jones & John Paton Ltd.	130
Alfred Hickman Ltd.	140	Llanelly Steel Company (1907) Ltd.	120		

Skinningrove Iron Co.	132	Lanarkshire Steel Co.	119	Llanelly Steel Company (1907) Ltd.	130
Vickers Ltd.	120	Patent Shaft & Axletree Co.	110	Hadfields Ltd.	120
Palmer's Shipbuilding & Iron Co.	120	James Dunlop & Co.	110	Patent Shaft & Axletree Co.	120
Llanelly Steel Company (1907) Ltd.	110	William Beardmore & Co.	110	Baldwin's Ltd.	110
William Beardmore & Co.	110	Hadfields Ltd.	100	Skinningrove Iron Co.	100
Patent Shaft & Axletree Co.	100	Partridge Jones & John Paton Ltd.	100	William Beardmore & Co.	100
Round Oak Co.	100	Barrow Hematite Steel Co.	93	Briton Ferry Steel Co, Ltd.	100
Blaenavon Iron & Steel Co.	100	Bynea Steel Works Ltd.	80	Bynea Steel Works Ltd.	90
Barrow Hematite Steel Co.	100	Briton Ferry Steel Co. Ltd.	80	Others	1,698
James Dunlop & Co.	95	Glasgow Iron & Steel Co.	80	Total	12,984
Grovesend Steel & Tinplate Co.	95	Others	1,777		
John Brown & Co.	90	Total	9,636		
Partridge Jones & John Paton Ltd.	90				
Bynea Steel Works Ltd.	90				
Briton Ferry Steel Co. Ltd.	90				
Glasgow Iron & Steel Co.	80				
Hadfields Ltd.	80				
Taylor Bros.	70				
Others	1,622				
Total	9,067				

Source: Company and Bank of England records.

Scottish reorganization in the 1930s with three exceptions. Two of them, Hickman and Grovesend, were strategic acquisitions by Stewarts & Lloyds and Richard Thomas respectively in the relatively expanding tube and tinplate sectors, the first largely to acquire a site and raw materials, the second to incorporate a small but dynamic competitor.[25] Only one merger, that of Dorman Long and Bolckow Vaughan, was a merger of major steel-producing rivals in an attempt to restructure and strengthen their competitive position.[26] The exit pattern demonstrates the rigidity of the industrial structure: reshaping was a slow process of attrition.

The persistence of a considerable number of firms does not mean that there was a competitive framework, however. Two main features increased the oligopolistic nature of the industry: regional and product segmentation. Thus in particular finished products there were far fewer firms. The largest ingot producer in the three sample years never produced more than 13% of national output, but in tinplate, for example, Richard Thomas increased its share of capacity from 22% to 49% between 1920 and 1939;[27] in tubes, Stewarts & Lloyds produced 72% of national output in 1932;[28] Lysaght produced 90% of high quality autobody sheet in the early 1930s;[29] Summers held 30% of national sheet steel output in the early 1930s;[30] and the Lancashire Steel Corporation dominated the market of certain wire products.[31] In these trades an undertow of expansion throughout the period facilitated concentration and technical change. But although important, they were only a limited part of national steel production; sheet, tinplate, wire, and tubes made up 28% of all finished steel in 1920, rising to 36% in 1937.[32]

Although the level of industrial concentration was highest in these sectors, the extent of monopoly power that this situation permitted was still limited. In tinplate, for instance, the persistence of foreign imports of semifinished steel combined with a long tail of small producers in the industry to exert strong potential downward pressure on prices. A considerable degree of informal cartelization restricted this in times of good trade, but cut-throat undercutting was common in slumps, and few cartelization attempts survived these periods. Richard Thomas & Co. was able to establish a position of dominance only by buying up small firms to reduce overcapacity—a task that was considerably eased when the small firms lost their access to cheap imported steel after the imposition of tariffs—and by introducing strip mill production, the major technological innovation of the interwar years.[33]

Elements of monopoly pricing are to be found in Lysaght's autobody steel sheet in the 1930s and in the tube industry, where Stewarts

& Lloyds dwarfed all its competitors. However, in all these trades high profits often drew other firms into those products—although problems of specialization, skill, and resources presented considerable barriers. Stewarts & Lloyds' tube monopoly power, for instance, was strongly bolstered by the scarcity of British producers of basic Bessemer steel, the grade of steel best suited to tubemaking.[34] With regard to Lancashire Steel's wire production and Summers' sheet trade, specialization and fairly limited markets meant that rivals preferred if possible to enter those trades through merger to acquire going knowledgeable concerns than to break in from the outside as complete newcomers.[35]

The product range of the British steel trade was, however, dominated by plates, rails, and structural steel. Their share of total production declined from 66% in 1920 to 58% in 1937—although plates declined more sharply, from 25% to 17%, whereas structural products rose slightly, from 32% in 1920 to 35% in 1937. In both cases the 1937 figure represented a considerable recovery after the slump of 1932.[36] In these sectors the pattern of competition and monopoly was rather different. Regionalization of production and demand was most intense, and in ship plates in particular customer linkages were of considerable importance: 73% of all plates were produced in Scotland and the Northeast Coast mainly for the local markets, and a similar proportion of structural steel was made in Scotland, the Northeast, and the Midlands.[37] As we shall see below, interregional competition was rare, and within districts direct price competition for markets was spasmodic, although when it came—as in the plate trade in the Northeast in the late 1920s—it could be fierce.[38] Generally, however, the division of the regional market between producers was fairly rigid. Prices were kept up somewhat against the downward pressure exerted by imports and overcapacity by a limited amount of price fixing, agreements with customers, and rebate schemes. This flexibility was possible because low profits and high capital costs were an effective barrier to potential entrants at least until the mid-1930s. Meanwhile, the oligopolistic features of the regional markets enabled most firms to resist competitive elimination by their larger rivals over very long periods.

In most sectors of steel production no firm enjoyed clear advantages of scale economies or lower costs based on technical leads. Competition always loomed in the background, and overcapacity was a constant pressure on prices. Market segmentation and a regime of self-regulation, however, enabled most firms in most major products to avoid life-and-death struggles because the costs of driving tenacious rivals out of the market could be high, whereas the alternative of buying them up was slow, and, except in tinplate, seemed to confer only uncertain future strategic advantages.[39] In Scotland, for instance, Colvilles for a long time felt that advantages were to be gained from merging with competitors to reduce competition and secure a larger share of the market during the slump. But in a period of expansion they expected to be able to develop more efficiently as an independent enterprise without having to deal with the problems of a rather disparate collection of assets which they would incorporate from other firms in an amalgamation.[40] Similar conditions underlay market stasis elsewhere in the heavy steel sector as well.

The segmentation of the market for steel had been crucially reinforced by the pre–First World War "Indian summer" of widening world demand for Britain's narrow range of products. High profits in the traditional sectors of armaments and shipbuilding reinforced further widening of capital in the old products, discouraged diversification, and encouraged steelmakers to forge links with other industries, usually in the same region and usually with the same cyclical demand pattern. In Scotland integration was with shipbuilding, in the Northeast with coal, in South Wales with coal, and in the Northwest with shipbuilding and armaments. Only in Sheffield and the Midlands was broader regional diversification possible. The problem of transition from old to new industries in Britain was a regional one as well as one of a transfer of capital. Hence, for instance, Stewarts & Lloyds' specialization in tubes was accompanied by migration from Scotland to Corby in Northamptonshire.[41]

Thus most of the diversifying links that were made actually accentuated existing problems. For firms involved in coal or shipbuilding or armaments, the downturn and losses were often even greater than in steel alone. One result was the process of de-merger of the armaments combines that led to the formation of the English Steel Corporation and the Lancashire Steel Corporation as separate steelmaking firms in the 1920s, the most notable shift in interindustry linkages connected with steel in the interwar years.[42] But even where large combines attempted to diversify into less closely related industries, success was problematic: Armstrong Whitworth's lack of a wide range of managerial skills led to ill-planned diversification and disaster;[43] Beardmore's venture into automobiles failed;[44] and Vickers' Wolseley venture was unsuccessful, although its involvement in electrical manufacturing brought more rewards.[45]

More feasible was "growing" from steel into other more highly finished products with potential expanding markets, but few of these existed and there were barriers to entry from regionalization, skills, and inadaptability of technology. Even firms that looked toward these sectors often had to buy up several smaller interests to obtain a market share, and this diversification was itself limited: Richard Thomas went into tinplate but not into cans, Stewarts & Lloyds into tubes but not into oil, motors, or engineering. GKN was more successful in offsetting declining steel profits by moving further into fabrication work, but GKN was a different sort of firm, a loose confederation with little internal integration achieving greater stability through a financial center holding a diverse portfolio of interests. It did not achieve many organizational economies but did spread its risks, although the firm was never really able to coordinate its investment policy. Its steel business behaved no differently from that of other steel firms, although the impact of its fortunes on its owners was modified.[46]

Thus steel was marked by elements of both competition and monopoly. The segmentation of markets by region, product, customer linkages, and specializations underlay the weak increase in concentration in the interwar years. This halfway-house structure of the industry was mirrored in the penalties of overcommitment and excess capacity within firms. Few firms were low-cost producers although many of them owned a number of best-practice and low-cost units, works, or plants. These, however, were combined with a mixed array of plants of other vintages with widely varying costs. As Tables 5 and 7 show, the cost of manufacturing steel ingots varied by more than 25% between different plants owned by multiplant concerns such as Richard Thomas and United Steel.

Part of the explanation for this situation lies in the intensely cyclical chronology of plant construction. Plants were constructed under certain configurations of technical knowledge, but factor prices and subsequent exogenous changes over time could make that technology less appropriate. Nevertheless, it could not be changed until the next cycle of new and replacement investment. In a depressed industry the rate of replacement investment was bound to be slower than in an expanding one, and the age of capital higher,[47] especially because best-practice plant was invariably larger scale and thus required a proportionately higher share of the market. For heavy steel between the wars one of these swings ended abruptly in 1920 and the next did not begin until 1934–1937. In sheet and tinplate, where the upswing to 1920 had been less sharp and where the downturn was more gradual, the date of plant obsolescence was relatively earlier which together with the availability of new technology provided the possibility of a much more drastic wave of replacement in the late 1930s.

Hence for most of the steel industry there was an interim period of fourteen years when the main relevant factor was the savings that could be made from modifications within the existing boundaries of

Table 5 Actual and obtainable costs of production of steel ingots in various regions, 1929 (£.s.d.)

Region/works	Actual cost	Optimum works	Obtainable cost
Lincolnshire			
United Steel: Appleby-Frodingham (open hearth)	79s. 2d.	Fully modernized Appleby-Frodingham/Redbourn plant utilizing some existing plant (basic Bessemer)	65s. 2d.
Richard Thomas: Redbourn (open hearth)	109s. 6d./92s. 1d.	New best-practice plant (basic Bessemer)	60s. 10d.
		Estimate for a program of remodeling and one new furnace	86s. 1d.
South Wales			
GKN: Dowlais (basic Bessemer)	99s. 10d.	New best-practice plant at Cardiff (open hearth)	69s. 1d.
GKN: Cardiff (open hearth)	105s. 6d.		
Baldwin's: Port Talbot (open hearth)	107s. 2d.		
Richard Thomas: Llanelly	93s. 9d.		
Richard Thomas: Cwmfelin	96s. 10d.		
Richard Thomas: Grovesend	90s. 2d.		
Richard Thomas: Bryngwyn	92s. 3d.		
Richard Thomas: Duffryn	90s. 1d.		

Location / Company	Description		
Northeast Coast			
Dorman Long, Cleveland (open hearth)	Cost after modernization and concentration of output in Dorman Long/Cargo Fleet merger (Cleveland)	93s. 4d.	88s. 7d.
Dorman Long, Acklam (open hearth)	As above (Redcar)	87s. 3d.	84s. 4d.
Dorman Long, Redcar (open hearth)	As above (Cargo Fleet)	91s. 2d.	82s. 7d.
Cargo Fleet		88s. 10d.	
South Durham, West Hartlepool (open hearth)		87s. 8d.	
Scotland			
D. Colville & Sons, Clydebridge	New best-practice plant at tidewater location	98s. 6d.	82s. 9d.
Stewarts & Lloyds, Clydesdale		102s. 3d.	
Staffordshire			
Shelton Iron & Steel Co. (open hearth)		79s. 8d.	
Northants			
Stewarts & Lloyds: Hickmans	New best-practice plant at Corby (basic Bessemer)	93s. 5d.	53/10
	As above (open hearth)		60/5
Lancashire			
Partington Iron & Steel Co. (open hearth)	Estimated costs for completion of Partington modernization scheme (open hearth)	105s.	84s. 6d.

Table 5, continued

Northwest Coast			
United Steel: Workington (basic Bessemer)	92s.	New best-practice plant at Workington (basic Bessemer)	66s. 6d.
United Steel: Workington (open hearth)	110s.	As above (open hearth)	85s.
		Existing Basic Bessemer plant with new Blast Furnaces and coke-ovens	80s.
Sheffield			
United Steel: Templeborough	102s. 1d.	As above (open hearth)	98s. 4d.
		New best-practice plant at United Steel Templeborough (open hearth)	82s. 1d.

Sources:

Lincolnshire: H. A. Brassert, Report on the Properties and Operations of the United Steel Companies Ltd., 9 Sept. 1929, SMT 2/153; H. A. Brassert and Co., Report on the Redbourn Iron and Steel Works of Richard Thomas & Co., 18 Oct. 1929, RT company records; H. Bond to H. A. Brassert, 30 Aug. 1929, RT, Blast Furnaces (general file, company records). Two figures are given for Redbourn. The higher is Brassert's based on actual current costs. The plant was, however, working only irregularly at this time. The lower figure is Bond's and is the cost he claimed could be achieved with the existing plant if it were to work regularly.

South Wales: P. Rintoul, Report on Proposals to Reorganize the plants of British (GKB) Iron and Steel Co., 13 March 1931; P. Rintoul, Comparison of Actual Costs with Estimated Costs of New Plant at Cardiff, 1931, SMT 3/168; Richard Thomas, Cost Sheets (company records).

Northeast Coast: Agreed Merger Costings, 1932, DL company records. These figures are derived from the 1932 figures. There were no significant changes in plant or production policy from 1929 to 1932 at the works concerned. Hence, it is reasonably accurate to deflate the 1932 figures by the changes in the costs of raw materials using Tew's index for raw materials prices as a basis. The resulting figures may be slightly low. Brassert, in assessing the Scottish scheme, referred to an average cost of ingots at all Dorman Long works in 1929 as 95s/2d. However, this confirms the general order of magnitude. For Tew's index see Brian Tew, "Costs, Prices and Investment in the British Iron and Steel Industries, 1924–37," Ph.D. diss., Cambridge University, 1940. Movements of average prime costs of production per unit output of steel, 1924-1937, table XXX, appendix E, pp. 466–468; for Brassert, see Comparative Statement of Costs of Production, BID 6/4.

Scotland: H. A. Brassert, Report to Lord Weir of Eastwood on the Manufacture of Iron and Steel, 16 May 1929, SL company records. For Clydebridge, see Report by Moores, Carson, and Watson on Clydebridge Manufacturing, 21 Dec. 1932, appendixes 2 and 4; and Clydebridge cost sheets, in file on Mr. Craig (Stewarts & Lloyds), Dec. 1932, DCS company records. (Clydebridge worked on 15% imported pig iron, 10% cast iron scrap, and 70% steel scrap.)

Staffordshire: P. Rintoul, Comparison of Actual Costs, 1931, SMT 3/168.

Northants: Proposals of Stewarts & Lloyds for Steel Manufacture in Northamptonshire as Basis for Reorganization of British Tube Industry, June 1931, SL company records.

Lancashire: H. A. Brassert, Report on Lancashire Steel, SMT 2/154. For Partington, see Notes on Evidence of J. Frater Taylor to Sankey Committee, 21 March 1930, CR(IS)74, CAB 58/129.

Northwest and Sheffield: H. A. Brassert, Report on the Properties and Operations of the United Steel Companies Ltd., 9 Sept. 1929, SMT 2/153. (Templeborough worked on cold pig iron from Workington and Appleby-Frodingham.) H. A. Brassert, Report on the rationalisation of the iron and steel industry in the North-West and Midlands, 11 Oct. 1930, SMT 2/159.

the productive unit. The flow of these modifications was continuous, and their cumulative effects could be very significant. But all such changes were by their nature short-term and limited by the nature of the equipment to be modified and its complex interrelatedness to other plant.[48]

The structure of plant at the end of the postwar boom was badly skewed. Most recent modernization had been concentrated at the steel rather than the ironmaking end of production, and integration and complementarity were poor. Much more spending was still needed when the boom collapsed. Thereafter patching was always patching an inadequate structure. Best-practice units in mixed vintage plants necessarily performed below potential, yet full modernization was prohibitively expensive.

Even during expansionary waves investment in new capacity came in sudden increments, whereas demand expanded more slowly. Earnings and profits from that new investment depended not so much on its potential technical economies but on the speed and extent to which the plant could be operated at its full planned capacity. In the 1920–1934 period contemporary estimates were that new integrated plant would generally have to operate at more than 80% of its capacity to cover new interest and depreciation and to realize the same rate of profit as existing plant could achieve at 40% capacity.[49] Yet in the 1920s few firms were able to work near that capacity in *any* year. National steel capacity utilization fell to as low as 30% in 1921 and 1927 and was 60% or below in 1922 and 1925 and around 70% in 1923–1924 and 1927–1928. The only time it neared 80% was in 1929, and thereafter it plunged abruptly again.[50] The position of heavy steel was even worse: in the relatively good year of 1924, only 27% of national rail capacity, 48% of plate capacity, and 45% of joist and angle capacity were utilized. The highest regional utilization of capacity for these products was 36% for rails, 62% for plates, and 46% for joists and angles, all in the Northeast.[51]

In this situation of excess capacity the relationship between technical best-practice and low-cost production was often sundered. Tables 5, 6, and 7 show the actual and obtainable costs at different works in various regions in 1929. The actual costs are based on works records and the forecasts on reliable estimates by engineering consultants. They reveal a considerable spectrum of costs and a major gap between costs being achieved and those that theoretically could be obtained. But this is deceptive. Costs rise sharply as capacity operation falls. The actual current costs given in the tables are for firms working between 65 and 80% capacity utilization, whereas the engineering estimates for obtainable costs assume 90% utilization. The gap

Table 6 Actual and obtainable costs of production of pig iron in various regions, 1929 (£.s.d.)

Region/works	Actual cost	Optimum works	Obtainable cost
Lincolnshire			
United Steel: Appleby-Frodingham (basic)	53s. 9d.	Fully modernized Appleby-Frodingham/Redbourn plant utilizing some existing plant	45s. 8.5d
Stewarts & Lloyds: North Lincolnshire	61s. 9d.	New best-practice, fully integrated works	39s. 4d.
South Wales			
GKN: Dowlais (hematite)	71s. 5d.	New best-practice plant at Cardiff (basic)	51s. 4d.
GKN: Cardiff (hematite)	70s. 1d.	New best-practice plant at Cardiff (hematite)	57s. 9d.
Baldwin's: Port Talbot (basic)	70s. 10d.		
Baldwin's: Briton Ferry (hematite)	75s. 2d.		
Northeast Coast			
Dorman Long, Cleveland	65s.	Cost after modernization and concentration of output in Dorman Long/Cargo Fleet merger (Cleveland)	63s. 7d.
Dorman Long, Acklam (basic and hematite)	67s. 1d.		
Cargo Fleet	67s. 9d.	As above (Cargo Fleet)	84s. 4d.
Scotland			
Average cost of production at existing Scottish blast furnaces (basic)	77s. 4d.	New best-practice plant at tidewater location	58s. 6d.

Staffordshire			
John Summers: Shelton Iron & Steel Co.	64s. 5d.		
Northants			
Stewarts & Lloyds: Corby (old blast furnaces)	53s.	New best-practice plant at Corby	41s. 5d.
Stewarts & Lloyds: Bilston	69s. 10d.		
Lancashire			
		Estimated costs for completion of Partington modernization scheme	60s. 2d.
Northwest Coast			
United Steel: Workington	66s.	New best-practice plant at Workington (hematite)	54s.
Sheffield			
United Steel: Templeborough		New best-practice plant at Templeborough (basic)	43s. 4d.

Sources: See Table 5.

Table 7 Indexes of production costs of nine leading iron and steel producers, 1929

Pig iron		Steel ingots	
Firm	Relative cost[a]	Firm	Relative cost[a]
United Steel (Appleby-Frodingham)	100	United Steel (Appleby-Frodingham)	100
Stewarts & Lloyds (Hickmans)	118	John Summers (Shelton)	101
John Summers (Shelton)	119	Dorman Long (Acklam)	110
Dorman Long (Cleveland)	121	South Durham (W. Hartlepool)	111
United Steel (Workington)	123	Cargo Fleet	112
Dorman Long (Acklam)	125	Richard Thomas (Duffryn)	114
Cargo Fleet	126	Richard Thomas (Grovesend)	114
Stewarts & Lloyds (Clydesdale)	129	Dorman Long (Redcar)	115
GKN (Cardiff)	130	United Steel (Workington-basic Bessemer)	116
Baldwin's (Port Talbot)	132	Dorman Long (Cleveland)	117
GKN (Dowlais)	133	Richard Thomas (Bryngwyn)	117
Baldwin's (Briton Ferry)	139	Richard Thomas (Llanelly)	118
Average of existing Scottish blast furnaces	144	Richard Thomas (Cwmfelin)	122
		Colvilles (Clydebridge)	124
		GKN (Dowlais)	126
		United Steel (Templeborough)	129
		Partington I. S. Co.	132
		GKN (Cardiff)	133
		Baldwin's (Port Talbot)	135
		Richard Thomas (Redbourn)	138
		United Steel (Workington-open hearth)	139

Sources: See Table 5.
a. Cost for lowest-cost producer set at 100.

between the costs in strict engineering terms, therefore, massively exaggerates the differences in real terms. The demise of schemes to introduce best-practice plant, such as the Brassert scheme for a new fully integrated plant in the west of Scotland, often resulted from this fact.[52] The overheads of best-practice new plants operating below capacity could be crippling, whereas old fully amortised plants could attain remarkable longevity.[53]

This tendency was reinforced by the fact that wages were not rising, which kept down the operating costs of more labor-intensive older plants. In depression the cost of new building fell, but so too did the costs of operating existing plant, especially because of falling wages, falling raw material prices, and scrap substitution. When orders were erratic, smaller units could be started up and closed down on a hand-to-mouth basis more cheaply than large units. At Steel, Peech and Tozer, for instance, the old hand-rolling mills were kept working at full capacity, whereas the new mills, theoretically intended to replace them, were kept idle in the late 1920s.[54]

Thus the penalties of overcommitment were rife and diseconomies of scale prevalent. The weak might survive and survivors might eventually prosper: the better would always be the enemy of the best. Many technical economies could not be realized. Demand could not be significantly enlarged by reducing prices because the market was highly segmented and insensitive to price changes. Even major cost reductions were unlikely to enable a firm to obtain the high level of capacity utilization it would need to realize profits through economies of scale. Price cutting could be used strategically to resist those who tried to introduce cost-reducing plant and to wreck the prospects of profits in the period immediately following investment. How did companies respond to these situations? Why were some submerged by the constraints of the market when others made headway? How important were the structures of ownership, control, and decision making in patterning responses to the ambiguities of the market? It is to these questions that we turn in the case studies that follow.

3.

The Northeast Coast Steel Firms, 1918–1939

By the 1920s Northeast Coast steelmaking was dominated by four major firms that produced more than 80% of the region's steel. Two of these companies, Bolckow Vaughan & Co. and the Consett Iron Co., had grown primarily through internal expansion and control of the best local raw materials. The third, Dorman Long & Co., evolved out of the malleable iron trade and had become a partially integrated iron and steel producer during a forty-year period of mergers with other local concerns. Charles Wilson rightly called it "an historic but haphazard collection of firms."[1] The fourth, the allied firms South Durham Steel & Iron Co. and the Cargo Fleet Iron Co., known as South Durham and Cargo Fleet, was a relative latecomer created when one of the region's largest shipbuilders moved into iron and steel production in the prosperous first decade of the twentieth century. Since the 1880s a rivalrous and overlapping industrial structure had built up. By and large the firms produced the same range of products and competed for the same classes of customers. Often they duplicated plant on adjacent sites. All had organizations that were strong at certain points in the chain of production and weak in others.

In the conditions of long-term overcapacity of the 1920s this structure might appear to be amenable to reorganization by merger in order to contract in size and reequip internally. Yet by and large this did not happen, and the structure of the industry in the region remained fragmented throughout the interwar years, even though its weaknesses and the desirability of structural changes were widely acknowledged. How did this come about? The main argument that follows is that the structures that grew up on the basis of nineteenth-century business strategies and market conditions inhibited radical modernization. This argument applies not only at the level of production, where overcommitment to technologically backward plant presented major difficulties, but also to institutional rigidities at the level of industrial organization. Management remained permeated with the perspectives of nineteenth-century individualistic competition, which generated intense personal hostility between the "captains" of the various industrial enterprises. At the same time their hands were tied by a complex network of conflicts of interest between creditors, shareholders, families, and customers *within* the various firms. Against this background the companies' bankers often emerged with powerful positions, but they lacked entrepreneurial experience or tradition, and their approach proved confused and indecisive. The result was a structure that proved remarkably resistant to change despite the demise of the conditions that had produced it.

The Development of Regional Oligopoly

Bolckow Vaughan and Bell Brothers had established their early lead on the basis of controlling the finest local coal and ores. These resources proved a mixed blessing, however, when these firms moved from iron to steelmaking in the 1880s. For the next thirty years both firms struggled to reconcile their old materials to their new techniques by constant improvisation.[2]

These difficulties allowed newcomers to carve out a position in the market. The North East Steel Co. (N. E. S. Co.) did not own local ironstone; instead it made much greater use of imported ores and pioneered the shift to open-hearth practice in the region in the 1890s.[3] Dorman Long, a firm of iron puddlers in the 1870s, grew to be the second largest steel firm in the country by 1913. As the demand for puddled iron diminished in the late 1880s, it was able at little expense to turn to steel production, still using its old rolling plant and keeping many of its old customers. But when the company wanted to integrate backward to gain control of earlier stages of production (coal and pig iron), it had to buy into a preexisting network of ownership of these resources.[4] It pursued this course vigorously, but the resulting mergers incorporated many undesirable features of the old firms into the new one.

Expansion came without serious integration or major economies of scale. Dorman Long merged with Bell to get coal and iron, but Bell was a notoriously overextended firm which in addition to its colliery interests became involved in chemicals in the 1850s, salt and soda ash in the 1870s, and even aluminium in the 1880s,[5] and it brought its problems into the merger. Struggles and disagreements between the two owning families delayed proper integration. The merged firm was known popularly not as Dorman Long but as Dorman versus Bell, and when steel production was expanded after the merger, Bell's Clarence site was developed as a concession to the Bell family and the question of centralization ignored.[6] Likewise Dorman Long purchased the Britannia steelworks from the family-owned firm of Sir Bernhard Samuelson & Co. in 1879 to increase its output of steel, but Samuelson refused to sell the neighboring Newport ironworks which supplied Britannia with pig iron. Instead Samuelson insisted on supplying Britannia with pig iron "under contracts usually of very short duration." To remedy this and effect integration by building its own blast furnaces would have cost Dorman Long £400,000 and would have resulted in a competitive confrontation with Samuelson; the Board opted instead for a working arrangement which, however, still precluded the proper integration of processes.[7]

By the 1890s the market for steel was expanding at what McCloskey calls "a miserably slow pace" of less than 1% per year. This low growth rate prevented British firms from building new plants on American lines. [8] Expansion had to come largely at the expense of competitors who had considerable defensive strength. Most were fairly prosperous; many were specialized in particular ranges of products and had developed close links with their consumers by offering speed of delivery, a reputation for quality, or an ability to supply special needs; and most were still the cherished offspring of founding families who were reluctant to relinquish control. Thus mergers were problematic. At the same time growth by internal expansion also faced serious barriers.

As Burn has noted, until 1900 the technical economies of scale in open-hearth steelmaking were somewhat limited and did not compare with those in basic Bessemer. Open-hearth technology was both conducive to less integrated production and far less capital intensive than basic Bessemer, which, with its faster throughput, required an extensive range of auxiliary equipment. Hence, there were limited opportunities for established producers to move to large-scale production. With slow growth of demand there was a fairly low rate of return to be expected from scrapping and new building. Incremental returns from improvements were more attractive, and both Bolckow Vaughan and Dorman Long committed themselves to this course. The major technical advances in the United States and Europe in this period, however, involved increased vertical integration—larger furnaces, mechanized materials handling, power generation from waste gas, mixers for molten pig, soaking pits, and the like—and the British firms were unable to take advantage of most of these modern practices.[9]

Thus, savings were not enough to justify replacing old open-hearth furnaces with large new ones integrated to hot metal, but they were sufficient to encourage new investment in best-practice plant where no scrapping and replacement were involved. This provided an opportunity for the big Northeast Coast shipbuilders, Furness, Withy & Co. of Hartlepool, to use the large liquid assets of the Furness family to integrate backward by creating a modern iron and steel plant around the turn of the century. Without having to write off expensive existing plant, Furness was able to buy the Stockton and Hartlepool works of the Weardale Steel Co., publicly float the South Durham Steel and Iron Co. in 1900 and link it to a wholly new best-practice plant at Cargo Fleet integrated from ironmaking to rolling mills. The modernity of the new Cargo Fleet works and the lack of any decisive modernization by Bolckow Vaughan or Dorman Long enabled Furness to carve out a place in the crowded and cartelized market in rails and angles by using aggressive underselling to compel the Rail Makers' Association to allocate him a substantial quota. Nevertheless, errors and delays in construction meant that in the period of falling prices that followed the plant's completion in 1907, such a policy was not very remunerative. The bulk of the Furness group's prewar steel profits came not from the modern Cargo Fleet works but from the less technically advanced South Durham works trading in the more favorable plate market and selling directly to the Hartlepool shipbuilders, especially Furness, Withy & Co.[10]

These were the problems of the Teesside firms. Fifty miles away, however, situated on an inland coalfield at Consett in County Durham, was another major iron and steel company. The Consett Iron Co. was a contrast to all the Teesside firms. It had been founded on the juncture of local ironstone and coal deposits in the 1860s, but the former were soon worked out and the advantages of the location passed away. Yet in the late nineteenth century it enjoyed a quite remarkable profit record: the average dividend from 1864 to 1914 was 23½%, and it was almost certainly the most profitable steelmaker of the period. Its specialization in plate production gave it an advantage over firms of a similar size producing a wider range of products. Profits fluctuated closely in relation to shipbuilding output, but this sector was growing throughout most of the period.[11] Cheap coal on its doorstep meant that in booms, when market prices surged forward, it was able to keep costs down, and its heavy involvement in Spanish ores ensured a good supply of cheap high iron content ore.[12] Consett reaped the benefits of specialized adaptation to market conditions.

Slow but positive growth until the war concealed many of the underlying problems of the region. The war and the postwar boom, however, entrenched the existing fragmentation, imbalances, and lack of integration still further. The chronology of wartime developments had important consequences for the industry's structure. The rush to expand capacity was heavily concentrated in the period from spring 1916 to summer 1917 and closely associated with the shell shortage and German damage to British shipping. The shortage of imported ores ensured that the expansion was largely in the basic process to which home ores were best adapted, but the massive schemes for new integrated production that were put forward in autumn 1916 were nearly all shelved because they would take so long to complete. Instead the urgency of the situation dictated a policy of piecemeal expansion for quick results and left the distribution of plant and location largely undisturbed. One department would be expanded to meet a bottleneck and new imbalances would thereby be created elsewhere. In particular, the expansion of steelmaking was not matched by equivalent extensions to blast furnace capacity.[13]

But the major wartime developments were not forced on the makers by munitions demand. Both Dorman Long and Bolckow Vaughan seized the opportunity of the war to move out of their contracting rail-centered markets to establish massive new ship-plate capacity, which they believed from prewar performance to be the most dynamic product. Dorman Long built the new and spacious Redcar works, one of the few of the large integrated projects put forward by planners in 1916 that was actually completed before the end of the war. It accelerated the firm's conversion to open-hearth practice and provided it with a best-practice plant feeding into the coveted plate market.[14] Bolckow Vaughan sought to take advantage of Ministry of Munitions loans to complete the rather belated transition from basic Bessemer to open-hearth steelmaking, which it initiated before the war because of customer resistance to the declining quality of its Bessemer steel. The Ministry, however, never committed itself to the project, which was not commenced until February 1918. Bolckow Vaughan expected the plant to be profitable anyway and pushed ahead with it. In the end neither profits nor Ministry aid materialized, and the firm was left with a heavy financial millstone in the 1920s.[15]

Thus, modern developments took place simultaneously with unsatisfactory improvisations on the cramped sites in the old Middlesborough ironmaster's district. Moreover, much of Dorman Long's 1914–1920 expansion took the form of accumulating a great deal of fairly old blast furnace capacity to balance its expanded steelmaking. It acquired Walker Maynard's blast furnaces, Samuelson's Newport Ironworks, and the Carlton Iron Co. to feed its steelworks at Acklam, Britannia, Clarence, and Redcar. This did nothing to improve integration of production and stretched the firm over a large, rather disconnected area without any clear center of production.[16] The most important of the old firms that were taken over—Bell, Samuelson, and N. E. S. Co.—remained intact as managerial units throughout the war and the wave of new spending that followed it, and the separate companies themselves were not wound up until 1923. As a result, all of the "old sacred things" that they brought with them tended to get a share of the new spending.[17] The old and rather decrepit Clarence works, for instance, were the recipient of a new blast furnace of high standard that was larger than the Redcar blast furnaces; but this was tacked onto inadequate facilities and was unsatisfactory throughout the 1920s.[18] Major work on integration did not follow. Instead there was a constant stream of modifications in design and practice that raised output per furnace from 837 to 1,105 tons per week between 1914 and 1925.[19] The period of expansion exacerbated Dorman Long's internal fragmentation and lack of control.

Only South Durham and Cargo Fleet on Teesside did not undertake large wartime or postwar expansion. Furness was unable to negotiate satisfactory agreements with the Ministry of Munitions either on the planning of new plant or on Excess Profit Duty Relief. As a new firm with very little previous profit history it was hard to assess for EPD, and company officials thought the Ministry most ungenerous. The breakdown of these negotiations pushed the firm toward a conservative expenditure policy. Furness was later to be thankful for this turn of events which kept the firm clear of large new commitments that would have come on stream only after the war and boom were past.[20]

As far as plant was concerned, the Teesside firms entered the 1920s with a motley collection of new and old plant and a clear need for a major shakedown, concentration, centralization, and reorganization. The contraction of their traditional product markets in the 1920s, however, made decisive action unlikely. All the Northeast firms were confined to the same narrow range of heavy rolled products. After their early concentration on rails they had moved into products such as plates, angles, joists, and sections, which served the heavy engineering, constructional, and shipbuilding industries. The firms differed only in the mix of these products that each made. In 1924, for instance, South Durham and Consett made almost solely plates; Cargo Fleet made 35% rails, 43% sections, and 15% joists; Dorman Long made 29% plates, 23% sections, 17% joists, 15% billets, and 5% rails; Bolckow Vaughan made 35% plates, 35% rails, and 17% billets.[21]

The contrast with South Wales is instructive. There, faced by the decline of rails in the late nineteenth century, the steelmakers were jolted into a move into the new tinplate and sheet markets. The Northeast had no such shock; shipbuilding and heavy engineering growth dovetailed fairly neatly with rail decline and provided continuously expanding outlets for the next forty years. Indeed, the boom of 1919–20 led to further consolidation of this orientation in anticipation of further growth in demand. The result in the 1920s was intense commitment to the slowest growing range of products of the period.[22] The firms faced each other at close quarters as direct antagonists for the same restricted markets, at times with the most modern and efficient plant on all sides.

Regional Specialization and Overcommitment in the 1920s

Faced with this legacy, the Northeast Coast steelmakers might have ruined each other by intensive competition, they might have come together in combines or cartels to restrict competition and manage contraction, they might have pursued internal retrenchment and cost reduction, or they might have attempted to diversify into new markets. In the event, although they nibbled at each option, they carried through none of them. But most of them survived, albeit precariously, to fight another day when trade revived in the 1930s. What accounts for this zero-sum outcome? The argument that follows is that a certain resilience and space remained in the traditional product market, even at quite low levels of demand, which restrained both the intensity of competition and the impulse to diversify. This in turn reinforced the overcommitment of the industry both to its existing plants and to institutional structures of management and ownership and placed major obstacles in the way of both effective retrenchment and reorganization by amalgamation. Against this background neither bankers nor entrepreneurs were able to use financial weaknesses as levers rather than encumbrances to push forward the sort of reorganization that observers both within and without the industry agreed was desirable.

Turning first to the product market, it was in plate production that there was the most prospect of direct confrontation and competitive elimination. Before the war the region's plate market had been dominated by Consett and South Durham. The latter was the largest plate maker on the Northeast Coast before the war, and despite the emergence of new competitors in the next ten years, it still made more than 50% of the Northeast plate output in 1924–25.[23] But although newcomers like Dorman Long and Bolckow Vaughan had broken into the market with modern but heavily overcapitalized plant during and

after the war, the counterpart of South Durham's more restrained expansion was that its plant was rather old and inefficient. The company did not have a really good modern unit. The Malleable Works at Stockton had plate mills far superior to those at their West Hartlepool works, but its open-hearth plant was nearly obsolete and far inferior to the one at Hartlepool. It was therefore hard for South Durham to concentrate operations at one efficient specialized plant.[24]

South Durham had a great advantage, however, in its well-established customer relationships. The Northeast makers sold nearly all their plates to the home market.[25] Winning and keeping big customers was vital. South Durham had established connections with the major Hartlepool shipbuilders like William Gray & Co. (the fourth largest British shipbuilder at the time) and the shipbuilding operations of the Furness combine. Through Furness it was linked to the Sperling group, which included the Fairfield Shipbuilding and Engineering Co. of Glasgow, the Northumberland Shipbuilding Co., and William Doxford & Sons of Sunderland. A dozen customers in Hartlepool and Tyneside took 85% of South Durham's plates in 1931.[26] Retaining customers by preferential treatment or even by price cutting was vital, and they were hard to recover by price cutting once lost.[27] But South Durham's dependence on plates was such that in 1931, even with one-third of Northeast Coast ship-plate orders, it could run at no more than 16% of capacity.[28]

Consett, too, specialized overwhelmingly in plates before the war. Its plant was modernized between 1900 and 1906; thereafter rising costs of construction and the threat of coal nationalization persuaded the board to defer major reconstruction and to concentrate on improvements and modifications. It specifically decided against building at high cost in the postwar boom, and boom demand still enabled them to reap record profits during 1918–1921.[29] But by then the existing plate mills were already forty years old, and the board reckoned that further profitable exploitation of them, even in relatively good conditions, was unlikely.[30]

The onset of the slump was interpreted by the firm as simply a cyclical downturn, which could provide "the opportunity we have been looking for to reconstruct the iron and steel part of our company's undertakings at the least cost possible in these times and to get ready for the large demand for iron and steel which is sure to come eventually."[31] The £5½ million reconstruction cost only two-thirds of what it would have cost if the order had been placed in 1920 and was easily financed out of retained profits.[32] The general feeling of the board was that plate demand would expand again in the medium term, and no serious consideration was given to any shift to

alternative product lines at this time. The development, therefore, was to double plate capacity from 4,000 to 8,000 tons per week. With this perspective, it accepted the necessity of virtually closing the works for two years to carry out the building work, even with the consequent risk of losing customer linkages, because it was confident of regaining them later.[33] For this reason, too, the Consett board did not attempt to shift the balance of the market by merger, rejecting proposals for linking up with United Steel in 1923.[34] Instead it continued to pursue the company's traditional aim of being a self-sufficient independent competitor.

Although the two largest producers delayed redevelopment, the high levels of prewar profits followed by the wartime and postwar boom superprofits (Consett earned £1.1 million profits on £3.5 million capital in 1919–20[35]) induced heavy new investment in this sector by other producers at what was in fact the tail of a long period of favorable demand conditions. Before the First World War, for instance, Dorman Long had not produced ship plates at all, but through the acquisition of the Redcar site and with the aid of EPD rebates, it took advantage of wartime conditions to build a new £5 million steelworks, a key feature of which was the production of plates for the first time. The company hoped for more aid from the Ministry of Munitions than in fact it got; nevertheless, the cost of building was fairly low, especially because the plant was in operation before the postwar boom. But its long-term future was explicitly predicated on an expanding ship-plate market.[36] When this market failed to materialize, the plant was too specialized to find an adequate load. In the 1920s it was often only kept in operation on work for structural engineering to which it was not best suited, at low profits.[37]

Simultaneously, Bolckow Vaughan was extending its Cleveland works plate capacity, and after Consett had rejected an alliance, United Steel went on to build new plate mills at its Appleby works, one hundred miles south down the coast in Lincolnshire, that were a model of best-practice technology.[38] When the boom tailed off in 1921, the result was an oversupplied and congested market, which was pushed to rock bottom by the completion of the belatedly undertaken developments of Consett and Appleby in 1925–1927.

A price-cutting war ensued. Both Consett and Appleby insisted that their special position of "coming into the market without a book" (that is, without regular customers) meant that they had to be allowed to sell below prices set by the Heavy Steelmakers' Association.[39] Consett was able to take several customers from South Durham who could not meet Consett's cut prices. It was able to establish links with Vickers-Armstrong Ltd. and Swan Hunter and Wigham Richardson, but

its approaches to William Gray & Co., one of South Durham's key Hartlepool customers, failed.[40] Dorman Long vigorously advocated continuing price maintenance despite the actions of the outsiders, but it was only able to make it effective in the Australian, Indian, and New Zealand markets where it held a dominant position.[41]

Plate prices during this period were driven down by internal and not foreign competition, but this was confined to a specific period of struggle for customers and did not ultimately prove ruinous. Prices fell from 125 in 1924 to 100 in 1926 (Index 1929 = 100) but from then until 1932 they fluctuated around 100 and never fell below 96, even though costs were falling during this period. In other words, profit margins were being held up effectively by the heavy steelmakers despite the recession. The fall of import prices from 108 in 1925 to 75 in 1932 (Index 1929 = 100) did not generally induce the Heavy Steelmakers' Association to reduce prices.[42] There was concealed undercutting by coupled bargains and other such maneuvers, but the trend of imports of foreign heavy steel as a proportion of the home market was downward from 1927 to 1932.[43]

This was because the plate and heavy steel markets were not wholly competitive but rather were segmented and strongly based on customer relationships. Transport costs and on-the-spot specifications and preferences were vital. When, for example, Lithgow was building the *Nerissa,* orders were taken to the steelworks "morning by morning as the plans were completed."[44] Speed and detailed consultation were highly valued by shipbuilders, which created, in effect, highly protected regional markets, the most notable being Clydeside, Tyneside, and Teesside. In Scotland this resulted in vertical integration and combined ownership; in the Northeast it meant tight customer networks. The cutthroat period of 1925–1927 ensued when two firms entering the market attempted to rearrange these relationships violently, but it did not shift the situation to one of long-term price competition; it just shifted the balance of power *within* the oligopoly. The fight was the result of the disastrous errors of entrepreneurial judgment by the Northeast firms in the early 1920s.

Underlying this market structure was the fact that elasticity of substitution between British and imported plates and sections was low. Continental competition was most intense in basic Bessemer steel which was not ideally suited to ship plates, and continental openhearth steel was likely to be unreliable in quantity and regularity. Heavy steel booms tended to by synchronized in Europe, and national customers got supplied first. Hence, in booms continental open-hearth steel was rapidly absorbed in European markets. Therefore, although heavy steel buyers could maneuver for advantage during depression, they felt it essential to safeguard secure local supply. Shipbuilders opposed steel tariffs not simply because British plate prices were substantially higher than continental export prices, but because apart from plates and sections, they particularly feared losing their access to forgings and castings used for stem frames, rudders, and brackets, which came almost entirely from continental producers at half the British price.[45]

Because of the lack of substitutability of continental steel, the price inducements to buy foreign steel were less dramatic than they might at first appear. Few shipbuilders could buy more than one-third of their plates and sections abroad. The rebate scheme introduced by the steelmakers in 1927 capitalized on this. Savings by buying British across the board and getting a rebate could balance out the alternative of saving a great deal on just one part of the purchase. For example, at the inception of the scheme the consumer could buy three tons of British joists at £7.5.0d per ton and one ton of foreign joists at £5.17.6d per ton for a total cost of £27.12.6d or an average price of £6.18.1½d per ton. Under the rebate scheme the shipbuilder could buy *all* its steel at £7 per ton or less, and the average cost could be very similar.[46] Moreover, even when the price differential between home and foreign plates was at its greatest—about £2 per ton in 1930—the extra cost for a 700-foot passenger liner was just £25,000, for a 10,000-ton tanker £10,000, and for an 8,000-ton cargo steamer £3,000. Most British shipbuilders did not find that these differentials cost them orders.[47] Thus, price inducements to buy foreign steel were limited and non-price inducements in the British market were of considerable significance. From 1927 onward, after the Northeast Coast battle of 1925–1927, the steelmakers' association restabilized the plate market, even though demand was low and profits remained small.

Thus, the most important product market did not, by and large, induce violent competition to the point of bankruptcy. It did, however, mean restricted demand and low levels of capacity utilization. It also made it very hard for firms with low levels of profits in their staple products to diversify or "evolve" into new products. Apart from shipbuilding there was a lack of local fabricating industries in the Northeast. The region rarely consumed half of its own steel production. Thus, in contrast to Clydeside, the Northeast steelmakers had a less rigid structure of consumers. Diversification also implied having to break into more distant markets. South Durham and Cargo Fleet's experience illustrates the difficulties of pursuing diversification. Its board was keenly aware in the early 1920s that it was over-reliant on plates and rails. Both products were under heavy pressure in the 1920s and slumped badly at the end of the decade. South

Durham's rail trade was heavily directed toward Japan, South Africa, Latin America, China, and Russia: in 1929, 80% of its rails went there. But by 1933 nearly all of these countries were virtually self-sufficient.[48] Diversification into tram rails in the early 1920s and withdrawal from all rail price-fixing schemes could not offset this drop in demand. In the end the company was saved only by the revival of rail demand in the 1930s, based in particular on big municipal tramway developments in Leeds, Liverpool, and Sunderland and major contracts from the London & North Eastern Railway for rails.[49]

South Durham made consistent efforts to move into a wider range of products throughout this period, but without success. In the 1920s it tried and failed to interest municipal consumers in switching from cast iron to its newly developed corrosion-resistant steel pipes.[50] It attempted to enter the galvanized sheet trade but could not get its ingot costs down low enough to be competitive.[51] In the 1930s it considered moving into tube making but was deterred by the range of specialized skills required and the competition of the expansionist Stewarts & Lloyds. They examined entering the special alloy market but again had no experience in this demanding Sheffield-dominated technology. It tried to expand its constructional steelwork, but Dorman Long, which dominated the field, was able to get the Structural Engineering Association to impose an embargo—to force South Durham to stop cutting prices to win orders.[52] The final alternative the firm considered was expansion in soft and special billets or the sheet trade, but it lacked the essential base of cheap steel, and this possibility was set aside once the traditional plate and rail markets began to revive in the mid-1930s.[53]

Dorman Long pursued a rather different strategy. It systematically developed its business in constructional steelwork fabricating, bridge building, dam making, and factory construction to open up new markets and to increase the outlets for its steel. In this effort the company was not wholly successful.[54] This strategy necessitated the development of an extensive and rather rambling worldwide organization which often severely drained managerial resources when leading managers were away for months traveling around the world on various projects.[55] Its greatest coup was winning the prestigious £4.2 million contract to build the Sydney Harbour Bridge; but the contract gave much of the common-grade steelwork to local firms, and Dorman had to concentrate on short runs of up to 113 complex specifications of shapes. In the end it lost £247,000 on the contract.[56] Moreover, here as in the Nile Dam project, the company found that it had to involve itself quite extensively in the local economy to compensate for inadequate infrastructures. The Sydney bridge necessitated setting up a Tasmanian concrete industry. Such expenditure was excessive and hard to sell off once the project was completed.[57]

The second arm of its policy in the early 1920s was to pursue increased outlets by setting up subsidiaries in Australia and South Africa. By the late 1920s, however, the development of domestic steelmaking in Australia was ousting British steel, and Dorman Long decided to sell its Australian subsidiary to an Australian firm and become investors in Australian companies instead.[58] In effect, it substituted searching for markets for its existing products for developing products to suit new markets, but the extent and relative success of its overseas involvement tended to encourage overcommitment to a fading market. It was able to keep a major proportion of a diminishing mass demand, and this may have generated a lack of incentive to diversify elsewhere. Between 1929 and 1931 the position of Dorman Long in this field was made impregnable by the acquisition of its structural rivals, Teesside Bridge and Engineering Co., which specialized in mechanical work like crane building, and Redpath Brown, which specialized in factory building. The management of these companies was not fully coordinated until Ellis Hunter's reforms in the mid-1930s. Nevertheless, the possession of these departments gave Dorman Long a considerable edge in structural contracts of all kinds, and this position was of particular value in the 1930s when structural steel began to expand. It gave the firm privileged access to a range of markets that were closed to its rival, South Durham and Cargo Fleet, who had no connections in this field.[59]

Thus neither the Dorman Long strategy of assiduously cultivating markets for existing products nor South Durham's greater willingness to look for new products and markets had much success. It is unlikely that any great feats of entrepreneurship could have created significant new opportunities in the 1920s. A potentially more productive strategy would have been to remodel firms for healthier future expansion by consolidating and reorganizing during the downturn. Here the problems were the inheritance of interrelated plant of widely varying vintages and the imbalance of productive capabilities at various stages of the production process.

None of the Teesside firms were strong at all stages of production—raw materials, blast furnaces and coke ovens, steelmaking, rolling, and finishing—but nearly every one of them had best-practice facilities at one stage or another. There therefore seemed to be some possibility of bringing together the best units in the region through mergers and concentration of production. The problems associated with that strategy will be considered fully in a later part of this chapter. A second-best solution appeared to be available in the form of internal rationalization within the boundaries of existing firms. In practice, however, pursuit of limited improvements without extensive new investment was severely constrained by the interrelatedness of existing facilities: improvements in one unit necessitated extensive changes in complementary areas of production; as a result, costs could become prohibitive. Although the combined effects of numerous changes could be of great significance in increasing productivity,[60] these opportunities were surprisingly scarce. The main avenues that might have been explored were the centralization of ore-handling facilities, the progressive enlargement of existing blast furnaces, the improvement of blast furnace auxiliary equipment, and the introduction of mechanical charging. Yet in each of these areas the Northeast Coast firms felt that the implications ramified so far that they were not worthwhile.

As far as ore handling was concerned, by 1922 Middlesborough was importing more than two million tons of ore a year, and expert contemporary estimates reckoned that best-practice discharging facilities could reduce the cost of handling from 1/10d to 4d per ton.[61] The proximity of local ironstone, however, had for a long time led them to neglect the problems of bulk ore handling, and a structure of assets had grown up over a long period based on scattered, privatized, and decentralized wharfage. Cooperative development to take advantage of economies of scale was needed, but there were weighty arguments against such proposals. As Outhwaite of Bolckow Vaughan put it, "There is a considerable advantage to the local ironmaker in having a ship at his own wharf. He is out to make money and he can handle his own material in a much more satisfactory way than the railway company can handle it for him. His works have been built or have grown to suit his requirements and everything is in keeping with that. His gantries, or 60% of them, will not carry anything like a 30–40 ton truck, and a 10–15 ton truck would have to be the figure to suit everybody in the district. Therefore the rail company would have to handle a larger number of smaller wagons for the same amount of ore to suit the people whom they cater for. The local ironmaster has got his own truck, his own wharf, and his own locomotives, and he does not get such a bad rate of discharge after all." Buying in small doses helped to keep stocks down, and Outhwaite concluded that "the old-fashioned way is more economical."[62]

The output and productivity of blast furnaces could be increased at relatively low capital cost by progressive enlargement and rebuilding of existing furnaces, but this course was already more or less exhausted by the major firms in the Cleveland area in the 1920s. At periods of peak demand they already worked their blast furnaces well above nominal capacity by straining both labor and auxiliary equipment to their limits. As Major H. G. Scott, Bolckow Vaughan's blast furnace manager, observed: "We have reached a point above which the only way to increase the make is to increase the diameter or cubic capacity of the hearth. This will demand a proportionate increase in the pressure of blast. I do not think that we can travel economically very far in this direction if at all."[63] Improvements of this sort would lead inevitably to a general scaling up of plant. Sir Francis Samuelson described the problems facing Dorman Long in this respect: "If we increase our engine power, we have not enough stove power; we may add new stoves, if we have room for them, which often we have not; we may raise the height of the old ones, if they are strong enough to carry the added weight—even then they are probably not strong enough for the new pressure. If we surmount the stove difficulty, we find our mains and connections are not large enough to take the increased volume of air. If, by partial scrapping, we get over all these difficulties, we find that our yard is not equal to the increase in traffic. So that there really seems no half-way house between letting moderately well alone and complete scrapping; we can get a certain distance on the road to improvement, but not as far as we would like."[64]

Similar problems arose when the installation of mechanical charging for blast furnaces was considered. For mechanical charging, ore bunkers had to be at right angles to the line of the furnaces; but in Cleveland they were nearly all parallel. Many felt that "it was not usually worthwhile to attempt to put a mechanical charging arrangement . . . on to an existing old plant which was arranged for hand-filling. There were so many things that had to be altered that by the time the work was finished, a satisfactory job was not obtained. It was far better to start afresh and to put in a new furnace plant entirely."[65]

In discussions of these sorts of innovations at the technical societies, works managers would very often agree about the abstract desirability of certain improvements but at the same time insist that they were not economically justified. Extensive alterations, they believed, were not feasible.[66] But their realism was also combined with a very real conservatism. Even improvements that involved no problems of interrelatedness were often tardily adopted. Gas cleaning was backward, as was the instrumentation of blast furnaces to allow precise evaluation of internal temperatures and pressures, and even the readily available tapping hole guns were only slowly introduced.[67]

The problems of most of the companies in relation to producing and selling steel were greatly exacerbated by their heavy involvement in another equally crisis-ridden sector. In 1930, 36 million tons of coal were produced in Durham by 97 undertakings from 237 mines. Of these undertakings, however, 21 produced 92% of total output, 15 produced 81%, and 7 produced 52%.[68] Of these 7, three (Bolckow Vaughan, Dorman Long, and Consett) were steel firms, one (Pease and Partners) wholly owned a steel subsidiary (Skinningrove), and one (Horden) was closely linked to Dorman Long. In 1930 Dorman Long produced 10% of the region's output.[69] The steel firms, however, owned very few of the really large mines and had only two of the twenty collieries in Durham in 1924 that employed more than two thousand workers.[70] The area witnessed little amalgamation in the 1920s, and even the largest concerns were often composed of numerous medium-sized mines. Two features stand out: first, although they were a major force on the coalfields, most steel and coal concerns were not highly rationalized; and second, the steel and coal complex was relatively autonomous from the field as a whole. Twenty-four percent of Durham coal went to the iron and steel industry in 1929, and the bulk of this moved internally through the integrated concerns.[71] At the same time, the steel firms often showed little interest or capacity for trading in coal on the open market.

The Teesside steel firms had acquired their coal holdings, mainly in Southwest Durham, as a largely incidental consequence of their policy of buying up iron and steel capacity. Dorman Long and Bolckow Vaughan, in particular, became heavily committed to those parts of the Durham coalfield that had been earliest, most intensively, and most wastefully exploited. By the 1920s underground conditions in many of their pits were becoming very difficult, and many of their assets were approaching exhaustion.[72] These pits had been acquired by iron-making firms in the years when cost advantages strongly favored moving from iron ore to coal.[73] Since then, however, as the weight of coal per ton of steel fell continuously with technical changes, the locational advantage had shifted dramatically away from inland sites toward the coast and imported ores. When world coal prices dropped in the 1920s, the potential advantages of coastal locations and buying coal on the world market were redoubled. Yet the 1919–20 boom saw a flurry of increased integration between coal and steel that tied the steelmakers into their local raw material suppliers and closed this option to them.

The steelmakers extended their coal ownership at this late stage because they believed that they were facing a period of intense competition for resources. On this basis there was some sense in their strategic calculations. In boom periods, when raw material prices rose sharply with demand, ownership of supplies could keep down coal prices, at least to the extent that production costs did not also rise, and thus enhance the profits of the boom. At the same time it would ensure that there would be no interruption of supplies and thus make possible securing maximum boom period profits. In an industry like steel, where profits in one boom year could be as much as those made in several ordinary years, this was of great importance. To a certain extent, therefore, it was to the advantage of the industry to bear certain losses in slump years in order to maximize profits at peaks.

However, the wisdom of buying into coal supplies during booms when prices were inflated was much more dubious. Dorman Long may well have paid twice as much for Carlton Iron Co. and its mines in 1920 than it might have done at another time. Colliery owners held out for high prices. Dorman Long was ready to buy more marginal collieries with shorter lives than it might otherwise have required.[74] Carlton's Mainsforth mines required the immediate expenditure of £600,000 to make them fully workable. But as Dorman Long itself admitted, it was only the possession of Mainsforth coal, as well as crucial supplies of ferro-manganese from the Carlton blast furnaces, that enabled the firm to operate at maximum capacity throughout the boom.[75]

Dorman Long further ensured its self-sufficiency in coal through shareholdings in the Kent coalfields[76] and was thus able to avoid the sorts of crises that beset Bolckow Vaughan, which was less than self-sufficient in the boom period and whose output of steel was seriously curtailed by shortages of coal in the boom years.[77]

Firms like South Durham and Cargo Fleet that did not control most of their coal supply could be hard hit by the market in booms. Before the war it relied significantly on purchases of coal from Bolckow Vaughan and Carlton, which more or less ceased by 1918. It was unable to purchase the extra tonnage that it required on the open market, and this had a direct and serious effect on profits.[78] It is impossible to quantify this fully, but in February 1919, with order books full, a working profit of £72,500 was made. In the following month coal shortages restricted production, and profit fell to £44,000. Further shortages in November 1919 restricted profits to £18,000, but the Christmas break enabled a stock of coal to be built up in December, which made possible capacity working in January and a monthly profit of £97,000.[79] The vulnerability of its coal supply remained a major area of management concern throughout the boom.

Once the boom was past, however, the steelmakers found themselves saddled with scattered high-cost collieries at a time when world coal prices were falling. In 1924 coke could be bought on the market at 25 shillings per ton. But Dorman Long was paying 25 shillings per ton delivered for *coal* from its own pits, and generally the firm used one-and-one-half tons of coal to manufacture one ton of coke.[80] These firms were, in effect, damaging their prospects at the higher level by being tied to a high-cost producer at a previous level. Yet the steelmakers were reluctant to shed their collieries. Most firms only slowly came to realize that the boom conditions of 1920 were not going to be repeated in the near future and that control of supply was therefore less vital. The Ruhr crisis in 1923 fostered this illusion for a while longer, and the reality was not fully acknowledged until the 1929–1933 slump.[81]

In the meantime, the steelmakers continued "defensive investment" in their mines. The rate of return on their investments might be low or negative, but the only alternative was closure; since the scrap value of mines was negligible, this would mean an almost total write-off of the large sums they had recently invested.[82] They made little headway in improving their mines. Often improvements required the acquisition of adjacent land, and the intricate pattern of ownership meant that such consolidation could involve complex negotiations with several parties, with pieces of land acquiring inflated strategic prices.[83] Similarly, much capital equipment such as coke ovens was linked to scattered pit-heads and could not easily be consolidated, and closures would entail major investment in the reorganization of coke ovens.[84] Nor did they have specialist management with knowledge of developing better marketing policies.[85] Before 1926 they also faced rigidity of wages. Strong union resistance to closures was broken only in the aftermath of the 1921 and 1926 strikes.[86]

The Teesside firms' collieries were a further drain on profits, and they accentuated fluctuations because their downturns coincided with those of steel. Losses were worst in 1922–1926 and were then moderated by wage cuts, pit closures, and a slight revival of demand.[87] Ownership of coal meant that the Teesside firms were generally paying more for their coal than they would have done on the open market. At the same time it overextended their management, required further "defensive" investment, and encouraged expensive "balancing" of suboptimal plant such as Bolckow Vaughan's coke ovens. Only Consett was able to derive much long-term benefit from integration. For the rest, although it is clear that control of supply during the boom raised profit peaks, this benefit was more than offset by the long-term effects of overcommitment to waning resources in a low-profit sector.

Consett, the exception to this picture, had genuinely low-cost coal which gave it significant advantages.[88] This consideration was a major determinant of Consett's strategy after the war. From as early as 1869 Consett's "isolated position was alleged to be fatal to its being any other than an ordinary coal producing establishment."[89] The firm could have ceased producing iron and steel and become a coal and coke company pure and simple. Its board, however, explicitly rejected this option when it decided to rebuild the steelworks in the early 1920s.[90]

Instead, the historical inheritance of integration was utilized as the basis for a strategy for the new cost conditions. With coal prices falling and markets contracting, a coal concern alone would have a poor future. As one leading figure on the board noted, "Coke and coal markets are bad, and these products have to be sold at low prices. If the Company is to do this, it had better sell as much as possible to itself . . . in sequence to the finished material—plates and sections."[91] Although little profit could be anticipated from coal, this could be offset by taking advantage of its cheapness as a raw material. The strategy depended on keeping costs below those of competitors, and this was one of the main reasons why Consett was a leader in the drive to raise productivity in the mines and a hawk in the attack on miners' wages, particularly with regard to replacing national by local wage bargaining, in the Northeast coalfields.

Consett consciously saw itself as the vanguard of the coal owners.[92] For almost five years, 1922–1927, it pursued the strategic goal of smashing the mineworkers' organization and slashing wages. In doing so, it engaged in a virtual local guerrilla war with the miners in the "Red Villages" of Chopwell and Consett. The most ruthless and hard-nosed tactics were used to destroy trade unionism in Consett pits as part of the reduction of its colliery costs to rock-bottom levels.[93]

Managers, Bankers, Creditors, and Shareholders: The Business Politics of Merger and Rationalization, 1929–1937

One solution to this depressed and deadlocked situation occupied the forefront of nearly all the discussions that took place in the late 1920s and early 1930s: rationalization through merger. Throughout the interwar years leading industrialists, bankers, and governments regularly argued that the success and competitive efficiency of the iron and steel industry could best be secured by "rationalization." The term was often used imprecisely, but it generally implied reorganizing the industry through amalgamations that would eliminate excess capacity, concentrate production, and realize economies of scale and best-practice methods. The potential of such solutions to achieve their goals will be touched on later. What is not in doubt, however, was that rationalization invariably headed the agenda in discussions on the reform of the industry and that, in practice, little was achieved.

Various mergers were discussed at some length, but only one, that between Dorman Long and Bolckow Vaughan in July 1929, actually took place, although negotiations on a subsequent merger of this new combine with South Durham and Cargo Fleet were carried to a very advanced stage before they broke down. Most of the participants agreed that, in a general sense, mergers appeared to be a logical and attractive solution to problems of excess capacity and rationalization. They were also the kind of activity that government and bankers wanted to see as an indication that steelmakers were getting their house in order, and as such an additional card in favor of tariff protection or the granting of exceptional financial assistance. But the case in their favor was rarely overwhelming. On close inspection the precise benefits of mergers were debatable, and even these invariably required additional expenditure that was hard to come by. In this situation the complex forces acting on the internal decision-making processes of the firms concerned often served to make decisive action in pursuit of calculated risks impossible.

Mergers might produce some market advantage or local monopoly power, but this was likely to be slight given the extent of national overcapacity. Initially the main benefits would accrue from the extent to which a merger could ease pressure on profits through better allocation of production between plants, concentration of output, and higher capacity utilization of the best plant. In the long term the major benefits would be those associated with the advantages of coordinated development in a period of expansion. However, different companies and different interests within those companies took varying strategic views of their long-term advantage. In a major expansion the old firms could hope to reap the benefits and undertake new building just as effectively as the rather cumbersome agglomerated combines with heavy debt burdens and inherited overcapitalization that would result from mergers. In this uncertain situation most firms were ready to face the problems of overlapping development as and when they arose. Only one firm, Bolckow Vaughan, was so weakened that it had to form an alliance in order to survive. For other firms the potential savings from a merger actually decreased as the depression deepened. The very depth of the trough made it hard to see how reorganization by merger could resolve current problems. Doing nothing seemed preferable.

When a merger did take place, even limited reorganization was impossible without finance. For example, the only substantive reorganization that the merged Dorman Long/Bolckow Vaughan was able to finance for several years was the closure of the Carlton ironworks and a number of other obsolete blast furnaces and collieries and the

coordination of their fabricating subsidiaries (Dorman Long Constructional, Redpath Brown, and the Teesside Bridge and Engineering
Co.).[94] Yet substantial further economies were potentially available.
In 1930 an internal report estimated the net savings arising from the
coordination and concentration of output within a comprehensive
regional amalgamation at £531,910. Of this, £307,597 was deemed to
arise from economies available from coordination within the existing
Dorman/Bolckow combine that had not yet been implemented,[95] but
the newly merged combine simply could not finance them.

The plan for a major regional amalgamation between Dorman/Bol-
ckow and South Durham/Cargo Fleet envisaged a two-stage program
of concentration and rebuilding. Initially South Durham's Malleable
Works at Stockton and Dorman Long's Britannia steelworks would
be closed and their output redistributed to other works. In the second
stage a new coking plant and modern finishing and auxiliary equipment would be introduced. But forecasting the results of this program
was a contentious matter, and estimates of the savings fluctuated
wildly. In 1929 Dorman Long estimated that the first stage would
yield £690,000 savings, rising to £1 million when the new building
was completed.[96] But in the following year the respective estimates
were revised downward to £355,000 and £700,000, and in 1932 the
estimated benefits of the first stage fell as low as £300,000 net savings.[97]

The problem of merger, however, went beyond the arithmetic of
production savings. Each firm consisted of a congerie of rival interests
each of which benefited differentially from alternative strategies and
had varying powers within the firm to exert influence over the outcome
of discussions. This power was more frequently the power to block
or forbid an option than to compel a particular outcome and generally
rested on a mix of financial and legal rights. The power was more
often negative than positive because most interests in the firm could
only defend the position of their capital. Only with the banks did
current debts imply to a certain extent privileged access to future
credit; bank capital was therefore strategically of the utmost significance. Bankers could back their judgments with cash in a way that
the debenture holders, for instance, as a group could not. The only
other source of finance was the capital market, but this was not a
viable option in conditions of low profitability.

The strategic significance of bank capital was recognized by all the
firms involved as a priority consideration in the formulation of a
merger. Access to bank funds when other sources of cash were tight
was a key factor. But the banks too had their strategies and desired
outcomes. In part they acted exactly as other creditors—that is, in
defense of their loaned capital. But at all times they had the potential

to offer inducements to restructure—although at the cost of taking risks and increasing their involvement. Only in the case of Bolckow Vaughan did their position as creditor actually extend so far as to give the banks direct power to enforce action. Elsewhere they had a powerful negative voice and were seen as an interest to be courted in all schemes. But they persistently sought to remain outsiders because only in that capacity could they retain the character of liquidity that gave their money its strategic power. Once they opted for investment in support of a strategy they bound themselves to that option; they would then be only one among the several groups whose capital was tied into the firm.

Largely as a result of the company's prewar financial practices the banks held a uniquely dominant position in Bolckow Vaughan. The firm had deliberately kept its share capital over which profits had to be divided as low as possible and opted instead to rely on the banks for regular working capital. By 1905 its share capital was £500,000 *less* than the value of its permanent assets. This made sense in the period before the war when profits were high in relation to fixed capital, but wartime extensions greatly increased the company's need for working capital, and the postwar capital issues barely kept abreast of the enlarged assets. In 1923 share capital was still only £4.3 million as against £4.8 million fixed capital.[98]

Moreover, excessively optimistic prognostications led Bolckow Vaughan to increase its debenture stock from £800,000 to £1.8 million in 1923, placing the new issue at 8% in the unfounded hope that it could pay off this issue over the next two years.[99] Instead, it had catastrophically escalated its burden of fixed charges.

This dependence on debt financing was a chronic weakness in the postwar depression. Kitson noted that until then "the banks have treated us with liberality" but that it was becoming clear that "that position cannot go on."[100] When the government refused to pay Bolckow Vaughan £600,000 that the company believed it was owed by the Ministry of Munitions for wartime extensions, a call on reserves to fill this gap depleted cash holdings, and a cash shortage and liquidity crisis became endemic.[101] Bank debt alone mounted rapidly from £838,000 in 1923 to £1,073,923 in 1924.

Ill-judged issues at the downturn had resulted in transforming Bolckow Vaughan from an undercapitalized firm to a massively overcapitalized one. In 1928 the company had £22.2.7 capital and debt per ton of output; its liabilities per ton stood at 10/5d and the profit per ton necessary to pay 5% on ordinary shares was 24/2d. As Table 8 shows, these figures dwarfed even those of Bolckow's competitors.

Not only was the cost of the debt itself crippling, but its structure

Table 8   Relationship between capital, output, and fixed charges for four Northeast Coast steelmakers, 1928

Firm	Capital (£m) Shares	Capital (£m) Debentures	Output of finished steel (tons)	Fixed charges per ton of output Capital (£.s.d.)	Fixed charges per ton of output Liabilities (s.d.)	Fixed charges per ton of output Profit[a] (s.d.)
Bolckow Vaughan	5.2	1.8	366,350	22.2.7	10/5	24/2
Dorman Long	8.0	4.3	872,700	14.16.9	9/6	16/5
South Durham	0.65	0.3	200,000	4.15.0	3/2	4/10
Cargo Fleet	1.0	0.79	234,000	7.4.8	3/8	7/7

Source: Company records and balance sheets.
a. Profit per ton to pay 5% on ordinary shares without provision for depreciation.

also placed the company's bankers in a commanding position of control vis-à-vis the shareholders. The company's overdraft was held roughly in the ratio of 3:2:1 by National Provincial, Midland, and Williams Deacon's through the 1920s. Midland was often hawklike in its demands for cash on the nail, but National Provincial was rather more accommodating. In 1924 Midland precipitated a crisis by threatening to demand repayment within one month of its loan unless it was immediately issued prior debenture stock as a security.[102] National Provincial put in the accountant Sir William Peat to conduct an investigation of the company's affairs, and as a result Bolckow Vaughan was forced to call up the balance of eight shillings per share remaining uncalled on their earlier £1.86 million issue. Coming in the depression, this demand was a considerable burden for many shareholders, backed up as it was by the threat of forfeiting the shares if the cash was not produced. Moreover, it was stipulated that *all* the £740,000 proceeds from this call should be used to reduce bank advances rather than to finance reorganization. Thus, even though in law the bankers had no entitlement to prior securities for existing overdrafts, they were able in effect to enforce a mortgage over the uncalled capital of the company, despite the fact that this was a clear incursion on the rights of the debenture holders and despite the opposition of shareholders and many directors. The Midland would settle for nothing less, and its position was so strong that it had to be paid off.[103]

To prevent any repetition of such losses, the shareholders under the leadership of Ben Walmsley, an ex-director of Redpath Brown, organized themselves to take a much more active role in the direction of the firm than was usual. After a period of "rather chilly" relations with the board, they were able to force the resignation of three directors and a managerial reshuffle. But they could not challenge the stranglehold of the banks. In fact this grip grew steadily stronger as Bolckow Vaughan found itself unable to meet the interest payments on its 8% debentures. Midland would allow further advances to prevent a receivership only in return for the most rigorous securities.[104] After a fruitless quest for alternatives, the bank's conditions were finally met, and in 1926 the three banks perfected their grip over the company by redeeming a part of the 8% debentures in return for the deposit of the redeemed bonds in the banks at 7% interest, thus giving the banks in addition most of the rights of the old 8% debenture holders.[105] Despite a slight revival of profitability after 1927 and the sale of some subsidiaries for cash, Bolckow Vaughan was never thereafter able to escape from this dependency on the bankers for its entire working capital.[106]

Thus Bolckow's bankers held a compelling position over the firm, and they also had a fairly clear idea of the best course for the company to pursue: they wanted an "amalgamation with some stronger concern" to restore Bolckow's fortunes. Some of the directors also favored such a move, but most of them and most shareholders feared that the firm would lose its identity and that they would get little out of it. The banks, therefore, found it wise to move cautiously behind the scenes to avoid treading on toes. When the National Provincial commissioned Peat and Plender to investigate possible mergers in 1924, the negotiations that followed were kept secret both from the shareholders and from the board as a whole.[107] But the power of foreclosure dictated that Bolckow Vaughan would ultimately have to come to terms with another company on the lines that the banks wanted.

The obvious candidate for such a merger was Dorman Long, but that firm also carried a heavy burden of fixed charges (see Table 8)— although Dorman's bankers, Barclays, did not hold nearly so powerful a position. But Dorman Long hesitated to involve itself with the overcapitalized Bolckow Vaughan unless it could get the guaranteed credit facilities from the banks that, in the absence of marketable securities, could alone make reconstruction following amalgamation effective. Barclays, however, took the position that it would not allow the future combine more than £2 million credit and stuck to it.[108] Bolckow's bankers were similarly adamant that their limit would be £1 million and even then only on strict conditions.[109] Dorman Long reckoned that £3 million was inadequate to carry through an effective amalgamation.[110] One of the major reasons that Dorman Long wanted to include South Durham and Cargo Fleet in a tripartite merger was that such "regional rationalization" could unlock the credit facilities of the Bank of England, which would be open to such a scheme although not to a bipartite merger.[111] In pursuit of these facilities, Dorman Long and Bolckow Vaughan made joint approaches to the Bank of England, initially keeping the moves a secret from their own bankers until the latter heard of the talks via the grapevine,[112] and they continued to lobby for Bank of England assistance even after the merger agreement had been signed, although without success.[113]

These approaches foundered because E. R. Peacock, Montagu Norman's principal adviser, and Deputy Governor Sir Ernest Harvey insisted on a larger scheme, preferably an operating company for the whole Northeast Coast.[114] They refused to consider a Dorman/Bolckow merger as a stepping-stone to the regional reorganization that they wanted to see.[115] Yet the Bank also refused to formulate its own proposals for such a scheme, as Kitson suggested it might. Harvey assured Kitson and Bolckow Vaughan that if the companies produced such a proposal the Bank would support it, although he avoided any commitment to provide finance. The Bank felt that any involvement in the formulation of a scheme and finding money for it would mean losing "the freedom of action which we now have in turning down any one scheme and forcing industry to bring forward a better one."[116]

Bolckow Vaughan had briefly hoped that Clarence Hatry's plan for a giant national steel combination (see below) might provide a new option,[117] but the collapse of the Hatry scheme meant that the company had to either merge with Dorman Long or go into the hands of the receivers. Thereafter the merger moved to a rapid denouement. But the agreement was concluded without adequate future finance being arranged beforehand. Both firms were aware for several months that reconstruction would inevitably overstep the credit limit approved by their bankers by as much as £1.73 million, but the banks would not budge. The new firm was enormously overcapitalized, and despite efforts to conceal the fact from shareholders, this situation necessarily implied that any further merger would require a massive writing down of capital.[118]

Nevertheless, the merger accomplished the first step in Dorman Long's recurrent aim in the 1920s to bring about a tripartite merger of the big three Northeast Coast companies which it, as the largest, hoped to dominate.[119] Bolckow Vaughan, the smallest firm, had generally feared that a tripartite merger would marginalize its position, and had therefore looked toward a simple merger with one of them, preferably Dorman Long, to precede any further scheme.[120] South Durham and Cargo Fleet, however, and especially Ben Talbot, its managing director, looked primarily to a national rather than a local combination as a means whereby it might outflank its neighbors. It rejected the idea of an all-inclusive regional merger of the type favored

by Dorman Long and the Bank of England. Strong personal animosity
between Talbot and "the two old gentlemen" (Dorman and Bell) reinforced this outlook.[121] Instead, in 1927 Talbot had engaged in prolonged but finally unsuccessful negotiations with Richard Thomas
and Co. and Colvilles about a large interregional merger, and a similar
project had been revived in the context of Hatry's plan for a giant
steel combination in 1928–29; but the Hatry crash cut short the discussions.[122]

Once the Dorman/Bolckow merger was completed, however, Dorman, on the initiative of Goodenough, the joint general manager of
Barclays, approached South Durham (the allied firm of Cargo Fleet
had been formally merged into South Durham during 1928) for extensive cooperation and joint work with a view to merger.[123] The next
three years saw a series of bewilderingly complex negotiations, involving five different schemes, several in many different versions,
ranging from regional reorganization schemes to operating companies
to outright purchase. All ran rapidly into a complex interlocking web
of sectional interests, and all proved abortive. The size and financial
complexity of the concerns precluded the direct personal bargaining
between owners that had characterized the mergers of the war and
postwar boom in the area. Careful conciliation and recomposition of
rival interests were now required in merger negotiations.

During 1930–31, Dorman Long, encouraged by Barclays, engaged
in a series of conspiratorial negotiations with Lord Furness about
buying out his shareholding behind the back of Talbot, the managing
director, and the rest of the company, possibly through a financial
group sponsored by the Bank of England's industrial investment organization, the Bankers' Industrial Development Co. (BID) and then
using this position to appoint Charles Mitchell of Dorman Long as
chairman, dispense with Talbot, and deliver South Durham on a plate
to Dorman Long.[124] Furness was cautious but "prepared to play."[125]
He had wanted to shed his steel commitments for several years and
had earlier contemplated selling out to Hatry. The sum considered
then was £576,000 against the new offer of £375,000[126] but Furness
realized that "the only way he is going to get any money out of the
steel industry is to sell out."[127] Above all he wanted cash and a clean
severance: "He does not want to spend any more money. He foresees
either an amalgamation or a fight and he wants to get out."[128]

There were two main obstacles to such a scheme. First, the high
price Furness wanted for his shares would inevitably push up the
price of other South Durham shares. Various subterfuges were considered to avert this—for instance, that Dorman Long would appear
to buy Furness's shares at a moderate price but would simultaneously

purchase from Furness other property in his Ormesby Estate worth
£70,000 at an artificially high price of £165,000.[129] But second and more
important, adequate concealment from the shareholders was almost
impossible. As Charles Bruce Gardner of the BID realized, Talbot
could easily organize the shareholders to resist such a maneuver. The
idea was a "wild-cat one."[130]

More generally, these difficulties confirmed that the question was
no longer one that could be settled by the heads of the companies.
Talbot's conservatism and opposition and the departure of the pro-
merger John E. James from the firm at a crucial time may have hampered negotiations,[131] and Dorman Long's octogenarian leadership
invested many of the negotiations with overtones of dynastic feud-
ing.[132] But even when, at Furness's instigation, Talbot was replaced
as managing director by McQuistan, and when, as a result of the
deaths of almost an entire generation of Dorman Long management
within a space of two years,[133] the "old deadheads" in both firms had
faded from the scene, the merger, even in the hands of two "old
friends" like McQuistan and Mitchell did not proceed much faster.[134]

Simple managerial conservatism was not the major problem of a
merger. Nor could an agreement among bosses circumvent the need
to conciliate and compose the diverse material interests that made up
the firms. The major barrier that any scheme had to face was the
problem of getting the debenture and preference shareholders to agree
to the necessary resolutions and writing down of capital.[135] The form
of merger that was finally pursued, that of purchase, was consequently that which involved getting the smallest number of assents
from the various classes of shareholders and creditors.[136]

To understand the nature of this problem, we have to look at the
capital structure of the firm and the interests that this embodied.
Dorman's capital had become heavily inflated in the postwar boom,
and the situation had then been exacerbated by an ill-judged issue of
£3½ million 5½% mortgage debentures in 1923. The company had
anticipated an imminent boom; instead it seriously increased its gearing just as the recession worsened. By the late 1920s its capital structure was dominated by the £5.2 million 5½% debenture holders, who
by 1930 were owed large arrears of interest and were in a powerful
position in terms of their rights to a full settlement of twenty shillings
in the pound in the event of a receivership. In fact, their rights preceded even those of the company's bankers, many of whose loans
were unsecured. The size of the debenture stock was such as to place
an enormous fixed levy on profits (see Table 8), which no merger
could contemplate incorporating with equanimity. Some form of reconstruction and reissue of this stock was a necessary part of any

amalgamation, but this would require the assent of the holders, and most of them took the view that this meant that "secured creditors were being asked to do something not merely to preserve their security . . . but to allow the Company to speculate with their money to purchase another undertaking."[137]

Dorman Long therefore had to persuade its debenture holders as a precondition of any merger that in the long run they would be better off with a reduced paper debt earning regular interest from a going amalgamated concern than with a large paper debt with arrears of interest in a concern with insufficient earning power to pay either in the foreseeable future. They also had to be convinced that in a receivership no one would buy the company outright for cash and that consequently the debenture holders would get only the breakup value of their assets and certainly less than twenty shillings in the pound.[138]

In 1933 Dorman Long was eventually able to persuade the majority of its debenture holders to accept the substitution of income shares for securities based on specific assets. As the board and its bankers had been aware, however, such a transaction was vulnerable to legal action by a dissenting minority.[139] A small group of £133,000 debenture holders were able to get Chancery to put aside the scheme on the grounds that their guaranteed security was being infringed, in particular with respect to the preferential treatment accorded to Barclay's unsecured loans.[140]

By the time this happened, however, the merger was already foundering on the rocks of other particular interests, and a resubmission to attempt to resolve this situation never took place. But this powerful position did enable the Dorman debenture holders to play a preponderant role in the reconstruction of the company following the failure of the merger proposals.

The other cluster of interests that occupied the foreground of the protracted period of negotiations were the South Durham debenture and preference shareholders, who had both a comparatively good current earnings record and important strengths in the event of a liquidation. None of the schemes that were put forward could guarantee them an assured earning power in a merger company sufficient to compensate them for surrendering these benefits.[141] Hence, in any successful scheme whereby Dorman Long was to acquire control, it would have to find cash to buy this group out, and that was something that it did not have.

Certain of the governor's industrial advisers within the Bank of England were prepared to consider the tactical application of their cash to resolve this deadlock. Nigel Campbell,[142] for instance, wanted to circumvent these obstacles by the establishment of an operating company in which the Bankers Industrial Development Co. would guarantee to buy out South Durham's stockholders who wanted to sell. This would additionally permit Dorman Long to avoid a comprehensive settlement with its bondholders as a precondition of merger. It would give South Durham "exactly the sauce at the end—namely cash" which was needed to push the scheme through. At the same time it would provide BID with a whip hand over Dorman Long during the period of reorganization.[143]

But Sir William McLintock, the Bank's chief accountancy adviser in this case, dismissed this idea as "hopeless."[144] Only a direct cash offer could, he considered, be effective. The BID had to decide "whether to sacrifice principle at an additional cost of £1m in order to evince progress."[145] But Campbell would not go so far as a direct initiative: "It would put BID in an impossible position if they were to make such a move now."[146] Bruce Gardner rejected McLintock's proposal from a more conservative position—"finding money to let people out was against our principles"—although he did concede that "in this case it might conceivably be considered at a later date."[147] When he discussed the principle with Montagu Norman, however, he found the latter adamantly "opposed to buying anyone out in any conditions"; Norman's preferred tactic was to let the matter "stew . . . it often happened the less keen one appeared to get people in, the more anxious they became."[148]

Norman's worldly-wise maxim was not apt. "Stewing" in this case was only a recipe for further retrenchment. In the absence of outside assistance the talks between Dorman Long and South Durham were broken off from the summer of 1930 until 1932. This delay critically damaged the prospect of a merger because of its impact on the rival companies' coke oven position. Both Dorman Long and South Durham had coke ovens that were nearing obsolescence and would have to be replaced shortly. The clear need was for centralized coking facilities between Redcar and Cargo Fleet.[149] The only alternative was the reinforcement of existing suboptimal competing structures through separate development. But any central coking plant would necessarily be on a Cleveland/Grangetown site, and as such it would greatly strengthen the position of Dorman Long vis-à-vis South Durham, even though it would neither "cut across, nor would it be altered by any future amalgamation."[150] Dorman's own coke oven plans were, in fact, more or less the same as the centralized scheme would be,[151] and it intended to implement them, whether or not South Durham participated.[152]

Hence, backing for a centralized plant would in effect be a scheme for one company alone. South Durham decided that its competitive interest was best served by unilateral building at its own works.[153]

When negotiations foundered in June 1930 the company commissioned these new ovens.[154] The BID tried to mediate to persuade both parties to agree to the formation of a separate operating company for a new coke plant, but neither party would cooperate.[155] As South Durham clearly realized, not only was this a damaging blow to the prospect of a merger, but it also reinforced overlapping capacity by the installation of a cramped and inadequate new plant.[156]

The final 1933 merger scheme that did go forward proposed to resolve the thorny questions that had held up progress for so long by, in effect, buying out the South Durham stockholders at the expense of the Dorman Long debenture holders.[157] Its shape was determined by combined pressure from Barclays, the City, and certain Dorman Long directors.

The Dorman Long board was for a long time unwilling to tackle the debenture holders.[158] South Durham did not press this issue at the start. During the spring of 1932 Mitchell and McQuistan were still seeking ways of leaving the debentures intact in a merger, but by April it was apparent to both sides that this could only be done at the cost of enormous overcapitalization, and McQuistan refused any longer "to be a party to bolstering up or perpetuating a situation that cannot possibly be run on commercial lines." In 1932 United Steel Companies Ltd. had set the pace for recapitalization at £7.10 per ton of output, a figure that implied that Dorman Long's £19 million capital had to come down to a maximum of £8 million. McQuistan insisted that although Dorman Long and its "City friends can juggle with the figures as much as they like . . . sooner or later they have got to come back to this basic principle." Its capital had to be written down.[159]

McQuistan forced this on Mitchell. He, in turn, pushed by Barclays, forced the debenture holders to accept that "the situation is going from bad to worse" and that they would have to "swallow the pill."[160] But even this did not satisfy the South Durham stockholders. Their active blocking and final rejection in the courts of even this relatively favorable scheme has to be understood in relation to the particular nature of their interests in the firm.

One group among them had a primarily rentier position; they viewed South Durham's stock as "gilt-edged" and their main interest was security. Another group feared involving themselves with what they regarded as a "rubbishy company" like Dorman Long, which they hoped would fall apart as a competitor.[161] But the core of the opposition was a lobby of local, primarily Hartlepool, capital, grouped around Cresswell Pyman, the managing director of William Gray and Co., shipbuilders of West Hartlepool, who feared that the merger would lead to the closure of South Durham's West Hartlepool works or else the subordination of Hartlepool to those of Middlesborough.

Firms like William Gray, which was South Durham's largest local customer, did not want to jeopardize their close customer relationship with the local steel firm.[162] These local interests had been very influential in the destruction of rival local concerns at Jarrow;[163] they now were able to defeat the merger proposal in 1933 and then delay resubmission by a lengthy suit in Chancery—a delay sufficiently prolonged effectively to wreck the scheme.[164]

They were largely correct in these fears, although their defense of local interests was not necessarily based on accurate economic calculations. The merger would result in the closure of the Stockton Plate Mills and the downgrading of the Hartlepool works. No new money was to be allocated to the Hartlepool plant under the merger.[165] John E. James, Talbot's deputy, concluded: "I think it is their intention to wreck South Durham."[166] Talbot recognized that one of the essential features of the merger was that excess plate capacity should be eliminated in order to facilitate diversification into other trades, which was one of South Durham's most pressing needs.[167]

Meanwhile, behind the scenes in all these maneuvers, Barclays Bank and the Bank of England were playing out an intricate parallel game. Barclays were bankers to both South Durham and Dorman Long, and Goodenough, its managing director, was anxious "not to lose any of the banking position which he has looked after for so long."[168] The bank had at risk unsecured overdrafts to Dorman Long of £2 million, but against this it was always clear that no postmerger investment program could be made effective in the depression without bank credit. More specifically, Barclays also held a significant power in the form of holding the ordinary share capital of Redpath Brown as security for a loan. This gave them the power to sell Redpath Brown to another firm and thereby seriously damage Dorman's structural steel business, which, although not very profitable in itself, provided important steel outlets.[169] In the eyes of the BID this meant that the bankers' position was essentially stronger than that of the debenture holders.[170]

In a sense this was correct, but Barclays was extremely sensitive to the formal weakness of its security in a reconstruction. Hence, in any scheme Goodenough was extremely anxious to secure a cash settlement of at least a significant part of the overdraft for the bank, or at least to get guarantees for its interest and rights in a restructured company. Its role as banker and creditor placed Barclays in a contradictory position with its role as trustees for the Dorman Long debenture holders. It was hardly compatible to demand and get a cash settlement for itself and at the same time persuade the debenture holders to accept less.[171] But unless it radically sorted out this position, the bank knew that no settlement would be acceptable to the BID that did not minimize the debt and rights encumbrances of the new company.[172]

Both Barclays and the BID wanted the other to take on the role of risk-bearing merger promoter. The BID, which represented central banking and the issuing houses, felt that it should only "supplement the efforts of Barclays,"[173] and that the clearing banks should bear the most risk. It wanted Barclays to fund its loans and give up its rights to foreclose on its specific securities, especially Redpath Brown. Unless this were done, the BID anticipated major problems in raising public capital for the merger.[174] It feared to give Barclays any hint that the Bank of England had a special interest in the Northeast Coast lest the bank try to take advantage of it.[175]

For a long time its complex interests made Barclays move hesitantly and were a difficulty in the way of any scheme.[176] In the end, however, it was Barclays who formulated Scheme Y on which the final scheme was based, drawing on a plan formulated by the Bank of England's solicitors for a Northeast regional merger. The scheme was very favorable to Barclays: £290,000 of its overdraft was paid off in preferred shares and £1.65 million of its debt remained outstanding. Interest on this would only be payable out of profits, but half the profits available after the payment of bank interest were to be used to repay the overdraft. Embarrassed by its position as trustees for the debenture holders, Barclays kept its role in this proposal secret and presented the scheme as coming from Mitchell.[177] In its capacity as trustees Barclays then advised the debenture holders to accept it. As Mr. Justice Maugham was later to point out when a minority of the debenture holders took the case to Chancery, in such a complex matter the shareholders' vote necessarily depended largely on the information they were given. Barclays' circular was deliberately misleading and unfairly conferred "substantial advantages" on the bankers.[178]

Barclays desperately wanted the BID to commit itself to backing the scheme,[179] but the BID would do so only if it minimized outstanding fixed charges. At present the BID felt that the level was so high as to imperil the scheme. The BID's initial survey indicated that the merger's earnings would provide only the "scantiest cover" for these charges, let alone for adequate depreciation.[180] Norman wanted fixed charges at almost nil for the first six years of merger, but Goodenough would not go beyond a three-year partial moratorium.[181]

The BID insisted on sacrifices all around and took a rigid position on its own terms for participation. It would not provide cash for buying anyone out.[182] It would provide cash only following an amalgamation for reconstruction; it would not buy out interests to secure one, even though it recognized that such a course "might mean the death of the scheme."[183] The BID implemented this policy rigorously.[184] Skinner, Norman's personal adviser, was even unhappy about the informal backing the BID was giving to the scheme, because the merger in itself—even though it was not using BID money—was violating the principle of "not buying people out" in the terms offered to the South Durham preference holders. He felt that the Bank was leaning too far toward a "get the work done at any price" attitude[185] and that it was being used by Barclays whom he did not trust. "Goodenough," he lamented, "always tries to implicate [BID] but only tells half the story."[186]

The Chancery cases effectively disrupted the amalgamation scheme. The Dorman Long debenture holders pressed for a receivership, and the board called a three-month moratorium to win time to prepare a reconstruction scheme.[187] The reconstruction that followed was dominated by the debenture holders.[188] The main feature of the new scheme when it emerged was the stress it laid on the preferential income rights of the debenture and preference holders. The company would have to divide its profits "up to the hilt" to pay these charges and initially even borrow to meet them. As *The Economist* concluded: "For the time being, therefore, the Company has secured the goodwill of its Debenture and banker creditors at the expense of its ability to create reserves or apply additional amounts of depreciation."[189]

The abandonment of amalgamation was accompanied and reinforced by the rapid revival of profits in 1933–34. Thus, although Goodenough persuaded the debenture holders to reopen talks with South Durham in early 1934, Talbot was not interested.[190] South Durham's profits were moving from £43,000 in 1933 to £105,000 in 1934, and it was in a position to demand still stiffer terms in any merger.[191]

Despite continued urging from the BID, rationalization by merger faded from view.[192] The debenture holders concentrated on internal reorganization. Their "watchdog" was Ellis Hunter, who as a partner in Peat, Marwick and Mitchell became secretary to the debenture holders in 1934.[193] Hunter was "behind what was happening long before it was seen that he was the fellow that was pulling the strings."[194] His aim was to clear out managerial "white elephants" and to establish more stringent managerial control at all levels.[195] So, in particular in alliance with the technocrat Laurence Ennis brought back from the Sydney side as a "strong man" across the group,[196] he whittled out the old guard, the businessmen of the old school like Mitchell and Walmsley,[197] restructured the commercial side of the business, and vigorously pruned corporate office administration.[198]

Although Hunter finally became managing director only in 1938 when Ennis retired, he was the real power behind the chairmanship of the figurehead Canadian financier and M.P., Hamar Greenwood. Greenwood "knew nothing about the iron and steel industry. He carried the AGMs by his own personality. He didn't understand what the people were talking about, but he got away with it." Hunter was formidable and difficult: "He didn't want to say 'no' to someone he was personally very friendly with, so, consequently, there were very few people he was very friendly with."[199]

Despite these internal changes, without combination the expansion and development of Dorman Long in the 1930s could not be based on fundamental reorganization but tended to continue along existing lines and perpetuate overlapping, bottlenecks, and dispersion. The most remote and old-fashioned blast furnaces and steelworks up river at Clarence and Newport were finally dismantled in the mid-1930s, thus making Dorman Long rather more geographically compact.[200] But otherwise development was ramshackle. A new battery of 136 coke ovens to produce thirteen thousand tons per week of coke was built at the Cleveland works for £600,000 and this was the biggest coke oven plant in Europe at the time.[201] But it was not part of any centralization program to achieve economies of integrated processes. By the late 1930s Dorman was producing 1.5 million tons of ingots per year from twenty blast furnaces and thirty-three steel furnaces at five works, four of which were literally within a stone's throw of each other.[202]

Plant expansion in the 1930s was dominated by the need to press every melting unit to its utmost capacity. Improvements made during the depression had not taken into account the problems of full capacity working, and bottlenecks were a persistent headache; charging and auxiliary equipment were often the main constricting factors.[203] Major blast furnace improvements were not planned until 1937 for Cleveland and Redcar, and until World War II nearly all of Dorman's blast furnaces remained hand charged and limited in scale by the need to fit in with the adjacent steelmaking and rolling plant.[204]

Thus, when expansion picked up in the 1930s it was channeled through old structures. The depression had produced no significant shake-out, and revival took place within the framework of regional oligopoly and overcommitment. Why did depression fail to clear the decks? It was rarely severe enough to *compel* merger or bankruptcy; most firms had the option to survive by sitting tight. Those that had been reasonably prudent in the 1920s like Consett and South Durham did not find it too hard to survive; but Dorman Long, which in terms of its size and facilities had a chance of dominating the region, had pursued unsound financial policies, which made survival harder than it was for its less potentially powerful rivals. Many of the firms might have benefited from mergers, but such moves were essentially forward-looking calculated risks rather than compelling necessities or bargains with obvious advantages. They depended on assessments of trends and perceptions of long-term advantages and involved decisions to take control of the market rather than merely reacting to it. The institutional structures of the firms blocked such developments. Within the firms shareholders, creditors, and customers took quite different views from managers as to where the balance of their interests lay vis-à-vis security, income, and growth. The defense of these positions created intractable problems. Managers were restricted in their decision making by the difficulties of forecasting, partial knowledge, and an aversion to unnecessary risks; beyond this the protracted survival of owner/manager structures built intense family and personal animosities into the economic conflicts. The banks might have overridden some of these conflicts if they had been able to work with powerful boardroom allies toward a clear goal. But the clearing banks were bogged down in preserving their "neutrality" between rival firms and nursing their loans, and the Bank of England, which did have a defined strategy, was unable to find a powerful grouping of entrepreneurs to push forward its ideas on the ground. Instead it was confined to external exhortation. In a situation of weak internal management, no one was able to win the confidence of wavering groups of shareholders and creditors to a program of positive proposals. The schemes foundered on legal actions, personal animosities, and pressures from important customers and local interests.

This is not to say that merger and rationalization were a panacea for the industry that the steelmakers missed out on. It is probable that a major shake-out of old and scattered plant and the concentration of control and investment in the 1930s would have produced a more profitable Northeast Coast industry in the 1930s. But the revival also showed that the steelmakers had been no fools in believing that they could do very nicely once revival came with the existing structure of production. Battening down the hatches and surviving was a reasonably low-risk strategy for this purpose. The weaknesses that remained made the steelmakers more vulnerable to new competition in expansion than they might otherwise have been; some of the consequences of this are examined in a later chapter in the context of the project for a steelworks at Jarrow. But in general, the complex and cramped decision-making structures of the firms were capable of no broader framework or horizon of decisions, and the line of least resistance was followed.

4.

The Scottish Steel Industry, 1918–1939

The interwar years saw the emergence of something akin to a regional steel monopoly in Scotland under the control of Colvilles Ltd. The contrast with the continuing multifirm fragmentation on the Northeast Coast is striking, but two qualifications to this picture must be made at once. First, the move toward quasi-monopoly was slow and erratic. As Table 9 and Figure 3 show, although Colvilles controlled 40% of Scottish steel output in the 1920s, the decisive breakthrough to 80% control did not come until 1936. Second, even when the concentration of ownership did come, the legacy of the previous fragmented structure persisted strongly within the new combine. Amalgamation did not provide a context for a radical resolution of underlying structural problems of a declining resource base, outdated locations, and restricted markets that were even more acute than on the Northeast Coast. Scottish combination was not the vehicle of large-scale reorganization so much as an alternative to it. Mergers were not the result of technical imperatives of production such as the pursuit of economies of scale, relocation, or the introduction of new processes or products. Nor can they be attributed, as Peter Payne has done in his recent book on Colvilles, [1] to the greater dynamism of that firm's leading entrepreneur. In fact the Scottish steel firms were as incapable of restructuring themselves by their own efforts and as crippled by the antagonisms of rival interests within and between firms as those on the Northeast Coast. Rather, the argument of this chapter is that the root of this contrast lies in the relationship between the steel firms and their regional industrial context and product market. It was this context that enabled giant shipbuilders in alliance with bankers to exert strategic control in reshaping the industry. Their influence was

Table 9   Steel ingot output of various Scottish steel companies, 1920–1940 (in thousands of tons)

Year	Colvilles[a]	Steel Company of Scotland	Lanarkshire Steel Co.[b]	James Dunlop & Co.	Stewarts & Lloyds	Scotland[c]
1920	829.5		163.9			2,074.4
1921	267.6		Nil			583.4
1922	267.4		73.4			768.1
1923	501.9		102.2			1,252.9
1924	588.6		113.6			1,241.4
1925	455.5		119.7			1,074.6
1926	166.4		32.1			423.7
1927	694.5		111.0			1,587.6
1928	626.3	237.3[d]	106.6	108.0[d]	162.0[d]	1,425.1
1929	697.6	249.5[e]	119.4	109.6[e]		1,581.6
1930	496.5	314.0[e]	105.4	98.2[e]		1,212.9
1931	349.4	157.6[e]	74.5			676.2
1932	275.5		68.6			552.7
1933	386.4		89.3			799.3
1934	693.2		130.0			1,220.3
1935	736.9	254.2[a]	141.8			1,326.0
1936	897.3[f]	326.8[a]	169.2			1,636.9
1937	1,029.1[f]	356.3[a]	170.5			1,895.1
1938	881.8[f]	294.3[a]	155.2			1,601.5
1939	1,544.4[g]		196.0			1,872.8
1940	1,608.4[g]		230.8			1,998.8

Sources: See footnotes a through e.
a. Colville records.
b. Lanarkshire Steel Co. Statistical Records, Output of Melting Furnaces.
c. BISF *Annual Statistics.*
d. Brassert *Report.*
e. Calculated from Notes on Steel Output, 4 Oct. 1932.
f. Glengarnock, Dalzell, and Clydebridge Works only.
g. Glengarnock, Dalzell, Clydebridge, Blochairn, and Hallside Works only.

by no means all-powerful, and the results were not always what they intended. Nevertheless, the interaction between these groups and the Scottish firms best explains the major changes in the structure of Scottish steel in this period: reorganization of firms without restructuring of production.

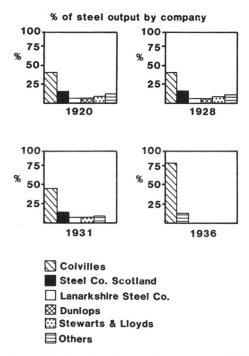

% of steel output by company

1920

1928

1931

1936

◩ Colvilles
■ Steel Co. Scotland
☐ Lanarkshire Steel Co.
▨ Dunlops
▦ Stewarts & Lloyds
▤ Others

Figure 3 Growth of Colvilles' Scottish steel monopoly, 1920–1936 (percentage of steel output by company). *Source:* See Table 9.

Structural Weakness and the Emergence of Shipbuilder Control, 1880–1923

The problems of the Scottish steel industry in the first half of the twentieth century can be traced to certain features of its nineteenth-century origins. Scotland was the home of the first and largest nineteenth-century iron industry, based on its local splint coal and iron ore resources. But although the geological conditions favored iron production, they did not fulfill the needs of steel. Scottish iron ores had a relatively high phosphorous content which was not suited to the production of either malleable iron or steel where it resulted in undue brittleness. Scottish puddlers eventually managed to use Scottish pig to make malleable iron by labor-intensive methods, but their early failures discouraged Scottish ironmasters from integrating forward into puddling. They remained specialized at the level of smelting pig iron, and it was separate firms that pioneered the development of malleable ironmaking in Scotland, largely as suppliers to the Clyde shipbuilders' enormous needs for forgings.[2]

Instead of linking themselves to the principal iron manufacturing trade, the Scottish ironmasters integrated backward. They developed a relatively self-contained and independent sector based on iron, coal, and by-products. The biggest ironmakers—William Baird & Co., William Dixon & Co., Coltness Iron Co., and Merry & Cunninghame—became also the largest coal owners. They used the local soft splint coal rather than coke in small blast furnaces, which in effect combined the functions of coke ovens and blast furnaces.[3] By driving these furnaces more slowly than the conventional British practice of the time, the ironmasters maximized their by-product yields. The low iron productivity of this practice was offset by the cheapness of the coal and the value of the by-products.[4] The ironmasters' by-product recovery plants attached to their furnaces were often their most important source of income, especially in depression years.[5] Pig iron became in many respects an outlet and epiphenomenon of an expanding coal sector, and its pattern of development was contingent on the needs of that sector. When steel began to rise in importance in the 1880s, there was no compelling reason for the ironmasters to look to imported ores and imported coke to serve the new sector. For the time being the old set-up remained viable. The long-term exhaustion of Scottish coal and ores inevitably meant eventual decline for these producers,[6] but before the war Scottish pig iron output carried on, rising to a record level of 1.4 million tons in 1910, and the underlying weaknesses remained masked.[7]

Hence, it is hardly surprising that it was not the Scottish ironmakers who took the initiative to develop steel production. The impetus came from the rapidly expanding shipbuilding industry, which had used malleable iron in the past but in the 1880s wanted steel. This pressing demand made it worthwhile for entrepreneurs to improvise production around the less than ideal raw material base. Early attempts to use Scottish ores to make basic Bessemer steel resulted in a traumatic failure,[8] and it was possible to use it in acid open-hearth furnaces only with considerable improvisation by skilled labor or in relatively small proportions in conjunction with scrap and imported hematite ores. Mostly the nucleus of the new industry was the existing malleable iron firms. These puddling businesses faced a twin crisis in the 1880s: their labor costs were rising sharply in a labor-intensive process, and at the same time their largest customers, the shipbuilders, were abandoning malleable iron for steel. To survive they had to move into steel.[9] This switch had long-lasting consequences. The malleable firms carried with them their practices of using a skilled labor force and local coal and coping with technical problems through labor-intensive methods in small-scale acid open-hearth furnaces. This made possible the use of a certain amount of Scottish iron along with imported ores and scrap. The location of the new steel industry also reflected that of the old malleable iron trade. The separation of ironmaking from malleable iron manufacture was perpetuated in the separation of iron from steel. In 1900 only three out of fifteen steelworks were integrated with blast furnaces.[10] Thus, paradoxically, although the impetus to create a steel industry came from consumer demand rather than geology, the locations of the new industry were the inland ones of the malleable iron producers and not the coastal ones of the shipbuilders. Nevertheless, in the buoyant trade conditions from 1880 to the war, few voices were heard urging relocation.

Until the war the scale of production of steel remained fairly small, and the lack of integration of processes meant that there was little hot-metal practice. But costs were kept down by the use of a high proportion of plentifully available cheap Scottish scrap and cheap imported Spanish hematite ore. These materials could be used along with a certain amount of Scottish pig in the closely controlled small open-hearth furnaces.[11] Before the war Scottish steel prices were above those of Cleveland steelmakers, who were the Scots' main competitors in their local markets; but Scottish prices were still below the average British price in 1913,[12] and through discounts and close customer relationships with the local shipbuilders the Scots were able to withstand competition from outside the region.[13]

By the outbreak of war the underlying weaknesses of Scottish steelmaking were clearly identifiable. It was a fragmented industry with small-scale units unable to take advantage of hot-metal practice and the available economies of scale. Its location was increasingly anachronistic, and its dependence on shipbuilding customers was suffocatingly close. At the same time the Scottish iron industry was locked into its own cycle of decline as its raw material base approached exhaustion. The war and the postwar boom brought major changes to the industry, but none resolved any of these problems. The war brought the rapid expansion of Scotland's steelmaking capacity—the largest firm, David Colville & Sons, increased its steel output by 250%—but no new blast furnaces were built in Scotland. Ministry of Munitions' demands were for immediate results with little scope for balanced long-term development, and the lack of integration between iron and steel was reinforced. There was also a considerable shift in the structure of firms during the war. David Colville & Sons moved from being a medium-sized firm producing 24% of Scottish ingot output to being clearly the largest firm with 46% of total output. The share of output of their nearest rival, the Steel Company of Scotland (SCS), fell over the same period, 1914–1919, from 18% to 16%.[14] Scotland emerged from the war with more concentrated ownership and considerable new steel capacity.

In the long run probably the most important changes took place in the postwar boom when, in a hectic two-year period, the Scottish shipbuilders took over all the major Scottish steel companies. The shipbuilders made their move under the intense but short-lived pressure of a shortage of steel supplies in 1919 and 1920 as the shipping lines initiated massive rebuilding programs under the influence of misguidedly optimistic prognostications of a renewed expansion of demand in the postwar world. Once shipbuilders started closing in on their suppliers, a follow-the-leader effect sent others scurrying to make sure they were not left out in the cold, and a scramble ensued in the overexcited atmosphere of the boom.

The most important initiative came from Lord Pirrie, the chairman of the Royal Mail Group of shipping lines and head of the giant Belfast shipbuilders Harland & Wolff, which built almost solely for the group, and a leading figure in John Brown & Co., of Clydebank. Pirrie's move to secure control of David Colville & Sons began in 1917 with attempts to guarantee supply through a 25% shareholding. But this fell through, and as supply pressures tightened in 1920, Pirrie finally bid successfully for outright purchase of all of Colvilles' ordinary share capital. This, Pirrie believed, would "enable us to get all the steel we required within another month or so."[15] Harland & Wolff thus secured ultimate control of Colvilles, and when, on the death of Lord Pirrie in 1924, Harland & Wolff was bought up by the Royal Mail shipping group, this control passed into the hands of Lord Kylsant, the head of the group who himself took on the chairmanship of the Belfast shipbuilders.

In the same month that Colvilles was bought by Harland & Wolff, the Steel Co. of Scotland rejected an approach from Barclay Curle for a three-year supply agreement.[16] But within weeks they were bought outright through a direct bid to their shareholders by a Clydebank syndicate comprising Alexander Stephen & Sons of Linthouse, Yarrow & Co. of Scotstoun, Scott & Son of Greenock, Campbeltown Shipbuilding Co., and several other smaller shipbuilding companies.[17] This consortium was originally formed around the idea of subscribing a fairly modest £100,000 each toward the purchase of the Glasgow Iron and Steel Co., but this firm was recognized to be backward and in need of major capital expenditure, and, at an asking price of £1.2 million, the consortium came to think that "the investment would not be a brilliant one." The companies thought the Glasgow firm was not worth more than £900,000, but the steel industry was being gobbled up rapidly, and rather than drop out of the chase for steel, they turned to the "much bigger proposition" of the Steel Co., even at an inflated £30 per share. As a result, as F. J. Stephen of Alexander Stephen & Sons realized, "now much more will be required and I am doubtful if some can rise to the bigger figure," which would perhaps be as much as £500,000 each.[18] Stephen & Sons had the financial resources of Lord Inchcape's P & O shipping group behind it, but others like William Denny of Dumbarton "who at first led us [Stephen's] to believe they would take the largest share of any of us, in the end dropped out." The price they finally paid is not known but although "fairly high" was not felt by the firms to be unreasonable as a price for getting desperately needed steel supplies at a time when order books looked full.[19]

The other three major Scottish steelmakers, Lanarkshire Steel Co., James Dunlop & Co., and the Glasgow Iron & Steel Co., were also swallowed up by shipbuilding groups as the wave of buying continued. The biggest purchaser was Clarence Hatry's Sperling Group of shipbuilding companies, which included the Northumberland Shipbuilding Co., Workman Clark of Belfast, William Doxford & Sons of Wearside, and 85% of the Fairfield Shipbuilding and Engineering Co. of Govan. The group was new and expanding fast. In February 1920 it attempted to buy up another major shipbuilder, Swan Hunter and Wigham Richardson of Newcastle-on-Tyne, which was itself trying to move in on steel firms through bids by their wholly owned subsidiary, Barclay Curle & Co. of Glasgow. Hunter, its chairman, suspected that the aim of the Sperling group was merely to "rob his companies of their ready money and then hoard it to buy other concerns," and the offer was refused.[20] To meet its enormous requirements for steel, the Sperling group established major supply contracts with Dorman Long and South Durham/Cargo Fleet on Teesside and bought the Lanarkshire Steel Co. through Workman Clark.[21] In late 1919 it also offered £900,000 for the Glasgow Iron & Steel Co. When this was refused, it made another abortive bid for the Steel Co. of Scotland.[22] It bought up all the ordinary shares of Baldwin's Ltd. of Port Talbot, which had been a major supplier of steel to Workman Clark before the war, at £3 per £1 share in a secretive deal in February 1920.[23] This deal had a knock-on effect. Before the war Russell & Co., (renamed Lithgows Ltd. of Port Glasgow in 1918) had relied on Baldwin's for large amounts of steel at peak times, buying through the steel merchants Peter MacCallum & Sons. Deprived of this source, it secured its supply of steel by purchase of a controlling interest in James Dunlop & Co.[24]

Swan Hunter and Wigham Richardson had failed in their attempts to acquire first Colvilles and then the Steel Co. of Scotland through their Barclay Curle subsidiary. When their renewed approaches to Colvilles were rejected, they joined 50/50 with Beardmore to buy the Glasgow Iron & Steel Co. They were scraping the barrel for steel acquisitions. Just a few months before, the SCS consortium had thought it unwise to go above an offer of £900,000 for the company; now, however, the group finally paid £1.5 million.[25]

This activity amounted to a remarkable regional concentration of capital. The two largest and most capital-intensive industries in the Belfast-Clydeside region were brought together into giant vertically integrated combines. The close interrelatedness of the two industries had a long history, and whether or not they were under common ownership their mutual dependence was bound to be great. What then were the effects of integration on two industries with such closely congruent production cycles? First, it is clear that no technical changes or economies of production arose from the mergers. Only one proposal, that of Barclay Curle to Colvilles in 1917 which mooted ambitious proposals for standardization and mass production of ships, went beyond the framework of securing supply.[26] The shipbuilders' sole concern seems to have been to ensure that they got the steel they needed. The steel firms were impressed by the inflated prices being offered for purchase, and both Colvilles and the Steel Co. of Scotland believed that these links would enable them to gain a disproportionate share of available demand.[27]

There was some truth in this, although important qualifications must be made. Once the slump was under way the shipbuilders could not create contracts out of nothing. The Steel Co. of Scotland had been purchased to satisfy desperate steel needs in April 1920, but by December the purchasing consortium was already aware that its orders would dry up within eight months.[28] As we shall see, the effectiveness of a link to a shipbuilder depended on that shipbuilder's order books and that in turn usually depended on that shipbuilder's further links to major shipping lines. Moreover, an ownership link could often not guarantee an order even when orders were to be had. For instance, Barclay Curle owned 50% of the Glasgow Iron & Steel Co., but when in 1923 P & O commissioned Barclay Curle to build two large steamships, it also compelled the company to buy its steel from the Steel Co. of Scotland with which P & O was linked, rather than from the Glasgow Iron & Steel Co.[29] Hence competition for orders continued in a disguised form within the framework of the new combines although with more rigidities and anomalies. Strategic interests within combines rather than price competition could determine the direction of orders. Consequently some steel firms did better from their ownership linkages than others. SCS sold 25% of its make to its own consortium in 1930.[30] But the links could cut both ways. In the mid-1920s Lord Kylsant's Royal Mail Group tried to cut out Lord Inchcape's P & O–controlled shipyards, which gave preference to SCS steel, as far as their ship repairing was concerned. In retaliation P & O did the same to the Royal Mail–controlled Harland & Wolff yards, which took Colvilles' steel, and considerable animus developed between the two combines.[31]

Integration with shipbuilders was therefore no panacea, but those firms that did not have links with strong shipbuilders had still greater difficulties. Beardmore, for instance, was not linked to any other large Clyde or Belfast shipbuilder, and, as we shall see, when its shipyards at Dalmuir slumped in the 1920s, the firm suffered acutely from lack of outlets for its Mossend plate mill. Likewise, the owners of Lanarkshire Steel Co., Workman Clark & Co. of Belfast, were in a state of collapse throughout the 1920s, and the consequent weakness of Lanarkshire's shipbuilding outlets meant that it looked much more to the export market than any of the other Scottish firms.[32] Possession of links to shipbuilders did not guarantee success, but lack of those links could be most detrimental.

A closer look at the position of Colvilles can amplify the position. Colvilles' most important trade was the production of plates at its Clydebridge works. The shipbuilders to which Colvilles were linked by ownership were Harland & Wolff and John Brown & Co., and in 1927–1931 these two firms took 37% of the Clydebridge plate production (250,859 out of 681,796 tons), although in the mid-1930s this fell back to an average of only 23%.[33] Harland & Wolff, the largest British shipbuilder, produced 10% of interwar British tonnage, and John Brown, which ranked twelfth, produced 2.6% of gross tonnage.[34] John Craig always felt that at these levels a guaranteed outlet to an additional shipbuilder was necessary to secure the consistent production runs that Clydebridge needed.[35] In the context of the depressed trade conditions of the 1920s and early 1930s the only other decisive source of purchasing power was Lithgows Ltd., the third largest British shipbuilder at that time, and this, as we shall see, was to prove a decisive force in the reshaping of the Scottish industry.

The influence that Sir James Lithgow was able to exert on development of the Scottish industry stemmed from his vital purchasing power as a shipbuilder and from his great financial strength. In the late 1920s, Lithgows of Port Glasgow and its associated yards produced more than one-third of Clyde tonnage, and with Harland & Wolff took more than half of the shipbuilding steel used on the Clyde and in Belfast combined.[36] Between 1919 and 1929 Lithgows built 1.8% of world tonnage, and as the market diminished in the slump it held

onto a disproportionate share. In 1932–1934 it built an average of 5½%
of world tonnage each year, almost one in every sixteen new vessels
in the world. In 1932 its output was a staggering 61.8% of Clyde
output.[37] While John Brown of Clydebank and Beardmore at Dalmuir,
Clyde giants that specialized in warships and liners, languished, the
Port Glasgow yards, where tramp shipping and cargo vessels were
being built, spearheaded the shipbuilding revival of the thirties. Tramp
shipping had held up better throughout the 1920s too. Lithgows Ltd.
made profits in every year of the 1920s—although only small profits
in the mid-1920s—and in 1927–1930 its output was climbing to prewar
levels. In 1929 it produced its greatest ever tonnage.[38] In a struggling
industry these were fine results, but they could not in themselves
have given Sir James Lithgow the financial muscle to intervene in
the steel industry. The roots of his strength lay in the enormous
reserves that he inherited before the war from his father's immense
personal fortune, which were greatly enhanced by wartime profits.
These resources were carefully husbanded in the postwar boom. Although acquisitions of both steel and shipbuilding firms were undertaken, this was done without incurring either heavy overdrafts or
costly debenture issues. Thereafter, as trade became difficult in the
1920s, financial resources were conserved within the company by not
paying out dividends to the family members and partners who held
the bulk of the shares and by concentrating on depreciation and reserves instead.[39] The depth of the Lithgow family's purse also enabled
the firm to make the most of the available business. Throughout the
1920s Lithgows continued the prewar practice of building "on spec"
when orders were scarce, and, as in the case of major customers like
the Lyle Shipping Co., would encourage shipping firms to build in
slack times by partly financing the construction of ships via the retention of shares in the completed ships.[40] With Lyle's business holding up profitably throughout the interwar years, this policy proved
an effective way of stimulating business.

Lithgow's commercial power was allied to a formidable personality.
Born in 1873, he exhibited a dauntingly energetic temperament allied
with a ruthlessness toward his workers. He was a great believer in
the virtues of wage-cutting. His biographer has argued that in his
commitment to work and production as well as to wealth Lithgow
was not an archetypal hard-faced capitalist,[41] and John Hume and
Michael Moss saw much of his business behavior as "essentially al-
truistic" and stemming from a deep Christian conviction in the moral
value of productive activity.[42] His religiosity is undoubted; he was a
traditionalist and fought against the revision of the Scottish hymn

book, and he gave enormous benefactions to religious causes. But there is no evidence of noneconomic motives in his business practice; rather it seems that his philosophy was that God's rewards were earmarked for those who were efficient in the cause of free enterprise. And in that cause he was a fiery champion. His colleagues remembered his habit of bursting into rooms and starting to talk at once even before he sat down. While he made the sparks fly, his brother Henry was cast as the moderating influence, ever present but always in James's shadow. Yet, as James Reid commented, "the partnership was so close that there could perhaps be a shade of make-believe in the contrast."[43]

A successful shipbuilder like Lithgow had great potential power over steelmakers—as to a lesser extent did the big shipbuilders that were linked to the resources of major shipping combines, as Harland & Wolff was to the Royal Mail Group and Alexander Stephen was to P & O. The less successful and smaller shipbuilders, however, could do little for their allied steel firms in the 1920s. For crisis-ridden firms like Workman Clark and Beardmore, probably the most significant effect of integration came from the significant loss in liquidity incurred by buying rather poor firms at a time of inflated prices. The £750,000 that Beardmore contributed to the purchase of the Glasgow Iron & Steel Co. lay in their books as an intractable part of their debt burden throughout the decade.[44]

The steelmakers, therefore, faced a market of a limited number of big and a few giant shipbuilding customers, nearly all of whom were linked to rival steel companies. The loss of such customers could mean disaster for a steel firm, and in the conditions of the 1920s it was not likely that major customers could be won by price competition. Moreover, other outlets were severely limited. Peter Payne has estimated that Clyde and Belfast shipyards swallowed 60% of all Scottish steel.[45] Hence, the potential influence of the large customers on shaping the organization and policy of the steel firms was considerable. Their actual influence, however, depended on whether they wanted to use their position, whether they were financially able to do so, and whether they had any clear idea of how they wanted to use it. In the absence of these factors the steelmakers would be largely left alone to pursue their own policies from their vantage point as rival firms with diverse internal interests. Reorganization, or the lack of it, in the 1920s was to be dominated by the latter considerations. It was only in the early 1930s that the power of the shipbuilders began to reemerge forcefully, primarily through the muscle of Sir James Lithgow who enjoyed considerable backing from the Bank of England, but also through the financiers and accountants who by that time controlled the remnants of Lord Kylsant's collapsed shipping and shipbuilding empire.

The problems of tackling the structural weaknesses of the industry have to be seen against this background. As we have seen, the inland locations of the industry were anachronistic. The iron industry was old-fashioned and declining fast, steel was excessively dependent on scrap as a raw material, and when imported ores were used they had to be freighted inland and the manufactured steel shipped back again to the coast. The industry as a whole was a patchwork of old and new, efficient and inefficient works. The results were high freight costs, high raw material assembly costs, poor fuel economy, and lack of economies of scale. Three issues were inseparable from any attempt to resolve these problems: the amalgamation of firms, the integration of different stages of production through the creation of modern blast furnace capacity, and the relocation of the industry on the coast. But who could carry such a program through? No single firm had the power to do it alone, but once questions of merger or cooperation were raised, all the myriad conflicts of interest between and within firms at once came to dominate the stage.

Stalemate on Rationalization, 1923–1931

Some talk about the possibility of mergers had taken place during the war—Colvilles had sympathetic discussions with Lanarkshire, the Steel Co. of Scotland, and Beardmore at various times[46]—but it was the slump of the early 1920s, the moves to amalgamation elsewhere in the country, and the failure of the Scottish Steelmakers' Association to maintain prices and profits[47] that really brought the issue to the fore. Even so, for most of the 1920s there was little enthusiasm to be found among the Scottish firms for a large regional amalgamation. In 1923 Lord Invernairn, the chairman of Beardmore, initiated a set of proposals and a round-table discussion with all the major Scottish steelmakers on the issue,[48] but his scheme got little support from other firms. Beardmore's interest in an amalgamation stemmed from its critical financial position, and the only other firm that showed sustained interest in the proposal was Lanarkshire Steel Co. (LSC), which was also looking for a buyer.

Colvilles sniffed around the scheme, but it was not really interested. The outlook of Lord Pirrie of Harland & Wolff and John Craig, the chairman of David Colville & Sons, was that a regional amalgamation could not possibly solve the problems of the Scottish industry; the Scottish makers were not equipped to be a self-contained unit and needed to link themselves with either South Wales or the Northeast Coast. The assembly of a Scottish combine did not offer immediate and sizeable advantages and was also fraught with local animosities and conflicts of interest. Hence, they would pursue a regional combination only if broader discussions failed and they were faced with a series of regional amalgamations in other districts.[49]

They were, however, interested in some sort of broader Anglo-Scottish amalgamation, and this remained a major theme of Colvilles' policy throughout the 1920s. In the mid-1920s Lord Pirrie and Lord Kylsant (who succeeded Pirrie at Harland & Wolff after the latter's death in 1924) made several approaches to the leaders of major British companies to formulate interregional amalgamation schemes, but without success.[50] In the late 1920s Craig continued to work on similar lines. However, sympathetic takers were to be found only in those quarters where regional combinations did not seem attractive, such as on the Northeast Coast where, as we have seen, Ben Talbot of South Durham and Cargo Fleet hoped to use a national amalgamation to circumvent Dorman Long's regional expansion.[51] Richard Thomas & Co., the big South Wales–based steel and tinplate firm, also showed an interest in a merger with South Durham and Colvilles as a way of enabling the firm to make better use of its modern but distant and unprofitable Redbourn works in Lincolnshire. But in late 1927 South Durham was pulled out by its chairman, Lord Furness, who was "getting very sceptical about a lot of these affairs" and who, unlike Talbot, was still open to further talks on a Northeast regional merger. After this, despite Richard Thomas's enthusiasm, the idea soon folded.[52]

While pursuing these broader schemes, Craig was also prepared to "proceed in a non-committal way" to discuss local merger proposals with other Scottish firms. In 1926–27 he had informal contacts with the SCS, Beardmore, Stewarts & Lloyds, Glasgow Iron and Steel Co., and Lanarkshire Steel Co.[53] Most of these initiatives did not amount to much more than turning over the problems, however. Only one local merger seems to have been an attractive and feasible proposition with definite commercial advantages, namely a Colvilles-Lanarkshire merger. The Colvilles board thought the ownership of this firm "most desirable."[54] The Flemington works were adjacent to Colvilles' Dalzell works at Motherwell, and it rolled a wider and largely complementary range of products so that the two plants could be run in conjunction effectively. Moreover, the Lanarkshire management was itself very much in favor of a merger. In depression it was able to utilize the low overheads of its old plant to win trade. It kept outside the Scottish Steelmakers' Association and frequently broke ranks in buying and selling agreements.[55] But a revival would not really help the firm, and

James Strain, the managing director and dominant figure in the firm, did not believe that it could be run successfully as an independent concern in the long run. As far as he was concerned personally, he had "no desire to enter into any further enterprises. He is a man of 62 years and seems to have plenty of money . . . though very much interested in coal as a hobby, he does not want to begin a new business."[56]

Yet despite these favorable conditions the merger talks broke down. Lanarkshire Steel Co. was not its own master; the real control lay in the hands of the shipbuilders Workman Clark & Co. of Belfast and Lanarkshire's bankers, Lloyds Bank. In 1926 the Northumberland Shipbuilding Co. went into the hands of the receivers; its wholly owned subsidiary Workman Clark wanted to sell Lanarkshire to Colvilles, but in this case ownership was not the same thing as control. Lloyds Bank held all the prior lien debenture stock of Lanarkshire Steel Co., and in this capacity it had also come to hold all the ordinary shares of the company and their collieries as security. As such it was the real seller and the management "cannot move without [its] authority."[57] Despite Strain's efforts to offer an acceptable price, Lloyds demanded £270,000, which it reckoned was the scrap value of the works.[58] Colvilles' estimates were that "its *full* market value to us is only £180,000."[59] It was prepared to go up to £200,000 to eliminate a "troublesome competitor" and because Colvilles believed it could considerably improve results by better management, but the plant was "unbalanced in layout with insufficient furnace capacity," and although "there is one excellent mill . . . it is not supported by the other necessary plant," and it would require £50,000 capital expenditure to rectify this deficiency.[60]

Lloyds was always likewarm about a sale that might mean writing off losses. Colvilles, however, took the attitude that "it might be a favour to [Lloyds Bank] to be freed of this liability."[61] This pattern recurred when negotiations were reopened in autumn 1928, with Strain again urging Colvilles to buy, Lloyds refusing to allow the price to fall below £200,000, and Colvilles refusing to go above £150,000.[62] Lloyds wanted to recover its capital; Colvilles wanted the increased earnings from a merger. But it would first have to find cash for Lloyds, and in the tight position of the late 1920s that was an unacceptable risk for a marginal increase in revenue.

The extra cash might have been forthcoming if discussions with Sir James Lithgow about a possible joint purchase had reached fruition. Lithgow assured Colvilles that if there was a joint purchase he would leave the running of the Flemington works solely in Colvilles' hands. Nevertheless, the Colville board still feared that Lithgow might impose restrictions on its freedom of action, and the deal fell through, even though Colvilles was aware of "the considerable benefits . . . in other directions" of some "definite connection with Messrs Lithgow."[63] The stalemate made a merger more and more difficult. Lloyds Bank, far from encouraging merger moves, allowed Lanarkshire extra loans for extensions in 1928–29, aiding the finance of a new furnace.[64]

Thus, bank control was a formidable barrier to the exit from the industry that the Lanarkshire management favored. In other firms, too, major company policies were often determined by a complex internal balance of personal, financial, and managerial forces, which could override the simple calculation of economic advantages in any particular transaction. The structure of authority and control in Colvilles was a multilayered cake of owners, managers, family, and creditors. Colvilles was owned by Harland & Wolff, which was a part of Lord Kylsant's Royal Mail Group. This was a large, loosely federated combine, and the top management's concern was primarily with the shipping end of the business.[65] As a result, the running of Colvilles was left almost entirely to the Colville board, which operated as a virtually autonomous enclave within the larger concern. Kylsant and his predecessor as chairman of Harland & Wolff, Lord Pirrie, both took a personal concern in overall policy and in particular were concerned to act as ultimate arbitrators in any merger questions, as their voluminous correspondence with John Craig testifies. But, by and large, in the 1920s the Royal Mail link was hardly visible. As we shall see, however, it was to emerge as a major complicating factor in reorganization moves in the 1930s.

Until that time, however, the decision-making structure in Colvilles was dominated by the slow ousting of the old family management by a rising independent managerial corps. The family had been the main active practical managers until its dominance was broken when Archibald and David Junior, who had run the firm since the death of their father, the founder, in 1897, both worked themselves to death in 1916.[66] The younger Colvilles were not equipped to take over. The most able of them, James Lusk, the founder's grandson, was killed in action in 1915. Norman Colville suffered from poor health as a result of a war wound, and he was also somewhat erratic: in 1921 he borrowed £10,000 from John Craig personally and lost it in a misguided oil fields deal.[67] Both he and David Junior became members of the board in 1920, but both lacked authority and experience.[68] This situation necessitated a promotion from the staff to fill the chair. The man appointed was John Craig who was to dominate the firm until his retirement in 1955 at the age of 82.

Craig was the son of a Colvilles blastfurnaceman who had worked his way to the top since starting as an office boy in 1888. He was a man of prodigious energy and deep religious convictions.[69] The personal credo by which he ordered his life combined the Protestant ethic and militant antisocialism: "I believe," he wrote in his personal notes, "the Lord helps those who help themselves and just as firmly that the Lord is on the side of the right."[70] Around him he gathered an able and accomplished management team, notably the new general manager G. P. West and the academically trained technical expert Dr. Andrew McCance, who was to figure second only to Craig in the interwar years.[71]

Initially the new management lived in the shadow of the family. Craig had a strong personal sense of loyalty to the family, and at first he conceived of his role as one of trusteeship for the younger members of the Colville family. But as sentimental ties to the deceased Colvilles grew more distant and none of the younger generation emerged as a forceful active manager, Craig and his board increasingly asserted their own and the firm's independent interests against the family. The family, however, for some time retained its old sense of a divine right to run the firm. Mrs. Colville constantly lobbied Craig to find positions in the firm for the Colville children: in 1926 she wanted John to be made a director because "it might cheer him up," and in 1924 she wanted Craig to invent a fictitious business mission in order to coax the unhealthy Norman to go out to the Colville rubber plantations in Ceylon.[72] Craig at first had a hard time resisting such pleas, but as day-to-day affairs came increasingly under the control of professional managers, the Colville family came to identify its interests with its role as rentiers and lenders of large cash loans to the firm rather than as the owners. From as early as 1921 the family was threatening that unless its present 6% interest rate was maintained, it would consider shifting its money to government securities,[73] and in the previous year Craig had unhappily noted that the attitude of the three younger Colvilles was that "if they give up control at all they would prefer to do so completely."[74]

Yet the continued involvement of the family had definite advantages to management. As Lord Pirrie noted, it kept the bulk of the company's loan stocks in amenable hands which could be more easily pressed to allow the business some leeway in difficult times. When the Colvilles were contemplating getting out of the business in 1920, Pirrie urged Craig to use his "judicious handling . . . to make the sons of my old friend realise what a sacrilege it would be to permit the business which was their father's pride to get into the hands of people who could not possibly take the same interest in it." He himself urged the family to look on the business as a "precious heritage."[75]

The family no longer controlled the board, but as cash lenders its position became of vital strategic importance in the years of depression. By 1931 the outstanding debt to the family lenders stood at £1,579,382, and Colvilles had been largely dependent on these loans for their working capital throughout the 1920s.[76] The family creditors constantly argued for more security and for the priority of their loans ahead of bank advances in the 1920s, but Colvilles faced none of the demands for repayment that other firms faced from outside lenders.[77] Nevertheless, some sort of settlement with these creditors was an essential precondition for any merger or reconstruction, and the family thereby retained a crucial blocking power, the same sort of ability to say no that we have seen Lloyds Bank exerting at Lanarkshire and which, as we shall see, the Treasury as guarantors of a Trade Facilities Loan could exert at SCS.

Colvilles' bankers were the National Bank of Scotland, which had been taken over by Lloyds Bank in 1918[78] but still operated autonomously in its advances to local industry. Throughout the 1920s its overdraft to Colvilles hovered between £500,000 and £800,000, a large figure in relation to the bank's capitalization to an extent which the bank found alarming.[79] All through the 1920s the NBS was pressing Colvilles to reduce its overdraft to more acceptable proportions and taking up shares of Colville subsidiaries as security.[80] Yet the size of the overdraft was such that the bank was as much dependent on Colvilles as Colvilles was on the bank, and it was in no position to compel action without incurring serious costs. Nor was it in any position to bear the risks of merger promotion. It favored the rationalization of the Scottish steel industry by merger and informally pressured Colvilles toward a big regional merger.[81] But by 1930 the floating debt of £2.25 million that the bank and the family held was a serious incubus to carry into any merger talks.

Colvilles' internal decision making was therefore essentially professional, hierarchical, and compact but subject to major external constraints in the form of the overriding policy goals of the big combine of which they were a peripheral part and the financial constraints arising from two powerful blocs of creditors. The Steel Co. of Scotland had a similar external constraint arising from a loan of £180,000 made by the Royal Exchange Assurance Co. and guaranteed by the Treasury through the Trade Facilities Act in 1927.[82] The loan was for the remodeling of its Hallside works, but the work was not completed until 1930 and no profits had been made on it when the trough of the interwar depression arrived.[83] The Treasury thus became SCS's most powerful creditor with a seat on the board for its nominee and the ability to veto proposals it did not like.

Internally, however, the structure of SCS was in sharp contrast to that of Colvilles. Whereas the Royal Mail Group had left the Colville management intact, the consortium that bought SCS dismissed the entire existing directorate and stacked the new board with representatives of the various shipbuilders. The only experienced steelmaker was the new managing director, W. G. Gray. Management remained weak throughout the 1920s; on several occasions board meetings were inquorate and unable to take decisions; and there were sharp disagreements among rival directors over policy. In 1921 Emile Aitken-Quack of the Ardrossan Dry Dock Co., one of the new directors, proposed a big bonus share distribution of £200,000 from reserves on the ground that the company's cash resources were beyond its immediate requirements. After sharp controversy the bonus distribution was finally cut back to £50,000,[84] but in 1923 a majority of the directors again insisted on a £19,000 dividend pay-out despite the fact that the company had a loss of £128,000 in that year.[85] Gray had the thankless task of presiding over this boardroom infighting, and as the years passed he developed a practice of keeping information away from three directors he thought unreliable.[86] Ownership by the consortium also had a damaging effect on commercial policy. One of the first acts of the new board was to close down SCS's Leeds and Birmingham agencies with the intention that SCS would act solely as a supplier to the shipbuilding owners.[87] The slump in ship construction rapidly made it clear that this was a short-sighted policy. Whereas Colvilles had a stable, experienced, and competent board running the firm as a fairly autonomous entity free from short-term outside interference by the wider group, SCS had almost the opposite. No single shipbuilder in the consortium was dominant. Alexander Stephen was the biggest, and it had the important resource of a link to P & O through Lord Inchcape's holding of 51% of its shares, but Inchcape's writ did not run through to the SCS board. Although Gray's authority seems to have increased over time, SCS remained a conspicuously weakly led firm.

Shipbuilding influence clearly pervaded all aspects of Scottish steel in the 1920s, but were there any precise objectives behind this influence? Most of the shipbuilders were very wary of the emergence of a giant Scottish steel combination or monopoly and were ready to prevent it even at the price of higher steel costs. As Craig observed to Lord Kylsant, "While the shipbuilders have not derived any profit from their [steel companies] and, in some cases have had to meet losses, still they have looked upon the actual possession of the works as an asset and will, we believe, continue to operate them irrespective of their results." Any merger, for instance, that would enable Colvilles to control 60% or more of the industry was likely to face undercutting competition from shipbuilding interests which "might consider it too great a risk to be at the mercy of our company."[88] In particular, SCS, the second largest Scottish steelmaker, under the control of its consortium was likely to be very wary of involvement in a merger dominated via Colvilles by Kylsant's Royal Mail Group. It was always the most prone to stand back from merger talks in the 1920s and refused even to attend discussions after the first meeting on Invernairn's scheme in 1923; during the talks on the Brassert scheme at the end of the decade it stayed largely on the sidelines.

At the same time, however, some shipbuilders at least were increasingly afraid of dependence on an ailing and backward industry. Andrew Duncan, the chairman of the Shipbuilding Employers' Federation, reported Sir James Lithgow's description of this contradictory position to Craig in 1925. At that time Lithgow had closed down Dunlop's steelworks and was purchasing half his steel from the Continent and the other half from England because "as he said, other people were stupid enough to be willing to make it for him in this country. But he realised, and believed the whole shipbuilding industry realised, that if the heavy steel industry was to collapse, cheap steel would not be available to the British shipbuilding industry from the Continent any longer and therefore that industry would itself collapse." Nevertheless, Lithgow insisted that in the current conditions he had no alternative to his current course of action if his costs were to be kept down.[89] Throughout the 1920s in talks with Colvilles on various merger matters, he had always refused any proposal that might involve confining his purchases of steel to any one company. He insisted on retaining his freedom to buy in the cheapest market. Gradually his position was to change to one of recognizing that rationalization by merger was of paramount importance to shipbuilders and steelmakers alike and to throw his weight behind that cause. In the 1920s, however, that was a thing of the future.

In the meantime, the main initiatives toward large-scale rationalization of Scottish steel came not from the shipbuilders or steel entrepreneurs but from elements of the wider industrial, political, and financial establishment. The first of these was a proposal put forward by the banker F. A. Szarvasy in early 1927 to form a giant holding company to take in Colvilles, Richard Thomas, United Steel, South Durham and Cargo Fleet, Baldwin's, Bolckow Vaughan, and Dorman Long.[90] The background to the scheme is not entirely clear. Szarvasy himself came from the British Foreign and Colonial Corporation, and he had important connections both with the Mond group and with the Kylsant group, for which he had acted as a key financial intermediary in the purchase of the White Star Line the previous year, although there is nothing to suggest that he was acting on Kylsant's behalf in this case.[91]

Whatever the actual origins of the scheme, steelmaking circles thought that they detected the hand of important financiers and bankers behind it. Craig suspected that the Rothschilds might be at the back of it, using Sir Harry Peat as their agent—although this suspicion was based only on a chat he had had with Peat in a train carriage coming back from Paris a few months earlier. With a scent of possible finance for reorganization in the air, the steelmakers "professed to be much interested" because, as Craig told Kylsant, "they felt that behind Mr. Szarvasy the banks were seeking to exercise some influence."[92] Sir William Larke of the National Federation of Iron and Steel Manufacturers saw the political significance of the initiative as a quid pro quo in the federation's tariff diplomacy at a time when the whisper going around was that the Cabinet was largely influenced in its attitude to the trade "by the feeling that those responsible . . . had not shown sufficient leadership."[93]

Szarvasy described his scheme to Larke as tentative and not "concrete positions which everyone can pull to pieces."[94] Craig thought it "largely academical." Nevertheless, an informal committee of steelmakers was formed to consider the proposals, but within three months talks petered out.[95] Szarvasy's idea was that a holding company could evolve gradually into an amalgamation, rather on the lines of the formation of Imperial Chemical Industries (ICI), and thus avoid some of the pitfalls of amalgamation. It could be created "without any reference to the shareholders of the existing companies, and all negotiations could be conducted privately, whereas if there was any attempt at amalgamation it would be so public and would take two years to carry through and would at this stage be somewhat easier to try."[96] The individual identities of the component companies would be retained, and they could, if they wished, resume independent operations at the expiry of the agreement. Craig was skeptical from the start: the scheme was "not worthy of support" because it did not face up to these problems and "no half measure can hope to succeed."[97] If the agreement were not permanent from the start, "the retention of the personal interest in any business would rob it of the benefits of a real wholehearted amalgamation." Within the holding company some firms would benefit at the expense of others; certain works would be maintained better, or skilled labor would be attracted away from those plants not fully employed. Firms were being asked to risk their competitive positions without any guarantee against disguised competition *within* the holding company or against reversion to competitive practices afterwards.[98]

More important than the specific proposal was the indication it gave to those in the industry interested in mergers that financial aid might be available for a major scheme. Henry Bond of Richard Thomas, who was president of the NFISM in 1926, reckoned that "whoever does make a start will have a good deal of outside support which will be given in the hope of inducing others to join." His own private talks with the merchant bankers Morgan Grenfell underlined the advantages of being "first in the field."[99] But he believed that an effective scheme could come only from the steelmakers themselves: "It is no use Sir Harry Peat or Szarvasy or anyone else to put their oar in at this stage," he told Craig.[100] Craig agreed; the way forward as he saw it was through delicate private talks among the leaders of industry: "Six or seven of the leading makers who have expressed sympathy with the idea of larger units in the trade being formed, should go into the country somewhere, to a quiet hotel, make up their minds that they would for a few days sit down to discuss in all its aspects the present situation of the industry, and, in an undisturbed manner, set themselves the task of endeavoring to evolve a practical scheme."[101]

What sort of support could the steelmakers have expected from outside financiers if they had devised such a scheme? Steel had not yet entirely lost its prewar aura of a large, successful, and profitable industry; that it was in a state of long-term decline was not yet widely recognized. Rather there was still a prevalent conviction in the City that some sort of scheme could cut the Gordian knot of the problems of the industry. The Szarvasy scheme was only one of a number of City approaches to the industry between 1926 and 1928, and in this context it is not so surprising that one of the largest financial speculations between the wars came in the form of Clarency Hatry's adventure into steel. In general, however, City figures flew kites in the direction of the industry while steelmakers talked in cabals, and little more than gestures came out of it on either side.[102]

Something rather different, however, began to emerge in 1928, although in its first stages it resembled the earlier kite-flying exercises. In April 1928 Lord Weir, the wealthy Glasgow industrialist, and Harry McGowan of ICI, acting for the newly formed Anglo-American Finance Corporation, approached John Craig about a merger for the whole Scottish steel trade. The inspiration for this activity was Weir's conviction, which Craig shared, that tariff protection for steel was being delayed by the steelmakers' inactivity with regard to reorganization. Craig saw the opportunity to use this finance to create a

Colville-controlled merger, and he urged that Anglo-American involvement be kept secret lest it "encourage statements of higher values than might otherwise have been made" by other companies and thus "create difficulties."[103] Sir James Lithgow was also approached, but he was suspicious of the scheme. He disliked the connection of the finance with Alfred Mond and ICI. He was bitterly hostile to Mond's involvement in the Mond-Turner talks at this time, and he referred to the employers participating in it as "blackleg employers."[104] Even more important, he distrusted what he called the "Mond Finance Scheme" because it represented the introduction of outside finance and control into the Scottish steel industry and awakened his fears that a Scottish steel monopoly could have a whip hand over the shipbuilders. In consequence, "as far as he was concerned, he would meantime enter into a shell and await developments as he had no particular love for such finance being introduced into the Scottish industry."[105]

Lithgow's attitude critically damaged the scheme's prospects of success. A press leak,[106] an indiscreet private conversation by Harry McGowan with Lord Invernairn of Beardmore,[107] and the crisis at Beardmore in the autumn of 1928[108] brought the proposals to a temporary halt. But in December 1928, with the backing of "leading members of government" and assurance that "government money would be available at a low rate of interest provided a suitable combined scheme was submitted,"[109] Weir reopened discussions with the major steelmakers and with William Baird & Co., the biggest ironmasters, and by February 1929 reached agreement that H. A. Brassert & Co., the leading American consulting engineers, should be commissioned to investigate the question of combination and the creation of modern blast furnaces in Scotland.[110]

With the commissioning of the Brassert report, for the first time in the decade the question of amalgamation was linked to the fundamental questions of production and industrial structure. Previous discussions had turned almost solely on commercial and financial matters, and even now many of the steelmakers were unhappy that Brassert, backed by Weir, used his brief to produce a comprehensive analysis of the structural ills of the industry. Craig later told Kylsant that Colvilles had "not anticipated that Brassert would suggest an entirely new steel plant; indeed the instructions were quite definitely to limit the preliminary report to pig iron."[111] The very idea that the pig iron question could be addressed separately from steelmaking is indicative of the narrowness of vision among the leaders of the Scottish industry. In fact, as noted earlier, the modernization of Scottish ironmaking raised the issues of location, integration of processes, and the raw material base, and these issues necessarily directed attention to the whole structural unsoundness of the Scottish industry.

Brassert went back to first principles in analyzing the Scottish industry. In effect he produced a blueprint for a best-practice iron and steel industry starting from two observations: first, that the old splint-coal blast furnace practice was obsolete; second, that the best-practice modern plant had to be a fully integrated chain of processes running from ore docks to finished products.[112] He noted that current demand for basic pig iron in Scotland far exceeded supply: in 1927 only 41,000 out of 298,000 tons used in Scotland were manufactured locally, and he noted that Scottish steel ingot output in 1927 fell 720,000 tons short of Scottish consumption. He concluded that to replace these imports and to reduce Scottish reliance on scrap for almost 70% of its steel-making raw materials, Scottish pig iron production should be increased from 692,000 tons per year to between 1.2 and 1.5 million tons per year—nearly all the increase being in basic pig.

The contents of Brassert's report have been thoroughly examined by Peter Payne and there is no need to go into detail here.[113] Briefly, Brassert proposed the construction of a new, fully integrated iron and steel works with modern ore docks and coke oven plant on the Clyde tidewater near Erskine Ferry. He rejected the pursuit of lower capital expenditure by using any of the existing sites as a basis for development: such a "temporary convenience" would prove to be a lasting handicap.[114] Although the makers' own examination of his report broadly upheld his costings, the committee of steelmakers finally rejected the scheme. Payne has laid great stress on personal antagonisms among the leaders of the industry in explaining this outcome—"they all hated each other," as he puts it.[115] This is quite true, but there were other circumstances that allowed these hatreds and jealousies full rein.

First, Brassert's report was weak in its analysis of competitive conditions. It made no attempt to estimate costs at less than full capacity operation. Yet Bird of the Steel Co. of Scotland argued that below 81.5% capacity it was cheaper to produce steel at an existing plant than at a new works because of the higher level of fixed charges on the latter, and Scottish output had never reached that level in the 1920s.[116] Similar arguments were common in the technical press.[117]

A more crucial flaw was that Brassert started from the premises that recent upward movements of scrap prices formed part of a continuing trend whereby scrap would become more expensive and scarcer and that imported pig iron would also become more expensive. The reliance of Scottish steel on imported pig and scrap therefore appeared to be a fatal weakness, and a domestic ironmaking sector was not merely desirable but essential.[118] But in fact the relative movements of prices in the following years undermined the basis of Brassert's scheme: depression gave a new lease on life to existing patterns of raw material use and procurement. Scrap prices, far from rising, plunged for the next seven years. Imported scrap was 68 shillings per ton in Scotland in 1929 but fell rapidly to a low of 43 shillings in 1933 and only exceeded the 1929 price again in 1936. In the downturn the price of scrap was below the prime *costs* of the best-practice British ironmakers.[119] Hence, Scottish scrap imports, far from declining, moved up from 325,000 tons (35% British scrap imports) in 1929 to a peak of 507,000 tons (47%) in 1936.[120] Imported pig prices followed a similar course. In the autumn of 1929 Tata Iron & Steel Co. announced that it could deliver one million tons of Indian pig iron to Colvilles over the next ten years at a cost even less than the cost of production envisaged for the new tidewater plant,[121] and in December 1930 the Steel Co. of Scotland was able to sign a contract for 24,000 tons of Indian pig per annum at 60 shillings delivered to works.[122] It was only in 1936–37 that reliance on scrap and imported pig began to produce the commercial problems that Brassert had thought imminent in 1928–29. By then the market price of scrap had soared to a ruinous 100 shillings per ton, and the Scottish steelmakers were saved from a serious crisis only by the BISF scrap levy, which cut the price to 65 shillings per ton.[123] Brassert's foresight was confirmed, but by then the tidewater scheme was aready dead and cold.

In the short run, however, the savings involved in the scheme were less marked than they appeared in Brassert's presentation. The relevant comparison for the steelmakers was not between existing works and Brassert's scheme but between modernized and improved works and the scheme. Many of the economies proposed by Brassert at stages of production later than the ingot stage were realizable by new investment at existing plant; hence, the savings up to the ingot stage were what really counted. Brassert intended to reduce the proportion of scrap used to 50% and charge Scottish basic pig iron from the new furnaces for the other 50%. The new furnaces could produce pig at 58/6d per ton, and the current Scottish ironmakers' average cost was 77/4d (see Table 10). But this comparison was somewhat misleading because barely any Scottish pig was currently used in basic steelmaking; the relevant comparison was with imported pig prices (which were 73/6d when Brassert drafted his report but which had fallen to about 60 shillings by late 1929) and with second-best solutions in Scotland. In late 1929 Bairds and SCS devised a joint plan to produce pig at a modernized Gartsherrie works for 61 shillings per ton.[124] Brassert reckoned the new works could produce plates at 119 shillings per ton

Table 10 Comparative costs of production at existing works in Scotland, at a new tidewater location, and at modernized inland sites, 1929

Product	Existing works[a]	New tidewater location[b]	Modernized works[c]	Imports[d]
Basic pig iron	77s. 4d.	58s. 6d.	60s.	60s.
Steel plates	165s. 2d.	119s. 0d.	135s.	130s.

Sources: See footnotes a through d.
a. Brassert *Report*, pp. 51, 153–155.
b. Brassert *Report*, pp. 139–145.
c. Figures are for Gartsherrie works producing iron for SCS steelmaking. See Note of a Meeting on Brassert Report, 14 April 1930 and 12 May 1930, Baird Papers.
d. For pig iron (Indian), DCS Minutes, vol V, p. 342, 15 Nov. 1929. For plates (German), ICTR monthly figures.

as compared with German imports at 130 shillings per ton and the current Scottish average of 165/2d per ton. This was impressive, but a modernized inland works feeding separate improved existing steelworks and working with a 65% scrap proportion could split the difference and produce plates at a level close to the import price at about 135 shillings.[125]

Hence, although the steelmakers found Brassert's cost estimate robust, they were skeptical about the level of savings involved. Brassert estimated that the savings obtainable from his full program amounted to £1.2 million or 22.7% of overall construction costs. But fixed charges on the £5.4 million cost of the scheme would be substantial: they would add 7/10d per ton to the cost of pig iron and 14/11d per ton to the cost of billets. These sums would cut sharply into the production savings, and the committee of steelmakers' final estimate was that the net savings would only be £157,745, out of which some compensation would have to be paid to close down certain works. They did not consider this an attractive proposition.[126]

Lithgow's attitude was typical. He was attracted by the technical excellence and scope of Brassert's plan and declared that "it was a pity something else had to be resorted to." But it was very costly, and after talks with SCS and Colvilles he believed that only £100,000 of savings could be guaranteed regardless of conditions,[127] and in that case "he would not spend a penny of anything; the industrial situation was too bad and what he had he would keep . . . The negotiators would have to become responsible for £5 (£6?) million backed by Government at 5½% and repayable over a term and that was not business."[128] As for W. G. Gray of SCS, he "was merely listening; he was not serious; he was seeing it through."[129] His board was split three ways between those like Gray who did not believe in a larger scheme and favored an alliance with Bairds to modernize existing Scottish ironmaking; those like Murray Stephen, the chairman, who strongly favored the Brassert scheme; and those who believed they should continue as they were until they were offered attractive terms for a merger.[130] By the beginning of 1930 SCS was much more involved in talks with Bairds about a development at Gartsherrie than in the Brassert proposals. But while the shipbuilding consortium owners of SCS feared a giant Scottish amalgamation that would be dominated by Colvilles and Lithgow, Bairds feared to go all out for an alliance with SCS because it did not want to get on the wrong side of Lithgow by going ahead independently.[131] The management of Bairds wanted to draw Lithgow into the Gartsherrie scheme, but Lithgow refused. As far as he was concerned, SCS would "bring nothing into the common pot," and Gray "was a man who took unreasonable views and would have to be kept in his place." He at once turned the proposal around and began to sound out whether Bairds might be usefully associated with the merger between Colvilles and Dunlop that he was trying to put together.[132]

Lithgow had opened discussions about closer relations between his own steel firm, Dunlop, and Colvilles at a fairly early stage of the discussions on the Brassert report in October 1929.[133] Lithgow had long been worried about the possibility of being marginalized in the course of any major reorganization of Scottish steel, especially if it meant a near monopoly under Colvilles or outside financial control. A merger of Dunlop and Colvilles would link him directly to the largest Scottish steel producer and also give him an inside position in any future large Scottish scheme. At the same time Colvilles looked very favorably on such a link; as Craig noted, not only did Lithgow have enormous personal and commercial influence and prestige, which in themselves were of great value, but also his custom was of immense value. "Indeed, personally, I indicated to our people time and again that Colvilles would gladly pay £15,000 a year to secure the Lithgow orders for steel; they would make all the difference in running Clyde-bridge and be a great help to Glengarnock."[134] These commercial considerations were given a sharper edge by wider developments in 1929–30. In late 1929 the affairs of Colvilles' ultimate owner Lord Kylsant and the Royal Mail Group were moving into a critical condition. If the group went into liquidation, the future of Colvilles' link with Harland & Wolff would no longer be secure, and it was known that Guest Keen Baldwin (GKB) of South Wales was very anxious to grab a share of Colvilles' Belfast market if the link were severed.[135] Hence, Craig was keen to secure a linkup with Lithgow, even at a price. In contrast with earlier negotiations, he was prepared to be very flexible about the terms of a merger and to allow Dunlop an "undue proportion" of preference shares in the merger company to sugar the deal for Lithgow.[136] Bairds and SCS thought that Lithgow was "crack(ing) a very noisy whip" and that Craig had "given way,"[137] but Craig was not prepared to push any point that might create the "risk of [Lithgow's] going off altogether."[138] He exerted all his influence to quash the doubts of the family lenders and succeeded in getting their assent, even though they probably got a poor deal from the merger.[139]

Was this scheme a first step in a major Scottish amalgamation and reorganization or was it an alternative to the wider discussions? Craig and Lithgow both claimed that their merger did not cut across a wider Scottish scheme, but other expert views disagreed. When the leading accountant Sir William McLintock analyzed the merger, he criticized the excessive capitalization of the new company which at £4.5 million would, he believed, foster later difficulties. "I must put it clearly on record," he said, "that when I come to advise on the larger question, I must in no way be held as having expressed approval of the present capitalisation of Colvilles Ltd." (the name given to the merger company). He felt that in any future merger it could result in considerable problems with the family cash lenders and Colvilles' preference shareholders. Both financially and technically "the present scheme cannot form the basis of the larger merger."[140]

McLintock's views were of more than just academic interest. In May 1930 the Royal Mail Group had finally crashed. Lord Kylsant disappeared from the scene, at first to South Africa and later to prison for fraud, and responsibility for untangling the mess was placed in the hands of a special committee of three voting trustees, McLintock (representing the Treasury), E. Hyde of the Midland Bank, and Arthur Maxwell of Glyn Mills. All the voting rights in the hundred companies in the wreckage of the group were transferred to a special overseeing voting trustee.[141] In the case of Harland & Wolff, the trustee was McLintock. As such he had the capacity to give or refuse assent to any merger proposals by Harland & Wolff's wholly owned subsidiary, Colvilles. He disliked the scheme but it was far advanced by the time he came on the scene. As McLintock described the situation, "Lord Kylsant had not mentioned the Colville and Dunlop negotiations until one day the proposed scheme was flung at the Committee by Kylsant who could not explain it, and they had been asked to approve it then and there."[142] In the end McLintock was railroaded into consent by Craig, who had a stronger claim to represent all classes of Colvilles' shareholders than anyone else in this confused situation.[143]

The creation of Colvilles Ltd. was the only concrete result of the discussions that followed the Brassert proposal. It did little to advance the technical reorganization of the Scottish industry that Brassert had deemed essential, however. It married Colvilles' three fairly efficient steelworks at Dalzell, Clydebridge, and Glengarnock to Dunlop's small and limited Calderbank works and its obsolete hand-filled open-topped blast furnaces at Clyde Ironworks. In one sense it was one more step in the postwar process of shipbuilders' tying up their steelmaking suppliers rather than an attempt to restructure the production of steel. Yet it also had a strategic significance for the future that went beyond its technical and commercial aspects: it brought together the financial power of the Lithgow group with the productive strength of Colvilles. The Royal Mail Group before its demise had had financial muscle, but Colvilles was an enterprise very much on the fringe of its main concerns. For Lithgow, however, the efficiency of steel was a principal concern. Until this time the antagonistic interests of shipbuilders had largely reinforced the separation and competition of steel firms in Scotland; now, with the power of both Harland & Wolff and Lithgows behind a single concern, there was the prospect of a turning point.

Yet in many respects the Brassert report had provided an opening for a much more decisive break with the past. There is evidence that if the steelmakers had gone ahead they would have enjoyed significant support in government and financial circles. Lord Weir had successfully negotiated with J. H. Thomas, the Lord Privy Seal, for a government guarantee of finance if the scheme went ahead,[144] and with the Labour government looking for some great achievement in fostering industrial reorganization, Kylsant and Craig believed that in many respects this was likely to be the most opportune moment for such an initiative.[145] Montagu Norman at the Bank of England was prepared to use his influence to ensure that developments at Beardmore and Lancashire Steel, where the Bank held considerable boardroom influence, "would not be allowed to impede possible developments."[146] And the National Bank of Scotland, the most important regional bank, considered a full-scale regional merger "essential" and was likely to give it an unusual amount of leeway.[147]

Despite this, none of the important entrepreneurs in Scotland believed that the scheme would succeed; as we have seen, the short-run costs of the scheme deterred them. But it is clear that if they had gone ahead and started to build in 1930, a time of low construction costs, the new works would have been coming on stream in 1933–34 just as the revival of demand for steel began to move into gear, and it would have been a gold mine. This was the experience of Stewarts & Lloyds' development at Corby, which was based on just the sort of locational and technical innovation that the Scottish makers declined to carry out.[148] But whereas Stewarts & Lloyds had to change or face impending disaster, the option of hanging on was viable for the Scottish firms, and in due course the unreformed industrial structure prospered in the boom of the later 1930s. A big scheme involved formidable uncertainties, and all concerned preferred safety first when the risk involved was not just one of financial losses but possibly gambling with the survival of the firm.

From the mid-1920s outsiders, whether the government, City financiers, or the Bank of England, had shown more enthusiasm for large-scale rationalization in Scotland than the Scottish makers. As we shall see, these outsiders were to continue to provide support in the 1930s even though by then it was the shadow rather than the substance of rationalization that was on the agenda. In the 1920s the shipbuilders had reinforced the steelmakers' reluctance to reorganize; in the 1930s, via Lithgow's influence, this position was to be reversed. At the time of the Brassert discussions, however, this change had not yet come, and the view from the boardroom won out.

Lithgow Takes Charge, 1931–1939

By 1931, with the depression at its nadir, no steelmakers believed that a full-scale reconstruction on the lines of Brassert's recommendations was still possible. For the time being imported pig was even cheaper than Brassert's estimates of production costs at a new plant. Even the Bank of England had resigned itself to forgoing its favored project. As Bruce Gardner of the BID put it, "This may not always be so, but I think you have to see the future a good deal clearer before you could show justification for a large expenditure to produce this iron."[149] No one believed that structural problems could feasibly be tackled at such a time, but merger discussions remained at the center of the stage. In September 1931 McLintock prepared a scheme for the merger of Scottish steelmakers at the request of those makers in the aftermath of the Brassert discussions (Table 11, col. b). When these proposals became stalled in a series of claims and counterclaims by the firms involved for different percentage allocations of the share capital of any proposed merger company (Table 11, cols. c, d, and e), Bruce Gardner himself made three further proposals in the course of 1933 in an attempt to break the deadlock (Table 11, cols. f, g, and h). The various proposals and claims, as tabulated in Table 11, all failed. In addition, Colvilles held unilateral merger talks at different times with the Steel Co. of Scotland, Lanarkshire Steel Co., Beardmore, and

Table 11 Claims for percentage allocations of share capital in various merger companies in Scotland, 1931–1933

Firm	Aggregate profits (4 years ending Dec. 1931) (a)	McLintock proposal (Sept. 1931) (b)	Colvilles claim (Dec. 1932) (c)	SCS claim (Dec. 1932) (d)	Lanarkshire claim (Dec. 1932) (e)	Bruce Gardner proposals (Jan. 1933) Proposal 1 (f)	Revised proposal (g)	Further revision (h)	Colvilles final offer (Sept. 1933) (i)
Colvilles Ltd.	86.5	67.0	80	—	—	70.8	75.6	83.4	73.5
Steel Company of Scotland	9.5	18.5	14	22	—	14.1	15.1	16.6	17.2
Lanarkshire	4.0	—	6	—	15	8.75	9.3	—	9.3
Stewarts & Lloyds	—	14.5	—	—	—	—	—	—	—
Beardmore	—	—	—	—	—	6.3	—	—	—

Sources: col. a, Colvilles Ltd. memo. to C. Bruce Gardner, 30 Dec. 1932; cols. b and c, minute of meeting of parties to the proposed merger, 4 Sept. 1931, and DCS minutes, VI, pp. 182-184, 11 Sept. 1931; cols. d and e, Considerations on Scottish Iron and Steel Merger, 17 Dec. 1932; cols. f-h, C. Bruce Gardner to J. Craig, 24 Jan. 1933, DCS minutes, VI, p. 279, 6 April 1933; col. i, DCS Minutes, 18 Oct. 1933.

Bairds also without success.[150] Why were these attempts so persistent and why did they fail?

Payne has attributed this result largely to Craig's dogged pursuit of his "grand design" for a big Scottish amalgamation: "Each new frustrating complication . . . seemed only to invigorate him . . . all were regarded simply as temporary obstacles in the way of his grand design."[151] This view involves Payne in a rather tortuous interpretation of the practice of Craig's merger diplomacy in these years, which often appeared to be itself the major barrier to the realization of a merger. Craig's obduracy in seeking to preserve intact the patrimony of the Colville enterprise, he argues, prevented the fulfillment of his own vision.[152] Payne's interpretation reflects the weakness of his central theme that in the personalities of "a handful of ambitious, single-minded, powerful and gifted men" can be found the central clue to the pattern of industrial development.[153] Although there can be no doubt of Craig's ambition for Colvilles to dominate a Scottish steel monopoly, there were good reasons for the contradictory nature of his energetic activity other than his personality alone. Part of the explanation lies in the activity of the shipbuilders and bankers.

From outside the firm the Bank of England and Lithgow were pressing Craig not to let the prospects of a merger pass by. Their view was that amalgamation was a precondition for the survival of the industry in a healthy form. Bruce Gardner's diagnosis of the condition of the Scottish industry was that it was "very acute and serious . . . There is so much dead wood that will have to be cut out. In order that the Scottish steel industry may in future be on a sound foundation, I see no possibility of avoidance of cutting deeply with the surgeon's knife and performing a serious amputation, which is necessary if the body is to be saved. It is going to be painful and pretty desperate. There are individuals we all know who, rather than going through the painful process of amputation, will hang on in the desperate hope that a tariff will save the position."[154] Until 1931 the Bank had seen rationalization as a way of avoiding a tariff; from 1932 with the tariff an accomplished fact, it shifted its position to insisting that a tariff alone unaccompanied by reorganization would not solve the problems of the Scottish industry. After all, even with a tariff, "a great deal of Scotland's output will have to come south, and this will bring them up against the most intensive competition if they are to hold their output."[155] Nor would their major customers, the shipbuilders, look kindly on the featherbedding of their major supplier if costs remained high. As Bruce Gardner put it, the Bank was extremely concerned about the political implications of any change of heart being "put down to the beneficial results of tariffs relieving the pressure" to

merge and reorganize.[156] Merger activity was an essential outward
sign that the steel industry was putting its house in order, and the
BID exerted a constant behind-the-scenes pressure in that direction.
It was highly critical of Craig's inflexibility in negotiations about percentage allocations in a merger. It felt that "it did not matter much
whether a few percentages more or less were obtained *provided one
could only get something done.*" Because in conditions of depression
no clear relationship existed between the value of assets and the
movements of profitability, endless holes could be picked in any valuation, but "though there may be injustices felt, far more money
would be lost by the delay in finessing for position rather than getting
on with the job."[157]

Colvilles' own analysis of the results of possible combinations did
not, however, correspond with the view from the Bank. Its financial
position was bad enough, but that of SCS was a good deal worse.
Colvilles' had averaged £225,244 trading profits over the four years
1927–1931; but after interest and depreciation its average net profit
was probably not more than £30,000. SCS trading profit had averaged
£24,601 per year, but its net profit was only half that amount, and
that figure was boosted by very good results for 1930 due to two
exceptional orders.[158] Moreover, SCS's Hallside works were a financial
hemorrhage, and from the beginning of 1931 the company was due
to commence repayments on its Trade Facilities Loan amounting to
£10,000 per year.[159] Colvilles was not anxious to take on board such
a sick partner. Had there been clear advantages in operating costs
arising from a merger to offset this, things might have been different,
but there were not. Savings in a tripartite merger with LSC and SCS
would come first from rolling an enlarged range of sizes in Lanarkshire's mills and second from reallocating SCS tonnage to Colvilles'
works and thus increasing the load factor at Clydebridge and Glengarnock.[160] From June 1931 Colvilles could have closed down both
SCS works, taken over all SCS tonnage, and still worked below capacity; but there would still be expenses arising from keeping SCS
plant on a care and maintenance basis.[161] Overall the net effect in bad
and moderate trade might be to slightly improve Colvilles' net profit
position (Table 12, lines 1–3). But the benefits resulting from reallo-
cation would disappear as soon as trade revived. As Colvilles recognized, linked to Harland & Wolff and Lithgows, "In busy times
we could do without contributed tonnage, by our strong connections
and 'goodwill.' "[162] As Table 12, line 8, shows, a tripartite merger
might raise the level of Colville profits in depression but it might
actually dampen them down in times of better trade. Colvilles' relatively strong potential cost position meant that management would

Table 12 Effect of a tripartite merger on the net income of Colvilles Ltd.[a] in various conditions of trade

Condition	Output (thousands of tons)	Profit per ton	Savings/profit from merger (£ 000)	Gross profit (£ 000)	Depreciation (£ 000)	Remainder (£ 000)	25% paid to partners (£ 000)	Colvilles Ltd. net profit (£ 000)
Bad trade								
Colvilles alone	300	6s. 8d.	—	100	80	20	—	20
Merger: estimate 1			80	180	120	60	15	45
Merger: estimate 2			50	150	120	30	7.5	22.5
Free prices and no profits								
Colvilles alone	300	1s. 0d.	—	15				—
Merger			−14.5[b]	0.5[c]				—
Moderate trade								
Colvilles alone	400	10s. 0d.	—	200	80	120	—	120
Merger			100	300	120	180	50	135
Good trade								
Colvilles alone	500	15s. 0d.	—	375	80	295	—	295
Merger			100	475	120	355	88	263

Source: Colvilles Ltd., Considerations on Scottish Iron and Steel Merger, 17 Dec. 1932.

a. Assuming that Colvilles Ltd. are allotted 75% of shares.

b. The document notes, "i.e. Colvilles carry burdens, but distribute nothing."

c. Made up of £15,000 profit at Colvilles; £17,000 loss at SCS; and £2,500 profit at Lanarkshire.

look very carefully at allying with firms whose long-term position might not be as strong.

Nor would Colvilles' creditors be prepared to accept a further impairment of their position. Following the merger with Dunlop the family creditors and the National Bank of Scotland had agreed to an eighteen-month moratorium on loans and overdrafts amounting to £1,680,948. Over this period the suspended interest payments amounted to £229,000.[163] No merger deal would be satisfactory that did not provide the necessary cash flow for these payments, but if the merger included SCS it would also have to make provision for a first charge to repay the Trades Facilities Loan. This charge directly conflicted with the claims of the Colville family, who had lent large sums without any debentures "on a very clear understanding that their security was not to be impaired." It was therefore impossible simply to take over the TFL debt in a merger.[164] Even if a solution to the question of rights and priorities could be found, the question of cash flow remained critical. Craig formulated the nub of the issue in his jottings: "Has DCS more chance of getting £63,000 per year as it is now, OR in a merger of which it owns 72% with Colvilles Ltd? *Now* it needs total profit of £150,000 (£160,000?) to pay £63,000 out to DCS . . . *as merger* what profit would do, and should it be more easily earned—with savings? ie, Could merger distribute £100,000 if it made £200,000? Could merger save £50,000 per year?"[165]

Thus, consideration of available production economies, cash flow for debt finance, and the rights of creditors makes it clearer why Craig was prepared to endlessly discuss mergers and yet at the same time constantly balk at the flexibility necessary to complete one. Craig took a position that would cover him in all these eventualities and stuck to it. As he told McLintock, "It is all very well to say that the big company is to reap the biggest rewards, but you must not ask them to sacrifice too much."[166] His target was an 80% allocation in a Colville/SCS/Lanarkshire merger, a figure closely in line with recent trading profits performance (Table 11, col. a) but well above McLintock's estimates based on the value of assets (Table 11, col. b). Yet each 1% advance by Colvilles on McLintock's percentage allocation required reducing SCS's share of the merger company by 5%, a prospect scarcely likely to entice SCS to participate. McLintock thought that the cost of a rather lower share for Colvilles was trivial against the advantage of bringing in SCS; he stressed that SCS had made substantial profits in the past and would no doubt do so again in the future.[167] But, as we have seen, Colvilles' own assessment of the prospects of a merger cast the issue in a rather different light.

SCS showed interest in a merger but stalled at Colvilles' essentially punitive terms. Lanarkshire, however, had found itself a market niche in the conditions of depression that made it quite comfortable for the time being. The bulk of its plant was thirty to forty years old, but the firm enjoyed a new lease on life because of its low capital charges and its ability to charge 95% abnormally cheap scrap (40 shillings per ton as against 67 shillings per ton for basic pig) in its steel furnaces, whereas the different qualities manufactured by Colvilles and SCS prohibited these firms from using more than 70%.[168] After 1929 Lanarkshire's costs decreased more rapidly than its output, and its output, based more on structural steel than ship plates, held up better than that of other firms.[169] At the same time, its ability to accept very small orders for immediate execution helped considerably. The firm became something of a jobbing steelmaker: the *average* rolling in its large mills in 1931 was only 21 tons and 15 tons in 1932; there were many rollings of two tons or less.[170] Andrew Gray, the managing director, believed that the company would do best in slack times when there was a plentiful supply of steel scrap but admitted that "in busy times, with their inability to expand output and having to face increased costs of scrap, they would find it difficult to make profits."[171] In the meantime, however, Lanarkshire was the only Scottish firm whose profits had been rising in 1930 and 1931.

These were the underpinnings of the stalemate of 1931–1933. The trade revival beginning in 1933–34 started to unravel some of these intricacies. The unique cost configuration of a firm like Lanarkshire was undermined, and the financial burdens of Colvilles eased. Thanks to Andrew McCance's skillful use of patching and cost-reducing improvisations at Clyde Iron and Dalzell, Colvilles also emerged as clearly the lowest cost producer.[172] But such developments were not necessarily conducive to mergers. SCS's weakening position meant that by April 1934 it was prepared to accept Bruce Gardner's merger percentage allocation of January 1933.[173] But, conversely, Colvilles felt that by this time it could afford to take a still harder line, and by summer 1934 it had "partially closed the door" on the question. Similar conditions on the Northeast Coast led to the abandonment of merger negotiations and the revival of separate competitive development. Yet in Scotland the period 1934–1936 was to see the consummation of a near regional monopoly under Colvilles. The crucial factor in linking revival with amalgamation was the intervention of Lithgow acting in collaboration with the BID and the Bank of England

Between 1929 and 1932 Lithgow's attitude toward Scottish reorganization had converged with that of the Bank. Both wanted large efficient units in the Scottish industry, and both saw centralized control as an essential step in securing effective reorganization. They took a view "from above," which sharply differentiated their position from Craig's cautious pragmatism based on a grudging assessment of the specific costs and advantages of particular mergers. The Bank of England had the same policy outlook elsewhere, but as we shall see later, nowhere else was it able to ally with a powerful entrepreneur capable of pushing its strategy into practice.[174]

By the end of 1931 Lithgow was growing impatient with the slow progress of merger talks. He told his friend Andrew Duncan at the BID that "one of my temperament gets 'fed up' with all these negotiations and talking," and he asked for a clear indication of what assistance he could expect from BID in pushing for mergers.[175] He saw collaboration with BID as a way of circumventing the deadlock. In particular, he felt that "the Colville element has had to play too prominent a part in the discussions,"[176] and in 1932–33 he was actively exploring with Bruce Gardner possible ways of getting around them. In particular, they discussed the possibility mentioned in the Brassert report of using Beardmore's Mossend steelworks as a primary plant for Scottish rationalization.[177] Lithgow had been on Beardmore's board since 1929, and in December 1932 Bruce Gardner outlined a scheme to him whereby Beardmore would sell Mossend to SCS, which would centralize its operations there and amalgamate with Lanarkshire, later developing its own blast furnaces at Mossend to produce a complete integrated plant near the tidewater.[178] The scheme was extremely ambitious and probably far-fetched, and Bruce Gardner probably saw it more as a way to spur Colvilles to action than anything else, but Lithgow did, as he later recalled, "spend infinite time and trouble" in exploring the possibilities of this sort of combination of "local companies."[179]

From early 1934 the revival of trade increased the anxiety of Lithgow and the BID to push through a regional amalgamation. The prospect of imminent expansion revived the possibility of new investment and therefore posed the question of how that money should be deployed. There was no certainty that development would take place on efficient lines. Duplication of plant might occur, backward plant would continue to yield profits in a protected industry, new competitors might be induced to enter the industry, and existing firms might not feel it worthwhile to buy up small competitors but rather bypass or "ghettoize" them in particular sectors of production. All of these possibilities seemed opposed to how Lithgow and the BID conceived of the rational ordering of large-scale production.

With SCS's position as a high-cost producer a weak one, Lithgow decided to take a direct initiative, with the collaboration of Bruce Gardner and the BID, to go past Craig's hesitations and break the deadlock in merger talks. Acting on Lithgow's behalf, Bruce Gardner carried out negotiations for the purchase of SCS and in June 1934 successfully made a firm cash offer of £13 per £10 share on a "take it or leave it" basis. Turnbull, the new managing director of SCS, Bruce Gardner told Lithgow, "put up a good fight and did his best to try to get better terms but I did not waver on the point."[180] Lithgow himself thought £13 too much; he originally wanted to pay only £10 and then a maximum of £12,10s, but Bruce Gardner had insisted that to make sure he had to go up to £13, and in the end Lithgow was both willing and able to pay what he regarded as over the odds.[181] Craig was told of the deal only at the last moment at a private meeting with Bruce Gardner and Lithgow at Bruce Gardner's home. There, as Bruce Gardner told Duncan, "The discussion really developed into an argument between Craig and myself with Craig endeavoring to substantiate a perfectly ridiculous price . . . After Craig had left, Sir James said that he was satisfied that Craig was wrong."[182]

Lithgow had acquired personal control of SCS, for £672,975 in July 1934. He at once set to work to coordinate SCS policy with Colvilles by putting in Peter Baxter as managing director, and the overall consolidation of SCS and Colvilles appeared imminent and straightforward.[183] Yet for well over a year this next step hung fire, and at times it began to look as if the Colville/SCS merger might after all not take place.

Behind this unlikely turn of events lay some awkward difficulties for Lithgow in reconciling his interests in the steel industry and his interests as a shipbuilder. It has to be remembered that Harland & Wolff was still the owner of all the ordinary share capital of David Colville & Sons, and as far as shipbuilding matters were concerned, its past relations with Lithgows Ltd. had not been amicable. Harland & Wolff, as a Belfast yard, had benefited considerably from the policy of the Northern Ireland government toward industry, an industrial policy that contrasted sharply with that of the British government and Treasury. Throughout the 1920s and early 1930s the Northern Ireland government pursued a policy of what Paul Bew has called "sectarian welfarism" designed to conciliate the Protestant working class by the maintenance of a certain discriminatory level of privileges vis-à-vis the Catholic working class.[184] One of the cornerstones of this policy was the maintenance of employment in the shipyards, especially at Harland & Wolff, which was something of a symbol for the Loyalist working class.[185] The instrument of this policy was the Loans Guarantee Act which, in effect, provided government aid to win orders for Belfast yards and thus maintain higher levels of employment and capacity utilization.

This policy was bitterly resented by the Clydeside shipbuilders as unfair competition,[186] and Lithgow was in the vanguard of this opposition as the chairman of National Shipbuilders Securities Ltd., the cooperative organization formed by shipbuilders to reduce excess capacity in the industry in 1930. As Lithgow pointed out to the president of the Board of Trade when he met him in October 1933, the NSS had scrapped a quarter of all English berths but had been able to scrap none in Belfast.[187] By the mid-1930s Harland & Wolff had government-guaranteed loans of more than £1 million and was resisting all attempts at rationalization.

In the early summer of 1935 a scheme for the merger of SCS and Colvilles was worked out whereby Colvilles Ltd. would increase its share capital to £4 million and use the resulting capital to purchase SCS, Lanarkshire Steel, and the remaining subsidiaries of David Colville & Sons all at once.[188] This proposal was jointly worked out by Sir William McLintock, representing Colvilles' family cash lenders and preference shareholders, and by Sir Reginald McKenna, the chairman of the Midland Bank, representing the control of Harland & Wolff. Since the collapse of the Kylsant group five years earlier, this control had been exercised jointly by the Northern Ireland government, the Treasury, and the Midland Bank, Harland & Wolff's biggest creditor. McLintock himself was the Treasury's representative on this control committee. One of the major objectives of this scheme, as far as McLintock and McKenna were concerned, was to carry through a major reconstruction of the finance of Harland & Wolff as part of its broader project of unraveling and reconstructing the Royal Mail Group. Cutting this particular knot by realizing the Harland & Wolff interest in Colvilles Ltd. would, they noted, "ease the situation very much and help in rearranging Harland & Wolff's capital." Indeed, as McLintock observed, until Harland & Wolff's shares in David Colville & Sons were disposed of and the cash realized, "I cannot see how we can hope to clear up the position of Harland & Wolff."[189]

Lithgow was naturally concerned about the effect of clearing up Harland & Wolff's financial position on its role as a shipbuilding competitor. It rapidly became clear that James Lithgow and his brother Henry (who had come onto the board of Colvilles Ltd. in 1931) were "allowing the future of Harland & Wolff to influence them very largely in their present attitude" to a Colville share issue in order to purchase SCS.[190] As James Lithgow told McLintock, his "concern quite clearly is, how are Harland & Wolff and Colvilles Ltd to be run after they are refloated on the public." He would "not willingly agree to steps which appear to us to be likely to check the progress which is now being steadily made" in rationalizing the shipbuilding industry. In the light of Harland & Wolff's past record, Lithgow wanted to have "some control or assurance that Harland & Wolff are going to work with us rather than against us in the larger sense as regards the shipbuilding industry" if he was going to help them reconstruct their financial position.[191]

In practice this meant that he wanted Harland & Wolff to allow NSS to "lop off" all but the repair functions of its D. & W. Henderson subsidiary and to "sterilise" its Glasgow subsidiary, A. & L. Inglis Ltd., against further shipbuilding. Also Harlands would have to agree not to build vessels below a certain size at either its Govan or Belfast yards. His condition of assent to a Colville scheme was a pact of nonaggression with Harlands: they would agree not to compete against each other; Harland & Wolff would have a clear run on passenger or warships but it would allow Lithgows Ltd. a clear run on all other types of ship.[192]

Lithgow's anxieties in this direction made him drag his feet on the scheme. By June 1935 Craig was convinced that Lithgow was trying to evade a decision and "playing for time." At a stormy board meeting Craig forced the issues into the open. An investigation by McCance of SCS's cost position had assured Craig that Lithgow "would be very disinclined to go on with the Steel Co on his hands" as a separate company. Armed with this, he called the Lithgows's bluff. He put Henry on the spot by demanding to know if there were any long-term alternative to a Colville/SCS agreement. According to Craig's notes, Henry replied: "Very definitely 'No,' they were bound to come together . . . I [Craig] said that I considered this statement so important that we were putting it in our minute."[193]

Ultimately Lithgow had gone too far to draw back now, but he was determined to use his strategic position to get the maximum guarantees from Harland & Wolff. In this he found a valuable ally in the Midland Bank, which, it must be remembered, was not only Harland & Wolff's principal creditor but also the Northern Ireland government's exchequer bank. As Sir Wilfred Spender, head of the Northern Ireland Civil Service put it, McKenna as chairman of the Midland Bank was to the Northern Ireland Ministry of Finance as the governor of the Bank of England was to the Treasury. Conflicts between the Midland Bank allied with the Ministry of Finance against the rest of the Northern Ireland government over economic policy had been a major theme of Northern Ireland history over the past fifteen years.[194] The bankers had frequently clashed with the government about the continuance of "unsound" financial policies embodied in welfarism and had demanded the more businesslike conduct of industry and the discontinuance of subsidies. Hence, the attitude of Midland to

Harland & Wolff tended to be bearish. Sir Ernest Clark, the Ulster government's representative on the Harland & Wolff board, later recalled having "to face the Midland Bank every month to beg for enough to carry on in bad times."[195] Thus in the Midland Bank Lithgow had a sympathizer inside the boardroom of Harland & Wolff who would help ensure that Harland acted "responsibly." During November 1935 McKenna, together with Hyde, the general manager of the Midland, negotiated with F. E. Rebbeck, the chairman of Harland & Wolff, to draw up guarantees to satisfy Lithgow. In the end Harland agreed not to sell any of its shares without Lithgow's consent during the next two years and that thereafter Lithgow himself should have the first option in any sale of Harland's shares.[196] Having received these assurances, Lithgow quickly completed the re-sale to Colvilles. He made a direct personal profit of £283,000 on the transaction over the eighteen-month period in which he owned the Steel Co., and he is reputed to have donated the entire profit to religious bodies in Scotland.[197]

No one else in Scotland had the financial resources to act in this way. Yet it is noteworthy that where his interests as a shipbuilder were concerned, Lithgow was as cautious and pragmatic as Craig had been about his steelmaking interests. Despite his hesitations about the shipbuilding position, however, Lithgow had in effect committed himself to the strategy of a big regional steel merger. Even while the SCS deal remained incomplete, he and Craig were moving toward a takeover of Lanarkshire to complete the project. As scrap prices moved forward in 1934–35, the production niche of LSC was undermined, and its unique ability to supply joists of the largest sizes, which had always given it outlets, was unlikely to be left intact for long by an expanding Colvilles.[198] Lloyds Bank took the opportunity of a reviving market to put in a receiver in April 1935.[199] Steel shares were buoyant on the stock exchange, and Craig at once realized that "if we are to keep Lanarkshire from being played with by other people" Colvilles would have to put in an offer. It offered £250,000 in May and increased this to £300,000 in June, "not because they like the price, but Lanarkshire in the hands of some outside people might undoubtedly prove troublesome."[200]

The BID too had an eye on this possibility, and it wanted Colvilles to act decisively. Bruce Gardner had already been approached by some London brokers who were interested in a purchase, and "though he did not interfere with any brokers or finance houses," he had put them off by saying that "if they acted as they proposed it would interfere with the proper organization of the steel trade of Scotland and would not be acceptable to some important authorities."[201] But in the absence of other developments by June, Bruce Gardner had to warn Craig in a late-night telephone call that renewed activity by the London brokers was imminent and that he could not hold them off longer. Despite the BID's sympathy, Colvilles' approach to LSC was indecisive. Craig resented Lloyds Bank's attempts to "force up the price" of Lanarkshire, and McLintock, to whom he had entrusted the negotiations, seemed by June 1935 to be "rather at his wit's end how to handle Lanarkshire."[202]

Colvilles was floundering about the question of price, and the possibility of outside acquisition remained. But with the SCS difficulties nearing resolution in October 1935, Lithgow intervened again to force the issue with a brusque piece of commercial warfare. He first went in person to see Sir Harry Peat, one of the receivers, and suggested that if the accountants Moores, Carson, and Watson would submit a price "as between a willing buyer and a willing seller," he would either get Colvilles to buy the company at that price or buy it himself for SCS. But if Peat or the other receiver hesitated, Lithgow told him, he would get Colvilles to commission new plant to make themselves completely independent of the range of joists made by Lanarkshire, "though it would from a national point of view be a regrettable redundancy in plant."[203] When, despite the agreement of the receivers, the debenture holders tried to hold out for a higher price, Lithgow at once had an order placed for such a mill at Glengarnock.[204] These moves were decisive, resistance crumbled, and the amalgamation finally went through in summer 1936 when Colvilles, using the proceeds of its March 1936 £1.5 million capital issue, exchanged 130,000 Colvilles ordinary shares for the whole of the Lanarkshire ordinary capital, a deal worth £215,000.[205]

With the completion of these mergers, Colvilles Ltd. accounted for more than 80% of Scottish steel production (see Table 9). What implications did this have for rationalization in a region where steel-making probably required more radical reorganization than anywhere else in Britain? Unification of ownership was the cornerstone of the rationalizing plans of Craig, Lithgow, and the BID, but they were plans with a form but no content. After the demise of the Brassert plan none of them reexplored the question of how the unification of ownership was going to lead into the reorganization of production. Instead, merger diplomacy filled the center of the stage and long-term planning was neglected. In the meantime, extensive improvements and patching operations went ahead. These developments represented an impressive catching-up operation, greatly reducing the relative inefficiency of Scottish works in comparison with those in Britain, and as Payne has shown it was a notable achievement largely due to the work of Andrew McCance, the leading figure on the technical side at Colvilles.[206] In a sense, however, his second-best solutions and improvisations were almost *too* effective. As Kenneth Warren has noted, in this sort of reorganization "the better was the enemy of the best."[207] The most brilliant improvisation was the modernization of the Clyde ironworks and linking them across the river Clyde with the Clydebridge steelworks as a close substitute for an integrated iron and steelworks. But it was a development built at the frontiers of its possibilities from the moment of its inception. In the long run the congested sites, the complex materials flows, and the use of already existing plant in remodeled forms severely restricted the prospects of future evolution.[208]

By the time unified control was established in 1936, the costs of new construction were soaring, and speed of expansion was the main priority to meet surging demand. Moreover, in contrast to 1929–30, the social costs of radical reorganization were on the agenda following the experience of Jarrow and Ebbw Vale. There is little evidence that steelmakers had been seriously affected by such considerations in the past—witness the wholesale removal of Stewarts & Lloyds from Scotland to Corby—but with their heightened political significance in the late 1930s they could no longer be ignored. The avoidance of social upheavals was one of the reasons why the BISF decided to sanction the Clyde/Clydebridge scheme rather than press for radical relocation.[209] Radical remedies were no longer on the agenda, and despite the contrast between near-monopoly control in Scotland and continuing multifirm operations on the Northeast Coast, the piecemeal development of production to meet pressing demand was characteristic of both areas. As a result the structural problems of Scottish steel remained untouched. By the end of the 1930s Scotland was still more dependent on scrap than any other district except Sheffield; Clydebridge was the *only* hot-metal steelworks; the old locations remained undisturbed, and the ironmasters were seizing the opportunity of expansion to modernize their blast furnaces on inland sites. As Warren has noted, "here, perhaps more clearly than anywhere else in Britain, the developments of the 1930's compromised the expansion to be followed over the next forty years through to the 1980's."[210]

It is therefore misleading to equate amalgamation and rationalization in the way that Peter Payne does. They were the same things only in the minds of businessmen, whose intentions may have been rationalizing ones but whose policy in practice did not go beyond the pursuit of amalgamation in its own right. But where is the driving force behind this policy to be located? Payne attributes these developments principally to the role of John Craig and his "sheer tenacity" in pursuit of a regional combine. In fact, as we have seen, his role was much more ambiguous, and the forces that pushed the aspiration into reality were to be found in Lithgow, the shipbuilder, backed by the BID and the Bank of England. It was Lithgow's strength as an independent entrepreneur, "a man entirely his own master,"[211] that enabled the BID and Craig to see their general policy aims carried out; without his resources neither would have been able to bring off a giant amalgamation. Yet he depended on them too in other ways. Craig played a vital role in curbing family resistance within Colvilles and creating a management team with sufficient authority to carry through difficult issues such as the merger with Dunlops; the internally divided and weakly managed Dorman Long, for instance, might well have foundered in that sort of crisis. At the same time the BID and the Midland Bank both played crucial parts by easing the path of amalgamation in wider political and financial circles and in reinforcing Lithgow's convictions at awkward moments. Together these forces reshaped the structure of firms, of competition and of decision making in Scottish steel; they did not, however, reshape the structure of production.

5.

Richard Thomas & Co. and the Tinplate Industry, 1918–1939

In Scotland and on the Northeast Coast little change in technology or market structure took place in the interwar years: the problems were those of rationalizing within a fairly stable framework. The structures of managerial and financial control combined with the legacy of overcommitment to prevent either an effective shake-out of the industry or the creation of new managerial and business structures capable of exploiting the existing opportunities for reorganization, innovation, and modernization. In marked contrast, the steel and tinplate industry based in South Wales experienced a major change in markets, technology, and industrial structure. In the nineteenth century the industry produced a limited range of conventional goods largely for export markets, but the emergence of new demands for a wide range of consumer goods in the interwar years provided new opportunities and requirements for higher quality and larger scale production oriented more and more toward the home market. This was accompanied by a fundamental challenge to the old pack-mill technology of tinplate making that had proved adequate for hundreds of years by the new technology of the continuous strip mill, large-scale investment, and mass production. In addition, the nineteenth-century world of teeming small producers was replaced by a world in which one industrial giant, Richard Thomas & Co., appeared for a time to have the possibility of taking a monopolistic grip on the sector.

Such changes would appear to offer an opportunity for a radical break from the old forms of industrial organization and for the emergence of Chandlerian modern enterprises that focused on greater control and coordination of all levels of production and pursued market-taking strategies. In fact, however, the way in which mass production emerged from the world of small production stamped it indelibly with the institutional legacy of the industry's past. In the first place, the limits of the product market were such that large-scale investment and mass production, although feasible and clearly the pattern of the future, were by no means the *only* possible option at that particular point in time; various intermediate strategies of improvements and modifications of the existing technology still had some profitable life in them. Second, the past structure of the industry placed powerful external constraints on the evolution of the firms and their capital development. Rival firms were able to impose severe limitations on the actions of the pioneering enterprise of Richard Thomas & Co. by exploiting the ambiguous positions of the national steelmakers' association (the BISF) and of the Bank of England and the company's bankers. Third, the result of these forces was to subvert the evolving managerial structures of Richard Thomas & Co. This company had moved from being a family firm to a managerial enterprise capable of conceiving and pursuing a strategy for transition to mass production of considerable sophistication, yet in the strain of the transformation effective control of the firm was lost to rivals and outsiders. Despite relatively dramatic changes in production techniques and product markets, old business rivalries and practices of defensive cartelization and restriction hedged in the leading company and made it pay a high cost for its role as innovator.

Families, Merchants, and the World of Small Producers

Until the First World War British tinplate firms had been able to expand and relocate within a more or less continuously growing world market. They had survived the shock of the 1890s when their former virtual world monopoly was dramatically broken by the closure of the American market by the McKinley tariffs. This outlet had accounted for 70% of British sales, and its loss, together with the development of native tinplate producers on the Continent in the next two decades, exerted severe pressure on an industry nurtured in a soft sales environment. From the 1890s world production growth was outpacing the growth of world demand, but Britain was still able to climb to an export peak in 1915. The watershed came with the expansion of world capacity during the First World War: by the 1920s world excess capacity had come to stay, and the British advantage of being first in the field had gone.[1]

In 1914 Britain had produced 45% of world output; by 1930 it produced 23%. This latter figure still represented 63.9% of world *trade* in tinplate, but this trade had shrunk as first America, then Germany,

Belgium, Italy, India, and Japan successively cornered their home markets. Privileged access to Empire markets significantly offset these losses, and the existence of a number of growing markets meant that tinplate performed relatively better than the rest of the steel industry in the 1920s.[2] This export orientation encouraged British firms to attach much less importance to their home market than their continental competitors attached to theirs. Yet from 1918 British home demand was expanding much faster than the export markets: in 1920 home consumption was less than a quarter of exports; by 1929 this proportion had risen to a third.[3] In both sectors the British tinplate industry supplied a rather scattered and diverse consumer market, quite unlike the big customers demanding more standard lines that the heavy steelmakers sold to. In the 1920s 60% of tinplate demand derived from tin boxes and open top cans for food, paint, medical supplies, tobacco, oil, and polishes. Other uses, such as toys, office furniture, roofing, and in the motor industry grew more slowly. Demand in these consumer goods held up much better than the demand for capital goods in the 1920s.[4]

Until the 1920s the production of tinplate was fragmented, dominated by small family firms and partnerships and almost completely regionalized in South Wales (Table 13). In its formative years the industry had drawn its capital from a wide range of small, primarily local investors who were attracted by the fairly low levels of capital provision required and the relatively short turnover time.[5] The industry developed primarily by grafting new finishing processes onto preexisting steel production, often simply buying bars from established producers. As such, until the 1920s tinplate remained an easy industry for small capital to enter.

In 1917 the total capital invested in tinplate was estimated at £6 million.[6] With five hundred mills in existence this averaged £12,000 per mill. Tinplate technology had changed little since the seventeenth century, and the existing pack-mill methods offered few available economies of scale. The main way of expanding and contracting capacity was not through enlarging the scale of production but by opening and closing mills with the trade cycle. Techniques were labor intensive, and during cyclical fluctuations labor could be laid off with far less cost than that of keeping fixed capital idle. As a result, average unemployment in the trade in the mid-1920s ranged from 2.7% in June to 45% in December.[7]

There was no technical imperative toward large-scale production, and as Table 14 shows, even when a number of large firms did begin to emerge, a very marked tail of small to tiny enterprises persisted. In the early 1920s more than 80% of tinplate firms had fewer than

Table 13 Concentration of tinplate ownership, 1919–1940

	Percentage of total capacity owned by the largest concerns							
Year	Richard Thomas & Co.	Grovesend Steel & Tinplate Co.	William Gilbertson & Co.	Baldwin's Ltd.	Briton Ferry Steel Co. Ltd.	Partridge Jones & John Paton Ltd.	Associated companies of the Llanelly Steel Co. (1907) Ltd.	Others
1919	21.8	4.0	3.2	7.2	1.8	—	—	62.0
1920	21.8	4.0	3.2	7.2	1.8	3.4	—	58.6
1921	21.8	4.0	3.2	8.6	2.6	4.2	—	55.6
1922	21.8	4.0	3.2	8.6	3.6	4.2	—	54.6
1923	30.7 ←	(8.9)	3.2	10.1	3.4	4.2	—	48.5
1924	30.8		3.1	10.1	4.8	4.1	—	47.1
1925	29.7		3.0	12.9	4.6	4.1	—	45.6
1926	29.6		3.0	12.9	7.1	4.0	—	43.4
1927	29.6		4.2	12.9	7.1	4.0	—	42.2
1928	29.6		4.2	12.9	7.1	4.0	—	42.2
1929	29.5		4.2	12.8	7.1	4.0	—	42.4
1930	29.3		4.1	12.7	7.0	4.0	—	42.9
1931	29.3		4.1	12.7	7.0	4.0	—	42.9
1932	29.7		4.1	12.7	7.0	4.0	—	42.5
1933	34.1 ←		(4.1)	12.7	7.0	4.0	—	42.2
1934	37.7			12.7	7.0	4.0	—	39.6
1935	38.9			12.7	7.0	4.0	—	38.4
1936	41.9			11.0	8.4	4.0	—	34.7
1937	41.9			11.0	9.1	4.0	—	34.0
1938	49.4			10.0	9.1	3.7	—	27.8
1939	49.4			10.0	8.2	3.7	7.3	21.4
1940	49.4			10.0	8.2	3.7	8.3	20.4

Sources: E. H. Brooke, *Chronology of the Tinplate Works of Great Britain*, 2 vols. (Cardiff, 1944-1949); Rylands' *Directory*.

Table 14 Distribution of ownership of tinplate mills, 1913–1940

Number of mills owned	Number of firms in—					
	1913	1920	1925	1930	1935	1940
0–5	39	28	23	23	16	12
5–10	16	20	15	13	15	9
10–15	5	3	2	1	—	—
15–20	3	3	3	2	2	1
25–30	—	2	1	—	—	—
35–40	1	1	1	1	1	1
40–45	—	—	—	1	1	1
50–55	—	—	—	—	—	1
70–75	—	—	1	—	—	1
75–80	—	—	—	1	1	1
80–	1	1	1	1	1	1
Total	65	58	47	43	37	28

Sources: E. H. Brooke, *Chronology of the Tinplate Works of Great Britain,* 2 vols. (Cardiff, 1944–1949); Rylands' Directory.

ten mills. This structure was propped up in the 1920s by the impact of the depressed world market for semifinished steel. Continental overcapacity resulted in the persistent dumping of tinplate bar and sheet bar in Britain. European producers made mainly Bessemer quality steel, which was probably better suited for tinplate manufacture than the open-hearth qualities that British steelmakers specialized in, and it was in Bessemer steel that European steel held its greatest price advantage over Britain.[8] Hence, the existence of cheap imported bars made it possible for unintegrated concerns with small mills, old plant, and low overheads to roll and finish tinplates and remain independent of British steelmakers. Re-rollers could maneuver between British and continental suppliers and retain a niche in the market. The influence exerted by this supply option shifted during the 1920s. In the early 1920s, while selling prices maintained their gross margins at reasonable levels, the pressure to take foreign bars was not strong and was more or less effectively counteracted by existing customer-supplier linkages with local steel producers. Until 1925 selling prices were maintained at a fairly high level, and a rapprochement and even several mergers between the steel firms and the re-rollers were possible. The changed circumstances of the late 1920s, however, reversed the picture and gave the re-rollers a new lease on life.

The changes of the early 1920s were significant but they did not fundamentally change the structure of the industry. The combined steelmaking and tinplate firm Richard Thomas & Co. increased its share of output from one-fifth to one-third of the total, and several other firms pushed their heads above the ranks of the small enterprises;[9] but little changed in terms of the production process or the physical integration of successive stages of production. Most of the mergers were the result of steelmakers' taking control of rolling business to ensure outlets for their greatly expanded steel production. During the war steel production in South Wales had increased from 1.15 to 1.5 million tons per year, and steelmakers were anxious to guarantee outlets for the extra steel.[10] During the early 1920s they were able to buy up many independent re-rollers who had been weakened by the wartime disruption of their imported semifinished steel supplies and who still faced irregular deliveries and erratic quality from those suppliers.[11] A number of these family firms were willing to leave the industry rather than attempt to modernize to meet the more rigid standards of production that were becoming prevalent or cope with more aggressive marketing.

For instance, the spendthrift Edwards family who were bought out by Grovesend had some potentially valuable plant. But before the war they had concentrated almost solely on selling inferior quality tinplates to Rumania, and when that country made itself self-sufficient during the war, they ended up in the hands of Barclays Bank. Likewise, the Lewis family who owned the Bryngwyn Co. had concentrated their sales on the "easy" Japanese sheet market and were left at a loss when Japan developed its own production in the 1920s;[12] they too sold to Grovesend. As small firms there were few obstacles of vested interests other than family chauvinism to their speedy disappearance. Thus, when F. W. Gibbins decided that after thirty-one years in the business he wanted to get out of his Eagle Works at Neath in 1921 "he put up to J. C. Davies, the managing director of Baldwin's, a memo running to six lines," proposing a sale price of £144,000. "After visiting the works, Davies suggested knocking off £10,000. Gibbins agreed."[13]

Such mergers resulted in little more than the agglomeration of old family-based enterprises and conferred no technical advantages. Baldwin's bought up fifteen mills between 1919 and 1924, and Briton Ferry also moved forward from steel into tinplate by increasing its ownership of mills from nine to thirty-seven between 1920 and 1926.[14] The Partridge, Jones, and Paton families, meanwhile, drew together twenty-two small Monmouth works in which they had interests around their Pontymister steelworks between 1919 and 1924.[15] In addition to the formal mergers, numerous other "understandings" or directorate connections were forged between steelmakers and independent tinplate firms in this period. The most notable were those involving the Lla-nelly Steel Co., which itself owned only eighteen mills but had financial or directorate links and supply agreements to a further sixty-three mills through eleven firms. Similarly, the Bynea Company, through the Tregonning and John families, was linked to twenty-four mills through four "independent" firms.[16] By the mid-1920s probably half of the "others" in column 8, Table 13, would have fallen into this "associated" category.

Only the merger between Richard Thomas and Grovesend, which we will consider in more detail below, had a more dynamic and strategic aspect. For the rest, the picture is one of families and small-scale producers clustered together under the umbrella of commercial alliances and supply linkages. The preponderance of these small firms, however, caused difficulties for the larger producers in the 1920s. The tail of small firms accentuated price fluctuations, because they could make good profits in booms and then keep alive in slumps by undercutting the bigger businesses with higher fixed costs. The larger firms like Richard Thomas, Baldwin's, Gilbertson, and Grovesend hoped to be able to restrain these fluctuations through cartelization or price agreements. For a while in 1922, when continental competition was weak and the supply and quality of imported semis erratic, the small makers benefited from the minimum prices offered in the first Stabilisation of Prices Agreement.[17] But as trade conditions shifted, this and subsequent agreements proved ineffective.

In order to poach trade and undercut effectively, the small firms depended on a large fringe of fairly speculative merchants to provide them with orders and outlets. Merchants had always played a central role in the tinplate industry, partly because of the high proportion of stockholding and working capital relative to fixed capital in the trade, and partly because of the scattered consumer market to which the industry sold. Many of the great tinplate names (such as Thomas, Bond, Paton, and Firth) came into the industry from merchant houses. By the First World War the merchants were beginning to be squeezed as large direct buyers appeared, and they depended more and more on consumer ignorance, transport differentials, and speculation for their profits.[18] By the early 1920s they had many common interests with the small re-rollers. Small makers like Theo Gibbins of Melyn, Hallowes of Byas, and G. Rowe of Upper Forest recognized that if the merchants were driven out, they too "would have to go with them for lack of trade."[19] The merchants and independents might, in the short term, agree to certain price maintenance schemes, but they drew back from any mechanism that would make possible effective policing of such an agreement—namely a central selling organization.[20]

Thus, when demand fell away in 1923–24, encouraged by what Gilbertson called the "lamentable tricks" of the merchants, they began to break away and undercut.[21] Richard Thomas found itself "acting as private detectives, coaxing information from potential customers, in order to use it against people with whom we are supposed to be cooperating."[22] As Walter Minchinton and E. E. Watkins showed, not one price agreement survived a period of bad trade.[23] William Firth of Grovesend, who was soon to become managing director of Richard Thomas, hoped to break the grip of the merchants by a system of discounts, linked to the Stabilisation of Prices scheme, which would separate the larger "legitimate" merchants from the three to four hundred smaller "tuppenny-halfpenny" speculative merchants and thus "about pay the price of a rope with which the merchants would hang."[24] Firth reckoned that central selling could reduce distribution costs from $2\frac{1}{2}$ to $\frac{1}{4}$% and saw streamlined marketing as a precondition for the modern organization of the industry: "Ford doesn't allow people to speculate or treble handle his cars. He fixes a price at which they must be sold and he studies world competition." Unfortunately, as Firth grudgingly admitted, tinplate "isn't on all fours with motors."[25]

The re-rollers and the merchants were able to hang on through the 1920s because of the advantages offered by continental imports and low overheads. They refused to be drawn into price maintenance schemes if this meant losing the ability to slip out of them as and when their advantage dictated.[26] Firth saw them as diehards, "slow-coaches with muddled brains," and Frank Thomas described their opposition as the attitude of somebody who says "I won't, I won't—I never have and I never will."[27] In fact, however, the market for tinplate still left plenty of room for the small producer, and those who aspired to mass production did not yet have the means at hand to make their aspirations effective.

In fact, in the late 1920s overcapacity and the ready availability of cheap semifinished steel produced a topsy-turvy economy of production with, in effect, marked diseconomies of scale. Continental dumping moved inversely with the state of trade in the European producer countries; it therefore peaked in the slumps of 1926–27 and 1930–31 and was at its lowest in the boom of 1928–29 when demand in the exporting countries rose to absorb a higher proportion of their own production.[28] Because British and European demand movements generally synchronized, these imports enabled re-rollers to win trade away from integrated producers in depressions, although not to make big profits in periods of better trade. Imported bar was never more than 23% of total bar used between 1925 and 1931, but it exercised a disproportionate effect in depressing the price of home bar and delaying a clear-out of small producers in the industry.[29]

The re-rollers, employing near-obsolete technology, were able to increase their share of the market significantly in the late 1920s. In 1925 East Wales, where the independents were clustered, produced 10.6% of tinplate exports; by 1930 they held 16%.[30] Almost no new construction of tinplate mills took place in the 1920s, and even within the largest firm, Richard Thomas & Co., production was skewed away from integration and toward makeshift adaptation to the pattern of current costs.

Richard Thomas was reluctant to use imports because savings on bar costs were considerably offset by the costs of restricting or closing its Lincolnshire or South Wales steelworks and because imports had a depressing effect on prices.[31] Thus in 1925 Henry Bond, the managing director, calculated that although the product composition of its eastern group of mills would enable the company to use seven hundred tons of imported bar at ten shillings per ton less than the cost of that delivered from its own works—a saving of £350—the impact on overall price levels would be such as to result in a net overall loss of £900 with diseconomies at works in addition. Imports, he argued, were worthwhile for his firm only if they could be kept secret from the rest of the trade.[32]

Richard Thomas's plant was an agglomeration of capital stock of widely varying vintages: some, like the works at Abercarn and Burry, dated from the 1870s and were so worn down that further expenditure was reckoned to be useless,[33] whereas other plant, like the steelworks at Redbourn in Lincolnshire and the Cwmfelin mills, were of modern design. Generally, its small works like Cwmbrwla, Aber, Cilfrew, and Cynon in the Swansea group were kept idle so as to keep the large Cwmfelin mills running at a high load and feed them with semis from Redbourn. From 1927 the company tolerated a considerable loss per ton on the Redbourn-Cwmfelin circuit in order to partly offset overheads there.[34] But with the gap between imported and domestic prices at its widest in 1930–31, it was forced to close Redbourn and Cwmfelin and switch to running the smaller mills, especially those in the eastern group, on imported bar. Thus, the impact of imports was to continue the fragmentation of production within the largest combine itself.[35]

Ownership, Management, and the Rise of Richard Thomas & Co.

Richard Thomas & Co. emerged from this milieu to become by far the largest single steel-tinplate firm in the interwar years. The company grew piecemeal, starting in 1871, through a series of personal and family alliances and through the growth, and later fusion, of two firms built up quite separately by different branches of the Thomas family. Between 1871 and 1917 the first two Richard Thomases developed a medium-sized South Wales tinplate firm which made its own steel but owned neither iron nor coal. These deficiencies were quite fortuitously complemented by the firm that Frank Treherne Thomas, another of the first Richard's sons, built up. In 1896 Frank bought the Cwmfelin steel and tinplate works and set up independent operations. In 1907 he bought the Redbourn Hill Ironworks in Lincolnshire as a source of basic pig iron for Cwmfelin.[36] Richard Thomas & Co. had drawn in the Bond family through its merger with Morewood and Co. in the 1890s, but its management still depended heavily on the guiding hand of the owner managers, and the firm was left rudderless with the death of Richard Beaumont Thomas in 1917. Henry Bond turned privately to Frank Thomas for an amalgamation agreement with his firm, partly to create a bigger and more broadly based unit and partly to resolve an internal managerial crisis. Because of personal tensions within the family and the boardroom, Bond intended to present a fait accompli to the board. But the other Thomas family directors (Wyndham, Harold, and Hubert) heard of it and objected to the procedure. Frank, who was a dynamic but autocratic character, declared that he was "startled . . . both at their manner and their insinuations" and decided to clear them out of the firm as his price for consummating the amalgamation. Wyndham and Hubert were barred from taking any further managerial role in the firm,[37] and an embittered Harold went off into the wilderness to run the Melingriffith works as the most obstinately independent of the small firms, undercutting and maneuvering against the larger makers until forced to submit by the changed conditions of trade under tariffs in the 1930s.

The amalgamation was followed by the consolidation of Frank Treherne Thomas's personal autocracy within the firm. He set up a sort of "kitchen cabinet" at his own personal headquarters, the Cwmfelin works at Swansea, which more and more abrogated to itself the decisions that were formally supposed to be taken by the full board.[38] He was widely acknowledged to be an impossible man to work with because of his "arrogant and overbearing disposition."[39] He resented any criticism of his management, but his ambitious policies of issuing more and more capital stock, expansion, and acquisitions generated opposition from within the family. This centered around Lord Bledisloe who favored a policy of slower growth and greater stress on keeping control of the firm in family hands.[40] During 1920 poor health forced Frank to resign from the chairmanship, but during the crisis resulting from the slump in tinplate demand and mounting difficulties at the Redbourn project, a shareholders' meeting called for his return to pilot the firm through its difficulties.[41] Frank Thomas took the opportunity to demand "supreme control" and the resignation of Bledisloe as the price of his return. "I cannot," he declared, "attend to the large questions of policy if I have to deal with carping criticisms and giving explanations." He accused Bledisloe of trying to use the general body of shareholders to block him;[42] Bledisloe retorted that Frank wanted to act as dictator and make the rest of the board "sham directors."[43] But Frank prevailed. Bledisloe was sacked and other family dissenters cowed into submission.[44]

The main restraint on Frank's autocracy was in fact his own poor health which forced him to retire briefly in 1920 and again in 1925. By 1923 he recognized that he was "getting a little bit too old for this kind of business," and this was one of his main motives in amalgamating with Grovesend so as to "bring in some younger men" from the managerial talent of that concern.[45] However, the fact that one of these men was the fledgling autocrat of the 1930s, William Firth, only heightened boardroom tensions and probably hastened Frank's retirement.[46]

Frank was ruthless, he had a personal command of managerial and productive resources which the firm needed, and he could draw on the status and legitimation of his family title. He was able to utilize these advantages to engineer a relatively centralized management and decision-making structure at Richard Thomas. Elsewhere families themselves might be awkward special interests as they were at Colvilles or the South Durham Co., or they might dominate management through inheritance rather than talent as at Dorman Long; at Richard Thomas they might have plunged the firm into factionalism, but Frank was able to exploit his opportunities to bring the family to heel and use them as a pliable constituency to bolster his authority in the firm. However, this strategy came close to backfiring. The price of preserving personal control within an expanding firm in the 1920s was a high-risk financial policy that in the late 1920s was on the verge of delivering the company into the hands of bankers and outsiders.

When Richard Thomas became a public company after the 1917 amalgamation, Frank secured a position of strategic dominance by acquiring substantial chunks of the newly issued stock. He personally held £670,000 of the £2 million ordinary shares (33.5%) and £287,000 of the £1 million preference shares (28.7%), and with his wife holding a further £171,000 (8.5%) ordinary and £73,000 (7.3%) preference, he and his immediate relatives held 72.8% of the ordinary and 58% of the preference shares.[47] Further issues were necessary to finance the expansion of the early 1920s, and they somewhat weakened this absolute family dominance. Frank, however, was at pains to engineer these issues so as to maximize the power exercised by his shareholdings. Thus, when £1 million 7½% debentures were issued in 1921–22, one of the conditions that he introduced watered down the voting powers of the preference shareholders to a third, so that the ordinary class where he retained a majority could outvote them.[48] By the late 1920s, even though he then held only £250,000 out of a total capital of several million, he still manipulated a strategic voting block of crucial importance.[49]

In order to keep this control intact, it had been necessary to restrict the expansion of the firm's share capital. Such a policy facilitated centralized control from the boardroom and also, in the context of a subordinated family, made possible a policy of keeping money in the firm for capital expenditure rather than paying large dividends out of profits.[50] But it also meant that the company had to turn to big debenture issues in the early 1920s, followed by loan and overdraft finance for further expansion and working capital. The result was excessive gearing. When expansion ceased in the middle 1920s, the company faced acute problems with its debt burden. By the late 1920s the company's overdraft from Lloyds and Martins banks hovered around the £2 million mark, and although debenture interest had generally been met, large arrears of preference share interest debt had built up.[51]

When major reconstruction became a pressing matter in the late 1920s, the banks had a powerful voice. In 1928 Lloyds Bank prompted the company to appoint an advisory committee, consisting of W. W. Paine (a joint general manager of Lloyds), Sir Gilbert Garnsey (see below), and the financier F. Szarvasy, to make recommendations on financial reconstruction.[52] They wanted to write down the firm's capital to facilitate new borrowing and spending.

At this point an aging and bitter Frank Thomas, now in retirement, appeared on the scene to use the shareholding power, which he had previously harnessed to support himself as an owner-manager, to defend his surviving interest as a creditor and shareholder. He was not prepared to make financial sacrifices for a firm being managed in a way that he did not approve, and he mobilized the preference shareholders, of which he was the largest, in his support. They were a relatively small group, but their extensive legal rights in the event of any reconstruction gave them a vital blocking power, and they used it to refuse to allow their assets to be written down or their debts written off.[53] Instead, they forced the advisory committee to turn back to the much slower policy of paying off the firm's debts as a preliminary to reorganization and thus effectively scotched any hope of a speedy reconstruction. If profitability had remained low, the preference shareholders might eventually have been brought into line by managerial and bank pressures; but a revival of profitability changed the picture. It was arranged that Richard Thomas would set aside the first £100,000 from profits each year to reduce its bank debt before any other payments should be made. Renewed profits enabled the company to do rather better than this: between 1929 and 1931 £1½ million profits made it possible to pay off £431,000 of the overdraft, redeem £127,000 debentures, and pay £540,000 in bank and debenture interest payments. By 1932 the overdraft was down to £923,000, by March 1933 it was £622,000, and by August 1933 it was "nearly negligible." A £1.7 million overdraft was repaid by 1927–1933, and fixed interest debts of £130,000 on the £1.8 million debenture stock was met every year throughout the period.[54] Thus, the company escaped from a heavy debt burden that had laid it open to outside intervention by bankers and committees of creditors and emerged in the early 1930s as a compactly controlled firm with relatively marketable stock. William Firth was able to step into Frank Thomas's shoes as managing director very much at the helm of the firm.

Firth was to dominate the tinplate industry until the Second World War. He came into the industry from his own merchant firm and along with Henry Folland led the Grovesend Steel and Tinplate Co. in its course of aggressive expansion in the early 1920s. They bought up a number of small companies and began to pose a threat of cut-throat competition to Richard Thomas & Co. Frank Thomas opted to eliminate these threatening rivals at an early stage by merging with them, thus both relieving the competitive pressure and bringing into the firm a profitable group of assets at a time when Richard Thomas's current earnings were rather depressed. Grovesend's current profits were sufficient in themselves to cover a 2½% dividend on *all* of Richard Thomas's ordinary share capital after the merger; such an injection would help Richard Thomas "tide ourselves over bad times." The merger also gave them, via Bryngwyn's sheet mills, an entrée into the sheet trade which was currently holding up better than tinplate. Moreover, it brought into the company Grovesend's dynamic management team.[55]

Grovesend too had reasons to desire the merger. Indeed, it took the initiative to open the discussions.[56] Its expansion had brought in the Bryngwyn and Duffryn works, which both had considerable potential but which had a history of neglect and poor management. Grovesend itself was too small to cope with the vigorous reorganization needed to realize its value. Thus at the time of the merger, although the Grovesend works were earning a return of 17% on its £606,000 capital, Bryngwyn was bringing in only 4.7% on its £598,000 and Duffryn 1.5% on its £612,000. The merger facilitated the spending of £135,000 at Duffryn, and £94,000 at Bryngwyn, and £98,000 at Grovesend in the next three years and also made possible an aggressive marketing policy and the rapid cutting of the labor force at the works. Firth deliberately closed down the Bryngwyn works for a period after the merger to destroy resistance to mass sackings.[57]

The merger confirmed Richard Thomas's position as the dominant tinplate firm. It had been the largest single tinplate firm since the merger with Frank Thomas's company, even though in 1919 it still owned less than 22% of total tinplate capacity, and with an estimated market value of £6.2 million it ranked as the twenty-sixth largest company in Britain at the time.[58] A merger between Grovesend and Baldwin's, Richard Thomas's closest rivals, would have created a company similar in size to Richard Thomas; instead, however, the Grovesend merger created a company with more than 30% of tinplate capacity, with no other company having even as much as 10%.[59]

The merger also helped to offset problems arising from other aspects of Richard Thomas's expansion in the early 1920s, particularly those deriving from its acquisition of collieries and its expansion of steelmaking at the big Redbourn works. Both of these operations were proving to be heavy financial drains in the early 1920s, and Grovesend's liquidity was of great value in this respect. Like many other firms Richard Thomas bought collieries at inflated prices during the postwar boom in order to safeguard its supplies. But once the boom passed, these collieries were a constant drain on liquidity: losses in 1925–1927 consumed about half of current trading profits.[60]

The large integrated iron and steel works at Redbourn in Lincolnshire was the other major headache of the 1920s. The works was a major part of Frank Thomas's legacy to the company—and it created both problems and important possibilities. Before the war Redbourn was solely an ironmaking plant, but Frank had long cherished plans to develop an integrated plant at Redbourn running from iron through steel to finished tinplates. He hoped to use wartime expansion for this purpose, but the Ministry of Munitions would only sanction a development as far as steel. The new steelworks was already under way at the time of the amalgamation between Frank's firm and Richard Thomas in 1917, but construction was dogged by delay, and the works was not completed until the summer of 1920. The boom was missed and, despite the arguments of Sir John Simon in the Ministry, the government refused to make its promised contribution to the cost of building.[61]

The plant provided the iron and steel capacity that Richard Thomas lacked in South Wales, where it owned only its Llanelly steelworks, but it also stretched a company formerly wholly centered in Wales across the entire country. The long freight of tinplate bars to South Wales from Lincolnshire was an obvious problem, especially because, unlike Lysaght, whose operations spanned the country in a similar fashion, Richard Thomas was unable to get cheap rates for railing its steel across the country.[62] The possession of the Redbourn works inevitably raised the question of where further development should take place and placed a question mark over the future of a Welsh location for tinplate. By the 1920s it was becoming clear that in the long run the future of tinplate rested with integration with iron and steel production. Although the timing of such a development was an awkward issue, the direction of change was apparent, and Richard Thomas's greatest potential in iron and steelmaking lay in Lincolnshire, not South Wales. The question of a major development at Redbourn was, however, fraught with technical and financial problems, and in the end the question was to remain hanging in the air until major developments in the 1930s shifted the position.

Redbourn was not the satisfactory modern integrated works that its owners and managers would have liked it to be. They had anticipated that it would be a low-cost producer contributing an estimated £½ million per annum to profits,[63] but this expectation was rapidly disappointed. In 1923 there was a £20,000 loss at Redbourn, and by the summer of 1924 a loss of £100,000 in that year was anticipated.[64] At the root of this lay the fact that Redbourn was a high-cost producer[65] as a result of poor planning, inadequate auxiliary equipment, poor layout, and lack of balance. Financial imperatives restricted weak management to a "patching" policy with profoundly unsatisfactory results.

The survival of technical data and works reports from Redbourn makes it possible to look at this question in some detail. The balance of the plant was poor: all the departments could not possibly run simultaneously at full capacity. The blast furnaces and coke plant could not meet the demands of the steel furnaces, whereas if the latter were run near capacity by outside purchases, their output exceeded the capacity of the rolling mills by 33%.[66] The rolling mills themselves were poorly designed for their tasks: in 1923 they were described as "acting as a steam hammer to crush walnuts."[67] Poor layout made handling and scrap arrangements wasteful. Although two of the blast furnaces were mechanically charged, poor ore-crushing facilities made this operation less efficient than hand-filling would have been: "The fines come out first and dribble down in the furnace, being followed by the rubble and finally by the lumps as the opening of the bell increases, and, as the rate of opening is very slow, this separation of the sizes must be very marked."[68] The inadequate coke batteries—two of which dated from 1906 and were deteriorating rapidly in the 1920s—were of old-style firebrick, worked below optimal temperatures, and produced an excessive moisture content as a result of hand-quenching with hoses. This reinforced the persistently poor performance of the blast furnaces.[69] These failings in capital equipment were compounded by poor management, which left many minor but costly defects untouched.[70]

Instead of being a major asset, therefore, Redbourn was a liability. The scale of the losses was such that as long as they existed, there was no prospect of paying any dividend on the company's ordinary shares[71]—an especially galling fact in view of the satisfactory performance of the other operations of the company. In view of this, Firth was by 1924 convinced that "THE ONLY SALVATION OF OUR COMPANY AS A WHOLE IS THE OUTRIGHT SALE OF REDBOURN, even if we could only secure £2m for it," which would represent a loss of £2 million on the initial investment. He asked the board to "visualise the difference between having £2m of cash available for expansion in Wales and finding another £1m or £1½m to bolster up our Redbourn property."[72] Its directors agreed that Richard Thomas's best course was to concentrate all its operations in South Wales, but no buyer could be found despite extensive efforts.[73]

Failing this, the board reverted to seeking ways to minimize losses during poor trade with a view to major modernization when trade recovered. In 1925, in consulation with the American engineering consultants H. A. Brassert and Co., the company devised a program of interim modifications to cut costs, concentrating on the raw materials end of production, especially crushing and handling improvements.[74] More comprehensive solutions had to await improved trade conditions. In May 1929, with these in prospect, the sort of integrated scheme at Redbourn that Frank Thomas had envisaged again became a possibility, and Firth commissioned Brassert to do a further broader report on the commercial possibilities of Redbourn.[75] Brassert outlined two options to the board. One was simply a scheme to modernize Redbourn's steelmaking capacity to produce 220,000 tons of bar per year, involving an investment of £780,000 but for the moment leaving aside the question of future integration with tinplate finishing. The other, which Brassert preferred, was a much larger project—a greatly enlarged plant producing 500,000 tons per year using the basic Bessemer process and costing £2.5 million. Such a plant, Brassert reckoned, could reduce costs for iron to £2.5s. 8d, ingots to £3.5s. 2d, and sheet bar to £3.19s. 3d per ton[76] (see Tables 5 and 6). To carry out such a large project, however, an amalgamation with other steel interests in the area would be required; in particular, United Steel would have to be drawn into a merger of its nearby Lincolnshire properties with those of Richard Thomas to make possible the most comprehensive development. Brassert proposed just such a merger in a report to United Steel on its properties submitted in September.[77] A merger would produce a combined demand adequate for best-practice basic Bessemer plant and rolling mills of about 500,000 tons of ingots and semis per year.[78] The ideal new development would start from new ore docks on the River Trent and finally run through in its third stage to the most modern finishing processes. But the capital cost of such a new site would be excessive, and Brassert preferred a combined Redbourn/Appleby-Frodingham development, building basic Bessemer plant as an extension to the existing Appleby melting shops, installing the new sheet bar rolling mills in the existing Redbourn mill buildings, and constructing a wholly new American style blast furnace/coke complex adjacent to the melting shop on a new site.[79] The savings in the new scheme would accrue primarily from major economies at the ironmaking stage.

However, Brassert noted, any merger or new construction had to be predicated on a plan to develop *complete* integration through to finishing. If such full integration "is not visualised and definitely planned at this time, we cannot recommend the Lincolnshire district as the logical location for producing Richard Thomas' sheet and tinplate bar requirements. On the contrary, if sheet and tin bar were wanted to supply existing sheet and tin mills in South Wales, we would recommend installing the new plant in Oxfordshire, thereby saving a large proportion of the freight on the semi-finished materials."[80]

Brassert urged combination because he believed that "the time is ripe for such a development,"[81] but the plan was never to get further than paper. The scale of the plan was intimidating, United Steel had just been through a period of internal turmoil, and, as we shall see below, the limitations of the market made Richard Thomas cautious in its approach to tinplate development.

The Strip Mill: New Technology and a Strategy for Growth

The new continuous strip mill technology was developed in America in the 1920s to serve an expanding mass market for sheet steel and, in particular, the demands of its largest customer, the automobile industry. The stamping presses of the automobile industry and of the metal furniture and household appliance trades required sheets with deep-drawing qualities and regular gauge and weight. The demands of the paint shop required extremely high surface quality.[82] Tinplate, which was less demanding of steel quality, was overshadowed and did not receive much attention in the United States. But in Britain the demand for sheet steel, particularly from the motor industry, was not comparable to that in America. The American automobile industry consumed 1.5 million tons of steel per annum in the early 1930s against a UK peak of 500,000 tons in 1933–34.[83] Tinplate was on a closer par with sheet in Britain, but it did not face the same sort of giant demanding customers. The canning sector exerted the most consistent pressure toward volume, regularity, and quality of supply, but canning did not dominate the demand horizon for tinplate in the way that autos did for sheet in America. The Metal Box Ltd. established a virtual monopoly over British canning in the early 1930s, and in 1933 it took 18% of home tinplate consumption. In the next four years its sales trebled from 115 to 335 million cans; it remained far and away tinplate's biggest customer but never neared monopsony. By 1937 can sales were worth only £1.2 million,[84] of which 45% were for milk and cream products, largely to United Dairies and the Co-Operative Wholesale Society. Of other products, only processed peas which took 19% of the total, mainly by Bachelors, had gained a significant hold on the market.[85]

Significant diversity of demand remained, and even in the late 1930s Britain, in contrast to its competitors, retained considerable export sales to the varied world markets.[86] The British markets before the war never exhibited the uniformity, the technical rigorousness, or the market power of giant hegemonic consumers that characterized the United States. Thus expert opinion in Britain in the 1920s had held that the limited size of the market ruled out the adoption of continuous rolling of either sheet or tinplate in Britain.[87] This remained the majority opinion in the early 1930s. G. A. V. Russell in a number of influential technical papers argued that an American-type installation of 500,000 tons per annum would cost nine shillings per ton in depreciation, interest, and standing charges even when working at 83% capacity. At 46% this would rise to a crippling seventeen shillings per ton. Yet currently few mills in Britain were able to work at more than 60%.[88] Such fears of an inadequate load for a strip mill were endemic in the trade; most makers feared that low running costs would be offset by a financial millstone. Hence, attention was directed primarily to looking for a compromise intermediate technology. E. R. Mort reckoned that a 100,000-ton per year strip mill was the optimal size for British conditions,[89] and Russell proposed 200,000 tons based on a wide range of products and located regionally to cater for the demands of local markets.[90]

The extension of this new mass production technology to Britain in the late 1930s was to transform both the sheet and tinplate industries, but initially at least the economic space for a strip mill was very narrow. The demand for either sheet or tinplate alone was not a broad enough base for a strip mill, and the British market could accommodate the new technology only under a certain fairly narrow range of conditions. The stucture of fragmented competition was frozen by cartelization under tariffs, and Richard Thomas had to undertake a tangled process of marshalling both supply and demand in order to make innovation a possibility. Even then the large-scale investment needed was a calculated risk, and because it broke the rules of the game in the cartelized sheet and tinplate industries and posed a threat of domination by a single market-taking firm, competitors were ready to use more or less desperate tactics to stifle the infant strip mill at birth while it was at its most vulnerable. Richard Thomas sought to guard against this by mobilizing wider political and financial support and enlisting tacit government backing; but the price of this support was the need to locate the new works at an unsatisfactory and costly location.

The introduction of the tariff in 1932 was followed by a fall in exports which was not immediately compensated by a rise in home demand. The slack market of the mid-1930s resulted in a revival of attempts at cartelization and pooling agreements. The tariff virtually eliminated the importing of semifinished bars—151,912 tons were imported in 1931 but only 3,068 in 1933—and this undermined the advantage of the nonintegrated re-rollers.[91] But it also made effective price maintenance and quota agreements possible. The 1932 pooling scheme limited the output of all tinplate firms to a quota allocated on the basis of previous output. No firm was allowed to work above 75% of its capacity unless the general level of tinplate demand was above that figure, and except for a brief period in 1937, prewar demand stayed persistently lower than that. This was combined with minimum prices and penalties for overproduction. Price maintenance protected tinplate makers dependent on relatively expensive steel from excessive competition, but it also perpetuated excess capacity.[92]

Firth, however, was keenly aware that technical possibilities existed that could transform the structure of costs and production in the trade, and that enormous potential advantages would accrue to the firm that would be first in the field, particularly if, as he expected, tinplate demand grew more and more rapidly. He had hoped that the tariff would drive out the independents and eliminate "wasteful" competition in that way, but the cartel protected them and Firth was soon highly discontented with the workings of the protected industry. By 1934 he was advocating the establishment of an effective central control in the industry, if necessary with government backing, to force amalgamation on unwilling participants and make possible the elimination of small producers and the concentration of production.[93] As long as the small producers survived and home demand remained at fairly limited levels, strip mill technology could be introduced only on the basis of the centralization of production and the aggregation of demand. To achieve the necessary scale of production, Richard Thomas's smaller rivals had to be either eliminated or taken over.

In 1934 Firth reckoned that a fully integrated tinplate works, probably at Redbourn, could reduce the cost of production of tinplate by thirty shillings per ton.[94] But the minimum efficient size for such plant was 80,000 boxes of tinplate per week or 25% of current aggregate demand, which was about 13.5 million boxes per year. The absorption of this production would require either the undercutting of existing competitors, the closure of 75% of Richard Thomas's existing capacity, or the buying up of other competitors' plants, closing them down, and retaining their quotas. In the summer of 1934 Firth gave extended consideration to these alternatives, and the survival of his notes on this question makes possible a clear assessment of the position of Richard Thomas at this time (see Table 15).[95]

In 1933–34, although working at only 60% of capacity, Richard Thomas was making a profit of £451,000 per annum.[96] But high interest and depreciation charges in the period immediately following the construction of new plant would make short-term profits unlikely.

Gross profits on production alone could be maximized by building a 160,000-box plant and closing down *all* the company's existing plant; this new mill alone could make all the eight million boxes that Richard Thomas's current plant made, and gross profit on production would be £1.2 million. But the new plant would cost £5 million to build— £3 million for the strip mill and £2 million for new steel plant—and even if this sum could be raised at 4½%, which Firth thought impossible, the initial interest and depreciation charges would be £750,000 per annum, the standing charges £200,000, and the overhead charges £65,000, reducing net profitability to £152,000. As Firth noted, "no financial house would look at the proposition."[97]

The minimum size mill (80,000 boxes weekly or 4.5 million boxes per annum) could be financed more easily, but it could not replace all other Richard Thomas plant and would have to run in conjunction with existing mills. If it was introduced in addition to existing capacity, it would enable Richard Thomas alone to produce all except 200,000

Table 15 Estimated profitability of various alternative conditions for the introduction of a strip mill by Richard Thomas & Co., 1934

Assumption	Profit (£ 000)
1. Works owned by the combine remain as at present and	
(a) we have same output as last year (trade 55%)	451
(b) we work 70% and trade works 55%	523
2. Construct strip plant at Redbourn for 80,000 boxes weekly and endeavor to work *fully* both there and in Wales; no Pool; trade demand as today, 55%	122
3. Construct 80,000 box plant at Redbourn and close corresponding number of mills in Wales and maintain the Pool;	
(a) trade at 70%	604
(b) trade at 60%	583
4. Purchase 80 tinplate mills in Wales and work 60% of our *new* quota	756
5. Extend strip plant at Redbourn to 160,000 boxes per week; close down all works in Wales; no Pool	152
6. If we decide to put up 80,000 box plant at Redbourn and competitors "fight";	
1st year *loss*	249
2nd year *loss*	196
3rd year *loss*	150
7. Purchase 170 mills to bring our allotment up to 80% of the trade and work 55% of *that* allotment	763

Source: W. J. Firth, Summary of Estimated Results under Various Conditions: Notes on Assumptions, 18 June 1934, Paper for RT board meeting.

boxes of current demand and leave the other 255 competitive mills wholly idle. On the "fantastic assumption" that these mills would become idle without a fight, Richard Thomas, working at 100% capacity, selling at bare production costs and making no allowance for depreciation, could earn gross profits of £722,000 per year, but interest and depreciation charges would slash this to £122,000.[98]

In practice, however, Richard Thomas's competitors could not be expected to give up quietly. They would fight, and to meet this, Richard Thomas would have to sell at sixpence to a shilling below cost, even excluding depreciation charges, and at current demand levels this would still only enable them to work at 70% capacity. With interest, overheads, and depreciation of £400,000 per year, this would involve a loss in the first year of £249,000 and a loss of £595,000 over the first three years, compared with an estimated £1.35 million *profit* in these years if current methods continued to be used. In other words, a *net loss* of £1.945 million would result. As Firth noted, "the prospects would be so alarming as to make it impossible to raise the money."[99]

One alternative was to build an 80,000-box plant and then close a corresponding number of mills in Wales so as to work near the company's existing quota of 130,000 boxes (70% of Richard Thomas's current 185,800 box per week capacity). At this level a Redbourn mill would produce 80,000 boxes at 3/6d profit per box, and the remaining Welsh mills would make 50,000 boxes at 2/- profit per box, an annual gross profit of £950,000. But pool penalties and idleness charges would reduce this amount by £234,000 per year, and depreciation and interest charges on the new plant would raise this figure to £632,000. Profits from coal and other subsidiaries would raise the overall net profit to £604,000, but to achieve this would require the rest of the tinplate trade to accept working at about 44% of their capacity without cutting their prices.[100]

Any of these schemes would be hard to finance, would involve heavy fixed charges, and would barely increase profitability above current levels. The only other way of proceeding was that of buying up the capacity and the quotas of competitors. Mills could be bought up at a going rate of £10,000 per mill where their owners could be persuaded to sell. Thus, for less than £1 million, an additional eighty mills could be purchased, and working 60% of the enlarged quota would realize net profits of £756,000 per year as against the current £451,000, even allowing for £150,000 interest and £150,000 depreciation each year on the newly purchased mills. This net profit would not, however, advance much further even if 80% of the trade were to be bought up.[101] Such purchases were a substitute for coordinated reorganization, a slower method of getting control of the required capacity to make integrated tinplate development possible. It was this path that Firth opted for.

The acquisition of Gilbertson in 1933 had given Richard Thomas 34% of tinplate capacity, and in 1934–36, by acquiring an additional forty-five mills, it had raised this to 42% (see Table 13). But the independents were becoming more and more aware of the value of their quotas and were increasingly prepared to resist. This created difficulties. A decisive shift in the balance of power within the industry could have come if Richard Thomas had succeeded in taking over Briton Ferry in 1933, but like many other smaller firms in the industry, Briton Ferry had established connections with Baldwin's Ltd., who feared the establishment of a Richard Thomas monopoly in the industry which would deprive them of valuable steel outlets. This consideration may well have been behind the rejection of Richard Thomas's offer by Briton Ferry shareholders, and similar concerns may have led to the rejection by Old Castle Tinplate Co., which was in the outlet orbit of the Llanelly Steel Co. (1907) Ltd.[102]

The expansion of Richard Thomas was regarded with apprehension by its tinplate rivals. It was also a cause for concern for the sheet steel firms who saw that a successful expansion by Richard Thomas in tinplate would inevitably result in its spilling over into sheet. The sheet firms were not ready themselves to venture into strip mill production, but they were very afraid of what might happen to them if Richard Thomas did so. What lay behind this defensive outlook?

The largest of the sheet-producing firms, John Summers and Sons, had produced only 262,000 tons of sheet in its best year in the 1920s (Table 16). Moreover, it was settled comfortably into the buoyant but fairly low-grade galvanized sheet trade and began to respond only

Table 16 British sheet makers: share in output, 1932

Firm	Number of mills	Actual output[a]	Estimated output per year (tons)	Percentage share in output
Baldwin's Ltd.	20	20,317	61,000	7.1
Dorman Long & Co.				
Bowesfield	15	15,081		5.3
Ayrton	7	10,633		3.7
Eston	6	10,212		3.6
Total	28	35,926	108,000	12.6
John Lysaght & Co.	35	32,284	97,000	11.3
Richard Thomas & Co.				
Ebbw Vale	6	4,986		1.7
Gilbertson	16	10,169		3.5
Grovesend	23	28,569		10.0
Total	45	43,724	131,000	15.2
Smith & McLean	9	11,505	34,500	4.0
(Colvilles Ltd.)				
John Summers & Sons	86	80,239	241,000	28.0
Others (13)	102	62,473	187,000	22.8
Total	325	286,468	859,000	100.0

Source: Sheet Makers Conference, output and allotments, 1932, Bank of England 3/3.
  a. Figures for actual output are for 17 weeks, Jan.-April 1932. Richard Thomas took over Gilbertson in 1933 and Ebbw Vale in 1935.

slowly to the newer demand by automobiles and other newer industries for higher quality sheet. When the company did begin to adjust to this in the late 1920s, it was beset with problems of producing adequate quality steel sheets because of its relatively poor steel. It called in the American expertise of the American Rolling Mill Co. (ARMCO) to help resolve this, but the resolution was protracted.[103] For a long time, Summers hoped to be able to use cold reduction as a less capital-intensive alternative to a strip mill, but ARMCO opposed this plan because, it argued, cold reduction could be valuable only if cheap high-quality semis were available. "Hot-strip steel is a *precondition* for cold reduction and the latter cannot *substitute* for the former . . . Anything short of a strip mill product which we may produce for subsequent cold reduction would be a palliative but not a remedy."[104] Thus, from the mid-1930s ARMCO was urging a hot strip development at Shotton. Summers, however, was deterred by the drastic nature of the change and only finally rather convulsively moved into strip in the late 1930s to avoid being left behind (see below).

John Lysaght & Co. probably produced 90% of British autobody requirements in the 1920s. Both here and in electric sheet it was the most advanced practitioner of the existing technology, pushing it to its limits in achieving fine deep-drawing qualities, and as a result developing strong customer relationships with the motor industry. This success made Lysaght optimistic about resisting strip mill competition and tended to encourage a policy of improvements rather than a radical change in the 1930s.[105] It judged that the market was not large enough for a strip development and therefore opted for cold reduction instead, a development that, with its high quality ingots, it could pursue more viably than Summers.[106] For a firm with only half of Summers' output and with no tinplate production, this view was realistic. Rolling the sort of autobody sheets that Lysaght produced on a continuous mill would require a massive 80" mill, which would require an enormous load to make it economic.[107]

Lysaght was not, however, an isolated firm. It had been taken over in 1920 by the Guest Keen and Nettlefolds group, and the aggregate demand for the products of the GKN-Baldwin's-Lysaght-Sankey group more nearly approximated a demand that could justify a strip mill. Baldwin's in particular owned 12.7% of tinplate capacity and 7.1% of sheet capacity in addition to Lysaght's share of 11.3% of the highest-value sheet output.[108] But the group was never really coordinated as a group or integrated,[109] and the problem was exacerbated by a considerable degree of animosity between the Beale family at the head of GKN and Sir Charles Wright at the head of Baldwin's during the 1930s. Lysaght continued to function more or less as an autonomous family-controlled enclave within the wider firm. Moreover, the group's sheet and tinplate interests were only one of a multitude of activities that they were involved in: in the mid-1930s they were particularly concerned with the extensive modernization of Margam and Port Talbot steelworks, and the finishing side received little managerial attention. Thus, although Guest Keen Baldwin's rebuilding of its Cardiff works in the early 1930s was stated to be designed "to be able to put down a strip mill for supplying hot strip coils for the manufacture of tinplate and sheets should this be required by the associated concerns,"[110] the idea was never really developed beyond that of a central producer of hot rolled products which would be finished in smaller existing scattered locations. The site was too cramped and lacked sufficient space to make the installation of a strip mill feasible. In the late 1930s the GKN group considered proposals for strip development at either Normanby Park (Lysaght) or Port Talbot, but no plan got off the drawing board before the Second World War.[111] In the mid-1930s Baldwin's was quite comfortably settled in the cartelized tinplate industry. It had the benefits of price maintenance and the guaranteed outlets of GKB steel to local re-rollers, and its fairly modern Elba works enjoyed a special position of exemption from the output restrictions of the pooling scheme because it sold its production solely to the petroleum industry to which it was linked by cross-shareholding. It was deterred from a strip development by the high capital cost and opted for improvements and cold reduction developments, but it was also aware of the potential danger presented by a large new development by Richard Thomas.

As Table 16 shows, besides these firms and Richard Thomas, Dorman Long was the largest of the other sheetmakers. The market for wide strip alone was, as Lysaght was aware, too restricted for large strip mill capital expenditure, but Dorman Long's large plate outlets presented the possibility of a combined sheet-plate development using a cold mill to roll sheet and strip up to 72", which would make possible sufficiently high levels of utilization.[112] Dorman Long was looking to diversify away from its existing heavy trades, and it investigated the possibilities of strip thoroughly. In 1935 it sent an investigative team to America, but this team recommended against strip and argued for basing diversification on Dorman's position as a structural engineer. Dorman Long finally opted to develop its abilities to roll the most advanced structural sections, the field in which most of its expertise and market advantages lay.[113]

United Steel also considered diversifying into strip in the early 1930s, but its large tilting furnaces at Scunthorpe working low-grade Frodingham ore could not produce steel of an adequate quality, and rather than pursue wholesale reconstruction, it turned its attention to the acquisition of existing sheet making firms.[114] This was the origin of United Steel's interest in Summers (see below).

Richard Thomas, however, possessed certain advantages over all these firms that made a strip development more viable. Its large output of tinplates, which required both narrower and lower grade strip than sheet, meant that it could operate and find outlets for a smaller 56" mill with its attendant lower capital costs. From its secure demand base in the tinplate trade, it could establish strip production and move from there into the sheet industry. Its large tinplate tonnage permitted cheaper installation than for those firms whose emphasis was on high-grade sheets. Richard Thomas had begun to study American strip mill practice in 1928,[115] when an integrated development at Redbourn was still in mind. Not surprisingly, A. W. Kieft, a director of Richard Thomas between 1932 and 1935, was one of the few who argued in the technical press in favor of an American-scale strip mill in Britain. He favored a cooperative development by the whole tinplate industry at a single optimal location. He reckoned that mechanized mills rolling strip breakdowns could save 18/6d. per ton over current hand mills and that strip mill products finished on three-high mills could save 23 shillings.[116]

But it was generally felt that this sort of development would require cooperation among existing producers, both to bring together adequate demand among tinplate producers and to avoid a trade war insofar as a Richard Thomas initiative in strip would imply making major incursions into the sheet trade. As far as the second of these points was concerned, Firth of Richard Thomas felt strongly the need for some sort of alliance to facilitate expansion into a trade in which it was a relative newcomer—its first sheet interests, at Grovesend, had only been acquired in 1923. He made approaches to both United Steel and Stewarts & Lloyds without success, but above all, he sought cooperation with Lysaght, which was likely to be Richard Thomas's principal competitor in the high-grade sheet market.

When Firth began to plan what was ultimately to be the Ebbw Vale project, its production was to include 250,000 tons per annum of high-grade sheet. Lysaght clearly feared that competition from this new plant would make its high-grade sheet plant at Newport redundant, even if it either amalgamated or cooperated with Richard Thomas. Firth wanted to get around this and eased the threat to Lysaght by his proposal that the Ebbw Vale output should be deducted from the total national sheet production figure before arriving at the tonnage on which each sheet conference member's quota was calculated.[117] Thus, both Richard Thomas and Lysaght would be allowed to work their existing mills at their current levels of output—130,000 tons per annum for Richard Thomas and 100,000 tons for Lysaght—less 15% and 12% respectively of 250,000 tons.[118]

But Lysaght discounted any possibility of Richard Thomas's being able to sell Ebbw Vale's 250,000 tons without making major inroads into its own, Summers's, and Baldwin's trade. Rather than just a loss of 12½% of existing production, Lysaght feared the loss of its entire high-grade sheet trade or very nearly two-thirds of its business. The problem, as D. C. Lysaght saw it, boiled down to a very simple question: "*Can* Firth raise his capital without our or Summers' help? If so, John Lysaght Ltd. would appear to be faced with severe competition at ruinous prices. If he can, is it better to co-operate with him and run the risk of the abandonment of some (probably a great part) of our Newport plant, or face the fight and inevitable loss resulting from the same?"[119]

Three factors decided Lysaght to "face the fight." First, even if Lysaght cooperated with Richard Thomas, unless Summers and Baldwin's were to do the same, there would be a ruinous battle between Richard Thomas and Lysaght, Summers, and Baldwin's. Second, Lysaght retained great confidence that its quality and costs could continue to compete with those of Richard Thomas. And third, it had detected the weak financial underbelly of the Richard Thomas scheme: determined opposition from other sheet interests might be able to prevent Richard Thomas from getting the financial support needed for the scheme.[120]

Until 1935 Richard Thomas was still only slowly disentangling itself from its earlier debts and overdrafts. It was not until July 1934 that a scheme of capital reorganization was approved, and not until January 1935 that the debenture interest burden was reduced substantially. During 1934–35 Richard Thomas's shares were still depressed: its 6/8d shares started 1935 at 4/9d During 1935 it began to recover, and shares reached a peak of 15/1½d in 1935–36 before climbing even higher in 1936–37.[121] Even so, in 1935–36, when the company was pushing to get the strip mill under way, the finance required was very large and the financial performance of the company relatively weak, and it was by no means clear that the company would succeed if it went to the public to get money for the scheme. Its rivals took advantage of this situation by launching an anti–Richard Thomas whispering campaign in the City, casting doubts on the feasibility of the scheme.[122] Firth had enormous confidence in the potential of a strip mill development and believed that the first in the field would very likely be able to dominate the trade. Difficulties about finance, however, posed dangers that others might move first.

The danger came not from the rival firms within the trade such as

Baldwin's, Lysaght, and Summers but from possible new entrants to the industry, in particular from the motor industry. Although they did not dominate the rolled steel product market in the same way that the American industry did, the motor manufacturers were a vocal and influential lobby, often bitterly critical of the steelmakers—who were, in Lord Nuffield's words, "all big cigars and nothing to do."[123] In 1934–35 both Nuffield and, more seriously, Austin threatened to set up their own steel plants unless the steel industry introduced modern rolled steel facilities.[124] What made their threat of incursion into steel serious was that there was no effective financial restraint on their entering the industry. As a leading stockbroker privately told Montagu Norman, "For the sum of money required, the Austin Co. has twice that amount of loose cash and could obtain credit any-where."[125] But conversely, Austin was unlikely, unless compelled by some urgent necessity, to diversify from a more to a less profitable trade, especially because it would have to fight its way in against the existing firms and contrary to the wishes of both the British Iron and Steel Federation and the Bank of England. Although such a project was given serious consideration, it was poorly thought out and Austin never committed itself to it.[126]

Austin's primary aim was probably a maneuver to put pressure on the steel firms.[127] By November 1935 Austin was in active discussion with Firth about his proposed development,[128] and the Bank of England noted that Firth "is handling the situation pretty well."[129] By December Firth had persuaded Austin that his scheme would satisfy its needs,[130] and in early 1936 Austin publicly abandoned its project.

The other possible entrant was the Metal Box Ltd. which had already acquired from Baldwin's its Eaglesbush tinplate works and put in American management there as a preliminary to further moves into tinplate. Metal Box was much smaller than Austin, and Firth was initially prepared to discuss the possibility of some sort of Richard Thomas/Metal Box merger with Robert Barlow, the managing director. But by 1935 Metal Box was already finding the problems of managing efficiently a vertical link with tinplate considerable and was easing up its pressure.[131]

Firth could ward off these challenges only if he could get his own scheme moving. For this he needed finance, and in 1935–36 it appeared as if this would be forthcoming only if he could counteract the pressures exerted by his rivals in the City. Firth saw the best way of doing this as enlisting a measure of public government support for the project. The lever to do this lay in the government's concern with the problems of the Special Areas, but the price was to be a compromise on the location of the new plant.

As we have seen, until 1934 Firth intended that an integrated strip mill should be developed at Redbourn in Lincolnshire. Richard Thomas's alliance with Whiteheads and the consequent removal of its Tredegar bar mill to Scunthorpe in 1934 underlined this intention,[132] and in July 1935 Firth announced that Richard Thomas would build its new works at Redbourn. Yet by the end of October the decision had been abandoned and Ebbw Vale designated as the site.

There can be no doubt that the relative cost positions favored Redbourn over Ebbw Vale. At one time Firth clearly accepted this in public: "It would be absurd and against the national interests to build modern works in South Wales. Northants and Lincolnshire are undoubtedly the natural centres for the economic production of British steel."[133] But at other times he argued exactly the contrary—that Ebbw Vale was an almost ideal site.[134] It is apparent that he was ready to change his stated opinions in order to suit his overall purpose, which was primarily to make sure that he would be able to pioneer the strip mill in Britain. He was confident that such a mill would produce sheet and tinplate so much cheaper than conventional methods that even at a suboptimal site it would enable him to dominate the trade once it was established. The major problem was, therefore, not where to build it but how to get the project off the ground quickly.

The unemployment problem in South Wales and the government's growing concern with the Special Areas gave Richard Thomas a lever in this direction.[135] The threat that the largest tinplate producer would leave South Wales had resulted in powerful labor agitation in connection with the closure of the old Ebbw Vale steelworks.[136] It is not clear to what extent the government actively pushed Firth to go to South Wales; Firth at times hinted at political pressure and at other times denied it. But Firth was certainly aware that the government was strongly in favor of a South Wales site and hostile to a move to Lincolnshire. Both Stanley Baldwin and Ramsay MacDonald wanted to be publicly associated with the decision to build in South Wales for political reasons: at the time of the 1935 election they wanted to appear to be doing something about unemployment, and Baldwin was publicly suggesting that the government had had a hand in keeping the work in South Wales.[137] It was also clear that government hostility to a Redbourn location would have made Firth's task in floating the scheme on the public doubly difficult. Firth had also hoped for a more positive quid pro quo in terms of pressure on his rivals to give the new works a clear run, but in this he was to be disappointed. Richard Thomas executives have since claimed that the government put pressure on others to stop their strip mills,[138] and there is evidence that the BISF dissuaded Briton Ferry from proceeding with a strip mill scheme in 1935, but it is unlikely that the Briton Ferry scheme was feasible in any case.[139] Firth was willing to make important concessions to the wishes of government in the hope of some wider political backing. When the Import Duties Advisory Committee (IDAC) put pressure on him to place orders for the new machinery for Ebbw Vale with British rather than German companies, he bowed to its wishes despite his own doubts. But then when contractors proved unable to produce the specified goods on time or to the specified price, he got very little sympathy from IDAC, and the resulting delays seriously damaged the project.[140] By late 1936 Firth felt that he had received the image rather than the reality of government backing, and he was seething with anger and resentment at his treatment.[141]

This was hardly surprising. Government policy, broadly speaking, was to back the BISF in the reorganization of the industry, not to sponsor individual firms, however progressive or dynamic they might be,[142] and within the BISF Richard Thomas was heavily outweighed by its rivals. Richard Thomas was able to go ahead with the scheme without the blessing of the BISF because by 1936–37 the revival of trade made the scheme a sufficiently attractive commercial prospect to be floated on the public, and £7 million was successfully raised in January 1937. The aim was to run Ebbw Vale at full capacity and cut into its rivals' trade if necessary to do so. Firth's only concession to his rivals was an agreement to restrict output at Richard Thomas's old plant on a pro rata basis with its rivals' works.[143]

But the Ebbw Vale location to which it had committed itself remained a compromise solution. In the short run it was bound to be by far the cheapest producer in the country through its new technology, but in the long run it was a hopeless location. The site was anachronistic, a "relic" location at an inland hill site with high freight and raw material assembly costs in comparison with a coastal location. Cheap local coal and an ample labor supply compensated partly for this, but site conditions were bad and were to massively inflate construction costs.[144]

There would have been problems with the Redbourn site too. As the earlier reports had stressed, full development there would have been possible only in a joint undertaking with the adjacent Appleby-Frodingham site, but such a merger went far beyond the perspectives of either firm.[145] In conjunction with this difficulty, the assistance that government approval for a South Wales project gave in promoting the idea, thus easing Richard Thomas's financial path around its competitors, was decisive. Once it was decided that the mill was to be in South Wales, the choice of Ebbw Vale followed as a necessary consequence. Ebbw Vale was the only plant in South Wales not owned by GKB that had blast furnaces of its own. Richard Thomas itself possessed none in this area, and since Baldwin's would not cooperate, short of building a wholly new integrated works at much higher cost and with problems of finding a site, there was no alternative Welsh location. Ebbw Vale's blast furnaces, although suitably large, were not ideal because they were not low-cost producers,[146] but it was Hobson's choice.

The political issue that provided the leverage for the location was unemployment. Yet the Ebbw Vale development was no real gain for employment except in the narrowest sense. Although it aided the local situation in Ebbw Vale, the new technology brought redundancies to the tinplate industry as a whole and did nothing for employment in South Wales generally. Ebbw Vale could not absorb the tinplate workers from the western areas made redundant by the impact of the new plant. The burden of unemployment was merely redistributed.[147] As far as many workers were concerned, "the line commonly taken in Cardiff and further west was that if the work was to go to Ebbw Vale it had better go to Lincolnshire."[148]

In the end, the Ebbw Vale development was undertaken as a calculated risk based on the willingness of the stock market to support it. In 1937 it appeared that the problems of the opposition of rival vested interests could be bypassed in a period of expansion; they were, however, to linger on and return with a vengeance when the tide of expansion was disrupted in the slump of 1938. Despite Firth's hopes, Richard Thomas had not been aided by the government in circumventing or neutralizing its opponents. Indeed, its wooing of the government had had double-edged consequences: it had resulted in the company's being pushed into a second-best location and in dependence on inadequate contractors. These problems were all to come home to roost and undermine the company's strategy when things began to go wrong with the project and its finance in 1938. The crisis that followed drew in the Bank of England in a vital role, and the outcome of the new situation can be fully understood only in the wider context of the evolution of banking intervention in the industry. The crisis is examined in detail in Chapter 10.

The rise of Richard Thomas up to the point of the launching of the Ebbw Vale scheme was the story of one firm's detaching itself from a world of small producers and establishing itself as the dominant firm in the industry. The old structure of production left the more backward firms with considerable resilience and an ability to "spoil" the position for Richard Thomas, even if they were unable to advance rapidly themselves. In particular, the scale of finance required by the technological leap involved in modernization gave the other producers a great opportunity to make life difficult for their rival. At the root of the problem was the fact that the new technology pressed against the limits of the extent of the market. In heavy steelmaking in Scotland and the Northeast Coast the domination of the industry by hegemonic consumers had contributed to stifling diversification and change; in tinplate it was the *lack* of a sufficiently rapidly expanding consumer demand that weakened the impulse to modernize. Richard Thomas had emerged from the demise of its family control with a fairly centralized leadership capable of maneuvering in pursuit of growth and modernization in a difficult and congested competitive field. For most of the 1930s these goals were fairly successfully pursued, but the final push for dominance of the market entailed a major risk. The risk seemed worth taking, although one element of it, the expectation of a significant degree of government support, proved misplaced and weakened the scheme. In the event, however, the company was accumulating a legacy of troubles that we will examine in a later chapter.

6.

Structure and Strategy in British Industries

The firms discussed in the preceding chapters were responsible for about one-third of British steel output in the interwar years, and together with the firms covered in detail in later chapters they accounted for two-thirds of all British steel production in this period. The most significant omission is a full-scale description of the United Steel Companies Ltd., which by the end of the period was the largest steel company in Britain. United Steel has been omitted largely because the company has been described in great detail by Andrews and Brunner in their book *Capital Development in Steel*; the material presented on the company later in this book (see Chapters 8, 9, and 10) relates to aspects of the company's history not covered there. Nevertheless, a few points should be made about this important company both for comparison with the preceding case studies and as background to the later discussion.

The multifirm combination that became United Steel between 1917 and 1920 emerged when two large Sheffield family firms (Steel, Peech & Tozer, and Samuel Fox & Co.), unintegrated steelmakers specializing in the rail and billet trades, pursued the strategic goal of securing their raw materials by merging with their traditional iron and coal suppliers. In the process much new and more diverse steelmaking capacity was also acquired, and the result was a widely scattered firm with little physical integration producing coal, iron, and acid and basic steel in Sheffield, Lincolnshire, and Workington. The merger brought together four major iron and steel firms, each with extensive interests at several levels of the production process; it produced a reasonably well-balanced and complementary range of products.[1]

In contrast to the Northeast Coast, the acquisition of coal and iron

156

came in a concentrated strategic burst and as a result was much less haphazard. At the same time, the key firms in the Sheffield area drew together to carry through the project rather than developing separate overlapping structures such as characterized the Northeast. The relative neglect of integration before the war avoided the accumulation of difficult cross-cutting interests in the region and made possible an easier accommodation between producers in pursuit of a mutually agreeable goal. The amalgamation also had certain similarities to a similar sized combine like Dorman Long. The various stages of production were by and large not physically integrated, and the firm became heavily overcapitalized as a result of its merger activity. By issuing £3½ million of debentures, preference shares, and other loans at 6%—not a particularly high rate of interest for the time—the firm incurred £650,000 per annum in fixed charges, whereas the constituent companies before the war had been virtually free of such encumbrances.[2]

There was also a similar continuity of "firm within a firm," in the management structure. Harry Steel, the initiator of the merger, wanted the constituent firms to maintain separate identities and to remain self-sufficient in their day-to-day affairs. He had much suprafirm authority, but he died soon after the consummation of the merger in 1920; his successor, Albert Peech, was much more closely identified with the Steel, Peech, Tozer branch of the amalgamation than with United Steel as a whole. Despite the growing need for centralization of decisions in the 1920s, it often proved difficult for him to push through decisions against the will of branches, and significant elements of interbranch competition also remained. The aim of the original merger was security and economy of supplies, not increased efficiency, and there was no conception of rationalization embodied in the new firm. Most of United Steel's investment projects in the 1920s had been embarked on *before* the completion of the merger, and the new central board had few opportunities to initiate others in the depressed years following the amalgamation. The main aim, therefore, was to complete the program of capital development already initiated.[3]

In its fragmented structure and lack of coordination United Steel bore some resemblance to Dorman Long: family interests lingered on, branch independence was perpetuated, and coordination was limited. In addition United Steel too suffered from a financial dead-hand on its shoulder. The lean years 1924–1927 drained the company because of its excess capacity, unamortized investment, and high fixed charges. Although the company made a trading profit every year except the last, its fixed charges meant that it lost £796,801 in the three-year period, and it was forced to negotiate a moratorium with its creditors in 1927.[4]

Its emergence from this situation to become the most conspicuously well-managed and financially balanced steel firm in the 1930s owed much to the appearance of a deus ex machina in the form of external intervention by a group of financiers. In 1929 Clarence Hatry's financial syndicate, the Austin Friars Trust, bought all the company's share and loan capital by direct bidding on the stock exchange with the intention of using the company as a nucleus for a giant rationalizing amalgamation. But the optimistic conditions of the stock exchange boom of 1929 soon faded and were quickly followed by the collapse of Hatry's adventuring financial empire.[5] The result was that Hatry's specially formed holding company became a convenient vehicle for the speedy reconstruction of United Steel's capital. In the aftermath the book value of United Steel's capital was virtually halved with little difficulty and the financial load of fixed charges almost eliminated.[6] Hatry was arguably the best thing that ever happened to United Steel: he took its financial sins on his shoulders and, when he was crucified, left it absolved of its financial guilt. The affair came at a crucial strategic moment. Faced by its heavy financial losses, the company had begun to look at centralizing its management in order to rationalize. In 1928 Walter Benton Jones replaced the sick Peech as chairman, and a man without any loyalty to particular branches—Robert S. Hilton from Metropolitan Vickers—was brought in as managing director to oversee a program of reorganization and coordination.[7] This managerial reorganization began before the Hatry intervention, but it was undoubtedly greatly assisted by it. The professional managers emerged from the debacle as the clear voice of the firm, and the sudden easing of the cash position made positive reorganization a possibility. The transformation of the capital structure removed at a stroke a great part of the network of vested interests, creditors, families, and branch identities that had so dogged attempts at reorganization on the Northeast Coast. The transformation was quite exceptional and possible only because the Hatry syndicate in effect absorbed the costs of the upheaval.

What light does this picture of the principal steel firms shed on the wider issues raised earlier? What perspective does it bring to bear on the various theories of the firm and on the pattern of interaction of institutional and market factors on the evolution of the industry? Despite the constraints of the market for steel, the case studies have shown in detail how certain opportunities existed for significant progress in particular sectors: consolidation and the avoidance of overlapping development in the Northeast; relocation, integration, and new building in Scotland; and new technology and volume production in tinplate. All of these options were, however, limited by the historical structure of firms and institutions of management and by the frozen, fragmented industry structure in which they operated. Long-term strategies were undercut by those with shorter term interests of salvaging investments, employment, local steel supplies, or managerial or ownership positions. Stock holders, debenture holders, and bankers exerted influence through the financial leverage they had over debt-ridden firms. Local consumers had financial as well as political leverage. Pressures for rationalization and merger heightened tensions between firm managers and family owners. Once regulatory policies were introduced, labor too exerted a certain amount of political leverage. The loosely oligopolistic structure of competition within the industry exacerbated the problem by heightening the defensive strengths of many enterprises. Strategic failures resulted from the interaction of competitive constraints and intrafirm institutions. For British steel firms, structure persistently determined strategy—the reverse of Chandler's classic formula.

This should not be taken to imply that rationalization was an ideal solution that guaranteed economic success. Its merits were focused narrowly on matters of industry efficiency and competitive advantage, and its social costs would have been high. Even within a narrow framework its success was bound to be contingent on the unfolding of subsequent decisions. Central purposiveness and large-scale reforms could have produced desirable benefits, but they might also have paved the way for major strategic errors. In the 1960s and 1970s, for instance, nationalization and centralized decision making opened the way for a disastrous policy of concentration in giant new steel plants. In the 1930s problems of monopoly control would have succeeded problems of industrial fragmentation. Large-scale amalgamations and best-practice investment depended for their success on major swings in the economy. If rearmament and war had not occurred and the sluggish economic climate of the depression had persisted, big new combines would probably have collapsed under their own weight.

It is not at all clear what historical criteria are best suited for assessing the success or failure of business performance. With hindsight it seems clear that certain opportunities existed for greater success in terms of efficiency, sales, and profits. Yet, even by muddling along, the industry equaled or bettered the performance of its European rivals and survived to serve the war economy and prosper in the postwar boom. The aim in this book is not to pursue this sort of complex economic assessment but rather to illuminate the conditions within which the actual economic choices were made. Market forces presented a variety of options and possibilities. The actual outcomes were the results of power relations within and between institutions and the historical structures of competition within the industry.

In this context this study clearly throws into doubt certain notions that recur in the theoretical literature on the firm, particularly those that treat it as a unitary locus of entrepreneurship allocating resources between alternative choices. In most of the firms discussed there was no *single* center of power; different groups had varying powers to influence particular outcomes, and these were more often powers to block unwanted policies than to shape strategies. Conflicts of interest permeated the firms themselves, and outcomes were conditioned by complex processes of internal bargaining. Even then, there was no necessary correspondence between who prevailed and whose interest the outcome finally served. Short-term and long-term interests were often contradictory, information was limited, and the actors operated in a world of "bounded rationality" and uncertainty.

One of the most striking features of this world was the ambiguous and only partial divorce of ownership from control that characterized the industry: the proportion of steel company directors who were members of owning families was 36% of the total in 1905–1925 and 28% in 1935–1947.[8] The founding families were still strongly represented at Dorman Long, United Steel, Colvilles, Summers, Stewarts & Lloyds, and Round Oak throughout the period. There were also managerial dynasties like the Furness family at South Durham & Cargo Fleet, who became predominant investors in a company founded by someone else and then perpetuated their family link, and dynasties like the Keens at GKN and the Hutchinsons at Skinningrove, where the father had worked his way up the ladder to the top and then passed on the inheritance to his sons. As Charlotte Erickson noted in the 1950s, "the steel industry has been governed to a very large extent by dynastic heirs or investors."[9] Yet in the interwar years the families were only one interest group among a series of manager, owner, shareholder, and creditor interests in the firm, and they could play a variety of roles in shaping the company structure. At Richard Thomas and United Steel the establishment of relatively centralized management owed much to the legacy of the families involved, but at Dorman Long and Colvilles the families were awkward barriers to major managerial reorganization. As we have shown, the distinctive interests and practices of the families and the other strategic owning groups had a direct effect on investment and merger strategy and on the structure of production.

In these conditions the professionalization of management and the elaboration of managerial hierarchies made little headway. Because new managerial skills were rarely needed, new functions rarely undertaken, and problems of growth rarely encountered, major administrative reorganization was slow to emerge. Even in a large combine like United Steel, the head office was not reorganized until ten years after the wave of amalgamation that brought the firm together.[10] Similarly, Ellis Hunter's reorganization at Dorman Long took place fifteen years after the creation of that combine.[11] The other notable managerial reorganizations were confined to those companies that were externally reconstructed by the banks. A remarkable continuity of both personnel and practices characterized most major firms like Colvilles, Stewarts & Lloyds, Consett, and Summers.

Generally a slow improvement of practices took place within existing management structures. There was a limited growth of professional nontechnical administrators, often by recruitment from outside the industry: senior administrators like Hilton of United Steel, John F. Beale of GKN, Holberry Mensforth of Bolckow Vaughan, and Walter Benton Jones of United Steel were imported respectively from Metropolitan Vickers, Midland Railways, British Westinghouse, and the Rother Vale collieries. More striking was the tightening of financial practices associated with the influx of accountants such as James B. Neilson (English Steel), Ellis Hunter (Dorman Long), Ernest Lever (Richard Thomas), and Mark Webster Jenkinson (Round Oak and English Steel) to the highest levels of management. Internal promotion ladders offered only limited opportunities for advancement, but exceptional figures like Craig at Colvilles, MacDiarmid at Stewarts & Lloyds, and E. J. George at Consett were able to reach the top in this way.[12]

Technical and production engineering management developed less fully. Figures like Andrew McCance (Colvilles), John E. James (South Durham, Lancashire Steel, and Richard Thomas), and Lawrence Ennis (Dorman Long), who rose to the top as technical managers, were rare. In the late 1930s James was almost the sole figure of this sort that the Bank of England could find to put in to rationalize the technical side of ailing firms, and most banks and firms turned to the American consultants H. A. Brassert & Co. for the most modern technical expertise. With the sole exception of the relationship between Sheffield University and United Steel in the 1930s, technical education did not feed directly into higher management in steel.[13] Consequently, stringent managerial control at the point of production was slow to develop.[14]

Was this sort of pattern a peculiar feature of the steel industry, or is it a specific instance of more general characteristics of the British economy in this period? Are these features of diffuse centers of control, persistence of family management, rivalry of interests within firms, consumer linkages, and the importance of external financial institutions necessarily characteristic of a period of transition from a competitive to a corporate economy? In the United States the transition from family to entrepreneurial to financial to managerial capitalism was expedited as a result of rapid technical and demand changes, but in the principal sectors of British capitalism the process seemed to have stopped halfway. As Chandler noted, "the relationship between ownership and management within the firm reflected the way it became large,"[15] and the diffuse structure of power within British steel might be seen as reflecting its history of a much slower and more diffuse course of growth. It is certainly true that where multi-divisional companies have emerged in Britain they have retained the marks of having evolved out of loose-knit, decentralized holding companies rather than, as in the American model, out of centralized companies seeking solutions to managerial problems arising from rapid expansion, diversification, and the need to cope with new products, new geographical areas, and new needs of mass distribution.[16]

But rather than looking at this feature of British corporate structure as a transitional phase, it is perhaps more useful to characterize the British economy in a different way altogether. Britain's industrial power was always a historically specific and limited preeminence based on an early start and a particular role in the world economy, which was always based on financial and military power as much as industrialism and technical innovation.[17] The economic center of gravity was not that of expanding corporations functioning as engines of growth and devising business structures capable of dealing with the problems of rapid expansion, as in America. Britain had never been simply a corporate economy, and the dynamics of business reflect this pattern.

One consequence is that, as we have noted, structure has tended to determine strategy across a wide range of British industries. Only in food, chemicals, and drugs was there much similiarity to American-style capital-intensive, high-volume, standardized production. For the rest, especially in the traditional sectors where technical change and demand shifted only slowly, the advantages of administrative coordination over the market were debatable. Hannah has argued that compact regional markets, long-established customer relationships and diverse specialized demand, highly developed commodity markets and financial services, and well-developed marketing and middlemen meant that the market generally proved adequate in the nineteenth century. By the time it was perceived to be inadequate, demand conditions in a whole range of traditional industries were deteriorating in such a way that very drastic reorganization was needed. The costs of the invisible hand of the market rose sharply, particularly the costs of excessive competition and surplus capacity.[18] This was partly true of steel and even more true of cotton where there existed what Lazonick has described as "a neo-classical economist's dream" of a hierarchy of extremely well-developed markets with horizontal competition and vertical specialization, which could expand and contract easily to meet demand fluctuations in the nineteenth century but which was paralyzed by the twentieth-century slump. New firms no longer entered, but old ones could survive by living off their capital, and the existence of inefficient firms destroyed the incentive of potentially progressive firms to reequip.[19]

Nor did the large multifirm mergers of 1885–1905 create any irresistible pressures for organizational changes and new business strategies. Most of these companies, like the Salt Union, the Calico Printers Association, Associated Portland Cement, and English Sewing Cotton, remained undiversified, single-product affairs, inspired primarily by defensive motives and the achievement of a measure of monopoly power. Many were like old trade associations in a new legal form, and restructuring was minimal.[20] The mergers of the early 1920s were likewise primarily defensive federations. Although it may be true to say that industrial concentration in Britain matched or surpassed that in America since the 1920s—although absolute size has been much lower—it is misleading to argue as Hannah does that Britain was "beginning to emulate the U.S. model from the 1930s."[21] Very different types of companies evolved from the British mergers.

These federations and other large British companies were permeated by internal conflicts of interest from the outset and lacked any dynamic central power to override or marginalize them. Peter Mathias has described the frequent conflicts of interest between these vertically integrated manufacturing firms and their retailing outlets, especially in margarine, shoes, and brewing: manufacturers wanted guaranteed outlets and the ability to impose buying, selling, and styling; the shops wanted to determine the mix of products and to transmit the discipline of the market as they perceived it to manufacturers.[22] In a large loose holding company like Imperial Tobacco, the central board had to tailor overall strategy to suit the desires of the individual branches; such firms grew not because of a centrally directed strategy but because while certain branches declined, others, like Players, which responded quickly to the opportunities for branded cigarettes, advanced rapidly.[23]

We have noted how in the steel industry consumer links constrained strategic options. This was particularly true of steelmakers' relations with shipbuilders, but it was even more true of the relations between the shipbuilders themselves and their major customers, the shipping lines. As Tony Slaven has shown, nineteen shipping lines ordered one-third of total British tonnage in the interwar years, and most British shipbuilders "obtained half or more of their orders . . . from a relatively small and clearly identified band of shipping companies who ordered regularly with them." Typically the largest shipbuilders sold half of their total output to between half a dozen and a dozen companies who ordered exclusively from them.[24] The "builder's friend" system was the foundation of shipbuilding production and marketing arrangements and operated through a highly personalized contact network in a strongly segmented market. The performance of shipbuilders has generally been explained by economic historians as a result of the conservatism of the builders, the effects of unfair foreign competition, and the influence of government policy on naval construction; but Slaven argues that the structural relationship between builders and owners was also crucial; shipping and shipbuilding had grown up in a symbiotic relationship of mutual dependence in the nineteenth century, and in the twentieth century builders had no mechanisms for seeking new orders outside their customary linkages and relied instead on the anticipated revivification of the British merchant marine for their salvation.[25]

Similar patterns can be seen at work in the papermaking industry, where the development of a business like Bowaters was critically shaped by the interests of its dominant customers, the newspaper proprietors, who for a long time held a major ownership role. William Reader has described how, for a considerable period, "the development of the business was conditional on Lord Rothermere's approval" and how Bowaters was pushed into a "long-drawn dance" to the proprietors' tune. Its options to pursue its commercial papermaking interests were restricted by the desire of Rothermere and Beaverbrook to use the firm solely as suppliers subordinate to their newsprint requirements, and by their practice of using one part of their empire to relieve financial pressures in other parts. Beaverbrook twice used his powerful holding to try to sell Bowaters over the family's head. The firm was pulled out of the orbit of these contending parties only when it was able to use growing prosperity to reestablish independent family control by buying out the newspaper proprietors in the early 1930s.[26]

Similarly, R. W. Ferrier has documented in great detail the restrictions imposed on the commercial policy of the Anglo-Persian Oil Corporation in the crucial period of the early 1920s by its principal consumer, the government. The government wanted regular cheap fuel oil supplies but did not wish to get involved in the development of the oil industry or in a concerted oil policy. Its intention was to secure this limited aim "without impairing the viability of the company or interfering with its managerial judgement."[27] In practice, however, the government's limited horizons ruled out key options for strategic expansion of the company. APOC knew that it could not remain healthy if it remained solely a procurement agency for the government, depending on crude oil alone, and its management wanted to move into refining and distribution. But the government blocked efforts to secure the capital necessary for this expansion; it feared that its own control would be diluted, and it prevented the company from using its strong position in the market to finance expansion through a public issue.[28] Government involvement precluded the acquisition of interests outside Persia, and its strategic priority of maintaining British control of supply made an effective and active amalgamation policy impossible. Only after 1922 was management able to counterbalance government influence by expanding public shareholding when the government retired to a position of "amicable indifference."[29]

At Bowaters and APOC the role of large consumer-shareholders was vital. In the case of the Rio Tinto Company, as with the Colville family interest in Scottish steel and the Furness family on the Northeast Coast, the role of a powerful rentier family was critical. Charles Harvey had shown how, until the mid 1920s, the Rothschilds, the major financial interest in the firm, treated it purely as a source of revenue and blocked the aspirations of management to diversify. A major shift in their attitude in the mid-1920s, when they swung their authority behind a new managing director committed to a policy of pursuing growth, led to the most important change of course in the company's history. In both phases of policy the rentiers were the ultimate determinants of policy.[30]

In a world of ambiguous markets and arguable options, diffuse entrepreneurship and power rivalries played pivotal roles in determining outcomes. Strategic decision making depended on a variety of contingent factors, and structural logjams were rife. In the context of these obstacles and the failure of industry's traditional mechanisms of adjustment, reorganization was too complex for individual companies to achieve in isolation. It was, as Bernard Alford has put it, "probably a matter for central action rather than something to be left to the forces of the market."[31] New forms of coordination and planning were needed, not to deal with expansionary economic pressures but to curb excessive and rapidly rising costs of the market—a different sort of visible hand, centering on an active role by the state or the banks to correct a perceived failure of the market. Most interpretations suggest that despite this situation the banks and the government remained fairly marginal. Lazonick, for instance, argues that "the banks stood aloof from industry" in this period,[32] and Hannah maintains that there is "little evidence of the influence of government on the evolution of the modern corporate economy."[33] The material presented in the next two sections, however, suggests that we may have to significantly revise these conclusions.

PART II

The Banks and the Steel Industry in the Interwar Years

7.

Banking and Industry in the Early Twentieth Century

Banking and government were both more extensively involved in promoting and shaping industrial reorganization in the interwar years than is often recognized. Although they were not always successful in achieving their aims, they were crucially important not only in steel but also in cotton textiles,[1] shipping,[2] electricity supply,[3] coal,[4] agriculture,[5] aircraft,[6] oil,[7] armaments,[8] and railways,[9] and of considerable significance in shipbuilding,[10] locomotives,[11] paper,[12] chemicals,[13] and sugar.[14] These interventions make up a vital part of the prehistory of developments such as nationalization, the growth of the mixed economy, and the growing role of financial institutions in industry since the Second World War. The failure of so many of these attempts highlights some intractable problems in making the transition from market to corporate forms in a mature economy. Britain's traditional industries were declining because their markets were breaking down, but the institutions that might have had the potential to generate effective reorganization of the economy had been formed by the same historical developments that had shaped the crisis in which they were intervening. Britain's early start and long, slow rhythm of industrial and commercial development had produced political, financial, and business institutions that were rooted in the structure of production and equally resistant to change. The visible hand of the banks and the state itself needed to be remodeled and to develop new functions and capabilities before it could operate effectively to reorganize the corporate economy.

In the meantime, their intervention proved to be clumsy and ill-directed and in practice often had effects the opposite of those intended. Thus, some of the most extensive and coherent notions of rationalization and coordinated development emanated from the banks, but at the same time banking interests represented some of the most stubborn obstacles to rationalization in practice. Extensive sets of controlling rights were in the hands of financial institutions, but they were unable to translate such control into effective managerial authority. Likewise, when the government followed the banks into the affairs of the steel industry, it appeared and saw itself as the partisan of reconstruction through supramarket cooperation, but in practice its contribution was to freeze the industrial structure and foster defensive federations under a state umbrella.

In order to understand the limitations of the British banking sector as an interventionist force in industry, it is necessary to place it in the context of the changing relationship between finance and industry from the mid-nineteenth century to the 1930s. The historical literature on bank-industry relations in Britain is somewhat limited with the exception of recent works by Philip Cottrell, Charles Goodhart, and William Kennedy, and much empirical groundwork remains to be done.[15] Nevertheless, this has not deterred historians, sociologists, and economists from taking forcefully argued positions on the issue. Both among Marxists and within the ranks of businessmen and bankers the relationship between finance and industry has been hotly debated. The debate within the business community in particular has sharpened since the speculative property boom of 1971–1973. But it has focused rather narrowly on the accusation (which the City denies) that finance has been diverting funds away from industry to unproductive uses, and it has noticeably lacked a historical dimension.[16]

A more historical approach is contained in the attempt at a long view of the trajectory of the British class structure from a Marxist perspective undertaken by Perry Anderson and Tom Nairn in the late 1960s. Their starting point was the premature and unfulfilled character of the seventeenth-century revolution and the ensuing "compromises" of 1688 and 1832, as a result of which the industrial bourgeoisie failed to attain an undisputed hegemony in society and to remake the ruling institutions of society in their own image. Rather a "deliberate systematized symbiosis" took place between the landed aristocracy and the industrial bourgeoisie in which the landed aristocracy was senior partner. The landed aristocracy from the seventeenth century colonized the City and, through its position in the political institutions, was the main beneficiary of imperialism; it carved out a niche for itself as the most decisive section of the ruling bloc, which it has retained to this day. From there, its "vices," especially its archaisms and its amateurism, have spread out and corrupted both industry and the whole political culture, including a pathological inability to modernize the state.[17]

Underlying this analysis is a view of the financial sector, "the City," as parasitic upon and a diversion from the full development of productive or industrial capital. This position is shared by Sidney Pollard in his review of monetary policy in the interwar years. He takes sides implicitly with industrial capital—which he sees in this case as tactically aligned with the interests of labor—against the City.[18] He argues that the City has enjoyed a "remarkable independence of the real industrial base of the economy," and as a result "the leaders of high finance [were] able to pursue their own narrow and selfish aims as financiers while recklessly damaging the productive capital of the nation."[19]

Two recent interpretative essays on the history of City-industry relations confirm the broad lines of this picture, although with differing emphases. Frank Longstreth argues that banking capital is a "political-economic fraction" of the dominant class which has dominated the British state since the decline of landed capital through its control of the key state bureaucracies, the Bank of England and the Treasury. Through these institutions it has set the parameters of economic policy, even though these have not necessarily been in the interests of "capital as a whole." This fraction continues to exert dominance over the state even though it has outlived its "world-historical role." Industrial capital had shown a surprising political weakness in failing to oust it, and its continuing political subordination has become more and more an anomaly.[20] Geoffrey Ingham accepts much of Longstreth's descriptive picture while rejecting his conceptual framework. In particular, he rejects the concept of "fractions of capital" as presenting impossible epistemological difficulties. No rigorous or meaningful definition of a fraction can be constructed, and in the absence of such a definition it becomes a misleading label for a contingent pressure group. The City, together with the Bank and the Treasury, he argues, should not be seen as the instrument of particular social forces but rather as an "institutional ensemble" that itself exercises power and pursues its own autonomous interests. These interests turn crucially on the City's role as an "international clearing house" and its commercial and financial intermediary roles, which have often been underrated but which are, in fact, more important than its role as investor. For a period under the gold standard the interests of these institutions complemented those of industry; since then, however, their material interests have diverged whereas the City managed to sustain its political control.[21]

The Anderson-Nairn thesis is based primarily on sociological and ideological aspects of the City and the state. Longstreth attempts to ground these features in social forces, but his methodology is open to serious objections. Ingham's argument that the institutions themselves have their own autonomous interests and powers leave unexplained the success of those institutions in defending their interests. Yet all of these writers are agreed that the problem to be explained is a major division within capital—the economic antagonism between different interests and the political subordination of one set of interests to another within a capitalist social formation.

In contrast, other interpretations draw more directly on the conception of "finance capital" as put forward by Lenin and Hilferding in the early twentieth century. The thrust of their work was to stress the supremacy of banking capital over industry.[22] The banks, according to Lenin, were transforming "scattered capitalists" into a single collective capitalist which could control industry through "restricting or enlarging, facilitating or hindering" credit and by extracting precise and extensive information about the workings of firms. In the end, banks can, he argued, *"entirely determine* their fate, determine their income, deprive them of capital, or permit them to increase their capital rapidly."* Banks were becoming "universal" institutions which could "terrorize" big monopolies just as the latter used to terrorize small capital.[23]

Clearly, both Lenin and Hilferding were to a large extent viewing the striking contemporary experience of the development of the large German and Austrian banks in the previous twenty years as a fragment of a universal movement. Yet, with certain qualifications, this view of the tendency of banking capital to supremacy or dominance over industry has remained highly influential: Ernest Mandel, in *Late Capitalism*, sees it as a long-term tendency of modern capitalist industry,[24] and Sam Aaronovitch and Hans Overbeck have applied the notion specifically to modern Britain, arguing in particular that there has been a "fusion" of banking and industrial capital in Britain through interlocking directorates and through financial institutions entering industry, and that banking capital has the dominant, central, or coordinating role in the process.[25] Although Nicos Poulantzas modifies the picture somewhat in his theorization of the relationship between different forms of capital, the underlying framework remains intact. Rather than Lenin's model, he draws more on Bukharin's variant of the "coalescence," fusion, or interpenetration of banking and industrial capital, a notion that does not attribute the same dominance to banking capital but sees the relationship more in terms of an alliance. Poulantzas emphasizes that the merger of banking and industrial capital does not necessarily take place under the aegis of banking capital, and above all he stresses that the process of merger does not *unify* the different fractions of capital but reproduces their contradictions in a new form. Thus, conflicts of interest continue to exist *within* monopolies as well as between monopoly and nonmonopoly capital.[26]

In two recent articles this tendency has been explicitly traced back into the history of the banks and industry in the interwar years. John Foster has argued that the boom after the First World War saw the arrival of the era of finance capital, which he defines as the fusion of monopoly and banking capital. At first, this was only partial, but certain finance capital groups had consolidated themselves in the early 1920s, and in the next two decades "the key institutions of state monopoly capitalism" were formed, within which banking capital had an especially dominant position.[27] W. D. Rubinstein traces a similar evolution, although with a different periodization. Between 1886 and 1922, he argues, the three separate financial, industrial, and landed elites were collapsed into a single "finance capital" dominated by the South of England and London finance. The shift was particularly rapid in 1929–1932 as opportunities for foreign investment declined and the merchant banks began to interest themselves on a large scale in British industry.[28]

Thus, while one view sees the City as essentially parasitic and its activities as a diversion from "real" or, in practice, industrial growth, the Leninist model sees the financial institutions as progressively dominating and directing the nature of economic growth. However, one problem of both lines of interpretation has been pointed out by Rubinstein: "It is a logical fallacy to infer from the central importance of industrial capitalism in the dialectical process the central importance of industrial capitalism for the bourgeoisie."[29] Anderson and Nairn tend to equate industrial capital with capitalism itself and to treat other capitals as inhibiting accretions around this core. This view indicates a misunderstanding of some of the central dynamics of the history of British capitalism. First, as E. P. Thompson has stressed, it seriously underestimates the socioeconomic significance of agrarian capitalism in eighteenth and nineteenth century British capitalist development.[30] Second, it distorts the nature of Britain's industrial power, which was always a historically specific and limited preeminence based on the conjunctural advantage of an early start and a particular role in the world economy and which was always based on a much thinner veneer of industrialism and technical innovation than is often presented.[31] Third, it does not recognize the autonomous economic power of British financial capital based on British imperialism, overseas investment, and financial services and the exceptional historical role of

Britain in the development of the world economy.[32] British central and merchant banks, in contrast to many European developments, were uniquely dependent on the development of the *world* economy and hence enjoyed a rare autonomy from the domestic industrial base—although that base, which was more strongly linked with the clearing banks, also prospered for a long time in the same relationship with the world economy. Hence, the dependency of British banks on economic development did not preclude a certain autonomy from their home base, for at least some banking sectors, for a prolonged period.[33] The picture is one of separate spheres of development with only limited points of interaction between the banking and industrial sectors. The crisis of the interwar years saw this division coming under pressure for the first time.

The origins of the banking sector's divorce from industry go back to the early nineteenth century. Alexander Gerschenkron and Rondo Cameron have stressed the contrast between the uniquely self-financing nature of early British industrialization with its relatively limited need for capital and the experience of later-starting economies where greater discontinuity at the takeoff stage required more systematic mobilization of funds.[34] In Britain the fixed capital needs of industry were low and as late as 1835 were only three times greater than inventory requirements.[35] Capital formation, therefore, in contrast to industrialization elsewhere, was regarded as something that occurred more or less automatically, and the financial system functioned to provide circulating capital and a regime of sound money as a stable background against which this process could continue, rather than as an engine to mobilize funds.[36]

The existing institutions were, however, unable to curb effectively the more pronounced economic disturbances that came with the acceleration of economic growth and the increased impact of industrial cyclical fluctuations within the economy. In these conditions the reform of central banking by the Bank Act of 1844 created the various mechanisms for regulating bills of exchange and bank deposits whereby the Bank of England was able in the long run to play a regulatory role in the financial system and operate as a massive force for stability.[37] Under this system it was the state of the Bank's reserves before all else that dictated policy. The aim was "sound money," and even after certain adjustments in the 1890s the active promotion of conditions for industrial growth were never seen as valid objectives for the Bank.[38]

Fundamental changes in clearing bank lending practices accompanied these developments. In the early nineteenth century strong bonds between the local banking system and industrial long-term finance had been developing,[39] but as the size of investment capital grew, much of this business became difficult for local banks to handle. The rash of mid-Victorian bank failures, culminating in those of 1875–1878, was a result of the banks' becoming too closely linked with local firms and overlending as these firms attempted to expand.[40] Rather than reorient and restructure in order to handle larger industrial requirements, the banks largely backed away from industrial investment. They had this option because Britain's world position enabled them to hold instead the more consistently lucrative, liquid, and marketable British and foreign government stocks, railway holdings, and gilt-edged bonds in their portfolios. Industrial stocks remained notable absentees from the portfolios of the big London clearing banks when, later in the century, they absorbed the local banks through amalgamation.[41] The discount houses, insurance companies, and other major financial institutions shared a similar pattern of development. The financial sector as a whole achieved its stability in the nineteenth century by specializing in low-risk assets, but it did not develop a position in long-term industrial capital formation.[42]

As Michael Edelstein has shown, the London capital market dealt in an unrivaled package of safe and lucrative shares. Safe investment often corresponded with overseas investment, and large profits could be made easily without having to turn to the riskier industrial sphere.[43] It was a self-reinforcing process, for noninvolvement meant that the City lacked the expertise and competence to handle industrial issues, and when they were made, they were often mishandled. The electrical and automobile industries are good examples here of what Kennedy has described as "waves of money carelessly supplied, followed by an equally unreflective withdrawal when problems appeared."[44] Little incentive existed for the sort of knowledgeable risk-taking that developed in Germany, Japan, and the United States, and so risk-taking capital markets did not develop.

The effectiveness of this system depended on Britain's unique position in the world economy. Central bank regulation in particular flourished because of British dominance of the world exchanges. It was not, as British bankers often came to assume, the result of some innate automatic process of the world monetary system. Rather, it was based on the superior productivity and long-term stability of British industry, British capital, and British sterling. Capitalists all over the world had faith in the stability of the pound sterling; pound notes could buy sought-after British goods, and government bonds held in pounds gave their owners a secure claim over the future surplus value of British capital. Hence, in effect, the world monetary economy operated on a gold-pound standard.[45]

Industrial capital formation, therefore, remained predominantly in the hands of friends, family, and business contacts, either through retained profits or through more or less informal tapping of pools of finance. Until at least 1900 the overwhelming majority of businesses raised their finance by private negotiations, and most long-term capital was drawn from a small business circle. Despite Kennedy's claims that the nonappearance of investment banking hindered growth, there is little evidence that British industry had any large, unsatisfied demand for capital from the London money market. The existing short-term and long-term financial services were sufficient, and even risky venture capital could be raised privately and informally without much difficulty.[46] In the newer industries, like motors and cycles, the money market in upswings provided capital freely; in downswings, as A. E. Harrison has shown, a variety of second-best solutions were at hand to fill the financial gaps.[47] There seems to be little evidence to support the view that the City was diverting badly needed resources away from domestic industry.

The concentration of British financial institutions on short-term business with highly mobile funds led to a pervasive emphasis on liquidity in all their dealings.[48] Insofar as banks related to industry, it was in the provision of short-term overdraft finance; they took pains to remain solely as financial intermediaries and to undertake no managerial responsibilities. The ideology of liquidity was probably more pure than its practice[49]—it is likely that many overdrafts became semi-permanent facilities—but there is no doubt about the overall shape of the system and the sharpness of the contrast between it and the roles of the German and Japanese banks, which, as we shall see below, developed considerable ownership roles and the skills to evaluate managerial performance and, where necessary, to intervene at managerial level.

During the late nineteenth and early twentieth centuries, however, the basis of this traditional arms-length relationship between industry and the banks was being eroded. As other states industrialized, Britain's international competitive position, especially in its staple industries, was undermined, and the First World War speeded the decline of the world gold standard system by hastening the emergence of rival world monetary centers in New York and Paris and eliminating the structure of gold flows around a single dominant world creditor.

Nineteenth-century conditions had produced what appeared to be a natural alliance between British financial interests and the capital goods exporting industries, centered on a common interest in maintaining the openness of the world market. Probably until the 1890s British exports of capital, mainly for social overhead investment in developing areas, directly fueled demand for British capital goods. But after 1900 it is hard to trace such a direct causal relationship any longer, although it was to remain an axiom in both business and banking circles for some time to come.[50]

The tradition that banking and industry were separate but happily complementary spheres was bound to come under stress in the aftermath of the First World War. What was not so predictable was that as the stresses developed, a number of banking concerns should find themselves with a higher level of industrial commitments than at any time in the past. Paradoxically, the 1919–20 boom, which represented the last spasm of Britain's primacy in the world economy, generated a violent deflection of banking capital toward domestic industry, including the staple industries, that had no parallel except perhaps in the brief domestic boom of the 1890s. The bankers shared the common euphoria of the industrialists in foreseeing a revival of the old patterns of the world economy and the collapse of Britain's European competitors.[51]

What was the impact of this shift in the relationship between the banks and the traditional industries? The flow of money mainly took the form of the expansion of public share capital and the extension of long-term debenture debt. The banks and issuing houses handled much of this business, but little of the stock finally came to rest in their hands. More important was the massive extension of overdraft finance that was associated with the wave of expansion: bank advances rose from £519 million (30% of bank assets) in 1918 to £926 million (42% of assets) in 1920.[52] Although large sums went to individuals and to stock exchange speculation, the bulk of this money went to companies. This policy was in keeping with the banks' traditional preference for advances and overdrafts rather than ownership; this type of business always made up their most lucrative outlet, and banks were generally very keen to find this kind of accommodation.

But the advances of 1919–20 differed in two important respects from the normal pattern. First, they were very freely given. As Thomas Balogh has noted, "advances were granted that should never have been permitted," especially to cotton but also to steel.[53] It was only the Lancashire banks' willingness to accommodate the speculative syndicates that made the reflotation boom in cotton spinning possible.[54] Second, contrary to a central tenet of banking orthodoxy that advances should be strictly based on the ability of a company to repay within a specified time so as to maintain liquidity, the lending at this time was characterized by high rates but with fairly slack provision for final repayments. The lure of high profits overcame traditional caution, and the banks' overdraft business, which was traditionally centered on a speedy turnover, became tied up as frozen loans in the downturn of the 1920s.

This position was exacerbated by additional lending to support the original loans and to nurse them through the depression. The effect of this situation on the banks was significant. By 1929, 14% of non-government overdrafts—£63 million—were to heavy industry, of which £16 million were to steel or predominantly steel companies.[55] More than 7³/₄% of Midland Bank overdrafts were in steel in 1928.[56] Lloyds Bank had 3.4% of their advances in steel in 1927,[57] and National Provincial probably had about 10% committed there.[58] Moreover, this pattern of lending was dominated by giant frozen overdrafts to a few large companies: a dozen steel companies held perhaps 40% of overdrafts to steel in 1929.[59]

Many of these debts were unlikely to be repaid in the near future, but the amount of cash loaned out was smaller than that loaned to cotton—Lloyds had 7% of its overdrafts in cotton in 1927 and Midland had 12.5% there in 1928,[60]—and the impact of these overdrafts on banking positions was by contrast less acute. The cotton crisis had an intense impact on the regionalized Lancashire banking sector, but most of the banks holding steel accounts had a much broader spread of holdings and therefore were not likely to be brought down by their steel positions. The most disturbing effect, therefore, was the rigidity that the situation introduced into their lending.[61] In particular, the frozen overdrafts narrowed cash ratios (the ratio of advances to deposits), the main indicator by which lending was extended or contracted and by which the banks assessed the soundness of their position.[62] Nevertheless, in the long term only a few of these debts were not repaid—only Ebbw Vale Iron and Steel Co. and Palmer's of the largest debtors were finally liquidated—and the policy of nursing the debts was to some extent vindicated by the fact that so many were fully paid off in the recovery of the 1930s.

For the steel companies this overdraft crisis had important ramifications. By the second half of the decade overdraft finance amounted to a sum almost equal to that from all other forms of loans held by the companies.[63] Consequently, many firms were dependent on the goodwill of their bankers not to foreclose on them to avoid a receivership and liquidation. In contrast to the position of the banks in Germany, however, this creditor position should not be confused with a position of real ownership. It is important to stress the limitations of their strategic power as creditors. This crucial difference was ignored, for instance, by Henry Clay, one of Norman's chief advisers at the Bank of England, when he stated that the British clearing banks are often "just as much implicated in the conduct of industry as the German banks, and differ only in never having faced systematically the responsibilities of the position into which they have slipped, the position of controlling partners in industry, and used their powers to compel a reorganisation of industry."[64] Although the British banks were powerful creditors, they were rarely controlling partners. As the chairman of the National Provincial Bank, which, with the accounts of thirteen of the thirty-six largest steel companies (see Table 17), was the clearing bank most deeply involved in steel, put it: "We often have the whip hand, but it is not alway desirable for us to use it."[65]

In part, this situation resulted from the intensifying competition between the major clearing banks in this period of bank amalgamations.[66] The competition did not take the form of differential rates for credit; rather as Sir James Lithgow noted, "the large banks look upon themselves as competitive with each other, not in the matter of rates, but in the treatment of their customers."[67] Above all, interference in the affairs of unprofitable clients was avoided lest business in more profitable areas should be transferred to banks that did not interfere.[68] When the Midland bank, for instance, refused increased overdraft facilities to United Steel in 1924 and to the Rover Motor Co. in 1929, both firms shifted their accounts to the more amenable National Provincial and Lloyds respectively.[69]

Banks were also reluctant to compel a reorganization of a firm in case they "put themselves in some sort of liability to their clients."[70] Their lack of expertise in industrial financing, consequent on the long history of self-financing by industry, reinforced their hesitancy to interfere. They lacked expert knowledge, and they and the Bank of England had to turn regularly to the American consulting engineers, Brasserts, for advice. When it came to schemes for reorganization, the lack of qualified agents who could exercise the necessary financial and technical control was even more acute. The banks continued to base themselves on the mobility of their credit rather than on detailed assessment of the long-run development of particular enterprises. They acted mainly as a specific creditor interest and in consequence often inhibited vigorous restructuring.

Pursuing maximum financial security without increased industrial involvement resulted in protracted, although unwilling, support for ailing firms in the depression. In order to keep the loans alive, overdrafts were steadily increased as the depression continued; often the banks sought to strengthen their position in the event of a liquidation by obtaining more and more security in terms of the specified asserts of firms.[71] Simultaneously, because the banks were operating

Table 17 The steel companies and their bankers

Company	B	BLB	BoE	BoS	CBS	D	GM	L	Ma	Mi	NBS	NP	RBS	UBS	W	WD
Sir W. G. Armstrong Whitworth & Co.			•													
Baldwin's Ltd.								•								
Barrow Hematite Steel Co.						•				•						
William Beardmore & Co.								•			•		•			
Blaenavon Iron & Steel Co.												•				
Bolckow Vaughan & Co.										•		•				•
John Brown & Co.							•			•		•		•		•
Brymbo Steel Co.															•	
Butterley Co.															•	
Cammell Laird & Co.									•	•		•				
South Durham Steel & Iron Co. and Cargo Fleet Iron Co.		•							•							
David Colville & Sons											•					
Consett Iron Co.		•					•									
Dorman Long & Co.		•										•				
James Dunlop & Co.					•							•		•		
Grovesend Steel & Tinplate Co.										•						
Guest Keen and Nettlefolds Ltd. (GKN)							•	•		•		•				
Robert Heath & Co.							•	•				•				
Lancashire Steel Corporation															•	
Lanarkshire Steel Co.																
John Lysaght & Co.								•								

Millom & Askam Hematite Iron Co.

Palmer's Shipbuilding & Iron Co.

Park Gate Iron & Steel Co.

Sheepbridge Iron Co.

Walter Scott and Co.

Skinningrove Iron Co.

Stanton & Staveley Iron & Coal Co.

Steel Co. of Scotland Ltd.

Stewarts & Lloyds Ltd.

John Summers & Sons

Richard Thomas & Co.

United Steel Companies Ltd.

Vickers Ltd

Sources: Stock Exchange Official Intelligence; company records.
Key: B, Barclays Bank; BLB, British Linen Bank; BoE, Bank of England; BoS, Bank of Scotland; CBS, Commercial Bank of Scotland; D, District Bank; GM, Glyn Mills Bank; L, Lloyds Bank; Ma, Martins Bank; Mi, Midland Bank; NBS, National Bank of Scotland; NP, National Provincial Bank; RBS, Royal Bank of Scotland; UBS, Union Bank of Scotland; W, Westminster Bank; WD, Williams Deacon's Bank.

on the basis of normal banking criteria, it was often bank overdrafts to small undercutting firms, which were often liquid and profitable, that enabled them to finance their stocks and work in progress and take advantage of the economies of depression.[72] Thus, the power of the clearing banks in the 1920s was limited and conjunctural; no structural or institutional changes resulted from the experience. Increases in overdrafts were associated with losses, but decreases followed rapidly on revived profits. Thus, in relation to steel in this period, Richard Sayers's observation that "bankers are entirely passive in the trade cycle" is quite accurate.[73] Even on the basis of a fairly cursory survey, it is apparent that there is little to justify the notion of Foster and Rubinstein of the emergence of a new bloc of finance capital in terms of new institutions or a coherent role for the banks at this level.

Central banking faced distinct but related problems to the clearing banks. The 1920s saw the Bank of England struggling to retain its world role, one corollary of which was that it had always perceived itself as less tied to the home base and to particular enterprises than the clearing banks. Its global view made it more willing to take a broad overall perspective and to contemplate a role in restructing industry; but at the same time its history meant that it lacked any institutional mechanisms whereby it could influence the clearing banks to take a given course, and its power over the banks through its financial regulatory means was both too blunt and indirect and constrained by its overriding concern with the restoration of the gold standard.

For most of the 1920s, therefore, the Bank was confined to exhortation and moral persuasion to encourage other bankers to face facts and not to relieve market pressures on lame ducks; firms should reorganize or go bankrupt.[74] But where the Bank was itself involved as a banker to industry, its conduct was not very different from that of the clearing banks.[75]

The continuous weakening of the international power of the City in the 1920s culminated in the collapse of the gold standard in the early 1930s. As a result the Bank of England imposed an informal embargo on overseas investment, partly to protect the pound from an outflow of gold and partly to safeguard the position of the government in the London capital market. Although this prohibition continued throughout most of the decade, it was never intended to be a permanent pillar of monetary policy and its implications were not fully faced. In 1920 the embargo fueled the new issue boom, and the policy thereafter put a greater premium on domestic investment. The Bank made little effort to shape domestic investment policy, however, largely because it had little faith in the ability of domestic industry to make profitable use of such investment, and because its long-term perspective remained a return to employing capital abroad to stimulate exports.[76]

By the late 1920s, however, the seriousness of the situation was forcing the Bank to look seriously for a time at a reorientation toward domestic industry and at whether more profitable outlets might not be available in Britain. This was the thinking behind the "German solution" of the integration of finance and industry that was canvassed before the MacMillan Committee. As Norman told the Sankey Committee at about the same time: "We have in London a great many famous and old banking houses who for 100 years have done a banking business almost entirely abroad. The conditions have changed, whereby they can no longer continue that foreign business owing to the financial and economic changes resulting from the war . . . I believe that the finance which for 100 years has been directed by them abroad can be directed by them into British industry, that a marriage can take place between the industry of the North and the finance of the South, provided that industry can satisfy finance that its house is in order."[77]

A second impetus in this direction was the effect of the reduction in foreign business done in London after the war on the established issuing houses. Baring Bros., N. M. Rothschild & Sons, Lazard Bros., J. Henry Schröder & Co., and Hambros Bank had all traditionally concentrated on high-quality overseas issues and made only a few very large domestic issues. With the decline of their traditional sphere of operations, they began a reluctant switch into home issues. The generally unimpressive record of home industrials and their lack of adequate investigative machinery made them proceed cautiously and concentrate on the larger companies in the 1920s, but after 1931 the switch accelerated.[78] In certain areas such as electrical manufacturing, houses like Morgan Grenfell & Co. at General Electric Company, Lazard at English Electric, and Higginson at Associated Electrical Industries had already begun to take on active roles in relation to company reorganization in the 1920s.[79]

The Bank of England's establishment of the Bankers' Industrial Development Corporation in cooperation with the major issuing houses at the low point of the interwar slump built on these developments. It was in 1929–1932 that most of the general discussion of redirecting existing financial institutions toward industry took place. But the Bank of England's interest was not sustained at this level; the industrial revival in the 1930s eased the urgency for bank financing for reconstruction, and Norman was glad to be freed of these responsibilities.

The reorientation of the issuing houses continued slowly but steadily, notably in the creation of new institutions to fill the "MacMillan Gap,"[80] but the role of the Bank of England remained unclear for the rest of the decade. During this time, however, as Susan Strange has shown, the abandonment of gold and the establishment of a new pattern of international capital flows, in particular in relation to the Empire, were laying the basis for the emergence of the new international role of the City, using the sterling areas, and for its new position as a financial entrepôt rather than as a capital exporter in the 1950s.[81]

Whereas the issuing houses began increasing their industrial involvement in the 1930s, the clearing banks were moving in the other direction. The most significant aspect of the industrial revival for the clearing banks was that very little of it was financed by overdrafts. Bank credit had a high floor, and it was generally cheaper for companies to reduce their bank debt and seek accommodation elsewhere, either by using undistributed profits, by replacing bank debt by issued capital, or by selling securities and using the proceeds. Heavy industries put a considerable volume of gilt-edged securities on the market in the 1930s, much of which was taken up by the banks, which thus became an indirect source of finance for industry.[82] In fact, liquidation of bank advances and debts was a priority in recovery, and such liquidation by steel companies was particularly heavy in 1935–36, especially for the large firms.[83] Bank loans to heavy industry fell from £63 million in 1929 to £40 million in 1936 and in steel they fell even more sharply from £16 million to £3½ million.[84]

Thus, by the mid-1930s, for steel at least, "whether they like it or not, industry has become largely independent of the banks."[85] By 1936 industry was largely self-financing, and the banks felt themselves to be losing out on a potentially profitable market and holding too high a proportion of low-yield securities.[86] By the mid-1930s the banks were finding it difficult to find profitable outlets for their loans.[87]

In the late 1930s, when, with new building, the scale of capital required began to increase rapidly, signs of a rallying demand for bank finance emerged. At the same time, insurance companies and other financial institutions were coming into the market offering credit for industrial reconstruction; they too had a large volume of funds in low-yield gilt-edged investments and were eager to find more lucrative outlets.[88] Although little research has been done on these activities of insurance companies, it seems that they took a more active interest in the management of their assets than bankers had been wont to do. The appearance of figures like E. H. Lever of the Prudential as a strong man put on the board in the reconstruction of Richard Thomas is indicative of these changes. The dominant pattern remained one of internal finance, with the funds serving essentially as strategic supplements, but this strategic bank financing also led to problems for the banks. As we shall see below, major clearing banks became involved in substantial loans for new technology and expansion in the new lighter steel product sector, where the centralization of capital and concentration of production were on a large scale relative to the size of the market. The consequent vulnerability to cyclical fluctuations was a heavy blow to the clearing banks, and once again the Bank of England was drawn in to unravel the situation. Because of the general strength of the upturn, this was to prove a conjunctural and limited involvement, although not without wider significance in the history of bank intervention in industry.

From what has already been said, it is clear that the various tiers of the financial sector responded differently to the breakdown of the nineteenth-century system in the interwar years. Our main concern in the following chapters is with central banking and the clearing banks. The involvement of the merchant banks remained slight throughout the period, and the emergence of a fourth layer—financial institutions such as insurance companies and pension funds—was barely perceptible before the war.

This overview of bank-industry relations clearly suggests that the rather simplistic notions of a process of fusion of banking and industrial capital, as put forward by Foster and Rubinstein, are wide of the mark for this period. Anderson and Nairn's stress on the sociology and ideology of bankers and industrialists is also an inadequate framework, and something other than the traditional concept of diversion of resources is needed to describe the banking sector's relationship to industry. In fact, it is not so much resources as the institutions and their strategic roles that are important.

We have already noted the structural contrast between the relations between banks and industry in Britain and the more interventionist systems that prevailed in Europe, Japan, and the United States. The statements by Henry Clay and Montagu Norman before the Mac-Millan and Sankey committees which have already been quoted are typical of the recurrent unfavorable comparisons that were made between the British system and its rivals in this period. Much lip service was paid to the potential of bank intervention as a strategic force in rationalization at the time, and recently Michael Best and Jane Humphries have echoed this position in arguing that rationalization was impeded in the interwar years because of the banks' failure to use their position of power to "coordinate industrial modernization" as, they argue, banks successfully did in Germany, other European countries, and the United States.[89]

This view, however, as we have already noted and shall see in more detail later, underestimates the constraints and limitations on the power of the banks in British industry. It also accepts rather uncritically certain conventional views about the extent and effectiveness of banking involvement in industrial finance and reorganization in other countries. It is true, as Best and Humphries note, that German banks were often instrumental in funding industrial ventures in the context of relative capital scarcity and state promotion of industrial development in the mid-nineteenth century.[90] But they ignore the doubts cast on the efficiency of the credit allocation policies of the *Kreditbanken* by recent research. According to Hugh Neuberger and Houston Stokes, the banks' bias toward heavy industry, export industry, and defense, partly resulting from pressure from the government, meant that "the industrial financing of the *Kreditbanken* in the period 1883–1913 was plagued by allocative inefficiency serious enough to have hampered the growth of non-agricultural output."[91]

Although this view remains controversial,[92] the previous view of the role of the German banks must be questioned. They undoubtedly were a fundamental force in the provision of short-term to medium-term start-up capital and in the public flotation of growing companies. Moreover, their knowledge and experience of industry were powerful elements in reorganization and the strategic development of new industrial sectors, and they often acted as important channels of communication fostering a "community of interest" between related firms.[93] But their dominance in industrial matters was probably declining from the turn of the century, especially in matters of combination and rationalization, and their strategic grasp was becoming less sure-footed. The peak of German bank involvement was in the period from 1870 to 1895 when large loans enabled steel, coal, and electrical engineering companies to make the large-scale investments in new technology that they required. At the same time the banks frequently took control of the companies concerned by taking up seats on the board.

Nevertheless, as Hans Pohl has shown, this picture was considerably modified after 1895. Both the wave of industrial mergers that followed and the increased scale of capital investment weakened bank control: mergers often dispersed bank control by bringing several different bankers on to the boards of enlarged companies, and at the same time the giant new loans were generally too large for individual banks to take on and tended to be financed by consortia of banks. Leading industrialists like Krupp and Thyssen were therefore able to deliberately restrain the influence of the bankers by spreading their major loans over several banks. Moreover, in the years before the First World War the proportion of industrial self-financing was rising rapidly, and the banks were not the main impetus in the period of industrial restructuring after 1900. The increased industrial concentration of the war years and the rationalization wave of the early 1920s took place largely independent of bank finance, and the mechanization of heavy industry in the late 1920s did not rely on bank credit. Both the German inflation and government credit allocation policies contributed to restricting the banks' role in these major developments.[94] This is not to deny that the German banks remained an important strategic force in German industry, but it does indicate that their role was less hegemonic than is often supposed and that their influence in twentieth-century restructuring was more problematic than it was in nineteenth-century industrialization.

Recent research also casts doubt on the earlier picture of the dominant role of Japanese banks in orchestrating industrial expansion. Kozo Yamamura has argued that the Japanese banks were much closer in practice to the British model than to Gerschenkron's model of the interventionist banking system of late industrializers, and it is important to remember that the *Zaibatsu* companies, which played the critical role in Japanese interwar industrial development, were not analogous to the *Kreditbanken* but were instead integrated industrial empires in which finance was only one branch of their broader manufacturing and commercial operations.[95]

Thus, the classic picture of the dominant role of German and Japanese banks in industrial modernization has been significantly questioned. Moreover, it is also apparent that in those cases where European banks did exercise a hegemonic role, the strategic purposiveness often imputed to them did not necessarily follow. We have already noted some of the criticisms made of the German banks in this respect. Herman Daems has shown that in Belgium, although the banks exerted direct control over large sectors of industry through their boardroom representatives, their investment practices were conservative. They confined themselves strictly to established industries, and their unwillingness to aid diversification seems to have contributed to the slow growth of newer sectors in Belgium.[96] Richard Rudolf has castigated the Austrian bankers for their attachment to "plump, juicy firms of sound prospects" and to policies of risk minimization.[97]

Furthermore, heavy banking commitments to industry could also jeopardize the stability of national banking systems. The classic case, of which Montagu Norman was acutely aware at the time of the Bank of England's most extensive industrial commitments between 1929 and 1932, was that of the Austrian banking system. Like the German and Belgian banks, the Austrian banks (most notably the Österreichische Kredit-Anstalt für Handel und Gewerbe) were deeply involved with domestic industrialization from its outset. They played a direct and dominant managerial role intensified by the fact that, unlike the German banks, they operated on the "exclusiveness principle" with only one bank lending to any major firm. The result was what Dieter Stiefel has called entwinement, an often excessive mutual dependence of the banks and their major industrial clients.[98] From the beginning of the twentieth century the Austrian banks were very concerned about this and sought to widen the equity base of their industrial clients, but the weaknesses of the Viennese capital markets frustrated them. Under the Hapsburg monarchy they were able to balance their industrial commitments with their transnational banking role within the Empire and also to restrain their industrial commitments by promoting flotations of their industrial clients, frequently placing the equity with foreign investors. But with the collapse of the Empire at the end of the First World War, their multinational aspirations were increasingly frustrated, and the Austrian inflation enhanced the dependence of industry on its bankers for investment funds and finally locked the banks into their industrial clients. The banks took on not only the leadership but also the risks of industry. The crash of Kredit-Anstalt, which destabilized the whole European financial system, was largely the result of its being dragged down by its industrial involvements.[99]

In contrast, the British banks benefited considerably from their relative noninvolvement in industry during the depression,[100] and the overdraft crisis and the experience of the Lancashire banks with the cotton industry underlined the perils of extensive involvement with industrial clients. The successes of the strategic role were given much attention, but in fact the experiences of the Continent did not constitute a wholly satisfying institutional formula to be emulated. The next section explores in detail the historical experience of the incursions of the various sectors of British banking into the steel industry and considers the opportunities and limitations involved. After this analysis we shall attempt a more precise evaluation of the dynamics of bank-industry relationships.

8.

The Political and Interventionist Role of Central Banking in Industry, 1920–1932

Before World War I connections between the Bank of England and industry were conspicuous by their absence. Yet, as the Bank's official historian has noted, industrial intervention was to become "one of the most characteristic activities of the Bank in the inter-war decades."[1] This change centered on involvement in two major industries, cotton and steel. By the late 1920s and early 1930s the engagement diary of Montagu Norman, the governor of the Bank of England, indicated that more time and priority were given to industrial matters than almost anything else, and this at a time of intense crisis in central banking's more traditional operations.[2] How did this change come about and what was its significance?

The Erosion of Abstention, 1920–1929

Until the late 1920s the Bank of England remained deliberately on the sidelines in discussions of industrial reorganization. Norman played the role of a conscience for other bankers, occasionally prodding banks in the direction of a receivership for their clients[3] or informally encouraging them to take action in the "national interest." Whether the clearing banks responded or not, inside the four walls of the Bank, both at this time and later, "industrial policy" was whatever Norman determined it should be, and Norman never met with any significant opposition to his evolving policies from his senior colleagues. At this time, however, there was no urgency or general cohesion to his policy, except to reject the notion of the systematic application of bank pressure in reorganization. When the idea of a bank trust was floated during the 1925 Balfour enquiry, Norman bluntly told the Chancellor that he had no intention of doing *anything* "until the enquiry into subsidies (i.e. tariffs) is ended and forgotten."[4] When Steel-Maitland reopened the question in 1928, Norman reiterated that such an idea was "impossible"' because the banks' fear "was too great of the charge of domineering over industry through money trusts."[5]

Although Norman clearly opposed direct bank pressure, he was more willing to give consideration to suggestions for schemes to mobilize the resources of the issuing houses or financial syndicates to provide extensive credit to the steel industry to promote rationalization. These ideas were mainly developed outside the Bank, but all were considered in some detail by Norman. The most significant, and the one that in many ways foreshadowed the later Bankers' Industrial Development Co. scheme, was put forward by E. Guy Ridpath, the chairman of the stock exchange, in 1927. During the course of a series of discussions about possible amalgamations involving Richard Thomas, Colvilles, United Steel, Bolckow Vaughan, Baldwin's, and South Durham, Ridpath proposed formation of a financial syndicate involving the major issuing houses, with Lord Revelstoke of the Bank of England as chairman, to break the logjam in the negotiations by providing finance and developing a general policy in conjunction with the National Federation of Iron and Steel Manufacturers (NFISM).[6] Norman himself was "very keen on the subject." He assured Ridpath that *"if necessary* he himself would be willing to serve on the Committee."[7] But Norman was also suspicious of the vague and general nature of the plans, and he pressed both Ridpath and Bond of the NFISM to produce concrete proposals. In the event, the scheme petered out over the next few months owing to the inability of the steelmasters to reach any measure of common agreement with each other.[8]

Soon after, similar proposals, put forward by Arthur Colegate for the formation of an iron and steel finance company on a profit-making basis, were received more doubtfully.[9] Norman feared that the prospect of fresh money, unless tied to definite schemes, would allow companies to avoid receiverships. He believed that the existing institutions were adequate to provide finance "once the individual concerns have been sufficiently deflated and once the position is so adjusted as to show a light at the end of the tunnel."[10]

Neither of these two proposals reached the stage of either concrete schemes or action. However, the proposals from Clarence Hatry that came before Norman in May 1929 were both more ambitious and actually in the process of realization. Hatry had developed a reputation for himself through the promotion of large local government issues, and he was now attracted to the possibilities of technical progress and reorganization in industry. His schemes were ambitious, but he was a respected and powerful figure in the City—and an extremely persuasive and charming man. He had a close personal association with several leading financiers, including Beaumont Pease, the chairman of Lloyds Bank, and before he turned to steel his projects had already received the backing of large loans from Lloyds, Barclays, National Provincial, and Kleinwort.[11] By 1929 Hatry's Austin Friars Trust had already acquired United Steel and was planning to develop a major holding company around it to acquire 60% of the steel industry by buying up all the major firms. Hatry by himself could not handle such a project, and he sought Norman's backing in order to get City support. But Norman, unlike Beaumont Pease, never trusted him. Norman doubted whether this sort of conglomerate merger could be as effective as regional groupings, and was keenly conscious of the speculative nature of the scheme. Hatry had pressed the urgency of the project: "At first he talked of the necessity of carrying through the main business within 19 days, though later he extended the period to two months."[12] Norman "expressed surprise" at the idea of funding an operation of that scale without any investigation of the plant involved and demanded further evidence that the project was feasible. His reservations led Norman to warn his associates against the scheme, which was already marked by dishonesty and suggestions of malpractice.[13] It was clear to him that Hatry had "already bitten off a scheme as large as (or larger) than he can chew; if he could further actualise a dream and join the two together on your and my backs, he would be relieved and also successful." They were seeing "a dangerous and perhaps an ailing Mr. Hatry."[14]

Within two months Hatry had crashed in a financial scandal that resulted in imprisonment.[15] The fiasco heightened the Bank's tendency to be cautious. Norman was hesitant about using the opportunities presented by the crash to use United Steel as a nucleus for reorganization. Herbert Lawrence, the managing director of Vickers and chairman of Glyn Mills Bank, felt that "the Hatry catastrophe may make a Steel Trust under proper auspices more feasible,"[16] and it was probably Lawrence and Webster Jenkinson, the leading accountant and another director of Vickers, who were behind the negotiations involving Sir Harry Goschen of Lloyds Bank, the Morgan Grenfell issuing house, and unnamed "American finance" to acquire United Steel and the options it had obtained on the South Durham and Cargo Fleet share capital, a transaction that would have created the nucleus of a large amalgamation in the Northeast region.[17] Norman, however, felt that Vickers was trying to ensure that in any rationalization of the steel industry the control would pass into the hands of Vickers, "a result which should be avoided at all costs."[18] As a result he refused to involve himself in such a scheme, and it subsequently fell through.

The Hatry scheme had been a speculation, and its aftermath was a complicated affair holding too many skeletons in too many cupboards for Norman to be prepared to use it as an opportunity to promote far-reaching reorganization. Nevertheless, by the time of the Hatry crash in 1929, Norman's earlier general interest in the rationalization of steel had begun to take a much more concrete form as the Bank's involvement in the industry began to expand for very different reasons.

The earliest direct involvement of the Bank of England with the steel industry came through its involvement with Armstrong Whitworth as an ordinary commercial customer whose business the Bank held as a result of its prewar practice of combining a commercial banking business with its functions as a central bank. Armstrong had become the largest customer of the Newcastle branch of the bank, and the latter had, as a matter of course, financed both its wartime and postwar expansion. With the curtailment of its armaments work, Armstrong had sought compensating outlets in commercial shipbuilding and locomotive building and in the creation of a large new pulp and paper manufacturing project in Newfoundland. In practice, however, these new enterprises only added to their problems; commercial ships were built that could not be sold, and the Newfoundland project proved a bottomless pit for funds.[19]

Norman's policy with regard to Armstrong was similar to that of other commercial banks in relation to their industrial clients. In the early 1920s he had decided that the Bank's commitments were too great for it to withdraw its support without precipitating collapse. He was, therefore, committed to propping up the firm.[20]

But despite an issue of £2.5 million debentures in December 1924, of which the Bank itself took up £500,000, the situation had become acute by mid-1925 and the Bank's advances to the company had risen to nearly £3 million.[21] Two months later it was £3.5 million.[22]

Until this time, however, despite its massive financial involvement, the Bank had not tried to exert any control over the firm's affairs or policies. Norman was reluctant to interfere with the management of Sir Glynn West who was "the one man on whose shoulders the whole burden of the various enterprises rested," even though "he had more to deal with than he could properly manage"[23] and was "overworked and overbothered."[24] This position was maintained by the Bank despite the fact that it was well aware of the ramshackle and inefficient organization of Armstrong. When Edward R. Peacock, Norman's personal adviser and confidant,[25] and Lord Revelstoke had tried to ascertain clearly the situation of the firm in spring 1925, it proved impossible for them to obtain accurate information "not because it was purposely withheld but because . . . there was no-one sufficiently versed in all the Company's undertakings to supply it."[26]

Only the dire situation of summer 1925 convinced the Bank that Armstrong's position was "too large, too complicated and too serious" for the company to be left alone any longer.[27] This position was one of overextension and lack of centralized management, unpaid debts and poor profits. The most pressing question was the disastrous Newfoundland project. It had been launched overhastily and without any real study of market conditions or any experience in how to run such a business.[28] By 1925 it was in "chaos," run by a scattered, cumbersome, and costly directorate in a most extravagant way.[29]

The man Norman turned to to deal with this state of affairs was J. Frater Taylor, who was to become a key figure in the Bank's intervention in steel and other industrial matters in the coming years. He had been born in Aberdeen, but like Peacock, who put his name forward to Norman, he had gained his experience in Canadian and international business as a "company doctor." He had reorganized several firms in India and Canada and had recently been put in to several concerns as the agent of the Bank of Canada and the Bank of Montreal.[30] As a person, he was "unimportant in appearance . . . not much given to talking but always very much to the point." He was also rather "difficult to get along with,"[31] but Peacock believed he had "an uncanny instinct for finding weak points and weak men."[32] On the basis of Frater Taylor's investigation, the Court of Treasury decided to allow the Newfoundland scheme to be carried through, because almost nothing could hope to be recovered unless the scheme was completed.[33] To do this and to sort out the rest of the organization, they would tighten their control over Armstrong through a committee of creditors, cut out any further dividend payments, severely restrict the Civil Engineering Department, which was making the largest losses, and, despite Norman's preference for a receivership in this case, make the Newfoundland company issue prior lien debentures to finance its completion.[34] Nevertheless, during the time of these investigations and organizations, the situation continued to deteriorate, and by December 1926 the Bank's commitment to Armstrong stood at £6½ million.[35]

Norman was thus thrust into the position of having to sort out the affairs of a complex and diverse business and find a long-term solution. The overall plan that emerged from the discussions of 1926 was first to combine Armstrong's heavy steel and armament section with Vickers in what he hoped would ultimately be a self-supporting company; second, to sell off or entrust to separate operating companies Armstrong's other assets and subsidiaries, including its major steelmaking subsidiary, the Pearson Knowles group; and third, to close down, scrap, or write off the remainder.

The key element in this plan was the scheme for a Vickers-Armstrong merger. The idea was first discussed and outlined by Webster Jenkinson of Vickers and Frater Taylor of Armstrong in December 1926, but Norman felt that these proposals favored Vickers too much and that it would "gobble up" the rest.[36] Norman saw this as a project of national interest and was most anxious to keep some measure of control over its development. Others, like Frater Taylor, however, were more pragmatic about the prospects of the Bank's exerting significant controlling influence in any merger by which it would salvage its ailing client. The shortage of armaments work was recognized to be fatal to Armstrong; only the concentration of Vickers and Armstrong's armament work in one place could make profitable operations possible. There was no way in which Armstrong could continue as an independent armaments firm. Vickers with its stronger position naturally wanted control in a merger, and, owing to its relative financial strength, "they can stand a prolonged siege where Armstrongs cannot." Although Frater Taylor believed that Armstrong could struggle for better terms, he discounted any possibility of outright or final rejection of the Vickers scheme.[37]

A number of difficulties were raised by the idea of merging a profitable and financially strong company with a sick and unprofitable one. Given the nature of the new company's markets, profitability under future peace conditions was unlikely.[38] Norman's first effort to get around this problem was to ask the government, in the national interest, to provide a guarantee of profits for the new company in order to maintain the arms industry. The government, however, refused. The alternative was to turn the original scheme around the other way: the Bank of England instead of the government would provide a guarantee of profits, but preserving the existing firms as integral units was not to be given priority; instead, all the assets of the merger company that could not be made remunerative under peace conditions would be abandoned—even if this meant that the new company would largely detach itself from the armaments business.[39]

Such a move by the Bank was unprecedented, and the Bank took good care to ensure that its role should not become public knowledge and encourage other firms to hope for similar aid. After considering and rejecting the idea of using Baring Brothers & Co., the merchant bankers, as trustees for an unknown guarantor, the Bank finally decided to put the required guarantee through the Sun Insurance Company "so that the camouflage should be complete."[40] This covert participation by the Bank was not publicly disclosed until 1935.[41]

The new company Vickers-Armstrong was controlled by Vickers through its two-thirds holding of the ordinary shares and an even larger proportion of preference shares. The Bank accepted Vickers-Armstrong ordinary shares in exchange for its entire holding of £5 million Armstrong Whitworth debentures.[42] The Bank's liability was changed from its loans to its guarantee of the new company's profits. It also wrote off considerable losses and bought out Armstrong's first debenture holders. Norman, however, found this position unsatisfactory. He was unhappy to cede control wholly to Vickers: "I have made sacrifices all round for moral reasons. I wish to retain control for rationalizing reasons."[43] He persisted in maintaining a quite unrealistic concept of partnership between Vickers and Armstrong, an idea that was inconsistent with the existing balance of power within the firm.[44]

Norman emphasized this concept of the new company largely because he wished to extend this merger into a broader amalgamation of all the armaments steel manufacturers. Although Herbert Lawrence, the chairman of Vickers, was sympathetic to the idea in general, he was reluctant to expand and take in new businesses too rapidly; hence, he had disagreed with Norman on the question of incorporating Beardmore in October 1927.[45] He did support the further merger of Vickers-Armstrong with Cammell Laird's steelmaking section that followed and created the English Steel Corporation (ESC), but he had sharp disagreements with Norman about its organization and management and especially about the role of Vickers in the new merger. They also differed sharply over the prospects of a further merger between the English Steel Corporation and Thomas Firth & Sons and John Brown Ltd. Norman felt that Lawrence was getting "more dug in, more static and less dynamic" as time went on, and that he was, therefore, "hindering the assembly of dynamic management for rationalisation."[46] In fact, however, Lawrence had a much firmer pragmatic grasp of the problems of assembling such a combination than did Norman.

The Bank wanted the management of ESC to be quite separate from that of Vickers-Armstrong. Lawrence wanted to put in George Taylor of Vickers to run the new concern but Norman resisted. Taylor was, he thought, "involved in secret hanky panky."[47] Lawrence in turn opposed Norman's first choice, Ernest Gowers.[48] Norman saw any intensification of Vickers's control as being opposed to a broader reorganization of this sector of the steel industry, but he had little actual power to resist the controlling role of Vickers's capital. Vickers owned £12½ million and Armstrong Whitworth £5 million of the £17.5 million Vickers-Armstrong capital. Vickers-Armstrong in turn held ten-sixteenths of ESC's £7.84 million capital, Cammell Laird owned five-sixteenths, and Vickers itself the remaining one-sixteenth.[49] Moreover, because the Bank would not undertake further investment in ESC, the influence it exerted through its profit guarantee to Vickers-Armstrong was steadily diluted. Thus, for instance, when ESC wanted fresh cash to buy Darlington Forge Company in 1929, it was Vickers and not the Bank who made a loan to ESC for the purpose, thus further strengthening its hold over the company.[50]

This pattern of control was finally consolidated when the capital of ESC was reconstructed and Vickers's loans were converted to ESC debentures, thus formalizing fully its dominant position.[51] The trend was particularly disheartening for Norman because he felt that Vickers-Armstrong and ESC were being developed on "wrong lines." He wanted properly managed "live" rationalized units and he did not feel that this was happening at ESC.[52] For him rationalization by industry was a clear guiding light to follow, and he felt balked by the more cautious approach of the industrialists.

Through Guy Dawnay and George Ionides, whom the Bank had appointed as chairman and vice-chairman of Armstrong Whitworth, the Bank had direct representation on the board of Vickers-Armstrong, but after Frater Taylor had "had enough" of Armstrong Whitworth and resigned from the board, the Bank had no one of dominant stature to provide the sort of policy direction it wanted to impose on the new combine.[53] Thus, in 1929 the ESC board went against the advice of the Bank's experts, who had advised the company that its Sheffield site could never be developed into a complete steelworks and proposed either a wholly new development on a new site or, alternatively, concentration of operations at the company's Openshaw works in Manchester. Instead of following either of these courses, the board decided to acquire the Darlington Forge Co. and develop and concentrate its forging work there.[54] In fact this money was never spent because of the slump in demand for the types of marine forgings and castings produced at Darlington. By 1931 the board realized that "any capital spent there would be thrown away."[55] Yet the alternative development strategy to which the company reverted was piecemeal development of the Sheffield site which the board now argued "could be done sufficiently for present prospects."[56] This expenditure was to be combined with writing down its capital.

The Bank's advisers were sharply critical of the lack of decisive rationalizing policy at ESC in its first two years. Bruce Gardner thought the new scheme inadequate; it lacked any serious analysis of profits and losses between various departments. In general, internal rationalization had still to be effected: "It is doubtful whether from the *practical* side, much thought was given as to the condition of the various works and their suitability or otherwise for the concentration necessary to give proper effect to the merger." Much pruning of obsolete plant still remained to be done.[57] E. H. D. Skinner, Norman's personal adviser, was even more critical: the plan was "shamefully drawn up" and "causes doubts" about whether the board has "too many financiers and accountants and quasi-financiers and not sufficient industrialists."[58] Despite this, however, the Bank had no locus standi in the matter. Its aim of an English Steel-Beardmore-John Brown linkup was not being pursued, and the developments that English Steel was in practice pursuing looked dangerously as if they might end up by cutting across the implications of the Bruce Gardner plan by resulting in English Steel's constructing blast furnaces in Sheffield.[59] The Bank had never exerted managerial or financial control over Vickers-Armstrong or English Steel; in the end it was merely an unwilling accomplice of those concerns' own development plans, which were not very much to the Bank's taste.

Moves toward Intervention, 1929–1932

These developments, deriving from the Bank's role as a branch banker, combined with the intractability of the crisis in the traditional industries and the growing demand for broader schemes of reconstruction, put pressure on the Bank's customary aloofness from industry. In one other respect, too, the industrial crisis held a prominent place in central bank attention: the crisis of the old industries was also a crisis for particular sectors of banking, which in turn involved the Bank's function of stabilizing the banking system and rescuing banks that were in trouble. This problem was felt most acutely in the cotton industry. Most major banks were able to cover their losses in depressed industries by profits elsewhere, but the local Lancashire banks did not have their interests spread so widely, and Williams Deacon's Bank's reserves in particular were almost exhausted by the coal, cotton, and steel depressions. The Bank's intervention to form the Lancashire Cotton Corporation was to a large extent a measure of "outdoor relief" for this and other ailing banks. Norman candidly described his attitude toward Lancashire cotton to the Court of Treasury: "He considered it necessary for the Bank to support and subscribe to a satisfactory scheme, partly to help the cotton industry, partly to keep the question away from politics but more especially to relieve certain of the banks from a dangerous position."[60]

Norman himself was the driving force behind the Bank's "industrial policy." By tradition the leading joint-stock bankers were unrepresented on the policy-making committees of the Bank of England, and Norman had carved out an unexampled position of authority for himself at the center of the Bank's decision-making apparatus. His dominance was reinforced by his personality. He was a cantankerous, aloof man. At one moment he would be plunged into black moods and deep anxiety; at another he would be almost euphoric and full of confidence. His difficult temperament was exacerbated by Carl Jung's misdiagnosis of him in 1913 as suffering from creeping paralysis of the insane. The doctor's verdict had been hushed up, but it preyed on Norman's mind.[61] His erratic personality, against the background of his financial prestige, invested him with an air of mystery and unapproachability that made his authority even more unchallengeable. The considerable degree of centralization and unification of decision making in Norman's hands at the Bank opened up the possibility of turning the Bank toward a new course in relation to industry. Conversely, however, the clearing banks, although they had little say over these decisions inside the Bank, in no way felt themselves bound by Bank policies. They could and did pursue independent policies with regard to industry, whether Norman approved or not.

Norman had hoped in the mid-1920s to develop a "Big Sixth" bank as a counterweight to the "megalomania" of the "Big Five." While blocking further expansion by amalgamation by the giant banks, he was simultaneously seeking to merge the Lancashire banks or to bring some of them together with either Glyn Mills or the Royal Bank of Scotland to form a new giant.[62] In 1926–27 he had devoted much attention to the Lancashire banks for this purpose, and although their industrial debts made it hard to bring them together, a major step had been taken with the creation of Martin's bank in December 1927. But when the auditors refused to sign the accounts of Williams Deacon's in late 1928, this major element of Norman's banking policy was severely jeopardized. Not only was the project set back, but a banking collapse that threatened confidence in the whole banking structure was also on the agenda.[63] In fact, one of Norman's objectives in pursuing a "Big Sixth" was precisely to resolve the problems of the small banks, lest the strain of rescuing them might threaten continued private ownership of the Bank.

The expensive rescue operation for Williams Deacon's and the pursuit of a solution to the problem of the local bank's industrial debts by rationalizing cotton through the Lancashire Cotton Corporation

moved ahead in tandem. Williams Deacon's was finally merged with
the Royal Bank of Scotland, but guaranteeing Williams Deacon's overdrafts to forty cotton firms—in secret, to prevent a crisis of confidence—and finding financial sweeteners to make Williams Deacon's
reasonably attractive to the Royal Bank of Scotland finally cost the
Bank between £3 and £4 million.[64] Once embroiled in cotton, Norman
was forced to turn his attention to industrial reorganization, but major
traditional banking concerns were clearly the prime impetus in this
case. Under these pressures Norman began to take a growing personal
interest in the wider questions of industrial reorganization and to
attempt to systematize Bank involvement in industry.

Norman did not have a clear policy, but he did have a consistent
approach to industrial questions. Like many others in the circles he
moved in, he believed in rationalization by industry as an idea, as an
elegant, efficient, and logical solution to the problems of industry,
and as a way of keeping the reorganization of industry in the hands
of right-thinking people and away from politicians—especially Labour
politicians. A number of leading industrial and banking figures shared
these ideas, and their names crop up recurrently in a wide range of
rationalization discussions in this period. Lord Weir, for instance, the
wealthy chairman of a Scottish engineering company who had been
a wartime business recruit to the coalition government and thereafter
moved easily in the corridors of power, was a key figure in the establishment of the Central Electricity Board and had close links with
the Mond group of employers[65] and with Harry McGowan of Imperial
Chemical Industries (ICI), who was also a director of the Midland
Bank. Acting on behalf of what Sir James Lithgow called the Mond
Finance Scheme, he and McGowan initiated negotiations for a Scottish
steel merger from which the Brassert scheme for Scottish steel reorganization emerged.[66] His closest banking connection was with Reginald McKenna, the chairman of the Midland Bank and fellow wartime
cabinet minister. McKenna had been deeply involved in the merger
which brought together ICI, and in the 1920s he was a major influence
behind the scenes in attempts to develop a British-Thompson-Hous-
ton/GEC merger in the electrical manufacturing industry.[67] In the steel
industry he shared responsibility for the McKenna-Larke proposals
for regional mergers that were put forward in 1927, and in the mid-
1930s he played an important role in the rationalization of Scottish
steel.[68] A further financial contact of the Mond group who operated
in a similar capacity was the financier F. A. Szarvasy, who had been
a key intermediary in the Royal Mail Group's purchase of the White
Star Line from the Americans, and who was closely involved in the
electrical manufacturing negotiations on rationalization in the 1920s,

in proposals for national steel reorganization, and, as we shall see, in the salvage of Beardmore.[69]

These figures inhabited the world surrounding politics, industry, and finance and moved easily in each of those circles. Their informal and overlapping connections created a rationalization milieu in which ICI, the electrical manufacturers, and Vickers (who spanned the electrical and steel industries) were prominent and with whom certain issuing houses such as Lazard Brothers (who were to be directly involved with the Bank at Beardmore) and Helbert Wagg & Co. (who played a similar role at Lancashire Steel) were also closely involved.[70] Their signficance was twofold: they created a current of ideas about rationalization, which matured in the less crisis-ridden chemical and electrical sectors and which were drawn on in thinking about steel reorganization; and they formed a pool from which Norman could draw in assembling an expert team to handle the Bank's industrial intervention.

In December 1928 Norman formed the Securities Management Trust (SMT) to deal with the problems of the Bank's industrial holdings which by this time included the Lancashire Cotton Corporation and the various interests deriving from the Armstrong Whitworth affair, notably the English Steel Corporation described above and the Lancashire Steel Corporation, which is discussed in detail in the next chapter. Six months later they were also to take on board the problems of the crumbling Scottish giant William Beardmore & Co.[71] Norman himself took the chair, with Andrew Duncan as vice-chairman. Duncan, who had been coal controller during the wartime government, had then headed the Shipbuilding Employers' Federation until he was brought in by the government to run the Central Electricity Board in January 1927. He was a classic product of the political/industrial/financial rationalizing milieu.[72] James Frater Taylor, who was the first managing director, the legal expert Hugh C. Bischoff, and the accountant Sir James Cooper were the practical men, and Frank Hodges, the ex-miners' leader, was put in as a political make-weight[73]—he too was a member of the Central Electricity Board. In 1930 the board was strengthened by the addition of Henry Clay, professor of social economics at Manchester University, who was particular expert on Lancashire cotton, and Charles Bruce Gardner, a former manager of the Shelton Iron and Steel Co. and a man with a wealth of experience in steel, coal, and chemicals.[74] In March 1930 Bruce Gardner replaced Frater Taylor as managing director.

The same personnel formed the basis of the Bankers' Industrial Development Corporation (BID), which was formed in April 1929 to run the Bank's wider intervention in industry. This new company, whose role was to draw in the issuing houses and merchant banks as partners with the Bank of England in the process of rationalization, was based on £6 million capital subscribed by all the major issuing houses and merchant banks.[75] Norman was the first chairman, and he brought in Sir Guy Granet, another important rationalizing figure as deputy chairman. Granet was an ex-chairman of the London, Midland & Scottish Railway and also a partner of the merchant banker Higginson & Co. and a director of AEI, the electrical manufacturers and one of Higginson & Co.'s leading industrial clients.[76] He was to be succeeded in 1932 by Nigel Campbell, a director of J. Henry Schröder & Co. and, as a director of Stewarts & Lloyds, one of the few banking figures to play an active managerial role in the steel industry in these years.

These two bodies, which were soon to become virtually indistinguishable, provided the institutional framework for the Bank's involvement in industry over the next decade. For the first time apparatuses for knowledgeable intervention were being developed. But would they confine their activities merely to managing the Bank's own investments and keeping a weather-eye on the industrial commitments of the clearing banks or would they throw the Bank's weight into industrial reorganization? These issues were to be fought out and by and large resolved over the next two years.

No sooner was the BID formed than a rapid series of developments gave it a heightened significance. In May 1929 a Labour government came to power in the general election, and the BID at once became an important part of the Bank's political response to the perceived threat to private industry posed by the Labour Party. A semblance of activity was calculated to keep the government satisfied that something was being done. After the Labour minister J. H. Thomas had called for more coordinated efforts at industrial reorganization in a speech at Manchester in January 1930, for instance, Norman had "felt it wise to support him in his efforts to restore industry."[77] The BID, therefore, would be "the outward and visible sign of what Mr. Thomas describes as 'the City.' "[78] Less guardedly, it was a commonplace in City circles that the BID was formed to "keep the government out of industry"[79] or "prevent government intervention in industry."[80] After eighteen months of existence, Nigel Campbell felt that it had at least done well in this respect: "As a bulwark to keep the Socialist government from tampering with industry it succeeded, though, had the Government stayed in power much longer, it is doubtful whether it could have held the fort."[81]

The Bank was forced to go beyond such defensive posturing by developments that accompanied the sharp worsening of the industrial and financial situation in late 1929 and early 1930. In June 1929 the Bank had to intervene to prevent the immediate collapse of Beardmore, and in the next six months it was faced with a series of crucial policy decisions both there and in the Lancashire Steel Corporation which forced it to consider its wider perspectives on rationalization.[82] Then in September 1929 came the Hatry crash, which contributed to a further deterioration of the sterling position and a rise in bank rate. On top of this, in October 1929 the government laid before the Bank for the first time the alarming position of Lord Kylsant's Royal Mail Group, the giant shipping conglomerate that controlled 15% of British shipping.[83]

A crash at the Royal Mail Group following the Hatry affair could have seriously jeopardized confidence in sterling. In addition it would almost certainly have undermined the confidence necessary for the bank to carry through its current commitments in industrial reorganization in the Lancashire Cotton Corporation, Lancashire Steel, Beardmore, and the big Scottish scheme, as well as in its nascent schemes for the locomotive and shipbuilding industries. But more than that it also highlighted major problems arising from various governments' ad hoc responses to industrial problems in the last decade. The government was involved with the Royal Mail Group as guarantors to substantial loans made to the group by the Midland Bank under the Trade Facilities Act. In the early 1920s this Act had made £75 million available to industry for capital investment projects, in the light of the contribution such schemes would make to employment in particular and trade in general. The loans were raised from banks or financial syndicates but were backed by government guarantees.[84] This legislation had resulted in the provision of new money for a number of crisis-ridden industries, and the government was therefore liable to find itself vulnerable to major calls on its guarantees. In early 1930 the British and Northern Ireland governments found themselves liable for calls of £4 million on account of the Royal Mail Group at a time of severe financial stringency.[85]

The loose system of control and supervision of TFA loans seemed to Norman to be a classic example of how *not* to handle such matters. It was not until the winter of 1929 that the Treasury became aware, much to its astonishment, of the extent to which Lord Kylsant had mishandled the group's affairs and of the depth of the crisis. Even then attempts to remedy the situation were ineffective because, despite Lord Kylsant's clear malfeasance, the government dared not openly challenge him for fear of torpedoing the Royal Mail Group by undermining public confidence. This inaction allowed Kylsant to carry on a protracted campaign of bluffing and stalling.[86] In March 1930

Norman bitterly attacked the government's handling of the situation: "Owing to Kylsant's ineptitude and the position of the Government in the matter, affairs had been going from bad to worse since last autumn. But for the position of the government in the matter steps would have been taken last August. At that stage some reconstruction might have been possible, but things are now so much worse that there is nothing for it but receivership in a number of companies."[87] Norman believed that Kylsant and his accountants proposed to make the government bear the costs of bailing them out, rather as Lord Invernairn had unsuccessfully hoped at Beardmore; but in contrast to Beardmore, with Kylsant the government was dealing with "bigger, stranger, more sinister, more cunning folk."[88] In the end, it was largely the ability of the Bank to coordinate the responses of various creditors and bankers that made it possible for the Treasury and the Midland Bank to insist on and dictate the form of an imposed reconstruction which narrowly averted a major public crash in May 1930.[89]

Against this background Norman began to develop more positive notions about the role of BID in reorganizations. By early 1930 he believed that rather than acting in a purely defensive way, the BID could undertake a limited and strategic intervention that could have a significant effect on the rationalization of British industries; he saw it as a "brief and particular object which could be accomplished within five years or never."[90] The BID therefore was at first formed for five years only, after which it was to be liquidated.[91]

Its declared aim was to stand above and outside industry as a national interest and to promote schemes of regional and sectoral reorganization in the basic industries. It would act as a "société des études," investigating projects and providing expertise, and it would provide capital that would not otherwise be obtainable. It could find cash "without such limitations as of necessity are attached to a policy, the main purpose of which is to procure profits for the company itself." Rather than direct generation of profits, "the attainment of success will bring satisfaction to the members of the Company by enabling them indirectly to obtain profits for their own businesses."[92]

As such, it would require "large credit but little money."[93] The Bank had no intention of tying up considerable funds in long-term investments. Moreover, this cash was specifically reserved for reorganization schemes and was not to be used to enable individual companies to sort out their affairs: "It is not the object of the BID to care for the individual interests of each unit of an industry, or section of an industry; its object is to care for the interests of the industry as a whole."[94]

As far as steel was concerned, the BID's program for reorganization was clearly spelled out. Two documents, the six-page Brassert memorandum on the regionalization of the iron and steel industry of January 1930[95] and the Bruce Gardner report of the following year[96] which extended this in more detail, set out the blueprint for reorganization that underlay Bank policy throughout the 1930s. Both reports advocated large vertical regional amalgamations of iron and steel in six major areas. The argument was based on the technical advantages of best-practice technology and large-scale operations. It was, however, as cursory as it was radical, a technical expert's blueprint. Norman had gone for advice to the top American experts, and they had, as John Vaizey noted, told their client "what he was already prepared to hear."[97]

Norman wanted a clear model on which to base his policy, and he got that, but, as one of Britain's leading steel experts noted, "at the cost of avoiding all the problems of the history of the industry." Both Brassert and Bruce Gardner were "cutting the roots and ignoring the consequences, in an effort to replant an ancient tree, after serious pruning and grafting on of new wood."[98] The general conceptions were sound enough, but the dynamics of transition to the desirable ends were not sufficiently mapped out. This deficiency was to dominate Bank intervention throughout the following decade.

Above all, any attempts to implement such a blueprint required the creation of new central banking practices compatible with a more interventionist and directive role. This in turn involved a fundamental reappraisal of what was involved in the long-term restructuring of capital in conditions of depression and recovery and, based on this, a reappraisal of banking criteria and the relations between the financial sector and the government. But how far were Norman and his BID staff prepared to go in taking on new responsibilities and carving out a new role for the Bank?

Norman's view in the 1920s had been that depression was an incentive to industrial reorganization. The Bank had hoped that the government could use the lure of a tariff to cajole the iron and steel industry into reorganizing itself—after which, in its official thinking, a tariff would no longer be necessary. Conversely, Norman also believed that either a tariff or the depreciation of sterling following the suspension of the gold standard would mean an end to rationalization. Hence, Bank diplomacy up to 1930 centered on resistance to protection and the consequent maintenance of pressure to reorganize from the invisible hand of the market. In July 1930 the BID held secret talks with the Tory party to encourage it to take a hard line on refusing to give the steel industry any promises about future protection, because the expectation of protection would put back reorganization "if not for many years, at least for a considerable time." The result was

disappointing; Cunliffe-Lister would go no further than undertaking
to stress to his steel friends that the *amount* of protection they would
get would depend on their efforts to reorganize.[99]

The extreme depth of the 1931 crisis undermined this view of reorganization by unhindered market forces. As Norman noted, the
effect of the crisis "had been to falsify the bases so far considered [for
rationalization], i.e. public issues and the possibility of getting money
through the banks. This last avenue was now closed for fear that two
or three countries in Europe would go off the deep end."[100] The
impending threat of European bank collapses meant that allowing
normal processes to take their course was no longer viable. Major
steel men like Beale of GKN and Craig of Colvilles were arguing that
no investment could be profitable at this time and that they would
not undertake it on any terms. For them the question was one of
returns on capital, not how to raise it, and therefore, they argued
that "no blame could at the moment be attributed to the City."[101]

In consequence, the original rationale of the BID as an improved
financial channel aiming to unblock an obstacle in the provision of
finance to industry became dubious. Andrew Duncan drew the logical
conclusion for BID: it should "give up pretending that it could fulfill
the functions for which it was formed," that is, financing combinations that would be profitable in the future but had to weather an
intervening unprofitable period, quite simply because "industry was
going down the slippery slope so fast that no-one knew where to put
in a peg to mark the basis of stabilisation."[102] As certain members of
BID had begun to realize soon after it was formed, "BID was not built
to function in such an emergency as the present; in fact, a source of
funds which was intended to meet the temporary failure of another
stream (public flotations) has itself dried up."[103]

This period of acute pessimism was fairly short lived, but it saw
the abandonment of gold and the acceptance of the principle of tariffs.
Thereafter a return to the old strategy was ruled out. Within the Bank
attention began to shift toward the scope for financial direction of
strategic investment. Should the Bank become a visible hand in industrial affairs? Bruce Gardner and Clay in particular tried to assess
the prospect for such strategic direction. There were, they argued,
three sets of trade conditions involved: "The first when trade was
bad and everyone too depressed to see a profit even in rationalisation;
the second when trade was a little better and profits were small and
people could see sufficiently far ahead to notice that by amalgamation
profits could be increased; the third when things were so good that
each man was willing to stand alone."[104] The current situation, for
them, corresponded to the second period, although as Bruce Gardner

saw it this period was likely to be a fragile flower. Unless tariffs for steel were temporary and conditional on reorganization, "as soon as conditions enable the industry to show slight profits, certain private interests in the City (though the City as a whole may be opposed to it) would again be inclined to venture into the steel industry," with the result of perpetuating duplication and conflicting developments.[105] The problems, therefore, was just as likely to be too readily available finance as a scarcity.

Thus, in the first two years of BID's existence its emphasis shifted from coping with a temporary incapacity of the City to provide finance for reorganization toward the acceptance of some sort of role in the strategic direction of investment. This development, however, exacerbated certain fundamental problems of how an exceptional role for the Bank was to be reconciled with its existing banking critieria and practices. Even in its first year of existence, Bruce Gardner had felt that "the tests we have been applying to all schemes are such as would be applied by any ordinary Issuing House and, if this is to be the accepted policy then the BID is not going to give any increased help to industry."[106] He wanted, therefore, to make provisions for finding large sums of new money for the future. Peacock, however, disagreed sharply; he argued that BID must make the same test as ordinary issuing houses or else it would mislead the public and industry and thus lead to competitive deformations. Its role had to be explicitly the same as that of the issuing houses in normal times, except that because its technical knowledge was greater, it could "come in earlier" and take larger risks.[107]

Such criteria, however, would make exceptional operations almost impossible. The BID wanted to hold as little direct investment as possible itself and to promote public issues at the earliest possible stage, thus shifting the burden to the issuing houses.[108] But, as in the case of the Lancashire Cotton Corporation, direct involvement of the Bank in issues was itself likely to give the issue in question an aura of being gilt-edged, with the consequent risk of damaging the Bank if the issue turned out to be unsuccessful. Thus, in the case of the Lancashire Cotton Corporation, although Norman made every effort to stress that the issue was an "adventure" and a "business risk,"[109] the Bank learned from that experience that "it must be acknowledged that it [BID] could never have done another business of that sort" without damaging consequences for its reputation.[110]

Retaining ownership of portfolios on which returns would be considerably deferred was also problematic. To do this the BID would require a much broader financial base, and over the next two years several possibilities in this direction were explored. In July 1930 Bischoff drew up a plan for a "Rationalisation investment trust company" which would supplement the BID and deal with securities that would have to be put into cold storage for the present and not issued to the public.[111] In November 1930 Norman proposed that the BID should itself raise finance for schemes where it could not make an immediate public issue by borrowing through its banker constituents. With the margin constituted by the BID's uncalled capital, the company would be able to offer adequate security to the joint stock banks for advances up to £20 million—although he did not think that much would be necessary.[112] Given that BID experts would vet the scheme, the banks "should be very willing" to lend. They might not want to become actual investors in the BID's securities, but they would be prepared to advance the BID money on the collateral security of such bonds. Likewise, the banks would not make long-term loans for this purpose, but they would almost certainly be prepared to grant extensions of advances from time to time as necessary.[113]

In July 1932 Bruce Gardner formulated the most extensive blueprint for such an approach in a proposal for the creation of a "BID Steel Finance Corporation." He proposed that, in return for protection, the steel industry should be made, by legislation if necessary, to pay a levy on all steel ingots of 2/6d per ton, which would be used by BIDSFC as the interest and sinking fund on large capital issues. BIDSFC would then gradually place these issues on the market. The company would exist only for seven to ten years by which time the steel industry should be properly reorganized. This scheme would have the double merit that it could be forced on the steelmasters and yet ultimately leave the industry under private control.[114]

These proposals for mobilizing and directing resources from the banks or from other credit institutions were more easily posed than implemented. Bruce Gardner's scheme represented an attempt to utilize systematically the traditional mode of generating investment—raising capital from retained profits—but doing it on a far broader and more centralized basis than before, but others doubted the feasibility of the compulsory element in this proposal and looked instead to the possibilities of other sources of external finance.

The conflicting interests of various sectors of finance became apparent in this regard. As Campbell noted, the shareholders of the BID—that is, the majority of the issuing houses in the City—only participated in the BID in the first place "under the distinct impression that it was more or less of a gesture" and that if the BID's credit were to be used it would only be for short-term financing. Any long-term financing could not, therefore, be undertaken without reviewing the commitment of the shareholders.[115] When the suggestion was raised that advances for investment could be obtained from the clearing banks against the uncalled capital of the BID, there were objections and demands that the BID be liquidated at once before any charge on the uncalled capital should be given. The strongest protests came from the smaller issuing houses who had subscribed to BID capital in equal proportion with larger houses and feared that they would have to carry a disproportionate burden in such a scheme.[116]

Even if this issue were resolved by reorganizing the capital of the BID, it would still only have sufficient finance to provide "long" capital for one or two large firms. Anything larger could not be attempted without government aid. The BID could therefore cope with only a few projects and would not be able to carry out a wholesale reorganization of the steel industry for which in 1930 the Bank had estimated that at least £13 million would be required.[117]

In this situation it appeared to some that the obvious source for the necessary funds was the government. Campbell, for instance, proposed the formation of a new company, which would acquire in the first instance the securities issued by various rationalizing undertakings and would find cash for this by issuing its own debentures and shares.[118] For him the scale of capital and risk involved implied recourse to the Treasury, but Norman insisted that this contradicted the political aims of the BID: "Up to the present, the project which had largely actuated the formation of the Company, viz. the prevention of government intervention in industry, had been singularly and unexpectedly successful. To invoke government aid now would be tantamount to an admission that it was indispensable to rationalisation and offer a dangerous weapon to that section of the Government and its supporters who were only too anxious to seize an opportunity to bring industry in some degree or other under State control."[119]

It is important that the formative years for these policies were under a Labour government that the Bank deeply mistrusted. Norman was hostile to the very principle of government involvement in industry, although some of those around him were more flexible. Nevertheless, in the summer of 1931 they were all prepared to block with brutal frankness a hesitant government turn toward public intervention in the steel industry through the creation of a public utility company.

William Graham, president of the Board of Trade, had raised the issue with Norman in discussions about Corby and then about the iron and steel industry in general. Norman and Bruce Gardner at once went personally to see the prime minister to nip the idea in the bud. They told Ramsay MacDonald that "we had been bound to explain the position to a few of our financial friends who were working with us and were immediately concerned and, therefore, for the time being we could not go on with the financial side of reorganisation." Norman suspected that Graham liked the idea and had exaggerated cabinet support for it and "gone far beyond his brief." MacDonald confirmed this and confided that the cabinet was treating the idea as important only because the iron and steel industries were inactive and because Ernest Bevin was supporting the idea and causing problems in the cabinet.[120]

Two days later, therefore, Bruce Gardner visited Graham and warned him that as long as his proposals persisted "everything was stopped" as far as the provision of bank finance to industry was concerned. Graham argued that this question involved one of the principles of the Labour Party and that he could not merely drop it. Bruce Gardner's reply was blunt: "I replied that I did not think that it would be necessary to recant what he looked upon as his principles, but could it not be said that, though he still believed in the principles, he and the Prime Minister might say to the Governor that we need not take any more notice of the suggested Public Utility Company as it would take many years before the social order would have so progressed that such principles could be satifactorily worked out . . . and, therefore, the Prime Minister would undertake that the matter would be dropped." It was, he went on, the principle of the public utility company that upset the confidence of the financiers and made it impossible to arrange finance in these circumstances: "I pointed out that financial credit was build up on not what one thought about things oneself, but on what the world thought. Already confidence in Britain had declined and, if, on top of this, it became known that it was intended to set up in this country Public Utility Companies for industries such as iron and steel, the rest of the world, who did not believe industry could be run in this way, would take fright and . . . we should see the flight from the pound."[121] Further discussion of a public utility company or other forms of government involvement in industrial financing for steel rapidly evaporated after this response.

Such pressure was sufficient to make the Labour government back away from direct intervention in industrial finance. Forestalling it was a major aim of Norman's policy. Yet as the debates in the Bank had revealed, once the Bank itself began to develop an industrial policy, the size, complexity, and political repercussions of its actions inevitably brought it into the sphere of traditional governmental action. The larger schemes required government sanction and financial guarantees, but the Bank would not accept a role that made it appear to be an agent of government policy. The alternative was a reversion to traditional fiduciary practices. Hence, Norman aspired to a role of strategic direction and began to reshape banking institutions for that purpose. The BID and SMT came to exercise considerable direct sway over large sections of the cotton and steel industries, yet they drew back from taking on the role of a visible guiding hand. The underlying principles of Bank activity came to the surface in the discussions of 1930–1932. Once the crisis was past, however, they were submerged again, although they lurked behind all the practical decisions that were taken in particular cases. It is to these cases that we now turn.

9.

Banks, Firms, and Industrial Rationalization

The involvement of the Bank of England with Armstrong Whitworth initially focused on the demerger and rationalization of the heavy and armament steel parts of that business. In the longer term, however, it was the problem of handling the other part of Armstrong's steel business, the Pearson Knowles Group of companies, that was to create the Bank's most extensive involvement in steel. Starting from this point of contact, the Bank became involved in the diverse and complex question of the reorganization of the steel industry in the whole Northern Corridor running from the Northwest Coast and Lancashire through to Sheffield and the Midlands ore fields.

Bankers, Companies, and Restructuring in the Northern Corridor, 1926–1932

The Pearson Knowles Group, of which Armstrong Whitworth owned 75% of the ordinary capital, included the steelmakers Partington Iron and Steel Company at Irlam near Manchester, the wiremaking firm Ryland Bros., and the coal companies Moss Hall Co. and the Wigan Junction Colliery Co. The combine made both steel and wire and fabricated products, but the production processes were not internally integrated. By the mid-1920s this group, like its parent, was in a precarious financial position and was itself putting a great strain on Armstrong Whitworth.[1]

Between 1920 and 1925 Pearson Knowles had financed £2.5 million capital expenditure at Partington at a time of inflated prices, and although the property thus developed was physically valuable, its earnings position was very unsatisfactory. Moreover, it had incurred massive bank debts to the Westminster Bank of £1 million in overdraft and £306,000 in 7½% five-year notes repayable in 1930. Pearson Knowles and through it Armstrong had agreed to guarantee these debts which were by this time a serious incubus on the whole operation. Armstrong had induced Westminster Bank to advance £1 million to Partington on the understanding that Armstrong would make an issue to cover that amount, but the deteriorating market position made this impossible. Reviewing the situation in March 1926, Frater Taylor recommended jettisoning the entire Partington operation by selling it off.[2]

The Westminster Bank, which was locked into this situation, felt that Pearson Knowles and Partington were being used "for the advantage of Armstrongs, very much to their [the bank's] disadvantage," and it was afraid that the Bank of England would pursue a solution to Armstrong's problem that would be very much at the bank's expense in regard to its involvement with Partington.[3] Norman was well aware of this; he feared that Westminster might use its influential position in Partington to cut across his own schemes, and he was unhappy that the situation should be subject to "the charges and chances of a couple of individuals"—that is, W. Ingles and John Rae, the general managers of the Westminster Bank.[4] Westminster's response to this situation was to devise its own plan for Partington and Pearson Knowles, and the bank commissioned Brassert to prepare a report.[5] If it did not act, it appeared clear from the drift of the situation that little would be done for Partington in any resolution of the Armstrong situation. Westminster's solicitors wrote to the Newcastle branch of the Bank of England to protest: "My impression is that the Bank of England are only concerned to see that Armstrongs stand to benefit by what is done."[6]

When Frater Taylor had made his investigation of the Pearson Knowles group in 1926, he had been very pessimistic about its prospects. However, Brassert was able to put forward an alternative scheme involving wholesale reconstruction and capital expenditure of £1 million. These proposals led to a shift of focus for Frater Taylor and Norman. Both came to see Partington as a potential nucleus for reorganization in the North and Northwest rather than as an obsolete asset. From the first, however, they differed in the emphasis they gave to Brassert's idea—a difference that was to evolve into a split between the two men. From spring 1929 Frater Taylor was keen to shift the center of his attention to the Pearson Knowles group. He had done the "ploughing" at Armstrong and now he wanted to move on to "seeding" at Pearson Knowles.[7] The Westminster Bank was very pleased to see him take a lead as the new chairman of the group appointed by the Bank of England, and it regarded his presence as something of a safeguard that its interests, which it identified with the well-being of Partington, were being protected.[8] Frater Taylor, basing his initiatives on the Brassert scheme, saw the opportunity of utilizing the locational advantages of Irlam where, by additions to the existing plant and concentration of production in wire products, a potential nucleus for reorganizaion could be developed.[9]

Norman was enthusiastic about the early stages of the project, and in regrouping the various interests of Partington, Ryland, and the Wigan Colliery Company into the new Lancashire Steel Corporation, he was particularly active in pressurizing the "small people" of Wigan to prevent them from carrying out independent developments.[10] At the same time he pushed forward a public issue for the new corporation through the issuing house J. Henry Schröder & Co. in order to involve the public and to give the scheme "a value outside the four walls of the Bank."[11] He and Frater Taylor were confident that the necessary £1 million could be obtained in the City, and if Schröder was able to raise this sum, the Securities Management Trust was prepared to subscribe £½ million as a junior security. Norman wanted the issue to be a model precedent for future rationalization schemes,[12] but he and Frater Taylor disagreed about what exactly rationalization meant in this case. For Frater Taylor the scheme was a valid development in its own right, but Norman was looking from the first to link it into a far larger reorganization scheme, and he remained wary that any short-term development might hinder a bigger arrangement.[13]

Norman's aim, basing his idea on the broad national rationalization scheme contained in the Brassert Memorandum, was to rationalize the whole of the Midlands and Northwest through a comprehensive arrangement drawing in the largest British steel company, United Steel, the Lancashire Steel Corporation, and the tube steel specialists Stewarts & Lloyds. Brassert himself envisaged the establishment of two regions: the Northwest would be focused on Partington as a steel producer and wire specialist with a subsidiary high-quality specialist plant at Workington; the Midland region would be based on two steel producing centers, the United Steel operations in Sheffield (Templeborough) and above all the cheap home ores of Scunthorpe. The Northwest group would be controlled from Partington and the Midland group by United Steel.[14]

However, at that time the interests of United Steel, which owned the Workington Iron and Steel Co., spanned both areas. The Northwest scheme implied building up Partington as a potential competitor with United Steel in the Lancashire area, and its management was therefore rather hostile to it. Norman's solution to this problem was to link the Lancashire Steel Corporation to United Steel and thus go one step further than the Brassert plan by having one giant firm controlling *both* adjacent regions.

Circumstances in 1930 provided Norman with a crucial opportunity to carry though his plan. With United Steel in the hands of the liquidators of the Austin Friars Trust after the Hatry crash, it was quite possible that control of it could be picked up quite easily by the Bank or its representatives.[15] Indeed in February 1930 Sir Gilbert Garnsey, who was the liquidator, actually offered control informally to the Bank, and Frater Taylor and Walter Benton Jones, a leading director of United Steel, discussed the possibilities of a United Steel/Lancashire Steel merger or trade agreement.[16]

For as long as the acquisition of United Steel was a possibility, Frater Taylor agreed with Norman that there was a good chance of rationalizing the whole area in one group.[17] When Garnsey brought the possibility of acquiring United Steel to Frater Taylor's attention, the latter "at once grasped the strategical significance of such control and advised the Governor to move in the matter . . . My aim was to have absolutely neutral control [of United Steel] so that all bias as regards proper rationalization could be eliminated. Just picture to yourself what a sale, in effect, of Lancashire Steel corporation to United Steel would mean. Why, Benton Jones frankly told me that he has 'expected' Partington would die, yet Brassert says, and I agree, that Irlam must be one of the pivotal points under any circumstances." The only people who could carry through such a plan, however, would have to be "someone impartial, from outside," and by that he meant the Bank of England.[18] But Norman did not take Frater Taylor's advice; the Bank did not take control and the United Steel situation remained unresolved.

Although he rejected the action necessary for a regional grouping, Norman retained the perspective of such an amalgamation as a guiding principle of his work. Consequently, by early 1930 he was becoming increasingly uneasy about the pattern of development being undertaken by the Lancashire Steel Corporation. Every step taken in carrying through the Brassert–Frater Taylor plan for Lancashire Steel in effect shored up the autonomy of that company as a competitor to United Steel. Hence, Norman tacitly began to try to put the brakes on the scheme in order that some larger agreement with United Steel could mature. Frater Taylor, sensing this drift, wrote to Bruce Gardner in the SMT in May that, "if in view of the lengths to which we have gone, you, as representing SMT, would like to pause, you must say so." He was doubtful if Schröder would be prepared to postpone the public issue for six months, and any delay might help the still reluctant Wigan Colliery Co. people to wriggle out of the merger; also opportunities for good terms from the Manchester Ship Canal might be lost. Frater Taylor bluntly warned the Bank that if it made such a request he would refuse it. Moreover, he argued, broader difficulties would be implied if the SMT was seen to be using its controlling position in this way.[19]

The SMT was also divided on the nature of the Partington scheme. Frater Taylor urged it not to pursue Norman's more ambitious project at the expense of jeopardizing a scheme that would be viable and profit-making in itself: "I should advise you and your colleagues not to throw away the substance for the shadow." Nor should they minimize the major difficulty involved in overcoming the jealousies of individual companies in a larger scheme. Instead, the carrying through of the Lancashire Steel Corporation scheme would in itself "prove to be an impelling force as regards bringing others into line."[20] Both Bruce Gardner and Brassert within the SMT accepted his contention about the need to press on, and during May and June Bruce Gardner continued to urge this while still trying to bring Lancashire Steel and United Steel together informally, although without success.[21]

The key to this stalemate lay in the strategy and market position of United Steel. United Steel had just passed through a major period of financial crisis and capital reorganization and was entering a period of internal managerial reorganization.[22] It was wary of overextending itself and as Benton Jones told Bruce Gardner "after several years of strenuous labour and great anxiety are naturally unwilling to undertake any new liabilities," or to ally itself with groups of uncertain earnings capabilities. "Left to its own policy, the Company would gradually absorb such other properties as might be of value to it, and as opportunity arose."[23] Hence, as Frater Taylor told Bruce Gardner, Benton Jones of United Steel would not "talk rationalization as you understand it; in other words he appears to believe that United Steel is making, and can make, progress independently of any other steel company."[24]

One of the vital bases of United Steel's relative prosperity was its uniquely low capitalization that had arisen out of the Hatry crash, and its management did not want to jeopardize this through an alliance with what it saw as an overcapitalized Lancashire Steel Corporation. Moreover, this reservation was combined with fundamental doubts about the profit potential of Lancashire Steel. The investment of £1.75 million at Irlam would only result in "putting on the market steel products which are already available in sufficient quantities and can only be sold by taking trade which companies at present operating already have."[25] It believed that "everything which they may make when their programme is completed can be made at a lower cost and delivered into the markets which they serve from our Lincolnshire or Sheffield works."[26] These doubts were heightened with the announcement of Stewarts & Lloyds' major development of tube-making capacity at Corby, because its management believed that the resulting loss of Partington's tube markets would further weaken the concern.[27] Above all, it disagreed with Brassert on the scope available in the market for developing integrated wire production. Brassert's prognosis of an expanding market for wire products lay at the heart of his decision to build new steelmaking capacity at Partington; without this expansion the danger of enlarging excess capacity in general steelmaking was considerable. The Lancashire Steel Corporation scheme would increase that company's capacity by a further 100,000 tons per year which, United Steel believed, would produce almost certain cutthroat competition with Appleby-Frodingham and Templeborough in sections and billets.[28]

At the heart of the problem was the fact that, as Brassert noted, in the North and Midlands, with the exception of Stewarts & Lloyds, "all the companies produce identical products; all are selling in the same markets and working below capacity and compete keenly against each other. At the same time, all have overlapping, inefficient and obsolete parts of plant" resulting in unremunerative operations.[29] He therefore wanted to cut out the dead wood.

But, unlike United Steel, he saw this dead wood located not primarily at Partington but rather at United Steel's own Workington works. This works, he argued, should cease to be a general tonnage plant and concentrate instead on the specialized market for acid steels. In his view, the general shift of world demand favored open-hearth rails rather than the acid Bessemer type made at Workington; thus the rail business would, if United Steel and Lancashire Steel were combined, "in the natural course of events drift into the Partington plant" and thus away from Workington. "Partington will also deliver Open Hearth billets and rods into its territory at a lower cost than they can be furnished from Workington (Acid Bessemer) or Sheffield." In addition, Partington would develop as the center of the Lancashire wire rod and ultimately wire finishing industries. Thus, Brassert felt that "if United Steel and the Lancashire Steel Corporation were combined, we would still recommend the present construction programme at Partington."[30]

United Steel, however, was keen to preserve Workington[31] and unwilling to face the redundancy of plant that a Brassert-style United Steel/Lancashire Steel merger would imply. It had its own view of regional mergers: with the minor exceptions of Millom & Askam and the North Lonsdale Co., United Steel was entirely dominant in the Cumberland area, and it wanted to treat this as a self-contained area for rationalization with Workington as its center. It wanted to exclude South Lancashire and Partington from this region and bring the Irlam works under its wing inside a Lancashire/Sheffield merger, demarcating it as a local producer with only limited general steelmaking; any expansion at the Lancashire Steel Corporation should be concentrated on providing material for the engineering side of the firm (Pearson Knowles) and for the wire side (Ryland), not on steelmaking. Any merger with Lancashire Steel would therefore take the form of breaking it up and absorbing units into United Steel rather than an amalgamation of the firms. Failing that, United Steel would prefer to see Lancashire Steel go ahead with its plans, preferably with some agreement to keep out of each other's ways and to threaten the possibility of a destructive trade war if the full Lancashire Steel scheme went ahead. Its low capitalization and low fixed charges provided a good position from which to conduct such a campaign if necessary.[32]

In the SMT Bruce Gardner had doubts about the Lancashire Steel scheme. He admitted that if he were manager of the corporation instead of Frater Taylor he would "hesitate to increase capacity to 300–350 thousand tons per annum at a time of depression." Perhaps influenced by Norman's unwillingness to commit himself fully to the scheme, he preferred some sort of phased expansion program.[33]

But Frater Taylor rejected such an intermediate proposal. He fully backed Brassert's original conception of the corporation as an integrated wire producer to come on stream in two years' time on the basis of likely market developments, and Brassert continued to maintain his technical and commercial judgment in this matter.[34] It was clear to him that the alternative being promoted by Norman and the SMT for restricting the scheme while waiting for outside developments would be a "thoroughly bad move." For him, "it must be all or nothing" in regard to a merger, and because Benton Jones was clearly not going to play the SMT's game, in practice this meant nothing.[35] If Bruce Gardner preferred a different policy, he would have to discharge Frater Taylor and put in his own man at the Lancashire Steel Corporation.[36]

By mid-1930 the confusion and hesitation of the SMT was accompanied by growing doubts on the part of Schröder, the issuing house handling the scheme. Probably in conjunction with Norman, Albert Pam, a leading director of Schröder, was urging the corporation to "restrict expenditure as much as possible" so as to ease the path of broader rationalization discussions.[37] Above all, Schröder feared that a hostile attitude by United Steel would jeopardize the viability of the Lancashire Steel scheme in the City. Pam did not believe that Benton Jones was likely to cooperate: "He is not a constructive minded individual." As the prospect of conflict rather than cooperation loomed, Schröder began to draw back farther: "We would never have invited our friends to put up money for Partington if we had realised then as we do now, that this was not really a rationalisation scheme for the benefit of the whole industry, but only a comparatively small local one which is more likely to postpone the agony than anything else, quite apart from the question as to whether Partington will be able to make the profits which were expected, if there is a trade war with United Steel."[38]

The SMT made a final attempt to impose its scheme on United Steel by threatening a trade war if it would not cooperate. Bruce Gardner warned Benton Jones that unless the two companies were brought together, "there will be a great deal of useless competition and waste of capital." He insisted that the Bank, having begun to back the Partington scheme, "will insist on their venture being a success. It therefore comes back to the old story—that the only way to obviate intensive warfare is to find some means of absorbing Partington. I am sure that it will cost you less in the long run."[39]

Frater Taylor, however, thought such moves hopeless. His priority was to put the Lancashire Steel Corporation on as competitive a footing as possible so as to ensure its success. Whatever was said to Benton Jones, he would regard Partington as "a menace to his company."[40] Hence, even while Pam was trying to urge upon him the fullest exchange of information in order to facilitate cooperation,[41] Frater Taylor was maneuvering to establish a strong position of competitive rivalry vis-à-vis United Steel. "Of course I have been vague with Benton Jones," he told Pam. "Do you think that as a possible rival I am going to give him intimate details?" Even a frank discussion of mutual product specialization would create difficulties because it would involve disclosing that Lancashire had a virtual option on the acquisition of the Whitecross Co., Ryland Bros.' most important local wire rival. Frater Taylor felt that the opportunity for merging Lancashire Steel and United Steel had been lost months ago, and he resented Schröder's and the SMT's dragging their feet.[42]

Thus, the split between the bankers and their managerial agent deepened rapidly in the summer of 1930. The break finally came over the issue of the purchase of the Whitecross Co. by the corporation. In order to strengthen the corporation's position as a specialist wire producer, Frater Taylor felt that this local competitor had to be bought up. This move would cost £150,000 and would require going beyond the initial subscription to raise the additional cash.[43] As in numerous other matters over the summer, the SMT hedged about allowing this to go forward. At the beginning of August, Frater Taylor wrote to Bruce Gardner: "Time is against you in this matter. Lancashire Steel Corporation plans are so complete that we cannot—dare not—dally. In saying this, I am not forgetting that the SMT is the controlling shareholder and up to a point will have its wishes met by the Board. To move slowly and incompletely with new construction would be costly and bad business. Lancashire Steel Corporation is not building for the present, but for the future. Once more I would remind you that the Lancashire Steel scheme *was* born before rationalisation became a subject for serious discussion. On its merits, I do not accept your somewhat pessimistic view on the outlook . . . We would expect to be supported in such a relatively small matter as the purchase of Whitecross and I cannot accept your hint of a refusal."[44]

The upshot was that Frater Taylor, who had been operating as acting chairman of the corporation, refused to become chairman because he felt that he did not have adequate support from Schröder and the SMT. Pam and Bruce Gardner were not unhappy about this; Frater Taylor, they felt, "has been far from helpful from the point of view of the SMT and BID" in their attempts to develop a Northwest/Midlands amalgamation.[45] The SMT view was that although the Lancashire Steel scheme was excellent in itself, it had been conceived before the BID was set up for broader rationalization and that it was now inadequate in this light.[46] Frater Taylor would not accept this and therefore had to go.

The Bank then had to find a replacement who would implement its policy, someone who would not identify too closely with the particular interests of the Lancashire Steel Corporation as a firm against those of a general amalgamation. As an interim measure, it appointed the Earl of Crawford as acting chairman, although his limitations were well known. He was a peer, a man primarily interested in coal rather than steel, and a rather erratic businessman, and, with his links with the old firms that made up the corporation, he might prove difficult to get rid of if he were unsatisfactory—an eventuality that might leave the SMT with no alternative but to bring Frater Taylor back again.[47] To cover itself in this move, the SMT put Andrew Boynton, one of Brassert's senior technical staff, on the Board both as a watchdog and to supervise the complex technical business of construction work at Irlam, which was being undertaken while the works were still in production.[48]

Crawford objected to this appointment from the first, and by the end of the year he was at loggerheads with the Bank. Like Frater

Taylor, he considered a United Steel merger premature, and he told Norman in February 1931 that "he and his Board demurred to an amalgamation of any kind."[49] Crawford also appeared to be excessively sympathetic to the interests of the Wigan Colliery Co., and he clashed sharply with Boynton about which tender to accept for coke ovens, only accepting Boynton's recommendation under pressure from the SMT.[50]

He wanted more freedom of action. Brasserts should be *"consulting engineers not* an overriding authority" as the SMT wanted it to be.[51] The SMT insisted that "Crawford must toe the line or go."[52] Relaxing its control over the corporation was out of the question, and on 17 February 1931 Norman gave Crawford a dressing down and told him that "in any matter in which he or his Board differed from the advice of Brasserts, the matters must be decided as required by Brasserts."[53]

The confidence of the City in the Lancashire Steel scheme had been shaken by Frater Taylor's departure, and the lack of confidence of financiers in the corporation's directors was becoming paralyzing.[54] On the suggestion of Bruce Gardner, but without consulting the corporation's board, Norman brought in John E. James of Cargo Fleet to be chairman and strongman.[55] Norman was not entirely sure that James would be a sufficiently powerful figure: "Can he dominate the fellows who are working there," he wondered.[56] But the discussions about a possible chairman had revealed an acute shortage of suitable talents. Duncan had favored promoting J. Sinclair Kerr within the firm. Bruce Gardner originally proposed the financier Dr. Herman Andreae of Sperlings who was "some connection of Kleinworts," but Norman was not impressed—he felt he had been "rather blown upon by the Sperling affair" (the Hatry crash). Others considered were Webster Jenkinson, the prominent accountant and director of Vickers, and Ionides of Armstrong. But in the end they decided that "if we were to have a Britisher, he (James) is no doubt the best we could get."[57]

Some of the problems were eased when this blatant interference by the SMT caused three Lancashire Steel Corporation directors to resign. But the Earl of Crawford remained "saucy and insolent,"[58] and the ex-directors remained on the boards of Pearson Knowles and Armstrong, and Norman still feared that "everything will go back to the old clique."[59] A more thorough shakedown of the old management was not achieved, and the influence of the supporters of Frater Taylor was not removed until Andrew Whyte, who with J. Sinclair Kerr had been Frater Taylor's chief assistant, resigned as a director to take up a job with Frater Taylor at Pease and Partners. John E. James, the Bank's new man at the helm, was delighted: "I get out of a certain FT [sic] atmosphere that I have never liked."[60]

The Bank's belated ability to stabilize the management of the corporation coincided with the de facto abandonment of its general strategy for the firm as a consequence both of the end of serious negotiations with United Steel and of the beginnings of steel revival and tariffs in 1931–32, which vindicated Brassert's judgment of the market value of integrated wire production, based on cheap steel production.[61] By August 1931 the demand for heavier wire coil was growing rapidly, and Brassert decided to use the currently cheap scrap and imported billets to reshuffle the development program, bringing forward the new rod mill from the second stage instead of building a new blast furnace, so as to maximize immediate wire production. With tariffs, this trend was fully confirmed. By March 1932 Ryland Bros. reckoned that it would have to double wire nail production by the end of the year, and its expectation was that it would soon have to expand still further as import substitution demand was supplemented by a revival in Britain's Empire markets.[62]

The Brassert–Frater Taylor strategy for the development of a strong independent wire producer had shown itself to be rooted in sound commercial judgment, whereas Norman's more ambitious wider perspectives on restructuring had proved abortive. Norman had pursued the shadow of a giant amalgamation and paid little attention to the practical schemes for adapting Lancashire Steel to market possibilities in which the men on the spot were more interested. But, paradoxically, his ambitious overall scheme was vitiated by his cautious, probably overcautious, practice: when he refused to take the gamble of taking control of United Steel when he had the chance, applying the traditional caution of a banker rather than the verve of a company promoter or entrepreneur, he lost any real chance of consummating the giant amalgamation. A strong central hand was needed to override local interests in the overlapping production and excessive competition of this region. Norman and the SMT had the aspirations and the opportunity to provide this direction, but in the end they lost their way. Norman and the SMT found themselves in control; but by 1932 their policy for the firm was drifting and increasingly confused.

Financial Constraints and Interfirm Competition: Corby, 1926–1934

This already difficult rationalization situation in the Northern Corridor was to be further complicated by the emergence of a new producer in the region in the early 1930s. As a result of regional migration and technical innovation almost unparalleled in the interwar years, Stewarts & Lloyds moved from almost wholly unintegrated methods of tube production straddling Scotland and the Midlands to become a fully integrated steel and tube producer concentrated at a new location at Corby. Its eruption onto the scene was to change the hole rationalization situation in the area; it was partly shaped by the hand of the Bank of England and was to add to the growing problems that the Bank already faced through its involvement in the steel industry of the region.

To understand the roots of the transformation of Stewarts & Lloyds and the origins of its incursion into the Northern Corridor, we have to return to the complex market and technical situation of the tube industry in the mid-1920s. Stewarts & Lloyds, at that time, was a prosperous tube-making concern earning fairly consistently just under £500,000 profits per year and with sizeable reserves. Its origin in a merger of the largest Scottish and the largest English tubemakers in 1903 resulted in its operations, being spread across two regions, and a rather scattered structure had persisted from then on.[63] It owned a rather inadequate steel plant in Scotland from before the war; it had purchased further iron and steel capacity in Lincolnshire and at Bilston in the Midlands between 1916 and 1920 but had not modernized this part of its business.[64] Nevertheless the company had avoided the overextension and depletion of resources that so many other firms fell into in this period.[65] In particular, it wisely decided not to commit itself to a new steel development in Lincolnshire in the postwar boom at a time of inflated building costs, which would have more than canceled out the advantages of the scheme.[66]

Hence, the iron and steel end of its business was conspicuously weak and remained so despite its expansion of share capital from £850,000 to £4,040,000 and its £5.9 million capital expenditure between 1919 and 1926. By the mid-1920s it was clear that the piecemeal policy of backward integration "has not paid its way" and had "not given the advantages expected and never will do so if steps are not taken to bring the works closer together."[67] As the scale of production increased, the economies of integrated production became more and more important.

By the mid-1920s the company that had evolved was riddled with inefficiencies and poor organization. It was made up of a large number of scattered high-cost works drifting toward technical obsolescence. At the steelmaking end, its Clydesdale works was handicapped by lack of access to cheap basic pig iron. Its Bilston works in Staffordshire had a pig supply, but it was expensively produced in obsolete blast furnaces, and the steel made there was used in Scotland, mainly for the rolled rounds produced at the Tollcross works, where the carriage was £1 per ton; those rounds then had to be shuttled back to the customers situated mainly in the Midlands. Clydesdale could be converted to produce steel for Tollcross to resolve part of the problem, but this move would still leave production remote from its market, and if less Bilston steel were freighted into Scotland, the company would lose its cheap railway rate concession on that tonnage.[68]

Reordering its steelmaking to suit its existing tubemaking setup also had major drawbacks. Its six Scottish tube works lay in the area of a triangle with ten-mile-long sides with Glasgow as the apex. Of these works, Calder had a very limited range, Tollcross lacked adequate finishing facilities, and although Clyde and Imperial were excellent plants of their type, they needed an enormous trade to run profitably. Both of them, moreover, were centered on the production of lapweld tubes mainly for the oil trade. The rapid technical development in weldless methods meant that by the late 1920s nearly all oil company demand was specified weldless.[69]

The existing scattered units could not be adapted to the new methods; none of the existing sites was suited to the erection of a large push-bench, Pilger, or weldless plant. Yet to establish a new unit on another site would increase the scattered nature and organizational problems of the works. In the mid-1920s Allan C. MacDiarmid, the chairman, made a detailed appraisal of the prospects of the firm and concluded that "if we do not develop the weldless side, we may be left hopelessly in the cold." He went on in a subsequent report to state that: "The main problems which Stewarts & Lloyds face are one and indivisible and cannot be resolved separately or one by one . . . an investigation into what appears to be the simple problem of providing plant for making weldless tube . . . involves a study of the whole policy of Stewarts & Lloyds."[70]

In addition to the internal condition of the firm, market developments meant that Stewarts & Lloyds' current relative prosperity was increasingly vulnerable, and the company faced the prospect of steadily falling behind best practice and opening up a gap that would be increasingly difficult to close unless action was taken. Throughout the 1920s its profits were modest but consistent,[71] but there was no prospect of rapid or immediate market expansion. The trend of aggregate world demand was only slightly upward, and continental competition was intensifying. The 1929 International Tube Cartel provided a breathing space,[72] but, as MacDiarmid recognized, it was likely to collapse at any minute and was no long-term solution.[73]

As was the case in tinplate, the available market was relatively small in relation to the minimum economic size for the new methods of production. Hence, in the late 1920s Stewarts & Lloyds concentrated on buying a number of small concerns to concentrate tonnage in its hands; as a result of this activity, by 1932 Stewarts & Lloyds controlled 80% of British tube output.[74] Even then, however, the combined ingot consumption of Stewarts & Lloyds averaged only 575,000 tons per year. In 1930 one-third of this was imported.[75] Nearly all of the imported material was of basic Bessemer quality which was ideally suited to tubemaking but of which only small amounts were made in Britain in the 1920s. Stewarts & Lloyds wanted to increase its Bessemer tube production, and the establishment of British Bessemer production was therefore the key target in reorganization. But the company used only 50% Bessemer in all its operations; it needed in addition large quantities of open-hearth steel for its seamless products in particular.

In moving into Bessemer steel, Stewarts & Lloyds possessed a major advantage in the largely fortuitous ownership of large tracts of Northamptonshire ironstone around Corby, which was particularly suited to Bessemer production. The company was aware of its potential since an internal report by C. G. Atha in 1927, and in 1930 Brasserts produced an authoritative report showing that a basic Bessemer plant could be built for £2.97 million and would result in savings of £341,000 per year, or a return on capital of 11.5%.[76]

But there was a superior alternative scheme. Stewarts & Lloyds needs were for both basic Bessemer and open hearth, and a plant based on larger steel output could achieve more economies of scale and higher profits. Encouraged by MacDiarmid, Atha, and others within the company, Brassert expanded his original scheme into a larger one including the simultaneous and interlinked development of basic Bessemer and open hearth based on an innovative resolution of certain technical problems.[77] Although Northants ores were ideally suited for basic Bessemer, open hearth usually required higher quality imported ore and hence, unlike basic Bessemer, was best located at coastal sites; a comprehensive development involving both qualities therefore implied two different locations. But, using recent German research, Brassert proposed the use of the basic duplexing process, which made it possible to use the same ores for both open hearth and basic Bessemer steel.[78] The implication of this was revolutionary: the "dormant national assets" of Northamptonshire ores could now be used in a large combined plant.[79]

The plant would cost cost £5.7 million and earn £1.2 million per year even before any concentration of tubemaking, the equivalent of a 21.5% return on new money. But the logic of such a development also required a much larger scale of production: Brassert reckoned that its profitability would decline rapidly at below 625,000 tons per year output. Under likely operating conditions, this meant that Stewarts & Lloyds would be putting 195,000 tons of cheap open-hearth steel onto the market each year (Table 18).[80] The full implementation of such a project would propel Stewarts & Lloyds beyond pure tube production and set it up in the Midlands as a major threat to existing steel producers in open-hearth steel. The consequence was that the scheme was bitterly opposed by rival steelmakers, and it encountered fundamental financial difficulties. The Bank of England, already deeply involved in the rationalization of Midland and Northern steel, was soon to be plunged into the center of this new issue.

Stewarts & Lloyds was able to break decisively from its past location and technology for two main reasons. First, unlike the situation at Colvilles and Dorman Long, control of decision making was fairly well unified in the hands of a strong and capable management team. Allan C. MacDiarmid, the chairman from 1926, was a tough driving character who had made his way to the top of the company on the accountancy side. The transition from family to professional management had proceeded gradually over twenty years, and the Stewart and Lloyd families now shared the board with professional managers to whom the main initiative had passed. The main local interest opposed to relocation was labor, and in the era before heightened political awareness of the Special Areas the unions could exert little pressure.[81] When the problems of the late 1920s loomed up, the firm was still relatively prosperous. It had avoided heavy debenture and debt encumbrances by its restrained financial policy in 1919–20. Faced with the prospect of imminent sharp decline, it was in a position to do something about it. Moreover, unlike the heavy steel firms that had fallen into the trap of overinvestment in the boom and overcapacity in the slump, it had a fairly good idea of the coming market conditions; hence, it had both the capability and the opportunity to shape its destiny rather than just ride up and down with the market. Its greatest weakness lay not in management or market strategy but in its ability to command the necessary capital to carry out its policy.

The opposition of Stewarts & Lloyds' competitors was powerful because it could make finance for the scheme, either from the public or via the BID, extremely difficult to obtain. The sum of nearly £6 million required for the full project was, as Bischoff of the BID noted, immense and "far too large a proportion against the existing assets valued at £3.5m." Without much security within the company's existing assets, some "satisfactory assurance of an earning capacity" for the new works was doubly important. A debenture issue to raise the new money would require £550,000 per year to pay it, and although Brassert reckoned that the plant could earn about £1 million, Bischoff feared that this gap might easily disappear.[82] For similar reasons, the market could not be expected to support an issue of this size, espe-

Table 18 The five major Corby schemes discussed, 1927–1932

Scheme	Ingot capacity (tons)	Pig cost (per ton, s. d.)	Ingot costs[a] (per ton, s. d.)		Billett costs[a] (per ton, s. d.)		Distribution	Plant cost (total, £m)
Atha, 1927[b]	100,000	60/—	88/1	BB	103/1	BB	All to SL	—
Brassert, Feb. 1930[c]	367,000	44/1	n.a.		n.a.		226,000 to SL; 141,000 outside	2.97
Brassert, Oct. 1930[d]	625,000	41/5	53/2 BB; 58/8 OH		66/— BB; 72/10 OH		430,000 to SL; 195,000 outside	5.7
Brassert, April 1931[e]	430,000	41/5	53/10 BB; 60/5 OH		68/— BB; 77/— OH		All to SL	4.2
Brassert, Sept. 1932[f]	200,000	(a) 41/—; (b) 44/—	54/3 BB; 57/5 BB		70/10 BB; 74/7 BB		All to SL; All to SL	1.8

a. BB, basic Bessemer; OH, open hearth; n.a., not available.
b. Scheme to use existing blast furnaces, build BB steelworks only and new Pilger plant.
c. Scheme to build two new 580-ton blast furnaces and 3 × 25 ton BB converters, and rolling facilities of 40″ blooming mill, 28″ reversing mill, and 12″ skelp mill. No new tubemaking facilities or coke plant at this stage. Cost estimates based on 1928 costs.
d. Scheme to build BB and OH steel plant, with two new blast furnaces and rolling facilities as above. No new tubemaking facilities or coke ovens at this stage. Cost estimates based on 1929 costs.
e. Reduced scheme to build BB and OH steel plant to produce 262,000 tons BB and 173,000 tons OH (by basic duplexing). Blast furnaces and rolling facilities as above.
f. Reduced scheme. BB steel plant only, and one blast furnace to be reconstructed. Provision of further £500,000 suggested for installation of the first stage of a new tubemaking plant. (a) and (b) show estimates for varying ore costs.

cially in depression. Brassert was optimistic from discussions with J.P. Morgan & Co. that he could get American finance for Corby,[83] thus enabling the project to proceed independently and compete in the open steel market regardless of the opposition of competitors.[84] The BID too was "all in favour of getting dollars into this country."[85] But MacDiarmid was not keen, and although this part of the story is obscure, the issues proved too complex.

The core of the hidden opposition to Corby was United Steel. Its opposition, it later became clear, "impeded to a greater extent than we [MacDiarmid] suspected" Stewarts & Lloyds' negotiations with the BID.[86] The other main opposition from within the industry came from Dorman Long and South Durham: Talbot of South Durham and Dorman both attacked the technical feasibility of steel production at Corby,[87] and by winning Peacock's ear on the question within the Bank, they forced the BID to bring in Edgar Lewis of the Bethlehem Steel Corporation as an independent expert to vet the Brassert scheme.[88] But United Steel was the firm most likely to want to enter tube steel production in the future, and it also dominated the common steel situation in the Midlands region. United Steel and the Lancashire Steel Corporation were the two pivotal firms in the Northern Corridor, and the former hoped to be able to dominate the latter in the near future.

However, the emergence of the Corby scheme came at the time when Frater Taylor was maneuvering to strengthen Lancashire Steel vis-à-vis United Steel. He saw a Stewarts & Lloyds/Lancashire Steel agreement as a way of giving the Corporation a "strong card" against United Steel. "Rightly or wrongly, I fancy that a Stewarts & Lloyds-Partington combination would give them [United Steel] something of a shock."[89] MacDiarmid realized that Frater Taylor's real aim was to "pinch" United Steel's wire business by getting a £500,000 joint Stewarts & Lloyds/Lancashire Steel investment in Partington wire developments.[90] Frater Taylor urged either a project to use Corby ores at a Partington steel works or a modification of the Partington scheme to use only Corby semis. Brassert, however, insisted that separate development was optimal,[91] and MacDiarmid agreed.

MacDiarmid thought that Frater Taylor's actions were an attempt to "force us into an amalgamation with Lancashire Steel Corporation" by the BID itself,[92] and he continued to talk to Frater Taylor at all "only out of deference to the Governor."[93] In thinking this he was quite mistaken, but he was unaware at the time of the gulf that had grown up within the Bank between Frater Taylor and the BID on the question of Lancashire Steel.

In fact, the BID's real objection to Stewarts & Lloyds' expansion was that it did not want to foster a common steel rival to United Steel in the Midlands in view of its plans for rationalization in the Northern Corridor. Stewarts & Lloyds gradually came to realize that "it is in fact impossible to obtain a 'fair field' for our Corby plans, including the necessary finance, unless we agree to restrict the admitted competitive strength of Corby in such a way as to safeguard the steel industry—and the bankers' loans involved—from its attacks."[94]

Hence, the company realized that "unless the demarcation principle is admitted, there is little chance of obtaining finance either through the BID or the banks,"[95] and so, in late 1930, MacDiarmid secretly contacted Benton Jones of United Steel without telling the Stewarts & Lloyds board of his intention.[96] He gave United Steel assurances that Corby would confine itself to the tube steel market if United Steel closed its opposition to the scheme. Bruce Gardner at the BID was "impressed and enthusiastic" about this contact: "It changed our position . . . from an 18-pounder to a 15 inch naval gun."[97]

To achieve the required changes, Brassert revised his proposals in April 1931 to produce a scheme confined to tube demand alone (see Table 18). This 430,000-ton plant would provide 75% of total British tube demand. Where necessary, long-term supply agreements would be negotiated to tie consumers to Corby. As a result, the plant could be sure to operate at 66% capacity, even if tube demand in Britain fell as low as half the 1929 level. It would still produce basic Bessemer and open hearth by duplexing and would earn £800,000 per year or a 20% return on capital.[98] On this basis Stewarts & Lloyds was able to negotiate a liaison agreement with United Steel in 1932 which, although it did not go far enough toward physical amalgamation to please Bruce Gardner, covered cooperation in marketing, research, and plan extensions.[99]

This demarcation, although strategically necessary, was not, in the opinion of many experts, the soundest commercial policy for Stewarts & Lloyds. Edgar Lewis of the Bethlehem Steel Corporation, whom the BID put in as a second independent technical expert to vet the Brassert scheme, knew nothing of Brassert's larger October 1930 scheme and assessed only the restricted April 1931 scheme (see Table 18). Yet after vindicating the technical bases of the scheme, he arrived independently at a position similar to Brassert's own. He criticized the more limited 430,000-ton tonnage as "insufficient for most economic production . . . Lewis has become more and more convinced of logic of our Corby position but on the basis of a large low cost plant having sufficient tonnage to warrant the capital expenditure."[100] Brassert and MacDiarmid found themselves in the position of having to try to win Lewis away from the ideas they themselves most favored and toward what was a strategically necessary compromise in the shorter term.[101]

Thus, Stewarts & Lloyds was forced to curtail its scheme in order to have any chance of getting BID and City finance and to placate other steelmakers. Once the principle of demarcation was accepted, two other demarcation agreements followed, with Colvilles about Clydesdale and with United Steel over the Midlands.

This alone did not solve the problem of finance, however. The interest rates that the BID demanded were felt to be "impossible."[102] The BID intended to arrange the issue rather than find the credit itself,[103] and it was seeking to place it at preference shares at $7\frac{1}{2}\%$ and debentures at $5\frac{1}{2}\%$ together with a $2\frac{1}{2}\%$ sinking fund. Stewarts & Lloyds felt that it "could not possibly afford this."[104] The high rate reflected the general market uncertainty about steel investment in general, especially in view of the current rapid fall in continental prices. By July 1931 continental tube strip could be delivered to Scotland at 88 shillings against a projected 81/7d Corby production cost. The BID's interest terms would add 18 shillings per ton, and freight from Corby to Scotland was about £1 per ton, pushing the total comparable cost up to 119/7d.[105] These factors cut into the apparently high rates of return on capital forecast by Brassert and made the scheme more problematic.

In consequence, Stewarts & Lloyds was beset with severe doubts about the whole scheme. Using the example of government credit provision to the sugar beet industry and to agriculture, it put forward the idea of applying to the government for finance at $3\frac{1}{2}$-4%, the sort of interest rate that industrial enterprises in more buoyant sectors of the economy could expect to get on the market. Following this approach, Graham at the Board of Trade touted the idea of running Corby through a public utility company.[106] Much of this was finessing for position, but the BID found it very disturbing. As a result, the BID refused to go on with the discussions. Stewarts & Lloyds in turn became thoroughly inhibited: "They felt the whole position had become so involved politically that they dare not move for fear of making a mistake. Their position was becoming desperate."[107] By January 1932 Bruce Gardner was telling MacDiarmid: "In my opinion, there can be no question of a sum of money of the magnitude required being arranged for from any source whatsoever in the immediate future."[108]

The imminent breakdown of the International Tube Cartel in 1932 made the issue even more pressing. The British home market was the only unreserved home market for tubes in Europe by this time, and South Africa and Japan were likely to become closed to Britain shortly. Protection for the British market would, it was hoped, offset such overseas losses, but also, with Corby, Britain could expect to *increase* its share of world tube trade.[109] Without protection, Corby had been urgently needed to maintain control of the home market; once protection was introduced, Corby was no less urgent because Stewarts & Lloyds' supplies of cheap imported Bessemer steel were thereby blocked.

Some immediate steps were therefore essential, and Stewarts & Lloyds moved to compress its project into an immediate plan for a 200,000-ton plant to produce basic Bessemer only, geared solely to its own tube needs and able to operate at 95% capacity even at only 60% of 1929 demand (see Table 18). This reduced scheme was consciously seen as a first stage, a nucleus around which further tubemaking and steelmaking could be consolidated and extended as demand increased. The capital cost of this plant would be £1.82 million, with a further £500,000 for the first stage of the tubemaking plant.[110]

The BID was willing to give full support to this restricted plan. It took action to secure loan capital of £3.3 million for Stewarts & Lloyds (£2.65 million for capital outlay and the rest for funding the existing overdraft incurred in the purchase of the Islip Iron Co.'s blast furnaces at Corby and additional ironstone reserves). It was instrumental in persuading the Union Bank of Scotland to allow a three-year £1.5 million overdraft to the firm; Lloyds Bank put up an additional £1 million, the Prudential Assurance Co. £250,000 and the BID itself the remaining £550,000.[111] In return, Stewarts & Lloyds agreed to bank solely with the Union Bank of Scotland and with Lloyds and to repay the loan via a public issue at a later date. The final decision to go ahead came in October 1932.[112]

The decision to invest came at the beginning of the upturn in the trade cycle. Site preparation began in January 1933, and building contracts were placed at rock bottom prices. As MacDiarmid noted in 1935: "It would be interesting to have an estimate prepared of the cost of Corby and the length of time it would take to complete the plant if the contracts were to be placed today."[113] The final scheme was based on the absolute minimum consistent with reasonable economy, but trade expansion made it feasible to expand the scheme to include reconstructing an extra blast furnace and to increase the ingot output from 200,000 to 290,000 tons in September 1933 while building was still in its early stages.[114] This additional work would cost £170,000 and the Union Bank of Scotland was dubious about whether the revival justified further expenditure, but building costs were so low that all the expenses of this expansion were met out of the original loan without requiring further demands on the bankers.[115]

Construction pressed ahead rapidly. No. 1 Blast Furnace was blown in on 8 May 1934, and the basic Bessemer plant was opened on 27

December 1934, even though MacDiarmid had earlier thought that even if the project commenced in February 1932 it could not be ready before January 1935.[116] In other words, the plant was built in just under two rather than three years, a striking contrast to the history of most other major steel construction projects in the interwar years.

The Difficulties of Disengagement

By the early 1930s the steel position in the Midlands and the Northern Corridor was deeply marked by the activity of the Bank of England and its financial connections. But far from acting as a coherent force for rationalization as Norman intended, the Bank was becoming more and more embroiled with the conflicting interests in the area and implicated in the development of several partially conflicting and potentially overlapping projects. At Lancashire Steel it exercised control over a firm that it was not wholly sure ought to be in existence. At Corby the Bank had been a strong influence in the containment of Stewarts & Lloyds to a technically suboptimal development marked by restrictions and demarcations as a corollary of the necessary finance for investment. In both cases tariffs and trade revival were to change considerably the positions and aspirations of the firms the Bank was involved with and to further limit the Bank's position to influence events.

The rapidity and extent of revival in the mid-1930s engendered shortages, and even many down-and-out firms were able to make big profits with old plant. Stewarts & Lloyds benefited from this too—even its old works which it had been planning to scrap earned enough during 1934 to pay the interest, depreciation, and dividends for the whole company—but Stewarts & Lloyds could take full advantage of this situation only by expanding its production. Yet Corby had been planned solely as a substitution plant to replace existing production. The reduced cost of production at Corby was designed to make the existing tonnage profitable. In the new situation, however, the company was blocked from expanding its tube production because it already virtually monopolized British demand and world markets were restricted by tariffs. Its most profitable course, therefore, would be to continue to use its old works for the tube trade at a profit and to use Corby to invade other steelmaking markets.

This policy required abandoning the principle of demarcation, which the firm had hitherto accepted. It had abided by this policy even though other steelmakers in other trades were seizing "piratical" tonnage from each other. Tube demarcation was something of an island in an industry where "the one word which is utterly taboo is the sacred word 'demarcation' " But with South Durham threatening to invade tubes, demarcation looked very precarious. In this situation Stewarts & Lloyds believed that its "proper defense is attack."

Tubemaking was too limited a market in itself and insecure. The National Committee, the embryo of the British Iron and Steel Federation, was moving in the post-tariff period toward tying up the steel trade in a system of quotas and rebates, and Stewarts & Lloyds feared that "if we sit down as demarked tubemakers with the negligible steel capacity of 200–250 thousand tons, all of which goes into tubes, we are likely to be ignored." Corby's cost advantages were likely to diminish as other firms invested in similar technology: "The matter brooks no delay. If we postpone, our position will be jeopardised." Stewarts & Lloyds would be in a better offensive-defensive position in relation to any negotiations about quotas or a Midland grouping once it was making 450,000 tons per year steel at the lowest cost with a surplus of easily marketed semis. This needed to be done before quotas were established, and finance for such a move was easily available through the overdraft facilities that had been provided by the Union Bank of Scotland.[117]

As Stewarts & Lloyds began more and more to see itself as a steel as well as a tube producer, the possibility of sharp conflict with United Steel about the pattern of future Midlands developments began to grow. One way in which Stewarts & Lloyds hoped to strengthen its position vis-à-vis United Steel was by building up its links with the Lancashire Steel Corporation. Lancashire Steel participated jointly with Stewarts & Lloyds in a new bar mill at Corby and made a supply agreement for billets with the Corby steelworks. It also formed a joint selling company to dipose of the products of the new mill.[118] Stewarts & Lloyds would have pushed for still stronger links with Lancashire Steel but for the opposition of John E. James.[119]

During 1935–36 Stewarts & Lloyds still hoped that some agreement might be reached with United Steel on mutual development. In 1935 it approached United Steel and Brassert investigated a joint Midlands scheme for them, but United Steel rejected the report he produced because it felt that Brassert was "too much Stewarts & Lloyds," and the latter was in any case afraid to go much further because it felt that United Steel wanted to acquire Corby, which was "outrageous."[120] Attempts to reach an agreement between the two firms were finally broken off by Stewarts & Lloyds in a "cavalier manner" in November 1936,[121] and in 1937 it went on to prepare to expand its steel production to 450,000 tons per year, a move that clearly threatened a Midlands trade war.[122]

United Steel's response was twofold. First, the company made preparations to fight Stewarts & Lloyds' invasion. In May 1936 it issued £2.2 million preference shares at 5 shillings premium, which gave them £2.7 million cash, for which they had at the time no declared plan. These funds could only be seen as a "war chest" by the Bank and others, and Stewarts & Lloyds and Lancashire Steel were afraid that "it is just the sort of thing to start a war."[123] Second, United Steel considered possible mergers—either a comprehensive amalgamation of all Midland steelmakers, possibly including Richard Thomas too, in a giant holding company or a renewed approach to the Lancashire Steel Corporation for a full merger.[124]

For the Bank, as controllers of Lancashire Steel, the position became both delicate and embarrassing. From the time recovery got under way it had begun to prepare the ground for withdrawal from the Lancashire Steel Corporation. By reducing the interest on the preference shares from 7% to 5% in early 1935, it aimed to pave the way for a further issue of preference shares to repay the Schröder loan.[125] But as yet the Bank did not think the situation ripe for relinquishing control.[126] As Stewarts & Lloyds became more of a threat, Benton Jones intimated to Bruce Gardner that United Steel was again interested in the acquisition of the corporation through share purchase. Bruce Gardner would not discuss this possibility until the Bank's new issue had taken place, and then he refused to negotiate on the ground that, having asked for money on the basis of existing results and structures, it would be wrong so quickly to dispose of control of the company, because Bank control was clearly seen as a major asset by prospective investors. With John E. James laid up in a nursing home for most of 1935, Bruce Gardner was not prepared to go any further with Benton Jones.[127]

As United Steel continued to press, the rationalization policy of the Bank became more and more intertwined with the development of an impending trade war in the Midlands. Norman's guiding policy was that any dealing in Lancashire Steel shares would only be for rationalizing purposes. The Bank would on no account engage in any merely market transactions,[128] particularly in the light of the effect that this would have on the balance of forces between rival companies. Hence, enormously complex diplomacy and conciliation became necessary. In May 1936 Bruce Gardner was engaged in extensive discussions with United Steel, Lancashire Steel, and Stewarts & Lloyds: "During the past fortnight he had almost daily interrogations by one or the other."[129]

In this situation the Bank's power to influence events was a grave embarrassment. On one hand, Norman was in a hurry to dispose of Lancashire shares, but on the other hand he dared not sell them to either of the most interested parties for fear of being represented as aiding one or the other.[130]

Six months earlier Norman had still hoped to use Lancashire Steel as a basis for a Northwest/Midlands amalgamation. But now United Steel was "greedy" and MacDiarmid "had become more rapacious," turning from defending his tube position to "invading" steelmaking.[131] It now seemed clear that the three firms "must either fight or agree," and Lancashire Steel would inevitably be drawn into any quarrel between the other two. Here were "rich industrialists each making £½m. per year who had been in the hands of the banks once and who did not intend to get in again, and who had violently fallen out with each other." If the Bank tried to interfere in this situation, it would no doubt be told to mind its own business.[132]

The Bank brought the three firms together for tripartite merger talks, but it soon became clear that Lancashire Steel's principle interest was in a linkup with Stewarts & Lloyds alone so that it could get access to the cheapest pig iron. United Steel saw this as a serious threat, and it was apparent that such a bilateral fait accompli would seriously compromise the Bank's good faith. Norman therefore had to back-pedal. He "would certainly feel inclined to veto" any Stewarts & Lloyds/Lancashire Steel arrangement, and he made it clear that he could not accept any agreement that did not include all three companies.[133]

Norman was able to freeze the situation by getting tripartite negotiations resumed during 1937, but disengagement remained a big problem. Lord Hyndley, a new member of the SMT, stressed that it "wanted to see the Bank out of this position as soon as possible," in particular because it felt that the boom "had realised the top for the time being" and that if the Bank did not get out soon it would be locked into Lancashire Steel in the next slump.[134] It remained imperative that in any sale of shares the equity should be so disposed as not to pass into the hands of any single controlling group and should be distributed as widely as possible. But this was not easy to arrange.[135] The classic solution of a sale to the highest bidder was in conflict with the Bank's perceived role as defending the national interest in steel by assembling the most efficient rationalizing combination.

The process of disengagement and devolution back to private capital was prolonged and became possible only when the tensions between United Steel and Stewarts & Lloyds eased.[136] High levels of demand meant that the potential confrontation between the two firms did not materialize. In these conditions the Bank had two main policy objectives, both very limited in comparison with its former grand aims. First, it remained anxious to get out of Lancashire Steel, particularly from 1939 when the Labour Party was using Bank control of the steel industry as a "formidable gun" against them.[137] This task of quiet extrication was finally completed only under the rather changed conditions prevailing during World War II.[138] Its second objective was to bring Stewarts & Lloyds, whom the Bank saw as a disruptive outsider, into some framework of control. Stewarts & Lloyds and the Tubemakers Association, which it dominated, had refused to enter the British Iron and Steel Federation before the Second World War.[139] The Bank therefore pursued an extended process of wooing Mac-Diarmid and his firm into the fold. Part of this process of conciliation was its action in putting MacDiarmid on the board of Richard Thomas in 1940 (see Chapter 10), but the final conclusion of this policy was not reached until MacDiarmid finally accepted an offer to become chairman of the Federation in 1944.[140]

It was a sorry story of decline from Norman's earlier aspirations to galvanize large-scale reorganization. The Bank ended up using its influence against mergers that, on paper, it favored. If it pushed for mergers, it was accused of unfair practices; if it tried to do nothing, it was pushed about by industrialists. And it could not even extricate itself because, in the delicate balance of the industry, that was as much of an intervention as throwing its weight behind a particular firm. Not surprisingly there was a growing sense of frustration, embarrassment, and helplessness within the BID.

The Bank was unable to develop strategies to link its pragmatic grasp of day-to-day realities to its blueprints for industrial reorganization. In particular, once it had failed to take control of United Steel it was always in a position where it needed United Steel's assistance more than United Steel needed the Bank. It could not carry through a major amalgamation plan without the active cooperation of United Steel, but in order to get that cooperation it would more or less have to allow United Steel to dictate the terms and the Bank would then be perceived as aiding one particular interest against other firms. As long as the Bank wanted to be a national interest, it had to restrict itself to arguing either for giant amalgamations involving *all* the relevant parties or nothing. The Bank was not prepared to step in as an active merger promoter itself, utilizing its resources to pursue its goals. It hoped to exert control at one remove by being able to say yes or no, and in the end this policy left it on the sidelines. The experience of the Northern Corridor was not unique; Bank involvement at Beardmore, to which we now turn, generated many similar problems.

William Beardmore & Co.: Control versus Management, 1926–1938

Simultaneous with its far-reaching involvement in the complex network of companies in the Midlands and Northern Corridor, the Bank of England was also becoming deeply involved in the affairs of William Beardmore & Co. In contrast with the Lancashire Steel Corporation, the Bank's initial involvement began purely as an "exceptional" operation, not through involvement with an existing industrial client. Hence, at Beardmore the Bank was less prone to deeper involvement in defense of its own interests. Nevertheless, even here, it was to encounter similar problems of management and control. Reliable managerial agents to carry out the Bank's policy were hard to come by, and management still tended to pursue the independent interests of the firm rather than the goals of the Bank. For a long time, although ultimately it was more successful here than at Lancashire Steel, the Bank was unable to translate its financial control into real managerial control.

In contrast too to its Lancashire Steel operation, the Bank's aims were far more limited, concentrating on liquidation and retrenchment rather than seeking to develop broader rationalization schemes. Beardmore was somewhat marginal to Scottish rationalization except in the specialized forging and castings sector and consequently involved fewer conflicts of interest with rival firms. The Bank did manage not to get drawn deeper and deeper into the industry and in the end managed to fulfill certain of its aims—although these had been formulated rapidly at the onset of its intervention and at times fitted in badly with its more general pursuit of rationalization. Moreover, once again, the process of disengagement proved arduous, with the Bank finding itself caught up in an invidious position between conflicting interests of rival firms and banking concerns. The Bank operated at Beardmore more in its capacity as a powerful banking creditor enforcing its rights than it did anywhere else, and its intervention was correspondingly more effective, although nonetheless problematic.

The steel, shipbuilding, and armaments combine William Beardmore & Co. of Glasgow had made average distributable profits of nearly £½ million per annum over the years 1916–1920. On this basis it ran up large quantities of short-term and unsecured debts, notably £1 million seven-year notes at 8% issued in 1920 to finance expansion and diversification. But heavy losses in every year after 1922 followed, making this debt position an enormous millstone. Attempts to regularize the position by replacing these debts by public debentures were unsuccessful in the following years, largely because inadequate security was available.[141] Hence, the company's bankers, primarily Lloyds, were faced with the prospect of either allowing their overdraft to increase, forcing bankruptcy, or reorganizing the firm.

In 1924 Lloyds increased its overdraft from £750,000 to £1¼ million, accepting in return admittedly inadequate securities of second charges on specific properties, in order to enable the firm to continue. It recognized that £310,000 of this would be swallowed up by redeeming debentures and paying fixed charges in the next two years and that the sum involved was inadequate for any reconstruction, but it allowed the position to hang fire in the hope of "a real profit earning period" in the next few years.[142]

By December 1926 Beardmore's position was critical. As well as the £1¼ million overdraft, there were £4 million debts and only £900,000 liquid resources. With repayment of the seven-year notes due, Lloyds refused to extend any further advances, and the company had to borrow £30,000 from the chairman's wife, Lady Invernairn, for working capital to pay wages.[143] With closure imminent, Beardmore & Co. appealed to the Treasury to give up some of its claims as creditors and to assist with fresh working capital.[144]

In the negotiations that followed, the Bank of England appeared on the scene for the first time. Norman contacted the government to urge it to refuse aid because this would only delay reorganization.[145] The Treasury, however, needed no such urging. Sir Otto Niemeyer, the chancellor's chief adviser at the Treasury, told Winston Churchill, the chancellor, that government aid would lead to a repeat experience of the subsidy to the coal industry in the months before the General Strike,[146] and Leith-Ross, another leading Treasury adviser, produced a damning report on Beardmore & Co.: the company had persistently "let liabilities accumulate and borrow more" rather than reorganizing. "The story is one of over-equipment and of borrowing to meet losses with a gradually worsening liquidity . . . Now they can borrow no more, they appeal to the government to take the place of the banks."[147] Churchill, who was bitterly opposed to subsidies to industry on principle, turned Beardmore down.

Norman's second approach was direct to Lloyds to urge it to take an active role in reorganizing the company. Under this carrot and stick, Lloyds allowed the firm to continue by agreeing to a further £270,000 overdraft in conjunction with the National Bank of Scotland and the Royal Bank of Scotland and set up an investigating committee consisting of F. A. Szarvasy the merchant banker, the accountants Gilbert Garnsey and P. E. Marmian, and William Paine, the general manager of Lloyds Bank.[148] Norman's notion was to reorganize Beardmore & Co. by incorporating it into Vickers-Armstrong. But that company's chairman, Sir Herbert Lawrence, rejected the proposal as likely to upset the current work of putting the newly formed company on a firm footing.[149] The investigating committee, and particularly Szarvasy, favored this too, and they urged Norman to put Frater Taylor on the Vickers-Armstrong board to "keep the matter warm,"[150] but after his earlier talks with Lawrence, Norman rejected such a move as premature and an excessive burden on the overworked Frater Taylor.[151] In the meantime, the Advisory Committee concentrated on financial reconstruction. By 1928 Lloyds was prepared to accept debenture stock ranking behind new money to facilitate an issue of debentures for cash,[152] but even so "for various reasons the market was missed,"[153] and the financial position remained overextended and unresolved.

In June 1929, with the situation of the company still deteriorating, imminent liquidation loomed up again. Norman's original intention was to allow liquidation, but the Bank believed that, under Scottish law, this would have meant immediate and complete closure,[154] a prospect that the new Labour government found alarming and which caused it to discuss government intervention. Largely to forestall such a move, Norman "for national reasons" but "very much against his will" had the Bank put up £750,000 to keep the firm alive. "It was all arranged in some 48 hours and was done on the understanding that he [Norman] had control and that the policy, in the national interest, was for Beardmore to be liquidated by rationalising the different sections of it."[155] Voting control was to be in the hands of a Control Committee of three (representing the Bank of England, the three clearing banks—N.B.S., R.B.S. and Lloyds—and Beardmore & Co.) nominated by the governor who would also approve the directors. The scheme became operative on 3 September 1929.

In the autumn of 1929, with a Labour government newly elected and the BID newly formed, Norman was perhaps somewhat prone to conjure up rationalization schemes on all fronts. The liquidation by rationalization envisaged in the 1929 scheme linked up with two other projects that Norman had in hand at the time. First, along with Sir James Lithgow, he was in the process of establishing a cooperative organization of shipbuilders to buy up and scrap excess shipyard capacity. (This was shortly to become the National Shipbuilders' Securities Co., or NSS.) Beardmore's Dalmuir shipyard would be the first sale to this proposed company.[156]

Simultaneously, Norman was working on a scheme for the merger of all the principal British locomotive manufacturers, a project that was abandoned some months later when the North British Locomotive Co., the biggest company, refused to be drawn in.[157] Beardmore's locomotive plant was to be sold to this combine and shut down as part of the rationalization plan. The feeling in the Bank was that these rationalization matters had to move with some urgency. In particular, action at Beardmore was seen to be vital in getting the NSS scheme off the ground. Norman, therefore, wanted to expedite rationalization plans by the appointment of Frater Taylor to the board.

But Frater Taylor did not want to get involved in Beardmore. He did not like the company and feared that association with it could damage his reputation. He and Norman had "sparred and abused one another" about the Control Committee job, until, after both Lord Weir and Andrew Duncan had refused it, Frater Taylor accepted the post, still stressing to Norman that "in this matter I am succumbing to you personally."[158]

Once in place, Frater Taylor rapidly ran into difficulties. The old Beardmore management group remained strongly represented on the new board. Lord Invernairn retired, but four of the old team remained, and, when Frater Taylor became chairman, the most prominent of these, Lewis Ord, who was also a director of Armstrong Whitworth, became managing director. He was a man with "a taciturn and furtive manner and a strange physiognomy," and his personal relationship with Frater Taylor was bitter from the start, but he was seen as a practical man with a grasp of the firm and its workings.[159] At first he and the Ord group of old Beardmore directors seemed to accept the Bank plan. But, as Frater Taylor noted, Ord was "very sanguine" that the savings from reorganization would be very considerable, perhaps amounting to £350,000 in the first year, and on this basis he hoped that it might be possible to do rather more than just run the firm down;[160] in particular, Ord still hoped to revive the shipyard and locomotive works as going concerns. It soon became clear that the ends he wanted to pursue "were not those contemplated when the Bank put in fresh money. He was all for saving the business and trying to build it up." Frater Taylor utterly rejected this: "No-one in the industry, other than Ord, thought that the business could be brought round."[161]

But Ord's detailed knowledge of the firm enabled him to exert considerable influence and persuasiveness. His arguments split both the SMT and the Control Committee down the middle. On the Control Committee, the accountant Sir James Cooper and Paine of Lloyds lined up with him, and in the SMT and on the board Frank Hodges also accepted his arguments, giving Ord a majority on the board. These developments, however, meant that Norman, Frater Taylor, and Duncan rapidly lost faith in Ord. They decided that the implementation of the original policy required them to put in a new man and "go nap" on him, and to wrest control back from the Ord group.[162]

But two things made this difficult. First, they had no alternative management team to put in, particularly if they were to clear out all those with a background with the firm. Moreover, kicking out Ord was likely to cause Paine, Cooper, and Hodges to resign in protest. Norman might have grasped this nettle if Frater Taylor were prepared to stay on and handle the matter, but the latter was loath to remain.[163] In the end as a compromise within the SMT, Frater Taylor was allowed to go, and Hans Reincke, formerly senior manager with John Brown & Co. and acquainted with the detailed problems of steel/shipbuilding/armaments combines, was put in as chairman in February 1930.[164]

Reincke was a professional manager, but also one who saw his role at Beardmore as explicitly to "safeguard the interests of the Bank" and to resume the policy of orderly liquidation. By the time he came in, Ord's strategy was already proving to be based on "representations impossible of fulfillment" and lack of foresight.[165] The Ord group had been in large part responsible for the sorry management record of the 1920s which had got Beardmore "looked on locally as kind of a ragtime crew,"[166] and they had remedied none of this under the Control. A technical investigation commissioned by Reincke in 1930 found that "it passes comprehension how any responsible head of a concern could permit such a disgraceful condition, however short of money the firm might be."[167] Reincke found the works in a state of "moral and material disintegration," and as a result in May 1930 he demanded and got Ord's resignation from the board.[168]

The result of this delay in the SMT's getting a proper understanding and grasp of the firm was that its early support for Ord was now seen to have worsened "an impossible situation." Of the original £750,000 bank loan, £516,000 had gone for repaying debts, and the necessary cash for immediate improvements prior to selling off assets had not been available. As a result of this situation, combined with Ord's prognostications, the burden of interest on Beardmore's debts had actually been increased during the first year of Control by £65,000 per annum.

By late November 1931 Hodges felt: "It is clear . . . that the Bank of England was wrongly advised when this money was put up. No scheme more calculated to thwart the attainment of the Governor's two objectives could have been devised than the one that came into operation."[169] As a result, difficulties in meeting interest payments had remained, and, because of the terms of the trust deed, Beardmore remained vulnerable to foreclosure by its creditors, even though its position was steadily improving. As Reincke noted, a less optimistic view in the first place would have resulted in the Bank's putting up either more money or none at all.[170]

The advent of Reincke as managing director rather belatedly brought management into line with Bank policy. In the course of the next year, with the assistance of the Bank, the disposal of Beardmore assets other than the main Parkhead forge proceeded fairly smoothly. Norman used his influence with Sir James Lithgow, the powerful West of Scotland shipbuilding magnate, to get National Shipbuilders' Securities to pay a good price for the Dalmuir shipyard under their scrapping program as "one way to . . . show his gratitude" to the governor for his interest in the shipbuilding industry,[171] and the locomotive department, which had been the other greatest drain on working capital, was soon closed too, after the collapse of Norman's plan for a giant locomotive holding company left no potential buyer.[172]

These moves prepared the ground for the next stage of the plan, that of using the conserved liquid resources to concentrate production and to modernize the melting shops and forge at Parkhead. Everything else would be closed or sold off. The continuation of depression, however, made this stage protracted. The experience of this period highlights the confusions that surrounded the exceptional role that the Bank had undertaken in its control of Beardmore.

First, despite the clearly abnormal conditions that had prompted Bank intervention, Norman never fully accepted that Beardmore could not be operated as a normal company while it carried its debt burden through the depression in the hope of renewed viability in a revival. Time and again, the Bank refused to commit itself any more deeply in order to ensure the rationalization that it wanted. In consequence, it came near to jeopardizing its own aims.

To set Parkhead on a viable footing, Reincke argued that it needed the Bank to put a further, comparatively modest sum of £250,000 on the table. But, as Reincke feared, Bruce Gardner replied flatly that there was no chance of extra capital from the Bank. He advocated instead dogged attrition. Norman would not provide more cash, and Bruce Gardner warned that even "to raise the question at an SMT meeting would only worry the governor."[173] Hodges did, however, grasp the nettle to the extent of proposing a further £100,000 cash injection on the grounds that "to close down now would be to take the type of action which any ordinary bank would take in similar circumstances, possessing no consciousness of any social obligations or any definite plan of rationalisation. It is just because the Governor of the Bank of England stands for something other than this that I recommend the above course be followed."[174]

In fact, many clearing banks were in practice more flexible toward the needs of their clients in nursing their investments through depression than the Bank proved to be with Beardmore. Bank policy recognized that even if the works were finally to be scrapped, the trough of the depression would be a bad time to do this, and it would be worth hanging on until the upturn. In late 1931 Bruce Gardner confirmed that this at least was what the Bank intended to do at Parkhead.[175] But the Bank had no clear banking criteria for dealing with such concerns, and Norman therefore tended to oscillate between a rigid actuarialism, which made the depressed firm hard to run in the short term, and exceptional semipolitical activity to determine policy in the long term.

The clearest example of this was the case of a major Admiralty contract for Beardmore in 1932.[176] Beardmore was still acutely short of orders, and Reincke felt, and Bruce Gardner agreed, that if it did not get this large contract, it would have to close. But the terms of the Admiralty contract created great difficulties: it was specified to be spread over three years, but no one could realistically guarantee that Beardmore would survive for three years; nor would the Admiralty accept an assurance from Beardmore that its contract would be completed, come what may. Bruce Gardner felt that at least an additional £100,000 new money for the firm was needed for working capital if potential losses for that period were to be covered. But Norman refused outright: "Work-in-progress ought to be financed by the bankers to the company and the Bank of England will not ever again put itself in the position of being bankers to anything but banking concerns."[177] In his capacity as banker to the Admiralty, Norman could not in banking terms fairly advise placing the contract with Beardmore, but he also knew the effect on Beardmore of not getting the contract. The company's commercial bankers, Lloyds, and their Scottish associate, the National Bank of Scotland, would not provide new money either, and the sale of assets alone would not be adequate to supply sufficient cash.[178]

In this crisis Norman finally devised a compromise to enable the Bank to stay within its principles and yet not, in effect, foreclose on the company: he agreed to reloan to Beardmore the interest that it had already repaid to the Bank on its previous loans and thus provide a minimum of new cash while only slightly stretching his actuarial framework.[179] Although admitting that Beardmore was kept alive only on the sufferance of the Bank, Norman was highly reluctant to accept any real responsibility for the fate of the firm, even though he clearly wanted to keep it alive on a reorganized basis rather than consign it to the hands of recievers.[180]

The second major area of confusion came where the case of Parkhead interacted with broader questions of regional and product rationalization. In two major areas the Parkhead scheme risked coming into conflict with the blueprints for product rationalization on which the Bank was basing its overall activity.

The first was in relation to the rationalization of castings and forgings and the wider context of Scottish rationalization. Parkhead's only point of contact with the other Scottish companies was in this sector where it overlapped with the Steel Company of Scotland's Tyre and Axle Department. In a 1931 investigation Hewitson Hall had recommended to Bruce Gardner that these departments should be brought together,[181] and Sir James Lithgow, who had come onto the board of Beardmore in June 1929, also strongly favored this course. In terms of Scottish reorganization he saw this merger "as of even more importance from the shipbuilders' point of view than is the amalgamation of the rolling businesses."[182] But the Steel Company of Scotland was unwilling to sell its department before a general Scottish merger, although it was ready to consider selling it to Beardmore after one. But it would give Lithgow no guarantee that it would not continue with its casting business inside a Scottish merger in competition with Beardmore outside. In face of this uncertainty, rival overlapping development continued despite the Bank's express wish to avoid it. In the end, the mating of the two firms' tire, wheel, and axle departments came about solely through the private initiatives of Lithgow himself between 1934 and 1936. Lithgow bought SCS, sold it to Colvilles, and then negotiated an amicable demarcation agreement on these products with Beardmore. Where the Bank had become enmeshed in endless diplomacy with the firms involved, Lithgow was able to act directly and cut the Gordian knot.[183]

Second, both of the guiding plans that had been drawn up by Brassert and Bruce Gardner for the Bank saw rationalization of armament steel as proceeding through the combination of Parkhead with the Sheffield arms firms John Brown & Co. and the English Steel Corporation. Parkhead was a superior unit to several of those in Sheffield, and in 1930 John Brown & Co. favored a merger with Beardmore rather than one with English Steel for that reason.[184] However, in 1931 John Brown & Co. resumed talks with English Steel, and the Bank feared that unless the three firms were speedily coordinated, the result of a Sheffield-only merger might be the construction of new blast furnace capacity in Sheffield that would cut across the lines of the Bruce Gardner plan.[185] A linkup and rationalization of Parkhead and Sheffield would prevent this and encourage what the Bank saw as the correct development. But they balked at what was involved in practice.

Reincke, himself a former manager at John Brown, argued that the "mating process" between Sheffield and Parkhead could not be left to the companies involved. English Steel, above all, was overcapitalized and "in no sense rationalised within itself, and the result of either Brown's or ourselves [Beardmore] rationalising with them would presumably be that they would expect to be the preponderating element with the power to close down our works and obtain a new lease of life for their own top-heavy organisation." Only Bank, SMT or government control over the proposed merger could prevent this outcome. For the SMT the implications of such a move went too far. Bruce Gardner scribbled curtly on Reincke's memorandum, "Can't be done,"[186] and in the event, despite the Bank's paper scheme, no attempts were made to use control of Parkhead to develop armament steel rationalization.

With the sale of Beardmore's Mossend steelworks to Colvilles in May 1934 and with the general revival in steel, Parkhead began to operate at a profit, and the completion of the Bank's strategy of rationalization by liquidation drew into sight. From March 1935 the government's stated defense policy meant that Parkhead forge had a guaranteed future, and by July 1935 Beardmore was able to redeem £150,000 debentures and allocate £100,000 for investment at Parkhead from profits and sales of assets. The situation was ripe for the Bank of England to consider disengagement.[187]

But the Bank had tied up the Beardmore management so effectively in 1929 through the Special Management Period and Voting Control Committee that by this time "the question of untieing it seems difficult." Norman wanted to relinquish the terminate control as soon as the future seemed reasonably assured; the Bank had never intended to become a permanent investor, and with the emerging prospect of buyers of "the control" it wanted to get out. But the sale of its holdings posed complex problems; it had no wish to exercise for the benefit of a third party the safeguards that were primarily instituted for the protection of its own position.[188]

Sir James Lithgow, the most powerful Scottish steelmaker, was the obvious buyer. The only other firm or group interested was Vickers, and it had no wish to compete with Lithgow for control—although if Lithgow was not interested "they would wish to be competitors with any other potential purchaser."[189] Lithgow was willing to put £700,000 to £800,000 into Beardmores as long as he got adequate security and control, and that, for him, meant the ownership of the entire debenture and preference stock currently held by the Bank.[190] But a simple substitution of Lithgow for the Bank would appear to other interests to be the Bank's getting out at the expense of Beardmore's rivals.

Moreover, because even after a sale to Lithgow the Bank would retain its legal control through the Control Committee, the Bank's position would be "invidious."[191] The other banks involved in Beardmore, for instance, had always seen their interests as being "practically identical" to those of the Bank of England, because their holding of income debenture stock would have been hit very hard by liquidation of the firm in 1929 or the years that followed.[192] Lloyds would not be happy, however, to see the role played by the Bank of England fall into the hands of Lithgow with whom it had a long history of wrangling hostility.[193] In consequence, Lloyds intended to block the Bank's withdrawal in Lithgow's favor through Paine on the Control Committee. It had, according to Skinner, "got used to consulting and receiving every consideration" from Norman, and it did not think it would enjoy a similar privileged relationship with Lithgow. It would prefer to see the company sold to a syndicate where it could still hope to exercise some control.[194]

The Scottish banks, however, welcomed the prospect of control by Lithgow, and Norman was able to utilize this support to circumvent the obstacle presented by Lloyds' £150,000 income debentures by buying them up and selling them half each to the National Bank of Scotland and the Union Bank of Scotland,[195] thus removing Lloyds' position on the Control Committee.

Once completed, the transfer of the Bank's shares in Beardmore to Lithgow revealed that he had a rather different idea of what the takeover was about. The Bank wanted the sale to be accompanied by a reconstruction of the firm's capital and a rapid normalization of the company.[196] But Lithgow and the other banks did not share the desires of the Bank of England. Paine of Lloyds opposed reconstruction and wanted to confine activity to reducing interest rates to create conditions in which Beardmore's stock could be marketed.[197] Lithgow too was "entirely opposed to reconstruction." He felt that the most it would do would be to reduce fixed charges, and the banks were ready to do that much voluntarily anyway. He feared that reconstruction would be a prelude to renewed demands for dividends by shareholders, which could conflict with his aim of conserving as much cash as possible within the firm for the present. The Bank of England, which still retained formal control but without any financial power, had grudgingly to agree to a much slower rate of normalization.[198]

This division became an angry split later when Lithgow finally did move to reconstruct. Lithgow put his profit estimates at as low a level as possible to avoid overcapitalization in what was still a precarious recovery.[199] For the accountants Deloitte Plender and for Norman this meant that both the Bank and the Treasury were being forced to make sacrifices in order to secure public support for Lithgow's scheme.[200] Norman, who saw himself as "a sort of public trustee or custodian of the rights of all classes" stubbornly argued the toss with Lithgow.[201] By October he declared that if Lithgow did not produce an acceptable scheme, "I will have nothing more to do with reorganisation, but will make things as difficult for Beardmore's as possible—both via the Control Committee and via Whitehall. I consider that Whitehall is entitled to ask or require that a leading and essential armaments company should, in these times, be able to publish a decent balance sheet and to enjoy a creditworthy position. Beardmores can do neither; and Lithgow doesn't wish them to!"[202]

In the end Norman was sufficiently pacified to recognize that Lithgow had to be allowed to go his own way. Lithgow's scheme finally went through in May 1938. By that time, as Skinner concluded, "by one means or another it seems to have been possible to satisfy everybody."[203] The Bank was free of Beardmore.

Had the Bank achieved its aims?[204] In one sense it had. Beardmore & Co. survived, slimmed down to a Parkhead which was profitable, better organized, and under strong Scottish management. But this conclusion conceals the major failings that occurred. The wider rationalization schemes—the locomotive merger, armaments merger, and Scottish forging amalgamation—into which the SMT sought to fit its work at Beardmore, came to nothing. These schemes could be seen as icing on the cake, but they were central to the Bank's own view of why it was involved in industry: it did not intend to be just a slightly more generous version of a clearing bank, keeping its client alive through depression. Nor could the Bank take most of the credit for the swelling profits of the late 1930s: under rearmament it would have been hard for the firm *not* to prosper. And in terms of management and policy, it had come to depend excessively on Lithgow. Where it had lacked such a forceful ally from the world of business the Bank had accomplished little. Yet the SMT would not recognize this in its policy. It refused to develop, for instance, an explicitly pro-Lithgow policy: it often liked what he achieved but not how he did it. At times he pulled the Bank in ways it did not want to go. The SMT could not itself act as a Lithgow, an active entrepreneur making decisions and backing them and making them effective by the use of Bank capital and expertise.

Could the Bank have tried to do so? One obvious set of factors made it unlikely. It has been argued earlier that there was a continuing tension between the Bank's new role and its conventional practices. In the Northern Corridor the broad strategic conceptions had dominated; at Beardmore, after the initial flurry of rationalizing ideas, the traditional actuarial framework was on top. Intervention emerged from a political crisis and was centered on strictly limited aims. Following this, there was a pervasive unwillingness to increase Bank involvement that at times seemed to come straight out of orthodox banking textbooks. Norman acted as almost any other banker might have done with all the attendant ills of a short-term cash flow perspective. Norman was genuinely interested in rationalization and at times obsessed with grand schemes; but perhaps the commitment was only skin deep—scratch the industrial strategist and you find the orthodox banker. The problems of Beardmore & Co. did not require a grand strategy for Scottish steel, but they did require a detailed grip on industrial management, a knowledgeable approach to asset stripping, and the sort of institutions that could give a strategic push to recalcitrant interests like Lloyds Bank or take on a big industrialist like Lithgow. Such resources did not exist, nor had the SMT or BID begun to discuss how they could acquire such powers. They relied on the "great influence" of the Bank, but here, as in so many other cases, it could not translate its prestige into action.

10.

Renewed Involvement in the Late Thirties

In many respects Bank involvement in Armstrong Whitworth, Lancashire Steel, English Steel, and Beardmore all stemmed directly from developments in the prewar and postwar booms: it was the restructuring of a number of old companies that were collapsing under their own weights in a changed market environment. These commitments also began to run more and more into problems of forward planning, particularly in the Bank's attempt in the Midlands and Northern Corridor to foster a rationalized industrial structure. Primarily, however, the Bank's role centered on taking exceptional measures to extricate itself from a pattern of involvement into which it had strayed and on assisting other bankers in similar positions, within an overall framework of rationalization, which seemed to mean in practice trying to get the steel industry to sort itself out before its deteriorating condition prompted government intervention.

The task of extrication, however, implied reconstructing the industry and hence a defined position on structural change in the industry. The Bank had slowly recognized this, for instance, by institutionalizing its planning in the BID. However, starting with Corby, the Bank was increasingly involved in a new range of problems—those of technical innovation in sectors of the industry that were expanding and which had good prospects for the future, but which were faced with rather constrained markets in the short term that were small in relation to the necessary economies of scale and the requirements of new technology, and where capital requirements were large in relation to the size of existing investment in the sector, the firm, and the market.

The full implications of this change were not immediately apparent. The secular movement of the economy, as we have seen, meant that recovery was rooted mainly in the more traditional heavy steel sector where the armaments and building-based revival of profitability and expansion of demand was most drastic in the mid and late 1930s (see Figure 2). In that sector no new technology was available and hence there was no demand for a sharply increased scale of investment. The heavy steel firms like Dorman Long and Colvilles were able to expand on the traditional basis of retained profits in the upswing through technical adaption and improvisation.

Nevertheless, lighter steel demand was also growing, although less rapidly. Here, however, new technology, largely the result of the economies of the American domestic market's size and demand pull, was exogenously available and set the pace for world competitive standards. The market for tinplate, sheet, and tubes was marginally able to sustain the levels of production required by this technology, but the financial base for these developments was narrow and given cyclical movements, somewhat precarious, notably in 1938.

The rather slow pace of development in these industries delayed the impact of this problem until the late 1930s, by which time the clearing banks, with some ease, and the Bank of England more slowly, rather embarrassedly and somewhat painfully, had extricated themselves from most of their rather complex involvements. But the fragile base of the new expansion, combined with its extremely good long-term prospects, made new investment imperative and also drew the Bank of England back in again, for political and strategic reasons, on a larger scale than before, at the very time when it was contemplating the completion of its withdrawal from steel.

All the old questions of criteria for investment and loans and relationships with competing enterprises reemerged in an even more acute form. But with the emergence of the British Iron and Steel Federation (BISF) as a government-backed industry-wide organization, the possibility of a new political strategy for the Bank also emerged: it could take up a position behind the national interest as embodied by the British Iron and Steel Federation, and this was the course it pursued. It was not unproblematic, however, because, as we shall see in a later chapter, the BISF was in itself a reflection of the internal conflicts and compromises within the industry and by no means an impartial regulating mechanism.

Competitors, Bankers, and the National Interest: Richard Thomas & Co., 1937–1940

This second wave of banking intervention was precipitated by the acute financial crisis of Richard Thomas & Co. in the short sharp slump of 1938. As we have already seen,[1] Richard Thomas's Ebbw Vale scheme, despite its long-term prospects, was inaugurated on a rather fragile demand base and in the face of great hostility from competitors. Nevertheless, in January 1937 Rothschilds had, after some initial difficulties, issued £7 million stock to finance the slabbing, hot and cold strip, and cross mills at Ebbw Vale and the new coke ovens at Redbourn, and it was then anticipated that a further issue of £2.5 million would be sufficient to complete the project.[2]

But within a year rising costs had undermined the earlier estimates, and it was clear that in fact a further £5–6 million would be needed to complete the scheme.[3] This cost inflation was accompanied by a sharp although short-lived fall in tinplate prices and a decline in motor car production in the slump of 1938.[4] Firth was also critical of the original estimates: H. A. Brassert & Co., he felt, was the greatest offender in not making adequate investigations beforehand of the cost of site preparation.[5] As a result Richard Thomas was consuming much of its working capital in carrying high stocks at the same time that the cost of the project was rising. By April 1938 the financial resources of the company were nearing exhaustion.

In February 1938 Firth had approached Lloyds Bank for some cash. He then estimated the need at £4 million, but an investigation for Lloyds by Binder showed that at least £7 million was needed.[6] Moreover, £1½–2 million of this was needed at once to pay bills and wages before July to avoid an immediate receivership. Lloyds would provide no more than £1 million on the available security, and Firth, left £500,000 short, felt he had been "left in the lurch."[7] Firth contacted Sir Andrew Duncan, the chairman of BISF, who unsuccessfully made representations to George Abell, Lloyds' general manager, and then approached Norman. With the Ebbw Vale scheme facing disaster, Norman agreed to lend £400,000 to Lloyds Bank for reloan to Richard Thomas.[8] At the same time, Lloyds asked Rothschild, the issuing house handling the project, to investigate a longer term solution, and the latter called in John E. James from Lancashire Steel as its technical expert.[9]

The Bank demanded no security for its loan to Lloyds, but it was aware that Lloyds "won't let us lose it if they can help it." In the long run Norman noted, "somehow we mean to save Thomas at all costs. So during James' examination we had better not worsen Thomas' credit by poking about for a charge."[10] This loan staved off the immediate crisis, but the Bank then faced the more complex question of putting the Ebbw Vale scheme on a sound footing.

A further £6 million was the minimum needed. A public issue

would not succeed, partly because of Richard Thomas's weak position and partly because rival companies had seized the opportunity to run a public campaign against the future prospects of Ebbw Vale.[11] A syndicate of banks and insurance companies to take up a new prior lien debenture issue was the preferred option, but nearly all the important insurance companies already held substantial lines of the existing debentures and would hardly be receptive to the idea of taking up shares in a further syndicate. The Prudential Assurance company, the trustees of the existing debenture stock, refused to involve itself in the creation of prior stock.[12] Norman, however, put a great deal of pressure on Ernest Lever, the Joint Secretary of the Prudential, and the latter agreed to allow the issue of prior stocks and in turn managed to persuade the other insurance companies, who wanted to enlist government assistance, not to do so.[13]

In establishing this new consortium, Norman wanted effective control. It could be either indirect as in the Lancashire Cotton Corporation or direct as in the Lancashire Steel Corporation; it "need not require absolute ascendancy in money," but it must be real control. Control was "really implicit in the Bank's policy of industrial rescue." Hitherto, "it had always been transitory in intention but permanent in the event except in Beardmore's." But, "since the Bank cannot escape responsibility for the future of any concern into which they go not for investment but on grounds of policy, they may as well have the best measure of control as they can get."[14]

In whose interests was the Bank to exert this control? It was insistent that "the Bank have no interest in Richard Thomas, nor in Baldwin's or Lysaght's, except as means to an end." That end was the development of the iron and steel industry in the national interest. The conclusion it drew was that aid had to be provided along the lines laid down by the BISF.[15]

The BISF was not, however, a unitary body but a congerie of interests that maintained its unity only by not intervening in the affairs of any particular concern but by concentrating on broad demands that were shared by all steelmakers. An attempt to focus on a particular firm was bound to create internal conflicts.

These conflicts rapidly emerged as the Bank sought to implement control. The Bank and the insurance consortium decided to establish a control committee with powers to appoint or remove directors; this was initially to be made up of Norman, Firth, Greenwood of Dorman Long representing the BISF, and Lever of the Prudential as nominee of the trustees for the existing debenture holders.[16] The actual running of the firm was to remain in the hands of a reconstructed board.

Duncan, who had moved on from the SMT to become chairman of the BISF, suggested on behalf of the BISF that Samuel R. Beale of GKN/Lysaght and Sir Charles Wright of Baldwin's should be put on the board; his aim was to strengthen the control of the BISF over the new project.[17] Although both Norman and Firth agreed with this proposal at this stage, they saw it in quite a different light from Duncan—as a first stage in cooperation between the principal sheet and tinplate concerns with a view to later association or amalgamation.[18] Their aim was a tripartite Richard Thomas/Baldwin's/Lysaght merger—possibly drawing Metal Box into a wider scheme—which could provide the cash the scheme now lacked and prepare the ground for a later strip development at one of Guest Keen Baldwin's coastal locations.[19] Beale and Wright, however, from the beginning saw the position in a third light: as a position from which to control a competitor.

Wright expressed this position clearly in an interview with Basil G. Catterns, the deputy governor, on 29 June 1938. He argued that the principal function of the new money put into the company, which he would represent on the board, was to "prevent Ebbw Vale being sold as a separate unit to some outside people at a cheap price, who might then work it in competition and outside BISF." He "could see no future for a considerable time for the company": Ebbw Vale was a liability and any work found for Ebbw Vale would merely serve to shift distress from Ebbw to Pontardulais and Llanelly. Beale in turn stressed that he and Wright were competitors of Richard Thomas and that "though they were perfectly willing to do everything they could to help in any way, they could not do anything which would be harmful to their own concerns." They were in no doubt about their position: "From this it will be seen that the matter was made perfectly clear to the Deputy Governor on these matters."[20]

Remarkably, despite this statement to Catterns, no one in the Bank paid serious attention to it.[21] Skinner recognized that they were competitors and that there might well be "arrières pensées" about it, but as far as he was concerned, "We are trying an experiment," and he hoped that despite appearances goodwill would breed real cooperation and perhaps even a prompt offer of reciprocal directorships as a token of sincerity about cooperation.[22]

These hopes were rapidly disappointed with the emergence of factions on the board. The Bank's position came under strain: "We are probably not too popular for having come to the rescue," Skinner told Norman. "Wright probably thinks that we are supporting Firth— that is how their minds work."[23] Norman was left trying to conciliate the parties. In particular, he hoped that James could be a force to draw the sides together.[24]

Firth rapidly came to feel that the presence of Beale and Wright on the board was neither conducive to the health of Richard Thomas nor a step toward cooperation in the tinplate industry. As he later put it, "in very dirty weather, some pirates pushed us on the rocks and boarded us disguised as 'National Interests' men."[25] Behind the disguises they were, however, competitors not colleagues and as such "on no ground can it be justified . . . It creates an atmosphere of resentment, suspicion and fear throughout the whole of the organisation." Once Beale and Wright had decided that amalgamation was "unacceptable to them, they . . . have no earthly right to a seat on our Board and should at once retire."[26]

In the summer of 1939 the question of managerial reorganization led to a decisive rupture. Firth wanted discussion of amalgamation to precede any consideration of management changes within Richard Thomas. Wright told him flatly that Baldwin's had no interest in amalgamation, and Beale complained that he was not getting sufficient information about Richard Thomas. Firth was furious that admitted competitors should be "telling me what the internal arrangement of our business should be."[27] In May he demanded their resignation, and Norman advised them to go.[28]

Beale and Wright had been using their position to ditch Richard Thomas. They had orchestrated a considerable propaganda campaign against the firm in the national and trade press and in the City.[29] Beale's firm, John Lysaght & Co., had been engaged in building a new sheet mill in Australia which would compete with Ebbw Vale at the same time as he had been criticizing the Ebbw expansion on grounds of overcapacity.[30] Moreover, they had not been above defending the markets of their own firms by sabotaging the quality of Richard Thomas's products. Beale and Wright feared that the lowest grades of steel strip made at Ebbw would be as good as their highest grades and would thus deny them the premium prices that they used to obtain for their "quality." The Metal Box Ltd., the largest single tinplate customer in Britain, found Ebbw ordinary sheets to be of better quality than those that went through an additional normalizing process at Baldwin's and Lysaght. These sorts of qualities were high-profit products with an average profit of £8 per ton being made by the established concerns on high-quality autobody sheets at this time.[31] To defend this interest, Beale, Wright, and Geoffrey Summers of John Summers & Sons, the leading sheet steel manufacturer, urged Richard Thomas to "spoil the surface of our sheets by deliberately letting air into our annealing furnaces and so causing a blue edge to form on our sheets and a scale to form on our surfaces."[32] Firth indignantly refused; it was an "outrageous" method of cooperation, and because the workers would be aware of what was happening, it could be used to discredit both the firm and capitalism.[33]

Over and beyond all this came intense personal antagonisms. Firth was an autocratic personality, and although the clashes with Beale and Wright were largely about policy, the continuation of vicious boardroom infighting after their departure suggests that personality was important too. J. Adamson, the accountant put in by the Bank, wanted to revamp the financial side of the firm.[34] Firth reacted violently against this outsider's ideas: he did not want any advice from this "vexatious small-brained accountant," this "conceited thick-skinned little man" whose "arrogant pomposity" was a "menace to the organisation."[35] While Beale and Wright had been on the board, Firth had insisted on his right to arrange management as he thought fit. Beale and Wright had wanted the firm to be run by departmental managers operating autonomously and reporting to the board, but Firth counterposed the need to integrate the firm. "If this policy were changed and the business now run departmentally, we should have a Grovesend man wanting to make a good showing vis-à-vis a Gilbertsons man and there would be a dog-fight between the one time competing businesses."[36] This was probably fair enough; old legacies had to be eliminated through centralization before effective coordinated decentralization could be pursued, but the theme of autocracy and conservatism ran parallel to this. In numerous squabbles about personnel, Firth always opposed proposals from James that Ebbw Vale needed American management and insisted on having local men from within the firm with xenophobic passion.[37] At the same time he guarded his own right to make overriding snap decisions and pursue his own policies,[38] and he showed considerable reluctance to let information on the firm out of his own hands.[39]

In this situation the Bank's aim was primarily one of conciliation. They hoped to use James, whose background in the wire trade made him more conspicuously neutral than the other outside directors, as a cat's paw within Richard Thomas to relegate Firth to a more limited role. His knowledge of the works and technical side, unlike that of Beale and Wright, matched Firth's, but he too was constantly balked by Firth's methods. When Firth had to go on a trip to the United States, in effect James complained, "he locked all the doors before he went and threw his keys in the river, so what can he expect? I am about the only friend he has, and he won't have me very much longer at this rate.''[40] In some ways he did manage to counterbalance Firth, and in August 1939 he became managing director, in effect pushing Firth upstairs to chairman, but further developments along these lines were frustrated by James's illness in autumn 1939.[41]

The strength of Firth's position derived from the fact that he had a much clearer idea of what he was doing than anyone else plus the immense loyalty he commanded among the Richard Thomas staff and the detailed works knowledge that enabled him to intervene at all levels of decision making, right down to the shop floor. In one four-day, almost nonstop stay at the works in March 1939, he checked out all aspects of production: he stopped workers from smoking in the plant; he ordered badges to be made for every worker so that all could be identifed and checks made to see that they were in the right place; he allowed the blast furnace manager to change the burden despite James's instructions; he ordered the conversion of an acid furnace at Gilbertson's and the reopening of another at Duffryn; and he decided on a shift to paying workers on tonnage rates.[42] Such activity indicates a management somewhere between a firm overall grasp of detail and something rather obsessional. In fact, as time passed, Firth's style became increasingly paranoid. As Skinner wrote to Norman in May 1939, ''I cannot believe he was always as he is now, unless Ebbw Vale is the product of a Frankenstein.''[43]

In the summer of 1939 the Bank tried to resolve the situation by the removal of Beale and Wright and the installation of more ''responsible'' outside directors, namely the Earl of Dudley (the owner of Round Oak steelworks), Sir James Lithgow, and MacDiarmid of Stewarts & Lloyds. Firth was initially delighted at seeing the backs of ''the men who have traduced me.''[44] But his desire to keep the reins firmly in his own hands soon led to new antagonisms, mainly directed at G. H. Latham from Whitehead Iron & Steel Co., who had been appointed to replace the sick James as managing director in December 1939 at Firth's own suggestion.[45] Firth's account of these developments was that the original ''Pirates'' were replaced by four others. The ''original one who remained (James) turned out to be treacherous,'' while Latham, ''swollen with his sudden importance as the leader of the gang was arrogant, greedy and stupid . . . The pirates with envy observed that it was a grand ship and sailing well despite their interference . . . so they asked me to hand the ship over to them . . . I refused, whereupon they threw me overboard.''[46]

By Spring 1940 Firth's antagonism to Latham was paralyzing the firm, and Lithgow, James, MacDiarmid, and Dudley threatened to resign unless Firth was removed.[47] Firth refused to go and alleged that Latham was using his position with Richard Thomas to divert orders to Whitehead & Co.[48] Norman finally settled the matter by utilizing the Bank's control to dismiss Firth in April 1940.[49]

Behind the complicated boardroom events lay a distinct evolution in the Bank's modus operandi in the steel industry. Norman and Skinner had recognized that their earlier efforts to reorganize firms by putting in their own agents as managers had a rather dismal record. Here therefore they sought to use the BISF as a representative of some notional national interest, only to find that the interests of diverse firms permeated and were reproduced by that organization as much as being resolved by it. The board reorganization of 1940 recognized this by selecting particular interests from within the BISF who would share with the Bank the common aim of making Ebbw Vale viable and who were not directly in competition with it. Unlike previous occasions, the Bank consciously rejected the option of devising its own rationalization plan and seeking to implement it.

The size of the Ebbw Vale project in relation to the rest of the tinplate industry meant that the future of that project inevitably had immense repercussions on the trade as a whole. Control of Richard Thomas meant control of the most powerful firm in an oligopolistic industry and posed the question of how to respond to the reactions of competitors.

Briton Ferry Steel Co. Ltd., one of the largest of the other tinplate firms (see Table 13), had announced early on that if Richard Thomas were to proceed at Redbourn, it too would convert its Albion works to strip production. The proposal was almost naive—its existing plant was much too poor to just tack on a strip mill, and the market was not large enough to support it.[50] But, as much as anything, Briton Ferry was trying to stake out its right to new construction: if Richard Thomas were to get preferential treatment in the form of Bank support, why not Briton Ferry?

This response was embarrassing to the BISF, and it was not structured to dispute its logic. The BISF did not like the idea and feared the creation of overcapacity, but it felt it had no right to block it.[51] Instead it resorted to dragging its feet, and Briton Ferry finally agreed to delay its scheme pending a general review of the South Wales steel and tinplate industry.[52] Meanwhile, five of the smaller Llanelly tinplate companies merged in 1938 with a view to taking action in response to the Ebbw Vale development.[53] In the end the war deferred the response of competing firms to the strip mill, but it was clear that in effect the rules of the game had been changed by the new plant and that the situation would not remain static. The prospect was that Richard Thomas would have an overwhelmingly dominant position in high-grade tinplate at the end of the war. As a result, the Bank feared in the period 1939–1941 that it would be held to be responsible in large part for this state of affairs and be subject to criticism as a result.[54] Norman was worried that the Bank might be pressured to help out in the situation of redundancy and quasi-monopoly that would result from a scheme it had backed.[55]

Some of the Bank's industrial advisers, especially James, saw the situation as an opportunity for the Bank to take the initiative in utilizing the new technical innovations to reorganize the entire sheet and tinplate sectors. "Such an opportunity is not likely to recur," he argued. He proposed a scheme to form a separate company to operate independently of Richard Thomas and to form a new Welsh Tinplate Corporation Ltd. to provide cold reduction plant and run a new hot strip mill as part of the wholesale rationalization of the rest of the trade.[56]

Norman and Skinner, however, shied away from such responsibilities. But although, as Norman later recalled, they were resolutely "unwilling to proceed as John E. James would like,"[57] at the same time they recognized that without some comprehensive scheme they would shortly face separate requests for money for a redundancy plan, a new plant for Briton Ferry, and a new mill for GKB. "In our own interests as well as those of the industry, we ought to stop giving piecemeal assistance." To get them out of this situation, their need was clear: as Skinner put it: "Could not the Bank take up a safe tactical position behind the BISF?"[58]

In 1939 this was a weak position. Duncan still felt tied by the tinplate association, which was dominated by the small plants and which was resisting any broad ideas for scrapping or reequipment. But in the next few years the situation changed considerably. First, the Bank consciously drew the BISF more and more into direct involvement in the management and running of Richard Thomas and Ebbw Vale. Second, under the impact of the war and in symbiosis with the government through the Ministry of Supply, the BISF began to develop a more conscious and deliberate control over development.

The Bank positioned itself firmly behind BISF, refused to take any further initiative, and left the task of taking action to others. In Norman's words, "if the BISF thus warned, chose to do nothing it might be a pity, but the Bank would have protected themselves as far as lay in their powers."[59] The wartime developments enabled the Bank to move steadily out of the limelight.[60]

The Bank's involvement had served its immediate purposes: Richard Thomas had been saved from collapse, and the government had been spared a politically costly crisis in South Wales. Moreover, Lloyds

Bank, Rothschild's, and the Prudential had been saved from the odium that would have attached to them if they had allowed one of the largest employers in a Depressed Area to collapse in the course of expansion for want of extra finance. But in terms of wider industrial policy, it remained an unsatisfactory experience. The Bank seems to have learned little from its previous experiences. The SMT remained very naive about the likelihood of goodwill from rival industrialists toward their competitors and failed to grasp the essential truth that industrialists looked first to their own firms' practical interests when confronted with broad reorganizing schemes—that the "wider view" came a very poor second. The Bank was still looking for solutions that would enable it to stay outside and above the industry, and its attitude to reorganization remained strongly in the mold of the late 1920s rationalization milieu. There was a notable lack of policy evolution, for instance, in the direction of nonmerger solutions; in this instance the Bank might have grasped the nettle of technical change by using the opportunity to back the most efficient single producers against the rest as the nucleus of reorganization. By the late 1930s the Bank had recoiled from the earlier strategy of taking the Brassert/ Bruce Gardner blueprint and sticking with it through thick and thin. Now it positively refused to put forward *any* blueprint. Instead of taking strategic control, the Bank merely devolved the responsibility for planning onto the BISF, whose inadequacy for the task was all too apparent.

Reorganization in the Sheet Steel Industry, 1938–1941

The Bank's last prewar involvement in steel came in the sheet trade. As in the Richard Thomas case, it was the financial problems associated with a major technical change that led to Bank intervention.

In an earlier chapter we saw how, as a result of contrasting market environments, the strip mill came to be pioneered in tinplate in Britain whereas in the United States it had emerged first in sheet. The impetus to technological change in sheet was less in Britain, but it still existed. John Summers & Sons, the largest British sheetmakers in the interwar years (see Table 16), had shifted from its specialization in corrugated sheet production in the 1920s to the production mainly of high-grade sheets by traditional methods at Shotton in the 1930s. During the 1930s the quality of American strip mill products was increasingly setting the pace, and the emergence of strip production in Britain at Ebbw Vale, even though not primarily directed toward sheet production, emphasized that in the long run Summers would have to produce strip mill quality to maintain its business.[61]

In the late 1930s Summers's profits were still fairly high, but like Stewarts & Lloyds in tubes ten years earlier, the company was facing a sharp prospective decline unless it acted. Its project to install a strip mill was, therefore, not a venture into a new market but a modernization scheme in order to supply an improved product to existing customers. Summers told Duncan and the BISF: "Any question of there not being room for two strip mills in the country could be ruled out, as we were planning to scrap much of our existing capacity." The new mills would produce 1.2 to 1.4 million tons per annum whereas the current total output was 2.2 million tons. BISF approval was given on this basis.[62]

But the necessary size of the new investment was large in relation to the size of the firm and its market. This created two problems, the provision of finance and the securing of an adequate high-quality steel supply for the new production. As far as finance was concerned, retained profits were inadequate for the size of investment required, and the City balked at the risks involved in the project. The cost of the scheme had been established as between £3.2 million and £4 million in an investigation in early 1938, and Summers initially hoped to raise this sum by £2 million debentures to be placed for them by Wagg's and overdraft facilities of £1.5 million from the District Bank. Despite the general keeness of banks to lend to industry in the late 1930s, the district felt that in the current uncertain conditions it could loan the amount required only if its security was to rank ahead of the debentures,[63] which would make it very hard to sell the debentures. As a result, as E. H. D. Skinner, Norman's private secretary, noted, the finance of the scheme was jeopardized "primarily through the inability of the company's bankers to take a further risk." It was not commercial doubts about the scheme that stalled District. Rather, it was "a question of magnitude and on this they (District) would seem to be correct; in fact the bankers have acted most reasonably."[64]

There was, however, an alternative avenue for raising the necessary cash—and one that would also secure at the same time a supply of steel—namely, an agreement with the expanding United Steel Co. United Steel was, indeed, ready to put up the necessary £2 million debentures, but in return it demanded 49% of Summers's equity free of charge. Summers rejected this; such harsh terms were incompatible with the Company's general solvency and with a scheme designed for expansion not for rescue. Despite this United Steel would not go below an unacceptable 25% of Summers's equity.[65] The question of equity ownership was very dear to the Summers family. In 1938 they still owned 100%, and only the younger Summers in the family was prepared to see any change in this state of affairs.[66]

The BID, chastened by what was going on at Richard Thomas, was wary of involvement in the Summers problem. Summers had in common with Richard Thomas the problem of the high initial fixed costs involved in entry into strip production, and, as Skinner had noted, both "have miscalculated their needs and both have left to chance the provision of the money."[67] Both, too, had "put themselves on the wrong foot" by planning their new mills first and asking for the money later.[68] But there were important contrasts. The Richard Thomas scheme involved £13 million and also, as far as the Bank was concerned, was a project to rationalize the whole tinplate industry as well. The Summers scheme involved only £4 million, and since Summers produced only 16% of sheets under 3 mm and 14% of galvanized sheets, its expansion was in no way pivotal to rationalization.[69] The Richard Thomas scheme also had important political ramifications concerning Ebbw Vale that Summers lacked. Finally, "in the Richard Thomas case no alternative money was available. John Summers can find the money but do not like the terms, and it is no part of our business to protect the necessitous from the strong."[70]

Involving the BID in Summers would make the Bank "shareholders in rival concerns without any prospect of those concerns ever amalgamating. An extension of this position might be extremely embarrassing."[71] These "fundamental questions . . . must always arise when financial assistance other than governmental, is sought by industry outside the normal channels."[72] Involvement would mean that the Bank would have to demand control in the Summers case "since we have demanded it in the Richard Thomas case. But there would probably be grave objections to the control of a company in the United Steel group." The preferred strategy was therefore to "keep any help we may give on a banking basis."[73]

The main pressure to change this position came from Duncan and the BISF. On 7 September Duncan saw Norman and the deputy governor and urged, on the analogy of the Corby project, that it would be proper for the BID to aid an individual firm. "He was convinced in his own mind that the John Summers scheme was a right one having regard to the future development of the industry, and, while he agreed that the occasion might be used to further regionalisation on the lines the Governor advocated, he thought the full step (i.e. amalgamation of Summers and United Steel) might not be possible and might even be dangerous and, if necessary, he would advocate helping Summers alone."[74] Coming from Duncan with his close acquaintance with the policy dilemmas and workings of the Bank, this was a powerful pressure; but Skinner had foreseen this and urged resisting it.[75]

Norman, however, was less cautious than his adviser and did not feel inclined to stand wholly aside. He wanted to take up the scheme and transform it into a real rationalizing one. To achieve this grander end, however, a Summers/United Steel merger would not be enough. Norman wanted to bring in Lancashire Steel too, and also, at first, Stewarts & Lloyds, although he withdrew the latter idea when Duncan objected strongly and insisted on continuing BISF policy of strictly segregating Stewarts & Lloyds into tubes.[76]

Discussion inside the Bank, therefore, included consideration of aid to an individual firm, an amalgamation, and a broad general movement of rationalization. But it was impossible to proceed step by step from one to another in sequence. Rationalization had different requirements from the other measures. For instance, a Lancashire Steel/Summers linkup was felt by Skinner to be a better starting point for a broad scheme than Summers/United Steel. It was regionally more correct, it would make James's technical expertise available to the new strip project, and it should be relatively easy to float it publicly in the near future.[77] Both Duncan and Skinner thought it very important to enlist the services of James for the Summers strip mill, but this was blocked by his Richard Thomas connections. The lack of available technical experts to manage similar schemes was such that, at a later stage, the Bank considered asking James to withdraw from both his Richard Thomas and his Lancashire Steel posts and accept employment directly from the Bank as a troubleshooter.[78]

Skinner's formulation of the problem was confused. Summers needed a steel supply, and the prospects of surplus ingots from either Partington or Corby were not good. The Summers/Lancashire Steel combine would still probably have to negotiate a buying agreement for steel from United Steel. There were, however, other more complex reasons behind Skinner's idea. One of his long-term aims was to shift the burden of financing Summers away from the Bank and into normal channels. By this he envisaged primarily overdraft financing from the clearing banks. From this perspective, one advantage of a combination with Lancashire Steel would be that it would bring in another bank to share the strain at Summers with the District, which although it had "acted most reasonably" was unable to involve itself any farther. This would reduce the likelihood that further aid from the Bank of England would be necessary. But even from this point of view Skinner's argument was flawed. Lancashire Steel's principal banker was Westminster (see Table 17) which was also banker to United Steel, and it was unlikely that it would wish to straddle such complex schemes. Such difficulties made Skinner aware that the Bank "would have to act alone for the time being" in financing any scheme.[79]

Norman and Duncan, too, were attracted by the idea of a Summers/ Lancashire Steel proposal. They wanted to secure cooperation among firms on the Richard Thomas model by cross-representation on the boards.[80] At a later stage United Steel would, they hoped, also be involved, through a similar arrangement. Geoffrey Summers and N. H. Rollason of Summers were prepared to accept almost any proposal from the Bank and would even, they said, welcome bank control, but they jibbed at the Lancashire Steel proposal. Partly this was because of the personnel involved: They did not want James on their board because of his Richard Thomas links, and they did not like Peter Ryland. But provided that Henry Summers could keep the chairmanship, they would be prepared to take Lancashire's Lord Crawford onto their board.[81] In terms of personal compatibility, Bruce Gardner thought that a Summers/United Steel scheme might be easier. Geoffrey Summers, since his Cambridge days, had been a close friend of Robert Hilton, the managing director of United Steel.[82]

In broader terms, whereas the Bank started from the point of view that it wanted to develop cooperation and rationalization, Summers's only real interest was in financing its own development. If it was interested in amalgamations per se, it would look for them among other sheetmakers.[83] Bruce Gardner had earlier made approaches on these lines to try to bring together Summers and Lysaght to build a joint strip mill,[84] but nothing had come of it. Summers was not really interested in this sort of rationalization, and Bruce Gardner's later argument that Summers was aiming at rationalizing "the South Lancashire Midlands and North Wales sheet trade: rationalisation by process so to speak," was stretching a point.[85]

The Bank's notion of rationalization became more and more of a pragmatic compromise. Its overall plan of reorganization and the development of optimum strip plant for sheet was subordinated to the practical effort of arbitrating between a choice of tactical amalgamations. Brassert had recommended, and Norman and the BID agreed in principle, that the best arrangement would be a Summers linkup with Stewarts & Lloyds so that the strip mill would be built at Corby. James also strongly favored this idea.[86] But as we have already seen, the strict demarcation of Corby to tubes was almost a fundamental tenet of BISF policy, and this option had to be ruled out.

In the absence of a decisive strategy of its own, the Bank could only act as a pressure group in connection with possible amalgamations. But in either a Summers/United Steel or a Summers/Lancashire Steel merger, the actual physical benefits would be comparatively slight. The Summers/United Steel merger was attractive to United Steel: it would enable the company to break into the sheet trade for the first time without having to construct plants or build up an organization and expertise of its own. United Steel wanted to share in the development potential of strip mills, but it did not want to have to find outlets for the entire output of one. It wanted complete control so that in the long run it could move the strip plant or develop new strip plant at its existing locations, probably at Appleby-Frodingham, and then close Shotton.[87] Hence, its emphasis was on digesting Summers. Summers was correspondingly unenthusiastic about a merger that would lead first to the dismembering of the existing firm by the closure of its Shelton works in favor of a steel supply from United Steel and later to the probable dismantling of the historic core of its enterprise at Shotton.[88] It still felt that it had a viable future as an independent operator if the company could survive this crisis of expansion.

The Lancashire Steel/Summers merger had a similar problem in that Partington considerably overlapped the current role of Summers's Shelton works,[89] but in broader terms, although regionally compact, it would be a patching amalgamation rather than rationalization. It would in effect be a diversifying rather than a consolidating merger, one that would produce a wire- and sheet-producing firm with no more than 25% of the British output of either product, and crucially, it would lack the high-quality steel production that both products needed.

From the start, one of the overriding considerations in the Bank's involvement was the need to give full political support to the BISF. It had come in largely because it was faced with the potential collapse of a project supported by the BISF, and its policy was to back the BISF to the hilt. The Bank accepted the BISF argument that in the current situation it was not so much the scheme itself that was at fault as the rigidities in financial provision through the clearing banks.[90]

As a result, the possibility of a special one-off intervention in this case began to be canvassed. After all, as Skinner observed, its analysis of the project revealed that "any commitment ought to be capable of unfreezing once things improve." If the Bank was going to follow this line it should do so sooner than later. "If we feel confident that the company's resources will not see them over the negotiations, ought we not to intervene at once?" either directly or by guaranteeing the District Bank.[91]

Pam of J. Schröder & Co., the issuing house that would be placing any issue involved in the Summers scheme, followed up this line of thought by preparing a scheme that would provide the conditions to make it possible for the bankers to advance the necessary £2 million. Because the bankers would not buy ordinary debentures, he proposed to tie up a loan so that Summers would be required to make repayments monthly at a rate of £1 per ton of output, basing his proposal on the assumption that the new mill would result in savings of £2–3 per ton on current costs. Thus, he argued, the banks would regard the loan as an advance on a commercial security which would be repaid within eight to ten years and thus avoid the objection to an ordinary long-term debenture.[92] Summers and Rollason found the proposal attractive,[93] but this was probably because they saw in it a way of keeping out of United Steel's hands.

For the BID "the ideal arrangement would have been the provision of new money by United Steel (and possibly Lancashire Steel) against ordinary shares in Summers, with a limited amount of borrowing in debentures" which could have been financed by the banks. But United Steel, which enjoyed a powerful cash position, was in a position to make conditions. It insisted on its capital being treated as a loan enjoying priority over existing preference shares; thus, if things went badly, it would get the strip mill cheap, whereas if things went well, it could exercise its conversion rights to obtain, hopefully, up to half the equity.[94]

United Steel's maneuvers were based on an analysis which showed that Summers's position was deteriorating and that, as a result United Steel might get a chance to take Summers over for very little. Summers was "a complete financial mess,"[95] according to a United Steel investigation of October 1938. The "poor and confusing accounting practices" of Summers had gravely understated depreciation, and when allowances were made for this, real returns on capital in 1935 and 1937 were shown to be 5% and 8½% respectively, considerably lower than Summers's own estimates and comparing badly with United Steel's 14% and Lancashire Steel's 11% in 1937.[96]

Henry Clay's conclusions from this evidence were sharp: "(1) John Summers ought to have seen the red light as soon as they made up their accounts. Perhaps they did; in which case they—and their advisers—have been very dilatory. (2) the group is short of working capital and should have been pulled up by their bankers long ago when the going was good. (3) The group as a whole has outgrown the capacity of the higher management."[97]

These underlying weaknesses heightened the significance of the uncertain trade prospects. The short-term outlook was poor, unless there was war. If £2 million were raised in debentures and £500,000 of existing plant scrapped, heavy amortization would produce heavy pressure on profits in the near future.[98] Yet the analysis made by Andrew Macharg, who replaced Adamson as Summers's accountant when the latter moved to Richard Thomas, showed that Summers's profits in the next few years were unlikely to exceed £330,000 after tax and depreciation. Because in the first five years, £300,000 would be needed to meet prior charges each year, this would not be sufficient inducement to attract the necessary ordinary capital.[99] Large-scale investment in Summers would be a gamble between the short-term risks and what were generally agreed to be good long-term prospects.[100] Macharg reckoned that profits of £2 per ton could be earned at 60% capacity, and that anything above 40% capacity would cover costs.[101] Nearer full capacity at 300,000 tons per year, the company could make £3 per ton, and at this rate the investment would pay for itself within five years. But this was unlikely to happen. The issue boiled down to assessing Summers's long-term prospects of cheapening its products and enlarging its markets.[102]

On these prospects United Steel, naturally enough, took a pessimistic and "bearish" attitude.[103] Spens, United Steel's financial adviser, pointed out that the adaptation of existing plants to the cold reduction process was undercutting the technological lead of the strip mills. United Steel "doubted the economies of the new process" and would therefore invest only if its capital stood at the head in terms of security.[104] Skinner and the BID recognized that although this view was exaggerated it contained a kernel of truth: "John Summers are going to double their capitalisation to do the same process, but they hope on a bigger scale and cheaper. They may be successful—I hope they will—but there is not going to be much available for the old capital unless they can do appreciably better than over the last eleven years."[105]

Everything turned on the estimates of savings and demand. James had doubts about whether an adequate level of sales could be achieved to make full economies of scale possible, because he believed that motor car demand was now reaching saturation point. In this perspective it was essential to keep fixed and prior charges to a minimum and make the equity component of the new capital as large as possible.[106] Yet it was precisely this type of capital structure that United Steel would not accept, and the Bank had no hold over United Steel in this situation. United Steel knew it, and Skinner and James had to recognize that they were dealing with "greedy people" in a strong situation.[107]

In the end, the need to back the BISF outweighed the Bank's reluctance to take the big risk: "It must be run, but in the present state of trade and investment the risk must fall on us and/or someone else in the industry who has the cash. If on us, let us not put the company in a form that will cripple it."[108] James still wanted to see a Summers/Lancashire Steel/United Steel arrangement,[109] but without control of

United Steel there was no prospect of that, and the Bank had no intention of involving itself in United Steel.[110]

The Bank wanted the reality of control without its appearance; in practice it was to get exactly the opposite. In October 1938, Peacock put forward a proposal for a capital structure that would relegate the family holdings behind a class of preferred ordinary shares and £2 million debentures. United Steel would invest in the preferred shares and the BID would take up the rest required to provide new capital. Control would be vested in the Bank until United Steel decided whether it wished to exercise an option to acquire complete or part control.[111] This policy aimed to commit United Steel to amalgamation by "holding the balance" between the parties.[112] Skinner, however, feared that this scheme would give the Bank little control.[113] James and Catterns, the deputy governor, shared these doubts. In particular, they felt that when, in due course, Sir Andrew Duncan with his close sympathy with the Bank's policy, no longer controlled the BISF, United Steel might well be hard to keep in line. Looking ahead, James feared the implications of this for the Ebbw Vale project too, because the latter "could not hold their own against an uncontrolled United Steel." To prevent such a development he wanted to establish BISF control committees to keep hold of and sustain both Richard Thomas and Summers. But, Skinner noted, "in saying this he probably does not realise the difficulty in the position from the public point of view. His fears are trade fears and the fact that the banks have put £X [sic] million into Richard Thomas on his recommendation."[114] Ultimately, real control was not possible unless the Bank went deep into the steel industry and confronted United Steel.

Norman told United Steel that he wanted the Bank to have the same control over Shotton as it had over Ebbw Vale. On paper his demands were substantial: Bank control of Summers for seven years "so that he [Norman] had the last word in the case of difficulties between Summers and Richard Thomas." Summers would have to come to an agreement with the BISF similar to that which Richard Thomas had made; in order to secure this "he would if necessary (though he hoped it would not be necessary) put up the whole of the £2m. required."[115]

In practice, United Steel realized that this put them in the driving seat, and it accepted without a murmur, having received the assurance that "bank control" meant "ultimate financial control not technical control."[116] The question of Summers versus Richard Thomas was, United Steel realized, a "red rag," a nonissue. Bank control was a convenient way for the Bank to reserve its commitment and leave Norman to "hold the ring." In this situation, as Skinner noted,

Walter Benton Jones of United Steel could afford to be no longer a wobbler."[117]

In effect, as it was soon to realize, the BID had "given United Steel the opportunity of having a look at the proposition before deciding whether to go further in." The United Steel investment could be easily sold if it changed its mind.[118] Summers felt that this was "pretty harsh" for them; United Steel was getting a gilt-edged deal with a good position in the capital structure, an entrée to a new trade, and no fixed commitments.[119]

Bank control meant very little. It was meaningful only if it could be used for rationalization, not just as a casting vote on a shareholders committee, which was what United Steel wanted it to be.[120] Duncan urged Skinner to make the control "real" and not let United Steel through their shareholding "boss the show." The Bank should take a definite stand against United Steel's "whittling away" control.[121]

This the Bank was not able to do. There was a limited extent to which the Bank could monitor developments, but in the long term, unless it was prepared to develop an ownership role, it had no sanctions against United Steel. All it could do was to state that the United Steel option to buy BID's Summers shares would be conditional on United Steel's carrying through a full amalgamation. This was the least the Bank could do in accordance with its general policy. "It would not be feasible for us to give preferential terms to an individual shareholder, unless in so doing we were acting in the public interest by bringing about an improved condition in the industry."[122] But without a choice of buyers, this power was very limited. The headlines might announce that Norman was a new steel dictator, but United Steel was the unseen power behind the throne.[123]

In practice "control" meant almost nothing. Summers and United Steel grew gradually closer together under the new arrangement, and in 1941 Rollason of Summers became managing director of United Steel, symbolizing these closer links. Norman was angry but impotent. The Bank had regarded Rollason as its man at Summers, but now "the Board gives away 50% of his time and just thumb their noses." Since the Bank had taken control, "this was the first occasion since they were here two years ago for protection, that any vital matter had arisen and all that happens is that he [Norman] gets a letter from the Chairman after he has read it in the newspaper." Norman felt that Summers and United Steel were "acting deliberately behind his back."[124] The episode throws an illuminating light on the sorry record of Bank control at Summers.

The outcome of the Summers story shows what a hollow shell the Bank's rationalization policy had become. By the late 1930s Norman and the BID no longer had any clear idea of what they meant by rationalization. Although it had always been somewhat abstract, by then it had become vacuous. It recurred as a theme and aspiration but it no longer had any purchase on the industrialists in charge on the ground. Lacking strategic clarity or effective institutions, the Bank was confined to acting as a pressure group. It would be wrong to suggest that it lacked any influence. Its role as a financial fire-brigade service meant that no company could leave the Bank out of its calculations, but the weaknesses of the Bank's position were often painfully clear, and United Steel exploited them skilfully in the case of Summers. The Bank tied itself in the late 1930s to building up the BISF as its institutional link with the industry. Politically it wanted to obviate direct intervention in difficult cases and to build up industrial self-government; in terms of industrial policy it was a recognition that the Bank's efforts at more direct involvement had been profoundly unsatisfactory. The Richard Thomas and Summers cases demonstrate some of the problems of this position. In the final part we shall examine some of the broader issues of the relationship of the BISF to the banks and the state.

11.

Banks and Industrial Restructuring in the Interwar Years

As we saw earlier, a much wider separation existed between the financial and industrial sectors in Britain than was the case in the United States and Europe. The economic crisis of the interwar years weakened this pattern of mutual autonomy and made many banks vitally interested in industrial decision making and restructuring in many sectors. Although this modified the prewar pattern, it did not overturn it, and the relative noninvolvement of British banking in industry meant that it enjoyed certain advantages in comparison to many European banks during the depression. What did come to the fore, however, was the potentiality of banking action as a strategic sector of capital in restructuring other parts of the economy.

In these conditions the Bank of England began to develop its political, strategic, and exceptional roles. The Bank recognized the need for planned reorganization both to prevent state intervention and in the interests of efficiency as it saw it. The appropriate path was perceived to center on enabling firms to achieve economies of scale via merger; this was invariably the core of rationalization proposals. Norman saw the Bank as a sort of neutral national interest group that could play an important intermediate technocratic role in restructuring industry by rationalization.

How valid was this as an industrial strategy? Some of the BID schemes for rationalization—for instance, in locomotives and motor manufacturing—were rather fanciful, and it is clear that the large amalgamation was Norman's panacea for all industrial ills. In cotton the schemes of the Bank seem to have been conspicuously poorly thought out, but in steel most of the SMT/BID schemes stand up fairly well to detailed examination. There can be little doubt that the Scottish scheme would have proved practicable and worthwhile in the long run if implemented, and effective consolidation on the Northeast coast had good prospects for success. The Bank's view of such reorganization schemes, however, was rather one-dimensional: it hoped that the schemes would carry the day through their own internal logic. Yet in the short term all such amalgamations were bound to be highly problematic, and it is not surprising that prudent, pragmatic steelmakers decided that the risks in the short term were too great, especially in the light of the complexities of decision making within firms that we have already noted. In such a context the banks might have stepped outside the conventional market framework to some effect: they might have offered not just guidance and a helping hand but some form of positive entrepreneurial leadership accompanied by a willingness to absorb some of the short-term risks themselves and a commitment to push forward the long-term plans that they favored. But the weight of central banking traditions was against this sort of intervention.

First, the Bank was profoundly orthodox in its economics, and for both economic and ideological reasons the Bank wanted to develop the ability of industry to stand on its own feet. It recognized that banking activity could stimulate the growth of firms, but to achieve overall economic growth the stimulus must result in genuine productivity advantages. Hence, by fostering amalgamations the Bank would make available to industry the potential advantages of scale economies, but industry itself would have to utilize this new structure. The Bank itself was not prepared to commit its own capital to a below-average rate of profit sector as the price of control in the short term in order to carry out restructuring and raise the level of profitability in the long term. This perspective resulted in a consistent gap between the Bank's enormous potential strength in industry and the actual influence it exerted.

Second, where banking involvement with industry became intricate, it required an extensive range of managerial capabilities that the Bank by and large lacked. Although Norman was able to assemble a powerful team of industrial advisers on general policy issues, he lacked the resources rigorously to reconstruct management at enterprise level; time and again bank involvement was hampered by conflict-ridden relationships between financial and managerial control within the enterprise, and the Bank got a bad press as a result of the attention that boardroom infighting attracted.

Third, the Bank of England was highly reluctant to change the nature of its relationship to the state. Large-scale industrial responsibility pointed toward political accountability, and the sheer size of broad industrial reorganization in a sector such as steel implied at the very least government consent and at most a government guarantee for the Bank's actions. It therefore cut across Norman's long-term determination to preserve the independence of the Bank as a private institution. Moreover, the political outlook of the Bank was also governed by a virulent anti-Labourism and, on Norman's part at least, opposition to government intervention in industry on principle. Hence, the Bank's involvement peaked in 1929–1931 as a way of forestalling Labour government action. Bank intervention was designed to prevent state intervention. The Bank did not accept that industrial reorganization required a central coordinating and guiding hand unless it arose from within the industry itself. One result of this was that the Bank continually got buffeted as a third party in struggles between conflicting capitalist interests. However, as we shall see in more detail in the final part, the situation began to change in the late 1930s; the beginning of a more coherent and representative employers' interest in the BISF in the political context of the National Government and the overshadowing of the Labour Party gave the Bank the possibility of putting its weight behind a unitary interest. The last few years before the war saw a very gradual beginning of a bank-industry-government rapprochement on industrial reorganization that the war and nationalization were to develop.

How did the Bank's involvement in steel affairs relate to its involvement in other industries? It is clear that the Bank was more deeply involved in steel than in any other sector; only in cotton was the Bank's involvement comparable. But there was also considerable activity in armaments, shipbuilding, and shipping, as well as more sketchy work in locomotives, film, automobiles, and small industries in Depressed Areas[1]—and this is probably not an exclusive list. Although a more detailed analysis of the Bank's overall role must await further research, some comparative points of interest can be made.

The Bank was instrumental in the formation of the Lancashire Cotton Corporation in 1928 largely, as has already been noted, to prop up the ailing Lancashire banking sector. In several respects the Bank seemed even less equipped and less able to cope with the problems of cotton than those of steel.[2] Henry Clay at the SMT was an expert on the global problems facing the cotton industry,[3] but there was no equivalent of the consulting engineers Brassert & Co. in cotton to conduct in-depth investigation and technical reorganization of existing units, and the LCC was notably weak on the technical side, at least until the appointment of Frank Platt in 1932.[4]

In addition, the problems of industry structure and management in cotton seem to have strained the Bank's capabilities. The cotton industry was characterized by highly fragmented ownership and highly

vertically specialized management. The LCC was a merger of forty
cotton firms, and it was therefore both an extremely large combine
in proportion to the preexisting managerial units and a very heterogeneous one. As Leslie Hannah has argued, these features are the
ones most likely to produce managerial diseconomies in mergers,[5]
and the Bank had no more success in resolving these sorts of problems
in the cotton industry than it had in steel.[6]

The problems of expertise and management were probably greater
for the Bank in cotton than in steel. In such a fragmented industry
the Bank was also bound to face allegations that it was promoting
unfair competition by, in effect, giving financial subsidies to weak
firms. This issue was inescapable for the banks in the cotton industry.
Henry Clay noted that as a result of the recapitalization boom of the
early 1920s the most modern firms were also the most indebted, with
consequent advantages for their less efficient competitors in the
depression. The Lancashire banks were, therefore, on one hand anxious to stave off bankruptcy for these more modern concerns whose
stock they held in large quantities as security for their advances. On
the other hand, because of their past overlending, they were very
unwilling to allow these firms more credit and relief from debt so that
they could use their potential lead in productivity. Clay called this a
process of "dysgenic selection," yet the Bank of England's involvement did little to remedy the situation. Norman did not want to create
widespread bankruptcies lest he put more pressure on the banks he
was trying to save. The banks in turn threw their weight into pro-
tecting heavily indebted and often inefficient firms from the pressures
of reorganization and amalgamation schemes. Their attitude was that
they preferred "scrap" to "scrip": they believed that they would get
more out of a liquidation if necessary than they would from obtaining
paper in an amalgamation, and they therefore preferred to sit tight.
The larger, more efficient, vertically integrated firms like Tootal,
Broadhurst, Lee denounced the banks' attitude as one that would
"enable the unable to disable the able." But there was no central
banking policy to override such local considerations.[7]

Why did the Bank become involved to such an extent in steel and
cotton and yet not in coal and shipbuilding? The question is easiest
to answer for coal, where the political complexity of the situation
made the Bank anxious to restrict its intervention. When in 1928
Vivian Smith, Edward Grenfell, and a third merchant banker tried to
interest Norman in a coal rationalization scheme, he resisted adamantly.[8] It was already too late in the 1920s for the Bank to forestall
government intervention by promoting reorganization, so it stayed
well out of it. By the 1930s the government itself was taking on many

reorganizing functions that might in other circumstances have de-volved on the Bank. In shipbuilding the Bank gave assistance to a scheme that enjoyed a fair degree of consensus among employers to scrap excess capacity through a cooperative levy administered by the NSS. Even though this scheme was limited, it was an attempt at indus-trial *self*-reorganization and the Bank preferred to support it rather than intervene directly.[9]

Further research should produce a better picture of the overall di-mensions of the Bank's industrial operations. It seems clear, however, that the issues arising in steel were fairly representative and that it is not a misleading case study in relation to the Bank's wider orien-tation to industry.

It is easier to outline the principal features of the Bank of England's involvement than that of the clearing banks. The lack of adequate research again makes it hard to place the experience in steel in context; there are as yet no substantial studies of the clearing banks' relations to their industrial clients after 1914. It is clear, however, from the case studies in steel that the clearing banks often differed with the Bank of England about industrial policies. Two features stand out. First, the clearing banks were regularly involved as a particular vested in-terest *within* the structure of particular firms and were therefore much more on the defensive than a central bank, which could more easily step back and take an overall view of policy. Their involvement con-sequently fluctuated sharply with their financial stake in the industry and was less politicized. They were most involved in the overdraft crisis of the 1920s, when the situation demonstrated the validity of Keynes's generalization that "a bank has power over you if you owe them £1, but you have power over them if you owe them £1 million." In order to salvage their money, the banks tended to identify fairly directly with the interests of particular companies.

It is not yet possible to draw up a profile of the varying policies and activities of the various clearing banks, but a brief consideration of some aspects of the policy and practices of the Midland Bank and Lloyds Bank reveals some of the most prominent features.

Midland had the most centralized decision-making structure with regard to advances of any of the Big Five: almost all major overdraft decisions went to the head office.[10] But this does not seem to have been associated with a particularly restrictive attitude to loans to in-dustrial and commercial clients; indeed, Midland had the largest pro-portion of such advances among the Big Five.[11] This relative flexibility of lending before World War I shaped some of the major problems with its biggest industrial clients in the 1920s. Before the war both Bolckow Vaughan and the Austin Motor Co. were highly undercapitalized and relied almost wholly on the Midland Bank for working capital: in fact, bank facilities were more important in Austin's finance than even retained profits before 1914.[12] When they wanted to expand rapidly in 1919–20, both companies had, therefore, to seek very large sums on an already saturated capital market, because the Midland could not provide the large-scale capital required. As a result, both firms were forced to issue large amounts of fixed interest stock at high rates in order to attract investors and in consequence incurred heavy debt service burdens in the depressed 1920s. In both cases Midland eventually reluctantly took up the firms' debentures as security for their overdrafts and thus became the most powerful vested interest in each firm. At Austin the bank was instrumental in forcing through a major reconstruction of management, and at Bolckow Vaughan it was probably the determining factor in that firm's decision to merge with Dorman Long.[13] Although the material is too thin to suggest that there was an overall pattern to Midland's policy, it seems that a similar situation of undercapitalization complimented by overdraft before World War I, followed by a swing to expensive overcapitalizaton with the bank picking up the tabs, may have characterized the Midland's cotton accounts, and it is possible that it may have been more generally true of the Lancashire banks in the cotton trade.

An example of a different, although probably fairly common, form of bank–industrial client relationship can be drawn from Lloyds. Lloyds had its origins in a big Birmingham bank which absorbed numerous Midlands and West Country banks, in the first instance, and later merged with various Scottish banks. Roy Church has shown how a Midlands' hardware firm like Kenricks, which had a close relatonship with Lloyds as its local banker, over a long period was able to obtain overdraft facilities with some ease before the war. When the firm ran into trouble in the 1930s, it survived while other smaller hardware firms did not because Lloyds was prepared to support it, mainly because of its long-standing ties with the firm but also because of the local social implications of precipitating the financial collapse of a family of leading public figures.[14] The story suggests the importance of certain nonfinancial considerations in local bank policy and also confirms the picture we have found in steel whereby certain banks acted as a barrier to exit and preserved firms that might otherwise have been eliminated by bankruptcy. This inhibition on restructuring recurs in Lloyds' role in Scotland. In the 1920s it owned all the ordinary shares and prior lien debentures of the Lanarkshire Steel Co. Its aim was to sell the firm for as much as possible, and it was prepared to maximize the company's nuisance value, even by allowing it further overdrafts, in pursuit of this end, despite impeding Scottish reorganization schemes in the process.[15] In a similar fashion, its wholly owned subsidiary, the National Bank of Scotland, found it prudent to keep its demands on its Colvilles' account to a minimum, because, as with the Lancashire banks and their cotton accounts, the sums involved were large in relation to the bank's capital.[16] The National Bank of Scotland was in a relationship of mutual dependence with its giant client, and it opted to take a passive role in relation to plans for rationalization.

Thus, Lloyds decided to nurse certain accounts through the depression—in one case to prop up the local social order which it was linked with through long-term personal and business ties; in another case to maximize its revenue by treating the firm purely as the subject of a market transaction; and in a third case to protect a vulnerable local banking position. These sorts of considerations were certainly not confined to Lloyds; they probably influenced the business of all of the major banks and demonstrate how the protection of banks' short-term assets could impede both bankruptcies and mergers.

There was, however, at least one area in which the clearing banks played a more positive role in relation to industrial reorganization. By and large, the banks were not able to use their position as powerful creditors to promote reorganization, but they were on occasion able to use it to discipline and reconstruct management. In sectors of business where the quality of management was an important determinant of performance, this could be a vital contribution. They could, for instance, play a decisive role in breaking the grip of founding families who were losing the sureness of their touch in a changing business environment; thus Lloyds pushed out Sir Thomas Lipton at Liptons and paved the way for a merger with Van den Bergh[17] and similarly put in Francis D'Arcy Cooper over William Lever at Unilever.[18] Midland removed control from Herbert Austin and put in the more professional Carl Engelbach at the Austin Motor Co.[19] Elsewhere, there are numerous cases of the banks making good use of advisory committees to promote managerial shake-ups, and Lloyds Bank's role at the Rover Co. is a good example of this sort of activity.[20] In most of these cases, however, the bankers were swimming with the tide of shareholders and other directors in the firms; they were able to apply vital strategic leverage to remove a managerial bottleneck. In the more internally confused affairs of the steel firms, there was rarely the opportunity for such simple decisive action.

Thus, the strategic view of the Bank of England was not shared by the clearing banks. The two sectors remained fairly autonomous. As Sayers notes, the Bank had to shape its relations with the clearers "on the basis that they were self-willed brothers with whom the Old

Lady must rub along."[21] Even in money market matters Norman was not always able to get the cooperation of the Big Five, and his ability to exert any institutional pressure on the banks was even less when it came to industrial matters. The history of the financial sector, as we have seen, laid the basis for this institutional weakness: dependency on a self-regulating money market provided no basis for a speedy development of interventionist financial institutions, and although Norman toyed with the idea for a while, no major financial grouping saw a need to create such institutions on a large scale.

Earlier we outlined some major criticisms of the fusion, dominance, and diversion theories of the relationship between banking and industry. A more adequate view has emerged from this study. Elements of *both* dominance *and* dependence characterized the relations between the banking sector and industry. In the long run British banking capital depended on productive capital for its prosperity; but as far as the British banks were concerned, *international* productive capital and profits were more important than domestic capital. Because of this international base, British banking could have fairly sharp conflicts of interest with British industrial capital. These conflicts are most obvious at a macroeconomic level: the strong exchange rate and deflationary economic policies that banking frequently favors often have deleterious effects on industry, and the powerful political influence of the financial sector has often enabled it to secure such goals. But the business of banking is more than its macroeconomic policies; the banking structure is multifaceted with crucial links of dependence with the industrial, regional, and national levels of the economy. The crisis of the domestic economy in the interwar years posed the issue of the extent to which the financial sector might take responsibility for restructuring industry and opened up questions that are still very much alive today about the traditional role of banking.

As long as the banks wanted to retain their ability to shift their resources freely across domestic and international economies, they had to forego any significant measure of direct control within the enterprise. The Bank of England considered briefly the task of remodeling institutions for a different role, but it backed away after bad experiences. It was not simply a question of channeling resources but one of deciding how those resources should be used, and it was at this level that the historic political and economic barriers were greatest. The banks lacked knowledge and expertise. Their industrial interests were diverse and pointed in different directions in different sections of industry and at different levels of the banking structure. Moreover, the complex industrial organization of the older industries persistently involved bankers in besetting conflicts of interest. Their roles in government and international finance remained more familiar and generally more lucrative. Above all, perhaps, they feared the political implications of an enhanced role in domestic industry. The revitalization of traditional modes of industrial finance in the 1930s relaxed the pressure for assuming new responsibilities, but the issues that came to the fore at that time lingered unresolved in the background and reemerged when the British economy once more faced a crisis in the 1960s and 1970s.

PART III

The State and the Steel Industry in the Interwar Years

12.

Government and Industry in the 1920s

The unquestioned primacy of Britain in the nineteenth-century world economy had produced an almost unique degree of government abstention from economic intervention, [1] and the flight from controls at the end of the First World War showed a nearly unanimous desire among industrialists and politicians to return to this situation. But the decade that followed demonstrated that there could be no viable return to the status quo; the changed economic situation pointed toward a far-reaching redefinition of the relationship between industry and the state based on the mutual reliance and support that characterize this relationship in most developed capitalist economies. In the interwar years the British state took the first steps in elaborating its role in such a relationship.

Ambiguities of State Intervention and Industrial Policy

Liberal and pluralist theorists have generally paid little attention to the relationship between the state and industry. The pluralist picture is one of a great weathervane of government slowly changing direction in response to the shifting winds of opinion.[2] The state is seen as something outside the economy that intervenes on an ad hoc basis to correct perceived malfunctions. Marxist and radical theorists have made the most extensive attempts to define the relationship. For a long time the predominant Marxist approach was to see the state as a tool of the ruling class, which is primarily coercive in its functions and represents an epiphenomenon of the economic base.[3] Recently, particularly in response to Poulantzas's work, these theories have moved away from deterministic formulations. Poulantzas argued that the state was not reducible to an immediate and direct expression of the strict economic-corporate interests of this or that class or fraction. Instead, his notion of relative autonomy defined the state as a "resultant" of the relationships of power between different classes in a capitalist social formation.[4] This severing of the state's deterministic anchor stimulated a flowering of theoretical debate, [5] but it is also arguable that it opened up an epistemological crisis for the Marxist approach to state theory. As Hindess, Hirst, and Cutler have noted, either the state is in fact subordinate to the requirements of capital, either through some instrumental mechanism or because the state is defined a priori in functional terms, or the state is genuinely autonomous, in which case there can be no theoretical guarantees that it will pursue the interests of capital.[6] Thus, history written from within such a framework is drawn toward casting its explanations in the form of a prolonged series of tautologies, premised on little more than an article of faith that the capitalist state is basically a vehicle of system-maintenance.

Douglas McEachern's recent historical study of the relationship between the steel industry and the government in Britain since the Second World War falls into this category.[7] A brief account of his argument shows some of the limitations of this kind of interpretation. He begins by noting, correctly, that success in the decision-making process does not mean that the outcome is necessarily in the subject's long-term interests. Thus, in the context of the first postwar nationalization of steel, although the will of the Labour government prevailed, the interest that prevailed was that of capital in general against that of the steel capitalists, despite the political doubts harbored by the wider manufacturing sector. The Labour government's project he argues, was to harmonize the relations between the steelmakers and the manufacturing industry by means of a change of ownership that would free management from the restrictions of profit seeking and the restraints of backward companies and make possible the single-minded pursuit of efficiency. Against this, the steelmakers believed that in the context of reviving demand, private enterprise could do the job just as well. In other words, their pursuit of their own sectional interests appeared compatible with the interests of capital as a whole. The debate was over "two different ways of advancing the interests of the capitalist class," and the outcome of the dispute was functional for capital: "As capital lacked effective procedures for the generation of class-wide policies and the state lacked internal arrangements to guarantee that its actions worked to advance the interests of capital, conflict between sections of capital and sections of the state was the only way in which the direction of social development could be established and politics roughly harmonised with the class interests of capital."[8]

When a Conservative government later denationalized the industry and supported the private owners they "reversed the line of advance of capital."[9] In the uncertain conditions of the late 1940s the Labour Party had opted for the more conscious unity of capital in order to plan and coordinate development through a mixed-economy strategy. In a more prosperous period the Conservatives felt it safe to return to a more traditional strategy. In the long term, however, their strategy failed; private steelmakers failed to take effective steps to modernize the industry, and their pursuit of their own sectional advantages between 1953 and 1966 was not in the long-term interests of the wider capitalist class. The result was a "growing tension between the class interests of capital and the short-term interests of the steel producers," and in 1966 when the Labour government renationalized the industry, capital as a whole did not rally to the defense of the steelmakers.[10] After the second nationalization the steel industry "was now owned and operated by the state in the collective interests of capital" and could pursue the necessary large-scale rationalization that private ownership had precluded. Thus, the class power of capital secured its own interests against the sectional interests of steel capital with the government acting as a "mediating institution, uniquely placed to effect changes in the relations between the various sections of capital when the class lacks internal arrangements capable of doing so in an organised and deliberate manner."[11]

In McEachern's schema government policies are in the long run compelled to be functional for capital even if, "given the unorganised state of the class of capital, the most appropriate government strategy can only be established by trial and error."[12] Allowing for this caveat, it seems that all is for the best in the capitalist world. But such an ultimatistic framework of analysis asks only very narrow questions and, in effect, knows all the answers in advance of history. But if, as Bob Jessop has noted, there are at any one time many viable paths toward capital accumulation, and the reproduction of capital "can be secured in different respects, over different time periods, to different extents,"[13] then any one of several contradictory possible outcomes could be seen as in the interests of capital in different ways. McEachern argues that denationalization was "against the long-term interests of capital," but his own material argues that continued nationalization would not have produced a substantially different conduct of the industry. In other words, *neither* option could have ensured what he takes to be the functionally optimal outcome for capital—

the effective technical transformation of the steel industry. However, he rejects the implication of such situations drawn, for instance, by Claus Offe, that the internal processes of the state cannot be adequate to the task of generating policies that will guarantee the interests of capital,[14] and insists that the immanent power of capital finally structures the outcome of state actions, even if this happens only "unconsciously and against the will and intentions of government."[15]

McEachern takes no account of the extent to which the later work of Poulantzas together with that of the "post-Althusserian" Marxists has gone a very long way in the direction of deconstructing deterministic Marxism. Once relative autonomy is taken seriously, there is no guarantee that assures the functionality of the state for capitalism. The capacity of a state to secure the "conditions of existence" of capital becomes a problem to be explored historically. Although the phenomenon of prevalent state support for major capitalist interests is undeniable, it is also apparent that state actions can have a variety of contingent effects; they are not necessarily system-sustaining and may be dysfunctional or have contradictory effects on the evolution of the system. It is these ambiguities that we shall investigate in the following chapters. Thus, Theda Skocpol is right to argue that "capitalism in general has no politics, only [extremely flexible] outer limits for the kinds of support for property ownership and controls of the labour force that it can tolerate."[16] The interests of social groups and of the state itself are invariably ambiguous and hard to identify, and they are as likely to be determined by ideological perceptions as by pragmatic calculus. The critical factors are the historical formation of institutions and the political constitution of interests. The state's capacity to represent interests depends crucially on the ability of interests to constitute themselves coherently and represent themselves politically. Unintended consequences of state actions are inevitable and often far-reaching.[17]

This chapter assesses the impact of state action on steel and other industries between the wars and the contradictory outcomes of these actions. For a long time historians of interwar Britain payed little attention to the role of the state in industry. Attention was focused mainly on financial and macroeconomic policies and their implications for business.[18] But some historians attributed more significance to state action. Eric Hobsbawm, for instance, dated to the 1930s the transformation of Britain from "one of the least into one of the most trustified and controlled economies, and largely through direct government action,"[19] and for Samuel H. Beer the 1930s were a decade of transition from a predominantly laissez-faire to a planned or man-

aged economy with "a pattern of economic policy that was comprehensive and radically different from that of previous generations."[20]
More recently, Sean Glynn and John Oxborrow have characterized
the interwar period as one of a dramatic reversal of previous policies
of the state toward industry.[21] During the last decade the state has
begun to figure more prominently in research. Historians have, however, varied in their interpretations. Some have stressed continuity
and interpreted changes in state policy as simply an accretion of ad
hoc responses to immediate difficulties, but others have begun to ask
whether there were more fundamental shifts in the internal dynamics
of state policy.[22]

In terms of international comparisons, Britain remained toward the
lower end of the spectrum of state intervention.[23] Nevertheless, in
iron and steel, coal, agriculture, and electricity supply, the state played
a crucial role, and there was also important direct government involvement in cotton textiles, shipbuilding, shipping, aircraft, and armaments. In a wider variety of industries, such as railways and
passenger transport, government was a significant factor in structur-
ing the economics of the industry. We shall examine some of these
cases in more detail later, but it should be clear that the problems in
the steel industry do not represent a special case but are part of wider
developments in business-government relations. These developments went beyond ad hoc responses and had wide implications for
the structural evolution of major sectors of the economy and for future
practices of the mixed economy: the way in which the institutions
and practices of the state evolved shaped their future functioning in
important ways. These developments were not, however, simply system-sustaining; they created their own contradictory effects. The effects were not those intended by the principal departments of
government involved; nor did they conform closely to the aspirations
of the major steelmakers. But they did have important determinant
effects on the structures of both business and government and on the
evolving pattern of their interaction. In particular, these developments contributed to a major restructuring of steelmakers as an interest group, shaped the growth of the state's interventionist capacities,
helped establish new channels and practices whereby state and industry could interact, and at the same time reinforced the backward
and fragmented structure of the industry.

The Growth of State Intervention

In both Britain and America the state played only a limited role in
the rise of the capitalist enterprise; by contrast, as Gerschenkron in

particular has stressed, all other capitalist countries have seen a much greater involvement of the state from the start of capitalist production. In the United States in the twentieth century the state has remained relatively little involved in production; Britain, however, provides a rare example of a transition from a little to a great deal of state intervention. In the United States Chandler's managerial revolution and the establishment of powerful corporate structures preceded the development of American state structures. W. H. Becker has described how in the early nineteenth century "the large-scale corporation was more highly developed bureaucratically than the executive departments of the federal government . . . the levels of bureaucratic control were greater and the scale of operations more complex than anything undertaken by the U.S. Government at the time."[24] Federal bureaucracies did not mature until the late 1930s, and only then did the revenues of the federal government begin to rival those of the largest corporations. Until then big business needed government much less than government needed big business, and even since then the U.S. government has remained relatively weak and fragmented faced by an already well-integrated system of capitalist business enterprise. Although there was more direct business-government collaboration in the arena of small producers trading in the world market where business needs were greater, big business before the Second World War turned to government only when necessary, usually in relation to political conditions favorable to the advance of foreign trade.[25] At the other end of the spectrum France combined a liberal economy with a protectionist state from the nineteenth century. Stephen Kuisel has argued that market capitalism was in much lower esteem in France because its triumph in the nineteenth century was less dramatic and its humiliation in war and depression much more severe. At the same time growth was especially motivated by competition among nations, and the catching-up effort usually implied a greater role for the state. As a result, as the social and political costs of the market rose in the twentieth century, the French state was able to move relatively smoothly into a more direct role in economic management.[26]

In Britain state institutions developed at one remove from the sphere of business. In a broad sense, the nineteenth-century British state developed erratically in response to particular economic and social shifts and crises. Widespread government activity clustered around primarily fiscal, legal, imperial, and military matters and subsequently expanded particularly in response to the political challenge of a growing working class. The state that emerged was a conglomeration of institutionalized functions and policies whose structure did not necessarily correspond to overt changes in government ideology or policy. In relation to industry, government activity was mainly confined to matters of industrial relations and industrial welfare and to guaranteeing financial stability through the gold standard and checks on the banking system. It was only with wartime mobilization in the First World War that the state became significantly involved in matters of production, and although state intervention decreased at the end of hostilities, the crisis of the postwar economy meant that production was bound to remain an important government concern thereafter.

The late arrival of government was seen by business as an indication of its inexperience and irrelevance to economic development. Politicians and civil servants themselves admitted that government was not equipped with the administrative and managerial skills to take an active part in the management and reorganization of industry. As Stanley Baldwin noted in the early 1920s, the civil service had developed as a "mere administrative service, and they would be the first to tell you that their training and position would not enable them to manage business. The businessman takes decisions, the official dare not. The businessman must come to a quick decision, he must be able to delegate responsibility. So long as you have management of business by the state, you will have to have responsibility to the House of Commons. Then you would find that every action can be criticised by the House of Commons, that business can only be run by a fixed rule. Business can never in these circumstances show the margin of profit that it can under private enterprise."[27] Particular rigidities within the state bureaucracy reinforced this inadaptability. Most notable was the entrenched dominance of the Treasury—and its very characteristic political persuasion—over other departments. Indeed, during the period 1919-1924 the hand of the Treasury over government policy was actually strengthened through its control of expenditure, its use of those powers to curb the growing Ministry of Labour, and the formal recognition of the permanent secretary at the Treasury as head of the civil service with the right to advise the prime minister on the appointment of senior officials to all departments.[28] However, the restrictions of limited administrative capabilities were not as absolute as Baldwin claimed: even before the First World War the Board of Trade had developed considerable business expertise in railway matters, and in the 1920s the Mines Department of the Board of Trade began to function as a coherent lobby for the organizational reform of the coal industry.[29] Moreover, the examples of the Central Electricity Board (CEB) and the London Passenger Transport Board showed that new forms of state corporation could be devised effectively where the need was felt.

However, Baldwin's broader point about the political problems involved in an enhanced role for government in economic management was partly substantiated by the history of government relations with the railway industry before the First World War. The government had always had a special regulatory role in railways based on the legal regulation of safety matters and the need for parliamentary bills to permit the building of lines and to protect consumers from the inevitable local monopolies that railway companies acquired.[30] This brought the supervision of railway companies—some of the largest companies in Britain—into the public arena, and the railways' big manufacturing customers, fearful of the size and potential monopoly power of the railway companies, organized effectively to use parliamentary control and the threat of hostile legislation to curb them. As P. J. Cain has observed, "When on occasion the basic antagonism between the companies and their consumers erupted into open conflict, the battle was often carried into Parliament where the chance of restrictive legislation reaching the statute book depended on the balance of forces between the 'railway interest' and those hostile to the companies in the legislature. This pull of interests hardly made for consistency."[31] Parliamentary approval was needed for amalgamations, and Parliament's attitude fluctuated between enthusiastic approval and bitter opposition.

In the late nineteenth century the balance between the railway interest and its opponents tilted sharply in favor of the latter. In an era of falling profits the railway companies found themselves blocked from either raising prices or pursuing amalgamations to curb competition. By 1907 Lloyd George's government and the Board of Trade in particular believed that amalgamations and agreements in restraint of competition could bring major improvements in productivity and industrial reorganization; but it proved impossible for them to devise safeguards on such combinations sufficient to satisfy consumers that did not also, in the opinion of the railway companies, hamstring the effective use of amalgamation and neutralize its advantages. In the resultant deadlock the necessary legislation collapsed in Parliament.[32]

Both here and in electricity supply, another "natural monopoly" that had become the object of a degree of state regulation from its inception, the politicization of the relationship between the industry and its consumers created grave problems for governmental attempts to mediate between the rival interests. By the turn of the century the problem facing the electricity supply industry was how to develop large-scale enterprises to take advantage of new techniques. Even though the public sector was considerably larger than the private sector by 1900, parochial feelings and political conflicts between public authorities and the private companies about the form of new enterprises held back the merger of franchises. Private firms would not surrender their rights over franchises, and municipalities would not accept bulk supply from private companies. In Germany private and municipal enterprises had allied to promote large-scale operations, with municipalities taking shareholdings and seats on the supervisory boards of the companies and the private companies working across groups of municipalities to achieve bulk supplies. But Britain lacked any similar tradition of technocratic cooperation between the state and private capitalists, and the result was a more politicized head-on clash and a deadlock that entrenched the status quo and resulted in the persistence of fragmentation and a high cost electricity supply into the late 1920s.[33]

In both railways and electricity supply by the 1920s the principal government departments had come to see excessive competition as a greater danger than monopolistic exploitation. But in neither case had they been able to formulate acceptable institutions either to fulfill perceived technical needs or to provide a framework within which the industries and their consumers could work out practical compromises rather than battle out entrenched positions on grounds of principle in Parliament. In both cases the issue was resolved when the economic dangers arising from private control effectively marginalized the private interests. In railways the wartime experience showed Parliament and manufacturers the advantages of combination, and the appalling financial state of the industry by 1921 gave the companies no choice but to accept compulsory amalgamation into four large companies as the price of decontrol and the survival of a degree of competition under the regulatory supervision of the Ministry. Government action was given added urgency by the industrial conflict that was resulting from the crisis of the industry.[34] In electricity there was widespread concern among industrialists about the manifest inefficiency of private control. Phillip Cunliffe-Lister, the Conservative president of the Board of Trade, noted that "electricity . . . is so inefficient today in this country that it has always been amazing to me that the Labour Government did not attempt to nationalise it".[35] The creation of the Central Electricity Board in the late 1920s had all-party support and broad approval from industrialists who wanted cheap power. The solution of a board run on a business basis without direct accountability to Parliament avoided nationalization and provided a workable compromise with private enterprise.[36]

Thus, concerns of national efficiency, the impact of industrial crises on labor relations, and the regulation of monopoly power in relation to powerful consuming interests pushed the government into some of its major steps into economic management in this period. Elsewhere, except in the coal industry, government intervention was fairly precisely delimited and selective. For instance, before the First World War Britain had been dependent on Germany for imported optical glass and key scientific instruments. Both here and in the case of cellulose manufacture, government support for nascent home industries was a matter of national strategic importance.[37] Tariffs and government assistance saved these industries from collapse in the early 1920s, and these measures were strongly supported by the trades themselves. The government's promotional role in the formation of the Imperial Chemical Industries amalgamation was likewise based on the state's traditional role of maintaining Britain's war potential; in this case the production of dyestuffs was a particular concern.[38] In armaments and naval fuel oil the government was forced to extend its activities to protect its special interests as a monopsonist customer with rigid quality and supply needs in a noncompetitive market.[39] Interventions here and in the creation of the BBC and Imperial Airways did not create far-reaching precedents or political implications.

But apart from these pragmatic adaptations, a deep suspicion of using the state was shared by most industrialists and Conservative politicians. One of the most powerful fears was that giving powers to the state was creating a hostage to fortune. As Roland Nugent, the secretary of the Federation of British Industries put it, a Labour government "might accept it with great pleasure and go much further than we should like."[40] At the same time, many employers were also concerned that particular individuals might be able to turn state action to their own benefit at the expense of others. Hence, there was much hostility to Alfred Mond's attempt to amend the Mining Industry Bill in 1926 in a way that many thought would assist him to create a West Wales anthracite monopoly, and Lord Ashfield's role in the creation of a passenger monopoly through the London Traffic Act of 1924 was regarded in a similar light.[41] Government initiatives were most broadly acceptable in areas such as optical glass, cellulose, and dyestuffs where a compact body of employers with a clear plan had been able to win the support of a specific government department for a specific course of action for a specific purpose; they were most problematic where they necessitated a complex involvement with rival capitalist interests. As John Turner has noted, the divided and backward structure of the British economy prevented the emergence of united political leadership among industrialists: "The political backwardness of British industry . . . was closely related to the much better known phenomenon of British industrial retardation."[42] This on one hand prevented the emergence of politically coherent demands from employers and on the other meant that the government risked embroilment in a complex set of rival vested interests if it began to involve itself with established industries. It was these sorts of complex intracapitalist divisions that virtually paralyzed the government in its dealing with the oil industry after the war. As R. W. Ferrier has shown, the government wanted to maintain effective control over the industry for strategic reasons. The oil producers believed that commercial expansion required larger companies, diversification, and either new developments or big amalgamations, but government officials feared that such a program would dangerously dilute their control or involve them in unacceptably large open-ended financial commitments to the industry. In the meantime, the rival oil companies played out a prolonged strategic game of trying to win government support for particular merger schemes that would operate most to their varying advantages. Faced with this situation, the government was unable either to devise a positive overall oil policy or to bring itself to wholeheartedly sponsor the interests of any one oil company in particular.[43]

In all of these cases governments balanced their concerns for competitiveness and national efficiency against political objections to moves in the direction of public ownership and their doubts about their capabilities of intervening to good purpose. In certain fields such as infant industries and security-related matters the ground was fairly clear. In others, such as electricity supply and the railways, the balance of arguments shifted fairly decisively and was recognized to have done so by a broad spectrum of industrial interests. The critical problems arose where an industry in crisis and needing reorganization raised sensitive political issues and where the possible courses of commercial reorganization were deeply controversial. In the 1920s the coal industry was the classic case. Before the General Strike the main concern of successive governments was either to negotiate a deal acceptable to both employers and miners or to disengage from the industry altogether so as to avoid the far-reaching political implications of any other course of action. The coal crisis was centered on the effects of the decline of the industry on labor and was a highly politicized conflict. As Susan Armitage has noted, the issues at stake in the future of the coalmining industry were "not so much an industrial question as it was the government's role in the total economy."[44] The government's role in such a situation was invidious, and officials sought to abdicate responsibility to the owners as far as possible. Baldwin rejected any form of compulsory reorganization that did not have the support of the employers, and his government's main priority was to escape from the mounting fiscal burden of the coal subsidy. Following the decisive defeat of the miners in 1926,

however, the Board of Trade at least was slowly converted to the
need for compulsion of the owners over the next three years. The
1927 Mining Industry Act sanctioned the principle of the coercion of
minorities in amalgamations; but the initiative for such amalgamations
had to come from within the industry itself. Cunliffe-Lister, president
of the Board of Trade, believed at the time that this was as far as the
state could go and yet avoid the threat of nationalization: "an industry
may not conduct its business in its own best interests," he said, "but
is it the function of government to force it to conduct its business on
lines which it is not prepared to accept voluntarily?" In this case he
believed that such a proposal was "perilously close to nationalisation."[45] In practice, however, the permissive powers of the 1927 Act
had little effect; the industry confined itself to toying fairly ineffec-
tively with further cartel schemes, and by 1929 the Board of Trade
had largely come round to believing that rationalization would proceed further only if the government took direct steps—a view that
the Mines Department had been urging for several years—and this
was close to becoming Conservative government policy when the 1929
election intervened. This movement came partly because the post-
1926 depoliticization of the coal issue made such action a less dangerous precedent, partly because the trend was running strongly in
favor of large-scale rationalization, partly because the expert staff of
the Department of Mines had formulated its ideas of the necessary
course of action more clearly, and also probably in part because the
experience of the formation of the CEB had nodified some of the
cruder objections from industrialists.[46]

In terms of their thinking about state intervention in peacetime,
politicians, administrators, and managers departed significantly from
orthodox laissez-faire notions in the 1920s and developed a new degree of pragmatic flexibility about government involvement. Outside
the CEB and the Mines Department of the Board of Trade, however,
there was little development of traditions of informed state supervision or direction, nor was there much progress in developing institutions within which government and business could interact to
formulate mutually advantageous compromises. The most striking
feature remained the persistent separateness of business and government institutions. Partly, as we have seen, mechanisms for implementing government involvement were not developed because the
government hoped that the banks might take on a more effective role
in industrial reorganization; but beyond this the situation also reflected the divided nature of industrial interests and their inability to
formulate programs for the government to support and the lack of a
state technocratic tradition. At the same time, the political weight of

labor and its access to government through the Labour Party made the state politically unreliable as far as industrialists and Conservative politicians were concerned and therefore an arena where new functions should be carefully weighed and new powers cautiously limited.

Thus, although the role of the state in production was expanding, it was doing so in a halting and contradictory fashion. The case of steel, where the relationship remained a difficult one throughout the 1920s, illustrates many of the important dilemmas in the piecemeal redefinition of state-industry relations. Like coal, steel was internally divided, represented a dangerous precedent for other industries, and involved a wide range of political issues, particularly insofar as the reorganization of the industry was bound up with the tariff question. The government felt that it was impossible to treat steel as a special case for protection and that it could not be isolated from the question of a general tariff.[47] But a general tariff was anathema to the City's financial interests, it cut across the Tory party itself, and it was an electoral maverick card which resulted in the Tories' electoral defeat of 1923.[48] The result was that in the 1920s the attitude toward intervention in steel was extremely hesitant and confused. Perhaps the guiding maxim for Conservative policy was Steel-Maitland's conclusion that "a policy of inaction . . . has a good deal to recommend it."[49] In this context government relations with the steelmakers remained firmly situated in the arena of informality, personal contact, and suasion—an array of tactics that was to have little significant effect.

Government and Steel in the 1920s: Suasion and Bargaining

The fragmentation and individualism of the steel industry described in the first part of this book made it inconceivable that it could deal with government with a unified voice. From the mid-1920s a clear majority within the industry believed that recovery would require some form of tariff protection or government assistance, and there was growing sympathy within the Board of Trade and certain other government circles for such a course of action. An industry united behind a program for reorganization in the context of protection might have succeeded in getting steel treated as a special case for assistance, but the internal divisions of the industry prevented the steel companies from formulating a coherent program of reorganization or acting as a sustained political lobby.[50]

It was only under government pressure during the First World War that the first serious national representative employers' association emerged in the steel industry. The National Federation of Iron and

Steel Manufacturers (NFISM), formed in September 1918, was a weak federal organization without much enthusiastic backing from within the industry, and the steel lobby remained a muted and internally divided affair.[51] There was a brief period of unity behind protectionist proposals during the war when a period of intense postwar economic nationalisms appeared likely, but the unexpectedly complete defeat of Germany and the prospects for a new buoyancy for British industry in a period of European reconstruction resulted in a sudden swingback against protection at the end of the war with free trade accepted as the corollary of the speedy decontrol of the industry.[52]

Thereafter, the reemergence of a coherent protectionist lobby was a slow process. Partly this was a result of the erratic economic fluctuations of the postwar years, notably the impact of the Ruhr crisis of 1923, which concealed the speed of the revival of European competition. Partly, it was only after the General Strike that many steelmakers abandoned the notion that cheap imports would force workers to accept wage cuts. Against this background, special interest groups like the re-rollers, who depended on cheap imported semifinished steel, were able to form a small but active lobby to exploit the broad political problems raised by the tariff issue.[53]

These divisions and uncertainties took pressure off successive governments who were themselves divided over the tariff question. In the 1920s the majority of the Conservative Party were sympathetic to tariffs, but few were prepared to commit the party to a tariff policy when to do so might jeopardize more important interests, particularly after the disastrous experience of the "tariff election" of 1923. In the aftermath of this defeat the free trade minority in the party were able to keep the protectionists on the defensive. Key figures like Baldwin, the prime minister, Phillip Cunliffe-Lister, and Arthur Steel-Maitland, the minister of labor, were personally committed to protection and, in particular, sympathetic to the claims of the steel industry, but from 1923 they accepted that it was politically unrealistic.[54] They spent considerable time and effort considering possible ways of offering assistance to the steelmakers within the framework of a pledge against a general tariff, including various proposals for subsidies,[55] but none of these proposals made much headway against Treasury opposition. The Treasury insisted that strict economic orthodoxy was more essential than ever in the years following the return to gold and that there was simply no alternative to the hard laws of economics to force reorganization on the steelmakers.[56] Moreover, Treasury officials feared that any subsidies would awaken the appetites of other industries— notably coal—and that it would then be hard to deny them similar treatment.[57]

In the face of the well-marshaled Treasury case the only possibility for steel to gain some special assistance would be if the government were firmly convinced that its involvement could be linked directly to an agreed program of active reconstruction, as in the case of the Central Electricity Board and the National Grid. For this the industry would have to show that a tariff or subsidy would definitely trigger industrial regeneration by rationalization. But the case that there was such a link did not emerge convincingly in either of the major government inquiries into the affairs of the industry in the 1920s (the Committee of Civil Research in 1925 and the Sankey Committee in 1929). It became clear that no clear understanding existed, even among the steelmakers who advocated tariffs, as to what exactly the linkages were between a tariff and the revival of the industry.[58]

The main argument put to the Committee of Civil Research (and to the Balfour Committee on Industry and Trade, which ran in parallel to it although with a rather wider brief) was that the exclusion of imports would give a new impetus to the industry by enabling it to operate its most modern equipment at full capacity.[59] The steelmakers suggested that with an import prohibition an additional two million tons of steel would be made in Britain, which would result in a cost reduction of 10 shillings per ton or about 10%. Amalgamation and the elimination of small makers alone, they argued, could not achieve such economies. As Sir William Larke, the president of the NFISM put it, "the small orders which are economically transferable to the big plants are not nearly enough . . . it is the orders for imported steel that can alone give the big plants what they need."[60] This argument for tariffs merged into arguments for the impossibility of reorganizing *before* tariffs: reorganization required increased loads which could be achieved only from a monopolized home market.

What could not be guaranteed, however, was that such protection would not be used to bolster inefficient production by reducing competition, raising prices and profits, and promoting malinvestment within the existing structure of the industry. The government wanted to see the elimination of excessive competition, but it feared the responsibility of creating monopoly conditions for an industry with such a wide variety of industrial customers. As a result, the aim of both Conservative and Labour governments between 1925 and 1931 was to foster private rationalization through merger with the aim of creating a slimmed-down, more efficient industry, which could justify protection once it had set its own house in order.

In this context both government inquiries rejected the view of an inverse relationship between protection and reorganization, contrary to the arguments of the industry. As Sankey noted, "Protection at the present time would, we believe, actually delay the reforms that are urgently required, as it would lead to the maintenance of a number of plants not designed for efficient production or suitable for amalgamation, which, in the interests of the country as a whole should not be encouraged to continue."[61] Both political parties had come to accept this view. Steel-Maitland, despite his general protariff outlook, believed that protection "would awake the old reactionary individualism of the industry."[62] As a result, if protection were introduced "at the present juncture . . . reorganisation would be indefinitely postponed."[63] The two Labour governments of the 1920s held this view even more firmly: tariffs, according to Ramsay MacDonald, were "a remedy that was no remedy at all,"[64] and Philip Snowden, his chancellor, was consistently adamant that, come what may, reorganization must precede any state aid to the steel industry.[65]

Consequently, in the late 1920s the government concluded that its best prospects of inducing reorganization lay in promoting the activity of the Bank of England and the clearing banks as intermediaries. During the 1925–1929 Conservative government the banking establishment was prepared to work autonomously along broadly similar lines to government thinking, but the complexities of banking interests in these industrial matters meant that such a strategy of indirect pressure was seriously flawed.[66] By December 1928 Steel-Maitland concluded: "I had hoped at one time to get them [the banks] to join in pressing the industry to reconstruct . . . But on further enquiry it seems hopeless to expect them to take this course."[67] From 1929, however, the tide in Conservative circles began to run more strongly in favor of protection, and the Bank of England became increasingly afraid that the party was wobbling on the issue. By the summer of 1930, as the trough of the depression neared, both political parties began to soften on the principle that reorganization must precede assistance, and the Bank took on the role of sole consistent guardian of this orthodoxy, now no longer hand in hand with government but increasingly in oppostion to it.[68]

The Bank was also very concerned about the interventionist ambitions of the Labour Party, but once in government, the party's position quickly converged on that of its Tory predecessors. The issue of compulsion was fought out and rejected early in the life of the Labour government around the Mosley memorandum. Mosley wanted a comprehensive government scheme for industrial reorganization and the provision of finance through an industrial bank.[69] His scheme was speedily defeated in the cabinet and although echoes were to be heard later from individuals such as Clement Attlee, Arthur Henderson, Vernon Hartshorn, and William Graham in the cabinet, the orthodoxies of evolutionary socialism as expounded by MacDonald and Snowden remained dominant.[70] Snowden believed that intervention was "contrary to all I have ever heard you [MacDonald] say about the steps to be taken in the direction of socialism."[71] The political framework of the labor leaders disarmed them before the prospect of a conflict with powerful vested interests involved in such a strategy. As Snowden and J. H. Thomas noted, moves toward compulsion would bring private sector efforts to a halt. Shareholders and creditors "would at once stiffen and you would be left to choose between extravagant claims and compulsion which would be called confiscation."[72] It would be "practically impossible for any government" to enforce "the essential sacrifices" from industry in terms of writing off losses.[73] In this situation the Labour government resigned itself to the same role that the Tory government had filled before it: "The best service which the government can render . . . is to continue to act as a bridge between industry and finance . . . At the same time, the great weight attaching to the public utterances of ministers affords a valuable opportunity of impressing on the industrial world the need for rationalisation."[74]

Thus, on the eve of tariff legislation the majority view in both parties remained the traditional one that the role of government was to do no more than oil the wheels of private industry. The failure of traditional market mechanisms to bring about structural reorganization had not produced any new thinking on the role of government or any significant attempts to formulate an industrial policy. Steel did not raise the sort of issues of national security or political stability that had forced governments to develop a more positive relationship with other industries. Instead, in confronting the problems of the steel industry, successive governments were aware that they would face a range of new problems. The structure of the steel industry was fragmented: divisions between and within firms and conflicting and overlapping interests prevented the emergence of positive programs from within the industry itself. Reorganization may have been favored generally, but in any particular case the conditions of depression made the immediate advantages to be gained by owners, managers, or creditors fairly marginal and often risky. If reorganization by amalgamation was to proceed speedily, some stimulus other than the invisible hand of the market would be needed; but the steel industrialists themselves had neither a coherent program nor the political unity to lobby effectively for a solution, and in the absence of such pressure internal divisions within the Conservative Party and the pledge against a general tariff ruled out protection for steel as a special case in the late 1920s. The steelmakers could not demonstrate any clear link between protection and reorganization, and government officials more and more took the view that, far from encouraging reorganization, protection would be one more barrier to it.

Hence, both Conservative and Labour governments turned to rationalization as an alternative to protection. They lacked any means to induce firms to reorganize, however, and did not themselves have any clear plan as to how reorganization should take place. The tariff was not a credible bargaining counter to promote reorganization, and both Conservative and Labour governments came to look toward the banks as their most valuable ally in promoting amalgamation schemes. As we have seen, however, the clearing banks had their own interests to defend, and the Bank of England itself, although sympathetic to government aims with regard to reorganization, did not want to be used as a cat's paw for government in industry. The main thrust of Bank of England activity in industrial reorganization under the Labour government was, in fact, directed to keeping government out of industry.

Both ideologically and organizationally, the government was unprepared for the power over and responsibility for the steel industry that the establishment of a tariff would thrust on them. All the issues that had been avoided through the 1920s would have to be resolved after the government had committed itself to assisting the industry, rather than before. The government knew that protection was no guarantee of the reorganization it wanted to see. Either the government would develop an industrial policy and find ways of implementing it, or as the politicians of the late 1920s feared, industrialists would use their newly strengthened position to seek their own salvation. The next few years would show who would be using whom.

13.

Government and Industry in the 1930s

When import duties finally were instituted with the legislation of 8 April 1932,[1] they were not associated with any strategy for reorganization but were simply a result of the recognition that the economic order of free international trade was defunct and that Britain had to come into line. It was openly admitted that although tariffs were necessary for economic progress and national security, they were in themselves inadequate to regenerate industry without extensive industrial reorganization. The government, and more particularly the Import Duties Advisory Committee (IDAC), the small specialist advisory committee of civil servants that was set up under Sir George May, a former director of the Prudential and a leading government financial adviser, to advise the Treasury and the Board of Trade on the progress of protected industries, hoped that reorganization would be eased by protection.[2] The chancellor of the Exchequer, Neville Chamberlain, shared these hopes: tariffs, he argued, "provide us with such a lever as has never been possessed before by any government for inducing, or, if you like, forcing industry to set its house in order."[3] In contrast, however, other Treasury officials and the Bank of England took a more pessimistic view that unless duties were explicitly temporary and conditional, they would hinder reorganization.

The events of the next three years justified the Bank's pessimism. Its broad strategy of regional amalgamations depended on resolving conflicts of interest within the industry in favor of the most efficient producers, but the Bank saw that by dealing with the industry as a whole a solution conciliating all interests became more likely and overall reorganization less likely. May and IDAC disagreed with this view, but they had no clear alternative strategy except to rely on the "good sense" of the industry. As we have seen, however, what was good sense for particular firms or particular interests within those firms did not necessarily correspond to reorganization of the industry. The starting point for May and IDAC was the need for some kind of central representational machinery which could put forward an overall policy for the steel industry. This position depended on generation of a workable consensus among industrialists. If such a consensus did not emerge, the government would find itself in a position of responsibility without power.

Government and Industrial Reorganization:
Conciliation and Compromise, 1932–1935

From the start, leading figures at the Bank of England foresaw the difficulties of promoting reorganization under tariffs. The most critical were Charles Bruce Gardner, the Bank's senior industrial adviser and former director of the Shelton Iron and Steel Co., and Andrew Duncan, the chairman of the Central Electricity Board and one of the most prominent of the industrialists involved in the SMT and the BID, who was to play a leading part in the history of the steel industry in the next two decades. They feared that IDAC's opening move, which was to make a direct approach to the principal steel employers' association, the NFISM, would shift attention from the development of practical amalgamation schemes to questions of the formal organization of the industry. They wanted instead to "get straight on to the people who were actually negotiating" and thus "keep Sir William Larke [the president of the NFISM] out," because he would tend to push to the fore compromises between the wide array of sectional interests represented in the NFISM. It was believed in the Bank that the first meeting between IDAC and the NFISM had been engineered by Larke who "had a very close friend in Mr. Ashley, the Secretary of IDAC," and that as a result discussion would at once be channeled into "going over the ground again" with minority interests in the industry "who had refused to play."[4]

Contrary to the worst fears of the Bank, however, it seems that May and IDAC did intend at first to insist on coupling the production of reorganization schemes with the establishment of representative machinery for the industry. Bruce Gardner thought that the steelmakers had expected to be able to "pat Sir George May on the back" and then get on with electing their own committee, and he was surprised that May acted to circumvent Larke by appointing Charles Mitchell of Dorman Long, who Montagu Norman respected and wanted to recruit to the BID, as chairman of the new National Committee that was set up to produce reorganization proposals. This, Bruce

Gardner felt was "a bombshell" which "told the steelmakers where to get off" and left the industry "scratching its head."[5] But although May's appointee was more dynamic than Larke, IDAC still had no real power, and in the next few months May's conciliatory speeches to the various trades associations within the industry amounted to a guarantee of the autonomy of the makers in working out their own solutions. As he put it to the sheetmakers, "The whole thing rests with you . . . I want you to do it all for yourselves . . . Why do you not all have a meeting and decide what you are going to do yourselves . . . It is your affair, it is not mine; honestly it is not. After all, you are all reasonably minded men. If you get together you will surely find a solution."[6]

The scheme agreed on at the June meeting of the NFISM envisaged a national plan being drawn up on the basis of district schemes formulated by regional and sectional committees based on the existing trades associations in the industry, which the National Committee would then fuse together. But, once established, despite the urgings of May and Alfred Hurst, the leading Treasury official with special responsbility for IDAC,[7] the committees relegated reorganization to the background and concentrated on their own arrangements of association and lobbying for higher tariffs. By July the SMT felt "the whole thing seems to be wrapped in fog," and May was unable to make any positive demands of the steelmakers.[8] By October he was ready to concede that he had no objection to schemes being made conditional on protection as long as there *were* schemes.[9]

This situation was exactly what a strong body of opinion in the Bank and a section of the government had feared. Duncan at the Bank, for instance, had argued for a tough line of making tariffs conditional on real action on physical amalgamations. In September 1932, seeing the drift of things, the SMT even discussed emphasizing this position by asking Norman to see May personally to "lodge a protest before it was too late" against his soft line.[10] Civil servants in IDAC committed to reorganization were likewise acutely dissatisfied with the National Committee's lack of progress. Nevertheless, they felt it impossible and undesirable not to renew the tariff for a further two years in October 1932. But they recognized that the devolved method of preparing schemes through regional and sectional committees had produced nothing, and it was abandoned. In its place a three-man subcommittee of Mitchell, Larke, and the Treasury official Sir Alfred W. Hurst was set up to draft proposals. It was hoped that the intimate involvement of Hurst would ensure serious pursuit of reorganization.[11]

The government's agreement to renew the tariff for steel in October

1932 was publicly declared to be based on "most definite assurances" on reorganization.[12] In fact, the government was well aware that these assurances were meaningless. Walter Runciman, the president of the Board of Trade, had already written to Neville Chamberlain at the Exchequer to tell him that "May could not tell me anything that I could say in the House to demonstrate that the iron and steel industry had in fact begun to reorganise itself . . . He is as convinced as I of the recalcitrant and procrastinatory nature of many people concerned." Steel had, in effect, "received protection which was beyond all its hopes a year ago and had done nothing."[13] Snowden meanwhile underlined the point to Prime Minister MacDonald: the assurances that May had got "are vague and not really worth much. It looks as if the Iron and Steel Committee are simply playing with him [May], and the difficulty is that a great deal of ammunition will be given to those who said that you must make protection conditional on reorganisation and that if you gave protection first you would never see reorganisation. In fact it is difficult to avoid the conclusion that May and Hurst have mishandled the business and been bamboozled and May continues to be bamboozled and the brunt of criticism and trouble will fall on you."[14]

The three-man subcommittee that followed tariff renewal prepared its schemes between October 1932 and March 1933. Its members did not even consider amalgamation of firms or concentration of production; such moves, they stated, could only have local or sectional impact. Instead they sought to develop national cooperation in the form of industry-wide price associations grouped around existing trades associations to stabilize the industry.[15] Hurst made some efforts to raise the issue of production and of a strong central reorganizing body funded from a levy and with statutory support, but as Bruce Gardner noted, the plan the committee drew up concentrated instead on "the much more seductive path of trying to placate the majority by means of making the price associations more comprehensive and powerful." Its references to reorganization were spurious; it just listed "a number of desirable functions of the Association, all of which are permissive" and never went further than "pious words."[16]

The SMT saw the scheme as an actual obstacle to regional amalgamations, and the Treasury agreed that it relaxed pressure to regroup.[17] Amalgamations would eliminate redundant plant and concentrate decision making and planning, but this scheme would have the opposite effect. By "placing every manufacturer within a Confederation of Associations" it would institutionalize the conflicts within the industry as conflicts between a number of elected representatives, all in competition with each other. Such a body could not promote rationalization but would be "a dead hand on outstanding initiative and enterprise." High-cost enterprises would resist investment by competitors to establish low-cost plant.[18]

The Bank of England, therefore, lamented that "the worst fears of six months ago had been realised"[19] but politically, like the government it accepted that the tariff had to stay. The absence of reorganization meant that, if the tariff were to be removed, the industry and its employment would be even more vulnerable than they were before. Both Bank and government were confined to coaxing and criticizing the recalcitrant industry. The BID, in fact, refused to cooperate with IDAC to provide finance for the development of the iron and steel industry within the framework of this confederation of associations.[20] But, as it predicted, the government rejected any recourse to compulsion, and Runciman admitted that, if the industry was agreed on what it wanted, the government had no alternative but to go along with it.[21] Meanwhile, despite the rancor and disillusionment in many government departments, in public the government continued to profess that the new scheme embodied in a white paper in February 1933 was a "real step forward" in reorganization.[22]

Why was the steel industry unwilling to move toward the sort of national reorganization that bankers and politicians were convinced was necessary? The main answer is to be found in how different firms and sections of the industry perceived the impact on their interests of a powerful central authority sponsored by government to promote reorganization. These clashes of interest can be traced in the debates of the two subcommittees of the National Committee that were established to translate the white paper into final proposals, which sat between July 1933 and April 1934.[23]

Three main currents existed. In the first stood the large, relatively prosperous, and expanding firms United Steel, Richard Thomas, and Stewarts & Lloyds. With their lower costs and favorable market positions, they wanted to strengthen their ability to expand at the expense of others, particularly because each saw the prospect of achieving either a regional or product monopoly. They saw themselves as the main beneficiaries of a particular type of increased legislative or government involvement. Hilton of United Steel, for example, was a vigorous advocate of a powerful central organization with large funds and of a flexible quota system, which would enable low-cost firms to increase their share of trade.[24] Firth of Richard Thomas, facing the problems of a growing firm and needing a whip hand against tenacious small enterprises, went further and proposed a body with statutory powers to enforce regional reorganization. He was a severe critic of IDAC for not setting duties high enough to drive out the small re-rolling firms which relied on cheap imported semifinished steel to undercut large integrated concerns like Richard Thomas which had higher overheads. These firms were sitting tight and waiting for imports to revive. Hence, Firth wanted a body with some coercive power.[25] A. C. MacDiarmid of Stewarts & Lloyds, which enjoyed a near-monopoly position in the expanding tube sector, also favored an enabling act to coerce small awkward rivals.[26]

The second and most powerful grouping which had the influential support of Larke of the NFISM, included the big heavy steelmakers that were still backward and depressed, represented by Dorman (Dorman Long), Talbot (South Durham), Beale (Guest, Keen, Baldwin), and Craig (Colvilles). It was their view that largely shaped the final scheme. Their main concerns were to revive profitability within existing company structures and current levels of demand. To do so, industry had to "discipline itself and restrict developments here and there." Even under tariffs internal competition could destroy profitability and so it must be restrained. If profits revived, this would probably generate "a new spate of competition in the more profitable parts of the industry and this competition must be regulated."[27] Hence, they wanted increased tariffs which would ensure their position of monopoly suppliers to home finishing trades by making possible long-term price-fixing arrangements with the finishers. Amalgamations should be left to natural market forces. At the same time, they resisted any strong central body, and they stubbornly resisted the proposal for a substantial central levy. For them, the advantages of a scheme were primarily in stability—to guarantee government favor and to clear the way for them to strengthen their own positions.[28]

The third group, numerically important but economically insignificant, were finishers, smaller firms, and re-rollers like Whitehead, Baird, Skinningrove, and the Steel of Scotland. They feared that a central organization would "put all the various sections under the domination of the heavy steel industry" (A. K. McCosh of Baird).[29] They resisted all apparatuses of control or quota schemes, loyalty rebates, and penalties because of the implications regarding the administration of control. As Alfred Hutchinson of Skinningrove noted, it raised "the grave question of where the control of each association is to be, especially if questions of efficiency and redundancy are to be raised."[30] Hence the latter two groups were prepared to make common cause to reject the quota proposals that Hurst and S. C. E. Lloyd of Stewarts & Lloyds pushed through one of the National Committee's subcommittees which allowed for an "auction" of a proportion of proposed annual quotas to enable progressive firms to expand at the expense of backward ones. This action implied "an automatically diminishing quota on the part of many firms and involve[d] their ultimate extinction."[31]

The only consensus within the industry was on the need to maintain the tariff, to maintain prices, and to develop a more effective national voice to bargain regarding tariff levels and negotiate with government. When it came to programs of reorganization all the latent conflicts of interest came to the fore and brought progress to a halt. Thus, when in February 1934 a constitution for a new central organization was passed 76-28 by the NFISM, it had only the most limited powers.[32] Although May assured the National Committee that such an organization was the best way to keep control of the industry and warned that public criticism would be aroused if the powers of the central body appeared too meager,[33] nevertheless the Revision Committee, which drew up the final constitution of the new central body, called the British Iron and Steel Federation (BISF), further safeguarded the autonomy of the associations. IDAC's original concept of a central supervisory body exerting control through a general policy of binding agreements on prices, quotas, and rebates was reduced to a shadow. The final scheme was not one of reorganization but solely one of price maintenance.[34]

IDAC accepted these developments more or less unhappily. Ideologically it rejected central planning and direction of the industry both as undesirable and as unenforceable and politically dangerous. It saw its role as "breaking down individualism and educating businessmen in many industries to work together."[35] Its intellectual rationale was that although free competition was the only effective long-term way to reorganize the industry, in the short term it would result in the industry's "bleeding to death." Hence, the position of IDAC was that the industry had to be kept alive through the depression by maintaining its profits at a reasonable level through price maintenance so that when recovery came, reorganization could follow in more favorable conditions. The development of central machinery was, therefore, primarily a way of developing channels to coordinate voluntary reorganization at a later stage.[36] IDAC was prepared to accept rather weak central structures and let it "play itself in" for the future.[37] Leading figures in the Treasury, however, did not like it; the situation left them "with an uncomfortable feeling that a defence is being made for being content with something rather ineffective."[38]

What of the other government departments? Runciman, president of the Board of Trade, and his officials saw the adoption of these proposals as putting the industry "into a straitjacket." The price maintenance and quota scheme was diametrically opposed to a merger policy and to them no more than "a seductive selling scheme." Yet, they concluded, if the industry was agreed on this policy "it is difficult to see what can be done to induce them to change their opinion." In this situation the government might have preferred to step back and leave the industry alone, but it could not. Whatever the new structures of the industry were, IDAC consent gave them the legitimation of government backing. Pragmatically, the National Government was prepared to make considerable departures from laissez-faire. Circumstances pushed it into a more active relationship with industry, but at the same time ministers and departments like Runciman and the Board of Trade wanted to maintain definite limits on such moves. Runciman feared the implications of getting involved in any scheme that had powers of central direction or that would make possible interference with the management of individual firms to such an extent as to cast into doubt the controlling role of shareholders. This would "lead pretty directly to the late [Labour] government's Public Utility Corporation."[39] The result of this attitude was a pervasive unwillingness to take any governmental initiative.

The BISF came into existence with a constitution but, because of the reluctance to define the terms of affiliation, without any members. Its continued existence depended on its getting the goodwill of the industry and persuading the various trades associations to affiliate. Both IDAC and steelmakers like Hilton, who saw a role for a central body, saw the credibility of the new BISF and its potential for evolving into something more positive as depending largely on the choice of a chairman. He had to be a "man of eminence" who could not be labeled a tool of the heavy steelmakers.[40] The choice of chairman reflected something of a government-industry convergence; both accepted that the BISF would be little more than an arena in which they could exert mutual influence and conciliate conflicting interests.

Meanwhile, as a result of a considerable shift within the SMT during 1933–34, the Bank of England also came to accept this as inevitable. The SMT majority, especially Bruce Gardner and Norman, originally wanted to have nothing to do with the National Committee Report of February 1933[41] or with the final report a year later, which was a "poor affair."[42] But during this period discussion was opening up within the SMT as Duncan began to shift away from his earlier highly critical position.[43] By March 1933 he was arguing "the report might not be what we wanted, but there it was, and in his view we should consider whether we could not turn it to good account." Although it did not contain a plan, it did contain machinery for a plan and "this was the only way the sanction of the industry could be obtained." By the time of the final draft he could see no alternative to the scheme except government control. Hence, the best way of working within the existing constraints was "to involve the right people" in the running of the machine, which boiled down by April 1934 to the need to get the right chairman.[44]

If the SMT were to follow Duncan's reasoning, it would have to acknowledge that its whole regional amalgamation strategy was defunct. The other members of the SMT accepted this rather more slowly and unwillingly, but once the option of using tariff changes as a bargaining counter disappeared, their options narrowed rapidly. During the summer of 1933 Sir William Larke at the NFISM had got wind of "a very strong movement in Bank of England circles to force Bruce Gardner into the position of chairman of our Corporation," and he suspected that the Bank might be prepared to exert financial pressure to get him in. MacDiarmid of Stewarts & Lloyds was arranging a dinner party the following week at which the Bank intended to float the idea. Larke felt that the prospect of cooperative organization among the producers might be jeopardized by such a "false step," and he circulated his friends to organize opposition. He told John Craig, the head of the largest Scottish steel firm, that "the best thing to do is to categorically show that it is *impossible* and *unthinkable* at the outset *now* before anyone is publicly committed to it. Just say, if asked, impossible no one would seriously entertain it." His own solution was for himself to be chairman at first, with Hurst as his deputy. In the meantime he would not "surrender my self-respect and reputation by succumbing to this horrible log-rolling pressure."[45]

Both this suggestion and a subsequent one to put in a hardliner like Sir Robert Horne as chairman of the Federation in order to bring governmental pressure to bear on the industry[46] got a cold reception and were not pursued. By 1934 the Bank had to recognize that the alternatives were either an unacceptable degree of far-ranging intervention or a compromise chairman who would have the goodwill of the industry and who would attempt to promote reorganization by voluntary methods.

Horace Wilson, the leading industrial adviser at the Treasury, outlined what the former strategy would involve. At the very least, the government would have to create legislative powers to enable it to buy up minorities in the industry at a fair valuation and resell them at the same price to merged interests. But if they did this, the demand to extend the legislation to coal and beyond "would be powerful." Moreover, debenture holders might hold out for better terms if they saw that the government intended to ensure mergers. Compulsory buying and scrapping would create politically difficult redundancies—which had been one of the main reasons for the reluctance to create compulsory amalgamations through the Coal Act. Or else, if a bought-up firm restarted new plant with its cash, the government might have to block this action and consequently become further involved.[47] In the cotton industry, where there was clear majority support for proposals formulated within the industry, the government was prepared to undertake a limited legislative intervention in the Spindles Act of 1936,[48] but in steel, where there was no such consensus within the industry about what was required, such an undertaking was too hazardous. The Treasury doubted the government's ability to deal effectively with the complex internal problems that would be generated by an attempt to force reorganization.

The Bank and the Treasury, therefore, came to recognize that they had to make the most of a bad job and pursue conciliation and suasion. Andrew Duncan of SMT was clearly the best candidate for chairman of the new Federation to carry out such a role. Norman had sounded him out in January 1934, and when the BISF committee selected him, Norman intervened behind the scenes to overcome Minister of Transport Leslie Hore Belisha's unwillingness to release him from his post as chairman of the Central Electricity Board. Duncan took office in January 1935 with Larke as his deputy. The choice of Duncan with his background in the CEB was highly significant. The CEB had been developed as a state-backed coordinator of existing private undertakings. It was conceived of by the government as a commercially minded and efficient excutive body "managed by practical men in close touch with industry" (Baldwin). Under Duncan it maintained rigorous independence from the government and was subject to only minimal Treasury or ministerial control; and during the period of Duncan's leadership it had concentrated on conciliating private interests within the electricity industry, employing personal contact and confidence as one of its main methods.[49] In all these features it established precedents for governmental thinking about the possible evolution of the BISF. In practice, Duncan was not able to repeat the successes of his CEB experience in steel, where he was faced with more powerfully entrenched interests and lacked the centralizing weapon of the national grid. Nevertheless, the CEB background was a powerful formative influence on his approach and strategy at the BISF.

The government was well aware that in the first few years under tariffs it had lost the initiative to the steelmakers who were taking advantage of the new structures to pursue their particular ends; nevertheless, it fairly soon resigned itself to accepting the position. The Bank of England did not acknowledge this situation so readily but in 1933-34 it too came to accept the strength of the position of the industry in relation to government as an accomplished fact. The appointment of Duncan as chairman of BISF in 1934 marked the acceptance by both the Bank and the government that industrialists in steel could not be forced against their wills. In the short term protection would not bring effective rationalization: the task now was to create an effective central organization with a certain authority in the industry which in the long term they could hope to influence in terms of overall policy and guidelines. The result was a state-sponsored cartel. Could this body be fashioned into a vehicle for effective reorganization?

Prices and Planning under Government Supervision

Sir Andrew Duncan was appointed chairman of the BISF in November 1934 and took office in January 1935. His appointment was the outcome of the individualistic resistance of the steelmakers to government attempts to steer them toward coordinated reorganization. Duncan represented an alternative to deadlock—a conciliator who would attempt to negotiate and put together a representative central authority in the industry in cooperation with its governmental supervisors. This was to prove a lengthy process, but Duncan had achieved a considerable measure of success by 1939, a success that laid the basis for the rapid consolidation of an industry-wide association during the war years. The relationship between such an association and industrial reorganization was, however, to remain highly problematic.

Duncan's arrival in office coincided with a decisive period in the British industry's relationship with the revived European steel cartel, and it was around this issue that the distinctive features of his approach and the developing relationship of the industry with the government began to take clearer form. A new situation had resulted from the revival of the European steel cartel by Germany, Belgium, France, and Luxemburg in February 1933. Previous cartel attempts had attempted to regulate production but this one concentrated solely on regulating export markets by apportioning the global tonnage. During 1933-34 the new cartel was systematically seeking to undercut the British tariff by pricing imports into Britain at up to £1 per ton less than its prices for other markets. In 1934 British imports of iron and steel increased 40% over the 1933 level.[50] At the same time the cartel was urging Britain to join, offering a trade-off of a lower allocated share of the British market in return for the higher prices obtainable on that quota. But whereas the cartel wanted to take 90% of the 1934 levels of imports as the basis for the quota allocation, the BISF was not inclined to go above 50% as the price of a deal.[51]

The 1932 levels of tariffs were clearly inadequate to keep out the cartel assault, and from the autumn of 1934 the steelmakers began to lobby IDAC for an increased tariff to enable them to bargain effectively with the cartel for an increased quota. From the time of the re-formation of the cartel leading figures in the BISF like Sir William Larke had been arguing that Britain should participate, and one motivation for the creation of a strong central organization shared by both the steelmakers and IDAC was to facilitate that participation.[52] Despite their doubts about the effectiveness of BISF's reorganizing, the important figures in IDAC believed that a higher tariff was essential for success in bargaining with the cartel. There were, however, political problems in simply endorsing BISF demands. It seemed that there were political disagreements in the cabinet about the level of protective tariffs being afforded to industry, and in the run-up to a general election in 1935 this was a sensitive matter. Sir George May was "exceedingly doubtful whether the Government would act on a recommendation [for higher duties] by the Committee at the present time." If the Federation insisted, he would be prepared to submit an application to the government, but he advised against it and instead urged the BISF to negotiate first with the cartel on the basis that if the negotiations failed an increased tariff would almost surely follow.[53]

IDAC wanted to avoid a position in which it would be seen to be making direct quid pro quo deals with the steelmakers. Hurst told Duncan privately that IDAC was afraid "that they (IDAC) would appear to have made an arrangement with us (BISF) to strengthen their own report and thus participate in internal discussions as between departments on a political basis." Duncan was aware from his discussions with IDAC of how important it was for the BISF to appear to act of its own volition so as not to endanger IDAC's prestige.[54] Although IDAC was prepared to play, in effect, a sponsoring role as a department, it had to be allowed the necessary room for maneuver in relation to other government departments.

The majority of the steelmakers were not, however, as convinced as Duncan of IDAC's capability and reliability in this matter. The leading heavy steelmakers—J. F. Beale, Craig, Dorman, I. F. L. Elliot (GKB), George, and Talbot—all wanted to force the issue and place the responsibility for continuing imports squarely on the government. J. Henderson, the president of the BISF, declared that he was "disgusted" that IDAC was reluctant to support an application. He and the others wanted IDAC to say that an increase in duties was essential, and that if the government rejected it, "then the Government took the risk and would have to take the consequences."[55] According to J. F. Beale, "the industry was being put off with excuses to avoid a clash of opinion within the Cabinet: this clash was inevitable sooner or later and he was in favor of it being settled as soon as possible."

Peaceful methods, he argued, would not get the industry what it wanted. A strong current around him favored a frontal attack through agitation in Parliament and the press.[56]

For Sir George May, however, "this was exactly the position he wished to avoid . . . Such an event would have the effect of making it extremely difficult, if not impossible, for the Committee to help the industry in the future." The danger of lobbying directly for increased duties was that "the details might become the subject of public debate. They could not settle terms for the industry on the floor of the House of Commons." At the same time such a campaign might risk spotlighting the lack of real reorganization among steelmakers to date. Beyond that there remained the undesirable political repercussions for the divided cabinet.[57] The steelmakers' traditions of individualistic and sectional bargaining seemed to both IDAC and Duncan to jeopardize their case. Herbert Hutchinson, a leading IDAC official, saw the steelmakers' behavior as "one of the last examples of the baronial system in British industry, but without an overlord to hold it together."[58]

Duncan and Larke were working to create a less conflictual relationship with the government, but at this stage, with the exception of support from Henry Summers, they were largely isolated in their outlook.[59] In the months before he formally took office Duncan put much effort into arguing the case that it would be counterproductive to be unfriendly to IDAC which was doing its best to help the industry, and in his first few months in office he was able to persuade the steelmakers to allow him and IDAC a certain measure of grace. After long discussions they agreed not to move precipitously and to at least negotiate with the cartel first before demanding higher tariffs.[60] Subsequent events moved much as Duncan had assured the Federation they would: in December 1934 the talks broke down when the cartel refused to go below its original quota demand; in the light of this breakdown IDAC recommended and the government granted an increase in duties, specifically as a bargaining counter against the cartel; and within a month the cartel backed down and accepted BISF's earlier demand for an import quota based on the 1933 figures.[61]

Duncan's success on this issue was an important first step in developing a framework of compromise between the industry and its supervisors. The negotiation of acceptable parameters of supervision required a new willingness to compromise among the steelmakers. IDAC placed the highest priority on suppressing the entrenched individualism of the industry which could endanger its wider aims of stability and controlled reorganization.[62] The choice, as IDAC saw it, was one "between edging the industry along the right path or passing the buck to the Government."[63] IDAC believed that a widespread consensus now existed among industrialists that unregulated competition was no longer desirable, and that as a result "the state cannot divest itself of all responsibility as to the conduct of an industry so far-reaching in its scope."[64] In practice, the consequence was that "the policy pursued by the State . . . has promoted . . . the formation of a comprehensive organisation capable of exercising a powerful influence on the conduct of the industry, and enabled it to negotiate with its foreign competitors on equal terms. This had only been achieved by giving the industry a quasi-monopolistic position in the home market."[65] Once the cartel arrangements were concluded, IDAC's task was the oversight of a central body whose rise it had fostered and the promotion of a framework of development through cooperation in price and planning policies. In public statements IDAC claimed a considerable degree of success in its pursuit of these objectives.[66] J. C. Carr and W. Taplin in their standard work on the industry, concur, but since Carr was himself at one time a senior official of IDAC this is perhaps hardly surprising.[67] More recently B. S. Keeling and A. E. G. Wright have restated this view, and Peter Payne has quoted their views on IDAC with approval.[68] These rather bland accounts, however, pass over the conflicts, contradictions, and inadequacies that were hinted at although not documented by many contemporary critics.[69] A study of price policy and cooperation in planning, however, reveals some of the key difficulties and limitations involved in the supervisory relationship.

The official view of tariffs and cartelization contained an implied price policy in the same way that it contained certain assumptions about reorganization. Publicly, both Runciman at the Board of Trade and the May committee in the first two years of protection argued that tariffs encouraged reequipment and made possible an increased scale of operations. It was a policy of high output and low prices. Any adverse price effects would be "transient disadvantages to a small section" while the effects of reorganization were working themselves out.[70] Duncan and the BISF gave the government specific assurances that this was their intention. This concept depended on effective reconstruction, however. As long as Britain remained a relatively high-cost producer, tariffs would keep prices high.

Initially, any price effects of tariffs were rather masked. In the 1929–1932 depression prices of finished steel products had fallen very little,[71] but costs had fallen as raw material prices fell and only the most efficient plant was utilized. Market imperfections, loyalty rebates, and the low elasticity of substitution between home and imported products that characterized the steel market outside semis meant that profits had been held up by price maintenance during a period of falling costs.[72] Hence, when tariffs were introduced, prices were not raised. Stabilization tended in itself to increase profitability. Merely enforcing existing prices rigorously tended to raise overall real price levels. This was the background to the relatively easygoing initial negotiations between IDAC and the steel industry on prices and the prominence of fairly vague assurances on the question. Until 1936 IDAC was fairly optimistic that price levels could soon be reduced with reorganization,[73] but the position changed sharply with the upward shift in the pattern of costs in 1936–37.

In the absence of reorganization rising demand did not mean falling costs; raw material prices increased rapidly, particularly the price of scrap on which Britain was heavily dependent, and much old plant that was out of date and had high running and maintenance costs was pressed into service. The absence of scale economies of integrated production came to the fore. There was a considerable lag before renewed profits worked their way through to investment, and the first wave of new investment was often in piecemeal expansion and in getting old capacity into speedy operation.[74] Best-practice investment did not commence until 1936–37. Hence, one of the upturn's early consequences was pressure of rising costs.

Most steelmakers were wary of responding to this situation merely by allowing prices to rise. They feared that rising prices might choke off demand at a time when recovery was still precarious, and many were anxious about allegations, particularly from motor manufacturers, that steelmakers were exploiting their protected position to bolster prices. Yet they were also naturally anxious to sustain profits. In consequence, the BISF and IDAC were agreed that the best course of action was to restrain the impact of certain costs, particularly those of scrap. We have already noted the persistently high utilization of scrap in British steelmaking in the depressed conditions of the 1920s. The proportion of scrap to pig iron used in British steelmaking rose from 40:60 in 1920 to 48:52 in 1929 to a peak of 60:40 in 1933, remaining at 55:45 in 1936–37.[75] This preponderance was based on its suitability to open-hearth production and above all on its relative price: in the early 1920s the price of scrap was generally close to but below that of pig; in the late 1920s and early 1930s it fell far below it.[76] The price movement was principally shaped by the sources of supply. Some firms had access to plentiful breakdown scrap from the shipbuilding and armaments concerns with which they were integrated. Most, however, was bought on the open market. Only 10% of scrap used was imported in 1934. As demand increased, it was at first relatively easy to go beyond British scrap supplies and to expand imports, which rose to 25% of the total in 1936.[77] Scrap was a fairly cheap and flexible raw material that in the short term could be expanded much more rapidly than pig iron production, but in the mid-1930s continental revival led to competition for scrap supplies. The precariousness of dependence on a raw material that characterizes depressed rather than expanding economies was manifested in scrap shortages and a rapid adverse movement in the price margin between scrap and pig iron.

The scrap problem of the mid-1930s therefore reflected the weaknesses of British iron production and lack of integrated iron and steel making. Scrap usage had been an empirical response to depression and covered a major structural flaw. In the short term the crisis of scrap supply threatened two unacceptable consequences: unless action was taken, steel prices would rocket upwards, and the expansion of demand might be interrupted at a time when the industry was facing its most favorable market for years. The political risks of such a price takeoff that would endanger the protected position of British producers just when IDAC was about to produce its major public review of the industry also pointed up the need for a centralized response.

Because a traditional antipathy existed between steelmakers and merchants, central action on buying was fairly readily acceptable in principle. The constituents of the BISF unanimously accepted the creation of a central "spreadover" levy of 5 shillings per ton on ingot output to subsidize losses incurred by the British Iron and Steel Corporation (BISC), BISF's commercial trading organization, in buying foreign scrap at high prices and reselling to British makers at lower fixed rates. This shortfall, initially reckoned at £3 million, rose to £5.5 million by November 1937, but these costs were sugared by exceptionally favorable financial conditions. IDAC allowed the levy to be treated as a charge on profits for tax purposes and at the same time as a cost in the determination of steel prices.[78]

However, the impact of the levy on rival firms and on the structure of the industry was not neutral. The levy was on all steel production rather than just on those who used scrap, because the significant effect that the policy was designed to control was the overall level of steel prices at the politically sensitive time of IDAC's first report. Hence, firms reliant on scrap benefited most. In 1935 Lincolnshire makers used only 26% scrap, the Northeast 36%, and the Northwest 23%, Welsh makers used 69%, Scottish 66%, and Sheffield, for rather different reasons, 72%.[79] At a time when the shortage of supply would have made the large scrap users the least favored producers, the scrap levy actually reversed the position. In 1937, instead of paying 100 shillings per ton for bought scrap as against 95 shillings per ton home price for pig iron, they were able through the scheme to buy scrap at 65 shillings per ton. Hence, steelmakers could get scrap cheaper than pig could be made anywhere except Corby and Lincolnshire.[80]

The scrap levy eased pressures to move toward lowest-cost practice and in particular took some of the urgency out of the position of the big Welsh and Scottish makers. The other steelmakers were ready to accept this as an interim solution because of the priority of short-term price stabilization for political reasons. Sir William Larke would have liked to develop the spreadover levy into a central stabilization fund which the BISF could use as an instrument of policy in directing development, but he got very little support for this scheme,[81] and the levy was temporarily halted in the sharp slump in 1938. Misjudgments by the BISF had resulted in heavy forward contracts for high-priced scrap at a time when trade entered an abrupt downturn, and this, together with the disappearance of the upward pressure on prices, meant a turn away from the scheme.[82] Within a year, however, the onset of war revived the idea, and the revised and extended scheme that followed was to be a major part of industry policy in the next decade.

In the prewar years, however, it was already clear that despite IDAC's rather vague notions of price policy as an element in the planning of development and expansion, the actual impact of this first experiment in centralized buying was to reinforce existing industrial structures. Similar problems arose in the elaboration of policies on overall price levels. These policies were major substantive issues in themselves, and the process of policy formation here also had widespread ramifications for the way in which the internal structures of the BISF took shape. From December 1935 Duncan and the BISF in conjunction with IDAC had to handle a series of applications for price increases.[83] No policy for price rises had been necessary when the structures of the BISF and IDAC were created to cope with depression conditions, and the new policy was formulated on a hand-to-mouth basis over a series of cases. From the beginning the direction that was taken was to attempt in some way to relate variations in prices to ascertained costs. This course implied certain infringements of strongly defended traditions of business secrecy within the industry, and it was of the utmost importance that Duncan was able to persuade the industrialists to identify him with their interests. He consistently approached the matter through personal confidential contact with the leaders of various trade associations, asking them to discuss any price increases with him while they were still in the pipeline. At the same time he stressed that he was not attempting to control price policy but to act as an intermediary between the industry and IDAC. His aim was to smooth the path with IDAC and to get a "common form of procedure." The final determination of the prices that the steelmakers would propose to IDAC, he continued to emphasize, remained the prerogative of the associations.[84]

The steelmakers came to have a considerable degree of confidence in Duncan, but his interest in the regulation of price increases was in tension with this relationship. From the summer of 1935 he feared that the autonomy of the associations might result in a situation in which prices were increased to such an extent that accusations of exploiting the protected position of the industry would be directed at the BISF. Alternatively, if he attempted to hold the line against the wishes of the major firms, it might result in the breakup of the Federation.[85]

Hence, Duncan needed not merely the general confidence that flowed from close personal involvement with the leaders of the industry but also a practice of price regulation that would be flexible enough to avoid provoking excessive discontent and allow fairly substantial profits yet at the same time curb pure profit maximization within the regulated regime of the cartel. This policy was embodied in the practices of cost calculation and price assessment that the BISF evolved. In developing these mechanisms Duncan relied largely on the work of J. T. Rankin, a senior accountant of Peat, Marwick and Mitchell, a firm with a long tradition of association with the steel industry. In time, Rankin became so closely associated with the industry that when the war came the government appointed another accountant to review and supervise his work in the belief that he was too closely involved with the steelmakers.[86]

Rankin developed the BISF's price policy in the course of a series of confidential audits undertaken for Duncan. The system he evolved was to produce a basic cost for any given product by taking sample costs of a number of "efficient and well-placed firms" and estimating the main variations in these costs at different levels of price or output during the period in which the price to be fixed was to be effective. This cost was below that of the highest-cost producers but above that of the most efficient makers. The basic cost, therefore, actually included a profit margin for more efficient producers. The price would be set by adding a fixed margin to cover interest, depreciation, obsolescence, and profit.[87]

Formally this embodied a general commitment to relate prices to costs, but it begged the question of exactly what costs were and how they were to be measured. Moreover, no simple relationship existed between movements in prices and costs; shifts in output, for instance, affected each differently. And when producers spanned a wide range of costs, the question of whose costs to relate prices to became of great significance. Even at the accounting level, different firms computed their costs in different ways. Practices of calculation in this area therefore made possible a pragmatic and almost indefinitely flexible mode of price regulation. The superficially impartial mechanism in fact incorporated wide scope for political adjustment and compromise.

One further implication of this method of cost assessment was the creation of an umbrella effect. It raised the profits of efficient producers but also took into account the lower level of efficiency in the sector as a whole and sheltered the inefficiency of other producers. Such a price policy could not and was not intended to effectively direct investment; it relied on giving high profits to the efficient and hoped that this would result in effective investment. However, within a cartelized regime the temptations to pursue maximum net revenue were strong, and in boom conditions patching and short-term investment for quick returns tended to be preferred to the BISF's proclaimed objective of broad restructuring.

Some examples can illustrate the political flexibility and nondirective nature of this price policy. In the case of the tube industry price increases were allowed in 1936 and again in 1937. In this period Stewarts & Lloyds' profits on tubes rose from 35 shillings per ton in April 1936 to 60 shillings per ton in August 1937. Corby produced 40% of home demand, Stewarts & Lloyds' other works produced 30%, and the independent tube makers, of whom only the Wellington Tube Co. was genuinely outside Stewarts & Lloyds' orbit, produced 30%. But the small producers were making profits of only 20 shillings per ton in August 1937; this reflected a spectrum of production costs from £11 per ton at Corby to £16 elsewhere. IDAC recognized that Stewarts & Lloyds' profits were abnormally high, yet the company demanded further price increases for the sector on the grounds of the narrow profit margins of the smaller producers. Attempts to get the firm to agree to voluntary dividend limitation in return for permitting a price increase were curtly rebutted. Politically, Stewarts & Lloyds had a strong hand. Duncan was very anxious to woo the firm into the Federation; its position half in and half out of the Federation was a source of discontent within the industry,[88] and Duncan felt that its refusal to participate in the new scrap levy was a threat to the success of that scheme. Hence, conciliation was of prime importance. IDAC was aware that the smaller, less efficient firms "existed only on sufferance by permission of Messrs. Stewarts & Lloyds" and that the company was using them as "a stalking horse to get higher prices." But it still felt it necessary to bow to the pricing demands and concede the increases.[89]

In the case of hematite pig iron, when there was an application for a price increase in late 1937, only two small firms, William Dixon & Co. and John Gjers & Co., were not making adequate profits according to a survey carried out by Rankin. Both had outdated plant and bought all their raw materials on the open market. These firms produced only 12% of total output, and no reasonable price increase could in any case solve their problems; Rankin therefore recommended against a price increase.[90] At this time, however, considerable tensions were developing within the BISF between the independent ironmaking sector and the steelmakers following the "undoubtedly liberal profit margins" that IDAC admitted that it had allowed to the latter in the 1937 price revisions. IDAC and the BISF now felt that it was very important, to "avoid any appearance of sacrificing the ironmasters to the steelmakers."[91] Already the Foundry Iron Association had refused to affiliate to the BISF, and the Hematite Association was intransigently uncooperative. The need to placate and woo these interests to strengthen the BISF suggested the desirability of searching for a compromise. There was room for maneuver in this area because only a minority of steelmakers bought their hematite pig iron on the open market and would suffer little from increased hematite prices, whereas the largest hematite producers were United Steel and Guest Keen Baldwin, who were also giant steelmakers. Hollins, the managing director of GKB, was also chairman of the Hematite Association.

To avoid a dangerous precedent it was necessary to present the concession to the small ironmasters as being within the apparently impartial framework of relating prices to costs. The solution that was found was a "flexible" recalculation of Rankin's original costings. The effect of forward *buying* of raw materials on keeping down costs was discounted; at the same time the effect of forward *selling* on reducing profits from a price increase were taken into account. The effect of falling freight rates was also removed, and additional flexibility was allowed for charging for extras—an old practice of price regulation maneuvers that had been a feature in steel for decades.[92] The juggled figures substantially raised the ironmasters' likely profits and represented a substantial concession to the iron sector while keeping intact the framework of price policy.

The political flexibility of the price policy was combined with extremely loose informational demands. Cost accounting before World War II was used by IDAC not as an instrument to organize and regulate production from the center, but as a framework for compromise between rival enterprises. When this framework was adapted for more conscious organization and evaluation of production during the war, these deficiencies of information were to be scathingly exposed. It emerged then that IDAC did not review the accounts of individual firms but relied on the cost investigations of the BISF's accountant, who based his figures on information supplied to him by the firms. As one member of the Commons Select Committee investigating wartime pricing noted, this "is not investigating; they depend entirely for checking Tweedledum on the figures supplied by Tweedledee."[93] When IDAC's own accountant, introduced in 1938, began to take a more active role, he found that the estimated costs had always been "to a large extent conjectural, some makers felt unable to furnish them, and they have not proved to be of any serious assistance."[94] The 1940 Public Accounts Committee found that "in the absence of knowledge of the basis on which the costs were founded or the details from which they were built up, [the Comptroller and Auditor General] was not in a position to express any opinion on the adequacy of the current arrangements for price determination."[95]

In the early years of the BISF some firms deliberately falsified their figures: in 1936 Lancashire Steel Corporation submitted costs that were so patently unreliable as to have to be excluded from Rankin's assessment,[96] and in 1937 Consett refused to submit figures at all.[97] Manipulation of figures by other firms made costing highly arbitrary. In part this problem derived from the limitations of firms' internal accountancy: before the war, for instance, there had been no accountancy discussion of the evaluation of blast furnace gases used in integrated processes,[98] and many small firms were unable to produce accurate costings because of a lack of weighing facilities and production control.[99] But the evolution of practice clearly followed the priorities of the system, and systematization of practices was not something to which the BISF and IDAC felt inclined to devote attention. Thus the "legitimate" scope for disparities on carriage costs, methods of charging for hot metal used in integrated works, and variations in stocking and dispatching costs remained wide.

One example will illustrate the scope for such manipulation. A prevalent practice was for producers to enter their raw materials costs at the full market price, even when they were getting their supplies much cheaper. Thus Bairds, which produced 96% of its own coke at 25 shillings per ton in 1937 and bought just 4% at 30/7d, submitted the latter figure as the cost of *all* their coke to the BISF. Similarly, United Steel (Workington) produced more than 70% of its own hematite ore at 8/6d per ton, yet it submitted a figure of 24 shillings per ton, the price it had paid for a small part of its outside purchases.

The effect of such practices could be considerable: the distortion of raw material costs alone raised the overall costs submitted to BISF for hematite pig by 16% for Bairds, 15% for United Steel, 13% for Consett, 6% for Colvilles, and 4% for GKB, thus seriously inflating profits.[100]

These more blatant practices declined as it became apparent that the BISF did not intend to use price policy for directive purposes and that price control tended to be a fairly generous framework. They persisted longest among the smaller firms who remained most suspicious of the Federation[101] and among firms that produced highly finished goods where profits were high, investment rapid, product differentiation considerable, and the charging of extras could be used by the associations concerned, as Duncan noted, to "virtually free themselves of price control by the Federation" as late as 1939,[102] especially in Sheffield where there were an enormous number of pseudo brands of steel.[103]

Nevertheless, for all firms the ability to conceal their actual costs continued to be regarded as a safeguard against more stringent control. When the war came the firms stubbornly resisted the inquiries of the Public Accounts Committee (PAC) for more rigorous disclosure over a three-year period before they revealed the actual bases of calculation of their costings—even though, when they were finally revealed, the PAC accepted that they were broadly acceptable.[104]

Price fixing based on average ascertained costs produced a wide spectrum of profits. The indicators used did not take account of the level of profits but only the trend of costs and margins within the industry. A price that allowed a small profit to one maker necessarily allowed big profits to others.[105] The existence of high-cost producers raised the profit level of low-cost producers, but the higher profits were gained only at the cost of the elimination of price competition. Hence, the relationship of the most dynamic corporations such as United Steel and Stewarts & Lloyds to the Federation was ambiguous, because stability was being traded off against the ability to win markets from competitors.

However, deliberate exploitation of the cartel position to produce inflated profits was constrained by two risks. On one hand, the formal involvement of government supervision heightened the political sensitivity of steel pricing and gave other manufacturers a potential lever to exert pressure on steelmakers. On the other, too high a level of profits and prices risked encouraging new entrants to the industry with the consequent increased risk of overcapacity if the new expansion of the market proved ephemeral. The BISF could to a certain extent discourage new entrants if profitability was only a little above average, but if the iron and steel industries were seen as an arena of inflated profits, capital would flow into it and the framework of regulation would be disrupted. Hence, profits were probably not too grossly exploitative for both political and economic reasons. Some firms could have made higher profits outside Federation control, but this risked increased competition in the longer run. One exception was Stewarts & Lloyds, which stayed outside the Federation precisely in order to make higher profits because it felt that in tubes increased competition was inevitable in the long run and that therefore in an expanding market it needed high profits and a high rate of investment.[106] For most makers, however, the objective of preventing excessive competition was dominant in the 1930s.

The actual level of profits cannot be exactly defined. Most steel firms also had coke, coal, or engineering interests, and profits and losses from these sectors were generally included in the overall profit figures of the firms. Moreover, profits themselves are a relation between income and costs, and both of these figures are problematic. However, the surveys undertaken by IDAC's accountant, Andrew Macharg, during the war showed the relationship between gross trading profit and capital employed. As Table 19 shows, they give an indication of the order of magnitude and spectrum of profitability within the industry. Comparison with Table 2 above shows that in 1936 steel profits, although rising, were still below the average rate of profit for all manufacturing industry. Although the gap narrowed rapidly in 1937, few of the big firms came close to the manufacturing average rate of just over 16%.[107] However, as Tables 19 and 20 show, profitability was considerably higher in more finished products than in heavy steel where the largest firms were concentrated. As a result, because of the impact of the profits of the specialist firms, the rate of profit in the industry as a whole was higher than that of many of the larger firms.

What neither of these tables tells us, however, is the extent to which these figures are higher than they would have been if prices had not been fixed. The revival of demand in itself was bound to revive profits, and it is hard to allot values to those parallel effects. Brian Tew and Duncan Burn suggest that prices and raw material costs moved closely together from 1932 to 1936 and that prices then, over the industry as a whole, began to move ahead faster than raw material prices.[108] Again it is not clear what caused this; it could as well have been the impact of demand on limited supplies as monopoly exploitation of prices.

Whatever the case, it does seem clear that cartelization guaranteed greater continuity of profits and gave steelmakers a bulwark against collapse even in the downturn of 1938-39.[109] By that time new cost-

Table 19   Profits of the major steel firms, 1936–37

Firm	Average capital employed (£)[a]	Profits (£)	Percentage of profit on capital
Baldwin's Ltd.	6,828,813	762,054	11.2
Barrow Hematite Steel Co.	1,832,907	90,000	4.4
South Durham Steel and Iron Co.	5,251,979	387,358	7.4
Colvilles Ltd.	10,478,880	1,362,514	13.0
Consett Iron Co.	8,219,719	788,267	9.6
Dorman Long & Co.	13,372,061	1,808,942	13.5
Guest Keen Baldwin's Ltd.	8,534,876	584,331	6.8
Lancashire Steel Corporation	6,945,588	733,507	10.6
Park Gate Iron & Steel Co.	2,328,057	107,622	4.6
Round Oak Co.	1,081,058	106,177	9.8
Skinningrove Iron Co.	1,583,125	101,244	6.4
John Summers & Sons	5,657,678	574,850	10.2
United Steel Companies Ltd.	14,668,989	1,845,675	12.6
Richard Thomas & Co.	16,181,977	1,544,775	9.6
Total	102,965,707	10,787,026	10.5

Source: A. S. Macharg, Memorandum on Profit Enquiry, 6 Jan. 1943, BISF Prices and Costs, 1939–1945.

a. Recorded book values of capital.

reducing investment was effectively coming on stream for the first time, and production costs were beginning to move downward more smoothly as output moved upward. Against a background of fear of allegations of profiteering on the rising tide of armaments contracts and despite "a certain amount of heart-burning in the industry," Duncan was able to persuade makers to reduce prices in anticipation of rapidly expanding future demand for the first time.[110]

Over the first four years of Duncan's office prices and profits had been stabilized within a framework of personal confidence and compromise between the firms, Duncan, and IDAC, but such stabilization was accomplished by optimizing certain short-term politically sensitive indicators rather than by developing broader overall policies. IDAC proved reluctant and ill-equipped to push any further in the latter direction beyond promoting cooperation and consensus among steelmakers. Such a policy produced little impetus toward structural changes, and in consequence, as profits stabilized in an industry that was not conspicuously efficient, the possibility emerged that outside firms might seek to enter the industry to pursue a low-cost strategy or that individual firms might try to break away in the same direction. Much of the contemporary criticism of the BISF and IDAC—notably that by Robert Brady, Henry Owen, and Ellen Wilkinson—stressed the role played by these institutions as barriers to such entry.[111] As we have already seen in the detailed case study of Richard Thomas & Co. and the new strip mill, these structures undeniably made it difficult for expansionist producers. New entrants could not win customers by pricing competitively because cartel policies more or less outlawed price competition. At the same time, the BISF refused to allocate a tonnage at existing fixed prices to new entrants, which raised the risks of entry to levels unacceptable to the capital market. The most famous test case on this issue was that of Jarrow.

Palmer's Shipbuilding and Iron Co. at Jarrow had been in acute trouble since the end of the First World War. The steel works had been closed in 1921 and thereafter worked only sporadically in 1923, 1927, and 1929. The shipyards closed finally in 1933.[112] Jarrow had depended almost solely on Palmer's for employment, and more than 80% of its workers were left unemployed. In 1933 National Ship-

Table 20   Comparison of profitability of different steel products, 1936–37

Product	Capital employed (£)	Profits (£)	Percentage of profit on capital
Heavy steel	74,297,239	7,905,337	10.6
Sheets	29,451,890	2,957,526	10.4
Hot rolled tubes	15,549,656	1,676,574	10.8
Cold drawn tubes	3,870,243	1,066,013	27.5
Re-rolled products	3,608,204	771,955	21.4
Steel castings	480,543	89,049	18.5
Forgings	495,916	92,181	18.6
Alloy steel	17,261,527	2,494,616	14.5
Wire	1,066,821	177,020	16.6
Wire rope	2,415,965	212,316	8.8
Bolts and nuts	1,498,982	362,204	18.1
Cast iron pipes	2,417,460	288,227	11.9
Total	152,914,726	18,093,018	11.8

Source: A. S. Macharg, Memorandum on the Financial Arrangements in Respect of Iron and Steel and Related Products during the War, 20 April 1943, Ministry of Supply, Iron and Steel Control, BISF Costs and Prices, 1939–1943.

builders Securities bought the shipyard and "sterilized" it under the national scheme, closing it down and banning any new purchaser from reopening it. But as trade revived, the Jarrow steel works regained a potential value with its excellent site and its plentiful cheap labor. Recognizing this, Consett in 1934 considered buying the site and scrapping the works to prevent its being bought and worked by a competitor; it did not do so only because it feared the repercussions of public opinion.[113] At the same time, an American financier, T. Vosper Salt, on the basis of a report prepared by Brassert, acquired an option to purchase for a syndicate he had formed. The syndicate approached city financial interests for backing through the stockbroker H. C. Arnold-Forster, and in due course it was referred for discussions to the BISF to see if other Northeast Coast interests would cooperate or participate. The individuals involved met Duncan in spring 1935, and Duncan commissioned a further report from Brassert for the Federation.

Brassert's investigations showed that a new integrated works at Tyneside (Jarrow) could produce open-hearth steel at 68 shillings per ton as against current Teesside costs of around 85-90 shillings.[114] A greenfield development on Teesside was not a feasible proposition, but complete modernization and extensions could, Brassert estimated, produce open-hearth steel at 71 shillings per ton at the existing sites.[115] (For details see Table 21.) However, Brassert's proposals went beyond adding to open-hearth capacity. He noted that the home ore basis of

Table 21 Estimates of attainable manufacturing costs on the Northeast Coast and in comparable regions under various conditions, 1935

Producing area	Cost of basic pig per ton	Cost of BB ingots per ton	Cost of OH ingots per ton
Northamptonshire	38s. 6d.	51s. 6d.	
Lincolnshire	42s.		59s.
Teesside (new integrated plant)	50s.	60s. 6d.	67s. 6d.
Tyneside (new integrated plant)	48s. 8d.	59s. 6d.	68s.
Teesside (existing plant modernized and extended)		70s. 6d.	71s.
Teesside (current costs)	65–68s.		85–90s.

Sources: Lines 1-4: H. A. Brassert & Co., Memorandum on the North East Coast Iron and Steel Industry, 1 Aug. 1935, SMT 3/78. *Line 5:* I. F. L. Elliott (commercial director, BISF) to Arthur Dorman, 21 Feb. 1936, Consett, Board Reports, Papers, and Agendas. *Line 6:* Estimates based on company records.

the Northeast iron and steel industry was becoming depleted and that in the long term development in the Northeast should be concentrated on coastal sites using foreign ores.[116] Within this framework he proposed that Jarrow should be developed as a pioneering basic Bessemer development in the area. He reckoned that total steel demand would be 10.5 million tons by 1940 and that of this at least 2.5 million tons of basic Bessemer would be required; yet Northamptonshire (Corby) output of basic Bessemer would not exceed one million tons. A Bessemer development could both fill this gap and provide a basis for the diversification of products in the Northeast away from its shrinking traditional plate and rail markets.[117]

This sort of development could also be constructed around the existing rolling mills at South Durham's Cargo Fleet site, although new docks, blast furnaces, and steel plant would be required and the congested site would prevent the attainment of lowest costs. South Durham considered this move but it was wary of the basic Bessemer process, which had only recently been revived at Corby, and above all it feared that such expansion would create excess capacity.[118] Like Dorman Long, South Durham saw the revival essentially as an opportunity to modernize and reorganize its existing works at minimal capital cost and thus hasten and maximize immediate profits. The urgency of diversification receded as the demand for traditional products revived in the late 1930s. As Table 21 shows, this attitude was not unreasonable as far as open-hearth production was concerned; modernization could produce costs comparable to new building at Jarrow. But this was not the case with basic Bessemer where a Jarrow development would retain a clear cost advantage over any modernized plant.

Given that they took a fairly cautious view about the prospects for expanding demand, neither Dorman Long nor South Durham was interested in fostering the development of new low-cost capacity or in participating in an enterprise that might make much of their plant obsolete. As Ben Talbot of South Durham frankly put it: "The position is simply that we are not interested. We are prepared to put our money into our existing works at Teesside and not on Tyneside. If anyone else wants to put their money in it, let them, that is all."[119] As the trade press noted, it was hardly realistic to expect the Tees manufacturers to cooperate in the establishment of a competitor.[120]

Consett's attitude, however, was rather different. Its geographical orientation was toward Tyne rather than Tees, and it was therefore more inclined to favor the scheme.[121] Brassert envisaged close cooperation between Jarrow and Consett; the latter's stationary open-hearth furnaces were ideal for the higher qualities of acid and basic steel and could easily be coordinated with a basic Bessemer program on Tyneside. Rolling could be distributed to best advantage between the works. Consett would also be directly involved in the management of the new works.[122]

Consett wanted Duncan to let Jarrow go forward as a joint Consett/ Stewarts & Lloyds' scheme with BID backing if the other Northeast makers would not cooperate.[123] But if Consett ran Jarrow, it would not be the cooperative project it would be if the Teesside makers were also involved. Instead, as E. J. George, Consett's managing director, stressed, it would have to pursue its own interests as a rival to the others.[124] To do this effectively, it needed the implementation of the original scheme in its entirety. The BISF's compromise proposal of mid-1936 to proceed on a "complementary" development based solely on 150,000 tons of basic Bessemer billets and bars for sale and 75,000 tons of basic Bessemer colliery arches, light rails, and sections would eliminate the duplexing facilities and hence Jarrow's potential for "cutting across the [Teesside firms'] quality trades" in conjunction with Consett.[125] Such a limited scheme offered no great attraction to Consett, and the company decided not to proceed further.[126]

The local membership of the BISF was therefore predominantly hostile to a Jarrow scheme. Only Consett believed that gains could be made from it, and, although competitive, it was one of the smaller firms. But Duncan, the chairman of the BISF, himself favored the Jarrow scheme. He was more concerned to expand national production than the local makers who had suffered reverses in the last wave of expansion. In addition, he was more sensitive to the political dimensions of the Jarrow employment question and to the public image of the industry, particularly with the Import Duties Advisory Committee's major public review of the workings of tariffs imminent. Hence, in January 1936 he told the BISF that Jarrow "had got to go forward."[127] Duncan feared just the sort of public scandal that Jarrow proved to be. He was able to persuade Colvilles to defer certain expansion plans for a time in view of a possible Jarrow development, but he had no machinery to force cooperation from recalcitrant makers.[128] He had to bow to the weight of the opposition of Teesside firms within the BISF.

If cooperation was not to be forthcoming, the alternative was competitive entry to the market. A new Tyne plant producing basic Bessemer would enjoy a cost advantage of more than 10 shillings per ton over its Teesside competitors after the latter had been modernized. But a Jarrow plant would not be able to use its price advantage to win customers; it would have to join the BISF and thus would be

bound by association prices, thereby losing its best weapon for obtaining trade. Hence, unless it had some sort of quota, it would have
difficulty in finding outlets, and the rival firms would not give it a
quota. To go outside the BISF would have been a risky commercial
proposition; finance would have been hard to raise for a project that
would have to fight a price-cutting war just to establish itself. Considerable financial sacrifices would have to be made even to enter the
market. The syndicate decided that the cost margin was not wide
enough to justify this risk. It took a less optimistic view than did
Brassert of the course of future demand in reaching this decision: it
calculated that to achieve lowest costs an output of 350-400,000 tons
was required, but that a demand of more than 250,000 tons basic
Bessemer by the time construction was completed was unlikely.[129] In
the light of the actual course of demand it is clear that the syndicate
overestimated the risks.[130]

Despite Duncan's apparent sympathy for the project, the structure
of the BISF made it impossible for it to proceed commercially without
cooperation. In effect, as Jarrow M. P. Ellen Wilkinson noted, the
BISF blocked the scheme and denied doing so at the same time, and
the Times pointed out that "There are more ways of killing a project
than expressly forbidding it." The government found it convenient
to stress the technically correct point that no one had formally blocked
it,[131] but Wilkinson is wrong to draw a picture of steel magnates'
pursuing private profits at the expense of national needs.[132] As E. J.
George noted, Arnold-Forster had no right to accuse the Northeast
steelmakers of selfishness, because his syndicate was only trying to
make a profit too.[133] Although the Jarrow workers were a political
embarrassment to the Federation and the government, their interests
were never a significant consideration. At Ebbw Vale labor agitation
had had a certain effect because it coincided with the interests of a
particular firm which had made use of it in their business strategy,[134]
but the Jarrow workers had no such leverage.

In fact the scheme generated a clash between two rival groups of
capitalists, and the strategic position of the Teesside BISF members
gave them the whip hand. The BISF as a representative organization
could not compel its members to act other than as they chose; in that
sense the real power resided in the regional associations rather than
the Federation itself. For the Teesside members who did not foresee
the length of the boom, immediate improvements to meet urgent
demand were more attractive than long-term projects slow to mature
which awakened fears of repeating the 1920s experience of overcapacity. As I. F. Elliott, commercial director of the BISF, put it, "While
a long-term policy of expansion must be borne in mind, the short-

term policy had become even more important—indeed a matter of national necessity." To meet these requirements, expenditure had to be concentrated on any serviceable plant that could be brought into operation within nine months. Thus, the proprietors of each plant, in incurring substantial expenditures to meet such needs "must be protected reasonably in regard to our long-term policy of expansion." Within this framework Jarrow could go forward only by consent of the Northeast makers and that was not forthcoming.[135]

The beginning of a new wave of expansion was clearly the vital time for long-term planning, but the BISF was not an organization that *could* plan. Duncan did not even have the same advisory resources that Norman, for instance, had had at the SMT and the BID, and he also lacked the overall blueprint for development that the Brassert and Bruce Gardner plans, despite their failings, had provided. Rather, the BISF was an organization that served to defend the interests of its existing membership as a whole and to impose a restrictive framework on the market for this purpose. The *Economist* correctly noted that "self-government of industry" in effect meant private monopoly, refusing entry to newcomers, and exploiting the imperfections of the market. The BISF's powers were exercised by a central body elected by individual producers and "the central body will have the conscience while the individual members have the power." The whole system, it concluded, was "an ossification of inefficiency, an endowment of selfishness."[136]

War and Nationalization: The Legacy of Intervention, 1939–1953

The developments of the 1930s had far-reaching implications, and to understand them fully it is necessary to look beyond the interwar years to the period of war and the first nationalization of the industry. The institutional and policy structures laid down in the period 1932-1939 were consolidated and became powerful determinants of the postwar history of the industry: the structures of industry-wide association and government supervision that the government had sponsored before the war became major barriers to changed governmental aims after the war, and institutions intended to advance the restructuring of the industry became the guarantors of its persistent inertia. Elements of this development were apparent before the war, and thereafter these tendencies were consistently reinforced.

The Second World War finally consolidated the BISF. Until 1939 divisions still existed among steelmakers as to how much power the organization should have. Important figures like Firth and MacDiarmid feared that a strong Federation would curb enterprising firms;

they saw a role for cooperation and association to eliminate violent price fluctuations and severe price competition, but they also wanted it to ensure the elimination of high-cost plants so that new modern works such as their own could run at full capacity, and before the war they had received little support for this point of view from the BISF. The war, however, led to the curbing of Firth and the effective absorption of MacDiarmid into the Federation, and by 1945 there remained no significant opposition among big firms to the BISF. At the same time the industry was viewed as functioning more or less as a quasi-autonomous department of government for the duration of the conflict—the "BISF in uniform." IDAC was absorbed into the Ministry of Supply as the Raw Materials Department to formulate steel policy and supervise its execution, and the BISF was absorbed into the Iron and Steel Control to administer its policies. Duncan became the first steel controller until he became president of the Board of Trade in early 1940 and later minister of supply; all the later controllers were drawn from steel firms and the administration largely from the BISF. Habits of cooperation increased, considerable experience of investment control accumulated, and the central technical staff made major advances. As the BISF gained universal acceptance among its membership, its structure also evolved: the Federation decentralized more and more authority to the sectional associations, and the idea of a strong independent chairman such as Duncan had been intended to be waned. More and more the associations came to run the Federation rather than vice versa. Finally, the practice of planning became more familiar as the Control and the Raw Materials Department forced the BISF to take responsibility for forward planning and licensing schemes during 1943–1945.[137]

By the end of the war the Federation had espoused as its own the role that IDAC would have liked it to play before the war, namely, one of a strong Federation undertaking more active planning and the elimination of price competition in the context of supervision by an impartial body appointed by government. In part, this was due to a pragmatic realization that the government's role of control would last for many years after the war and that unless steelmakers devised voluntary schemes of self-control the government would impose its own priorities on them. Postwar investment would inevitably take place against a background of shortages and restrictions and scarcity of plant and labor and they recognized the need to plan and formulate priorities. As the war drew to a close, there was also greater sympathy for notions of wholesale modernization and doubts about the viability of continued patching policies. In the face of envisaged intensified competition, the Federation would need, as IDAC had suggested in its report before the war, to both veto certain schemes and devise schemes of its own which no individual maker would be capable of. Meanwhile, the increased political pressure of a Labour government created a greater need for the steelmakers to demonstrate their efficiency and enthusiasm for reform. The big firms were quite happy to have the continuation of some IDAC-style supervision—partly to give smaller firms confidence that they would not be dominated by the larger ones, partly to legitimize the collective action of employers in the eyes of both consumers and the public, and partly because they realized that major social issues were bound to be involved in questions of the future of the industry that went far beyond their own perspectives and responsibilities. Nevertheless, they were determined that scrutiny should remain at one remove from decision making: they did not want the government to take any active role in planning.[138]

The continuing active relationship with government had transformed the weak and fragmented and obstinately individualistic steelmakers into a coherent and effective lobby capable of coordinating resistance to government policies. In 1946 the BISF refused to cooperate with the Iron and Steel Board until the Ministry of Supply guaranteed that the board would not be expected to advise the ministry on nationalization: the ministry backed down. Through the long buildup to nationalization the BISF organized sustained and influential propaganda and lobbying and argued the political case for the status quo in close alliance with the Conservative Party. When nationalization did come, the BISF doggedly refused to cooperate with the nationalizing body, the Iron and Steel Corporation of Great Britain (ISCGB). An uneasy truce between the two bodies severely curtailed the corporation's authority during the brief period of its existence, and no steelmaker of note ever agreed to serve on it.[139]

As the industry-wide institutions consolidated their internal coherence and autonomy, their price and planning policies had increased effects on the evolution of the industry. The spreadover schemes of 1936–37 had distributed the burdens of high marginal costs over the whole of production by levies. Until the war this system, combined with minimum prices based on the average costs of all but the most and least efficient producers, had prevented low-cost firms from attracting business by charging less and at the same time ensured stable and moderately high profits for the most efficient. During the war, however, wider government priorities meant that the main aim of wartime policy was to keep prices low and stable even if this meant a subsidy. In this context prewar cost-spreading practices were combined with a price *ceiling* and therefore tended to equalize profits among more and less efficient producers, and prices ceased to be in any definable sense a mechanism to induce efficiency. Firms could allow their costs to rise within very wide limits without suffering any decrease in profits and therefore had no financial motives to reduce costs.[140] The Select Committee on National Expenditure in 1942–43 recognized this as a problem but chose to assume that in practice firms would strive to maximize their performance both for reasons of patriotism and in order to safeguard their long-run competitive positions.[141]

This overriding priority of price restraint subdued the relative advantages of many firms. As Burn put it, the real problem was that stabilization came at the expense of "any rational distribution of profits."[142] The effect of stabilization was to redistribute profits in a fairly contingent manner first toward heavy steel users, which benefited disproportionately from the control of coal; second, toward those firms that used other raw materials that qualified for subsidies; and third, toward those firms that were most adapted for war work. The main contemporary criticisms, however, focused not on this inequity but on the overall level of profits, which were argued to be too high.[143] As we have seen, however, although prewar profits and prices on which the wartime standards were based had been fixed in such a way as to protect marginal producers, they were generally below the manufacturing average before the war. It was not the level of profits so much as their distribution that was the main problem.

The attempt to maintain prices at artificially low levels did not end following the war. The BISF and the Iron and Steel Board continued the practice of equalizing raw materials costs of all firms by administrative intervention. This policy particularly benefited firms using a high percentage of scrap and imported ore and eliminated many of the cost advantages of the most efficient home-ore based firms like Stewarts & Lloyds and United Steel. The advantages of shifting to best-practice relative to the existing cost structures were curbed.

What was the logic of this policy for the BISF? Some of the most efficient firms opposed it, but these were few. The low-price feature meant that it enjoyed the blessing of the Iron and Steel Board and the government, but there is no evidence that they exerted pressure on the BISF to achieve this; rather, as Burn noted, the BISF was very much "the mind behind the price structure."[144] Partly the thinking was based on the idea that current costs were exceptional and that they would return to a more normal configuration in the long run. Possibly there was some validity in this notion, an adequate analysis of this issue is beyond our scope here. But the policy was not based on careful long-run assessments of relative cost movements; rather, it represented a negotiated compromise among existing steelmakers about the desirable relationship between scrap and pig-iron costs. As such it both reflected the inertia of the industry and reinforced it. Price control, raw material subsidies, and profit equalization diminished the advantages of those seeking to introduce best-practice relative to long-term advantages, but it did not discourage *all* investment. Demand was high and the industry desired to counter the campaign for nationalization by demonstrating its capacity to raise output. As a result investment was considerable, but it followed the course of short-run advantages.[145]

During the war both the Federation and the Iron and Steel Control had come to recognize that misinvestment because of short-term considerations was a serious danger. At the end of the war the White Paper developed by the BISF and the Ministry of Supply argued forcefully that even though new plant might have only marginal advantages in the short term, it was essential to move to best-practice plants and locations to ensure the long-run health of the industry. Despite this affirmation, however, considerable tensions existed within the report: it argued for overall reconstruction and cooperation in the regions to avoid a "patchwork job," yet it remained biased toward the old locations, and it planned to modernize so many existing works that major scale economies could not really be achieved.[146] It was a plan for "re-equipment de-luxe" based on aggregating the different aims and aspirations put forward by the different firms. No overall policy was adopted about long-term costs and locations, and the Federation backed the "practical planning" of the individual firms with the outcome that the existing pattern of production was perpetuated and merely scaled up. The 1946 scheme at first included both short-term patching and three large long-term schemes (at Lackenby, in Northamptonshire, and on the Clyde tidewater) to be built in the next five years; but although the firms ensured that the former were quickly under way, they had no real confidence in the advantages of the latter. As Payne has shown in his analysis of the Scottish tidewater scheme, the plan had been wished upon Colvilles by the Federation, and the company gradually slipped out of it. The abandonment of these schemes was largely a rationalization of pressure from individual firms pragmatically responding in isolation to the tempting pressures of demand for steel and at the same time trying to expand cautiously to avoid a repetition of the overcapacity of the interwar years.[147] It was a fail-safe policy that produced consistently high, although not the highest possible, profits. Piecemeal expansion could relatively easily attain the forecasted levels of demand—although not in the event the actual levels of demand—and in a period of boom no dramatic repercussions resulted from not building lowest-cost plants.

No significant conflict arose between the industry and either the wartime coalition or the Labour government about these policies. From 1944, the Ministry of Supply took the attitude that if firms thought projects necessary and profitable, they were generally uncritically accepted. The coalition believed that it should "try to avoid holding too many things up or turning too many things down." If proposals would reduce costs, even though not by as much as possible, the government was prepared to take what was on offer.[148] Broadly speaking, the Labour government too approved of the postwar record of the steelmakers; conflict was largely confined to issues of public ownership.[149] The Labour Party stressed the potential harmful effects of private control but its own policy for the management of the industry was not very different from that of the Federation and the board themselves: indeed, many inside the leadership of the Labour Party, like Herbert Morrison and Arthur Greenwood, were lukewarm about nationalization because they were not confident that a state body could run the industry better than the BISF.[150] As Burn observed, the Iron and Steel Bill itself showed a desire to maintain continuity in the management of the firms so that the recent "record of success" should not be disturbed: "The harmony in the outlook of the government and the Federation . . . on the proper pattern of policy to be pursued was almost complete . . . the only tangible object of the Bill was to transfer power."[151] Despite government arguments about the need for public ownership to facilitate radical change, it had no policies for such change. In fact, the government leaned as strongly toward piecemeal adaptation as the steelmakers. For social reasons it was at least as anxious as the industry to confine developments within locational limits that did not produce painful social upheavals, and in the case of the new Margam works in particular it encouraged the industry to ignore the locational drawbacks of the site for these reasons. At the same time, it gave priority to the quantity of output rather than the cost structure: in general it saw the crux of the problem as inadequate investment and the restriction of output to bolster profits. But in practice, in the late 1940s at least, the real problem was not the aggregate level of investment but its maldistribution, resulting partly from a policy that kept prices artificially low.

The Labour government's commitment to public ownership did not come to terms with the problems of industrial structure. In an industry where the scale of low-cost operations had for a long time been growing faster than the market, there were no obvious opportunities to strengthen its position by the introduction of large new projects from the outside. In the brief life of the ISCGB the continuity of price and planning policies that damped down pressures for structural change was the dominant feature. When denationalization came, it restored the prenationalization form of regulated competition with something akin to the IDAC system of government supervision, thus perpetuating a remarkable institutional continuity from the 1930s to the 1950s. The failures of this system did not penalize the industry as long as international competition remained weak—until the late 1950s. The industry remained strong internationally via piecemeal adaptation, and its structural problems hit it with a vengeance only when decline set in in the 1960s and the weaknesses of the "fair-weather edifice" were revealed. By the mid-1960s there was very widespread acceptance that only nationalization could achieve the sort of restructuring that now seemed inevitable.[152]

14.

The Limits of State Intervention

In the 1920s successive governments tried to keep out of the steel industry both because of their principles and their political concerns and because they believed that intervention would delay reorganization. In the crisis of 1932, however, the National government decided that limited action was necessary to aid recovery and promote reorganization. The core of the new policy was "industrial self-government" and the fostering of business collectivism. By stimulating the creation of an effective central employers' association, the government hoped to avoid embroiling itself in discriminating between rival private interests and to push forward reorganization while leaving the responsibility for it in the hands of industrialists. This policy contrasted with the growing willingness of the Bank of England to deal directly with firms and plant and to support the most efficient producers to facilitate their expansion at the expense of weaker firms. The Bank and its advisers never resolved the difficult problems generated by such an orientation, and the government had no desire to grapple with these issues. In the end, however, self-government fairly predictably failed to produce reorganization of the kind the government envisaged; it foundered on the lack of any positive consensus on restructuring in the industry which resulted from the internal divisions and fragmentation of the producers. The industry was willing to band together to protect existing vested interests but it would not move beyond that position without a more vigorous push than the state was inclined to give. Actual rationalization would have torn the BISF apart, and the government both lacked the bureaucratic apparatus and expertise to proffer technocratic solutions and retained a deep moral and ideological resistance to the extension of compul-

335

sion. It hoped to develop a strong and institutionalized persuasive influence over the industry through IDAC, but it never wanted real control: the aim was industrial autonomy under the umbrella of the state, and insofar as the industry really was autonomous this implied the possibility that it could act contrary to the wishes of the government. There were no significant advocates in government circles of the view that the government could run industry better than the industrialists. Far from the concept of the state's "acting in the true interests of capital as a whole," the National government basically acknowledged that it did not know what the true interests of capital were.

Does this mean that the impact of the state on the industry was insignificant? On the contrary, as we have seen, it had fundamental economic and political consequences. In effect, the state sponsored a cartel over which it had little control. The government wanted reorganization, but in practice it helped to reinforce old structures with a new layer of powerful institutions that embodied existing structural problems rather than counteracting them. At the same time, the government played a major role in making possible the emergence of an organized and coherent corporate interest group from among the individualistic steelmakers. The organization that emerged in the 1930s was the basis of the vigorous and effective resistance to nationalization in the 1940s. Although this most striking manifestation of employer organization was in conflict with the government, this outcome should not obscure underlying cooperative developments of equal significance. A new framework of compromise between the steelmakers and the government was emerging as familiarity and consultation developed, symbolized by the emergence of a "national interest" figure like Duncan, somewhere between business and politics, politically reliable, and capable of mediating between government interests and the constituency of industrialists. In particular, substantial cooperation could develop around common ground such as price stability and locational inertia where there was a convergence of at least short-term interests, and both sides were prepared to shelve consideration of the long-term implications of these moves. When nationalization ended, this cooperative relationship became the basis for supervised private ownership in the 1950s and 1960s.

The visible hand of the state reinforced the structural deadlock of the industry. The traditions, organizational forms, and political ideologies of both National and Labour governments made them inadequate to the task of reorganizing a major declining industry. In the event, the state was less committed to maximizing efficiency in the industry than in pursuing a variety of different concerns, such as the prevention of the collapse of the industry and the preservation of national self-sufficiency, the mitigation of the social effects of the crisis, and preserving some balance between steelmakers and other manufacturing interests. Its only positive industrial policies were concerned with prices and locations, and by and large such policies worked against rationalization. The lack of any serious alternative strategy on the part of government was palpably demonstrated in the weaknesses and fragility of the nationalization initiative after the war.

Was the steel industry typical of wider changes in the relationship between industry and the state, or was it a special case? There was no single pattern of increasing government involvement in industry; the state responded in different ways in the face of the varying economic circumstances of different industries. In relation to the newer sectors of large-scale manufacturing industry, as Hannah has noted, the government eschewed either a trust-busting or a trust-promoting role and remained committed to unfettered private control and nonintervention.[1] But across a wide swath of British industries the government played a much larger role, and in government circles the ideal of laissez-faire coexisted with major and persistent departures from the framework. In mining and agriculture government conduct mirrored important elements of its involvement in steel. In electricity supply, railways, cotton, and shipbuilding considerable departures from laissez-faire ideas and practices also took place. Was there any identifiable pattern of either motivation or consequences behind these interventions?

M. W. Kirby has argued that the extensive legislative intervention in coal in the 1930s was an exceptional case arising from the "uniquely disastrous labour relations" of the industry and, above all, conditioned by the associated social and political issues. Only cartelization could prevent cutthroat price competition with dire effects on wages and jobs, and the government gave consistent backing to the tightening of price and market controls. On paper at least, the government was also committed to the pursuit of amalgamations, by compulsion if necessary, but it became apparent soon after the Coal Mines Act of 1930 that cartelization made amalgamations less rather than more likely. Although the goal of amalgamations remained in the minds of policy makers throughout the decade, in practice the government opted to maintain employment through the restrictive elements of its legislation rather than to pursue efficiency by amalgamations that would leave large numbers out of work.[2] "By the mid-1930s," Kirby notes, "the cartel system, successively strengthened and modified at the dictates of government, had come to be accepted by the Mining Association as a vital factor in the campaign against compulsory amalgamations."[3]

In coal, as in steel, government intervention reinforced the old industrial structure that it was intended to reform. The coal owners were even more fragmented and parochial than the steelmakers and were less able to take advantage of the government's desire for industrial self-government to develop effective self-organization. No equivalent of Duncan emerged to aid the development of a regime of sustained compromise between government and the industry, and the relationship that resulted was more conflictual. But the weakness of the coal-owners' organization was compensated for by the convergence of their interests with the threat of industrial conflict and social disruption that would arise from a vigorous amalgamation policy. Compulsory powers reached the statute book largely because of the effective lobbying of the Liberal Party during the genesis of the Coal Mines Act and remained in effect because of the insistent pressure of the Department of Mines thereafter.[4] These political pressures were quite different from anything attempted by IDAC, and they made considerable inroads against the government's general reluctance to use compulsion. But a change at the level of legislation could not be easily translated into practice, and the coal owners were largely able to negate these provisions by resort to the courts. The issue of compulsion remained a major irritant and barrier to a cooperative relationship between the coal owners and their supervisory agency, and unlike the steel industry there was not the same sustained recovery from the early 1930s to ease the evolution of practical compromises. Despite a lack of mutual trust between the owners and the government, however, the legislative framework in practice permitted autonomous self-regulation: the government had little voice in fixing prices and the administration of the quota system completely escaped control.

Although it was more marked by legislation and more conflictual, government-backed self-organization in coal was exceptional in its particular features rather than in kind, and it shared much common ground with the relationship between steel and the state. A similar pattern recurred in agriculture. The lack of historical research in this field makes a sustained comparison difficult, but it is clear that in agriculture nineteenth-century policies were completely reversed with the establishment of a regime of tariffs and subsidies operating through marketing boards. These boards were producers' associations set up in conjunction with the National Farmers' Union, which raised prices and stabilized levels of output, thus enabling the less efficient producers to stay in production while the more efficient achieved handsome profits. Despite certain disputes with government about detailed regulation and administration, government policy took the form of fairly uncritical backing for collective organization among farmers. It was only in the late 1930s that the government began to push for more supervision of the marketing boards, and there was no governmental attempt to develop an overall policy on production or prices. As in steel and coal, the autonomy of the existing producers was confirmed and the existing structure of production reinforced: the new institutions stimulated by government provided a defensive umbrella and not a framework for change.[5]

In cotton the pattern was somewhat different. The government was less ready to take the initiative, and no legislative intervention took place until 1936. The social and economic position in the cotton manufacturing areas was less acute than in coal or steel, its overwhelming export base made it unsuitable for solutions that sheltered it from foreign competition, and until the mid-1930s the bankers were still active, through the Lancashire Cotton Corporation, in trying to engineer private reorganization. When it came, the Spindles Act was a measure for a compulsory levy to buy and scrap spindles and was in effect government backing for a proposal formulated within the industry with clear majority support.[6] This was rather similar to the National Shipbuilders' Securities scheme where the Bank of England provided the external backing for the industry's own scheme. In cotton and shipbuilding there was sufficient agreement among a majority of producers to make the coercion of a minority feasible on a limited basis; in coal, steel, and agriculture it was necessary to devise negotiated compromises that safeguarded both the weak and the strong.

These cases do not exhaust the spectrum of state interventions. Important developments that began in the 1920s, particularly public corporations like the CEB and the BBC, have already been noted. In the 1930s this nodel was confirmed and strengthened. The CEB provided a legislative framework for a rapid catching-up operation in the efficiency of electricity supply in the 1930s and was widely approved by the Conservative as well as the Labour government.[7] In the early 1930s the London Passenger Transport Board was set up on a similar model, devised by Herbert Morrison under Labour and implemented in legislation under the National government. State action encompassed public corporations, industrial self-government, and traditional laissez-faire. By and large the boundary seemed to be drawn only at the point of direct intervention at the level of particular companies. Perhaps the most significant exception to this rule was the Cunard/White Star shipping merger about which Francis Hyde has concluded that "it was the government . . . who imposed the terms which ultimately resulted in a merger."[8] The rather exceptional conduct of the government in offering direct financial inducements to promote a merger resulted from three interlinked circumstances. First, the Treasury already had a direct role as one of the principal creditors of White Star as the unforeseen outcome of Trade Facilities Act transactions of the 1920s; second, for similar reasons and because of its distinct industrial and employment policies, the Northern Ireland government was the largest single creditor; and third, the Bank of England was pursuing a complex strategy of breaking up and re-merging companies in alliance with other major banks in the aftermath of the collapse of the Royal Mail Group. In this context government intervention was partly to safeguard its own particular financial interest, partly a measure of support for the Northern Ireland government, and partly a form of assistance for the work of the Bank of England.[9] In addition, the consummation of the merger made possible the speedy resumption of work on the giant liner No. 534 (Queen Mary) at John Brown's and as such was a matter of national prestige and employment policy. The huge uncompleted hull had become a symbol of depression, and renewed construction activity was likely to have an impact out of proportion to its economic significance in persuading public opinion that the tide of recovery was beginning to flow. Such a conjunction of circumstances did not appear elsewhere.

This rough taxonomy of government interventions indicates that the state was a crucial determinant of the pattern of industrial change in some of the most important sectors of the economy. This does not mean, however, that we should resurrect the rather caricatured picture drawn by the trades unions and the Left in the 1930s of the National government as a government of businessmen. Walter Citrine, for example, described the Federation of British Industries as "a most sinister organisation always working behind the scenes to dictate the policy of employers" and in league with the government,[10] and similar views have recurred in modern textbooks.[11] Clearly the government had a great deal of sympathy for industrialists, but the relationship between industry and government was a much more complex one. S. H. Beer has described the relationship as "neither one of business pressure groups dictating to government nor of government agencies planning the activities of business. Decisions were made, rather, in a process of bargaining and negotiation."[12] There is much truth in this, but the interaction involved more than a series of disconnected ad hoc responses. We have analyzed the process of bargaining and negotiation in relation to steel in detail, and it is clear that the constraints and structures of this process had determinant effects on the development of the industry. The most important of these structures was the government's self-denying ordnance embodied in the notion of industrial self-government.

The government opted to confer legal privileges and protection on the organized producers already established in crisis-ridden industries. Keynes termed this "a return . . . towards medieval conceptions of separate autonomies,"[13] and Brady echoed this view in his description of the workings of the National government as "the new feudalism."[14] The underlying ideas, however, were only weakly elaborated, and although they moved in certain common directions, they were largely pragmatic adaptations to the perceived failure of supply and demand to cope with the problems of the market. Old laissez-faire ideas were not yet dead, and no new philosophy accompanied the extension of government involvement in industry. Industrial self-government was seen as a practical way of regulating production in accordance with effective demand. It had an immediate commonsense appeal as a way of correcting a malfunction in supply and demand while retaining most of the old framework of ideas.[15] As Harold MacMillan put it in 1933, this type of planning "is not a new or strange idea. It is, in fact, what every producer must attempt in order to sell his products at a profit rather than a loss. What *is* new is the set of circumstances which requires the co-ordination of the efforts of private individuals and groups to achieve and maintain an equilibrium which in former times could well be preserved by an automatic reaction to the indicator of price fluctuations."[16] Most Conservatives did not see beyond this framework of self-government and self-regulation, understand its implications, or seek to develop an industrial policy to accompany it. This activity was confined to a minority of "corporatist" thinkers in the 1930s who, as L. P. Carpenter has shown, started from this common ground and moved outward to formulate wider economic and political proposals either for "industrial parliaments" to coordinate the activity of separate industries, or, as in the case of Political and Economic Planning (PEP), for national planning by the state so that national priorities could be imposed on the planning undertaken by each industry. But relatively few went far along these paths.[17]

In the main, most leading Conservatives, including those like Baldwin, Steel-Maitland, and Cunliffe-Lister, who had been prepared to consider increased state intervention in the 1920s, were ready to take up self-government as an acceptable minimum interference with the market. In the 1920s they had hoped that the state could stand behind the banks; in the 1930s they hoped to stand behind producers' associations. In order to do that they had to establish the preconditions, if need be by legislation, for effective associations to exist. The aim was to set industries on a self-governing basis and then exert a persuasive advisory influence. In practice, the more effective the self-government, the less effective was the persuasion, and the new state-backed structures often meant responsibility without power. The government ended up sponsoring autonomous groups in steel, coal, and agriculture whose conduct it regarded as dubious and reluctantly propping up industrial structures that experts regarded as anachronistic. The lack of an alternative industrial policy and a limited convergence of labor and producer interests around minimizing the disruption of rationalization meant that the government was often prepared to acquiesce, even though the situation was unsatisfactory. One way out would have been the development of a detailed policy for each industry to be pursued by a mixture or orders and incentives through technocratic departments. The lack of suitable administrative traditions made this course unlikely, but more important, neither party advocated the extension of microeconomic planning: Labour sought an organic change in the conduct of industry which would arise from the transformation of ownership and the control of disinterested managers; the Conservatives believed that if industrial self-government could effectively stabilize private ownership, in the long run the effective management that they imputed to that form of ownership would reemerge.

With the war and the postwar boom the issues of industrial self-government and microeconomic planning became historical dead ends. Expansion and Keynesianism made it possible to adjust demand rather than supply and to ignore the long-term problems of industrial structure. Macroeconomic solutions provided, for the time being, a workable alternative to the unsolved problems of microeconomic intervention that had come onto the agenda in the 1930s.

Thus, the outcomes of state actions in the field of industrial organization were persistently contradictory. The state and its departments pursued a variety of aims, many of which were imcompatible, with limited capabilities, and unintended consequences were an inevitable feature of this activity. As a result, state action cannot be tied in any deterministic way to the furtherance of the interests of capital or to a system-maintaining role. In terms of modernization or the increase of capitalist efficiency, the actions of the state probably had a regressive effect, strengthening and confirming the worst faults of the existing system. At the same time, the state stimulated the organization of corporate groups, but insofar as it bolstered their autonomy, state power was itself diminished in the face of the growth of large oligopolies and powerful institutions. The political coherence of capitalist interests was rearranged but not significantly advanced. But it would be wrong to assess state actions primarily in the light of broad systematic goals. The state did not want to control or order industry and did not really believe that it could. Government intervention flowed from more specific political and economic concerns ranging from national recovery to the avoidance of social upheavals, and it pursued these aims within the constraints of limited capabilities and resources. We have seen how the historical structures of power relations within companies and banks were imbued with contradictions that restricted or even paralyzed efforts at restructuring; these historical limitations apply equally to the state. State structures were evolving in a symbiotic relationship with the existing structure of British industry—as indeed the wider structures of the state related to the structures of British society—and they came to embody and reinforce many of its problems themselves. The visible hands of banks and the state themselves needed to be remodeled and to develop new functions and capabilities before they could operate effectively to reorganize the economy. In the meantime, their interventions proved to be clumsy and ill-directed and in practice often had effects directly the opposite of those intended.

Conclusion

The concluding sections of each of the parts of this study contain brief synopses of the various stages of my argument. At this point I wish to indicate some omissions and to point up some of the general issues resulting from the approach and findings. Because the study has been thematic, certain areas have been neglected that should receive more detailed coverage in a more comprehensive treatment of the industry. Perhaps the most striking of these is the absence of any sustained account of the role of labor in the economic development of the industry.

The main concern of the book has been conflict among capitalists and its impact on policy. It has largely ignored conflict between capital and labor except where this has appeared as an important element in intercapitalist struggles, notably through the impact of labor concerns on government policy. Labor was not a major determinant of the shaping of the interwar steel industry; in general, its position in a depressed industry was too fragile for it to be a powerful bargaining force. It is probable, however, that it did at least reinforce certain trends. Labor organization at the workplace level invariably takes the existing structure of production as its starting point and seeks to take advantage of bargaining opportunities arising from, and to defend its position within, the existing labor process. In a period of expansion this may lead to certain resistances to innovation, but in a period of retrenchment it may well result in convergences of interest with industrialists pursuing particular adaptations to the market.

Thus, for example, the existence of pools of relatively cheap skilled labor may well have influenced choice of technique. This was clear in the persistence of labor-intensive pack mills in the tinplate industry where employers were able to use skill-intensive processes with flexible costs to counterbalance the advantages of innovators with high fixed-cost capital-intensive technologies in order to carry on a prolonged rearguard action.[1] Elsewhere it may have been an important consideration in the continuing preference for open-hearth over basic Bessemer production in Britain and the bias away from production based on home ores. Open-hearth production was a much slower, more labor-intensive process, and high inputs of experience, skill, and improvisation made it a much more flexible technology than the basic Bessemer converters with their fast throughput and much more rigid requirements for uniform inputs.[2] Jackson has described the dependence of open-hearth techniques on labor skills in this period and the ability of senior operatives with experienced eyes, instincts, and manual skills to maximize output from their furnaces. Such workers could make effective use of technology that would otherwise be well past its point of obsolescence and fit only to be scrapped.[3]

Parallel to this, the wage and union structure may have had important effects on the resilience of the industrial structure. Because wages were based on a sliding scale and tonnage bonuses, they were much more flexible—particularly downward—with shifts in selling prices and output than wages in mining and other manufacturing sectors. At the same time, the prevalence of tonnage bonuses meant that low-productivity plants were compensated for their poor performance by low wage levels. Wide interplant wage differentials existed, and high wages were concentrated in a very small number of steelworks in the 1920s. The seniority system reinforced these differentials: promotion was confined to a *plant*-based seniority ladder, which effectively locked workers into their own plants and virtually prohibited mobility between plants, thus easing the pressure on low-wage low-productivity plants to bring their wage levels into line with those of more efficient plants. A major shift in the wage structure in the late 1920s cut the rates of the higher-paid workers and increased those of the lower-paid hands. This change disproportionately benefited workers in low-productivity firms and disadvantaged the more marginal producers, but any effect it may have had in squeezing inefficient employers was more than likely offset by its simultaneous effect on more efficient firms with higher-paid workers, where it increased the share of the employers from incremental increases in productivity from existing fixed capital and curbed some of the wage drift that had previously been associated with patching policies. Certain elements of the wage structure clearly reinforced other diseconomies of scale discussed earlier, although a more detailed assessment must await more comprehensive studies. Moreover, it should also be noted that the industry's wage and seniority structures had a relationship of both cause and effect with the relatively cooperative framework of relations between the steelmakers and the largest steel union, the Iron and Steel Trades Confederation (ISTC). As Frank Wilkinson has shown, the generally harmonious structure of industrial relations in the industry owed much to the self-adjusting nature of the wage mechanism on one hand and the vertically disintegrated structure of plant-based branches on the other, which gave great strength to a central leadership who broadly accepted the steelmakers' contention that there was a limited wage fund related to the performance of the industry out of which all wage claims had to be met.[4]

Beyond this, it is arguable that some employers were affected by considerations of welfare or social policy in considering production and location decisions, especially those where entire communities seemed at stake. There are indications that this factor may have been significant in United Steel's decision to maintain steelmaking in West Cumberland, and Payne hints, although he does not document, that similar considerations were operative in the continuation of production in Glengarnock in Scotland in this period.[5] However, labor interests were ridden over roughshod in the decision of Stewarts & Lloyds to uproot the bulk of its Scottish operations and move to Corby in Northamptonshire, and, as we have seen, they were opportunistically used by Richard Thomas in its campaign to initiate strip mill production without any real concern for the welfare of the communities directly involved.[6] Labor issues may have been of greater significance for some of the smaller localized firms,[7] but in general they seem to have been a subordinate concern more often than not used as a matter of rhetoric than as a substantive force. Nevertheless, this is an area that remains to be examined historically.

Perhaps of more importance is the lack of adequate broader studies of the impact of labor matters on the overall development of industrial, regional, and employment policies of the National Government in the 1930s. The political implications of mass unemployment and the threat of social upheaval seem at times to have been taken very seriously, despite the weakness of politically organized labor and the demoralization of the unemployed and the regionalization of unemployment. More background is needed before we can assess the importance of these forces in government acquiescence with respect to locational rigidity and the patching policies of large employers in areas of high unemployment: How important were labor concerns in Conservative political thinking? How much did they contribute to the habit of following the line of least resistance?

Another area that has received only limited attention in this study is an attempt to define what would have been the optimally efficient course of development for the industry or to prescribe alternative courses of development. Partly this is because, in keeping with the stress on the constraints acting on the decision-making environment, most alternatives were not real possibilities. My focus on the power relations of decision making inevitably involves actual and implied criticisms of particular decisions and the correctness of the reasoning behind them, but this sort of assessment is not the main object of the study. With hindsight, and in view of the sustained wave of expansion from the 1930s to the 1960s, it is fairly clear that the advantages of large best-practice plants at low-cost locations would have been enormous in terms of efficiency of production, output, and employment if it had proved possible to wholeheartedly follow this course; despite short-run difficulties, long-run advantages were clearly on the side of the reorganizers. But who could have reasonably forecast thirty years of continuous expansion in 1932? Indeed, would that expansion have been sustained had it not been for the exogenous and unpredictable factors of global war and subsequent shifts in the world economy? The subsequent trend of the market does provide a yardstick by which to measure the decisions of the firms, and it is compatible with how the subjects of the study understood things in their own terms, but it does not imply three cheers for the reorganizers. First, industrial reorganization required developing new forms of political and economic organization to cope with the restructuring task, but such a project barely figured on the agenda. Ironically, the one proposal for radical institutional reform, that of nationalization, in effect skated around the problems of industrial structure and production strategy; it assumed that institutional change was a sufficient stimulus to industrial regeneration rather than one of several necessary ones. Second, insofar as reorganization implied major social and economic upheavals, it required new dimensions of social and economic planning which the actors at the time were not remotely prepared to define or implement. Third, it would not be correct to argue that there was only *one* correct route to success even within the old framework. A more detailed study of special-quality steelmaking or the Sheffield area would have raised interesting questions about whether Britain should have pursued skilled specialization and the comparative advantages enjoyed in these specialized fields as well as concentrating on the reform of bulk steelmaking. The point is that even though bulk steelmaking in Britain had a long future, other adaptations could also have been effectively pursued that might have proved advantageous in the long run.

What of the wider implications of the sort of analysis undertaken here? One question that arises is the adequacy of looking at Britain in terms of an industrial society or corporate economy. In reality Britain has been a much more hybrid society, with financial and imperial interests on a par with those of industry for much of the time. Industrialists had no powerful voice in political affairs, and politicians did not depend on business support. Even when they might have exerted political influence, businessmen were frequently divided on economic issues and consciously sought to eschew taking a stand on overt political matters. It is therefore questionable to place industry at the center of all British economic equations and to see, for instance, the success of finance as coming at the expense of industry. What is needed is a much more differentiated picture of where power lay between industry, finance, empire, land, and for that matter, labor, and the lines of convergence, overlap, and division within and between such groupings. The congruence between the aims of the state and those of any one of these social groups was inevitably only partial, and the pursuit of political goals involved complex and changing alliances.

At the same time, we cannot take business decisions or political choices as simple proxies for the outcome of market or social forces. Power relations and institutions are major determining factors in their own right: the behavior of firms cannot be understood merely as responses to market forces; banking institutions exhibit an array of political as well as financial aims; and government policies are not functional outcomes of the needs of the economy at any given time. All of these institutions shape the range of possible solutions to economic problems, all of which may have unforeseen outcomes. The power relations involved cannot be seen to derive from underlying economic forces in a deterministic way nor understood as part of the universal experience of advanced capitalist societies. It is now commonly accepted that the possibilities of language shape what is thinkable; in the same way institutions condition responses to economic problems. Their structures are embedded in the past, and their effects are continuously inscribed in the present and the future.

Abbreviations

AGM	Annual General Meeting	JC.B	File B, John Craig Papers, Colville Archives
AS	Alexander Stephen & Sons		
BID	Bankers' Industrial Development Company	JC.F	File F, John Craig Papers, Colville Archives
BISF	British Iron and Steel Federation	*JISI*	*Journal of the Iron and Steel Institute*
BSC	British Steel Corporation	JSA	Joint Steelmakers Association
BT Marine Dept.	Board of Trade, Marine Department	*JWSISI*	*Journal of the West of Scotland Iron and Steel Institute*
BT 56	papers of Sir Horace Wilson	MT	Ministry of Transport files, PRO
BV	Bolckow Vaughan & Co.		
BV PRIV	Bolckow Vaughan Private Minute Books	MUN 4,5	Ministry of Munitions, files 4 and 5, PRO
CA	Colville Archives	NCEO	National Confederation of Employers' Organizations
CAB 24	Committee for Civil Research, 1925–1930	NFISM	National Federation of Iron and Steel Manufacturers
CAB 58	Economic Advisory Committee	NIESR	National Institute of Economic and Social Research
CF	Cargo Fleet Iron Company		
Cmd.	Command Paper	NLB	New Left Books
CON	Consett Iron Company	P & O	Peninsular & Orient Shipping Co.
CP	Committee Paper		
DCS	David Colville & Sons	PRO	Public Record Office
DL	Dorman Long & Co.	Q	Question
DL DTR	Dorman Long Directors' Files	RT	Richard Thomas and Company
DL MTG	Dorman Long Directors' Meetings papers	SCS	Steel Company of Scotland
		SD	South Durham Steel and Iron Company
EAC	Economic Advisory Committee		
EcHR	*Economic History Review*	SISM	Scottish Iron and Steel Makers' papers
FBI	Federation of British Industries		
GD 193	File number in Steel-Maitland papers	SL	Stewarts & Lloyds
		SMT	Securities Management Trust
GKB	Guest Keen Baldwins Ltd.	SMT 2	papers of E. H. D. Skinner
GKN	Guest Keen & Nettlefolds Ltd.	SMT 3	papers of C. Bruce Gardner
HMSO	Her Majesty's Stationery Office	SMT 8	Branch Banks Office files
ICTR	*Iron and Coal Trades Review*	SMTHM	minutes of weekly House Committee meetings, SMT
IDAC	Import Duties Advisory Committee	T.172	Chancellor of the Exchequer's office, iron and steel files, PRO
ISTC	Iron and Steel Trades Confederation		
JB	John Brown & Company	T.175	papers of Sir Richard Hopkins, PRO

Note on Sources

Company Records

Northeast Coast

All the company records for this region used in this study are housed in the British Steel Corporation Northern Records Centre at Middlesborough. They consist mainly of minute books and annual general meeting reports together with a limited amount of correspondence and reports. There are also extensive works ledgers and contract books. The company records concerned are those of Dorman Long & Co., Bolckow Vaughan & Co., Bell Bros. and Co., Sir B. Samuelson & Co., Carlton Iron Co., South Durham Steel and Iron Co., Cargo Fleet Iron Co., and the Consett Iron Co.

Scotland

The main company records used for this region are the voluminous records of David Colville and Sons and their successors Colvilles Ltd. Extensive correspondence and board reports have been preserved covering the whole range of the company's activities. (A description of the records can be found in P. L. Payne, *Colvilles*.) These records are housed in the BSC Regional Records Centre in Irthlingborough, Northants, together with the papers of the Steel Co. of Scotland, Ltd., which are more limited and consist mainly of minute books. Other important records of Scottish iron and steel makers and their allied shipbuilding concerns are held in the Colquhoun Collection of Business Records in the University of Glasgow. The most extensive of these are the papers of William Beardmore & Co., but I have also drawn extensively on the papers of John Brown and Co., William Dixon and Co., A. Stephen & Co., W. Baird and Co., and Lithgows Ltd.

South Wales

The records of Richard Thomas & Co. are held at the BSC Strip Products Group Record Centre at Shotton on Deeside, together with some surviving papers of the Redbourn Hill Iron and Coal Co., and the Grovesend Steel and Tinplate Co. Most of this material is minute books, but the Richard Thomas papers also contain some correspondence and reports.

Stewarts & Lloyds

The records of Stewarts & Lloyds Ltd. are at Irthlingborough, Northants. These contain minute books and some extensive company reports pertaining to the Corby decision. The minute books of the Oxfordshire Ironstone Co. are also kept in this collection.

Employers' Organizations

The minutes and papers of the National Federation of Iron and Steel Manufacturers and of the British Iron and Steel Federation along with their various subcommittees are held at the BSC Midlands Record Centre: some of these documents are on microfilm. These papers are very extensive and include detailed minutes of discussions in subcommittees as well as the heads of discussions in more formal minutes. There are also extensive reports prepared for specialist subcommittees. The papers of the regional bodies, notably the Scottish Steelmakers' Association, the North-East Coast Steelmakers' Association, and the Tinplate Stabilisation of Prices Committee are also held here. The records of the first two associations are only minute books, but the Tinplate committee papers contain correspondence, too.

As far as national employers' organizations are concerned, I have also used the archives of the Confederation of British Industries, which contain the records of its predecessor bodies, the Federation of British Industries and the National Confederation of Employers' Organisations.

Bank of England

These records, which form the basis of Part II, are held in the Bank of England in Threadneedle Street. From these records I have drawn on the papers of E. H. D. Skinner, the papers of C. Bruce Gardner, the Branch Banks Office Files, the Securities Management Trust papers and the Minutes of Weekly House Committee Meetings, and the papers of the Bankers' Industrial Develoment Co. Each of these groups of papers contains voluminous files on the various steel companies that came in contact with the Bank in this period, including correspondence, reports from consulting engineers, and contemporaneous notes on discussions and telephone calls.

Government Papers

All of these are to be found in the Public Record Office at Kew. I have drawn mainly on the following files: the papers of the Committee for Civil Research, 1925–1930 and the Economic Advisory Committee; the iron and steel files of the Chancellor of the Exchequer's office; the papers of Sir Richard Hopkins; the papers of Sir Horace Wilson; and Ministry of Munitions files. All of these are open to the public. I was also allowed access to the files of the Import Duties Advisory Committee, which were not at that time usually open to the public: some have now been made generally available.

Trade Union Papers

The most useful papers are the records of the Iron and Steel Trades Confederation which include inter alia verbatim reports of proceedings at conferences with the Iron and Steel Trades Employers' Association. These are now held at the Warwick University Modern Records Centre. I also made use of the papers of ISTC Division No. 5, which are held at the Swansea University Archives.

Private Papers

The J. R. MacDonald Papers were consulted courtesy of David Marquand; the Baldwin Papers are in the University Library, Cambridge; the papers of Lord Weir are in the Churchill College Library, Cambridge; and the papers of A. Steel-Maitland are in the Scottish Record Office.

Notes

The place of publication for all works is London unless otherwise stated.

Introduction

1. Martin J. Wiener, *English Culture and the Decline of the Industrial Spirit, 1850–1980* (Cambridge University Press, 1981); Perry Anderson, "The Origins of the Present Crisis," in Perry Anderson and Robin Blackburn, eds., *Towards Socialism* (Ithaca, N.Y.: Cornell University Press, 1965).

2. Derek H. Aldcroft, *The Interwar Economy: Britain, 1919–1939* (Batsford, 1970); Derek H. Aldcroft and Peter Fearon, eds., *Economic Growth in Twentieth Century Britain* (Macmillan, 1969); Derek H. Aldcroft and Harry W. Richardson, *The British Economy, 1870–1939* (Macmillan, 1969); Alexander J. Youngson, *Britain's Economic Growth, 1920–1966* (Allen & Unwin, 1967); William Ashworth, *An Economic History of England, 1870–1939* (Methuen, 1960); Bernard W. E. Alford, *Depression and Recovery? British Economic Growth, 1918–1939* (Macmillan, 1972).

3. Alfred D. Chandler, *The Visible Hand: The Managerial Revolution in American Business* (Cambridge, Mass.: Harvard University Press, 1977); and A. D. Chandler, *Strategy and Structure: Chapters in the History of the Industrial Enterprise* (Cambridge, Mass.: MIT Press, 1962).

4. See, for example, the essays in Leslie Hannah, ed., *Management Strategy and Business Development: An Historical and Comparative Study* (Macmillan, 1976); and Alfred D. Chandler and Herman Daems, eds., *Managerial Hierarchies: Comparative Perspectives on the Rise of the Modern Industrial Enterprise* (Cambridge, Mass.: Harvard University Press, 1980).

1. Decision Making, Entrepreneurship, and the Theory of the Firm

1. The best known include Bernard W. E. Alford, *W. D. & H. O. Wills and the Development of the U.K. Tobacco Industry, 1786–1965* (Methuen, 1973);

356

Theo C. Barker, *The Glassmakers: Pilkington, The Rise of an International Company, 1826–1976* (Allen & Unwin, 1977); Donald C. Coleman, *Courtaulds: An Economic and Social History*, 3 vols. (Oxford University Press, 1969–1981); R. W. Ferrier, *The History of the British Petroleum Company*, vol. 1, *The Developing Years, 1901–1932* (Cambridge University Press, 1982); Charles E. Harvey, *The Rio Tinto Company: An Economic History of a Leading International Mining Concern, 1873–1954* (Penzance, Alison Hodge, 1981); William J. Reader, *Imperial Chemical Industries: A History*, 2 vols. (Oxford University Press, 1970–1975); William J. Reader, *Bowater: A History* (Cambridge University Press, 1982); Charles Wilson, *The History of Unilever*, 2 vols. (Cassell, 1954). Studies that deal with smaller or less successful firms include Peter L. Payne, *Colvilles and the Scottish Steel Industry* (Oxford University Press, 1979); Roy A. Church, *Kenricks in Hardware: A Family Business, 1791–1966* (Newton Abbot, David & Charles, 1969); Stanley D. Chapman, *Stanton and Staveley: A Business History* (Cambridge, Woodhead-Faulkner, 1981).

2. Leslie Hannah, "Business Development and Economic Structure in Britain since 1880," in L. Hannah, ed., *Management Strategy and Business Development: An Historical and Comparative Study* (Macmillan, 1976), pp. 1–2.

3. George C. Archibald, ed., Introduction to *The Theory of the Firm* (Penguin, 1971), p. 10.

4. Mark Blaug, *The Methodology of Economics* (Cambridge University Press, 1980); P. J. Devine, "The Firm," in P. J. Devine, R. M. Jones, N. Lee, and W. J. Tyson, *An Introduction to Industrial Economics* (Allen & Unwin, 1974).

5. Donald N. McCloskey and Lars Sandberg, "From Damnation to Redemption: Judgements on the Late Victorian Entrepreneur," *Explorations in Economic History* 9 (1971), 89–108, reprinted in D. N. McCloskey, *Enterprise and Trade in Victorian Britain* (Allen & Unwin, 1981), pp. 55–72; D. N. McCloskey, *Economic Maturity and Entrepreneurial Decline: British Iron and Steel, 1870–1913* (Cambridge, Mass.: Harvard University Press, 1973); Lars Sandberg, "The Entrepreneur and Technological Change," in Roderick Floud and D. N. McCloskey, eds., *The Economic History of Britain since 1700*, II (Cambridge University Press, 1981), pp. 99–120.

6. McCloskey, *Economic Maturity*, p. 38; McCloskey, "Damnation to Redemption," p. 66.

7. Stephen Nicholas, "Total Factor Productivity Growth and the Revision of Post–1870 British Economic History," *Ec.H.R.* 35 (1982), 83–90.

8. See George L. S. Shackle, *The Years of High Theory* (Cambridge University Press, 1967), pp. 2–6, 18; Donald Winch, *Economics and Policy: A Historical Study* (Collins/Fontana, 1969), pp. 75–79; Piero Sraffa, "The Laws of Return under Competitive Conditions," *Economic Journal* 36 (Dec. 1926), 535–550.

9. Brian J. Loasby, "Hypothesis and Paradigm in the Theory of the Firm," *Economic Journal* 81 (Dec. 1971), 863–885; B. J. Loasby, *Choice, Complexity, and Ignorance: An Enquiry into Economic Theory and the Practice of Decision-Making* (Cambridge University Press, 1976).

10. M. Bauer and E. Cohen, "The Invisibility of Power in Economics: Beyond Markets and Hierarchies," in Arthur Francis, J. Turk, and Paul Will-

man, eds., *Power, Efficiency, and Institutions: A Critical Appraisal of the Markets and Hierarchies Paradigm* (Heinemann, 1983).

11. John R. Hicks, *Value and Capital* (Oxford University Press, 1939; 1946 ed.), pp. 83–85.

12. Fritz Machlup, *The Methodology of Economics and Other Social Sciences* (New York: Academic Press, 1978), chaps. 16 and 28.

13. Philip W. S. Andrews and Elizabeth Brunner, *Capital Development in Steel: A Study of the United Steel Companies Ltd.* (Oxford University Press, 1952), p. 11.

14. Shackle, *High Theory*; Loasby, "Hypothesis and paradigm."

15. Herbert A. Simon, *A Behavioural Model of Rational Choice* (Santa Monica, Calif.: Rand Corporation, 1953); Robin L. Marris, *The Economic Theory of Managerial Capitalism* (Macmillan, 1967); Richard M. Cyert and James G. March, *A Behavioural Theory of the Firm* (Englewood Cliffs, N.J.: Prentice-Hall, 1963).

16. Oliver E. Williamson and W. O. Ouchi, "The Markets and Hierarchies Programme of Research: Origins, Implications, Prospects," in A. van de Ven and W. Joyce, eds., *Perspectives on Organisation Design and Behaviour* (New York: Wiley, 1981).

17. Bauer and Cohen, "Invisibility."

18. Francis et al., Introduction, in *Power, Efficiency, and Institutions.*

19. Joseph A. Schumpeter, *The Theory of Economic Development* (Cambridge, Mass.: Harvard University Press, 1934) chaps. 1 and 2; J. Schumpeter, *Business Cycles: A Theoretical, Historical, and Statistical Analysis of the Capitalist Process* (New York: McGraw-Hill, 1939), chaps. 2 and 3.

20. Derek H. Aldcroft, "The Entrepreneur and the British Economy, 1870–1914," *EcHR* 17 (Aug. 1964), 166; D. H. Aldcroft and Henry W. Richardson, *The British Economy, 1870–1939* (Macmillan, 1969).

21. McCloskey, *Economic Maturity*, p. 127.

22. William Lazonick, "Competition, Specialization, and Industrial Decline," *Journal of Economic History* 41(March 1981), 37–38; W. Lazonick, "Factor Costs and the Diffusion of Ring Spinning in Britain prior to World War I," *Quarterly Journal of Economics* (Feb. 1981), 91; W. Lazonick and William Mass, "The Performance of the British Cotton Industry, 1870–1913," *Research in Economic History* 9 (Spring 1984), 1–38.

23. Alfred D. Chandler, *The Visible Hand: The Managerial Revolution in American Business* (Cambridge, Mass.: Harvard University Press, 1977).

24. Bernard Elbaum and William Lazonick, "An Institutional Perspective on British Decline," in B. Elbaum and W. Lazonick, eds., *The Decline of the British Economy* (Oxford University Press, 1986), pp. 1–17.

25. See in particular Hannah, *Management Strategy*; Derek F. Channon, *The Strategy and Structure of British Enterprise* (Macmillan, 1973); and the essays by Elbaum, Lazonick, and Michael Best and Jane Humphries in Elbaum and Lazonick, eds., *Decline of the British Economy.*

26. Chandler, *Visible Hand*; Channon, *Strategy and Structure*; A. D. Chandler, "The Development of Modern Management Structures in the United States and the U.K.," in Hannah, *Management Strategy*; B. W. Alford, "The Chandler Thesis: Some General Observations," in ibid., pp. 52–60.

27. Chandler, "The Development of Modern Management Structures," pp. 23–52; A. D. Chandler, "The United States: Seedbed of Managerial Capitalism," in Chandler and Daems, *Managerial Hierarchies;* Chandler and Daems, "Administrative Co-ordination, Allocation, and Monitoring: Concepts and Comparisons," in Norbert Horn and Jurgen Kocka, eds., *Law and the Formation of Big Enterprises in the Nineteenth and Early Twentieth Centuries* (Göttingen: Vandenhock & Ruprecht, 1979), esp. pp. 46–52; A. D. Chandler, "The Emergence of Managerial Capitalism," *Business History Review* 58 (Winter 1984), 502–503.

28. Charles F. Sabel and Jonathan Zeitlin, "Historical Alternatives to Mass Production: Politics, Markets and Technology in Nineteenth Century Industrialization," *Past and Present* no. 108 (Aug. 1985), 133–176; Michael J. Piore and C. F. Sabel, *The Second Industrial Divide: Possibilities for Prosperity* (New York: Basic Books, 1984); Steven Tolliday and Jonathan Zeitlin, "Between Fordism and Flexibility," in S. Tolliday and J. Zeitlin, eds., *The Automobile Industry and Its Workers: Between Fordism and Flexibility* (Cambridge: Basil Blackwell/Polity Press, 1987), pp. 1–25.

29. Barry Supple, Comment, in Harold F. Williamson, ed., *The Evolution of International Management Structures* (Newark: University of Delaware Press, 1975), p. 63.

2. The Economics of Steelmaking

1. There is an enormous historical literature on the performance of the British steel industry before the First World War. The classic account is in Duncan L. Burn, *The Economic History of Steelmaking, 1867–1939* (Cambridge University Press, 1940). Later critiques of the performance of the industry are contained in Derek H. Aldcroft, "The Entrepreneur and the British Economy, 1870–1914," *Ec.H.R.* 17 (Aug. 1964), 113–134; David S. Landes, *The Unbound Prometheus: Technological Change and Industrial Development in Western Europe from 1750 to the Present* (Cambridge University Press, 1970). The rehabilitation of entrepreneurial performance is argued most fully in Donald N. McCloskey, *Economic Maturity and Industrial Decline: British Iron and Steel, 1870–1913* (Cambridge, Mass.: Harvard University Press, 1973). Other accounts have argued a case of relative decline within the context of serious structural constraints on the industry, notably Peter Temin, "The Relative Decline of the British Steel Industry, 1880–1913," in Henry Rosovsky, ed., *Industrialisation in Two Systems* (New York: John Wiley, 1966), esp. pp. 144–149. Recent work has revived the case for relative failure arguing that a lag in the adoption of best-practice technology resulted from the interaction of problems of slowly growing and segmented markets and the fragmentation of the industrial structure; the result was serious constraints on entrepreneurial action and a pattern of suboptimal and defensive investment. See esp. Bernard Elbaum, "The Steel Industry before World War I," in Bernard Elbaum and William Lazonick, eds., *The Decline of the British Economy* (Oxford University Press, 1986), pp. 51–81; Robert C. Allen, "International Competition in Iron and Steel, 1850–1913," *Journal of Economic History* 39 (Dec. 1979),

911–937. See also Stephen B. Webb, "Tariffs, Cartels, Technology and Growth in the German Steel Industry, 1879–1914," *Journal of Economic History* 40 (June 1980), 309–329.

2. The important role of productivity growth in the staple industries in British interwar economic performance has recently been stressed by G. N. Von Tunzelmann, "Structural change and leading sectors in British manufacturing, 1907–1968," in Charles P. Kindleberger and Guido di Tella, eds., *Economics in the Long View: Essays in Honour of W. W. Rostow*, 3 vols., (Macmillan, 1982), III, pp. 1–49; and N. F. R. Crafts and Mark Thomas, "Comparative advantage in UK manufacturing trade, 1910–1935," *Economic Journal* 96 (Sept. 1986), 629–645.

3. Ingvar Svennilson, *Growth and Stagnation in the European Economy* (Geneva: United Nations Economic Commission for Europe, 1954), pp. 120–121.

4. Norman J. G. Pounds and William N. Parker, *Coal and Steel in Western Europe: The Influence of Resources and Techniques on Production* (Faber, 1957).

5. Svennilson, *Growth and Stagnation*, p. 119; Henry W. Richardson, *Economic Recovery in Britain, 1932–1939* (Weidenfeld & Nicolson, 1967), pp. 18, 66; H. W. Richardson, "Overcommitment in Britain before 1930," *Oxford Economic Papers* 17 (July 1965), 240.

6. Outside the United States, USSR, Western Europe, and Japan, global production increased threefold from 1925–1929 to 1935–1939 while consumption increased by 40%. Net imports decreased by 25%. United Nations Economic Commission for Europe (Steel Division), *European Steel Trends in the Setting of the World Market* (Geneva, United Nations Economic Commission for Europe, 1949), p. 9; Svennilson, *Growth and Stagnation*, table 32.

7. Kenneth Warren, *World Steel: An Economic Geography* (Newton Abbot: David & Charles, 1975), pp. 27–49.

8. On European ores, see Pounds and Parker, *Coal and Steel*, pp. 287–289; and Peter Temin, "Relative Decline," pp. 144–146. On the world market, see Gerald Manners, *The Changing World Market for Iron Ore, 1950–1980* (Baltimore: Johns Hopkins University Press, 1971).

9. William A. Johnson, *The Steel Industry of India* (Cambridge, Mass.: Harvard University Press, 1966); Dileep M. Wagle, "Imperial Preference and the Indian Steel Industry, 1924–1939," *EcHR* 34 (Feb. 1981), 120–131; T. Gulilat, "Protection and Infant Industry Promotion: A Case Study of the Indian Iron and Steel Industry." Ph.D. diss., University of California, 1967; Brian R. Tomlinson, *The Political Economy of the Raj, 1914–1947* (Macmillan, 1979).

10. Colin Forster, *Industrial Development in Australia, 1920–1930* (Canberra: Australian National University, 1964); Werner Baer, *The Development of the Brazilian Steel Industry* (Nashville, Tenn.: Vanderbilt University Press, 1969).

11. NFISM *Annual Statistics*.

12. Alice Teichova, *An Economic Background to Munich: International Business and Czechoslovakia, 1918–38* (Cambridge University Press, 1974), pp. 153, 37.

13. Svennilson, *Growth and Stagnation*, pp. 127–130.

14. Ervin Hexner, *The International Steel Cartel* (Chapel Hill: University of North Carolina Press, 1943) pp. 120, 175, 198, 244.

15. Alfred E. Kahn, *Great Britain in the World Economy* (Pitman, 1946), p. 61.

16. Richardson, *Economic Recovery,* p. 80.

17. Maurice Dobb, *Studies in the Development of Capitalism,* 8th ed. (Routledge and Kegan Paul, 1963); for some of the political implications of this see Alastair Reid and Steven Tolliday, "The General Strike, 1926," *Historical Journal* 20 (Dec. 1977), 1001–12.

18. NFISM and BISF *Annual Statistics.*

19. United Nations Economic Commission for Europe (Industry Division), *The European Steel Industry and the Wide Strip Mill* (Geneva: United Nations Economic Commission for Europe, 1953), pp. 9–10, 40–52.

20. All these figures are derived from BISF *Annual Statistics.*

21. Thus, in 1929, for instance, the Ebbw Vale Steel, Iron & Coal Co. stood as one of the largest steel companies in terms of capital, even though it was producing nothing. Similarly, the financial upheaval of the Hatry affair almost halved United Steel's capitalization, yet its production remained unaffected and its financial position was actually strengthened. In Hannah's capitalization table of the fifty largest companies, however, United Steel falls from tenth to forty-seventh. Leslie Hannah, *The Rise of the Corporate Economy* (Methuen, 1976), pp. 118–121.

22. Ingot values are fairly uniform, except for special steels.

23. 1913 figures: from Dorman Long company records; from David Colville and Sons company records; estimated for South Durham and Cargo Fleet; extrapolated from Philip W. S. Andrews and Elizabeth Brunner, *Capital Development in Steel: A Study of the United Steel Companies Ltd.* (Oxford University Press, 1952), for Steel, Peech and Tozer; estimated for John Summers.

24. See Chapter 8.

25. See Chapter 5 for Richard Thomas and Chapter 9 for Stewarts & Lloyds.

26. See Chapter 3.

27. See Chapter 5.

28. See Chapter 9.

29. See Chapter 10.

30. See Chapter 10.

31. See Chapter 8.

32. BISF *Annual Statistics.*

33. See Chapters 5 and 10.

34. See Chapter 9.

35. See Chapter 10.

36. BISF *Annual Statistics.*

37. P. Cunliffe-Lister, "Possibility of Amalgamations," 21 July 1925, Appendix C, CR(H)16, CAB 58/9.

38. See Chapter 3.

39. See Chapter 5.

40. See Chapter 4.

41. See Chapter 9.

42. See Chapter 8.

43. See Chapter 8.

44. John R. Hume and Michael S. Moss, *Beardmore: The History of a Scottish Industrial Giant* (Heinemann, 1979).

45. Robert Jones and Oliver Marriott, *Anatomy of a Merger: A History of GEC, AEI, and English Electric* (Pan, 1970), pp. 60–64, 137–138, 148–149, 190–192.

46. On Guest, Keen, Nettlefold (GKN), see Chapter 10.

47. Temin, "Relative Decline," pp. 144–146; Elbaum, "Steel Industry before World War I," pp. 63–64.

48. For case studies of these problems in Lincolnshire and on Teeside, see Chapters 3 and 5.

49. See, for example, J. Bird, "Presidential Address," *JWSISI* 39 (1931–32), 1–16; T. W. Hand, "Progress in British Rolling Mill Practice," *JISI* 111, no. 1 (1925), 43–112.

50. Company records, Ryland's Directory, NFISM *Annual Statistics*.

51. Appendix to P. Cunliffe-Lister, "Possibility of Amalgamations," 21 July 1925, CR(H)16, CAB 58/9.

52. See Chapter 4.

53. For a case study, see Chapter 5.

54. Andrews and Brunner, *Capital Development*, p. 169. For another example, see the case study of Richard Thomas & Co., Chapter 5.

3. The Northeast Coast Steel Firms, 1918–1939

1. Charles Wilson, "Company Histories I: Dorman Long," *Steel Review* 6 (April 1957), 19.

2. See the comments by Bolckow's managing director, Windsor Richards, in the discussion of a paper by J. Hand, "Changing Open Hearth Furnaces by Machinery," *JISI* 51, no. 1, (1897), 106. Duncan Burn, *The Economic History of Steelmaking, 1867–1939: A Study in Competition* (Cambridge University Press, 1940), pp. 200–216.

3. A. Cooper, "Metal Mixers as Used at the Works of NESCO," *JISI* 47, no. 1 (1895), 66–76.

4. DL, AGM, 1898; Burn, *Economic History*, p. 272. See also Jonathan S. Boswell, *Business Policies in the Making: Three Steel Companies Compared* (Allen & Unwin, 1983), pp. 35–42.

5. Kenneth Warren, *The Geography of British Heavy Industry since 1800* (Oxford University Press, 1976), p. 48; DL, AGM, 1899.

6. Burn, *Economic History*, pp. 249–273.

7. DL, AGMs, 1899, 1904, and 1911.

8. McCloskey, *Economic Maturity*, pp. 40–46; R. C. Allen, "Entrepreneurship and Technical Progress in the North-East Coast Pig Iron Industry, 1850–1913," *Research in Economic History* 6 (1981), 42–50.

9. Burn, *Economic History*, pp. 183–219, 362–370; Bernard Elbaum, "Labour and Uneven Development: Unions, Management, and Wage Structure

in UK and U.S. Iron and Steel, 1870–1970," Ph.D. diss., Harvard University, 1981.

10. W. G. Willis, *South Durham Steel and Iron Co.: A History* (Portsmouth: Eyre & Spotiswoode, 1969), p. 6; SD and CF, AGMs, 1907–1913; Gordon H. Boyce, "The Growth and Dissolution of a Large-scale Business Enterprise: The Furness Interest, 1892–1919," Ph.D. diss., London School of Economics, 1984, pp. 64–69, 144–145, 173–175, 233–237.

11. Henry W. Richardson and J. M. Bass, "The Profitability of the Consett Iron Company before 1914," *Business History* 7 (July 1965), 72–75, 78–80, 84–88.

12. Michael W. Flinn, "British Steel and Spanish Ore, 1871–1914," *EcHR* 8 (Aug. 1955), 84–90.

13. J. C. Carr and W. Taplin, *History of the British Steel Industry* (Oxford: Basil Blackwell, 1962), pp. 320–337; Burn, *Economic History*, pp. 350–393.

14. Arthur Dorman, "Development of the Basic Open Hearth Process in Cleveland," *Proceedings of the Cleveland Institute of Engineers* (Nov. 1925); *ICTR*, 15 Sept. 1922, p. 377; ibid., 8 Oct. 1920, pp. 471–472.

15. BV Minutes, Jan. 1917 to Dec. 1919. See also the report of the later court case in *ICTR*, 23 Nov. 1923, p. 782.

16. *ICTR*, 5 Aug. 1921; D. C. D. Pocock, "A Comparative Study of Three Steel Towns: Middlesborough, Scunthorpe, and Corby," Ph.D. diss., Dundee University, 1969.

17. Author's interview with Edward T. Judge; Report on the Future Policy of NESCO by Mr. Grant, Mr. Cooper, and Mr. Mason, 9 Oct. 1917; DL Minutes, passim.

18. Cf. "New Blast Furnaces at Clarence Ironworks," *ICTR*, 26 Jan. 1923; R. A. Sharp, "The Future of Blast Furnace Practice in Cleveland," *ICTR*, 10 Feb. 1922; DL Minutes, 15 March 1927.

19. Dorman, "Development."

20. SD Minutes, 23 Oct. 1917 and 28 Nov. 1917.

21. "Comparison of Balance Sheets and Information on North East Coast Firms Prepared for Mr. Caddick," CF Papers, 1925, box 02607.

22. Kenneth Warren, "Iron and Steel in the North East: Regional Implications of Development in a Basic Industry," *Regional Studies* 3 (1969), pp. 49–50.

23. See note 21.

24. SD Minutes, 27 Oct. 1927 and 14 Dec. 1927.

25. DL, "Deliveries of Year Ended 30th September 1929," corrected statement of 9 Dec. 1929.

26. SD, current contracts file.

27. On price cutting to retain customers, see SD Minutes, esp. 26 May 1920 to 24 Oct. 1920.

28. SD Minutes, 24 June 1931.

29. CON Directors' Report 1900–1921.

30. R. M. Hornsby, *History of Consett Iron Co. Ltd.* (Consett, n.d.), p. 32.

31. C. Smith, Memorandum, 7 March 1922, CON Minutes. The remark-

able technical ingenuity of the reconstruction on Consett's restricted site, honeycombed by old mineworkings, is described in Steven Tolliday, "Industry, Finance, and the State: The Case of British Steel," Ph.D. diss., Cambridge University, 1980 (cited as "British Steel"), pp. 118–119.

32. E. J. George, Memorandum on the Question of Financing Reconstruction and Additional Capital Expenditure, 1 May 1922, CON Minutes.

33. CON Minutes, 9 Jan. 1923 and 6 March 1923. Cf. also Mr. Scholes's (Chief Engineer) Report to Board, 3 Jan. 1923.

34. CON Minutes, 5 April 1921 and 6 April 1923.

35. CON, Balance Sheets.

36. DL, AGM, 17 April 1923; DL Minutes, Jan. 1916 to March 1923, passim.

37. DL, AGMs, 1928 and 1932.

38. Andrews and Brunner, *Capital Development*, pp. 136, 151–152.

39. CON Minutes, 24 Sept. 1925; ibid., Nov. 1925; and letter from Frodingham Iron and Steel Company to North East Coast Steelmakers Association, JSA Minutes, no. 3926, p. 1877, 14 March 1924.

40. CON Minutes, 5 Oct. 1926; SD Minutes, 24 March 1926.

41. JSA Minutes, nos. 3999, 4242, 4506, 4546, 4816, and 4661, 1924–1928.

42. *ICTR*, monthly price lists.

43. Brian Tew, "Costs, Prices, and Investment in the British Iron and Steel Industries, 1924–37," Ph.D. diss., Cambridge University, 1940, table XXXa, p. 156.

44. James M. Reid, *James Lithgow: Master of Work* (Hutchinson, 1964), p. 108.

45. Evidence of Sir James Lithgow (president of the Shipbuilding Federation) to the Sankey Committee, 8 Oct. 1929, CR(IS)33, CAB 58/129, p. 8.

46. *ICTR*, 2 Sept. 1927.

47. E. L. Champness, "Are We Justified in Using Steel and Other Materials of Foreign Manufacture in the British Engineering Industry?" *Transactions of the North East Coast Institution of Engineers and Shipbuilders* 47 (1930–31), 389–390.

48. CF, Report to Executive Committee, 28 Sept. 1934.

49. CF Minutes, Oct. to Nov. 1923 and Current Contract Lists, 1929–1935.

50. Willis, SD, pp. 18–20; CF, Report to Executive Committee, 23 Feb. 1932.

51. SD Minutes, 28 June 1922, 31 Oct. 1923, and 28 Oct. 1925.

52. CF, Report to the Executive Committee, 4 Oct. 1932; ibid., 23 Feb. 1932; CF, Managing Director's Report, 3 Nov. 1931; CF Minutes, 30 Jan. 1935.

53. CF, Report to the Executive Committee, 28 Sept. 1934; ibid., Jan. 1935. On the context of this in the sheet trade, see Chapter 5.

54. DL, AGM, 16 Dec. 1928.

55. Cf. DL Minutes, 12 May 1924 and 12 July 1927; DL, AGM, 1932. After the Nile Dam project in 1926, Dorman Long decided to discontinue dam making, DL Minutes, 14 Dec. 1926.

56. J. J. C. Bradfield, "The Sydney Harbour Bridge," *Proceedings of the Cleveland Institute of Engineers* (9 Oct. 1924), 7–8; Ralph Freeman, Lawrence Ennis, J. J. C. Bradfield, and J. F. Pain, "The Sydney Harbour Bridge," *Minutes*

of the Institution of Civil Engineers, 238, Part 2 (1933–1934) 153–475 (reprinted as a pamphlet in 1935).

57. DL, AGM, 1928–1931.

58. Colin Forster, ed., *Australian Economic Development in the Twentieth Century* (Allen & Unwin, 1970), pp. 158–166.

59. CF Minutes, Cargo Fleet Sales Conference, 28 Dec. 1933; CF File 03174 DL Minutes, 17 Jan. 1936, 26 June 1936, and 3 April 1936.

60. W. E. G. Salter, *Productivity and Technical Change* (Cambridge University Press, 1966).

61. F. G. Smith, "The Mechanical Handling of Iron Ore and Similar Bulk Material," *Proceedings of the Cleveland Institute of Engineers* (6 March 1922).

62. Outhwaite in discussion on F. G. Smith, "Mechanical handling."

63. H. G. Scott, "The Practical Management of Blast Furnace Plants in Cleveland," *Proceedings of the Cleveland Institute of Engineers* (10 Nov. 1924), 41.

64. F. Samuelson, "Presidential Address," *JISI* 105, no. 1 (1922), 36–37. And cf. also R. A. Sharp, "Future of Blast Furnace."

65. Discussion of D. E. Roberts, "Notes on Blast Furnace Filling," *JISI* 105, no. 1 (1922), 74.

66. See, for example, the contributions of Scott (Bolckow Vaughan) and Wilson (Skinningrove) in the discussion of Sharp's paper, "Future of Blast Furnace."

67. R. Sharp (Blast Furnace Manager of Clarence Works), "Future of Blast Furnace."

68. Coal Mines Reorganisation Commission, Memorandum on Colliery Amalgamations, August 1931. Reprinted in Andrew M. Neumann, *Economic Organisation of the British Coal Industry* (Routledge, 1934), appendix.

69. D. AGMs, 1931–1934.

70. Ryland's Directory, 1920–1930, and cf. ownership diagram in Tolliday, "British Steel," p. 90; Armstrong College, University of Durham, Newcastle-on-Tyne, *The Industrial Position of the North East Coast of England* (Board of Trade, Newcastle-on-Tyne, 1935).

71. DL, AGM, 1929.

72. Much workable coal became inaccessible because bad methods of working coal produced dangerous conditions. Cf. Thomas Sharp, *A Derelict Area: A Study of the South West Durham Coalfield* (Hogarth Press, 1935).

73. P. G. Craig, "Location Factors in the Development of Steel Centres," *Papers and Proceedings of the Regional Science Association,* vol. 3 (Cambridge, Mass.: Regional Science Association, 1957), p. 252.

74. DL, AGM, 1920; Palmer's of Jarrow, for instance, acquired the South Pelaw collieries in 1920 "at abnormal prices" and thus dissipated reserves that would have been very valuable in the slump. See Ellen Wilkinson, *The Town That Was Murdered* (Gollancz, 1939), p. 132.

75. DL, AGM, 1921.

76. Royal Commission on the Coal Industry, 1925. Appendix 16, pp. 117–120.

77. BV Minutes, 25 Feb. 1919 and 20 Aug. 1920.

78. SD Minutes, 18 Dec. 1918.

79. SD Minutes, 30 April 1919 and 14 Feb. 1920.

80. DL, MTG, IV J. H. Pizey, Notes of a Visit to Four Works of Dorman Long & Co., 3 March 1924; DL, MTG, IV, J. A. Roelofsen to T. H. D. Stubbs, 19 March 1924.

81. Firms like Bolckow Vaughan remained obsessed with the idea of self-sufficiency. BV Minutes, 22 Dec. 1921 and 26 Jan. 1922.

82. This argument is based on the notion of "defensive investment" elaborated in Alexandre Lamfalussy, *Investment and Growth in a Mature Economy: The Case of Belgium* (Macmillan, 1961), pp. 79–94.

83. DL Minutes, 9 Oct. 1928; Carlton Iron Co., Minutes, April to July 1922.

84. BV Minutes, 12 Jan. 1926; cf. Report by Mr. Hare, BV Minutes, July 1926.

85. Bolckow Vaughn itself eventually realized that coal policy was handled "altogether too much from the point of view that they (the mines) were there in order to supply fuel for steel." Cf. BV PRIV Minutes, Feb. to July 1928.

86. See the plan drawn up by Mensforth during the general strike; BV Minutes, 13 July 1926, and W. R. Garside, *The Durham Miners, 1919–1960* (Allen & Unwin, 1971), esp. p. 212.

87. Detailed figures are not available. The general movements are,, however, indicated in BV, AGMs, 1923 and 1925; Report by Peat, Marwick, and Mitchell to DL on proposed merger, 20 June 1932 and in SD/CF Minute Books.

88. Hornsby, *History*, pp. 27–32; Richardson and Bass, "Profitability," p. 82; CON, AGMs, passim.

89. L. George Neasham, *The History and Biography of West Durham* (privately printed by the author, 1881), p. 3.

90. CON, AGM, 1926.

91. E. J. George, Memorandum as to the Present and Probable Financial Position, CON Minutes, 24 Sept. 1924.

92. Memorandum by E. J. George on the Stoppage at the Collieries, CON Minutes, 16 Feb. 1926.

93. This episode is described in Tolliday, "British Steel," pp. 105–110.

94. DL Minutes, Feb. to June 1930.

95. DL, Merger File, Schedules A to C, "Proposals under Unified Control," April 1930.

96. Ibid.; Report of the Joint Committee, April 1930, schedule 6.

97. CF, Merger File, "Estimated Results," Sept. 1932.

98. BV, Balance Sheets and AGM, 1924.

99. BV, AGM, 1923.

100. BV, AGM, 1924.

101. Bolckow Vaughan took the case through the courts as far as a Petition of Right; see *ICTR*, 23 Nov. 1923, p. 782.

102. E. Woolley (joint managing director, Midland Bank) to J. E. Johnsonn-Fergusson, 17 July 1924, BV PRIV Minutes.

103. BV Minutes, BV PRIV Minutes, April to Oct. 1924.

104. BV Minutes, 8 April 1925, 13 May 1925, and 25 June 1925.

105. BV PRIV Minutes, 27 Nov. 1925 and Dec. 1925; BV, AGM, 1926.

106. For example, it had to borrow to reopen its open-hearth furnaces after the General Strike. BV Minutes, 13 Oct. 1926.

107. BV PRIV Minutes, 4 April 1924 and 13 Aug. 1924.

108. C. F. Goodenough (joint general manager, Barclays) to A. Dorman, DL Minutes, 12 Dec. 1928 and 24 Jan. 1929.

109. DL Minutes, 19 March 1929.

110. DL Minutes, 15 Feb. 1929.

111. Cf. E. R. Peacock, Memorandum on McLintock's Report on the Dorman/Bolckow Amalgamation, 11 July 1929; and Peacock, Memorandum Regarding the Proposal to Form a New Operating Company in Order to Effect an Amalgamation of Steel Manufacturers, 26 Oct. 1928, SMT 2/93.

112. BV PRIV Minutes, 25 June 1929.

113. E. R. Peacock, Memo on Dorman/Bolckow Merger, SMT 2/93, 25 July 1929; Kitson to Harvey, SMT 2/93 19 July 1929; DL Minutes, 23 July 1929.

114. Peacock, Memo, 25 July 1929, SMT 2/93.

115. Harvey to Kitson, SMT 2/93, 17 July 1929, Harvey to Peacock, 18 July 1929, SMT 2/93.

116. N. L. Campbell, Memorandum on the North East Coast, 23 June 1920, SMT 3/107; DL Minutes, 8 July 1920.

117. BV PRIV Minutes, 25 June 1929; BV Minutes, 12 June 1929.

118. DL Minutes, 23 April to Dec. 1929.

119. Cf. DL Minutes, 15 Nov. 1928 and 13 March 1929: A. Dorman to C. Bruce Gardner, 18 Sept. 1928, SMT 3/107.

120. DL Minutes, 13 Nov. 1928.

121. J. Craig to H. Bond, 22 July 1927. CA (British Steelmakers) File.

122. M. Norman (governor of the Bank of England) to R. Kitson, Sept. 1929, SMT 2/93; C. Mithcell, Memorandum re: Further Meeting with Ethelbert Furness, 28 July 1930, SMT 3/107; Craig to Lord Kylsant, 22 July 1929. Kylsant Correspondence, CA.

123. DL Minutes, 19 Nov. to 17 Dec. 1929.

124. C. Bruce Gardner to A. Duncan, 19 March 1931, BID 1/74. C. Mitchell, Memorandum on North East Coast Rationalisation, 21st May 1930, SMT 3/107. Lord Furness had a considerable, although not preponderant, shareholding interest. He controlled in all £429,784 out of £1,755,753 ordinary shares of South Durham (24%) and £98,548 out of £980,000 debentures (10%), plus £134,000 out of £610,000 ordinary and £122,000 out of £885,000 preference shares of subsidiary coal companies. "Furness Share Interests," CF, Miscellaneous, File.

125. E. H. D. Skinner (senior adviser to the governor of the Bank of England) "Iron and Steel, North East Coast," 2 May 1931, SMT 2/93.

126. C. Mitchell, Memorandum re: Further Meeting with Ethelbert Furness (manager of the Furness estate), 28 July 1930, SMT 3/107.

127. Skinner to Peacock, 2 May 1931, SMT 3/93.

128. Skinner, "Iron and Steel, North East Coast," 2 May 1931, SMT 2/93.

129. C. Mitchell, Memo, 28 July 1930, SMT 3/107.

130. Bruce Gardner to Duncan, 10 March 1931, BID 1/79.

131. James departed in a hurry to run the Lancashire Steel Corporation without even giving the required six months' notice, Furness to Talbot, 2 March 1931, CF File No. 03175.

132. Boswell, *Business Policies,* pp. 77–82, 108–110.

133. Charles Dorman, Colonel Byrne, and J. F. Mason all died in the spring of 1929. In Oct. 1929 Arthur Cooper retired; Sir Arthur Dorman died in Feb. 1930, aged 84; and Sir Hugh Bell died in July 1931, aged 87. DL Minutes, passim.

134. SMTHM Minutes, 5 Oct. 1931 and 21 March 1931. The BID told Bruce Gardner to tell them that "we were ashamed of the pair of them" for not progressing faster.

135. H. C. Bischoff to Bruce Gardner, 5 Nov. 1931, BID 1/82.

136. Goodenough to Mitchell, 31 March 1932, BID 1/82.

137. *ICTR,* 1 Dec. 1933.

138. *ICTR,* 28 July 1933, p. 152.

139. Goodenough to Mitchell, 31 March 1932, Mitchell, Memorandum on Proposed Amalgamation, 23 Dec. 1931, BID 1/82.

140. *Financial Times,* 1 Dec. 1933; *ICTR,* 1 Dec. 1933, p. 854.

141. McQuistan to Mitchell, 10 Nov. 1931, BID 1/82.

142. See Chapter 8.

143. N. L. Campbell to Bruce Gardner, 9 Aug. 1930, SMT 3/107.

144. Sir W. McLintock to Campbell, 5 Aug. 1930, SMT 3/107.

145. SMTHM, 25 Aug. 1930.

146. Campbell to McLintock, 6 Aug. 1930, SMT 3/107.

147. Bruce Gardner to Campbell, 12 Aug. 1930, SMT 3/107.

148. Norman speaking at SMTHM, 23 June 1930.

149. Sir H. Mensforth to Sir Horace Wilson, 25 Nov. 1930, BID 1/79.

150. Bruce Gardner to Sir Gilbert Garnsey, 4 Dec. 1930, BID 1/79.

151. Bruce Gardner, Notes on North East Coke Ovens, 16 Dec. 1930, BID 1/79.

152. DL Minutes, 8 July 1930.

153. Talbot to Peacock, 22 Dec. 1930, BID 1/79.

154. CF, Managing Director's Report, 23 June 1930.

155. A. Pam, Memorandum on the Provision of Coke-Ovens for Dorman Long and Cargo Fleet, 3 Dec. 1930, BID 1/79.

156. C. Mitchell, Memorandum re: Meeting with Ethelbert Furness, 15 July 1930, SMT 3/107. On the new plant, see "The Gibbons-Kogag Coke-Ovens at the Works of Cargo Fleet Iron Co.," *ICTR,* 20 Jan. 1933; and "Coke-Oven Installation at Cargo Fleet Iron Works," *ICTR,* 7 Dec. 1934, p. 890.

157. In a simultaneous capital reconstruction the Dorman debenture holders were to see the value of their stock halved and reduced to preferred stock, taking second place to a new £2.5 million prior lien stock, which would be floated publicly to pay for carrying through the amalgamation and to provide new money for capital expenditure. In return, the old debenture holders would hold a "special management share" with a majority vote until dividends had been paid for three consecutive years. Half the proceeds of the

issue would go to buy out the South Durham stockholders. *Economist*, 8 July 1933, p. 82; *ICTR* 7 July 1933, p. 33.

158. McQuistan to A. M. McColl, 1 April 1932, BID 1/82.

159. Goodenough to Mitchell, 31 March 1932, BID 1/82.

160. Goodenough to Mitchell, 31 March 1932, BID 1/82.

161. Minutes of Meeting of SD Preference Shareholders, 19 July 1933. SD Archive.

162. The opposition was coordinated by Alderman Hyde of West Hartlepool. Cf. letter from Hyde to shareholders, 10 July 1933. W. G. Willis, *South Durham Steel and Iron Co. Ltd.*, p. 22. *ICTR*, 17 Nov. 1933.

163. Wilkinson, *Town That Was Murdered*, pp. 161–162.

164. Cf. Results of Voting on a Scheme of Arrangement Dated 30 June 1933. The vote was close but the opposition of the preference shareholders was decisive.

165. See DL/SD Merger File, passim.

166. J. E. James to Furness, 14 April 1930. Quoted in Willis, *South Durham Steel and Iron Co. Ltd.*, p. 6.

167. Minutes of meeting of preference shareholders, South Durham, 19 July 1933. SD Archive.

168. Peacock, Memorandum on Interview with Goodenough, 12 May 1931, BID 1/79.

169. BID 1/84 Memorandum on North East Coast Amalgamation, 23 March 1933.

170. Bruce Gardner, Notes, 16 June 1930, SMT 3/107.

171. Goodenough to Mitchell, 5 Nov. 1931, BID 1/82.

172. BID 1/84 Memorandum on North East Coast Amalgamation Scheme, 23 March 1933.

173. Peacock, Memorandum on Interview with Goodenough, 12 May 1931, BID 1/79.

174. Campbell, Memorandum on Proposed £2m. Prior Lien Debenture Issue, 30 March 1933, BID 1/84.

175. Norman to Bruce Gardner, 29 March 1930, SMT 2/73.

176. Cf. managing director's report to the executive committee, 28 June 1932. In his opinion this was the major obstacle to the scheme.

177. Goodenough to Bruce Gardner, 19 May 1932, BID 1/82.

178. Chancery Division: before Mr. Justice Maugham. Reported in *ICTR*, 24 Nov. 1933, p. 818, and 1 Dec. 1933, p. 854; and in *Financial Times*, 23 Nov. and 1 Dec. 1933. The judgment largely upheld the case of the dissenting debenture holders that "this was not the company's scheme at all; it was a bankers' scheme. It had been devised in the interest of Barclays Bank and [their] submission was that Barclays Bank had wholly failed in its position as Trustee and had used its position to induce the company to adopt a scheme which was particularly favourable to the bank."

179. Norman, Remarks, 21 March 1933, SMT 2/93.

180. BID, Memorandum on North East Coast Amalgamation Scheme, 23 March 1933, BID 1/84.

181. Ellis Hunter, "Dorman Long: Points Outstanding with BID," 4 May 1933, BID 1/84.

182. Norman to SMTHM, 23 June 1930.

183. Bruce Gardner, Interview with Mitchell, 11 Sept. 1930, SMT 3/18. Peacock to Goodenough, 24 June 1931, SMT 2/55. SMTHM, 8 May 1933.

184. It refused to provide £150,000 in May 1933 to buy up a loan from the Midland Bank to Redpath Brown that was holding up the whole scheme. Campbell to Norman, 3 May 1933, SMT 2/93.

185. Skinner, Note, 4 July 1933, SMT 2/93.

186. SMTHM, 2 July 1934.

187. *ICTR*, 15 and 22 Dec. 1933.

188. Vaizey wrongly attributes the dominant role to Barclays. As we have seen, its own scheme had already been defeated. In this matter it acted only nominally as trustees to the debenture holders. John Vaizey, *History of British Steel* (Weidenfeld & Nicolson, 1974), pp. 62, 84.

189. *Economist*, 3 Nov. 1934, p. 837; and *Investor's Review*, 3 Nov. 1934.

190. Campbell, Memorandum on Dorman Long, 8 Feb. 1934, BID 1/86.

191. Willis, *South Durham Steel and Iron Co. Ltd.*, p. 24.

192. SMTHM, 18 June 1934.

193. Charles Wilson, *A Man and His Time: A Memoir of Sir Ellis Hunter* (Newman Neame, 1962), p. 12.

194. Author's interview with E. T. Judge.

195. Ellis Hunter to J. H. B. Forster, 31 Jan. 1934, CF File no. 03175.

196. On Ennis's background in engineering, see Charlotte Erickson, *British Industrialists: Steel and Hosiery, 1850–1950* (National Institute of Economic and Social Research, Economic and Social Studies, Vol. 18, Cambridge, 1959).

197. SMTHM, 4 June 1943.

198. Walmsley to Mitchell, 16 March 1934; DL, DTR, XXI and DL Minutes, March 1934, passim.

199. Author's interview with E. T. Judge.

200. DL Minutes, 1935, passim.

201. A. Hutchinson, "Presidential Address," *JISI* 135, no. 1 (1937), 75–77; DL Minutes, 25 Jan. 1935.

202. See James Henderson in discussion on W. Geary, "Hot Metal Practice in Five Melting Shops on the North East Coast," *JISI* 136, no. 2 (1937), 281, and in BISF *Annual Statistics*.

203. Geary, "Hot Metal," p. 282.

204. See "Review of Blast Furnace Plants in England and Wales," National Union of Blastfurnacemen report, Feb. 1944, Iron and Steel Trades Confederation Archives.

4. The Scottish Steel Industry, 1918–1939

1. Peter L. Payne, *Colvilles and the Scottish Steel Industry* (Oxford University Press, 1979), pp. 52–53.

2. R. H. Campbell, "Early Malleable Iron Production in Scotland," *Business History* 4, no. 1 (1961) 23, 26–33.

3. Kenneth Warren, "Locational Problems of the Scottish Iron and Steel Industry since 1780," *Scottish Geographical Magazine* 81 (April 1965), 18–36; 81 (Sept. 1965), 87–103. H. Bumby, W. Wylie, and H. Archibald, "On the Iron and Steel Industries of the West of Scotland," *JISI* 60, no. 2 (1901), 12.

4. Neil K. Buxton, "Efficiency and Organisation in Scotland's Iron and Steel Industry during the Interwar Period." *EcHR* 29, no. 1 (1976), 118; Anthony Slaven, *The Development of the West of Scotland, 1750–1960* (Routledge and Kegan Paul, 1975), pp. 170–171.

5. Bumby et al., "Iron and Steel," pp. 12–13; W. Jones, "Present Position and Prospects of Processes for the Recovery of Tar and Ammonia from Blast Furnaces." *JISI* 2 (1885), 410–447.

6. H. A. Brassert & Co. Report to the Lord Weir of Eastwood on the manufacture of iron and steel by Wm. Baird and Co. Ltd., David Colville and Sons Ltd., Jas. Dunlop & Co., Steel Company of Scotland, Ltd., and Stewarts & Lloyds Ltd., CA, 16 May 1929—hereafter *Brassert Report (Scotland)*, p. 43; Slaven, *Development*, pp. 169–170; E. H. Lewis, "Presidential Address," *JWSISI* 31 (1923–24), 5.

7. I. F. Gibson, "The Establishment of the Scottish Steel Industry," *Scottish Journal of Political Economy* 5, no. 1 (Feb. 1958), 37.

8. Payne, *Colvilles*, pp. 32–34, 19–21.

9. R. H. Campbell, *The Rise and Fall of Scottish Industry, 1707–1939* (Edinburgh: Donald, 1980), pp. 118–122.

10. Slaven, *Development*, p. 177; Campbell, *Rise and Fall*, p. 122.

11. Slaven, *Development*, p. 177.

12. Warren, "Locational Problems," p. 26.

13. Slaven, *Development*, p. 178.

14. For the war period see Payne, *Colvilles*, pp. 125–150. Output figures are from table 6.2., p. 136; see also Peter L. Payne, "Rationality and Personality: A Study of Mergers in the Scottish Iron and Steel Industry, 1916–1936," *Business History* 19 (July 1977), 163–166.

15. DCS Minutes, 17 April 1917 and 9 March 1920. See also Edwin Green and Michael Moss, *A Business of National Importance: The Royal Mail Shipping Group, 1902–1937* (Methuen, 1982), pp. 46–49. JB Minutes, Report of a committee meeting, Lord Pirrie to Sir Thomas Bell (director of John Brown), 17 March 1920.

16. SCS Minutes, 3 March 1920.

17. SCS Minutes, 1 and 20 April 1920.

18. AS Letter Books, F. J. Stephen to Lord Inchcape, 24 Dec. 1919 to 16 April 1920.

19. AS, AGM Report, 1919; and F. J. Stephen to Lord Inchcape, 16 April 1920, AS Letter Books.

20. W. Russell to J. R. Craig, 10 Feb. 1920, JC.B.II(vii), CA.

21. W. E. Coe, *The Engineering Industry of Northern Ireland* (Newton Abbot: David & Charles, 1969), pp. 84–86.

22. AS Minute Books, UGD 4, F. J. Stephen to Lord Inchcape, 20 Dec. 1919 and 23 Jan. 1920.

23. H. Robertson to J. Craig, 20 Feb. 1920, JC.B.VIII(i), CA.

24. John R. Hume and Michael S. Moss, *A Bed of Nails: The History of P. MacCallum & Sons Ltd. of Greenock, 1781–1981* (Greenock, Lang & Fulton, 1983), pp. 25–67.

25. W. Russell to J. Craig, 10 Feb. 1920, JC.B.II(vii), CA.

26. W. R. Fergusson to J. Craig, 22 March 1917, JC.F.II(17), CA.

27. Moore, the Colville auditor in DCS Minutes 9 Dec. 1918. For SCS, see F. J. Stephen to Sir Duncan Carmichael, 7 Nov. 1922, AS Letter Books, concerning Peninsular & Orient line orders.

28. F. J. Stephen to Lord Inchcape, 8 Dec. 1920, AS Letter Books.

29. Lord Pirrie to Sir Thomas Bell, JB Minutes, 17 March 1920.

30. J. Morton, Memo on a Meeting with W. G. Gray (managing director of SCS), January 1930, Baird Papers.

31. John Philip to J. Craig, 28 April 1936, JC.F.IV, CA; and AS Minute Books, 7 Nov. 1921 and 26 Feb. 1923.

32. Andrew Gray, Memorandum on the Position of Lanarkshire Steel Co. in a Proposed Merger with Colvilles and SCS for Submission to Bruce Gardner, 29 Dec. 1932, BID 1/61.

33. Quarterly Deliveries from Each Works to Customers, 1927–1936, CA.

34. Anthony Slaven, "British Shipbuilders: Market Trends and Order Book Patterns between the Wars," *Journal of Transport History* 3 (Nov. 1982), 47.

35. J. Craig to Sir W. McLintock, 16 June 1930, CA.

36. James M. Reid, *James Lithgow Master of Work* (Hutchinson, 1964), p. 110; Notes of a Conversation between A. J. H. Mowbray and A. K. McCosh, 15 May 1930, Baird Papers.

37. Reid, *Lithgow*, p. 142.

38. Lithgows Ltd: Summary of Margins from 1911 to 1938, Lithgow Papers, GD 320, File 4.6.1.

39. Lithgow Papers, Financial Papers, GD 320, passim.

40. John Orbell, *From Cape to Cape: The History of Lyle Shipping Co.* (Edinburgh: P. Harris, 1978), pp. 74–77; Slaven, "British Shipbuilders," p. 51.

41. Reid, *Lithgow*, p. 75.

42. John R. Hume and Michael Moss, *Beardmore: The History of a Scottish Industrial Giant* (Heinemann, 1979), p. 7.

43. Reid, *Lithgow*, p. 88.

44.. C. Bruce Gardner, Report on William Beardmore and Co., 21 Nov. 1931, SMT 3/137.

45. Payne, *Colvilles*, p. 117.

46. DCS Minutes, 9 April 1918, 15 Jan. 1918, 18 Feb. 1918; SCS Minutes, 15 Oct. 1918; 18 March 1918.

47. See SSA Minutes for various attempts to control the price of supply by buying agreements. The most recent scheme collapsed in Aug. 1922.

48. Lord Invernairn to Craig, 29 Jan. 1923, Invernairn Amalgamation Papers, CA.

49. J. Craig to Lord Pirrie, 8 Nov. 1923, CA.

50. DCS Minutes, Dec. 1923 to July 1925.

51. J. Craig to H. Bond, 22 July 1927, 17 Dec. 1927, and 20 Dec. 1927; B. Talbot to J. Craig, 19 Dec. 1927. CA.

52. B. Talbot to J. Craig, 2 Feb. 1928, CA; and correspondence between H. Bond and J. Craig, 26 Oct. 1927 to 28 Jan. 1928, CA.

53. Payne, *Colvilles*, pp. 163–164.

54. DCS Minutes, 13 Nov. 1928.

55. For example, SSA Minutes, 20 June 1919 and 11 March 1920.

56. J. Craig to Lord Kylsant, 6 Jan. 1927, CA.

57. Correspondence between Sir W. McLintock and J. Craig, 15 Jan. to 7 Feb. 1927, CA.

58. J. Craig to Lord Kylsant, 8 Sept. 1926 and 29 May 1926, CA.

59. DCS Minutes, 13 July 1926.

60. J. Craig to Lord Kylsant, 11 Feb. 1927, CA.

61. Sir W. McLintock to J. Craig, 11 Feb. 1927.

62. DCS Minutes, 14 Aug. to 30 Oct. 1928.

63. Ibid., 13 Nov. 1928 and 11 Dec. 1928.

64. Ibid., 13 Nov. 1928 and 15 Jan. 1929.

65. Green and Moss, *Business of National Importance*. See also Peter N. Davies, *The Trade Makers: Elder Dempster in West Africa, 1852–1972* (Allen & Unwin, 1973), pp. 251–260.

66. Payne, "Rationality and Personality," p. 164.

67. N. R. Colville to J. Craig, 23 Nov. 1921, JC.B.XIX(iv), CA.

68. David Colville, Jr., to J. Craig, 14 February 1918, JC.B.XX(iii), CA.

69. Payne, *Colvilles*, p. 133.

70. See Craig's Credo, JC.B.XXI(i–iv), CA.

71. Payne gives full details of Colvilles's management, *Colvilles*, pp. 133–134, 241–249, 141–142.

72. Mrs. M. S. Colville to J. Craig, 26 Nov. 1926, JC.B.XIV.(iii),CA. Ibid., 26 Jan. 1924, JC.B.XIX.(xiii) and (xiv), CA.

73. DCS Minutes, 9 Aug. 1921.

74. J. Craig to Lord Pirrie, 9 Feb. 1920, JC.F.I, CA.

75. Lord Pirrie to J. Craig, 14 Feb. 1920, JC.F.I, CA.

76. "Summary of Cash Position as at 21st September 1931," CA.

77. DCS Minutes, 13 Sept. 1927 and 16 May 1929.

78. Sidney G. Checkland, *Scottish Banking: A History 1695–1973* (Glasgow: Collins, 1975), pp. 562–563.

79. National Bank of Scotland to J. B. Allan (Colvilles), 29 Dec. 1921, CA.

80. W. Carnegie (general manager, National Bank of Scotland) to J. B. Allan, 29 Sept. 1927, 18 Oct. 1928, and 18 May 1929. CA.

81. DCS Minutes, 19 and 1 May 1930.

82. SCS Trade Facilities Act Files, T.190/242.

83. Memo by A. M. Stephen, 28 Oct. 1931, DCS Minutes.

84. SCS Minutes, 31 Aug. 1921.

85. SCS Minutes, 31 Oct. 1923.

86. J. Morton, Handwritten Note on a Talk with W. G. Gray, 4 March 1930, Baird Papers.

87. SCS Minutes, 23 June 1920.

88. J. Craig to Lord Kylsant, 5 Dec. 1929.

89. J. Craig, Note of an Interview with Sir Andrew Duncan, 29 Sept. 1925, JC.F.I(14), CA.

90. F. A. Szarvasy to W. J. Larke, 23 Feb. 1927, CA.

91. Francis E. Hyde, *Cunard and the North Atlantic, 1840–1973: A History of Shipping Management* (Macmillan, 1975), pp. 191–219; Robert Jones and Oliver Marriott, *Anatomy of a Merger: A History of GEC, AEI, and English Electric* (Pan, 1970), pp. 122, 127–128.

92. J. Craig to Lord Kylsant, 20 Jan. 1927; and correspondence between J. Craig and H. Pear, 29 Sept. to 11 Oct. 1926, CA.

93. W. J. Larke to J. Craig, 3 Jan. 1927, CA; and J. Craig to H. Bond, 14 May 1927, CA.

94. F. A. Szarvasy to W. J. Larke, 13 Jan. 1927, CA.

95. H. Bond to F. A. Szarvasy, 5 May 1927, CA.

96. J. Craig to Lord Kylsant, 20 Jan. 1927 (reporting Szarvasy's ideas), CA.

97. J. Craig to Lord Kylsant, 9 Feb. 1927, 15 Jan. 1927, CA.

98. J. Craig to W. J. Larke, 6 Jan. 1927, CA.

99. H. Bond to J. Craig, 11 and 28 Jan. 1928, CA.

100. H. Bond to J. Craig, 7 July 1927, CA.

101. J. Craig to H. Bond, 14 May 1927, CA. Marked "not sent."

102. For the Ridpath, Colegate, McKenna-Larke, Szarvasy, Weir, and Hatry schemes, see Chapter 8.

103. Correspondence between Lord Kylsant and J. Craig, 20 May 1928, CA.

104. National Confederation of Employers' Organisations, General Purposes Committee Minutes, 11 June 1928, p. 7, NCEO, C.66/1.

105. J. Craig to Lord Kylsant, 13 June 1928 and 24 May 1928.

106. *Financial News*, 5 June 1928.

107. J. Craig to Lord Kylsant, 11 June 1928, CA.

108. See Chapter 8.

109. DCS Minutes, 11 Dec. 1928.

110. DCS Minutes, 12 Feb. 1929. The five companies that participated were David Colville and Sons, SCS, Dunlops, Stewarts & Lloyds, and Bairds.

111. J. Craig to Lord Kylsant, 3 July 1929, CA.

112. *Brassert Report (Scotland)*, p. 43.

113. Payne, *Colvilles*, pp. 170–180.

114. *Brassert Report (Scotland)*, pp. 121–124.

115. Payne, *Colvilles*, p. 180.

116. J. Bird, "Presidential Address,"*JWSISI* 39 (1931–32), 1–16.

117. R. Hamilton, "Presidential Address," *JWSISI* 37 (1929–30), 1–14. Hamilton was a manager at Colvilles' Glengarnock works.

118. *Brassert Report (Scotland)*, p. 50.

119. Burn, *Economic History*, pp. 474–477.

120. BISF Statistics; Buxton, "Efficiency and Organisation," p. 111. Between 1931 and 1935, Colvilles used an average of 75% scrap in their steel-

making. Memorandum as Basis for Discussion on Future Requirements and Supply of Raw Materials, Colvilles Minutes, 9 April 1936.

121. DCS Minutes, 15 Nov. 1929.

122. SCS Minutes, 9 Dec. 1930.

123. See Chapter 13.

124. Notes of a Meeting on the Brassert Report, 14 April 1930, Baird Papers.

125. Notes of a Meeting on the Brassert Scheme, 12 May 1930, Baird Papers.

126. Payne, *Colvilles*, p. 178.

127. Notes of a Meeting between J. Morton and Sir James Lithgow, 17 April 1930, Baird Papers.

128. J. Morton, Handwritten note, 13 Feb. 1930, Baird Papers.

129. Ibid.

130. J. Morton, Memorandum, 7 April 1930, Baird Papers.

131. J. Morton, Note, 6 March 1930, Baird Papers.

132. Note of a Meeting between J. Morton and Sir James Lithgow, 17 April 1930, Baird Papers.

133. DCS Minutes, 11 Oct. 1929.

134. J. Craig to Sir W. McLintock, 16 June 1930, CA.

135. Note of a Meeting between J. Morton and Sir James Lithgow, 17 April 1930, Baird Papers.

136. DCS Minutes, 21 March 1930.

137. J. Morton, Notes on a Talk with W. G. Gray, 4 March 1930, Baird Papers.

138. J. Craig to Sir W. McLintock, 30 June and 8 July 1930, CA.

139. DCS Minutes, 11 June 1930.

140. Sir W. McLintock to J. Craig, 30 Oct. 1930, CA.

141. Green and Moss, *Business of National Importance*, chap. 7.

142. Notes of a Meeting between Sir. W. McLintock, R. L. Angus, and A. K. McCosh, 4 July 1930, Baird Papers.

143. Sir W. McLintock to J. Craig, 30 Oct. 1930, CA; J. Craig to Sir W. McLintock, 8 July 1930, CA.

144. J. Craig to Lord Kylsant ,5 July 1929, CA.

145. J. Craig to Lord Kylsant, 5 Dec. 1929, CA.

146. DCS Minutes, 9 July 1929.

147. National Bank of Scotland to J. B. Allan, 1 May 1930, CA; DCS Minutes, 9 May 1930.

148. See Chapter 9 for Stewarts & Lloyds.

149. C. Bruce Gardner to J. Craig, 27 Feb. 1932, CA.

150. DCS Minutes, 9 Oct. 1931 to July 1932.

151. Payne, *Colvilles*, pp. 201, 190.

152. Payne, *Colvilles*, p. 203.

153. Payne, *Colvilles*, Preface, pp. ix–x.

154. C. Bruce Gardner to J. Craig, 27 Feb. 1932, CA.

155. Ibid.

156. C. Bruce Gardner to J. Craig, 21 March 1934, CA.

157. C. Bruce Gardner to J. Craig, 27 Feb. 1932, CA.

158. Payne, *Colvilles*, table 8.3, p. 203, confuses *net* profits with trading profits. See SCS and Colville accounts in CA.

159. For Hallside, see Payne, *Colvilles*, table 8.4, p. 205; and SCS Trade Facilities Act File, T.190/242–243.

160. Considerations for Colvilles in Possible Merger, 16 Dec. 1932, CA; Reasons Why 75% Would Not Be Enough, n.d., CA.

161. Report on Estimated Benefits, 1 June 1932, CA.

162. Reasons Why 75% Would Not Be Enough, n.d., CA.

163. DCS Minutes, 8 Sept. 1933, 18 Oct. 1933, and 27 April 1934.

164. Sir J. Lithgow to Sir A. Duncan, 2 Nov. 1931, SMT 3/101; A. M. Stephen to David Colville, 9 Dec. 1931, SISM Files, CA.

165. J. Craig, Handwritten Note on SISM, n.d., CA.

166. J. Craig to Sir W. McLintock, 7 Aug. 1931, CA.

167. Sir W. McLintock to J. Craig, 18 Aug. 1931, CA.

168. Memorandum to Bruce Gardner on Colvilles' Claim to 80%, 30 Dec. 1932, CA.

169. A. Gray, Memorandum on the Position of Lanarkshire in a Proposed Merger with Colvilles and S.C.S. for Submission to Bruce Gardner, 29 Dec. 1932, BID 1/61.

170. List of rollings 27″/36″ mill for week ending 17 Dec. 1932, BID 1/61.

171. Gray, Memorandum, ibid.

172. Payne, *Colvilles*, pp. 204, 216–219, for details.

173. DCS Minutes, 27 April 1934.

174. See Part II.

175. Sir J. Lithgow to Sir A. Duncan, 2 Nov. 1931, SMT 3/101.

176. Sir J. Lithgow to Sir A. Duncan, 15 Nov. 1932, SMT 3/121.

177. *Brassert Report (Scotland)*, pp. 119–120.

178. C. Bruce Gardner to Sir James Lithgow, 9 Dec. 1932, CA; C. Bruce Gardner, Report on Wm. Beardmore and Co., 21 Nov. 1931, SMT 3/137.

179. Sir J. Lithgow to H. A. Reincke, 11 Dec. 1934, SMT 3/129.

180. C. Bruce Gardner to Sir A. Duncan, 7 June 1934, BID 1/56.

181. Sir J. Lithgow to C. Bruce Gardner, 4 May 1934, BID 1/58; C. Bruce Gardner to Sir James Lithgow, 9 May 1934, ibid.

182. C. Bruce Gardner to Sir A. Duncan, 7 June 1934, BID 1/56.

183. DCS Minutes, 30 Nov. 1934.

184. Paul Bew, Peter Gibbon, and Henry Patterson, *The State in Northern Ireland, 1921–1972: Political Forces and Social Classes* (Manchester University Press, 1979), pp. 75–102.

185. Sir Wilfred Spender to S. D. Waley (Treasury), 29 Feb. 1932, MT. 9/2560. See also Patrick Buckland, *The Factory of Grievances: Devolved Government in Northern Ireland, 1921–1939* (Dublin: Gill and Macmillan, 1979), pp. 116–117.

186. For example, A. M. Stephen to C. G. MacAndrew (Clydeside M.P.), 18 Feb. 1932, BT Marine Dept., MT 9/2560.

187. Note on a Call of Sir James Lithgow to the President of the Board of Trade Regarding Unfair Competition of Northern Ireland Shipyards Subsi-

dised in Various Ways by the Northern Ireland Government, 17 Oct. 1933, BT Marine Dept., MT 9/2560.

188. Colvilles Minutes, 24 June 1935.

189. Sir W. McLintock to J. Craig, 26 June 1935, CA.

190. J. Craig to F. E. Rebbeck, 20 June 1935, CA.

191. Sir J. Lithgow to Sir W. McLintock, 29 Oct. 1935, CA.

192. Sir J. Lithgow to F. E. Rebbeck, 26 Jan. 1935, JC.F.IV, CA.

193. J. Craig to F. E. Rebbeck, 25 June 1935, CA; J. Craig to Sir W. McLintock, 27 June 1935, CA.

194. Bew et al., *State in Northern Ireland*, pp. 79–82, 92–93.

195. E. Clark to W. Spender, 12 Nov. 1943, W. Spender Financial Diary; quoted by Bew et al., *State in Northern Ireland,* p. 91.

196. Minute of a Meeting on 7th November 1935, CA.

197. Payne, *Colvilles*, p. 214.

198. Memorandum on Lanarkshire Steel Co., 8 April 1936; A. McCance, Report on the Lanarkshire Steel Co., 14 Nov. 1935; Sir J. Lithgow to J. R. Maskell (of Lescher, Stephens & Co. Receivers), 11 Dec. 1935, CA.

199. G. F. Abell (chief general manager of Lloyds Bank) to Sir W. McLintock, 29 April 1935, CA.

200. J. Craig to F. E. Rebbeck, 18 and 17 May 1935, CA.

201. J. Craig to F. E. Rebbeck, 17 May 1935, CA.

202. J. Craig to F. E. Rebbeck, 8 June 1935, CA.

203. Sir J. Lithgow to J. H. Stephens (Receiver), 18 Oct. 1935, CA; W. H. Peat to Sir J. Lithgow, 17 Oct. 1935, CA. Colvilles Ltd. Minutes, 18th October 1935.

204. Minutes of an Informal Meeting, 8 Nov. 1935, CA; Sir J. Lithgow to J. R. Maskell, 8 Nov. 1935, CA.

205. Maclay, Murray, and Spens Ltd. to Colvilles Ltd., 15 July 1936, CA; J. Craig to Sir W. McLintock, 23 March 1936, CA.

206. Payne, *Colvilles*, pp. 216–222.

207. Warren, "Locational Problems," p. 87.

208. Warren, ibid.; David W. Heal, *The Steel Industry in Post-War Britain* (Newton Abbot: David & Charles, 1974), pp. 99–103.

209. Import Duties Advisory Committee, *Report on the Present Position and Future Development of the Iron and Steel Industry,* Cmd. 5507. HMSO 1937, pp. 33, 37, 38.

210. Kenneth Warren, "Iron and Steel," in Neil K. Buxton and Derek H. Aldcroft, eds., *British Industry between the Wars: Instability and Indusrial Development, 1919–1939* (Scolar Press, 1979), p. 122.

211. The phrase is that of F. E. Rebbeck; F. E. Rebbeck to J. Craig, 26 June 1935, CA.

5. Richard Thomas & Co. and the Tinplate Industry, 1918–1939

1. See Walter E. Minchinton, *The British Tinplate Industry: A History* (Oxford University Press, 1957), pp. 120–139; Kenneth Warren, *The British Iron and Steel Sheet Industry since 1840: An Economic Geography* (Bell, 1970), pp. 71–

104, 106; R. C. Allen, "International Competition in Iron and Steel, 1850–1913," *Journal of Economic History* 39 (Dec. 1979), 914.

2. Thomas H. Burnham and George O. Hoskins, *Iron and Steel in Great Britain, 1870–1930* (Allen & Unwin, 1943), p. 171.

3. E. E. Watkins, "The Development of the South Wales Tinplate Industry, 1919–1939," M.A. thesis, University of Wales, 1948, pp. 114–115; E. H. Brooke, *Chronology of the Tinplate Works of Great Britain*, 2 vols. (Cardiff: William Lewis, 1944–1949), pp. 1–3.

4. Minchinton, *Tinplate Industry*, pp. 178–180.

5. A 2- to 3-mill plant cost only £3,000–4,000 and tinplate products spent only 14 days in the factory compared with a six-month turnover period in the iron industry. Watkins, "South Wales Tinplate," pp. 12–18.

6. *Report of the Departmental Committee Appointed by the Board of Trade to Consider the Position of the Iron and Steel Trades after the War*, (Scoby-Smith Committee), Cmd. 9071, HMSO 1918, p. 10.

7. *Report of the Committee on Industry and Trade: Survey of Industrial Relations* (HMSO, 1929), p. 35.

8. See Warren, *Steel Sheet Industry*, p. 105.

9. See Tables 13 and 14.

10. Cmd. 9071, HMSO 1918, *Scoby-Smith Report*, p. 10; F. H. Hatch, *The Iron and Steel Industry of Great Britain under War Conditions* (Harrison & Sons, 1919), p. 41.

11. *ICTR*, 19 Jan. 1923.

12. W. J. Firth, Report on Grovesend Steel and Tinplate Co., 10 June 1926, RT Minutes.

13. Leslie Hannah, "Takeover Bids in Britain before 1950: An Exercise in Business Pre-History," *Business History* 16 (January 1974), 66. Hannah confuses this sale with Gibbins's sale of Melyn Works three years later to Briton Ferry in a rather similar manner.

14. E. H. Brooke, *Chronology*, pp. 20–28.

15. Ibid., pp. 93–98.

16. These links can be traced in company records and Brooke, *Chronology*. And see List of Welsh Steel and Tinplate Works Compiled for SMT, Sept. 1929, SMT 28/3.

17. *ICTR*, Nov. 1923.

18. Minchinton, *Tinplate Industry*, pp. 81–82.

19. Firth to Henry Bond, 7 Sept. 1923, and Firth to F. W. Gilbertson, 11 Dec. 1924, RT, Stabilisation File.

20. F. T. Thomas to Gilbertson, 13 Sept. 1923, RT, Stabilisation File; and see also editorial in *The Ironmonger*, 15 Sept. 1923.

21. Gilbertson, in *ICTR*, 8 May 1935.

22. Firth to Gilbertson, 11 Dec. 1924, RT, Stabilisation File.

23. The four main attempts at regulation ran from Oct. 1922 to 9 May 1925; Dec. 1925 to the general strike (the Tinplate Conference); March 1927 to Dec. 1927; after that regulation was intermittent from 1928 to 1932. Details in Watkins, "South Wales Tinplate," pp. 69–71, and Minchinton, *Tinplate Industry*, pp. 145–148.

24. Firth to H. C. Thomas, 7 Sept. 1923; Firth to F. T. Thomas, 21 Feb. 1925. RT, Stabilisation File.

25. Firth to J. Bevan, 7 Sept. 1923, ibid.

26. Cf. W. Isaac Williams to Firth, 13 Sept. 1923, ibid.; Gilbertson to F. T. Thomas, 18 Sept. 1923, ibid.

27. Firth to F. T. Thomas, 14 Sept. 1923, ibid.

28. Minchinton, *Tinplate Industry*, table on p. 158.

29. Bruce Gardner to J. A. C. Osborne, 3 Dec. 1931, SMT 3/75.

30. Board of Trade, *Industrial Survey of North Wales* (HMSO 1932), pp. 76–77.

31. M. Falcoln to H. C. Bond, 29 Nov. 1928; T. I. Jones, Reports on the Position at the Collieries, monthly, 1925–1927. Whenever Redbourn was restricted, less coal was needed from the collieries; and as output fell, mining costs rose sharply.

32. H. C. Bond, Report, 2 Sept. 1925, RT Minutes; see also RT, AGM, 1931. Duncan L. Burn, *The Economic History of Steelmaking, 1867–1939: A Study in Competition* (Cambridge University Press, 1940), p. 431, has a rather different interpretation.

33. T. F. Davies to F. T. Thomas, 13 Aug. 1925, Grovesend Files. T. O. Lewis (Manager, Burry Works) to Bond, 14 Oct. 1925, RT Minutes.

34. Bond, Monthly Reports to the Board, 1927–1928, especially 23 April and 22 August 1928.

35. The contents of this paragraph are based on a detailed analysis of the changing capacity utilization of each of Richard Thomas's various plants 1927–1936, RT Archives.

36. Warren, *Steel Sheet Industry*, p. 112.

37. F. T. Thomas to Bond, 16 Aug. 1917, Redbourn Hill Iron Co. Minute Books.

38. RT Minutes, Board Meeting, 6 Jan. 1919.

39. RT, AGM, Directors' Report, 1929.

40. Lord Bledisloe to David Jones, 2 Jan. 1919, RT Board Papers.

41. RT Minutes, Board Meeting, 2 June 1921.

42. F. T. Thomas to Bond, 29 June 1921, RT Board Papers; Bond to F. T. Thomas, 28 June 1921, ibid.

43. Lord Bledisloe to Bond, 6 July 1921, RT Board Papers.

44. RT Minutes, 7 July 1921; and David Jones to F. T. Thomas, RT Board Papers.

45. F. T. Thomas, Address to Meeting of Shareholders, 23 Oct. 1923, RT Board Papers.

46. RT, AGM, 1929.

47. Ordinary and Preference Shareholders of Richard Thomas and Co., 26 June 1919, RT Board Papers.

48. Cf. Minutes of Meeting of Preference Shareholders, 22 Jan. 1930. The preference shareholders later regretted their lack of vigilance in letting him get away with this maneuver.

49. RT, AGM, 1929.

50. RT, AGM, 1929. Ironically this policy came under pressure only when

Frank Thomas added his support to the call for a higher rate of disbursement in the late 1920s. See Bond to Firth, 28 Feb. 1930, RT Board Papers.

51. Minutes of Meeting of Preference Shareholders, 22 Jan. 1930.

52. Meeting between Paine, Garnsey, and Szarvasy and the Board, 16 July 1930, RT Board Papers.

53. Minutes of Meeting of Preference Shareholders, 22 Jan. 1930.

54. RT, AGMs, 1930–1934.

55. F. T. Thomas. Address to RT AGM. 23 Oct. 1923. For Grovesend's expansion, see Tables 13 and 14.

56. RT Minutes, Special Board Meeting, 25 Sept. 1923.

57. W. J. Firth, Report on the Grovesend Steel and Tinplate Co., RT Archives, 10 June 1926.

58. Leslie Hannah, *The Rise of the Corporate Economy* (Methuen, 1976), pp. 118–119.

59. See Tables 13 and 14.

60. T. Ivor Jones, Report on Collieries, Sept. 1925 and 18 July 1927, RT Minutes.

61. Warren, *Steel Sheet Industry,* p. 134.

62. RT, AGM, 1928.

63. Bond to W. Peat, 8 Jan. 1920, RT, Profit and Loss File.

64. RT, Finance Committee Minutes, 3 July 1924.

65. In 1924 Redbourn sheet bars cost at least £1 more than the average commercial price for such bars in South Wales of £8.8.2d. Notes by W. J. Firth on Redbourn, 7 July 1924, RT, Redbourn File.

66. H. A. Brassert, Report on the Redbourn Iron and Steel Works of Richard Thomas and Co., 18 Oct. 1929, pp. 19–20.

67. RT, Redbourn Hill: Works Report, 30 Nov. 1923.

68. Data Concerning the Nos. 3 and 4 Blast Furnaces at the Redbourn Works, 9 Nov. 1925, RT, Blast Furnaces (General) File, and Redbourn Hill: Works Reports, passim.

69. Ibid.

70. See Redbourn Hill: Works Reports, passim; and Steven Tolliday, "Industry, Finance, and the State: The Case of British Steel," Ph.D. diss., Cambridge University, 1980, pp. 195–197.

71. RT, Finance Committee Minutes, 3 July 1924.

72. Firth, Notes, 7 July 1924, RT, Redbourn File.

73. Report by Messrs. T. Ivor Jones, David Jones, and F. Hole on Richard Thomas and Redbourn, 1 Sept. 1924, RT, Redbourn File.

74. Mr. Guy Barratt's report to Mr. T. Ivor Jones on the remodelling of Redbourn works, 10 April 1926, ibid.

75. Firth to Brassert, 23 May 1929, RT, Redbourn File.

76. H. A. Brassert, Report to Richard Thomas and Co., RT Archives, pp. 22–28; and H. A. Brassert, Report on the Properties and Operations of the United Steel Companies Ltd., 9 Sept. 1929, SMT 2/153, pp. 16–19.

77. Brassert, Report on United Steel, passim.

78. Ibid., p. 11. United Steel at Appleby-Frodingham already produced

the cheapest open-hearth steel in Britain, but this would enable the company to combine it with basic Bessemer production.

79. Ibid., pp. 13–14.

80. Ibid., pp. 11, 12.

81. H. A. Brassert, Covering Note on Report on United Steel.

82. S. E. Graeff, "The Development of Continuous Hot and Cold Rolling of Flat Rolled Iron and Steel Products," *Proceedings of the South Wales Institute of Engineers* 83 (April 1948), 186; E. R. Mort, "The Manufacture of Full-Finished Steel Sheets," *JISI* 129, no. 1 (1934), 187; Warren, *Steel Sheet Industry*, pp. 141–150.

83. Report of Mr. Pagnamenta on the Weight and Cost of Iron and Steel Used in the Manufacture of Representative Motor Vehicles and Their Effect on the Export Trade, July 1936, BISF, Executive Agendas; R. A. Solberg (managing director of ARMCo. Ltd.), Aide-Memoire on Some Salient Facts Pertaining to the Advisability of the Creation in England of Another Quality Sheet Manufacturing Unit, 4 Dec. 1934, BID 1/124; J. Malborn, "Hot Strip Rolling Mills," *Sheet Metal Industries,* 24 (July 1950) 581–594.

84. William J. Reader, *Metal Box: A History* (Heinemann, 1976), pp. 50–58, 80. In 1937, 110,000 tons of tinplate went to open-top cans, 280,000 to other containers, and 86,000 to other uses. Minchinton, *Tinplate Industry,* p. 181.

85. Cf. A. Plummer, *New British Industries of the Twentieth Century: A Survey of Development and Structure* (Pitman & Sons, 1937), p. 231; Reader, *Metal Box,* pp. 67–73.

86. Erwin Hexner, *The International Steel Cartel* (Chapel Hill: University of North Carolina Press, 1943), pp. 160–161. During the International Tinplate Cartel, 1934–1939, the United Kingdom was allocated 55% of the world market as against 22% for the United States, 16% for Germany, and 7% for Italy and France.

87. J. P. Bedson, "Continuous Rolling Mills: Their Growth and Development," *JISI* 109, no. 1 (1924), 43–66, especially pp. 61–62.

88. G. A. V. Russell, "Some Considerations Influencing Plant Facilities for Strip Sheet Production under British Conditions," *JISI* 133, no. 1 (1936).

89. E. R. Mort, "The Manufacture of Full-Finished Steel Sheets," *JISI* 129, no. 1 (1934).

90. G. A. V. Russell, "Flexibility as a Factor in the Economic Exploitation of Rolling Mills and Some Technical Means for Its Realisation," *JISI* 130, no. 2, (1934), 26–126; and Russell, "Some Considerations," *JISI* 133, no. 1 (1936), 53, 83, 89.

91. BISF *Annual Statistics.*

92. Minchinton, *Tinplate Industry,* pp. 164–166.

93. W. J. Firth, letters to the *Times,* 22 Feb. 1934, p. 10, and 16 April 1934, p. 7; and Letter to the *Engineer,* 2 March 1934, p. 225.

94. Ibid.

95. Firth's notes on this are to be found in "Summary of Estimated Results under Various Conditions: Notes on Assumptions," 18 June 1934 (henceforth "Assumptions"). The contents are summarized in Table 15.

96. Profit and loss accounts and works records, RT Archives.

97. Firth, "Assumptions," no. 5.

98. Firth, "Assumptions," no. 2.

99. Firth, "Assumptions," no. 6.

100. Firth, "Assumptions," no. 3.

101. Firth, "Assumptions," nos. 4 and 7.

102. N. L. Campbell (director of Baldwin's), Memorandum on Richard Thomas and the Briton Ferry Group, 13 Nov. 1933, BID 1/52.

103. Warren, *Steel Sheet Industry*, pp. 151–152.

104. R. A. Solberg (American Rolling Mill Company) to Henry Summers, 21 March 1935, BID 1/124.

105. Warren, *Steel Sheet Industry*, p. 170.

106. W. R. Lysaght, Presidential Address, *JISI* 127, no. 1, (1933), 44–45; and G. C. Richer in *ICTR*, 24 Jan. 1936, p. 211.

107. Warren, *Steel Sheet Industry*, pp. 131, 170.

108. See Table 16.

109. Although taken over by Guest Keen and Nettlefolds Ltd., Lysaght continued to be under family management. GKN held a 54% controlling interest in Guest Keen Baldwin. The unintegrated nature of the combine was to be an important factor in wartime developments and in the formation of Richard Thomas Baldwin after the war. See Warren, *Steel Sheet Industry*, pp. 220, 225–226.

110. Sir Charles Wright (Baldwin's), in *Sheet Metal Industries* 11 (May 1937), 456.

111. Warren, *Steel Sheet Industry*, p. 191.

112. Ibid., p. 168.

113. DL Minutes, July 1934 to Sept. 1935, interview with E. T. Judge. He was one of the team that went to America.

114. Philip W. S. Andrews and Elizabeth Brunner, *Capital Development in Steel: A Study of the United Steel Companies Ltd.* (Oxford University Press, 1952), p. 170.

115. Warren, *Steel Sheet Industry*, p. 173.

116. Kieft in discussion on Russell, "Some Considerations," p. 76.

117. D. C. Lysaght, Notes of an Interview with Sir William Firth, 30 Nov. 1936, SMT 3/113.

118. Sheet Makers' Conference, Allotment of Output, Bank of England 3/3. See Table 16.

119. D. C. Lysaght, Notes of an Interview with Sir William Firth, 30 Nov. 1936, SMT 3/113.

120. Ibid.

121. J. C. Carr and W. Taplin, *History of the British Steel Industry* (Oxford: Basil Blackwell, 1962), pp. 542–543.

122. RT, AGMs, 1935–36; W. J. Firth, Memo to IDAC, 20 Dec. 1937, RT Archives.

123. E. Payton to A. Duncan, 7 Nov. 1935, SMT 2/161.

124. In early 1935 Austin went as far as having discussions with the Commissioner for Special Areas about the possibility of taking over the old Ebbw

Vale Steel and Iron Co. works to make its own autobody sheet, and later in the year it formed the Tunstal Steel Co. Ltd., proposing to build a four-high reversing mill and cold reduction plant near Wolverhampton for £5 million to roll bought slabs for its own and neighboring motor company uses. See *News Chronicle*, 18 Nov. 1935.

125. M. S. Myers (stockbroker) to Montagu Norman, 31 Oct. 1935, SMT 2/161.

126. E. H. D. Skinner, Memorandum on Austin Motors Ltd., 10 Oct. 1935, SMT 2/161.

127. It never explicitly admitted this, however. See E. Payton (Austins) to A. Duncan, 7 Nov. 1935, SMT 2/161.

128. E. H. D. Skinner, Note, 19 Nov. 1935, SMT 2/161.

129. Ibid.

130. Duncan to Skinner, 20 Dec. 1935, SMT 2/161.

131. Reader, *Metal Box*, pp. 80–82.

132. I.F.L. Elliott to J. F. Beale, 7 April 1935, BID 1/70.

133. Firth, Letter to the *Times*, 27 May 1936, p. 13.

134. Firth, Letter to the *Times*, 29 July 1938.

135. On the development of government policy in relation to the general question of the relocation of the iron and steel industry, see Commissioners' First Report for the Special Areas (England and Wales) *Parliamentary Papers*, (HMSO, 1935–36), XII, paras. 19–27.

136. Alan Bullock, *The Life and Times of Ernest Bevin*, vol. I, *Trade Union Leader, 1881–1940* (Heinemann, 1960), p. 540; David E. Pitfield, "Regional Economic Policy and the Long Run: Innovation and Location in the Iron and Steel Industry," *Business History* 16 (July 1974), 162–163; Michael Foot, *Aneurin Bevan: A Biography* (Davis-Poynter, 1962), I, 217–219.

137. The *Times*, 13 Nov. 1935, p. 6.

138. Warren, *Steel Sheet Industry*, p. 181.

139. J. M. Bevan (Briton Ferry) in *Sheet Metal Industries* (July 1938), 25–30.

140. Memorandum by IDAC Secretary on Richard Thomas Continuous Strip Mill, 29 Dec. 1937, IDAC Papers.

141. W. J. Firth to A. W. Hurst, 13 Aug. 1936, IDAC Papers.

142. See Chapter 13.

143. Minchinton, *Tinplate Industry*, pp. 204–209.

144. David W. Heal, *The Steel Industry in Post-War Britain* (Newton Abbot: David & Charles, 1974), p. 34. On the works and site, see H. H. Mardon and J. S. Terrington, "The Layout of Integrated Iron and Steel Works: A Survey of Some Civil Engineering Aspects," *JISI* 141, no. 1 (1949), table X; see also the German aerial photograph of Ebbw Vale in 1940, reproduced in John Vaizey, *History of British Steel* (Weidenfeld & Nicolson, 1974), pp. 102–103.

145. Vaizey, *History*, p. 79.

146. "Ebbw Vale Reawakes," *Iron and Steel Industry*, no. 12, 1938–39, p. 413; and Memorandum on Ebbw Vale Steel Works, 24 May 1934, SMT 3/113.

147. Hilary A. Marquand, *South Wales Needs a Plan* (Allen & Unwin, 1936), pp. 49–57.

148. Burn, *Economic History*, p. 460.

6. Structure and Strategy in British Industries

1. Philip W. S. Andrews and Elizabeth Brunner, *Capital Development in Steel: A Study of the United Steel Companies, Ltd.* (Oxford University Press, 1952), pp. 102–115. See also Jonathan S. Boswell, *Business Policies in the Making: Three Steel Companies Compared* (Allen & Unwin, 1983), for additional material on United Steel.

2. Andrews and Brunner, *Capital Development*, pp. 112–115, 117–118.

3. Ibid., pp. 119–121; Boswell, *Business Policies*, pp. 70–76.

4. Andrews and Brunner, *Capital Development*, p. 157.

5. See Chapter 8.

6. Andrews and Brunner, *Capital Development*, p. 157.

7. Ibid., pp. 162–166.

8. Charlotte Erickson, *British Industrialists: Steel and Hosiery, 1850–1950* (NIESR, Economic and Social Studies, vol. 18, Cambridge, 1959), p. 22.

9. Ibid., p. 51.

10. Andrews and Brunner, *Capital Development*, pp. 163–166.

11. See Chapter 3.

12. Erickson, *British Industrialists*, pp. 61–78; and company records.

13. Michael Sanderson, *The Universities and British Industry, 1850–1970* (Routledge & Kegan Paul, 1972) p. 270; cf. also Sanderson, "The Universities in Industry in England, 1919–39," *Yorkshire Bulletin of Economic and Social Research*, 21 (May 1969), 39–65.

14. For some interesting comments, see Albert A. Jackson, "The Rise and Fall of the Open Hearth," *Ironmaking and Steelmaking* 3 (1976), 1–9.

15. Alfred D. Chandler, *The Visible Hand: The Managerial Revolution in American Business* (Cambridge, Mass.: Harvard University Press, 1977), p. 491.

16. Alfred D. Chandler, "The Development of Modern Management Structures in the United States and the U.K.," in Leslie Hannah, ed., *Management Strategy and Business Development: An Historical and Comparative Study* (Macmillan, 1976), p. 25.

17. Raphael Samuel, "The Workshop of the World: Steam Power and Hand Technology in Mid-Victorian Britain," *History Workshop* (Spring 1977), 6–72.

18. Leslie Hannah, "Visible and Invisible Hands in Great Britain," in Chandler and Daems, eds., *Managerial Hierarchies: Comparative Perspectives on the Rise of the Modern Industrial Enterprise* (Cambridge, Mass.: Harvard University Press, 1980), pp. 41–77.

19. William Lazonick, "Competition, Specialization, and Industrial Decline," *Journal of Economic History* 41 (March 1981), 31–38.

20. Peter L. Payne, "Industrial Entrepreneurship and Management in Great Britain," in Peter Mathias and Michael Postan, eds., *The Cambridge Economic History of Europe*, vol. 7 (Cambridge University Press, 1978), pp. 204–220.

21. Hannah, "Visible and Invisible Hands," p. 42.

22. Peter Mathias, "Conflicts of Function in the Rise of Big Business: The

British Experience," in Harold F. Williamson, ed., *The Evolution of International Management Structures* (Newark: University of Delaware Press, 1975), pp. 47–49.

23. Bernard W. Alford, *W. D. & H. O. Wills and the Development of the U.K. Tobacco Industry, 1786–1965* (Methuen, 1973), pp. 324–325, 358–370; and "Strategy and Structure in the U.K. Tobacco Industry," in Leslie Hannah, ed., *Management Strategy and Business Development* (Macmillan, 1976), pp. 73–79.

24. Anthony Slaven, "British Shipbuilders: Market Trends and Order Book Patterns between the Wars," *Journal of Transport History* 3 (Dec. 1982), pp. 50–53.

25. Ibid., pp. 57–58. See also Anthony Slaven, "A Shipyard in Depression: John Brown's of Clydebank, 1919–30," *Business History* 19 (1977), 192–217.

26. William J. Reader, *Bowater: A History* (Cambridge University Press, 1982), esp. pp. 60–80.

27. R. W. Ferrier, *The History of the British Petroleum Company*, vol. 1, *The Developing Years, 1901–1932* (Cambridge University Press, 1982), p. 207.

28. Ibid., p. 384.

29. Ibid., p. 373.

30. Charles E. Harvey, *The Rio Tinto Company: An Economic History of a Leading International Mining Concern, 1873–1954* (Penzance: Alison Hodge, 1981), pp. 187–227.

31. Bernard W. Alford, *Depression and Recovery: British Economic Growth, 1918–1939* (Macmillan, 1972), p. 48.

32. William Lazonick, "Production, Productivity and Development: Theoretical Implications of Some Historical Research," Harvard Institute of Economic Research, discussion paper 876, Jan. 1982, p. 61.

33. Hannah, "Visible and Invisible Hands," p. 60.

7. Banking and Industry in the Early Twentieth Century

1. Maurice W. Kirby, "The Lancashire Cotton Industry in the Interwar Years: A Study in Organisational Change," *Business History*, vol. 16 (July 1974), 145–159; Richard S. Sayers, *The Bank of England, 1891–1944*, 3 vols. (Cambridge University Press, 1976), pp. 318–320; James Bamberg, "The Government, the Banks, and the Lancashire Cotton Industry, 1918–39," Ph.D. diss., Cambridge University, 1984.

2. Edwin Green and Michael Moss, *A Business of National Importance: The Royal Mail Shipping Group, 1902–37* (Methuen, 1982), chaps. 6–9; Francis E. Hyde, *Cunard and the North Atlantic, 1840–1973: A History of Shipping and Financial Management* (Macmillan, 1975), pp. 200–217.

3. Leslie Hannah, *Electricity before Nationalisation* (Macmillan, 1979).

4. Maurice W. Kirby, *The British Coalmining Industry, 1870–1946: A Political and Economic History* (Macmillan, 1977); M. W. Kirby, "The Politics of State Coercion in Interwar Britain: The Mines Department of the Board of Trade, 1920–42," *Historical Journal* 22 (June 1979), 373–396; M. W. Kirby, "The Control of Competition in the British Coal Mining Industry in the Thirties," *EcHR* 26 (1973), 273–284.

5. Arthur F. Lucas, *Industrial Reconstruction and the Control of Competition: The British Experiments* (Longmans, 1937), pp. 232–257.

6. Robert P. Shay, *British Rearmament in the 1930s: Politics and Profits* (Princeton, 1977); Keith Middlemas, *Politics in Industrial Society: The Experience of the British System since 1911* (Andre Deutsch, 1979), pp. 248–259; D. E. H. Edgerton, "Technical Innovation, Industrial Capacity, and Efficiency: Public Ownership and the British Military Aircraft Industry, 1935–48," *Business History* 26 (Nov. 1984).

7. Geoffrey Jones, *The State and the Emergence of the British Oil Industry* (Macmillan, 1981); R. W. Ferrier, *The History of the British Petroleum Company*, vol. 1, *The Developing Years, 1901–32* (Cambridge University Press, 1982).

8. Clive Trebilcock, "A Special Relationship: Government Rearmament and the Cordite Firms," *EcHR* 29 (1966), 364–379; C. Trebilcock, *The Vickers Brothers: Armaments and Enterprise, 1854–1914* (Europa, 1977).

9. Geoffrey Channon, "The Great Western Railway under the British Railways Act of 1921." *Business History Review* 40 (Summer 1981), 188–216; P. J. Cain, "Railway Combination and Government, 1900–14," *EcHR* 25 (Nov. 1972), 623–641.

10. Sayers, *Bank of England*, pp. 320–321; Anthony Slaven, "Self-Liquidation: The National Shipbuilders' Security Ltd. and British Shipbuilding in the 1930s," in Sarah Palmer and Glyndwr Williams, eds., *Charted and Uncharted Waters* (National Maritime Museum, 1982), pp. 125–147.

11. R. H. Campbell, *The Rise and Fall of Scottish Industry, 1707–1939* (Edinburgh: Donald, 1980), pp. 170–172.

12. William J. Reader, *Bowaters: A History* (Cambridge University Press, 1982), pp. 47–58, 179–183.

13. William J. Reader, *Imperial Chemical Industries: A History*, 2 vols. (Oxford University Press, 1970–1975); W. J. Reader, "ICI and the State," in Barry Supple, ed., *Essays in British Business History* (Oxford University Press, 1977), pp. 227–243.

14. Philippe Chalmin, *Tate and Lyle, géant du sucre* (Paris: Economica, 1983).

15. Philip L. Cottrell, *Industrial Finance, 1830–1914: The Finance and Organisation of English Manufacturing Industry* (Methuen, 1980); Charles A. E. Goodhart, *The Business of Banking, 1891–1914* (London School of Economics, 1972); William P. Kennedy, "Institutional Response to Economic Growth: Capital Markets in Britain to 1914," in Leslie Hannah, ed., *Management Strategy and Business Development* (Macmillan, 1976), pp. 151–183.

16. The principal texts are National Economic Development Organisation, *Finance for Industry* (NEDO, 1975); "An Approach to Industrial Strategy," Cmd. 6315 (HMSO, Nov. 1975); *Report of the Committee to Review the Functioning of Financial Institutions* (Wilson Report), Cmd. 7937 (HMSO, 1980); *Evidence by the Committee of London Clearing Banks to the Committee to Review the Functioning of Financial Institutions* (HMSO, 1977); Richard Minns, *Take over the City: The Case for Public Ownership of Financial Institutions* (Pluto Press, 1982); Yao-Su Hu, *National Attitudes and the Financing of Industry* (Political and Economic Planning, 1975).

17. Perry Anderson, "The Origins of the Present Crisis," *New Left Review*,

no. 23, reprinted in *Towards Socialism,* ed. Perry Anderson and Robin Blackburn (Fontana, 1965); Tom Nairn, "The British Political Elite," ibid., pp. 21–22; T. Nairn, *The Break-Up of Britain* (New Left Books, 1978); T. Nairn, *The Left against Europe* (Penguin, 1970).

18. Sidney Pollard, "The Great Disillusion," *Bulletin of the Society for the Study of Labour History* (Spring 1968), p. 34.

19. Sidney Pollard, "Introduction" to *The Gold Standard and Employment Policies between the Wars* (Methuen, 1970).

20. Frank Longstreth, "The City, Industry, and the State," in Colin Crouch, ed., *State and Economy in Contemporary Capitalism* (Croom Helm, 1979).

21. Geoffrey Ingham, *Capitalism Divided? The City and Industry in British Social Development* (Macmillan, 1984).

22. R. Hilferding, *Finance Capital: A Study of the Latest Phase of Capitalist Development,* ed. Tom Bottomore (Routledge & Kegan Paul, 1981).

23. V. I. Lenin, "Imperialism: The Highest Stage of Capitalism," in Progress Publishers, ed., *Selected Works* (Lawrence and Wishart, 1969), pp. 176–263.

24. Ernest Mandel, *Late Capitalism* (New Left Books, 1978), p. 594.

25. Hans Overbeek, "Finance Capital and the Crisis in Britain," *Capital and Class,* no. 11, 1980; Sam Aaronvitch, *The Ruling Class* (Lawrence and Wishart, 1961).

26. Nicos Poulantzas, *Classes in Contemporary Capitalism* (New Left Books, 1975), pp. 91–116; N. Poulantzas, *Political Power and Social Classes* (New Left Books, 1973), pp. 190–195, 229–254; for useful comments on his use of the notion of "fractions of capital," see Doreen B. Massey and Alejandrina Catalano, *Capital and Land* (Edward Arnold, 1978), pp. 29–49. See also Nikolai Bukharin, *The Economics of the Transition Period* (New York: Bergman, 1978), pp. 15–19.

27. John Foster, "Imperialism and the Labour Aristocracy," in Jeffrey Skelley, ed., *The General Strike* (Lawrence and Wishart, 1976), pp. 10–12.

28. W. D. Rubinstein, "Wealth, Elites, and Class Structure of Modern Britain," *Past and Present,* no. 76 (Aug. 1977), pp. 124–125.

29. Rubinstein, "Wealth, Elites," p. 126.

30. Edward P. Thompson, "The Peculiarities of the English," *Socialist Register,* no. 2 (1965), ed. Ralph Miliband and John Saville; reprinted in E. P. Thompson, *The Poverty of Theory* (Merlin, 1978).

31. Raphael Samuel, "The Workshop of the World: Steam Power and Hand Technology in Mid-Victorian Britain," *History Workshop,* no. 3 (Spring 1977), 6–72; C. H. Lee, "Regional Growth and Structural Change in Victorian Britain," *EcHR* 34 (Aug. 1981), 438–452; Dolores Greenberg, "Reassessing the Power Patterns of the Industrial Revolution: An Anglo-American Comparison," *American History Review* 87 (Dec. 1982) 1237–61; E. Hopkins, "Working Hours and Conditions during the Industrial Revolution," *EcHR* 35 (Feb. 1982) 52–66.

32. On the significance of this role see Eric J. Hobsbawm, *Industry and Empire* (Penguin, 1968).

33. For a useful discussion of this issue see Richard Minns, "A Comment

on Finance Capital and the Crisis in Britain," *Capital and Class*, no. 14 (Summer 1981), 98–109.

34. Alexander Gerschenkron, *Economic Backwardness in Historical Perspective* (Cambridge, Mass.: Harvard University Press, 1966), esp. pp. 15–16, 353–354; for some important qualifications of Gerschenkron's generalizations see Rondo Cameron, ed., "Introduction" to *Banking and Economic Development: Some Lessons of History* (Oxford University Press, 1972); D. Good, "Backwardness and the Role of Banking in Nineteenth Century European Industrialisation," *Journal of Economic History* 33 (Dec. 1973), 845–850; W. A. Ashworth, "Typologies and Evidence: Has Nineteenth Century Europe a Typology of Economic Growth?" *EcHR* 30 (Feb. 1977), 140–158.

35. Francois Crouzet, ed., *Capital Formation in the Industrial Revolution* (Methuen, 1972), p. 32; Peter Mathias, "Capital, Credit and Entrepreneurs in the Industrial Revolution," *Journal of European Economic History* 2 (Spring 1973), 121–143.

36. Edward V. Morgan and W. A. Thomas, *The Stock Exchange: Its History and Function* (Elek, 1962), pp. 38–40; W. P. Kennedy, "Institutional Response," pp. 151–183.

37. Jonathan R. T. Hughes, *Fluctuations in Trade, Industry, and Finance: A Study of British Economic Development, 1850–1860* (Oxford University Press, 1960), pp. 229–231, 283–284.

38. Richard S. Sayers, *Bank of England Operations, 1890–1914* (Cambridge University Press, 1936), pp. 116–117, 125–126.

39. Cottrell, *Industrial Finance*, pp. 15–22.

40. James B. Jeffereys, "Trends in Business Organisation in Britain since 1856," Ph.D. diss., London University, 1938, pp. 17–18, 119, 142; and Kennedy, "Institutional Response," pp. 159–160.

41. Goodhart, *Business of Banking*, p. 135.

42. Kennedy, "Institutional Response," pp. 165–168.

43. Michael Edelstein, "Realised Rates of Return on UK Home and Overseas Portfolio Investment in the Age of High Imperialism," *Explorations in Economic History* 13 (1976), pp. 283–329; M. Edelstein, "Foreign Investment and Empire," in Roderick Floud and Donald McCloskey, eds., *The Economic History of Britain since 1700*, vol. 2 (Cambridge University Press, 1981).

44. Kennedy, "Institutional Response," pp. 164, 173–174.

45. M. de Cecco, *Money and Empire: The International Gold Standard, 1873–1914* (Oxford: Blackwell, 1974), pp. 145–149; Mandel, *Late Capitalism*, p. 461.

46. R. C. Michie, "Options, Concessions, Syndicates, and the Provision of Venture Capital, 1880–1913," *Business History* 23, no. 2. (July 1981) 147–164; Wayne Lewchuk, "The Return to Capital in the British Vehicle Industry," *Business History* 27 (1985), 3–25.

47. A. E. Harrison, "Joint-Stock Company Flotation in the Cycle, Motor Vehicle, and Related Industries, 1882–1914," *Business History* 23 (July 1981), 165–190; Cottrell, *Industrial Finance*, pp. 169–183; for a contrary example of a viable company experiencing consistent difficulty in raising capital see A. E. Harrison, "F. Hopper & Co. The Problems of Capital Supply in the Cycle Manufacturing Industry, 1891–1914," *Business History* 24 (March 1983), 3–23.

48. The classic statement of these attitudes is in the book by Walter Leaf (chairman of the Westminster Bank), *Banking* (Thornton Butterworth, 1926).

49. Cottrell, *Industrial Finance*, pp. 210–238; for other examples, see Chapter 3 for Bolckow Vaughan; Roy A. Church, *Herbert Austin, The British Motor Car Industry to 1941* (Europa, 1979), pp. 55–67; John R. Hume and Michael S. Moss, *Beardmore: The History of a Scottish Industrial Giant* (Heinemann, 1979), chap. 4; Augustus Muir, *The History of Baker Perkins* (Cambridge: H. Heffer & Sons, 1968), p. 53.

50. Philip L. Cottrell, *British Overseas Investment in the Nineteenth Century* (Macmillan, 1975), chap. 5; S. B. Saul, *Studies in British Overseas Trade, 1870–1914* (Liverpool University Press, 1960), chap. 2.

51. For another example of bank euphoria in lending to industry, see the case of Lloyds Bank and Unilever described in Charles Wilson, "Management and Policy in Large-Scale Enterprise: Lever Brothers and Unilever, 1918–1938," in Barry E. Supple, ed., *Essays in British Business History* (Oxford University Press, 1977), pp. 127–128.

52. Thomas Balogh, *Studies in Financial Organisation* (Cambridge University Press, 1947).

53. Balogh, *Financial Organisation*, p. 77.

54. G. W. Daniels and J. Jewkes, "The Post-War Depression in the Lancashire Cotton Industry," *Journal of the Royal Statistical Society* 91 (1928), 170–177.

55. *Report of the Committee on Finance and Industry* (Macmillan Committee), HMSO 1931.

56. R. McKenna to Midland Bank, AGM, 1928.

57. R. W. Wilson, (joint managing director of Lloyds Bank), Memorandum, 30 Jan. 1930, EAC(IS)92, CAB 58/131.

58. Sir H. Goschen, Evidence to the MacMillan Committee, Q. 1809–Q.1958, *Report of the Committee on Finance and Industry*, Minutes of Evidence, HMSO, 1931 (cited as MacMillan Committee, *Evidence*).

59. Figures for overdrafts are not regularly given in published company accounts and not all company records have been available or inspected. However, it is likely that the twelve largest overdrafts in 1929 were held by the following firms: over £500,000—United Steel, Bolckow Vaughan, Dorman Long, Richard Thomas, Pease and Partners, David Colville and Sons, and Ebbw Vale Iron and Steel Co.; £200,000–£500,000—Beardmore, Steel Co. of Scotland, Partington, Palmer's, Lanarkshire Steel Co., Barrow Hematite, and Baldwin's. For details of the companies' bankers, see Table 17. The positions of the banks in Bolckow Vaughan, Dorman Long, Richard Thomas, Beardmore, Partington, Lanarkshire, Colvilles, and the Steel Co. of Scotland are described elsewhere in the book. For United Steel, see John Vaizey, *History of British Steel* (Weidenfeld & Nicolson, 1974), pp. 42–43; Philip W. S. Andrews and Elizabeth Brunner, *Capital Development in Steel: A Study of the United Steel Companies Ltd.* (Oxford University Press, 1952), passim. For Palmers, see Wilkinson, *The Town That Was Murdered* (1939), pp. 120–124; and Sir James Lithgow to N. L. Campbell, 19 Feb. 1932, SMT 3/5. For Barrow, see SMT File 3/238. For Ebbw Vale and Baldwin's, see J. P. Addis, "The Heavy Iron and

Steel Industry in South Wales, 1870–1950." Ph.D. diss., University of Wales, 1957, pp. 210–213. For Steel Co. of Scotland, see Trade Facilities Act Files, T.190/242/3. For Pease and Partners, see Treasury File, T.175/10.

60. W. A. Thomas, *The Finance of British Industry, 1918–76* (Methuen, 1978), pp. 76–77.

61. Susan Howson, *Domestic Monetary Management in Great Britain, 1919–38* (Cambridge University Press, 1975), pp. 88–90.

62. Samuel E. Thomas, *British Banks and the Finance of Industry* (P. S. King, 1931) p. 261; and MacMillan Committee, *Evidence*, Q. 624.

63. Ronald H. Coase, R. S. Edwards, and R. F. Fowler, *The Iron and Steel Industry 1926–35: An Investigation Based on the Accounts of Published Companies*, London and Cambridge Economic Service, Special Memorandum no. 49.

64. Henry Clay, *The Unemployment Problem* (Macmillan, 1929), p. 83.

65. Sir H. Goschen, MacMillan Committee, *Evidence*, Q.1809 and Q.1822.

66. See evidence of Goodenough to MacMillan Committee, Q.780–Q.781; and S. E. Thomas, *British Banks*, passim.

67. Sir James Lithgow to N. L. Campbell, 19 Feb. 1932, SMT 3/5.

68. R. Holland Martin, Presidential Address to the Institute of Bankers, 6 Nov. 1929.

69. Vaizey, *History*, p. 42; James Foreman-Peck, "Exit, Voice, and Loyalty as Responses to Decline: The Rover Co. in the Inter-War Years," *Business History* 23 (July 1981), 199.

70. Sir H. Goschen, MacMillan Committee, *Evidence*, Q.1809 and Q.1822.

71. For example, the Midland Bank obtained shares in Bolckow Vaughan's Redpath Brown subsidiary and the National Bank of Scotland took Colvilles' coal subsidiary shares as securities. For a similar pattern in cotton, see Bamberg, "Government, Banks, and Lancashire Cotton Industry," pp. 24–28.

72. F. J. Lewcock, "The Power of the Overdraft," *Financial Times: International Banking Supplement*, 30 March 1931. See the case study of Lanarkshire Steel Co. and Colvilles, Chapter 4.

73. Richard S. Sayers, *Modern Banking* (Oxford: Clarendon Press, 1938), p. 25.

74. Montagu Norman, Evidence to the Sankey Committee, EAC(IS)100, CAB 58/131.

75. See Chapter 11.

76. J. Atkin, "Official Regulation of British Overseas Investment, 1924–1931," *Economic History Review* 23 (Aug. 1970), 325–333; Henry Clay, *Lord Norman* (Macmillan, 1957), p. 130.

77. Norman, Evidence to the Sankey Committee, 21 March 1930, EAC(IS)100, CAB 58/131.

78. Thomas, *Finance of British Industry*, pp. 48–49.

79. Robert Jones and Oliver Marriott, *Anatomy of a Merger: A History of GEC, AEI, and English Electric* (Pan, 1970), esp. pp. 102–105.

80. Thomas, *Finance of British Industry*, p. 120.

81. Susan Strange, *Sterling and British Policy: A Political Study of an International Currency in Decline* (Oxford University Press, 1971), pp. 55–80.

82. R. E. Catterall, "Attitudes to and Impact of British Monetary Policy

in the 1920s," *Revue internationale d' histoire de la banque*, no. 12, 1976, 29–53; Derek H. Aldcroft, *The Inter-War Economy, 1919–1939* (Batsford, 1970), pp. 337–339; Edward Nevin, *The Mechanism of Cheap Money: A Study of British Monetary Policy, 1931–1939* (Cardiff: University of Wales Press, 1935), pp. 202–203, 251.

83. Nevin, *Mechanism of Cheap Money*, pp. 225–226. For cases, see the studies of Richard Thomas and Dorman Long in Chapters 3 and 5.

84. Alexander T. K. Grant, *A Study of the Capital Market in Britain from 1919 to 1936* (Frank Cass, 1937; new edition, 1967), p. 187; Coase et al., *Iron and Steel Industry*, p. 16.

85. Grant, *Capital Market*, p. 187.

86. R. McKenna to Midland Bank, AGMs, 1935–1937.

87. Roger J. Truptil, *British Banks and the London Money Market* (Cape, 1936), p. 306.

88. Thomas, *Finance of British Industry*, pp. 69–70; Nevin, *Mechanism of Cheap Money*, pp. 264–267.

89. Michael Best and Jane Humphries, "The City and Industrial Decline," in B. Elbaum and W. Lazonick, eds., *The Decline of the British Economy*, pp. 223–239.

90. Best and Humphries, "City and Industrial Decline," p. 224; and see J. Riesser, *The German Great Banks and Their Concentration* (Washington, D.C.: Government Printing Office, 1911), pp. 364, 473–476; K. E. Born, *International Banking in the Nineteenth and Twentieth Centuries* (Leamington Spa: Berg, 1983).

91. Hugh M. Neuberger and Houston H. Stokes, "German Banks and German Growth, 1883–1913: An Empirical View," *Journal of Economic History* 34 (Sept. 1974), 710–731, esp. p. 729; Hugh M. Neuberger and Houson H. Stokes, "German Banking and Japanese Banking: A Comparative Analysis," *Journal of Economic History* 35 (March 1975), 238–252. For other critical views on the German banks see Bertrand Gille, "Banking and Industrialization in Europe, 1730–1914," in Carlo M. Cipolla, ed., *The Fontana Economic History of Europe*, vol. 3, *The Industrial Revolution* (Fontana, 1973), pp. 285–297; Udo E. G. Heyn, *Private Banking and Industrialization: The Case of Frankfurt am Main, 1825–1875* (New York: Arno, 1981), esp. pp. 375–400.

92. Rainer Fremdling and Richard Tilly, "German Banks, German Growth and Econometric History," *Journal of Economic History* 36 (June 1976), 416–424; Richard Sylla, "Financial Intermediaries in Economic History: Quantitative Research on the Seminal Hypotheses of Lance Davis and Alexander Gerschenkron," in Robert E. Gallman, ed., *Recent Developments in Business and Economic History: Essays in Memory of Herman E. Krooss* (Greenwich, Conn.: JAI Press, 1977), pp. 55–80; Clive Trebilcock, *The Industrialisation of the Continental Powers, 1780–1914* (Longman, 1981), pp. 92–106.

93. Clifford N. Smith, "Motivation and Ownership: History of the Ownership of the Gelsenkirchen Bergwerks A.G.," *Business History* 12 (1970), esp. pp. 10–11; Trebilcock, *Industrialisation of Continental Powers*, pp. 98–104.

94. Hans Pohl, "Forms and Phases of Industry Finance up to the Second World War," in Wolfram Engels and Hans Pohl, eds., *German Yearbook on Business History, 1984* (Berlin: Springer-Verlag, 1985), pp. 79–90; W. Felden-

kirchen, "The Banks and the Steel Industry in the Ruhr: Developments in Relations from 1873 to 1914," in W. Engels and H. Pohl, eds., *German Yearbook on Business History, 1981* (Berlin: Springer-Verlag, 1982).

95. On Japan see Kozo Yamamura, "Japan 1868–1939: A Revised View," in R. Cameron, ed., *Banking and Economic Development: Some Lessons of History* (Oxford University Press, 1972), pp. 168–198; Hugh T. Patrick, "Japan, 1868–1914," in Rondo E. Cameron, ed., *Banking in the Early Stages of Industrialization: A Study in Comparative Economic History* (Oxford University Press, 1967), pp. 239–289; Kazuo Sugiyama, "Business Finance in Japanese Business," in Keiichiro Nakagawa and Hidemasa Morikawa, eds., *Japanese Yearbook on Business History, 1984* (Tokyo: Japan Business History Institute, 1985); Neuberger and Stokes, "German Banking and Japanese Banking."

96. Hermann Daems, *The Holding Company and Corporate Control* (Leiden: Martinus Nijhoff, 1977).

97. Richard Rudolf, "Austrian Banking, 1800–1914" in Rondo Cameron, *Banking in Economic Development*, pp. 47ff. Recent work, however, suggests that in contrast the Swedish banks played a dynamic and innovative role in the Swedish industrial revolution of 1895–1910: see Lars Sandberg, "Banking and Economic Growth in Sweden before World War I," *Journal of Economic History* 38 (Sept. 1978), 650–680; Ingemar Nygren, "Transformation of Bank Structures in the Industrial Period. The Case of Sweden, 1820–1913," *Journal of European Economic History* 12 (Spring 1983), 29–68, esp. pp. 61–63.

98. Dieter Stiefel, "Austrian Banks at the Zenith of Power and Influence: System and Problems of the Austrian Finance Capital from the 1890s to the International Economic Crisis of the 1930s," in Hans Pohl and B. Rudolph, eds., *German Yearbook on Business History, 1985* (Berlin: Springer-Verlag, 1986), p. 82.

99. Stiefel, "Austrian Banks," pp. 80–93; Hans Kernbauer and Fritz Weber, "Multinational Banking in the Danube Basin: The Business Strategy of the Viennese Banks after the Collapse of the Hapsburg Monarchy, in Alice Teichova, Maurice Levy-Leboyer, and Helga Nussbaum, eds., *Multinational Enterprise in Historical Perspective* (Cambridge University Press, 1986).

100. R. S. Sayers, *Modern Banking*, pp. 188–189.

8. The Political and Interventionist Role of Central Banking in Industry, 1920–1932

1. Richard S. Sayers, *The Bank of England, 1891–1944*, 3 vols. (Cambridge University Press, 1976), p. 314.

2. Ibid., p. 315.

3. See for instance the case of National Provincial and Robert Heath and Low Moor.

4. M. Norman, marginal note on a letter from E. R. Peacock to Norman, 21 Aug. 1925, SMT 2/72, reporting his conversation with the chancellor.

5. A. Steel-Maitland to Norman, 21 Nov. 1928, Steel-Maitland Papers, GD 193; and Norman to Steel-Maitland, 28 Nov. 1928, ibid.

6. E. Guy Ridpath, Memorandum on the Iron and Steel Industry, 10

May 1927, SMT 2/72. The financial syndicate was to comprise Baring Bros., Robert Fleming, Hambros, Higginsons, Lazard, Morgan Grenfell, Rothschild, Schröder, and Helbert Wagg.

7. Ridpath to H. C. Bond, 20 May 1927, SMT 2/72.

8. Correspondence between Ridpath and Norman, May to Sept. 1927, SMT 2/72.

9. Arthur Colegate, Memorandum on the Modernization of the British Iron and Steel Industry, 9 Feb. 1928, SMT 2/72. Colegate had been financial manager of Brunner Mond for seven years and was currently a director of Robert Heath and Low Moor; Norman to E. R. Peacock, 3 Dec. 1926, SMT 2/126.

10. Norman to Colegate, 25 Feb. 1928, SMT 2/72.

11. William J. Reader, *A House in the City* (Batsford, 1972), pp. 146–154.

12. Note of a Conversation between Mr. Hatry and the Governor, 29 May 1929; and Memorandum on an Interview between the Governor and Mr. Hatry, 11 June 1929, SMT 2/147.

13. Both Peacock and Norman wrote separately to Frater Taylor, warning him not to touch Hatry; E. R. Peacock to Norman, 4 June 1929, SMT 2/147. Hatry was already suspected in the Bank of having invented a story of an approach to him by Dorman Long concerning a possible sale, in order to put pressure on Bolckow Vaughan to do a deal with him. See C. S. Mahon, Note, 31 May 1929, and Sir Guy Granet to Norman, 31 May 1929, SMT 2/147.

14. Norman to Peacock, 1 June 1929, SMT 2/147.

15. For the details of the Hatry case, see Peter N. Davies and A. M. Bourn, "Lord Kylsant and the Royal Mail," *Business History* 24 (July 1972), 103–123; and Reader, *House in the City*, pp. 146–154.

16. H. Lawrence to Norman, 23 Sept. 1929, SMT 2/147.

17. Norman to Peacock, 25 Sept. 1929, Memorandum on the Steel Industry; see also Memorandum of a Meeting between Messrs. Brassert, Baring, Lockhart, Keefer, and Norman, 24 Sept. 1929, SMT 2/147.

18. Norman, Note, 21 Sept. 1929, SMT 2/147.

19. Henry Clay, *Lord Norman* (Macmillan, 1957), pp. 318–319.

20. Ibid., p. 319.

21. Deputy Governor, Interview with Mr. Harrison (financial secretary of Armstrong), 18 June 1925, SMT 8/3.

22. Court of Treasury Minutes, 28 Aug. 1925.

23. Branch Banks Office, Memorandum respecting E. R. Peacock's Call on the Governor, 30 March 1925, SMT 8/1.

24. Notes on a Visit from Sir Glynn West, 24 April 1925, SMT 8/1.

25. Edward R. Peacock came from a Canadian and international business background. He was a director of the Bank of England from 1921 to 1924 and again from 1929 to 1946, and between these dates he remained a close personal adviser and associate of Norman. He was a director of Baring Brothers, the merchant bank, from 1924 to 1956.

26. Branch Banks Office, Memorandum respecting E. R. Peacock's Call on the Governor, 30 March 1925, SMT 8/1.

27. Notes, 24 April 1925, SMT 8/1.

28. J. Frater Taylor to E. R. Peacock, 13 July 1925, SMT 8/3; cf. William J. Reader, *Bowater: A History* (Cambridge University Press, 1981), pp. 55–57.

29. J. Frater Taylor, Confidential Memorandum on the Newfoundland Power and Paper Company, 15 Sept. 1925, SMT 8/3.

30. See W. K. Wigham to Sir Glynn West, 28 April 1930, SMT 8/1; and F. Williams Taylor (Bank of Montreal) to Peacock, 16 Feb. 1925, ibid.

31. Ibid.; and Peacock to Norman, 13 March 1925, SMT 8/1.

32. Quoted in John D. Scott, *Vickers: A History* (Weidenfeld & Nicholson, 1962), pp. 161–162.

33. Sir W. G. Armstrong-Whitworth and Co. Ltd., Report to the Directors by J. Frater Taylor and Sir Gilbert Garnsey, 30 March 1926; and Reader, *Bowater*, pp. 55–57.

34. Court of Treasury Minutes, 13 Aug. 1926; and Memorandum of a Meeting at Barings, 6 Oct. 1925, SMT 8/3.

35. Clay, *Norman*, p. 320.

36. Correspondence between Peacock and Norman, Dec. 1926, SMT 2/126.

37. Frater Taylor to Peacock, 27 Dec. 1926, SMT 2/126.

38. Sir William Plender, Memorandum on Vickers and Armstrong, 8 Aug. 1927, SMT 2/126.

39. Plender, Memo, ibid.; and Norman to Peacock, 30 July 1927, SMT 2/126.

40. Norman to Peacock (a director of Barings), 26 Aug. 1927, SMT 2/126.

41. Cf. Evidence of Lawrence (Vickers) to *Royal Commission on Private Trading and Manufacturing of Arms* (1935), SMT 2/131.

42. See Clay, *Norman*, p. 322. The shipbuilding and paper companies were sold off, and the cash went to the Bank in partial settlement of debts.

43. Quoted in Clay, *Norman*, p. 323.

44. Frater Taylor to Peacock, 24 March 1929, SMT 2/95.

45. Correspondence between Norman and Lawrence, Oct. 1927, SMT 2/126.

46. Norman to Peacock, 16 March 1929, SMT 2/131.

47. Norman, marginal note on letter from Peacock to Norman, 4 Dec. 1928, SMT 2/127.

48. Norman to Peacock, 16 March 1929, SMT 2/131.

49. O. E. Niemeyer, Notes on ESC, 5 Dec. 1931; and cf. also *Financial News*, 31 Jan. 1931.

50. C. F. Sim to General Manager Sun Insurance Company, 13 Aug. 1929; and Memorandum of terms, 20 Sept. 1929, SMT 3/88. On the wider context of Vickers policy, see Richard Davenport-Hines, *Dudley Docker: The Life and Times of a Trade Warrior* (Cambridge University Press, 1984), pp. 178–185.

51. For these terms, cf. Linklaters and Paines, and Freshfields, Leese, and Munn, Scheme for the Reconstruction of the Capital of ESC, 14 Dec. 1931, SMT 2/95.

52. Norman to Peacock, 11 May 1929, SMT 2/95.

53. Frater Taylor to Peacock, 23 March 1929; Gen. Dawnay to Norman, 1 Nov. 1929, SMT 2/95.

54. O. E. Niemeyer, Memorandum on Darlington Forge Co. Acquisition, 13 Sept. 1929, SMT 8/38.

55. C. Bruce Gardner, Memorandum on ESC, 10 Dec. 1931, SMT 2/131.

56. O. E. Niemeyer, Note on ESC, 5 Dec. 1931, SMT 2/131.

57. C. Bruce Gardner, Memorandum to J. A. Cooper and O. E. Niemeyer, 10 Dec. 1931, SMT 2/131.

58. E. H. D. Skinner, Notes on English Steel Corporation, 11 Dec. 1931, SMT 2/131.

59. SMT. House Committee meeting minutes, 7, 14, and 28 Dec. 1931.

60. Court of Treasury Minutes, 19 Sept. 1928. See also Sayers, *Bank of England*, vol. 1, and M. W. Kirby, "The Lancashire Cotton Industry in the Inter-War Years: A Study in Organisational Change," *Business History* 25 (July 1974), 145–159.

61. Andrew Boyle, *Montagu Norman* (Cassell, 1967).

62. Sayers, *Bank of England*, pp. 249–250.

63. Ibid., p. 253.

64. Ibid., pp. 255–258.

65. Leslie Hannah, *Electricity before Nationalisation* (Macmillan, 1979), esp. pp. 90–93; Geoffrey W. MacDonald and Howard F. Gospel, "The Mond-Turner Talks 1927–1933: A Study in Industrial Co-operation," *Historical Journal* 16, no. 4 (1973), 807–829.

66. See Chapter 4.

67. Reader, "Imperial Chemical Industries and the State," in B. Supple, ed., *Essays in British Business History*, pp. 227–231; Robert Jones and Oliver Marriott, *Anatomy of a Merger: A History of GEC, AEI, and English Electric* (Pan, 1970), p. 102.

68. See Chapter 4.

69. See Jones and Marriott, *Anatomy of a Merger*, pp. 122, 127–128.

70. See Chapter 9.

71. See Chapter 9.

72. See Leslie Hannah, "A Pioneer of Public Enterprise: The Central Electricity Board and the National Grid, 1927–40," in B. Supple, ed., *Essays in British Business History* (Oxford University Press, 1977), p. 212.

73. By this time Hodges had been repudiated by the miners and was thought of as "a hanger-on of the directors of capitalist industry." Margaret Cole, ed., *Beatrice Webb's Diaries, 1924–1932* (Longmans, 1956), pp. 147–149.

74. See Sayers, *Bank of England*, pp. 324–327, for further details on SMT.

75. The following issuing houses and merchant banks were involved in BID: J. Henry Schröder & Co., Baring Bros., N. M. Rothschild & Sons, Morgan Grenfell & Co., Lazard Bros., Glyn Mills (a private bank), Hambros Bank Ltd., M. Samuel and Co., Brown Shipley & Co., Robert Benson & Sons, Samuel Montagu & Co., Helbert, Wagg & Co., Guinness, Mahon & Co., Erlanger & Co., Higginson & Co., Seligman Bros., Stern Bros.

76. Jones and Marriott, *Anatomy of a Merger*, p. 135.

77. Court of Treasury Minutes, 15 Jan. 1930.

78. Norman to W. Fisher, 22 Feb. 1930, SMT 2/55.

79. Norman to Sir Guy Granet, 18 Dec. 1930, SMT 2/55.

80. BID Minutes, 18 Nov. 1930, BID 1/4.

81. N. L. Campbell, Memorandum, 28 Oct. 1931, BID 1/10; and cf. also Norman to Duncan, 7 May 1930, SMT 2/53.

82. See Chapter 9.

83. Edwin Green and Michael Moss, *A Business of National Importance: The Royal Mail Shipping Group, 1902–1937* (Methuen, 1982).

84. PRO, Introduction to the Trade Facilities Act Files T.190. See, in particular, Files T.190/79 and T.190/124.

85. Green and Moss, *Business of National Importance*, p. 104.

86. Ibid., pp. 91–120.

87. E. S. Morland, Memorandum on a Meeting at the Treasury on 7th March about the Kylsant Group, 10 March 1930, T.190/124.

88. M. Norman to Sir Warren Fisher, 20 March 1930, cited in Green and Moss, *Business of National Importance*, p. 108.

89. Ibid., pp. 110–117.

90. Norman to Fisher, 22 Feb. 1930, SMT 2/55.

91. H. C. Bischoff, Memorandum on BID, 10 Feb. 1930, SMT 2/55; and cf. also Sir Guy Granet, Evidence to MacMillan Committee.

92. Bischoff, Memorandum on BID, 10 Feb. 1930, SMT 2/55.

93. Norman to Fisher, 22 Feb. 1930, SMT 2/55.

94. Bischoff, Memorandum on BID, 16 Feb. 1930, SMT 3/39.

95. H. A. Brassert, Memorandum on the Regionalisation of the British Iron and Steel Industry, 10 Jan. 1930, SMT 2/154.

96. C. Bruce Gardner, Confidential Report on the Structure of the Iron and Steel Industry of Great Britain, Incorporating Plans for Rationalisation, n.d., BSC Archives.

97. John Vaizey, *History of British Steel* (Weidenfeld & Nicolson, 1974), p. 53.

98. F. Clements (manager of Park Gate Iron and Steel Co. and leading technical expert in the Iron and Steel Institute), Comments on the Bruce Gardner Report, Feb. 1931, SMT 3/75.

99. Private Meeting between Sir Guy Granet, Bruce Gardner, and Cunliffe-Lister at 7 Lygon Place, 30 July 1930, SMT 3/19. At the same time Cunliffe-Lister was giving various steelmakers personal assurances that the Tories would introduce tariffs when elected. See A. Pam to A. Dorman, 29 July 1930, SMT 3/19.

100. SMTHM Minutes, 15 June 1931.

101. Ibid., 30 March 1931.

102. Ibid., 11 May 1931.

103. Private meeting, 30 July 1930, SMT 3/19.

104. SMTHM Minutes, 5 Oct. 1931.

105. Bruce Gardner to E. J. George, 22 Sept. 1931, SMT 3/75; and SMTHM Minutes, 23 Nov. 1931.

106. Bruce Gardner, Memorandum on BID, 17 April 1931, SMT 2/53.

107. Peacock to Bruce Gardner, 20 April 1931, SMT 2/53.

108. Campbell, Memorandum on BID, 28 Oct. 1931, BID 1/10.

109. BID Minutes, 6 Jan. 1931, BID 1/4.

110. Campbell, Memorandum on BID, 28 Oct. 1931, BID 1/10.

111. Bischoff, Memorandum, 9 July 1930; Campbell to Bischoff, 10 July 1930; Campbell, Memorandum, 3 Nov. 1930, SMT 4/42.

112. BID Minutes, 18 Nov. 1930, BID 1/4.

113. BID Minutes, 16 Dec. 1930, BID 1/4.

114. Bruce Gardner, Memorandum on Finance for the Steel Industry, 27 July 1932, SMT 2/73.

115. Campbell, Memorandum on BID, 4 July 1932, SMT 2/56.

116. Campbell, Memorandum on BID, 18 July 1932, SMT 2/56.

117. Campbell, Memorandum on BID, 22 July 1932, SMT 2/56; E. H. D. Skinner, "Rationalisation: A Perspective," 7 Oct. 1930, SMT 2/53.

118. BID Minutes, 4 Nov. 1930, BID 1/4.

119. BID Minutes, 18 Nov. 1930, BID 1/4.

120. Bruce Gardner, Notes on an Interview at 10 Downing Street, 11 June 1931, SMT 3/19.

121. Bruce Gardner, Memorandum on Visit to the President of the Board of Trade, 13 July 1931, SMT 2/73.

9. Banks, Firms, and Industrial Rationalization

1. J. Frater Taylor and Sir Gilbert Garnsey, Report to the Directors of Sir W. G. Armstrong Whitworth and Co. Ltd., 30 March 1926, SMT 3/118.

2. Ibid.

3. Peacock to Norman, 30 Sept. 1925, SMT 8/3, quoting Mr. John Rae, joint general manager of Westminster Bank.

4. Norman to Peacock, 11 Dec. 1926, SMT 2/126; cf. Rae, Memorandum on the Pearson Knowles Group, 13 Dec. 1926, SMT 2/126 on the extent of Westminster's involvement in Partington and its desire to have some share in the control in any reconstruction scheme.

5. H. A. Brassert, Report for the Westminster Bank and Sir W. G. Armstrong Whitworth and Co. Ltd. on the Properties of the Pearson Knowles Group, 10 Dec. 1927, SMT 8/33.

6. W. H. Leese to Mr. Stevenson, 3 July 1928, SMT 8/33.

7. Frater Taylor to Peacock, 25 March 1929, SMT 2/95.

8. Cf., for example, John Rae (director and chief general manager Westminster Bank) to Peacock, 29 Sept. 1930, SMT 2/132.

9. Brassert Report, ibid.; Frater Taylor to Norman, 30 Oct. 1929, SMT 2/132.

10. Correspondence between Frater Taylor and Norman, Oct. 1928 to Aug. 1929, SMT 2/132.

11. Norman, Notes on Frater Taylor's Visit, 4 Nov. 1929, SMT 2/132.

12. The sums were finally raised to £1.65 million of which Schröder was to raise £1.5 million. Draft proposals, 14 Jan. 1930, and correspondence between Norman and A. Pam (Schröder), Nov. 1929 to Jan. 1930, SMT 2/132.

13. Correspondence between Norman and Frater Taylor, Oct. 1928 to Aug. 1929, SMT 2/132.

14. H. A. Brassert, Memorandum on the Regionalization of the British Iron and Steel Industry, 10 Jan. 1930, SMT 2/154; and Brassert to Norman, 24 Oct. 1930, SMT 3/109.

15. See Chapter 6.

16. Memorandum of a Conversation between Sir Andrew Duncan and Norman, 6 Feb. 1930, SMT 2/132; and W. Benton Jones to C. Bruce Gardner, 25 Nov. 1930, SMT 3/109.

17. Frater Taylor to Bruce Gardner, 9 May 1930, SMT 3/199.

18. Frater Taylor to Peacock, 5 Nov. 1930, SMT 2/159.

19. Frater Taylor to Bruce Gardner, 12 May 1930, SMT 3/199.

20. Ibid.

21. Correspondence between Norman, Brassert, Bruce Gardner, and Frater Taylor, Feb. to June 1930, SMT 3/199.

22. Philip W. S. Andrews and Elizabeth Brunner, *Capital Development in Steel: A Study of the United Steel Companies Ltd.* (Oxford University Press, 1952), pp. 162–166.

23. W. Benton Jones, Memorandum to Bruce Gardner, 10 July 1930, SMT 3/73.

24. Frater Taylor to Bruce Gardner, 18 July 1930, SMT 3/199.

25. Extract from Benton Jones' Notes on an Interview with Frater Taylor, 18 July 1930, SMT 3/109.

26. Benton Jones to Bruce Gardner, 25 Nov. 1930, SMT 3/109.

27. Bruce Gardner to Brassert, 6 Nov. 1930, SMT 3/109.

28. R. S. Hilton, Memorandum on the Rationalisation of the Midlands Steel Industry, 6 Sept. 1930, SMT 3/109.

29. H. A. Brassert, Report on the Rationalisation of the Iron and Steel Industry in the North-West and Midlands, 11 Oct. 1930, SMT 2/159.

30. Brassert to Norman, 24 Oct. 1930, SMT 3/109.

31. Jonathan S. Boswell, *Business Policies in the Making: Three Steel Companies Compared* (Allen & Unwin, 1983), pp. 174–176.

32. Benton Jones, Memorandum on the Consolidation of the North-West Coast Iron and Steel Works, 25 Oct. 1930, SMT 3/109; and correspondence between R. S. Hilton, Brenton Jones, Frater Taylor, and Bruce Gardner, July to Oct. 1930, SMT 3/100, 3/109, and 3/199.

33. Bruce Gardner, Memorandum of Meeting with Frater Taylor, 31 July 1930, SMT 3/18.

34. Andrew Boynton (Brassert & Co.) to Lancashire Steel Corporation, 9 Oct. 1930, SMT 3/207.

35. Frater Taylor to Bruce Gardner, 2 Aug. 1930; and Frater Taylor to A. Pam (Schröder), 23 Aug. 1930, SMT 3/199.

36. Bruce Gardner, Memorandum of a Meeting with Frater Taylor, 31 July 1930, SMT 3/18.

37. Frater Taylor to Bruce Gardner, 26 Aug. 1930; cf. also Bruce Gardner, Memorandum, 1 Aug. 1930, SMT 3/199.

38. A. Pam to Frater Taylor, 22 and 26 Aug. 1930, SMT 3/18.

39. Bruce Gardner to Benton Jones, 26 Aug. 1930, SMT 3/199.

40. Frater Taylor to Pam, 23 Aug. 1930, SMT 3/199.

41. Pam to Frater Taylor, 22 Aug. 1930, SMT 3/199.

42. Frater Taylor to Pam, 23 Aug. 1930, and to Bruce Gardner, 26 Aug. 1930, SMT 3/199. Even when Pam insisted on disclosure, Frater Taylor withheld important details of Partington's expansion plans. Benton Jones to Bruce Gardner, 25 Nov. 1930, SMT 3/199.

43. Frater Taylor to Bruce Gardner, 29 July 1930, SMT 3/199; and H. A. Brassert, Report on the Whitecross Co., SMT 3/206.

44. Frater Taylor to Bruce Gardner, 2 Aug. 1930, SMT 3/199.

45. Pam and Bruce Gardner, Memorandum for Norman, 3 Sept. 1930, SMT 3/199.

46. BID Minutes of Meeting between Committee of Directors, 9 Sept. 1930. BID 1/100.

47. Bruce Gardner, Notes on Chairman, n.d., SMT 3/199. See also John Vincent, ed., *The Crawford Papers: The Journals of David Lindsay, 27th Earl of Crawford, 1892–1940* (Manchester University Press, 1984), pp. 530–531.

48. Pam to Earl of Crawford, 16 Oct. 1930, SMT 3/199.

49. Earl of Crawford to Bruce Gardner, 30 Dec. 1930; H. C. Bischoff, Notes of an Interview on the 17th February between the Governor and Lord Crawford, SMT 3/199.

50. Correspondence between Crawford and SMT, Dec. 1930, SMT 3/199.

51. Crawford to Pam, 15 Dec. 1930, SMT 3/199.

52. Bruce Gardner to Duncan, 4 Dec. 1930, SMT 3/199.

53. Bischoff, Notes of an Interview between Governor and Crawford, 17 Feb. 1930, SMT 3/199.

54. See the attitude of the Westminster Bank; C. Lindbury (chief general manager of Westminster Bank) to Peacock, 20 March 1931, SMT 3/199.

55. Correspondence between Bruce Gardner, Crawford, and Norman, March to April 1931, SMT 3/200 and 3/199.

56. Norman, Notes on John E. James, 17 March 1931, SMT 2/132. Later Norman deleted the word *dominate* and substituted *conciliate*.

57. SMTHM Minutes, 23 Feb. 1931; Peacock to Bruce Gardner, 31 March 1931, SMT 3/199.

58. SMTHM Minutes, 27 April 1931.

59. Bruce Gardner, Notes on an Interview with Sir Ernest Roney, 17 June 1931, SMT 3/200.

60. J. E. James to Bruce Gardner, 29 Aug. 1932, SMT 3/202.

61. Brassert to James, 10 Sept. 1931, SMT 3/211.

62. Correspondence between Brassert and James, Aug. to Sept. 1931, SMT 3/211; and Revised Development Plan, 30 March 1932, SMT 3/211.

63. See Sir Frederick Scopes, *The Development of Corby Works* (Corby: Stewarts & Lloyds, 1968), pp. 5–8, 13–15, for the early history of the firm.

64. Scopes, *Corby Works*, pp. 15–60.

65. It narrowly decided not to buy new collieries for more than £600,000 at inflated prices in 1920. SL Minutes, 18 May 1920 and 4 Nov. 1920.

66. Mitchell, North Lincolnshire Iron Co. Preliminary Memorandum on Proposed Steelworks, 23 Jan. 1920, SL Minutes.

67. A. C. MacDiarmid, Report to the Board, 15 July 1926; and Letter to Directors, 10 Sept. 1927, SL Minutes.

68. H. A. Brassert & Co., Report on the Properties and Future Manufacturing Policy of Stewarts & Lloyds, 12 Feb. 1930, SMT 2/156.

69. MacDiarmid, Report to Board and Letter to Directors, SL Minutes; and Brassert, Report, pp. 109–122.

70. MacDiarmid, Chairman's Review, 28 April 1927; and MacDiarmid, Report to the Board, 15 July 1926, SL Minutes.

71. They were able to pay out dividends of 12½% in 1924, 5% in 1927 and 1928, 7½% in 1929, and 3¾% in 1930. G. R. Denton, "Investment and Location in the Steel Industry—Corby," Oxford Economic Papers 7 (Oct. 1955), 272–273.

72. Proposals of Stewarts & Lloyds for Steel Manufacture in Northamptonshire as Basis for Reorganisation of British Tube Industry, June 1931, SL Minutes. On the tube cartel, see Ervin Hexner, The International Steel Cartel (Chapel Hill: University of North Carolina Press, 1943).

73. MacDiarmid, Report to the Board 15 July 1929, SL Minutes.

74. Proposals of Stewarts & Lloyds, June 1931.

75. Brassert, Report, and Brassert, Concluding Memorandum, 11 Oct. 1930. SL Minutes.

76. Ibid.

77. Ibid.; and C. G. Atha, Memorandum, 24 March 1930, SL Minutes.

78. T. P. Colclough, "The Constitution of Blast Furnace Slags in Relation to the Manufacture of Pig Iron," JISI 134, no. 2 (1936), 548–580. Colclough was Brassert's senior chemical engineer.

79. Stewarts & Lloyds Proposals, September 1932, SL Minutes.

80. Brassert, Concluding Memorandum.

81. David E. Pitfield, "Regional Economic Policy and the Long-Run: Innovation and Location in the Iron and Steel Industry," Business History 16 (July 1974), 160–174.

82. H. C. Bischoff to Bruce Gardner, 10 April 1931, BID 1/100.

83. H. A. Brassert to MacDiarmid, 9 Dec. 1930, BID 1/100.

84. Cf. Bruce Gardner, Interview with MacDiarmid, 4 Sept. 1930, SMT 3/18.

85. Sir Guy Granet to Bruce Gardner, 7 Jan. 1931, BID 1/100.

86. MacDiarmid, Notes Read by Chairman, 10 Nov. 1931, BID 1/100.

87. B. Talbot to Bruce Gardner, 20 July 1931, BID 1/101.

88. Correspondence between Sir Guy Granet and Bruce Gardner, July to Aug. 1931, BID 1/101.

89. Frater Taylor to Pam, 19 June 1930, SMT 2/147.

90. Bruce Gardner, Interview with MacDiarmid, 4 Sept. 1930, SMT 3/18.

91. Frater Taylor and MacDiarmid to Brassert, 17 June 1930, BID 1/101; SL General Purposes Committee Minutes, 28 July 1930.

92. MacDiarmid, Comments on the Position, Jan. 1935, SL Minutes.

93. Bruce Gardner, Interview with MacDiarmid, 4 Sept. 1930. SMT 3/18.

94. MacDiarmid, Notes Read by Chairman to the Board, 10 Nov. 1931, SL Minutes.

95. Ibid.

96. MacDiarmid to Bruce Gardner, 21 Nov. 1930, BID 1/100.

97. Bruce Gardner, Notes on an Interview with MacDiarmid and Atha, 10 Dec. 1930, BID 1/100.

98. Brassert, Memorandum on Proposed Scheme for New Works at Corby, April 1931; Proposed Plan of Stewarts and Lloyds for Steel Manufacture in Northamptonshire as Basis for Reorganisation to Tube Industry, 17 April 1931, SL Minutes.

99. Bruce Gardner, Notes, 2 June 1932, SMT 3/90.

100. Telegram Brassert USA to Brassert London, 18 Oct. 1931, SL Minutes.

101. Cf. ibid. and Brassert London to Brassert USA, 19 Oct. 1931, SL Minutes.

102. MacDiarmid, Comments on the Position, Jan. 1935, SL Minutes.

103. Bruce Gardner to Sir Horace Wilson, 2 July 1931, BID 1/101.

104. Bruce Gardner, Memorandum of Interview with Maclay (director of Stewarts & Lloyds), 3 June 1931, BID 1/101.

105. Bruce Gardner, Memorandum on Visit to the President of the Board of Trade, 13 July 1931; and Memorandum of Interview with MacDiarmid and Granet, 15 July 1931, BID 1/101.

106. Peacock, Notes on Conversation with MacDiarmid and Maclay, 11 May 1931, BID 1/100.

107. Bruce Gardner, Memorandum on Visit to the President of the Board of Trade, 13 July 1931, and letter to Peacock, 12 May 1931, BID 1/100; Memorandum of Interview with Maclay, 30 June 1931, BID 1/101.

108. Bruce Gardner to MacDiarmid, 21 June 1932, BID 1/101.

109. MacDiarmid to Bruce Gardner, 15 Feb. 1932, BID 1/101.

110. Proposals of Stewarts and Lloyds, Sept. 1932.

111. Bruce Gardner, Notes on Meeting with Mr. Hird (Union Bank of Scotland), 14 Sept. 1932; Hird to Bruce Gardner, 27 Oct. 1932, BID 1/102.

112. Bruce Gardner, Notes on a Meeting at Lloyds Bank, 16 Nov. 1932, BID 1/102.

113. MacDiarmid, Comments on the Position, Jan. 1935, SL Minutes.

114. MacDiarmid, Proposed Increase of Corby Steelworks Capacity from 200 to 290 Thousand Tons, 26 Sept. 1933, BID 1/104; MacDiarmid to Bruce Gardner, 15 Feb. 1932, BID 1/104.

115. MacDiarmid, Comments on the Position, Jan. 1935, SL Minutes.

116. Ibid.

117. MacDiarmid, Letter to the Directors, 23 Oct. 1935. SL Minutes.

118. A. R. Duncan, Notes on Midlands Rationalisation, 10 Nov. 1936, SMT 2/149; and Draft Agreement, July 1936, SMT 3/215.

119. N. L. Campbell to Norman, 6 Jan. 1937, SMT 2/149.

120. Campbell to Norman, 6 Jan. 1937, SMT 2/149.

121. Bruce Gardner, Notes on Meeting with Hilton, 3 Nov. 1936, SMT 2/149.

122. SL, AGM, 1937.

123. SMTHM Minutes, 18 May 1936.

124. Norman, Note, 22 Dec. 1936; W. Benton Jones, Suggested Method of Amalgamation, 26 Jan. 1937, SMT 2/149.

125. W. P. Rylands to Mr. Hawson, 30 Nov. 1934, SMT 3/209.

126. Skinner to Bruce Gardner, 15 April 1935, SMT 3/209.

127. Correspondence between Bruce Gardner, Norman, and J. E. James, April to Oct. 1935, SMT 3/203 and 3/214.

128. Norman, Memorandum on Lancashire Steel, 11 June 1936, SMT 3/204.

129. SMTHM Minutes, 18 May 1936.

130. SMTHM Minutes, 19 Oct. 1936.

131. Duncan, Memorandum, 10 Nov. 1936, in SMTHM Minutes, 6 Sept. 1937.

132. SMTHM Minutes, 19 Oct. 1936.

133. SMTHM Minutes, 5 April 1937.

134. SMTHM Minutes, 1 Nov. 1937.

135. Bruce Gardner, Memorandum of Meeting with J. E. James, Lord Crawford, and Sir Peter Ryland, 24 Nov. 1937, SMT 3/205.

136. Norman to Bruce Gardner, 17 March 1938, SMT 2/138.

137. Skinner to Norman, 8 June 1939, SMT 2/138.

138. SMT 2/138, passim 1939–1943.

139. Import Duties Advisory Committee, *Report on the Present Position and Future Development of the Iron and Steel Industry*, Cmd. 5507, HMSO 1937, p. 116.

140. Duncan L. Burn, *The Steel Industry, 1939–1959: A Study in Competition and Planning* (Cambridge University Press, 1961), p. 62.

141. Beardmore Minutes, passim, esp. 29 Feb. 1924 and 14 May 1924. For a detailed history of the whole Beardmore enterprise, see John R. Hume and Michael S. Moss, *Beardmore: The History of a Scottish Industrial Giant* (Heinemann, 1979).

142. Beardmore Minutes, 9 May 1924.

143. Beardmore Minutes, 13 Dec. 1926; cf. for further details Hume and Moss, *Beardmore*, pp. 196–200.

144. The Treasury held a first mortgage on Beardmore's Mossend works.

145. Henry Clay, *Lord Norman* (Macmillan, 1957), p. 323.

146. Niemeyer to Churchill, 12 Dec. 1926, T.175/10. Niemeyer remained at the Treasury until 1927, when he left to become comptroller at the Bank of England. He was largely responsible for the shape of Treasury policy in this period and was throughout in close personal contact with Norman. He became a director of the Bank of England in 1938.

147. H. Leith-Ross, Memorandum on Beardmore, 7 Dec. 1926, SMT 2/79.

148. Beardmore Minutes, 4 March 1927; Memorandum on Beardmore, May 1930, SMT 3/121.

149. Correspondence between Norman and Lawrence, Oct. 1927, SMT 2/126; and see Chapter 8.

150. Peacock to Norman, 15 Oct. 1928, SMT 2/126.

151. Norman, marginal note on Peacock to Norman, 15 Oct. 1928, SMT 2/126.

152. W. W. Paine (Lloyds Bank) to Norman, 14 June 1929, SMT 3/121.

153. This was probably because current losses were too high to make an issue feasible. Memorandum on Beardmore, May 1930, SMT 3/121.

154. This was, in fact, untrue. Beardmore was not a Scottish firm but was registered in England and therefore did not come under Scottish company law. In February 1932 a legal investigation by Douglas Jamieson disproved "everything that has been believed previously as to the difficulty of appointing a Receiver; the misconception was due to the error of believing that Beardmore is a Scottish company." A receiver could have been placed in control *and* the business continued. (Cf. D. Jamieson, Opinion, 11 Feb. 1932, SMT 3/138, and SMTHM Minutes, 4 Jan. 1932.) Clearly, though, in 1929, Norman *thought* that a receivership meant closure.

155. Memorandum of an Interview between Lord Brentford (Lord Invernairn's legal adviser) and Norman and Bruce Gardner, 24 June 1931, SMT 3/138. Cf. for further details, Hume and Moss, *Beardmore*, pp. 208–211.

156. Frater Taylor to Norman, 19 June 1929, SMT 2/82; for further details see Slaven, "Self-Liquidation," p. 135.

157. Hume and Moss, *Beardmore*, p. 222.

158. Correspondence between Frater Taylor and Norman, 6 Aug. to 15 Sept. 1929; Norman to Peacock, 15 Aug. 1929, SMT 2/79.

159. Report on Wm. Beardmore and Co., 17 Jan. 1930, SMT 2/80; Meeting of Norman, Paine, Cooper, Hodges, and Duncan, 20 Jan. 1930, ibid.

160. L. Ord to Norman, 21 June 1929, SMT 2/79; Memorandum on Beardmore, May 1930, SMT 3/121; Frater Taylor to Norman, 19 June 1929, SMT 2/79.

161. Meeting of Norman, Duncan, Paine, and Cooper, 31 Dec. 1929, SMT 2/80.

162. Frater Taylor to Norman, 26 Nov. 1929, SMT 2/80; Frater Taylor, Memorandum to Sir Andrew Duncan, 21 Dec. 1929, SMT 2/80.

163. Norman to Duncan, 21 Jan. 1930, SMT 2/80.

164. Skinner to E. Harvey (deputy governor of the bank), 29 Nov. 1929; Duncan to Norman, 22 Jan. 1930, SMT 2/80.

165. H. A. Reincke, Memorandum to Bruce Gardner, 6 July 1931, SMT 3/121. In particular, Ord had taken on a number of unprofitable contracts for the Dalmuir locomotive department, contracts that had necessitated further spending in a department that had a bad record of losses and that Norman wanted sold off.

166. Sir James Lithgow to Duncan, 15 Nov. 1932, SMT 3/121.

167. T. G. Rose, Preliminary Notes on the Personnel and Layout of Messrs. Beardmore's Parkhead Works, 6 June 1930, SMT 3/121.

168. Reincke to Bruce Gardner, 19 May 1931, SMT 3/138; Reincke to Ord, 29 May 1930, SMT 2/80. Hume and Moss, *Beardmore*, give a surprisingly uncritical account of Ord's period of management.

169. F. Hodges, Memorandum on Beardmore, 11 Nov. 1931, SMT 3/121.

170. H. A. Reincke, Memorandum to Bruce Gardner, 6 July 1931, SMT 3/121.

171. Skinner, Note on Beardmore's shipbuilding, 30 May 1930, SMT 2/80.

For further details on the rationalization and liquidation of Beardmore's various interests, see Hume and Moss, *Beardmore*, pp. 215–231.

172. Hume and Moss, *Beardmore*, p. 222; R. H. Campbell, *The Rise and Fall of Scottish Industry, 1707–1939* (Edinburgh: Donald, 1980), pp. 170–172.

173. Bruce Gardner to Reincke and to Duncan, 23 July 1931, SMT 3/121.

174. Hodges, Memorandum on Beardmore, 11 Nov. 1931, SMT 3/121.

175. Bruce Gardner, Report on Wm. Beardmore & Co., 21 Nov. 1931, SMT 3/137.

176. Skinner, Memorandum on Beardmore, Aug. 1932; Bruce Gardner to Skinner, 6 Aug. 1932, SMT 3/125.

177. Skinner, Note on Beardmore, 10 Aug. 1932, SMT 3/125.

178. Skinner, Memorandum, ibid.

179. Bruce Gardner to Norman, 27 June 1933, SMT 3/126.

180. For Norman's reply to complaints from the Admiralty see Norman to A. P. Waterfield (Admiralty), 3 Aug. 1933, SMT 3/124.

181. Bruce Gardner to Duncan, 21 July 1931, SMT 3/121.

182. Lithgow to Duncan, 15 Nov. 1932, SMT 3/121.

183. The details can be followed in Hume and Moss, *Beardmore*, pp. 234–239; see Chapter 4 for the context of Scottish reorganization.

184. Reincke to Bruce Gardner, 19 May 1931, SMT 3/138.

185. SMTHM M 7 Dec. 1931. See also Chapter 8.

186. Reincke to Bruce Gardner, 8 July 1931, Bruce Gardner's marginal notes, SMT 3/121.

187. Reincke, Memorandum on Beardmore, 20 July 1935, SMT 3/130.

188. Skinner to L. E. Peppiatt, 22 November 1935, SMT 3/130.

189. Norman to Bruce Gardner, 25 Nov. 1935, SMT 3/130.

190. Lithgow to Norman, 15 Feb. 1936, SMT 3/85.

191. V. Smith (Freshfields, solicitors) to Skinner, 17 Feb. 1936, SMT 2/85.

192. Voting Control Committee to Lord Invernairn, 29 Jan. 1935, SMT 3/129.

193. Cf. Norman, marginal note on letter from Lithgow to Skinner, 29 Dec. 1936, SMT 2/86, referring to Lithgow's relationship with Lloyds: "This feud will never be appeased! alas! no! "

194. See Skinner, Memorandum on Beardmore, 13 Feb. 1936, SMT 2/85.

195. Mr. Whyte (Royal Bank of Scotland) to Norman, 11 March 1936; and correspondence between Skinner and Lithgow, March to Nov. 1936, SMT 2/86.

196. Correspondence between A. S. Macharg (accountant) and Bruce Gardner, Jan. 1936, SMT 3/130 and 3/131.

197. Paine to Skinner, 23 Dec. 1935, SMT 3/130.

198. Macharg, Report on Beardmore, 18 Jan. 1936, SMT 3/131; Skinner, Memorandum on scheme of reconstruction, 28 Feb. 1936, SMT 2/88.

199. Skinner, Memorandum, 29 Oct. 1937, SMT 2/88.

200. Cf. H. Read (Deloitte Plender), Comments on Proposed Scheme of Reconstruction Submitted by the Chairman of the Bank of England, 18 May 1937.

201. Norman, Note, 2 July 1937, SMT 2/87; Lithgow to Norman, 25 Oct. 1937, SMT 2/87.

202. Norman, Note, 28 Oct. 1937, SMT 2/87.

203. Skinner to Lithgow, 21 June 1938, SMT 2/89.

204. Hume and Moss, *Beardmore*, conclude that the Bank had been almost wholly successful. Their account differs extensively in interpretation from that presented here.

10. Renewed Involvment in the Late Thirties

1. See Chapter 5.

2. W. J. Firth, Circular to shareholders, 4 July 1938, SMT 3/219.

3. J. E. James, Report on the Present Position, 24 May 1938, SMT 3/220; Peat, Marwick, and Mitchell, Report on the Financial Requirements of Richard Thomas, 26 May 1938, SMT 2/162.

4. Kenneth Warren, *The British Iron and Steel Sheet Industry since 1840: An Economic Geography* (Bell, 1970), table 27, p. 197.

5. Firth to Abell, 25 April 1938, SMT 2/192; and cf. Development at Ebbw Vale and Irthlingborough, 1938, Schedule K. Estimates of construction costs rose from an original £7.4 million to £10.2 million. The layout of the works and site preparation costs rose from £786,000 to £1.53 million, and the strip mill cost £500,000 more than originally planned.

6. Skinner to Norman, 30 April 1938, SMT 2/162; Binder Hamlyn Report, 25 April 1938, SMT 2/192.

7. Firth to Chamberlain, 11 July 1938, SMT 2/164.

8. Skinner to Norman, 30 April 1938, SMT 2/162.

9. J. E. James to Norman, 2 May 1938, SMT 2/162.

10. Norman, Note, 15 May 1938, SMT 2/162.

11. Press cuttings in SMT 2/162.

12. Memorandum on Alternative Suggestions for Raising Fresh Capital for Richard Thomas & Co., 26 May 1938, SMT 2/162.

13. Skinner, Note, 3 June 1938, SMT 2/163.

14. Skinner, Memorandum on Control, 26 May 1938, SMT 2/188.

15. Skinner, Memorandum on Richard Thomas, 5 Dec. 1938, SMT 2/188.

16. Firth, Circular, 4 July 1938, SMT 3/219.

17. Skinner, Memorandum, 25 Nov. 1938, SMT 2/188.

18. Firth to Beale, 18 May 1939, SMT 3/219.

19. Skinner to Norman, 24 April 1939, SMT 2/188; William J. Reader, *Metal Box: A History* (Heinemann, 1976), p. 82.

20. Beale and Wright, Memorandum of Interview with B. G. Catterns (deputy governor of the Bank of England), 29 June 1938, SMT 2/188.

21. Beale to Norman, 12 July 1939, SMT 2/188.

22. Skinner, Memorandum, 25 Nov. 1938; Skinner, Memorandum on Richard Thomas, 5 Dec. 1938, SMT 2/188.

23. Skinner to Norman, 6 Dec. 1938, SMT 2/188.

24. Skinner, Memorandum, 5 Dec. 1938, ibid.

25. RT, AGM, 1940.

26. Firth to James, 26 April 1939, SMT 3/219.

27. Notes on a Meeting between Adamson, Beale, Wright, James, and Firth, 11 May 1939, SMT 3/219; and Memorandum by Norman, 8 Feb. 1939, SMT 3/219.

28. Correspondence between Beale, Wright, and Adamson and Norman, 1939, SMT 3/219.

29. Firth to Chamberlain, 11 July 1938, SMT 2/163.

30. Correspondence between Firth and Skinner, May 1939, SMT 3/219.

31. Firth to Skinner, 17 March 1939, SMT 2/164.

32. Firth to Skinner, 20 March 1939, SMT 2/164.

33. Firth to Skinner, 17 March 1939; Firth to Spencer Summers, 24 March 1939, SMT 2/164.

34. Firth to Beale, 18 May 1939, SMT 3/219.

35. Firth to Skinner, 19 April 1939, SMT 2/188.

36. Firth to Beale, 22 May 1939, SMT 3/219.

37. Cf. Wright to Norman, 7 Feb. 1939, SMT 3/219; Memorandum by Norman, 8 Feb. 1939, about a dispute over the appointment of a general manager for Ebbw Vale, ibid.

38. While his staff were negotiating with one party to sell the New Sharlston collieries, Firth was unilaterally negotiating elsewhere; Adamson to Beale, 25 May 1939, SMT 3/219. He also unilaterally authorized special expenditure to reopen plant for ARP work without consultation; ibid.

39. See Wright to Norman, 7 Feb. 1939, SMT 3/219.

40. Skinner to Norman, 6 March 1939, SMT 3/219—quoting James's "obiter dicta" about Firth.

41. Skinner to Norman, 4 Oct. 1939, SMT 3/219.

42. Firth to James, 15 March 1939, SMT 3/219; Skinner to Norman, 18 April 1939, SMT 2/188.

43. Skinner to Norman, 25 May 1939, SMT 2/188.

44. Firth to Catterns, 24 June 1939, SMT 2/163.

45. Memorandum on Firth's removal, May 1940, SMT 2/166.

46. RT, AGM, 1940.

47. Lithgow, James, MacDiarmid, and Earl of Dudley to Norman, 1 April 1940, SMT 3/219.

48. Firth to Control Committee, 9 April 1940; Notes on a Discussion Held by the Board "in camera," 28 March 1940, SMT 3/219.

49. Norman, Memorandum, 15 April 1940, SMT 3/219.

50. BISF Expansion Committee, Notes of a Meeting on 4th March 1938, BISF files; J. Bevan (managing director Briton Ferry) to Duncan, 7 March 1938, SMT 2/218.

51. BISF Expansion Committee, Notes of a Meeting 21st January 1938, and Notes of Meeting between Bevan and Duncan, 28 Nov. 1938, BISF Files.

52. Bevan to Duncan, 6 March 1939, SMT 2/218.

53. Warren, *Steel Sheet Industry*, p. 195.

54. Skinner, Memorandum on South Wales, 11 Dec. 1940, SMT 2/218.

55. Norman, Memorandum on Tinplate Industry, 22 Jan. 1941, SMT 2/218.

56. James, Memorandum on the Tinplate and Sheet Trades, 22 Jan. 1939, SMT 2/218.

57. Norman, Memorandum on the Tinplate Industry, 22 Jan. 1941, SMT 2/218.

58. Skinner, Memorandum on South Wales, 8 March 1939, SMT 2/218.

59. Norman, Memorandum on the Tinplate Industry, 22 Jan. 1941, SMT 2/218.

60. On wartime and postwar developments, see Warren, *Steel Sheet Industry*, chap. 12; Duncan Burn, *The Steel Industry, 1939–59: A Study in Competition and Planning* (Cambridge University Press, 1961), pp. 3–51.

61. W. H. Scott, A. H. Halsey, J. A. Banks, and T. Lupton, *Technical Change and Industrial Relations: A study of the Relations between Technical Change and the Social Structure of a Large Steelworks* (Liverpool University Press, 1952), p. 35.

62. Memorandum as to the General Position of John Summers & Co., 8 Sept. 1938; J. Adamson to J. I. Spens, 29 July 1938, SMT 2/63.

63. Skinner, Memorandum on Summers, 8 Sept. 1938, SMT 2/63.

64. Skinner, Memorandum on Summers, 15 Sept. 1938, SMT 2/63.

65. Cf. J. Adamson to J. I. Spens, 29 July 1938, SMT 2/63, on Summers's profit record.

66. Memorandum on John Summers, 13 Sept. 1938, SMT 2/63; Scott et al., *Technical Change*, pp. 380–389.

67. Skinner, Memorandum on Richard Thomas and John Summers: Points of Similarity and Difference, 29 July 1938, SMT 2/63.

68. Memorandum on John Summers, 13 Sept. 1938, SMT 2/63.

69. Sheet Makers Conference: Output and Allotments, 1932, BID, 3/3.

70. Skinner, Points of Similarity and Difference.

71. Ibid.

72. Skinner, Memorandum on Summers, 15 Sept. 1938, SMT 2/63.

73. Skinner, Points of Similarity and Difference.

74. Memorandum on Meeting between Duncan, Norman, and Catterns, 13 Sept. 1938, SMT 2/63.

75. Skinner, Points of Similarity and Difference.

76. Memorandum on meeting between Duncan, Norman and Catterns, 13 Sept. 1938, SMT 2/63.

77. Skinner, Memorandum on Summers, 15 Sept. 1938, SMT 2/63.

78. Skinner, Memo on Summers' Financial Position. 26 Sept. 1938, SMT 2/63.

79. Skinner, Memorandum on Summers, 15 Sept. 1938, SMT 2/63.

80. H. Clay, Notes of a Discussion on John Summers, 16 Sept. 1938, SMT 2/63.

81. H. Clay, Notes on Conservation with Peacock and Duncan about John Summers, 22 Sept. 1938, SMT 2/63.

82. Notes on Lunch with Bruce Gardner, 19 Sept. 1938, SMT 2/63.

83. H. Clay, Memorandum on John Summers, 23 Sept. 1938, SMT 2/63.

84. Notes on Lunch with Bruce Gardner, 19 Sept. 1938, SMT 2/63.

85. Skinner, Memorandum on Rationalisation, 17 Sept. 1938, SMT 2/63.

86. Skinner, Notes on Conversation with James, 30 Sept. 1938, SMT 2/63.

87. BID Minutes, 1 Nov. 1938, confidential information from Benton Jones to the BID.

88. Memorandum as to the General Position of John Summers & Co., 8 Sept. 1938, SMT 2/63.

89. H. Clay, Memorandum on John Summers, 23 Sept. 1938, SMT 2/63.

90. Skinner, Memorandum on Summers, 15 Sept. 1938, SMT 2/63.

91. Memorandum as to the General Position of John Summers & Co., 8 Sept. 1938, SMT 2/63.

92. H. Clay, Notes on a Discussion with Pam on John Summers, 16 Sept. 1938, SMT 2/63.

93. H. Clay. Notes on Conversations with Peacock and Duncan about John Summers, 22 Sept. 1938, SMT 2/63.

94. Clay, Memorandum on John Summers, 23 Sept. 1938, SMT 2/63.

95. Clay, Note on an Interview between BID and Mr. Spens (United Steel), 3 Oct. 1938, SMT 2/63.

96. Deloitte Plender, Report on Summers, May 1938, SMT 2/63; Skinner, Report to the Deputy Governor, 19 Oct. 1938, ibid.

97. Clay, marginal notes on Skinner, Report to the Deputy Governor, 19 Oct. 1938, SMT 2/63.

98. Skinner, Memorandum on Summers' Financial Position, 26 Sept. 1938, SMT 2/63.

99. Clay to Skinner, 28 Sept. 1938, SMT 2/63.

100. Clay, Note on an Interview between BID and Mr. Spens, 3 Oct. 1938, SMT 2/63.

101. Clay, Notes on a Meeting between Mr. Macharg and BID, 28 Oct. 1938, SMT 2/63.

102. Clay to Skinner, 28 Sept. 1938, SMT 2/63.

103. Skinner, Note on John Summers, 4 Oct. 1938, SMT 2/63.

104. Clay, Note on an Interview between BID and Mr. Spens, 3 Oct. 1938, SMT 2/63.

105. Skinner, marginal note on letter from Clay to Skinner, 28 Sept. 1938, SMT 2/63.

106. Ibid.

107. Skinner to Catterns (deputy governor of bank), 29 Sept. 1938, SMT 2/63.

108. Skinner, marginal note on letter from Clay to Skinner, 28 Sept. 1938, SMT 2/63.

109. Skinner, Notes on Conversation with James, 29 Sept. 1938, SMT 2/63.

110. Skinner, Memorandum on John Summers, 31 Oct. 1938, SMT 2/63.

111. Clay, Note on an Interview between BID and Mr. Spens, 3 Oct. 1938, SMT 2/63.

112. Skinner, Memorandum on John Summers, 31 Oct. 1938, SMT 2/63.

113. Skinner, John Summers: Methods of Control, 4 Nov. 1938, SMT 2/63.

114. Skinner, Private Note, 4 Nov. 1938, SMT 2/63.

115. BID Minutes, 10 Nov. 1938.

116. Ibid.

117. Skinner, Aide-Memoire on Talk with Walter Benton Jones and Ivor Spens, 17 Nov. 1938, SMT 2/63.

118. Skinner, Note on John Summers, 7 Dec. 1938, SMT 2/63.

119. BID Minutes, 7 Dec. 1938.

120. Skinner to Peacock, 2 Jan. 1939, SMT 2/63.

121. Skinner, Telephone Conversation with Andrew Duncan, 30 Dec. 1938, SMT 2/63.

122. Skinner to Peacock, 2 Jan. 1939, SMT 2/63.

123. Press cuttings in SMT 2/70: E. G. Daily Express, "One Share Makes Norman Steel Dictator"; Daily Herald, "Montagu Norman Takes Control of Steel"; etc.; 10 Jan. 1939.

124. Minutes of Meeting at Bank of England about John Summers & Co., 15 April 1941, SMT 2/66.

11. Banks and Industrial Restructuring in the Interwar Years

1. On Bank involvement in the Depressed Areas see Carol E. Heim, "Limits to Intervention: The Bank of England and Industrial Diversification in the Depressed Areas," EcHR 37, no. 4 (1984), 533–550.

2. James Bamberg, "The Government, the Banks and the Lancashire Cotton Industry, 1918–39," Ph.D. diss., Cambridge University, 1984, passim.

3. Henry Clay, Report on the Position of the English Cotton Industry (SMT, 29 Oct. 1931).

4. M. W. Kirby, "The Lancashire Cotton Industry in the Interwar Years: A Study in Organisational Change," Business History 16 (July 1974), 145–189; Bamberg, "Government, Banks and the Lancashire Cotton Industry," pp. 234–266.

5. Leslie Hannah, "Managerial Innovation and the Rise of the Large-Scale Company in Interwar Britain," EcHR 27 (May 1974), 252–270.

6. Bamberg, "Government, Banks and the Lancashire Cotton Industry," pp. 100–155.

7. Clay, Report, p. 78; Bamberg, "Government, Banks and the Lancashire Cotton Industry," pp. 255, 370.

8. Andrew Boyle, Montagu Norman (Cassell, 1967), p. 208.

9. For Norman's views, see M. Norman to J. Frater Taylor, 4 June 1929, SMT 2/280; see also Anthony Slaven, "Self-Liquidation: The National Shipbuilders Security Ltd. and British Shipbuilding in the 1930s," in Sarah Palmer and Glyndwr Williams, Charted and Uncharted Waters (National Maritime Museum, 1982), pp. 125–47.

10. W. A. Thomas, The Finance of British Industry, 1918–1976 (Methuen, 1978), p. 57.

11. See Chapter 7.

12. Roy A. Church, *Herbert Austin: The British Motor Car Industry to 1941* (Europa, 1979), p. 18; for a similar pattern in several firms in the Coventry motor and cycle industries before 1914 see David Thoms and Tom Donnelly, *The Motor Car Industry in Coventry since the 1890s* (Croom Helm, 1985), pp. 57–59; A. E. Harrison, "F. Hopper & Co. The Problems of Capital Supply in the Cycle Manufacturing Industry, 1891–1914," *Business History* 24 (March 1982), 3–23.

13. For Bolckow Vaughan see Chapter 3; for Austin see Church, *Austin*, pp. 55–67.

14. Roy A. Church, *Kenricks in Hardware: A Family Business, 1791–1966* (Newton Abbot: David & Charles, 1969), pp. 183–189, 220–221. For another case of Lloyds supporting a firm because of local social links see the case of Siddeley-Deasy in Coventry: Thoms and Donnelly, *Coventry Motor Industry*, p. 59.

15. See Chapter 4.

16. See Chapter 4.

17. Peter Mathias, *Retailing Revolution* (Longmans, 1967), pp. 247–250.

18. Charles Wilson, "Management and Policy in Large-Scale Enterprise: Lever Brothers and Unilever, 1918–1939," in Barry Supple, ed., *Essays in British Business History* (Oxford University Press, 1977), p. 128; idem, *The History of Unilever*, 2 vols. (Cassell, 1954), II, 259–260.

19. Church, *Austin*, pp. 65–66.

20. James Foreman-Peck, "Exit, Voice and Loyalty as Responses to Decline: The Rover Co. in the Interwar Years," *Business History* 23 (July 1981), pp. 195–202; Richard Langworth and Graham Robson, *Triumph Cars: The Complete 75-Year History* (Motor Racing Publications, 1979), pp. 53, 96, 111.

21. Richard S. Sayers, *The Bank of England, 1891–1944*, 3 vols. (Cambridge University Press, 1976), p. 552.

12. Government and Industry in the 1920s

1. Eric Hobsbawm, *Industry and Empire* (Penguin, 1968), p. 225; Barry E. Supple, "The State and the Industrial Revolution 1700–1914," in Carlo M. Cipolla, ed., *The Fontana Economic History of Europe*, vol. 3 (Fontana, 1973). As Arthur J. Taylor, in *Laissez-Faire and State Intervention in Nineteenth Century Britain* (Macmillan, 1972), points out, this did not preclude a certain amount of selective state intervention.

2. For some of the classic formulations see Robert A. Dahl, Mason Haire, and Paul F. Lazarsfeld, *Social Science Research on Business: Product and Potential* (New York: Columbia University Press, 1959), esp. p. 36. For a critical review see Eric A. Nordlinger, *On the Autonomy of the Democratic State* (Cambridge, Mass.: Harvard University Press, 1981).

3. For critiques of this "instrumental" view of the state, see Jairus Banaji, "Modes of Production in a Materialist Conception of History," *Capital and Class*, no. 2 (Autumn 1977), 1–44; David A. Gold, Clarence Y. H. Lo, and Eric Olin Wright, "Recent Developments in the Marxist Theory of the State," *Monthly Review* 27 (Oct. 1975), 29–43, and (Nov. 1975), 36–51.

4. Nicos Poulantzas, *Political Power and Social Classes* (New Left Books,

1973); *Classes in Contemporary Capitalism* (New Left Books, 1975); *State, Power, Socialism* (New Left Books, 1978). For a discussion of these ideas see Bob Jessop, *Nicos Poulantzas, Marxist Theory and Political Strategy* (Macmillan, 1985), pp. 53–148.

5. Simon Clarke, "Marxism, Sociology and Poulantzas' Theory of the State," *Capital and Class*, no. 2 (Summer 1977), 1–31.

6. Anthony Cutler, Barry Hindess, and Paul Hirst, *Marx's Capital and Capitalism Today* (Routledge & Kegan Paul, 1977).

7. Douglas McEachern, *A Class against Itself: Power and the Nationalisation of the British Steel Industry* (Cambridge University Press, 1980).

8. Ibid., pp. 76–102.

9. Ibid., p. 116.

10. Ibid., pp. 145–170.

11. Ibid., p. 174.

12. Ibid., pp. 176–198.

13. Bob Jessop, *The Capitalist State* (Oxford: Martin Robertson, 1982), p. 226.

14. Claus Offe, "The Theory of the Capitalist State and the Problem of Policy Formation," in Leon N. Lindberg, Richard Alford, Colin Crouch, and Claus Offe, eds., *Stress and Contradiction in Modern Capitalism: Public Policy and the Theory of the State* (Lexington, Mass.: Council for European Studies, 1975); Claus Offe, *Disorganised Capitalism: Contemporary Transformations of Work and Politics* (Cambridge: Basil Blackwell/Polity Press, 1985), pp. 170–259.

15. McEachern, *Class against Itself*, pp. 177–182.

16. Theda Skocpol, "Political Response to Capitalist Crisis: Neo-Marxist Theories of the State and the Case of the New Deal, *Politics and Society* 10, no. 2 (1980), 200.

17. For further development of these points, see Steven Tolliday and Jonathan Zeitlin, eds., *Shopfloor Bargaining and the State: Historical and Comparative Perspectives* (Cambridge University Press, 1985), esp. the essay by Zeitlin, "Shopfloor Bargaining and the State: A Contradictory Relationship," pp. 1–45.

18. Derek H. Aldcroft, *The Interwar Economy: Britain, 1919–1939* (Batsford, 1970); Alexander J. Youngson, *Britain's Economic Growth, 1920–1966* (Allen & Unwin, 1967), pp. 23–140; G. A. Phillips and R. T. Maddock, *The Growth of The British Economy, 1919–1968* (Allen & Unwin, 1973), pp. 150–158; S. N. Broadberry, *The British Economy between the Wars* (Basil Blackwell, 1986), esp. pp. 111–168.

19. Hobsbawm, *Industry and Empire*, p. 242; see also Sidney Pollard, *The Development of the British Economy, 1914–1967* (Edward Arnold, 1972), p. 172.

20. Samuel H. Beer, *Modern British Politics: A Study of Parties and Pressure Groups* (Faber, 1965), p. 279.

21. Sean Glynn and John Oxborrow, *Inter-War Britain: A Social and Economic History* (Allen & Unwin, 1976), p. 141.

22. For examples of these newer views see the essays collected in John Turner, ed., *Businessmen and Politics: Studies of Business Behaviour in British Politics, 1900–1945* (Heinemann, 1984).

23. Peter A. Gourevitch, "Breaking with Orthodoxy: The Politics of Eco-

nomic Policy Responses to the Depression of the 1930s," *International Organisation* 38, no. 1. (1984), 95–130.

24. W. H. Becker, *The Dynamics of Business-Government Relations: Industry and Exports, 1893–1921* (Chicago: University of Chicago Press, 1982), p. 183.

25. Ibid., passim; Skocpol, "Political Response," p. 176.

26. Stephen Kuisel, *Capitalism and the State in Modern France* (Cambridge University Press, 1981), pp. 273–280.

27. Quoted in Keith Middlemas and John Barnes, *Baldwin: A Biography* (Weidenfeld & Nicolson, 1969), p. 379.

28. Rodney Lowe, "The Erosion of State Intervention in Britain, 1917–24," *EcHR* 31 (May 1978), 270–286.

29. Henry Parris, *Government and the Railways in Nineteenth Century Britain* (Routledge and Kegan Paul, 1965), 212–230; P. J. Cain, "Railway Combination and Government, 1900–1914," *EcHR* 25 (Nov. 1972), 623–641; M. W. Kirby, "The Politics of State Coercion in Inter-War Britain: The Mines Department of the Board of Trade, 1920–1942," *Historical Journal* 22 (June 1979), 373–396.

30. Parris, *Government and Railways*; Cain, "Railway Combination," pp. 623–641.

31. Cain, "Railway Combination," p. 624.

32. Ibid., pp. 623–641; Geoffrey Alderman, *The Railway Interest* (Leicester University Press, 1975).

33. Leslie Hannah, "Public Policy and the Advent of Large-Scale Technology: The Case of Electricity Supply in the USA, Germany, and Britain," in Norbert Horn and Jurgen Kocka, eds., *Law and the Formation of Big Enterprises in the Nineteenth and Early Twentieth Centuries* (Göttingen: Vanderhoek & Ruprecht, 1979), pp. 579–586.

34. Geoffrey Channon, "The Great Western Railway under the British Railways Act of 1921," *Business History Review* 55 (Summer 1981), pp. 188–190; Derek H. Aldcroft, "The Decontrol of Shipping and Railways after the First World War," in Derek H. Aldcroft, *Studies in British Transport History, 1870–1970* (Newton Abbot: David & Charles, 1974), pp. 117, 122–125; Michael Bonavia, *The Organisation of British Railways* (Ian Allan, 1971), pp. 3–35.

35. Leslie Hannah, *Electricity before Nationalisation* (Macmillan, 1979), p. 89.

36. Ibid., pp. 75–149.

37. On optical glass, see R. MacLeod and K. MacLeod, "War and Economic Development: Government and the Optical Industry in Britain, 1914–1918," in Jay M. Winter, ed., *War and Economic Development* (Cambridge University Press, 1975); on cellulose, see Donald C. Coleman, "War Demand and Industrial Supply: The 'Dope Scandal,' 1915–1919," ibid.

38. William J. Reader, "ICI and the State," in B. Supple, ed., *Essays in British Business History* (Oxford University Press, 1977), pp. 227–243.

39. Clive Trebilcock, "A 'Special Relationship'—Government, Rearmament, and the Cordite Firms," *EcHr* 29 (1966), 364–379; Geoffrey Jones, *The State and the Emergence of the British Oil Industry* (Macmillan, 1980).

40. Minutes of the FBI Committee on Industry and Finance, 23 Oct. 1929. FBI/W/Walker/25.

41. Kirby, *British Coal-mining Industry*, p. 83.

42. John A. Turner, "The British Commonwealth Union and the General Election of 1918," *English Historical Review* 93 (July 1978), 551–553.

43. R. W. Ferrier, *The History of the British Petroleum Company*, vol. 1, *The Developing Years, 1901–1932* (Cambridge University Press, 1982).

44. Susan M. H. Armitage, *The Politics of Decontrol of Industry* (Weidenfeld and Nicolson, 1969). See also Alastair Reid and Steven Tolliday, "The General Strike," *Historical Journal* 20 (Dec. 1977), 1001–12.

45. M. W. Kirby, "The Politics of State Coercion in Interwar Britain: The Mines Department of the Board of Trade, 1920–1942," *Historical Journal* 22 (June 1979), 383.

46. On the Mines Dept., see Kirby, "Politics of State Coercion," 373–396.

47. Churchill, Memorandum on the Iron and Steel Industry, 30 Oct. 1925, CR(H)34, CAB 58/10, p. 10.

48. Maurice Cowling, *The Impact of Labour, 1920–1924. The Beginnings of Modern British Politics* (Cambridge University Press, 1971), on the internal debate within the Conservative Party, esp. pp. 304–305.

49. A. Steel-Maitland, Draft Memorandum, Dec. 1928, p. 60, Steel-Maitland Papers.

50. This section is based on a more comprehensive analysis presented in Steven Tolliday, "Tariffs and Steel, 1916–34: The Politics of Industrial Decline," in John Turner, ed., *Businessmen and Politics*, esp. pp. 50–63.

51. On the war, see J. C. Carr and W. Taplin, *History of the British Steel Industry* (Oxford: Basil Blackwell, 1962), pp. 299–346; Duncan Burn, *The Economic History of Steelmaking, 1867–1939: A Study in Competition* (Cambridge University Press, 1940), pp. 350–392.

52. *Report of the Departmental Committee Appointed by the Board of Trade to Consider the Position of the Iron and Steel Trade after the War*, Scoby-Smith Report, Cmd. 9071, HMSO 1918; P. Cline, "Winding Down the War Economy: British Plans for Peacetime Recovery, 1916–19," in Kathy Burk, ed., *War and the State: The Transformation of British Government, 1914–19* (Allen & Unwin, 1982), pp. 164–165, 167.

53. Tolliday, "Tariffs and Steel," pp. 53–54.

54. See Christopher P. Cook, *The Age of Alignment* (Macmillan, 1975); Cowling, *Impact of Labour*; J. Ramsden, *The Age of Balfour and Baldwin, 1902–40* (Longman, 1978); A. J. Sykes, *Tariff Reform in British Politics, 1903–13* (Oxford University Press, 1979).

55. For instance, P. Cunliffe-Lister, Proposals on Steel Industry, 1 Dec. 1926, T.175/10.

56. F. Leith-Ross, Review of Cunliffe-Lister's proposals, 7 Dec. 1926, T.175/10.

57. O. E. Niemayer to W. S. Churchill, 5 July 1927, T.175/10.

58. W. S. Churchill (chancellor of the Exchequer), Memorandum on Steel Industry, 30 Oct. 1925, CR(H)34, CAB 58/10, pp. 4, 9.

59. Summary of Evidence and of Memoranda Submitted to the CCR, 16 Nov. 1925, CR(H)41, CAB 58/10.

60. Larke to Balfour Committee, Q.6200, "We have never had a full run on that new plant."

61. Sankey Committee Report, p. 35. CAB 58/10.

62. A. Steel-Maitland, Memorandum, July 1928, CP.255(28), CAB 24/197.

63. A. Steel-Maitland, Draft Memorandum on the Iron and Steel Trades, 18 Dec. 1928, Baldwin Papers, vol. 29, p. 56.

64. Minutes of the second meeting of the Economic Advisory Committee, 21 July 1930, EAC(ISC), CAB 58/143.

65. Snowden to MacDonald, 3 July 1930, MacDonald Papers 1/164.

66. See Chapter 8.

67. Steel-Maitland, Draft Memorandum, 10 Dec. 1928, pp. 56–57; Steel-Maitland to Baldwin, July 1928, Steel-Maitland Papers; and G. H. Goschen (Lloyds Bank) to Steel-Maitland, 7 Dec. 1928, ibid., for Steel-Maitland's contacts with bankers.

68. See Chapter 8; for shifts within the Conservative Party, see Susan Howson and Donald Winch, *The Economic Advisory Council, 1930–1939* (Cambridge University Press, 1977), p. 96; Lord Swinton, *I Remember* (Hutchinson, 1948), p. 38; Leopold Amery, *My Political Life*, 3 vols. (Hutchinson, 1953–55), III, 20–31.

69. Mosley Memorandum, 23 Jan. 1930, CP 31 (30), CAB 24/209), esp. p. 13 and Appendix 1.

70. Cf. C. Attlee, "The Problems of British Industry," 29 July 1930, CP 283 (30), CAB 24/124; and discussions in the Unemployment Committee, UP (30), 25 Oct. 1930, ibid.

71. Snowden to MacDonald, 1 May 1931, T.172/1772; and cf. also Ralph Miliband, *Parliamentary Socialism: A Study in the Politics of Labour* (Weidenfeld & Nicolson, 1969); Ross McKibbin, "The Economic Policy of the Second Labour Government, 1929–31," *Past and Present*, no. 68 (August 1975), 95–123; Sidney Pollard, "The Great Disillusion," *Bulletin of the Society for the Study of Labour History*, no. 16 (Spring 1968), 34–40. For a contrasting view, see Robert Skidelsky, *Politicians and the Slump* (Penguin, 1967).

72. Snowden to MacDonald, 1 May 1931, T.172/1772.

73. Unsigned memorandum, The Rationalisation of Industry, 1931, T.175/41, Hopkins Papers. The content makes it clear that it was prepared in close conjunction with Snowden and Thomas.

74. Ibid.

13. Government and Industry in the 1930s

1. See *Recommendations of the Import Duties Advisory Committee*, Cmd. 4066, April 1932, pp. 10–11, for details.

2. SMTHM Minutes, 23 Nov. 1931; on May, see Herbert Hutchinson, *Tariff-Making and Industrial Reconstruction: An Account of the Working of IDAC, 1932–1939* (Harrap, 1965), pp. 26–27.

3. Keith Feiling, *The Life of Neville Chamberlain* (Macmillan, 1946), p. 203.

4. SMTHM Minutes, 30 May 1932.

5. SMTHM Minutes, 6 June 1932.

6. Note of a Meeting of the IDAC with the Sheet Conference at Caxton House, 7 Sept. 1932, T.172/1772; and cf. also IDAC, Report of Conference with Representatives of the Iron and Steel Industry, 3 June 1932, T.172/1773.

7. Minutes of meeting of the Executive Committee of the National Committee, 14 Sept. 1932, T.172/1773; and A. Hurst, Reorganisation of the Iron and Steel Industry: An Analysis of the Present Position, 9 Feb. 1933, ibid.

8. SMTHM Minutes, 18 July 1932.

9. Minutes of meeting of Executive Committee of National Committee, 10 Oct. 1932, T.172/1773.

10. SMTHM Minutes, 19 Sept. 1932.

11. A. Hurst, Reorganisation of the Iron and Steel Industry: An Analysis of the Present Position, 9 Feb. 1933, T.172/1773.

12. Recommendations of IDAC, Cmd. 4181, Oct. 1932, pp. 4–5.

13. W. Runciman to N. Chamberlain, 5 Oct. 1932, T.172/1772.

14. P. Snowden to R. MacDonald, n.d., Oct. 1932, T.172/1772.

15. Minutes of the Executive Committee of the National Committee, 27 Oct. 1932, T.172/1773.

16. C. Bruce Gardner, Notes on the Iron and Steel Industry, 24 Feb. 1933, SMT 3/89.

17. Horace Wilson (Treasury), Memorandum on Iron and Steel Organisation scheme, 6 March 1933, T.172/1773.

18. C. Bruce Gardner, Notes on the Iron and Steel Industry, 24 Feb. 1933, SMT 3/89.

19. SMTHM Minutes, 17 Oct. 1932.

20. SMTHM Minutes, 20 Feb. 1933.

21. C. Bruce Gardner, Notes on the Iron and Steel Industry, 24 Feb. 1933, SMT 3/89; W. Runciman to N. Chamberlain, 30 March 1933, T.172/1773.

22. White Paper on proposals for reorganization of the iron and steel industry, Feb. 1933. HMSO 63-9999, 1933.

23. A joint drafting committee with two subcommittees (A and B) sat from July to Nov. 1933. In Nov. 1933, their proposals were partially adopted by the National Committee. In Feb. 1934, a Revision Committee was set up and produced the final BISF Constitution, which was adopted in April 1934.

24. Minutes of Subcommittee A, 21 July, 1 Aug., and 21 Sept. 1933, NFISM Papers.

25. E. H. D. Skinner, Note on William Firth's views, June 1934, SMT 2/73.

26. Stewart & Lloyds was represented on Subcommittee B by S. C. E. Lloyd. For his views, see Minutes of Subcommittee B, 11 Aug. 1933. NFISM Papers.

27. J. Craig in minutes of NFISM Executive Committee, 18 May 1933, p. 7, NFISM Papers.

28. Minutes of Special General Meeting of NFISM, 22 Feb. 1934, NFISM Papers; and Minutes of Subcommittee A, ibid.

29. A. McCosh in minutes of National Committee, 10 March 1933, NFISM Papers.

30. Minutes of Joint Meeting of Executive and General Standing Committees of NFISM, 21 Dec. 1933, NFISM Papers.

31. Minutes of Subcommittee B, 11 Aug. 1933, NFISM Papers.

32. Minutes of Special General Meeting, 22 Feb. 1934, NFISM Papers.

33. Cf. A. W. Hurst, Reorganisation of the Iron and Steel Industry: Report on the Present Position, 31 Oct. 1933, T.172/1773.

34. See comments of C. Bruce Gardner to A. Pam, 21 April 1934, and Notes, n.d., SMT 3/89.

35. Hutchinson, *Tariff-Making*, p. 78.

36. Cf. Record of a Conversation between the Chancellor of the Exchequer and Sir George May, 2 Nov. 1933, T.172/1773.

37. A. W. Hurst, Reorganisation of the Iron and Steel Industry: Report on the Present Position, 31 Oct. 1933, T.172/1773.

38. D. Ferguson, Note Accompanying Hurst's Report to the Chancellor of the Exchequer, 1 Nov. 1933, T.172/1773.

39. W. Runciman, Memorandum, 11 Nov. 1933, T.172/1773.

40. Report of the Independent Chairman Committee, 11 July 1934, NFISM Papers.

41. SMTHM Minutes, 20 Feb. 1933.

42. C. Bruce Gardner in SMTHM Minutes, 14 April 1934.

43. For example, SMTHM Minutes, 19 Sept. 1932.

44. SMTHM Minutes, 13 March and 16 April 1934.

45. W. Larke to J. Craig, 6 June 1933, JCB XVIII (iv) Craig personal papers, Colville Archive.

46. SMTHM Minutes, 17 July 1933.

47. Sir Horace Wilson, Iron and Steel Trade—Chairman, 26 June 1934, SMT 2/73; and Wilson, Memorandum on Iron and Steel Reorganisation, 6 March 1933, SMT 2/215.

48. M. W. Kirby, "The Lancashire Cotton Industry in the Inter-War Years: A Study in Organisational Change," *Business History* 26 (July 1974), 145–159.

49. Leslie Hannah, *Electricity before Nationalization* (Macmillan, 1979), pp. 150–186, 213–256.

50. Ervin Hexner, *The International Steel Cartel* (Chapel Hill: University of North Carolina Press, 1943), pp. 82–88.

51. J. C. Carr and W. Taplin, *History of the British Steel Industry* (Oxford: Basil Blackwell, 1962), pp. 518–521.

52. BISF Tariff Committee Minutes, 1933–1934, passim; IDAC Statement, 13 Oct. 1932, BISF Microfilm no. 13.

53. Notes on a Meeting between Sir George May and BISF Delegates, 15 Nov. 1934 and 6 Dec. 1934, BISF Microfilm no. 13.

54. A. Duncan, Note on a Discussion with Sir Alfred Hurst, 18 Dec. 1934, ibid.

55. Minutes of a Meeting between BISF and IDAC, 15 Nov. 1934, ibid.

56. Minutes of BISF Foreign Relations Committee, 19 Dec. 1934, ibid.

57. Minutes of a Meeting between BISF and IDAC, 15 Nov. 1934, ibid.; and 1 Nov. 1934, ibid.

58. Hutchinson, *Tariff-Making*, p. 131.

59. Minutes of BISF Foreign Relations Committee, 19 Dec. 1934, BISF Microfilm no. 13; and 13 Dec. 1934, ibid.

60. BISF Tariff Committee Minutes, 12 Dec. 1934.

61. Carr and Taplin, *History of British Steel*, pp. 519–521.

62. Import Duties Advisory Committee, *Report on the Present Position and Future Development of the Iron and Steel Industry.* Cmd. 5507, HMSO 1937 (henceforth IDAC *Report*) pp. 1–20; Hutchinson, *Tariff-Making*, pp. 77–78.

63. Hutchinson, *Tariff-Making*, p. 132.

64. IDAC *Report*, p. 29.

65. Ibid., p. 23.

66. Ibid., passim.

67. Carr and Taplin, *History of British Steel*, esp. preface.

68. B. S. Keeling and A. E. G. Wright, *The Development of the Modern British Steel Industry* (Longmans, 1964), p. 22; Peter L. Payne, *Colvilles and the Scottish Steel Industry* (Oxford University Press, 1979), p. 239.

69. Cf. Duncan Burn, *The Economic History of Steelmaking, 1867–1939: A Study in Competition* (Cambridge University Press, 1940); R. A. Brady, *Business as a System of Power* (New York: Columbia University Press, 1943).

70. Cmds. 5201 and 4851, (HMSO, 1932–33).

71. Brian Tew, "Costs, Prices, and Investment in the British Iron and Steel Industries, 1924–1937," Ph.D. diss., Cambridge University, 1940, table on p. 150.

72. See Chapter 3 for the example of ship plates.

73. Cmd. 5201 (HMSO, 1936), pp. 6–7.

74. For examples, see the Northeast and Scottish case studies.

75. BISF *Annual Statistics*, 1920–1938.

76. For price data, see monthly figures in *ICTR*.

77. I. F. L. Elliott, Memorandum on Scrap Imports, 24 Aug. 1937, BISF "Spreadover" File, 011485.

78. Details of the scheme are in Burn, *Economic History*, pp. 473–477, and in IDAC *Report*.

79. Draft Information for IDAC, 6 Nov. 1936, BISF Agendas for Finance and Emergency Committee.

80. Ibid.

81. Sir W. Larke, Memorandum to Emergency Committee, 16 Sept. 1936, ibid.

82. Carr and Taplin, *History of British Steel*, pp. 567–572; Burn, *Economic History*, pp. 473–477.

83. These were basic billets, 1935; acid billets and basic pig iron, 1936; rails, joists, angles, plates, tubes, and hematite pig iron, 1937.

84. BISF Executive Minutes, 18 June 1935 and 20 Feb. 1936.

85. BISF Executive Minutes, 1935, passim.

86. IDAC had recognized the lack of its own accountant to crosscheck the BISF for several years before it put in Macharg of M'clelland and Ker. See for example, IDAC, CP.174/37. Iron and Steel Prices: Tubes, 30 Aug. 1937.

87. On the basic cost method, see Peat, Marwick, and Mitchell to Duncan, 19 May 1936, BISF Executive Agendas. The price was fixed by estimating firms' depreciation costs and working capital costs and then adding on a figure that would yield an average annual return of 7½% on debentures,

5½% on preference, and 9% on ordinary shares for a company with a "typical" capital structure. Burn, *Economic History,* p. 496, argues that this was a very generous assessment of costs.

88. See Chapters 9 and 10.

89. Iron and Steel Prices: Tubes, 30 Aug. 1937, IDAC, CP.174/37.

90. J. T. Rankin, Iron and Steel Prices: Hematite Pig Iron, 1 Nov. 1937, IDAC, CP.228/37; and Rankin, Report to Duncan, 23 Oct. 1937.

91. Rankin, Iron and Steel Prices, 19 Nov. 1937, IDAC, CP.244/37.

92. Meeting between IDAC and Hematite Pig Association, 17 Nov. 1937, IDAC, CP.244/37; and Iron and Steel Prices: Hematite Pig, 19 Nov. 1937, IDAC, CP.244/37.

93. Mr. Benson, Q.817, First Report of the Public Accounts Committee, July 1940.

94. A. Macharg, Cost Procedure, 31 March 1939, IDAC Prices and Costs File.

95. Second Report of the Public Accounts Committee, July 1941, p. xxv and also Q.3550.

96. Peat, Marwick, and Mitchell to Duncan, 19 March 1936, IDAC, CP.97/36.

97. Rankin, Iron and Steel Prices: Hematite Pig, 1 Nov. 1937, IDAC, CP.228/37.

98. Memorandum by Messrs. Wintle, Johnson, and Barfield, 1940, n.d., BISF Prices and Costs File, 1939–1945.

99. J. H. Hale, Report to R. M. Shone, 10 April 1947, BISF Standing Costs Committee.

100. Rankin, Report to Duncan, 23 Oct. 1937; Rankin, Iron and Steel Prices: Hematite Pig, 1 Nov. 1937, IDAC, CP.228/37.

101. Iron and Steel Prices: Basic and Hematite Pig, Soft Billets, and Heavy Steel, 26 Nov. 1938, IDAC, CP.175/38.

102. Duncan, Iron and Steel Prices: Extras, 13 March 1939, IDAC, CP.48/39.

103. Iron and Steel Prices: Re-Rolled Steel Products, 18 Oct. 1938, IDAC, CP.152/38.

104. Third Report of the Public Accounts Committee, Nov. 1942, Q.4947; Fourteenth Report of the Select Committee on National Expenditure, (HMSO 1942–3). War Production: Methods of Settling Prices for War Stores; G. D. N. Worswick, "Steel Prices," *Bulletin of the Institute of Statistics,* Oxford, 5 (June 1943), 151–155; and Worswick, "Note on Steel Prices," *Institute of Statistics Bulletin* 5 (Dec. 1943), 284–288.

105. J. C. Carr, Iron and Steel Prices: Black and Galvanised Sheets, 3 Dec. 1938, IDAC, CP.178/38.

106. See Chapter 9.

107. The overall picture is understated by the omission of Stewarts & Lloyds, who were outside the BISF. The tube sector in which it operated had an average rate of return of more than 14%, and this could be taken as a minimum for Stewarts & Lloyds' profit rate, which would make it the most profitable of the big steel firms.

108. Burn, *Economic History*, pp. 476–477; Tew, "British Iron and Steel Industries," Appendixes.

109. Burn, *Economic History*, pp. 499–502.

110. Iron and Steel Prices: Position after 30th June Next, 17 April 1939, IDAC, CP.61/39.

111. Henry Owen, *Steel: The Facts about Monopoly and Nationalisation* (Lawrence & Wishart, 1946); Ellen Wilkinson, *The Town That Was Murdered* (Gollanz, 1939); Robert A. Brady, *Business as a System of Power*.

112. Wilkinson, *Town That Was Murdered*, p. 134.

113. CON Minutes, 31 July 1934.

114. Current costs are estimates based on company figures and details for 1929–1932 in DL/SD & CF merger files.

115. H. C. Arnold-Forster, letter to the *Times*, 8 July 1936.

116. H. A. Brassert and Co., Memorandum on the North-East Coast Iron and Steel Industry, 1 Aug. 1935, SMT 3/78.

117. Brassert, ibid., p. 14. On the problem of diversification in the Northeast, see Chapter 3.

118. CF Minutes, 15 Jan. 1936.

119. *Financial Times*, 7 July 1936.

120. *ICTR*, 24 July 1936.

121. CON Minutes, 5 Nov. 1935 and 4 Feb. 1936.

122. Brassert, Memorandum, pp. 12, 15, SMT 3/78.

123. CON Minutes, 4 Feb. 1936. Stewarts & Lloyds was interested in an outlet for Corby iron; IDAC *Report*, p. 26.

124. E. J. George to I. F. L. Elliott (commercial director of BISF), 24 Feb. 1936, CON Board Reports, Agendas and Papers.

125. I. F. L. Elliott to A. Dorman, 21 Feb. 1936, CON Board Papers.

126. C. Cookson to H. Arnold-Forster, 27 May 1936, CON Minutes; and Jarrow Steelworks: Position as It Affects Consett, 17 July 1936, CON Board Reports, Agendas and Papers.

127. H. Arnold-Forster, letter to the *Times*, 6 July 1936.

128. IDAC *Report*, p. 28.

129. Ibid., p. 27.

130. See BISF *Statistics* for basic Bessemer production in 1937.

131. Wilkinson, *Town That Was Murdered*, p. 184; and *Hansard*, 30 June 1936.

132. Wilkinson, *Town That Was Murdered*, p. 174.

133. Memorandum of Meeting between E. J. George and H. Arnold-Forster, 26 Sept. 1936, CON Board Reports, Agendas and Papers.

134. See Chapter 4.

135. I. F. L. Elliott to A. Dorman, 21 Feb. 1936, CON Board Papers.

136. *Economist*, 18 July 1936.

137. Duncan L. Burn, *The Steel Industry, 1939–1959: A Study in Competition and Planning* (Cambridge University Press, 1961), chap. 1.

138. Burn, *Steel Industry*, chap. 3.

139. George W. Ross, *The Nationalisation of Steel* (MacGibbon and Kee, 1965).

140. Burn, *Steel Industry*, chaps. 2 and 3.

141. Fourteenth Report of the Select Committee on National Expenditure, (Session 1942–43).

142. Burn, *Steel Industry*, pp. 30–50.

143. Henry Owen, *Steel: The Facts about Monopoly and Nationalization* (Lawrence & Wishart, 1946); Wilfred Fienburgh and Richard Evely, *Steel Is Power* (Gollancz, 1948).

144. Burn, *Steel Industry*, p. 212.

145. David W. Heal, *The Steel Industry in Post-War Britain* (Newton Abbot: David & Charles, 1974).

146. Reports by BISF and the Joint Iron Council to the Ministry of Supply, HMSO, Cmd. 6811, May 1946.

147. Payne, *Colvilles*, pp. 275–310; Burn, *Steel Industry*, chap. 4; Heal, *Post-War Steel Industry*, pp. 50–73.

148. Burn, *Steel Industry*, p. 105.

149. John Vaizey, *History of British Steel* (Weidenfeld & Nicolson, 1974), p. 100; Douglas McEachern, *A Class against Itself: Power and the Nationalisation of the British Steel Industry* (Cambridge University Press, 1980), pp. 76–102.

150. Ross, *Nationalisation of Steel*, pp. 38–46.

151. Burn, *Steel Industry*, p. 308.

152. See esp. Heal, *Post-War Steel Industry*, pp. 107–145, and McEachern, *Class against Itself*, pp. 156–172.

14. The Limits of State Intervention

1. Leslie Hannah, *The Rise of the Corporate Economy* (Methuen, 1976), pp. 45–60.

2. M. W. Kirby, *The British Coalmining Industry, 1870–1946: A Political and Economic History* (Macmillan, 1977); M. W. Kirby, "The Control of Competition in the British Coal-Mining Industry in the Thirties," *EcHR* 26 (May 1973), 273–284; M. W. Kirby, "Government Intervention in Industrial Organisation: Coal-Mining in the 1930s," *Business History* 15 (July 1973), 160–173; M. W. Kirby, "The Politics of State Coercion in Interwar Britain: The Mines Department of the Board of Trade, 1920–1942," *Historical Journal* 22 (June 1979), 373–396.

3. Kirby, *British Coalmining Industry*, p. 163.

4. Kirby, "Politics of State Coercion," pp. 373–396.

5. E. H. Whetham, *The Agrarian History of England and Wales*, vol. 8. *1914–1939* (Cambridge University Press, 1978), pp. 244–260; Arthur F. Lucas, *Industrial Reconstruction and the Control of Competition: The British Experiments* (Longmans, 1937), pp. 232–235.

6. M. W. Kirby, "The Lancashire Cotton Industry in the Inter-War Years: A Study in Organisational Change," *Business History* 16 (July 1974), 145–159.

7. Leslie Hannah, "Public Policy and the Advent of Large Scale Technology: The Case of Electricity Supply in the USA, Germany and Britain," in Norbert Horn and Jurgen Kocka, eds., *Law and the Formation of Big Enterprises in the Nineteenth and Early Twentieth Centuries* (Göttingen: Vandenhock & Ruprecht, 1979).

8. Francis E. Hyde, *Cunard and the North Atlantic, 1840–1973: A History of Shipping and Financial Management* (Macmillan, 1975), p. 217.

9. See the Treasury files on Cunard/White Star merger, esp. T.190/79.

10. Walter Citrine, *Men and Work* (Hutchinson, 1960), p. 87: see also Owen, *Steel*; Nicholas E. H. Davenport, *Vested Interests or Common Pool* (Gollancz, 1942), passim.

11. Noreen Branson and Margo Heinemann, *Britain in the Nineteen-Thirties* (Fontana, 1971), chap. 1.

12. Samuel H. Beer, *Modern British Politics: A Study of Parties and Pressure Groups* (Faber, 1965), p. 297.

13. John M. Keynes, *The End of Laissez-Faire* (Oxford University Press, 1926), pp. 41–42.

14. Robert A. Brady, *Business as a System of Power* (New York: Columbia University Press, 1943), pp. 153–182.

15. Donald Winch, *Economics and Policy* (Fontana, 1969), pp. 223–229.

16. Harold MacMillan, *Reconstruction: A Plea for a National Policy* (Macmillan, 1933), p. 16.

17. L. P. Carpenter, "Corporatism in Great Britain, 1930–45," *Journal of Contemporary History* 11 (1976), 3–34.

Conclusion

1. On this issue generally see C. Knick Harley, "Skilled Labor and Choice of Technique in Edwardian Industry," *Explorations in Economic History* 11 (1974), 391–414.

2. Bernard Elbaum, "Labor and Uneven Development: Unions, Management, and Wage Structure in U.K. and U.S. Iron and Steel, 1870–1970," Ph.D. diss., Harvard University, 1982.

3. Albert A. Jackson, "The Rise and Fall of the Open Hearth," *Ironmaking and Steelmaking* 3, no. 1 (1976), 1–9; Helen Gintz, "Effects of Technological Change on Labour in Selected Sections of the Iron and Steel Industries of Great Britain, the United States, and Germany, 1901–1939," Ph.D. diss., University of London, 1954.

4. Frank Wilkinson, "Collective Bargaining in the Steel Industry in the 1920s," in Asa Briggs and John Saville, eds., *Essays in Labour History*, vol. 3, *1918–1939* (Macmillan, 1977).

5. Jonathan S. Boswell, "Hope, Inefficiency or Public Duty? The United Steel Companies in West Cumberland, 1918–1939," *Business History* 22 (Jan. 1980); Peter L. Payne, *Colvilles and the Scottish Steel Industry* (Oxford University Press, 1979), p. 144.

6. David E. Pitfield, "Regional Economic Policy and the Long-Run: Innovation and Location in the Iron and Steel Industry," *Business History* 16 (July 1974), 165–174; see also Chapter 4.

7. Stanley D. Chapman, *Stanton and Staveley* (Cambridge: Woodhead-Faulkner, 1981); C. Knox, *Steel at Brierley Hill: The Story of Round Oak Steel Works, 1857–1957* (Round Oak, 1957).

Index

HARVARD STUDIES IN BUSINESS HISTORY

(Some of these titles may be out of print. Write to Harvard University Press for information and ordering.)